the new
BELIEVERS

the new BELIEVERS

A SURVEY OF SECTS, CULTS AND ALTERNATIVE RELIGIONS

DAVID V. BARRETT

CASSELL&CO

This book is for those who ask questions,
rather than for those who already have all the answers.

'There is a principle which is a buffer against any information, which is proof
against all argument and which does not fail to keep every human being in
constant ignorance. This principle is to condemn before researching.'

Herbert Spencer (1820–1903)

First published in the United Kingdom in 2001 by Cassell & Co
A Member of the Orion Publishing Group

Distributed in the United States of America by Sterling Publishing Co., Inc.
387 Park Avenue South, New York, NY 10016-8810

A CIP catalogue record for this book is available from the British Library

ISBN 0 304 35592 5

Edited by Stuart Booth
Text editor Sarah Widdicombe
Designed by Richard Carr
Printed and bound in Great Britain by
Creative Print and Design (Wales)

Cassell & Co
Wellington House
125 Strand
London WC2R 0BB

Contents

Acknowledgements

I would like to express my thanks to all those who have helped me with this book, in many different ways: by making comments on and criticisms of the earlier edition, and for spotting errors in that book which I had missed; by suggesting additional movements to be included in this edition; by giving encouragement, advice and assistance; and by giving generously of their time and their own specialist knowledge. In particular I would like to thank Harry Coney and Morag Traynor for reading through portions of the manuscript, correcting errors and infelicities, and making invaluable suggestions for improvement; any errors which remain are my responsibility. Thanks also to my editor at Cassell, Stuart Booth, and my agent, Liz Puttick, both for helping to make this book possible, and for their patience at my delays and their calmness when we encountered problems.

Some of the chapters in Part One contain material first presented at a number of seminars and conferences.[1] I would like to thank the relevant organizers and chairs, and particularly all those in the audiences who contributed questions, comments and criticisms.

Finally, my thanks must go to the representatives of all the movements covered in this book for the information (and in many cases photographs) which they supplied. Although a very few movements created difficulties, the vast majority understood the purpose of this book, and were co-operative in both correspondence and conversations. They may not agree with everything I have said about their movements, but I hope that all will accept that I have tried throughout to be fair and objective.

All quotations are copyright their original authors and publishers, and all photographs are copyright their originators.

Every effort has been made to ensure the accuracy of the entries in this book. Any factual errors should be reported to the author via the publishers.

Notes

[1] Graduate seminars in Sociology of Religion, and in Cults, Sects and New Religions, Department of Sociology, London School of Economics, 1997–9; conference on new religions at the School of Oriental and African Studies, April 1998; European Fantasy Literature Conference, 'The Disreputable Attractions of the Supernatural', Senate House, University of London, March 1998; UnConvention, University of London Union, April 1998, and Commonwealth Institute, April 1999; graduate seminar, Department of Anthropology, Goldsmiths College, London, October 1999; Willesden Green Library, November 1999; South-East London Folklore Society, Charlton House, London, May 2000.

Introduction

WHAT is a cult? What is a sect? Are they as dangerous as they are often portrayed in the tabloid press? Do we need to be on our guard against their devious ways? Or are they all honest, straightforward religions which have Truth, Beauty and Light, and which have never set a foot wrong? The answer, as usual, lies somewhere between the two extremes – and there isn't a single answer which applies to all religious movements. One of the points which should become apparent throughout this book is that generalizations tend not to be very helpful.

This book is a revised and greatly expanded edition of my earlier book *Sects, 'Cults' & Alternative Religions* (Blandford 1996).[1] Every entry has been thoroughly checked; some have had only minor alterations, but many have been changed considerably, mainly to reflect changes in the movements over the last five years. Around 20 new entries have been added. Note that the information about movements in this book supersedes that in the earlier book.

In addition, many matters which were touched on briefly in the Conclusion of the previous book are now dealt with in some depth in separate chapters:

- Why do people join alternative religions?
- How do they join – of their own free will, or are they tricked, even brainwashed, into joining?
- What are the genuine problems (rather than the tabloid scare stories) that members might face?
- How can families and friends of 'cult' members deal with their loved one being in a strange religion?
- Why do some members find it enormously difficult to leave a movement?
- What went wrong at Waco, and Jonestown, and with Heaven's Gate, the Solar Temple and Aum Shinrikyo – and should we fear more of the same?
- Now that 1 January 2000 has passed, have we seen an end to Millennial Fever?
- Who are the 'cult-watchers', and should we trust everything that anti-cultists say?

These questions, and more, are covered in Part One of the book, which is all new material. Part Two is a revision and expansion of the earlier book, with entries on over 60 individual movements organized into various categories: Christian origins, Eastern origins, and so on. This is followed by a major case study on how and why a particular modern religion exploded into hundreds of fragments. In itself this is a fascinating story; it also illustrates some of the themes discussed in Part One.

Notes

[1] Since writing *Sects, 'Cults' & Alternative Religions* I have had the opportunity to conduct deeper study into such movements, including beginning research for a PhD in this area at the London School of Economics. For nearly three years I worked one day a week as an Information Officer at INFORM (see Chapter 9), which provides information about new religions to a wide variety of enquirers. Both through seminars and conferences and through my own researches, I have met current and former members of many different movements, and have had many long conversations with them about their beliefs and practices. Families and friends of members have provided other insights into movements.

Although I have learnt much from them, especially from my doctoral supervisor Professor Eileen Barker, OBE, FBA, it must be emphasized that this book should not be taken to represent the views of any other scholar of religion, except where explicitly quoted; neither, although it has benefited from my working experience at INFORM, should it be seen in any way as representing or sanctioned by INFORM. As with my previous books, the authorial and editorial stance is entirely my own.

major issues of
alternative religions

CHAPTER 1

Who, What and Why

The purpose of this book

THIS is not intended to be an academic textbook. It is written for anyone who wants to know more about new religious movements. I hope that it will be useful to clergy, university chaplains, teachers, youth workers, counsellors, advice centres, and also the media, as a handy reference text giving straightforward factual information about movements. And I hope that it will be particularly useful to the families and friends of members of these religions – and also to members themselves, to help them see their own religions in the context of others. It is also intended to be of use to students of Religious Studies, Sociology of Religion, etc., both as a source book on several dozen movements and as an introductory text to the study of new religious movements in general.

WHO IS IN THIS BOOK, AND WHY

The inclusion of any movement in this book does not mean that I consider it to be a cult. It may, however, mean that other people consider it to be a cult – or a sect, or a heresy; depending on their own agenda, people might criticize movements in this book for being either dangerous ('cultish') or deviant ('heretical').

How have the movements included in this book been selected, out of the thousands of small or unusual or new religious movements which exist?[1] Briefly, the criteria for inclusion include: those movements which have a significant presence in the UK, Europe and the USA; those which have attracted attention from anti-cultists or the media; and those which are criticized by the Christian counter-cult movement for being 'counterfeit Christianity'. This last category explains the presence here of large and well-established religions such as Unitarianism and Mormonism, which might otherwise seem out of place next to some of the movements which have sprung up in the last few decades, with memberships only in four figures.

The book also includes several organizations such as NLP, Insight and Landmark Education, which are not religions at all but are usually categorized as 'personal development movements'. They are included for three reasons. First, even though the organizations are not religions, personal development or self-improvement is a common religious aim, so there is some overlap in the perceived benefits which members gain from them. Second, some of the techniques of these organizations are used in movements which are religious. And third, some of these organizations have met criticisms similar to those made of new religions by anti-cult groups. However, it should be stressed that this book is not suggesting that they are sects or cults, nor classing them as religions.

THE STANCE OF THIS BOOK

This book treats no theological position as more 'true' or 'valid' or 'sound' than any other. It is immaterial to this book whether a Christian-based movement accepts the doctrine of the Trinity or not, or indeed whether a religion believes in One Creator God, or several gods, or no god at all. There have been plenty of books opposing 'cults' on the grounds that their beliefs are wrong, or differ from the Nicene Creed or the Westminster Confession, or that they add a new Scripture to the complete revelation of the Bible. Such authors have every right to defend the truth of their own beliefs, and to point out the 'heresies' of others, so long as they make their own position clear; what is not acceptable is if they pretend that they are being objective.

So far as this book is concerned, the approach taken is much the same as that of Comparative Religion, or Sociology or Phenomenology of Religion: this is what these people believe and do, as described by themselves and as observed by others. The objective truth of the beliefs is not a concern; the subjective truth, as believed by the members, is respected.

There is no doubt that religious experiences occur – or experiences which, either because of their immediate context or from a later religious perspective, are *interpreted* as religious. These may be visions, auditory hallucinations, apparently meaningful dreams, out-of-body-experiences, an overwhelming sense of unity with the whole cosmos, or just a general feeling of well-being. For the person they happen to, such experiences are undeniably real, though for a disinterested observer, nothing much may seem to be going on.

Some of these experiences, and some of the beliefs of religions covered in this book, outsiders might find difficult to credit – but that is no reason to disbelieve or doubt the integrity or rationality of those who have them. Most non-Mormons find Joseph Smith's golden plates pretty hard to accept. Most people who aren't Neo-Pagans or members of esoteric groups scoff at the idea of real magic. As for those who believe in extra-terrestrials bringing religious and moral messages to mankind, many people would quietly tap the side of their heads.

But people – intelligent, sensible, rational, well-educated people – do believe in all these things. For them, these 'unbelievable beliefs' are absolutely real. And so, in this book, both the beliefs and the believers are treated with respect.

RESPECT FOR SINCERITY

My view of the honesty and integrity of the spokespeople for the many movements in this book is rather different from that of many anti- and counter-cultists. Some of these will not meet or talk with 'cult leaders'; one told me, 'There's no point; they'll only lie to me.' When I suggested that a spokesperson for a movement might actually tell the truth about what they believe and practise, the response was, 'It would take a lot to convince me of that.'

In contrast, I give the same credence to a spokesperson for a religious movement as I would to anyone else with strong beliefs or opinions: I accept that they are telling me the truth *as they see it*, while also accepting that they will put the best possible 'spin' on any debatable issues, and that they will be unlikely to volunteer negative information. In other words, I treat their statements just the same as I would those of a politician, a businessman, a social worker, a school teacher – or my next-door neighbour. There is a world of difference between listening with caution and careful judgement to what someone says, and assuming that they will automatically lie.

Normally, we would assume that our local Methodist minister is reasonably honourable and truthful, unless there is evidence to the contrary; here the same courtesy is extended to ministers (and their equivalents) of new religious movements.

I have been accused by leaders of some anti-cult organizations of being a cult apologist, even pro-cult, because I allow movements to speak for themselves about what they believe and do, and because I don't automatically condemn them as cults. If I am an apologist for anything, it is for freedom of religious belief and practice, as enshrined in the United Nations Universal Declaration of Human Rights, the US Constitution, and elsewhere. I may, for all sorts of reasons, personally dislike a particular movement, but, with Voltaire, I defend their right to exist, and their members' right to belong and believe.

However, this tolerance does *not* extend to illegal or immoral behaviour, or to sexual or financial abuse, which I condemn unreservedly wherever they occur, whether in a modern religion, business, government or police force. Such behaviour, when it occurs, should not be covered up or 'explained away'; it should be exposed and stopped, and its perpetrators dealt with by whatever legal means are available.

This book aims not just for fairness but for accuracy; not all observers of new religions appear to do so. One Christian website, *Cult Catalog Of The 'Other' Jesus*,[2] a collection of brief notes on 75 religions old and new, uses source material on the Family (which it calls the Children of God) that is 23 years old. Its entry on Eckankar lists its leader as Sri Darwin Gross, who actually left that position in 1981. Similarly, an attractively produced popular book on the subject, *Cults: Prophecies, Practices and Personalities*, perpetuates several fallacies. For example, it states, 'To what extent modern Satanism can be linked with child abuse is yet to be determined...',[3] two years after a report commissioned by the UK government found that there was no such link. (This book, which contained several factual errors, acknowledged by name the assistance of four British anti- or counter-cult leaders.)

These are examples of what too often occurs in such literature – from where such inaccuracies can be picked up by the tabloid press, so maintaining public ignorance and reinforcing public prejudice.

Simply by being prepared to talk to the movements, it is possible to avoid such incorrect criticisms. To refuse to talk to them means deliberately maintaining ignorance about them; ignorance breeds fear; and fear breeds intolerance and prejudice.

However, it would be equally inexcusable to ignore all the criticisms of movements. This book is not a whitewash job. Some of the new religions, or their leaders or members, have gone badly wrong over the last few decades. Quite a few of the entries, then, do include criticisms – and the movements have been invited to respond to the charges.

Some movements were unhappy about criticisms being included in their entries. They are included for several reasons. First, if my account of a religion is to be objective, then 'objective' doesn't mean a one-sided glowing account such as could have been written by the movement itself. Second, in some cases the criticisms have become part of the 'mythology' associated with the religion. Just because a myth may not have a factual basis doesn't diminish its power in the public mind; these criticisms in particular need to be addressed. Third, if the criticisms are untrue or inaccurate, this is an opportunity for the movement to put the story right. And fourth, if the criticism is valid, then the best thing a religion can do is to be up front and honest, and admit it made mistakes, and show how it has moved on from them. Religions are human organizations, and humans are imperfect. Sometimes human pride, lust for sex or power, carelessness or honest mistakes, have caused leaders of certain religious movements to behave appallingly; this applies, both historically and now, to mainstream religions just as much as to new religious movements – a point easily forgotten.

STRUCTURE OF THE BOOK

The next chapter examines just what is meant by the word 'cult', why it is not a helpful word, and why other terms such as 'alternative religions' might be preferred. The chapters which follow deal with a number of issues related to alternative religions. They are intended to be informative, and also to be challenging: to challenge the way we often automatically think about such matters, and to suggest new ways of looking at things – hence the deliberate 'irreverence' of the chapter titles in what is a serious book. Because these chapters deal with controversial and often contentious issues where there is a wide range of viewpoints, my own voice will be more apparent here than in the remainder of the book.

The last chapter in Part One is a very brief introduction to the main religious traditions of the world, to provide a context for the entries on individual modern movements.

Part Two contains entries on individual movements, organized into five sections:

- Christian origins
- Other 'Religions of the Book' origins
- Eastern origins
- Esoteric and Neo-Pagan movements
- Personal development movements

Any categorization of this type is arbitrary. There can be no argument that, for example, the International Church of Christ fits into the Christian section, that the Hare Krishna movement fits into the Eastern section, and that Wicca fits into Neo-Paganism. But not all movements are so easily placed. Transcendental Meditation, for example, although sometimes thought of as a personal development movement, began with a Hindu guru, and so is in the Eastern section. Although the Church Universal and Triumphant has Christian elements, its focus on Ascended Masters puts it in the Esoteric section; however, the Liberal Catholic Church, though it is strongly Theosophical, is placed in the Christian section because of its roots in the European Old Catholic Church.

In several cases, the placing of movements in particular sections might be debated; but despite its drawbacks, readers have said that they find the classification system helpful. To aid the locating of individual entries, an alphabetical listing of all the movements in the book has been provided in the Appendix on page 534.

Each section begins with a brief introduction, to provide an historical context and to draw together some common themes from the section.

The entries themselves discuss the origins and history, and the beliefs and practices, of the movement concerned. Much of the information came from the movements themselves, from their literature and from correspondence and interviews with spokespeople. Some information came from secondary sources: books, articles or academic studies about the movements.

The next section of the book consists of an extended case study of a Church which fell apart after its founder died; at the latest count it has over 200 offshoots. To the best of my knowledge, this chapter is the only widely available, objective, in-depth study of this fascinating family of Churches. But it is not just a study of one relatively small group of heterodox Christian Churches: it is an examination of a microcosm of ideas and events which occur throughout the macrocosm of alternative religions – authority problems, abuse, scandal, millenarian theology, schism and much more can be seen in this one group of Churches, perhaps more than in any other.

DEFINITIONS

I have provided a whole chapter on definitions of the words 'cult', 'sect', 'new religious movement', 'alternative religion' and so on, which demonstrates how these terms mean different things to different people, and the dangers of using such terms loosely. Throughout the book I use 'new religious movement' (NRM) and 'alternative religion' more or less interchangeably. I also use 'religion', 'movement', 'organization', 'group' and 'Church' almost interchangeably, obviously depending on context.

The way that the word 'myth' is used in this book should be explained. In normal everyday usage it tends to mean a story that is not true, a made-up fable. In this book, in common with many other books on comparative religion, it is used to mean a story whose value doesn't depend on its historicity. A myth in this sense may or may not have a factual basis, but what is important is the way that the story has endured, and is used for teaching, and contains power. Evangelical Christians object to the word 'myth' being applied to any part of the story of Jesus; but the ideas of the virgin birth, and healing miracles, and even a god dying and coming back to life, are very common myths in other religions. Applying the word 'myth' to the virgin birth of Jesus, or to Joseph Smith's golden plates in Mormonism, or to the travels to the mysterious East of Madame Blavatsky, G.I. Gurdjieff or L. Ron Hubbard, does *not* mean that I am suggesting that these accounts are factually untrue. They are important parts of the narrative of the religions; they are myths of the religions.

Christ spark is a term sometimes used to refer to the spark of the divine flame, or the tiny fragment of God, which some believe is within each human being.

Esoteric comes from the Greek for 'inner' or 'within', and applies to something taught to or understood by the initiated only.

Exoteric, from the Greek for 'outside' or 'the outward form', applies to knowledge available to the uninitiated.

Evangelical means a Bible-believing (usually Protestant) Christian who stresses the need individually to be 'born again' for salvation.

Evangelistic means preaching the Gospel, spreading the word, openly taking the message to others.

Fundamentalists are those who have absolute conviction of belief in the fundamental precepts of their faith, to the extent that they will not even consider the possible validity of other beliefs.

Heresy and heretical beliefs are always defined as such by the establishment Church (of whatever religion), usually as a means of enforcing their control over spiritual dissidents. The word actually comes from the Greek for 'choice' which, historically, many religious hierarchies have tended to deny to individuals.

Occult comes from the Latin for 'hidden'; it is used in that sense in both astrology and astronomy today, without any devilish connotations.

Rite and ritual are used to refer to any religious ceremony or formal observance, whether communal or individual.

Note that the word 'orthodox', unless it is used with a capital letter to refer to the

Eastern Orthodox Churches, is used throughout in the sense of mainstream, establishment beliefs, in contradistinction to unorthodox, heterodox, unusual and perhaps heretical beliefs.

The capitalized word 'Church' refers to a (usually Christian) denomination or sect, however large or small; in lower case it means a religious building.

The word 'God' is capitalized when referring to belief in one God (monotheism), and in lower case when referring to belief in several gods (polytheism); no judgement on the truth of the belief is implied. In common with modern practice, pronouns relating to the deity are not capitalized.

The capitalized word 'Charismatic' refers to Churches and believers who emphasize the (Pentecostalist) Gifts of the Holy Spirit, including speaking in tongues and prophecy; in lower case it refers to an individual's personal charisma, the powerful personality which attracts followers.

Founders and leaders of movements are referred to by the most usual or the most convenient name (often simply the surname) rather than by the honorifics members of the movement may use. Thus Moon rather than Reverend Moon, King rather than His Eminence Sir George King, Prabhupada rather than A.C. Bhaktivedanta Swami Prabhupada, etc. No disrespect is intended. Similarly for convenience, the Church of Jesus Christ of Latter-day Saints, for example, is generally referred to as the Mormons.

In recognition of the facts that we live in a multi-cultural society, that not all readers of this book will be Christians, and that many of the movements included in this book are not Christian, the terms CE and BCE (Common Era, and Before the Common Era) are used instead of the Christian-specific AD and BC (*Anno Domini*, In the Year of the Lord, and Before Christ).

Biblical quotations are taken from the Authorized Version of the Bible unless otherwise stated.

To avoid awkward grammatical constructions, the word 'he' is sometimes used instead of 'he or she', when speaking generally of founders or leaders of movements.

Notes

[1] J. Gordon Melton's *Encyclopedia of American Religions* has 1,730 detailed entries; Benjamin Beit-Hallahmi's *The Illustrated Encyclopedia of Active New Religions, Sects and Cults* has 2,200 brief entries. Also strongly recommended is the Religious Movements Homepage of the University of Virginia, established by Professor Jeffrey K. Hadden, which may be found at http://cti.itc.virginia.edu/~jkh8x/soc257/welcome. This website, and Melton's massive encyclopedia, are essential resources for the serious study of 'new' or 'alternative' religious movements.

[2] Computers for Christ website at http://www.seii.com/ccn/cults/fal10.txt.

[3] Michael Jordan, London: Carlton Books, 1996: 98. This book is extremely unusual in that the publisher's name does not appear anywhere in it; the only indication is the ISBN.

CHAPTER 2

Is it a cult, or a real religion?

The problem of definition

EVERY cult-watcher will hear this question just about every working day. The question contains an unexamined assumption: that there is a difference in kind between a cult and a real religion, a proper religion. On the one hand, you have the bad guys in black hats; on the other, the good guys in white hats.

LIFE ISN'T THAT STRAIGHTFORWARD.

Is it a cult, or a real religion? That all depends on what the speaker means by 'cult', 'religion', and, for that matter, 'real'. But surely, the questioner will say, we all know what we mean by 'cult': one of those fake religions that brainwashes people into joining, takes all their money, then commits all sorts of abuse on them, and then they all commit suicide.

If that is indeed what the word 'cult' means, then there have been mercifully few of them. In later chapters we'll look at brainwashing, abuse, and suicide; for now, let's look at what different people mean by the word 'cult'.

WHO IS SPEAKING?

Lewis Carroll's Humpty Dumpty said, 'When *I* use a word... it means just what I choose it to mean – neither more nor less.'[1] The words people use can sometimes tell us more about the speakers' own agenda than what they are talking about.

In the field of religion, the use of words is complicated by beliefs and emotions, both those of the speaker, and those which speakers wish to arouse in their audience. With such terms as 'cult' or 'sect', the intended meaning can be quite different depending on whether the speaker is, for example, a tabloid newspaper headline writer, an anti-cultist, a lawyer, a psychologist, a theologian, a religious teacher, or a sociologist of religion. Both journalists and the anti-cultists tend to use the word 'cult' more than 'sect', probably because it carries more emotive 'baggage', and so its use furthers their aims; in general parlance, 'cult' is almost always a strongly disapproving term, whereas 'sect', though often also having pejorative overtones, is closer to a neutral term.

☼

'Evil cult stole my daughter!' It's a great tabloid headline. You hardly need the story beneath it. The word 'cult' is ideal for a sub-editor on a tabloid paper; it is short, punchy and emotive. It can also readily take powerful adjectives: 'sex cult', 'suicide cult', 'evil cult'. It is an excellent word for both playing off and reinforcing the readers' existing prejudices. The word is rarely defined; newspapers make use of readers' stereotyped assumptions.

The word is a gift. In four letters it can contain a paragraph's worth of implied information: the story is about a movement which is probably religious, but very definitely peculiar in its beliefs; it has dubious, probably unseemly practices; it entices people into itself through a combination of lies and promises; it takes their money; it has a powerful and unscrupulous leader; it manipulates members' minds and their lives; it breaks up families; it does great psychological harm to its members; it is most certainly not what your Great Aunt Maude would recognize as a religion. The rest of the story simply fills in the details: who, where, what, etc. Whatever the protestations of the movement concerned, or of cult-watching academics, no journalist is going to waste valuable headline space on the cumbersome term 'new religious movement'. The journalist's ultimate aim is to write stories which will sell newspapers, and so enhance his reputation and ensure his livelihood. Balance and objectivity might actually be detrimental to those aims.

Many of the associations of the word 'cult' in the minds of both journalists and the general public are encouraged by opponents of new religions, who in some cases will have fed the story to the newspapers in the first place.

The London-based Cult Information Centre, according to its general secretary Ian Haworth, defines a cult as:

a group having *all* of the following five characteristics:
1 It uses psychological coercion to recruit and indoctrinate potential members.
2 It forms an elitist totalitarian society.
3 Its founder leader is self-appointed, dogmatic, messianic, not accountable and has charisma.
4 It believes 'the end justifies the means' in order to solicit funds or recruit people.
5 Its wealth does not benefit its members or society.[2]

One technique sometimes used by anti-cultists is to explain carefully that cults, by definition, use deception in their recruitment techniques, and some form of mind control over their members; their aim is not spiritual (in fact, they say, many cults are nothing to do with religion) but all to do with power, control, and taking as much money as possible from their members as quickly as possible. To avoid the possibility of legal action, anti-cultists are usually careful not to state explicitly that, for example, the Hare Krishna movement or the Family or Scientology are cults, but they leave listeners in no doubt that such movements are cults – and therefore, *by definition*, have the characteristics they have already specified.

But it was they who defined 'cult' in those terms in the first place.

'CULT' OR 'RELIGION'?

It has been said, not entirely tongue-in-cheek, that the difference between a cult and a religion is about a million members. Consider Christianity, for example. Jesus' group of followers, when he was still alive, might be described as a Jewish sect; the same could probably be said, after his death, of the Jerusalem church led by his brother James. Under Paul the focus changed, and the reformist Jewish sect became the cult of Christ. In terms of numbers and influence, it was only under the Emperor Constantine that Christianity, with state recognition, became a full-blown religion.

It has also been said that 'a cult is a religion that I don't like.' This is hardly a definition, but it does contain an element of truth. Some anti-cultists, including some MPs, argue that all cults should be registered. When pressed, they are rarely prepared to say which sorts of movements should be registered and which shouldn't, or even what the criteria for such a choice should be – or who should decide. If we register, for example, the Unification Church and the Family, what about that rather exuberant Pentecostal church down the road? What about the Baptist Church? Or the Methodists? Where do you draw the line?

If you make such a choice, it will necessarily be arbitrary. The choice of which movements to include in this book as alternative religions, and which to leave out as mainstream religions, although based on several criteria, was ultimately an arbitrary decision (see page 12). There are no straightforward dividing lines.

OTHER USES OF 'CULT'

In popular usage the word 'cult' is usually seen in negative terms: mindless devotion to an unscrupulous cult leader. But it has many other usages, often emotively neutral. Historians speak of the mystery religions of ancient Greece and Rome as cults. Among other meanings, the word 'cult' can refer to a movement which emphasizes devotion, dedication, a deep focusing on a particular person or place. Within the Roman Catholic Church, for example, it is quite acceptable to speak of the cult of

Mary, or the cult of Medjugorje or Knock.

The word 'cult' is used in non-religious contexts as well. *The X-Files* and *Buffy, the Vampire Slayer* are often described as cult TV programmes. This isn't just an American phenomenon; the British TV series *The Avengers* (especially with Diana Rigg) and *The Prisoner*, with its powerful slogan 'I am not a number, I am a free man', had 'cult' status. So do certain rock stars, film stars, football stars. A 'cult novel' has a readership which may initially be small, but which is dedicated, sometimes obsessive; think of Tolkien fans, or readers of Terry Pratchett's *Discworld* books. The word 'fan', after all, is short for 'fanatic': the former is socially acceptable; the latter brings us back full circle to the popular conception of a 'cult'.

The point can also be made here that even the negative connotations of religious 'cults' are to be found in everyday society.[3] The much-criticized deceptive practices supposedly used to recruit members of new religions are not too different from the manipulations used to persuade us to vote for one political party or another. New religions are often accused of only being after their members' money. Perhaps some are. But the 'Get Rich Quick' schemes advertised daily in newspapers and magazines generally mean that a few get rich at the expense of the many who send in their application fee. Banks, building societies, life assurance schemes: all of them entice us with promises of increased wealth, but all of them, as businesses, are primarily concerned with making profits for themselves. Religious movements are often criticized for the commitment of time and energy they demand from their members; but in some 'high flier' professions such as management consultancies, it is not uncommon to see people putting in 60-hour weeks and burning out by the age of 35.

All organizations which expect a commitment from us put on a smiling face, or have other inducements to attract us in, and minimize the inconvenience, expense and sheer hard work which will be involved. We accept this as part of life. But it may be that with religious movements we expect too much from them, and then judge them too harshly when they fail to deliver perfection.

As for sexual abuse, which is one of the most common accusations made against 'cults', there is no doubt that, in some cases, it has happened. But when a Catholic bishop is discovered to have 'love-children' from a long-term mistress, it is noticeable that it is he who is criticized, not the Church of which he is a leader. Paedophiles working in children's homes are rightly condemned; but it isn't argued that all children's homes should be closed down. How many female secretaries have been taken advantage of by their bosses? In the film industry, for decades, the cliché that pretty young actresses started their career on the casting couch had an element of truth.

None of this is right behaviour, wherever it occurs. It is equally wrong if such abuse occurs within a business, or a mainstream religion, or an alternative religion – though one might reasonably expect a higher standard of behaviour from a self-proclaimed religious person or organization. But to characterize 'cults' as 'religions that abuse', and then to imply that most if not all new religions are *de facto* cults, is simply bad reasoning. Yet if it's said quickly enough, and firmly enough, and often enough, such an insult to our intelligence can slip through what has crudely (but perhaps not inaccurately) been called our crap-detection system, and embed itself in that area of our mind which harbours irrational prejudices.

SOCIOLOGICAL DEFINITIONS

The words 'cult' and 'sect' are not only used for pejorative purposes. They have been used by sociologists, in very precise ways, for over a hundred years.

Sociologists of religion, like other academics, write mainly for each other and for their students: an ivory-tower audience, rather than the general public. They usually aim to be methodologically agnostic, not judging the truth of movements' beliefs or the efficacy of their practices, and so are generally anxious to avoid any emotive overtones in their use of language. Because of their popular pejorative usage, such words as 'cult' and 'sect' would, perhaps, be better avoided altogether. But both have a long history of use within sociology, and it is likely that they will continue to be used.[4]

Ernst Troeltsch (1865–1923) distinguished between Churches and sects. The former, he said, have members from all social strata, with perhaps an emphasis on higher-status groups, while the latter tend to be predominantly lower class and socially disadvantaged; members are born into a Church, but they are recruited, probably with a conversion experience, into a sect; a Church is a large, formal, hierarchical organization; a sect is small, with (at least in theory) more equality between members; the Church is the repository of authority and salvation through the priesthood; a sect takes its authority directly from the Bible and/or God, and believes (in principle) in the priesthood of all believers. These are what sociologists call 'ideal types', subject to variation in reality; but the distinction is clear.

However, early sociologists, when writing of Churches and sects, were generally thinking only of distinctions within the Christian religion in the West, at their own time. Although movements with non-Christian origins certainly existed in the West in the late nineteenth and early twentieth centuries, they were not as prominent as they are today. There have been other cultural changes which make earlier sociological typologies less useful today than they once were; for example, the wave of NRMs from the late 1960s onwards has tended, with some exceptions, to appeal to middle-class, well-educated people; although they may be *disaffected* with mainstream society, they are not socially *disadvantaged* in the way meant by earlier sociologists when describing the typical membership of sects, i.e. low income, low educational level, and working class.

William Sims Bainbridge, discussing the problems of terminology, points out that in ordinary usage 'a denomination is a moderate, respectable religious organization, whereas a sect is a troublesome one.'[5] Sociologists, he says, have tended to use the term 'sect' to mean a schismatic movement[6] and/or a religiously intense movement, within the traditions of a more mainstream religious culture (e.g. the early Methodist and Baptist Churches were Christian sects). In distinction, he says, a 'cult' is a 'culturally innovative new group', one that stands out from its milieu.[7]

The term 'new religious movement' (NRM) is used by most present-day sociologists of religion to avoid the pejorative overtones of 'sect' and 'cult'. This might seem a good solution, but once again there are problems of definition. Not all NRMs are new; the Hare Krishna movement strongly objects to the term because, it says, its beliefs and practices can be traced back for several centuries. Rodney Stark avoids this problem by redefining an NRM as a 'novel religious movement',[8] thus neatly distinguishing it from a sect, which is seen as an intense offshoot within the tradition of its parent body. Eileen Barker proposes an arbitrary cut-off point at World War II; new religious movements are those founded, in their present form, since then.[9] A further refinement might be to consider an NRM within its present cultural environment; so the Hare Krishna movement might well be a centuries-old variant of Hinduism in the East, but ISKCON is a new religious movement in the West. There are further problems with the term NRM. Some movements labelled NRMs are to do with psychology or self-help, rather than religion; should these so-called 'human potential movements' be classed as new *religious* movements?

The term 'alternative religion' avoids the 'newness' problem of 'NRM' by simply and arbitrarily distinguishing between mainstream, established religions and movements which are an alternative to the mainstream. Again this depends on social context; there is nothing alternative about being a Mormon in Salt Lake City, but there might well be in Welwyn Garden City. And again the dividing lines can be debated endlessly; this division, just like the others discussed above, perhaps says more about the speaker's *perceptions* of the movements than about the movements themselves. It's relatively easy to decide, for example, that Methodists and Baptists are mainstream, while Jehovah's Witnesses and Christadelphians are alternative religions, but what about Unitarians, Quakers and the Salvation Army? This distinction tends to depend partly on an intuitive and individual understanding of what is generally socially acceptable as 'standard' or 'normal', and partly on how far the beliefs of a movement have changed from the spectrum of 'mainstream' beliefs within the parent religion.

The term 'alternative religion' thus ties in rather well with how mainstream Christians write about 'sects and cults', but without being pejorative. Generally they make their decision on theological grounds, including whether the movement is Trinitarian or not – and many of the 'alternative' Christian movements are not. It's irrelevant that, as we shall see, some of them are centuries old, and sometimes well respected. If they don't believe in the Father, Son and Holy Spirit as distinct and equal persons of the Godhood, as set out in the historical creeds of Christianity, or if they deviate from other long-established mainstream Christian beliefs, then Christians label them sects or cults. This is why certain well-established Churches, clearly not *new* religious movements, are included in this book: not because I think of them as 'cults', but because they are treated in this way by Christian counter-cult writers. Put simply, books on cults by Evangelical Christians tend to use words such as 'cult' and 'sect' to show that such movements are, in contrast with their own true faith, false religions.

Terminology, then, is a minefield. If words such as 'sect' and 'cult' are used, it is necessary to explain what one means by them, to distinguish one's usage from the popular pejorative perception of the words.

And whenever one encounters any of these terms, it is vital to look at who is using it, and why, and to ask what *they* mean by it, and what their agenda might be.

WHAT IS A RELIGION?

The answer to this question is far more complicated than it might appear at first sight. For example, any definition that includes the idea of God immediately excludes most varieties of Buddhism. If you open it up wider, to something as vague as 'a philosophy of life', it would include Marxism – and indeed, arguments have been made for Marxism being considered as a religion. Open up the definition just a little wider and football matches, rock concerts and science fiction conventions could be considered as religious activities. In the Bible we find 'Ye cannot serve God and mammon' (Matthew 6:24); the *Shorter Oxford English Dictionary* defines mammon as 'A term of approbrium for wealth regarded as an idol or an evil influence. Usually more or less personified.' In these terms, 'serving mammom' is almost seen as religious.

Most of us would probably shy away from describing football, rock music or science-fiction fandom as religions – but in the devotion of their followers, and in some of their joint activities, they certainly have aspects which are analogous to 'religious'. When 50,000 rock fans hold up their lit cigarette lighters during their band's anthem (note the word), this is effectively a religious moment. Anyone who has been in that situation, freezing in a field at midnight, will recognize the feeling of fellowship or communion or oneness with each other, and the sense of loving identity with the band. It may not be religion, but it is undoubtedly religious.

In more conventional terms, a useful definition of religion might be something like: 'A social construct encompassing beliefs and practices which enable people, individually and collectively, to make some sense of the Great Questions of life and death.'

For most purposes, the common-sense approach is as useful as any: if it looks like a duck and quacks like a duck, then we might as well call it a duck. But it isn't always that straightforward. In this book, for example, Neuro-Linguistic Programming (NLP) is included, but *not* as a religion; it is described as a technique, or a series of techniques, or a process. It is used by some religions, and NLP as a philosophy does exhibit some characteristics which are sometimes found in some religions, but overall the balance comes down against it being labelled a religion.

But what about Transcendental Meditation? It too would describe itself in terms of a technique, or a series of techniques, or a process. Many people who use TM are members of other religions, or of none; they use it because they find it a useful technique, not for any spiritual or religious reasons. And yet it is usually thought of as religious, by the same reasoning that NLP isn't: a matter of balance. By its origins, by its initiation ceremony, by some of its teachings and practices, TM tips the balance the other way.

There has been a great deal of controversy, for several decades, over whether or not Scientology is a religion. Leaving to one side the fact that it calls itself a religion – indeed, its correct name is the Church of Scientology – academics have argued persuasively both for and against it being a religion (see page 447).

This is not simply academic game-playing: there can be practical consequences from all this quibbling about definitions and terms. In most countries there are distinct tax advantages for religions. Whilst critics of the Church of Scientology have long alleged that one of the reasons for Scientology's decades-long attempts in many countries to be classed as a religion was these not inconsiderable tax benefits, the Church of Scientology strongly denies this. TM, in contrast, didn't want to be classed as a religion. For some years it had been running very successful courses in American schools, when it was challenged on the grounds that religion may not be taught in American public (i.e. state) schools. TM argued that it was not a religion; it fought a long and hard battle in the courts, and lost.

SUMMARY

Throughout this book, the terms 'alternative religion' and 'new religious movement' (NRM) are used almost interchangeably, but there are differences. The first is used to mean a religious movement which is an alternative to the mainstream religions (and so would include, for example, Jehovah's Witnesses); the second refers specifically to movements founded in their present form and within their present cultural environment, since World War II (and so wouldn't).

The word 'sect' is used to mean an enthusiastic splinter group with much the same beliefs but with different emphases from its parent religion. And on the occasions when the word 'cult' is used, it is usually within the context of negative public perception, or of the anti-cult movement.

No movement discussed in this book thinks of itself as a cult. Some see themselves as religions, or religious groups, others more as philosophical schools, and others as self-help or personal development systems. Many are not happy about being in 'a book about cults', and about being included side by side with groups which perhaps *they* consider to be 'cults'.

'Cult' really has become a four-letter word. In popular usage it is nearly always pejorative. The question 'Is it a cult, or a *real* religion?' simply isn't a useful question; it has nothing to do with the movement itself, and everything to do with the beliefs and preconceptions of the questioner. More useful questions are, 'What does this movement believe? What does it do? Where did it come from? What is its context?' These are the sorts of questions which this book addresses.

Notes

[1] Lewis Carroll, *Through the Looking Glass*, Chapter 6.

[2] Article distributed by CIC, first published in *Assignation* (ASLIB Social Sciences Information Group Newsletter), vol. 11, no. 4, July 1994.

[3] For a full-length discussion of this, see Deikman 1994.

[4] The following discussion is a very brief summary of some of the terms and definitions which have arisen during a century of Sociology of Religion. For more detail, see Scharf, Towler, Robertson, Wilson 1970 and 1990, and other texts listed in the Bibliography under Religion and New Religious Movements (General).

[5] Bainbridge 1997: 23.

[6] It is tempting to see a connection between 'sect' and 'section', but there is in fact no etymological connection; 'sect' is from the Latin *secta* = 'follow', while 'section', 'bisect' etc. are from the Latin *secare* = 'cut'.

[7] There is an indirect etymological connection between 'cult' and 'culture'; 'cult' is from the Latin *cultus* = worship, from *colere* = inhabit, cultivate, protect, honour with worship; 'culture' is more linked to 'cultivate'.

[8] In Bainbridge 1997: 24.

[9] Barker 1989, 1992: 145.

CHAPTER 3

Sects appeal

*Conversion, recruitment, mind control
or brainwashing?*

'PEOPLE do not join cults. They are recruited,' says Ian Haworth, general secretary of the Cult Information Centre.[1] 'People are recruited by a method not a message.' According to Audrey Chaytor, chairperson of FAIR (Family Action Information and Resource):

> Most people are recruited into cults, sects or groups, and my organization would never agree that they 'join'. This is done by deceitful practices and promises which put pressure upon the victim to make a quick decision and once that has been achieved it is very difficult for them to leave.[2]

These statements are fairly representative of the anti-cultist stance.

There are several assumptions implicit in such statements. First, 'cults' are deceitful by their very nature. Second, they trick people into joining. Third, this is the reason people join, rather than their wanting to join and making a conscious decision to do so. Fourth, there is the implicit assumption that 'cult recruits' are weak-willed people, easily seduced by the cults. And leading from that is the underlying belief that no one in their right mind would ever join such a movement.

As was seen in the previous chapter, statements of this nature can show more about the motivations and assumptions of the speaker than about the subject under discussion. For example, is it actually the case that 'cults' are deceitful by their very nature, or is this simply someone's definition – in which case we need to ask, whose definition?

Should we, as some anti-cultists do, distinguish between 'cults' and 'real religions' largely on their techniques of recruitment? After all, people are born into, say, the Anglican Church, or choose to join, for example, the Baptist Church; they're not actively recruited into them. This takes us back to early sociological distinctions between a 'Church' and a 'sect', which are far less clear cut now than they were in the early twentieth century. It also ignores the facts that today many people change from one denomination to another, just as they change careers, sometimes several times; and also that many people today *are* born into alternative religions – any religion that has been around for more than a couple of decades will have not only second- but third-generation members. And there is recruitment into mainstream Christianity, in the form of evangelistic crusades. Billy Graham's crusades are the obvious headline example, but such crusades, large or small, are an inseparable part of Evangelical Christianity on both an organizational and a personal level. Telling other people the 'Good News' in the hope of their salvation is a vital part of being an Evangelical; Jesus did, after all, tell his disciples to be fishers of men (Mark 1:17).

But surely mainstream religion doesn't use 'deceitful practices and promises which put pressure upon the victim to make a quick decision'? Anyone who has been urged to get up out of their seat and ask Jesus into their heart *before it's too late*, after a hell-fire and damnation sermon, might disagree.

That's an extreme example, of course, deliberately couched in extreme language to make the point of comparison; but many of the criticisms of 'cult' recruitment also use extreme cases. The point is that high-pressure recruitment techniques are not unique to 'cults'.

It is often assumed, as mentioned above, that 'cult recruits' are weak-willed people, easily duped into joining such a movement. Cults, we are told, prey on the lonely, the vulnerable, the insecure. In her study on recruitment into the Unification Church, *The Making of a Moonie*, Eileen Barker examines the possibility that cult recruits are more 'inadequate' than the rest of us. Using standard criteria for assessing social and psychological vulnerability, she compares the characteristics of Moonie recruits with a control group, and concludes:

> most Moonies do not differ significantly from their peers with respect to characteristics which could form independent criteria for assessing whether or not a person could be classified as prone to 'passive suggestibility'.[3]

Most of us, at some point in our lives, are lonely, vulnerable, insecure. Most of us don't join alternative religions, even when the opportunity is offered to us. In fact, Barker found that even of those people who went to Moonie weekend workshops – i.e. people who were already interested – 90 per cent didn't join. And of those who did join, more than half left within two years.

THE BRAINWASHING HYPOTHESIS

After the Korean War, psychologist Robert J. Lifton examined the phenomenon of American captives who had 'gone over' to the beliefs of their Chinese Communist captors. He found that under extreme conditions, including captivity, torture or the threat of torture, sleep deprivation and so on, some captives appeared to have been converted to their captors' ideology. The popular term 'brainwashing', though often incorrectly associated with Lipton, was actually coined by a journalist, Edward Hunter; apparently it is a poor translation of the term *hsi nao*, 'to cleanse thoughts'.[4] Hunter's description of the effects of brainwashing is rather sensationalist:

> The intent is to change a mind radically so that its owner becomes a living puppet – a human robot – without the atrocity being visible from the outside. The aim is to create a mechanism in flesh and blood, with new beliefs and new thought processes inserted into a captive body.[5]

It is this model which was taken on board by anti-cultists, with the *cachet* of Lifton's name attached, despite Lifton's own doubts about its applicability. It is obvious that the recruitment techniques of religions bear little if any resemblance to the terrible conditions under which some soldiers ended up making pro-Communist statements (in fact, even under those circumstances it was no more than one in 50[6]).

One of the main proponents of the brainwashing theory, Margaret Singer, is a clinical psychologist at Berkeley, California. In the 1980s she frequently appeared in court on behalf of members' families or ex-members, arguing that movements had used brainwashing or 'coercive persuasion' to remove the free will of members. Singer conducted a study for the American Psychological Association (APA) on Deceptive and Indirect Methods of Persuasion and Control (DIMPAC), but in 1987 the APA rejected it as 'unacceptable' on the grounds of 'significant deficiencies', saying that 'the report lacks the scientific rigor and evenhanded critical approach necessary for the APA imprimatur.' Several academic studies showed that Singer's position on coercive persuasion was unsound and 'was not generally accepted in the relevant scientific communities',[7] and courts began to pay less attention to her testimony. In one court case, *US vs Fishman*, the court concluded that Singer's theories 'regarding the coercive persuasion practised by religious cults are not sufficiently established to be admitted as evidence in federal law courts.' Because Singer and her colleague, sociologist Richard Ofshe, spent much of their time testifying in court cases as paid expert witnesses, they twice attempted to file a lawsuit claiming they had been 'the victims of a conspiracy by the APA and a number of individual scholars to destroy their reputations and income.' The cases were thrown out of court before coming to trial.

With the discrediting of the brainwashing hypothesis, the majority of anti-cult and counter-cult spokesmen have now stopped using the term 'brainwashing' in their public pronouncements, in favour of 'mind control' or Lifton's own preferred term, 'thought reform'. However, the damage has been done: tabloid newspapers still use the word, and in the popular consciousness 'cults' are still associated with 'brainwashing'.

Ian Haworth, General Secretary of the Cult Information Centre (see Chapter 9), often uses the term 'mind control':

> More than 500 cults that use mind control to recruit and keep members are operating in the United Kingdom, with many registered as religious orders, therapy groups or management training organizations, an anti-cult expert [Haworth] warned yesterday.[8]

A CIC leaflet[9] lists 26 'mind control techniques', including hypnosis, love bombing, time sense deprivation, verbal abuse and change of diet, as well as less obviously negative 'techniques' such as dress code, chanting and singing, and games. The explanation of 'chanting and singing' as a mind control technique is 'Eliminating non-cult ideas through group repetition of mind-narrowing chants or phrases'; it might be thought that this could apply equally to the congregational recitation of the Creed or the Lord's Prayer in any Christian church.

As for hypnosis, there are some psychologists who dispute its very existence. The generally accepted view is that hypnosis is a state of relaxation leading to heightened suggestibility; but also, that no hypnotist can make someone do something they don't want to. The Svengali-like hypnotist forcing his victims to do his evil will, so familiar from films, is a fiction. However, this is not to say that a charismatic leader can't have a powerful influence on followers.

WHY SUCH EMPHASIS ON DECEPTION?

Why is it that Haworth, Chater and others put so much emphasis on the actively deceptive techniques of movements in the recruitment/conversion process? There may be many reasons, but two possible ones will be considered here.

First, there seems to be a deep, underlying belief that no one in their right mind would ever join such a movement, with its strange beliefs and odd practices. A moment's reflection will reveal the inherent conservatism of such an attitude. Millions of people believe weird and wonderful things which more sane and sensible people (note the assumptions!) 'know' to be rubbish. Who decides what is an acceptable belief and what is a crazy one? What is unconventional in one context is perfectly natural in another. There might even be a certain cultural prejudice here, with echoes of imperialism; at its extreme, it might be called racism. It's all right for an Indian to be a Hindu, but not for a white Surrey stockbroker who has had a good English education, dammit, to start chanting 'Hare Krishna'.

Second, we all have a natural tendency to want to blame someone else. To be able to point an accusatory finger at the brainwashing, mind control or thought reform techniques of a movement removes any element of self-blame from an ex-member who might now wonder how they devoted so many months or years of their life to a movement or an ideology with which they have now become disenchanted. (Much the same process leads ex-lovers, after a relationship has ended acrimoniously, to absolve themselves of 'blame' by accusing the other person of deceiving, seducing or otherwise enchanting them. It is much more comforting to say 'I was fooled' than 'I was such a fool.') It can be difficult for an ex-member simply to admit, 'Yes, I did believe that, then.' It takes real guts to say, 'Perhaps I was naïve; perhaps I made a mistake.' It's so much easier to say, 'I was conned; I was deliberately tricked, cynically manipulated and deceived.'

There are probably as many reasons why people join movements as there are members themselves; some of these will be considered shortly. But for anti-cultists, a new member's personal reasons for wanting to join are less important than the alleged deceptive recruitment techniques of the movement that recruited him or her. Here is a brief analysis of how the common anti-cultist stereotype of cult recruitment – and of cults – is formed:

1 In a specific case – a particular individual joining a particular movement – make an assertion of mind-control, deception, etc.
2 Add this assertion to a list of dubious recruitment techniques of cults.
3 Define a cult, at least in part, as a movement which practises any of these techniques.
4 Use the word 'cult' when talking about the 'dangers' of movements such as Scientology, the Moonies, ISKCON, the Family, etc.
5 Therefore these movements 'by definition' practise mind control, deception, etc.

The fact that logically this is an invalid train of reasoning is irrelevant; it works perfectly well in practice, as a glance at any tabloid story about cults will confirm. And note that the initial assertion (1) need not be objectively verified; it could come from the testimony of a disgruntled ex-member in the course of exit counselling, or from the exit counsellor himself or herself, or from a concerned parent whose child is in a movement. Indeed, this sort of 'reasoning' depends for its emotive power on such individual anecdotes. In contrast, Barker's study, referred to above, examined 1,000 potential Moonie recruits.

The Moonies, the tabloids tell us, are a dangerous organization because as a cult they practise mind control when enticing people to join. There are around 500 Moonies (members of the Unification Church) in Britain. People join and people leave – they have quite a high turnover of members – but the number has stayed fairly constant for some years. One UK Moonie has said wistfully – and jokingly – that he almost wished mind control *did* work.[10]

WHEN DECEPTION DOES OCCUR

Even if mind control, like coercive hypnotism, is a fiction, and even if the anti-cultist/tabloid arguments about cult-recruitment are largely fallacious, it shouldn't blind us to the possibility that not all recruitment is completely above board. Sometimes there is deception, at one level or another. A potential recruit might be invited for a meal, or to a discussion group, without being told that it is a meeting of a particular movement. If the Mormons come to your door they immediately identify themselves and their Church; many other movements don't. The author has twice been stopped in the street by complete strangers and invited to a church service, and only by very persistent questioning extracted the information that it was the London Church of Christ. Withholding information which might put someone off is probably seen as common sense by the movement concerned, but in reality it is a form of deception. (This isn't only practised by *new* religious movements; for some years the Seventh-day Adventist Church, to avoid alienating potential enquirers, deliberately adopted a policy of anonymity, presenting its books, magazines and meetings simply as Christian rather than Seventh-day Adventist. This practice attracted claims of deception, and was eventually dropped.)

Another form of 'passive' deception is letting someone believe that joining a movement means fun and fellowship once a week, and neglecting to mention the hours and hours of commitment expected of you once you have actually become a member. And another is proclaiming that a movement will set you free, when in reality it may impose strict restrictions on how you spend your money, on your social life, even on whom you may marry.

These are all common deceptions practised by some new religious movements when recruiting new members, and there are many more. This book certainly does not seek to excuse them. Neither do academics specializing in new religions. But as Barker points out:

> Recruitment that employs deception should, however, be distinguished from 'brainwashing' or 'mind control'. If people are the victims of mind control, they are rendered *incapable* of themselves making the decision as to whether or not to join a movement – the decision is made for them. If, on the other hand, it is just deception that is being practised, converts will be perfectly capable of *making* a decision – although they might make a different decision were they basing their choice on more accurate information.[11]

Religious movements, preaching Truth, Purity and other ideals, are understandably sensitive to accusations of deception. It still goes on, certainly, but 'Heavenly Deception', where some movements considered it acceptable actually to lie in the furtherance of the greater Truth, is far less common now than it was in the 1970s.

As will be seen throughout this book, a lot of the over-enthusiastic new movements of the 1960s and 1970s have matured in recent years – though this is disputed by some cult-watching organizations:

> Religious movements may say they have moved on in their practices, and may even appear to have done so, but it is not generally found that this moving on is anything other than a shallow approach. Most people respond to criticism by changing their front image, do they not?[12]

This may be so; but such comments appear to carry the implicit assumption that new religions aren't to be trusted, that they are not honest or sincere. Is this an assumption that we are entitled to make?

To finish this chapter, let's look at some fictional examples of how and why people join new religions. These are fictional in that they are not real-life case histories, nor even based on real cases; neither are the movements based on any specific groups – but these stories contain elements which frequently occur.

CHRISTINE

It's Christine's second term at university. She's missing her home desperately: her parents; her sister Anne, with whom she's shared a room, confidences, mutual support, and growing up, for most of her life; her friends, especially her boyfriend from school. She's found it really difficult to settle in, and hasn't made many friends. She knows she's to blame; she's not into sports, she doesn't enjoy clubbing, she doesn't see the point in getting drunk and then throwing up, and she was horrified by the boast on the front page of the student newspaper that there wouldn't be a virgin left on campus by the end of Freshers' week. There was certainly one, she knows.

She's just not fitting in.

And then the work: she'd never realized how much reading she would need to do for each essay; she'd meant to catch up with it over the Christmas vacation, but it was so great being back home again, she hardly did any, and now she's four essays behind.

And then this second-year student picked her up, and she drank too much (or maybe he put something in her drink), and now she wasn't a virgin any more, and she was terrified she might be pregnant, or have caught something, and she felt really grubby and *ashamed*.

She thought of going to the chaplain. She used to go to church back home, not all that often, but Christmas and Easter and a few other times, and she'd been really involved for a while when she was 14, and she knew that priests were good at listening. But the chaplain was official, he was part of the university, and he might report back to the authorities, and what would happen then?

She's sitting, miserable, on her own as always, in one of the campus cafés, and somehow she gets talking to someone, and she doesn't know how it happened, but suddenly she's pouring it all out, and pouring out the tears as well, and she feels so embarrassed; but this other girl is so calm about it all, so sympathetic, and suggests that Christine comes over to her place that evening; she knows someone who's really good at listening, and he might be able to help.

'Is he a priest or something?'

'No, he's not a priest. He's really great. Understanding.'

Christine goes along, and the guy is really great, and understanding, and then half a dozen others turn up, and then (she doesn't know how this happened either) they're all praying for her – and suddenly it feels as if a great burden's been lifted off her, and she's crying again, but this time it's with relief, and she's actually smiling and laughing, for the first time in ages.

She gives her hall of residence phone number to the girl she first met, Fiona, and she's invited to go over there again a few days later, and soon she's going two or three or four times a week. They're fantastic people, they genuinely care about her; they're not into clubs and drugs and getting drunk either; with a shock she realizes *she's fitting in!*

After a few weeks she moves out of her student room, and moves into her new friends' shared house. It makes sense; she's spending a lot of time there anyway, and now she won't have to get a bus across town for every Bible study and prayer meeting. They're every evening now, and sometimes there are things on during the day as well.

She still goes to lectures; well, sometimes. They just don't seem important any more, compared to what she's learning in the group.

One day she happens to go past her old hall of residence, and thinks she'd better check her pigeon hole (she'd forgotten to leave her new address for forwarding mail), and there are over a dozen letters from her sister, each one more desperately asking why she hasn't written back. She *had* written to her, saying she'd be moving in with these new friends, so what was she getting so upset about? Christine mentions Anne's letters to Peter, the leader at the house, and he says there's probably no point her writing back, because her sister wouldn't understand, and anyway, it's better if her new life is kept separate from her old. Christine feels a bit of a twinge; it is a long time since she's seen her sister – in fact, it must be months now, because Easter's been and gone, but with being so busy all the time, and not going to lectures any more, she simply hadn't noticed when term changed to vacation and back to term again. It would be nice to see Anne again, but Peter's probably right. He usually is.

This scenario – or variations on it – is quite common at universities and colleges all over the country. There are several different Christian movements, with more or less standard Evangelical theology, which specifically target university students. A few might be affiliated to local mainstream churches; others are smaller, newer movements, which have attracted a certain amount of controversy in recent years.

TONY

Tony is 29. He has a good job with a management consultancy, and his salary is way above the average. He earns it: he's usually at the office by 7.30, and he often doesn't leave till 9 or 10 at night. He spends his weekends writing up reports. But it seems to be getting harder for him to achieve what he used to be able to do, as he remembers, almost effortlessly. There are kids coming up behind him, a year or two out of university, and they're the ones getting commendations for their work, not him. By now he'd have expected to be an associate, on track to partnership; but he's stuck at his level, and others are beginning to overtake him.

He sees an advert for a personal development course: only £350 for a long weekend, Friday evening through to Sunday. He works like crazy to give himself a clear weekend (when did he last have one of those?), and does the course. The difference is phenomenal; he's turbo-charged when he returns to work on Monday. His confidence, his authority, his decision-making abilities – all of them pretty good to start off with, he has to admit – shoot through the ceiling. Over the next few weeks he knows he's back on track; two different partners have stopped by his desk and complimented him on his work – one of them hinted about him joining the golf club.

A few months later Tony is beginning to flag a bit, when the personal development company contacts him. There's a one-week course coming up, with just a few vacancies left; normally it would cost £2,500, but because he did so well on his earlier course, they're prepared to make him an unrepeatable offer at £1,795, if he sends a deposit of £595 right now.

Tony reaches for his chequebook.

SOPHIE

Sophie is 43 and divorced, with three children in their late teens. She's fairly happy with her secretarial job, has a pretty good social life, and is generally quite content with her life. She's been using Tarot since she was a teenager, and occasionally does readings for friends; she's also pretty good at interpreting dreams.

For the last four or five years she's been going to Mind, Body, Spirit festivals, and has been making a real effort to deepen her personal spirituality. She spent nearly a year attached to a Wiccan group, but decided not to go through initiation to become a full member of the coven. There were probably several reasons for this, but one was that she'd never lost weight after her third kid, and when her marriage split up she had a chocolate binge for a few months, and she'd never lost that weight either, and there was no way she was going to take part in a skyclad ritual, even though the members of the coven were really nice people whom she knew wouldn't mind; but she just couldn't do it.

After she left the Wiccan group she signed on for a course on 'Shamanism in the City' at her local college. It was fascinating, and she learnt a lot, but she found it difficult going into a trance state, and when the course finished she decided not to continue with the advanced course.

Recently Sophie went to a Pagan conference, which she really enjoyed, and where she met a group of druids whose meetings were only a few miles away from her home. She's always been sort-of interested in environmentalism – she once carried a placard at an anti-bypass demo – and she likes the idea of integrating this with a spiritual approach. She's started going to the druid moot, and thinks she's finally found the right path for herself.

RICHARD

Richard was brought up in a regular church-going family. He's 22, he's just left university and started his first job, and he's living on his own in a town where he hardly knows anyone.

Richard began with the best of intentions, to go to church every Sunday, and he found a good church of the same sort of flavour as he was brought up in. But there's no one to encourage him to go there every single week. One Sunday morning it's raining, or he wakes up with a hangover, or with a new girlfriend, or he just can't be bothered; and he doesn't go. It can be very easy to break the habits of a lifetime, when you're in a different environment. Once he's skipped church one Sunday, and then again the next week, by the third week he's established a new habit, of not going.

The new habit is easier, and the freedom of the new lifestyle is more fun – but Richard feels guilty about it. He knows his parents would disapprove if they knew, so he doesn't mention it; and if they mention church he hedges, or even lies.

Richard rationalizes it to himself. He's learnt a lot in recent years; he's learnt something about other religions, so he no longer accepts that his own is unique, even though he may still believe that it's *right*. But he's learnt of some of the weaknesses or uncertainties or fallacies of the religion he was brought up in, and he's actually a little angry that these were hidden from him as a child. He begins to intellectualize his turning away from practising the faith of his fathers.

But Richard hasn't actually stopped believing in God. With a child-like belief, he knows that God is missing him in his church; and strangely, Richard is missing God as well. There's an old cliché about everyone having a God-shaped hole inside themselves; if you've been brought up in a religion, and you've now turned your back on it, you become very aware of that hole. It might be something missing deep inside yourself, if you had a real faith before; or it might be something missing in your life, if your church-going was more of a habit than a deep commitment.

What Richard misses most of all is the companionship, the fellowship, of being with other people whom he's known for years, singing hymns together, praying together, going to Bible study together – having fun together in a spiritual setting.

He misses all of this, though he doesn't really admit it, even to himself. He's turned away, and it's now very difficult to turn back. It's like saying sorry after a serious argument; he would have to admit that he was wrong.

But there's still that hole. It's empty, and it's yearning to be filled.

And then Richard meets someone who seems so much more alive than him; the guy is bubbling with it; there's a visible joy in him; it's shining in his eyes. The two of them get talking. Richard becomes more aware of the *something* that he's missing, and he realizes that this other person has it.

The guy's going to a meeting that night; why doesn't Richard come along? 'It's just a few friends. I'm sure you'll get on with them.'

Richard realizes very quickly that they're religious, and that it's not a religion he's familiar with; in fact, it's one of those peculiar cults. He's deeply suspicious of the whole thing. It turns out it's not even Christian; they've got some sort of Eastern beliefs, Buddhist or Hindu or something, but they don't wear robes or anything, and they all seem to be both decent and intelligent people (not at all like he'd have expected them to be), and Richard's not stupid; he's not going to fall for a religious con; he's sensible enough not to get sucked in.

Within a couple of months he's inviting other people along. It's the most important thing in his life. It is his life. People can see it shining in his eyes.

These are fictional scenarios; they are not based on any individual cases or groups. They show four very different people, joining four very different movements for very different, individual sets of reasons. We'll meet up with Christine, Tony, Sophie and Richard in a later chapter, and see how they're doing a few years later.

Notes

[1] Article distributed by CIC, first published in *Assignation* (ASLIB Social Sciences Information Group Newsletter), vol. 11, no. 4, July 1994.

[2] Audrey Chaytor, chairperson of FAIR, in correspondence with the author, 18 September 1995.

[3] Barker 1984: 203.

[4]Shupe, Bromley and Oliver 1984: 83. I am grateful to Jane M. Cooper for drawing my attention to this in her BA dissertation *From Thought Reform to Mind Control: The Cultivation of the 'Brainwashing' Model*, School of Oriental and African Studies, University of London, 1999 (unpublished).

[5]Hunter 1956: 309.

[6]Alan W. Scheflin and Edward M. Opton, *The Mind Manipulators*, cited in Shupe, Bromley and Oliver 1984.

[7]Quotations in this paragraph are from J. Gordon Melton, 'Brainwashing and the Cults: The Rise and Fall of a Theory', Introduction to the forthcoming *The Brainwashing Controversy: An Anthology of Essential Documents*, edited by Melton and Massimo Introvigne, available on the CESNUR website, http://www.cesnur.org/testi/melton.htm. See also Wilson and Cresswell 1999: 226–8.

[8]*The Independent*, 19 April 1994.

[9]*Cults on Campus*, Cult Information Centre, 1993.

[10]Conversation with the author.

[11]Barker 1989: 17.

[12]Joy Caton of Deo Gloria, in correspondence with the author, 19 September 1995.

CHAPTER 4

Would you let your daughter marry one?

Problems for families of members

THE resonances in the title of this chapter are quite deliberate. Twenty or so years ago it was not uncommon to hear someone say, 'I've got nothing against Blacks, or Indians, or Pakistanis, but I wouldn't want my daughter to marry one.' Racial prejudice still occurs, but a combination of legislation, children of different races and cultures going to school together, and no doubt many other factors, has made it socially unacceptable. For many it has been a very real change in attitude; walk down any city street in Britain, and you'll see plenty of young couples of mixed race.

Racial prejudice and discrimination haven't gone away entirely, of course. They still occur in the workplace, in all sorts of social environments, and on the front pages of tabloid newspapers every time there's a trade war or an international football match. It's more open, perhaps more widespread, in some continental European countries, where ultra-right-wing political parties attract disturbingly large followings. But for many people, there is now a strong awareness that racial discrimination is not only illegal, but also morally wrong. In contrast, *religious* discrimination is not illegal in most countries, and in some it is actually enshrined in law.

Discrimination is the outcome of prejudice; prejudice often stems from fear, and fear often comes from ignorance; and sometimes ignorance is deliberately sustained by misrepresentation, if not actual lies.

Of course, it is not possible, or in any way desirable, to force people to like other people, or to agree with other people's beliefs. Multi-culturalism, including religious pluralism, is not about totalitarian conformity; it is about accepting someone else's right to be different from you, but to be entitled to equal treatment.

Ignorance, fear and prejudice operate on both an individual and a social level. In Britain and the US in the 1990s, social workers enlisted the aid of the police when accusing parents of 'Satanic Ritual Abuse', an astoundingly successful moral panic engineered by a small group of Evangelical Christians (see page 339). In some parts of Germany, Scientologists are barred from taking any government office.

With alternative religions one should not pretend that everything in the garden is lovely – sometimes, very evidently, it isn't. But if factual information about movements can be presented in a fair and objective manner, the level of ignorance about such movements could be reduced, so perhaps defusing some of the fear, and thereby decreasing the unthinking prejudice against them.

THE DISTRESS OF FAMILIES

For some parents, the fear is not that their daughter might marry one, but that she might become one. 'Evil cult stole my daughter' may well be a great tabloid scare-story headline, clichéd and pandering to prejudice – but when it is your daughter, the fear and pain and upset are very real.

The distress of parents, siblings, friends and colleagues of those who have joined NRMs, and who have vanished from their lives, is very real. Simply telling them that the vast majority of people who join will leave within a few months, or at most a year or so, doesn't take away the pain. Neither does telling them that everyone has the right to belong to whichever religion they choose. Most friends, even most parents, accept that. But this is *their* son, *their* daughter, *their* close friend. It's personal. It's immediate. In a way, it's analogous to a bereavement. We all know that everyone has to die some day. We all know that hundreds of people die every day even in our own county, thousands in our own country. That doesn't lessen the pain when it's someone close to us who dies. One is abstract knowledge; the other is personal grief.

In some cases, sadly, losing someone to a new religion can be like losing them to death: they go off, perhaps abroad, leaving no way to contact them, and their families and friends don't know if they will ever see them again. Sometimes they never do.

This does still happen, but very rarely.

It happened far more in the 1960s and 1970s. Movements were new, young, idealistic, enthusiastic – and, in some cases, astonishingly naïve, even culpably stupid. Sometimes movements behaved like thoughtless adolescents. Most parents must know what it is like when their teenager goes to a party, decides to stay overnight, and doesn't think to phone home to let them know. Some movements were like this. They were full of excitement: they knew that Jesus was going to return at any moment, or that their guru was leading them to a fantastically high plane of spiritual fulfilment. This was what was real; their old lives (if they ever thought of them) were pale, hollow, pointless, dead. And after all, didn't Jesus say to leave your father and mother and follow him?

Well, yes; but he didn't say not to leave a forwarding address.

The cult-watching organizations have played their part in helping such movements to realize just how incredibly thoughtless they were being. Many movements, including some of the former worst offenders in this respect, now actively encourage their members to keep in touch with their families, by letters, by phone, by visiting home from time to time. Some even encourage families to visit them, to see how their son, daughter, brother or sister is living. It's sometimes been a slow process, but progress has very definitely been made.

There's another factor worth noting. Back in the 1960s and 1970s, a lot of movements had communal living of one sort or another: community homes, ashrams, live-in temples. Far fewer do so now. From the Family to ISKCON, a new recruit has to work pretty hard to persuade the movement to let them live in-house. The great majority of members of the great majority of movements today live in their own homes, hold down jobs in the outside world, and are generally part of the wider community. As movements have matured from their adolescence, as their longer-term members have reached their forties and raised their own children, a lot of movements have at least started to become, in Bryan Wilson's ungainly term, denominationalized.[1]

Rather than filling distressed parents with even more fear, by telling 20-year-old stories as if they happened yesterday, it is far more helpful, far more constructive, to look at movements as they often actually are today.

FERVENT EVANGELICALS

It is worth noting at this point that it is not just alternative religions which have been the cause of parental concern. There are parents and friends of 18-year-olds who have gone off with, for instance, Operation Mobilization (OM) or Youth With a Mission (YWAM) who have been just as concerned as those whose youngsters have joined ISKCON, the Moonies or the Family. OM and YWAM are Christian 'youth mission' organizations, and both are well respected within the 'normal' Evangelical community. The Anglican, Methodist or Baptist church on the corner of your street might well sponsor one of their young people to work for a year or so with either of these organizations or similar ones, doing a combination of volunteer social work and evangelism in a host of countries around the world.

For parents and friends, though, even if they are church-goers themselves, such whole-hearted commitment to 'working for the Lord' can come as a shock. Adults in their forties and fifties easily forget the energy and enthusiasm which 18- or 25-year-olds can pour into something they believe in; and when that belief is the deep, loving relationship of a born-again Christian with their Lord, it can fill their hearts and minds to the exclusion of everything else – some would say, to the exclusion of common sense, tact and consideration for others. It's more important for them to go out and serve the Lord than to go to college or university to gain qualifications for their own future. 'What if' – and this is a genuine question sometimes asked by young, enthusiastic Christians – 'what if Jesus returns, and because I didn't go out to Africa or India, someone isn't saved who might have been, while there was yet time? The fate of their soul was in my hands, and I failed them because I was selfishly thinking about my own life rather than about their soul.'

Because they are within the mainstream Evangelical Christian community, organizations such as OM and YWAM would probably never even consider that some people might be concerned about their activities, especially their influence over young people. They're respectable; they're members of the Evangelical Alliance; they have support from most of the denominations. It's very easy for fervent Evangelicals to forget that a lot of people, even a lot of Christians, might find the level of their spiritual commitment disturbing; because it's outside their own experience, such zeal can be alien and frightening. Worried relatives of 18-year-olds have asked whether OM or YWAM are cults. The effects can be just the same.

WHAT CAN PARENTS DO?

What can be done by parents of children (who may, of course, be in their twenties or thirties) who have joined NRMs? First of all, let's look at how *not* to do it. For simplicity of grammar, let's assume that it's your daughter who has joined a movement.

If you know where she is, you could go there, and bang on the door, and demand that they let your daughter go immediately, or else... Or else what? Will you take her by force, against her will? Apart from the fact that this is kidnapping, and illegal, it would almost certainly antagonize your daughter, and strengthen her resolve to stay with the movement.

You could phone every day and demand to speak to her. If she, for whatever reason, doesn't want to speak to you, this will probably only strengthen your belief that either she's being held against her will, or else she's been brainwashed.

You could try to take legal action. Some parents have actually tried to gain legal custody of their adult child by persuading the court that the child is mentally unsound, unfit to take her own decisions; after all, no one in their right mind would join a cult. Even in the highly unlikely event that you win (in some American cases the parents did win), you'll end up with a highly resentful daughter who will never trust you again; you've publicly branded her mentally incompetent.

You could take your story to the newspapers. No one likes bad publicity; surely they'll let your daughter go now? But that's assuming that the movement has effectively abducted your daughter; it's ignoring the fact that she's joined them of her own free will (whether you can believe that or not). And after you've splashed her story all over the tabloids, do you really think she'll want to come back to you? The only benefit (if you can call it that) from such a story is the titillation of a million or so readers.

All that you've managed to achieve, from any of these actions, is to drive a deeper wedge between you and your daughter. Is that what you wanted? If you go in with all guns blazing, you've lost before you start. If you argue with her, it becomes confrontational; your positions will be polarized; you are likely to achieve exactly what you don't want – a strengthening of her resolve to stay in the movement.

☼

There are better ways, ways that at least stand a chance of keeping you in touch with your daughter, even if they don't fetch her out of the movement straight away.[2]

Write to her, gently explaining that you're worried, partly because you don't know anything about this movement she's joined, but mainly because she's not been in touch: could she at least drop you a line, just to let you know she's okay? Don't go overboard; don't let her think you're bullying her with emotional blackmail. Tell her that you love her, that you're not trying to force her to change her mind, that what-ever happens now or in the future you'll be here for her.

If she doesn't want to meet you, talk to you, write to you (and there may be all sorts of reasons why – children of all ages do fall out with their parents), see if you can find an intermediary, someone she trusts – maybe her brother, maybe an old schoolfriend – simply to pass on your message to her, and to bring back reassurance to you that she's all right.

Find out about the movement. If it's not described in this book, check your local library and major bookshops to see if you can find anything about them. You might not; they may be too small and obscure, or too new. This is where the 'cult-watching' organizations can be tremendously useful. They may have access to information from the movements themselves; to academic studies; to press cuttings about them; to accounts by members and ex-members, both favourable and unfavourable. They may also have contacts within the movement, senior people who may well be concerned that their movement is causing distress, and who may themselves be willing to mediate. Even if not, they are likely to have useful contact addresses, phone numbers, names. They should also be able to tell you something about the movement: what they believe, what they do, whether there has been any cause for concern in the recent past – or, just as important, whether there hasn't been. It's important to learn something about the movement's beliefs, and where they fit into the wider religious scene. Are they radical Evangelical Christians? Are they a Buddhist or Hindu-based group? Do they have a living guru? Where are they coming from? What makes them tick?

If you are able to learn something about the movement's beliefs and practices, you'll be in a better position to talk with your daughter – *not* in order to convince her that the movement is wrong, but to understand better why she has felt drawn to them, what it might be that they offer that answers a need in her.

If you are able to talk with her, don't be antagonistic. Ask questions, about the group's beliefs, about their lifestyle, about what it is that attracts her to them. She might be living in her own home and have a job, and just spend her evenings with them; or she might be living in a communal home, full-time with the movement, in which case she might not have much money; you could also ask if there's anything she needs: clothes, toiletries, etc.

It will probably be obvious to her that you'd rather she hadn't joined the movement, and that you'd be much happier if she left; but try to let her know that you respect her right to choose her own religion, her own lifestyle.

If she's abroad, whether living in an ashram in India or doing missionary work in South America, you're more likely to communicate by letter than to meet her. Again, you could check if she has everything she needs. You might not be happy about sending her money, in case she gives it all straight to the movement, but you could offer to send her clothes, or other things she might need. You could also pay for an open-date air ticket back home, and leave this at her nearest airport – but be careful how you put this idea to her. If she thinks you're trying to bribe her out, she won't thank you for it; you need, instead, to let her know that the ticket is there for her *if* she needs it, *if* she decides at any point that she wants to leave.

Whether you meet her, talk on the phone, write to her, or contact her through an intermediary, don't let her feel you're putting on any pressure for her to leave. She's an adult. You love her, and you also respect her. It is her choice to stay or to leave, and no one else's. You'll still love her, and respect her, and be here for her, whatever she chooses to do.

This all looks fine in theory; but when it comes down to reality, when it is your daughter, it won't be that easy for you. It will be even more difficult if it's a movement about which you've heard bad things, or if you're a firm believer in your own religion, and your daughter (or nephew or friend or whatever) has joined a religion you believe is wrong theologically. Don't argue. Don't preach. You only need to look at Northern Ireland to see what can be the effects of deeply entrenched opposing beliefs. Trying to prove that your beliefs are right and hers are wrong will get you nowhere except either side of an ever-higher wall between you.

It is distressing when any family is split on any issue. Sadly, it happens all the time, for all sorts of reasons. It doesn't need a 'cult' to separate a lively 19-year-old from his stultifyingly boring family, or a sensitive child from two parents who are always arguing, or from an aggressive or drunken or abusive father, or from an over-protective mother who won't accept that her little girl has grown up. Even if it's a perfectly well-adjusted, happy, normal family (whatever 'normal' means when applied to something as complex as the relationships to be found in families), kids move on. University, a job in another part of the country, a boyfriend or girlfriend – all these (and many other things) can separate a young person from their family, and sometimes permanently. How many parents think that their daughter's choice of partner 'isn't good enough for her'? And how often does this create such tension that the daughter really doesn't want to visit her family any more? Or the young person could marry someone from another country and move there, or simply get a job abroad. They have their own life; they start their own family. Travelling thousands of miles to see parents who are from their 'old' life isn't always an appealing option, even if it's financially possible. People go their separate ways. Grandparents don't always get to see their grandchildren growing up.

All of these separations are common occurrences. It doesn't need a 'cult' to divide offspring from their parents, temporarily or permanently. But if a religion, particularly a new religion, is part of the picture, it will often be seen as the cause of the split, when it might instead be the effect, or the means, or be quite unconnected. We all look for something or someone else to blame, and 'one of those weird cults' is an excellent scapegoat.

One further thought on this subject. An 18-year-old girl decides to go off and join a movement. She's given a new name, maybe even a male name. She has her beautiful long flowing hair shorn off; she wears old-fashioned clothes which, among other things, completely desexualize her. In fact, she'll never know the joys of sex, or of having children; she's gone through a bizarre ritual in which she's symbolically married the founder of her movement, even though he's long dead. She gets up before dawn every day. She spends long hours every day chanting and praying. She's cut off from the outside world. Her family will rarely, if ever, see her again.

And her family are proud of her because, of course, they're a traditional Catholic family and their daughter has become a nun.

It's all a matter of perception.

Notes

[1]Wilson 1990:109. See also page 59.

[2]Some of the ideas in the next few paragraphs are discussed in more detail in 'A Middle Way', chapter 12 of *New Religious Movements: A Practical Introduction* by Eileen Barker, which is strongly recommended.

CHAPTER 5

So hard to say 'Goodbye'

Problems of leaving a movement

THERE are many members of NRMs who are clearly very happy to be members. There are many ex-members who have few or no ill feelings about their time in a movement; they have moved on, for whatever reason, but in many cases they remain in friendly touch with people who are still members. But there are also ex-members who for various reasons are unhappy with their time in a movement. The mistake of some cult-watching groups is to generalize from these specific cases, and to make the leap of logic that the bad experiences of a minority of members make all members 'victims'.

For some members of alternative religions, the real problems don't come with their joining, or even with their time in the movement, but when they decide to leave. First of all we'll return to our four characters from Chapter 3, and see what's been happening to them over the next year or so. Remember that these cases are fictional, as are both the movements and the cult-watching organizations involved; but these stories are examples of some of the problems that people can encounter in a movement, or when they're leaving.

Following the four stories, we'll look more generally at some of the things that can go wrong within religious movements, and why members might want to leave, and some of the practical difficulties they might encounter.

CHRISTINE

After she's been living with the others for a month or so, Peter suggests that Christine should get a job; someone has to pay the rent on the shared house, and most of the others work full time for the Lord. Sometimes Christine feels she's doing that as well; somehow she ends up doing most of the cooking and other housework when she returns from her job in the evenings. But as Peter says, whatever part you play, it's all the Lord's work.

Her university work has gone completely by the board, but that doesn't matter. Jesus is returning soon, and she's helping to spread the word – isn't that more important than studying for a degree? Anyway, what use will a degree be when the Lord and King is ruling his earthly kingdom, with her as one of his handmaidens? That's what Peter says. Anyway, a woman's place shouldn't be at university; she should be serving the Lord at home, raising children for him if she's married, supporting his workers if she isn't.

It takes a surprisingly long time before Christine realizes she's become an unpaid servant, and is paying for the privilege. All the money she earns goes into the communal pot, not just for the rent, but for feeding six people. She has to do the grocery shopping as well; she's given a fixed amount, and has to return any change, and Peter checks the receipts.

When she gets a small pay rise at work, she doesn't tell Peter, hiding the extra few pounds a month. She hasn't had any new clothes for over a year; the shoes she wears to work are almost worn through. One day, in her lunch hour, she buys a new pair of shoes. She keeps them at work, changing into them when she gets there, but one day when she leaves work she forgets, and goes home in them, and Peter notices, and explodes at her. *Does she not realize that she has been stealing God's money?* He tears the shoes off her feet and takes them into the back yard and pours petrol over them and burns them, making her stand in her bare feet to watch.

The next day Christine goes to work and doesn't come back. A girl in her office lets her sleep on her couch for a while. But, despite everything, she misses the group of people she's lived with for over a year; she misses the fellowship, the prayer meetings and worship, the Bible studies. At least she's taken her Bible with her.

A week or two later she comes out of work, and Fiona, the girl she first met in the campus café, is waiting for her, and suggests they go for a coffee. They all miss her, Fiona says, and Peter's sorry he upset her, and they'd love her to come back. Christine's tempted – she misses them as well – but it crosses her mind that what *they* are missing is her money, her cooking, cleaning and washing up. It takes an effort, but she says no. Okay, says Fiona, but let's at least keep in touch, I mean, we're friends, aren't we? She persuades Christine to give her the phone number of the place she's staying.

Every evening, sometimes three or four times, they phone her: Fiona, or Peter, or one of the others. The girl she's staying with has had enough; she asks Christine to go. But where *can* she go? She's not been in touch with her family all this time; she couldn't possibly go back to them now. She's dropped out of university, so that avenue's closed as well. Where can she go?

She goes back, and everyone is really nice to her for a while; but it's not long before everything is as it was before. She's determined that she's going to leave, but she just can't see how to do it. And worse, Peter is now making it very clear, in their daily Bible studies, that anyone who turns their back on the Truth is committing the unforgivable sin against the Holy Spirit. If she leaves, she'll be risking her salvation.

Eventually she goes to speak to a local priest, and he phones his diocesan adviser on new religions, and he phones a cult-watching organization which, from the various clues Christine is able to provide, eventually manages to track down the movement that Peter's little house-group is part of. The movement has a track record of over-zealous 'shepherding' by some of its leaders, where leadership has become control. The cult-watching organization is able to give the priest sufficient information about the movement that he has some understanding of the environment Christine has been living in for the last year or so. With Christine's permission, they also let her university chaplain know that the movement is recruiting there.

Christine returns to her family while she considers whether to resume her university career. Through discussions with other Christians she is reassured that attending her local Church of England church won't condemn her to damnation.

TONY

Over the last year Tony has been on several personal development courses, and there's no doubt that they've had an effect. He's sure that it's partly due to them that he's finally gained the promotion to associate that had been eluding him for so long. But he's begun to have some doubts about the courses. Each one promises new personal skills, new revelations about how he can increase his personal power and his interpersonal skills; but as a management consultant who has done this many times himself with expensive reports for companies, he realizes that each course is really just a recycling of ideas from previous courses he's been on: different words, but the same principles, with a couple of new specific applications each time. The basic ideas are fine; the techniques *do* work; but is each new course really worth what they charge for it? Especially as each one costs more than the one before.

He's beginning to think that he's got just about as much as he can out of these courses; he doesn't think he'll take any more. Then he's sent an invitation to take a course at a much higher level. This is the big one, and not everyone is invited to do it. It promises real personal empowerment and advancement. With this under his belt he could become a trainer himself, if he wanted to. It's a ten-day course, and it costs £4,325. Tony decides to do it.

It turns out that the secret of personal empowerment and advancement, which is kept until the final day, is something he'd first read in a self-help paperback he'd bought several years ago. Tony asks for his money back. They refuse, pointing to the small print. Tony storms out, furious.

Over the next few days he calms down a bit. True, he's spent thousands on these courses, but he'd been able to afford it, and he had gained a lot from them, in self-belief, assertiveness, presentational abilities, and much more. And he still has all his course packs; he could give himself refresher training whenever he needed to. But he still feels he's been conned.

Then he meets a former colleague, who had also done some of the courses, and who starts talking to him about the cult. 'What cult?' asks Tony. The training company. 'But it's not a cult; there's nothing religious about it,' says Tony. But his former colleague is adamant. He knows someone in a cult-watching organization, and they've got massive files on this company; all it's concerned with is making as much money as possible, as quickly as it can, out of gullible people. Tony protests that he wasn't gullible; yes, it was expensive, but he'd taken what he wanted from the courses, and then left, and he'd found a lot of it useful. 'No, you've been fooled into thinking that,' says his former colleague. He persuades Tony to go and look at the files, and to talk to people who *really* know all about it.

The files, and the cult-watching counsellor, are very convincing. The more Tony reads, the more he hears, the more angry he becomes about how much money they'd suckered out of him.

Once he has been taught the truth about the cult and what they did to him, everything he had gained from them turns to ashes. The presentational skills, the sharper decision-making, the incisive insights: all gone. His self-belief withers; the only way he can hang on to any self-respect at all is by putting all the blame on the cult, which had obviously used mind control techniques to suck him in.

Tony has become a professional victim.

Three years on, Tony now spends all his spare time campaigning against the company, 'this wicked cult'. He is bitter against them, for what they did to him. They cheated him out of thousands of pounds, for false promises and a load of psychobabble. Cults like this are deceptive, destructive, evil. They must be stopped.

SOPHIE

Sophie stayed with the druid group for nearly a year, before moving on to something else. She's a searcher, a joiner. Maybe one day she'll find a movement which satisfies all her spiritual and social needs; maybe not. It doesn't worry her too much. She's decided to spend a week of her holiday at Glastonbury; she's heard there are some really interesting groups there, and someone's teaching how to use crystals to get to know your inner self. She'll give it a try.

RICHARD

The longer Richard stays with the group he's joined, the deeper he gets into their teachings. Initially, of course, he wasn't going to 'join' anything, but he got on well with the other people, and he particularly liked the sort of relaxed intensity of their teaching sessions, their discussions, their meditations. He didn't feel they were putting any pressure on him to commit himself and, completely contrary to everything he'd ever heard about groups like this, they never once asked him for money. Oh, they'd pass the hat around for contributions to a communal meal, and he bought a few magazines and a couple of books, but that was all.

They followed the teachings of a guru (though they didn't call him that) who'd been born in America to Hindu parents. His teachings had some aspects of Hinduism, but really only as a background to the core teaching on approaching the transcendent God through focusing on the immanent 'godness' within each person.

Once Richard knew where the group was coming from, and who their guru was, he went to the library and borrowed a few books and checked them out. The history, the teachings, the practices, all were as he'd already discovered; they'd developed over the 30-odd years the movement had been around, but not markedly. There was some negative stuff as well: a sex scandal back in the early 1970s, some accusations of financial mismanagement, some domineering leaders, a couple of case histories of people who had wanted to leave their ashram, and had found it difficult to do so.

Richard made notes on all this, and at the next meeting questioned the leader.

'That's right: we screwed up. The Founder made some fairly serious mistakes early on – he is human, after all! – including putting people into positions of authority who simply weren't ready for it.'

What had happened, and in later research Richard found this had happened in several of the new religions of the 1960s and 1970s, was that the movement had grown too quickly, too soon. At that time, partly because of the Founder's Hindu background and partly because of the whole 'Spirit of the Sixties', he'd thought that living in communal groups was the best way of doing things. But some of the leaders of these communes had been members for less than a year themselves; they might know the *information* that the Founder taught, but they hadn't all fully internalized it into their lives. And some of them were far too young, far too immature, to have been put in a position of such authority. The worst case was a guy of 21 who'd been fairly heavily into drugs before encountering the Founder's teachings, but who had embraced everything about the movement wholeheartedly, and really seemed to understand what it was all about, in spiritual truths, way of life, everything. By the time the Founder heard about it through the newspapers, this leader had had sex with over a dozen of the most attractive girls in his commune, telling them it was the best way to achieve Oneness; he'd also appropriated the funds of his commune and gone back to drugs in a big way. He was the worst, but there had been several others who had 'gone bad' in similar ways: too much power too young, without the maturity to handle it, and abusing that power to their own advantage.

It had shaken the Founder to the core, had even made him, for a while, doubt his own teachings. He had spent over a year working on repairing the damage, first to the individual members who had been abused, and then to the movement itself. He completely rethought the practicalities of his movement. He scrapped the commune system, encouraging members to live in their own homes and have jobs and a life outside the movement. He set up a training centre where he, and eventually a few of his most trusted, older, more mature followers, taught potential leaders not just how to teach the truths, but how to lead. As the movement became more established, he set up a management structure with checks and balances, with job rotation and elections, so that no one person could become too powerful. And then he stepped back from leadership himself, to concentrate solely on developing the Teachings, and making them more relevant to the Western world.

Richard decides to continue going to the group. Over the next few years he attends training sessions at the movement's spiritual retreat; he becomes a local leader, and eventually becomes the UK leader. In that time he's also married, bought a house, started raising a family, moved on in his career. He still has a normal job, four days a week. He devotes one day a week to visiting local groups; they pay his expenses, so he is neither out of pocket nor making anything financially from his work for the movement.

The past never goes away. One Sunday a tabloid newspaper runs a story about the 'secretive sex sect'. Almost every detail in it is wrong. By careful misdirection it gives the impression that the particularly juicy sex scandal at the heart of the story has just happened, and is symptomatic of the movement. The paper hadn't contacted the movement when writing the story; Richard contacts them now, giving them the actual facts. As a result of this incident Richard writes an introductory booklet, to be given to anyone who comes to their meetings, and to be sent to religious affairs journalists. Whatever accusations might be flung at them in the future, secrecy wouldn't be one of them.

Critics would say that Richard has been successfully sucked into the movement, and that he's now sucking others into it; he would say he's found a belief that works for him, and that whether other people join or not is up to them.

OTHER PROBLEMS OF MEMBERSHIP

In Chapter 3 it was argued that 'brainwashing' or 'mind control' in the recruitment of members is at best a dubious concept, with no evidence to support it. But we mustn't throw the baby out with the bathwater. There is such a thing as indoctrination, or conditioning, and this can help a movement to keep a hold on members, and make it more difficult for them to leave. First, the extreme case.

There has been some evidence, in some movements, and far more so in the past than today, that new recruits were sometimes kept on a poor diet and kept awake late into every night being fed the teachings of the religion. Physically and emotionally weakened, they would begin to accept everything they were told. They would learn to obey the leader of the group which recruited them, in every tiny detail; his word would be absolute law. How much more, then, must they revere the founder of the religion, or if the founder has passed on to greater things, his or her chosen successor?

As they progress through the ranks, members would be careful not to voice any doubts they might have, about doctrine or practices. They would see the example that is made of those who do open their mouths. They would be encouraged to watch each other for signs of weakness, and report them. Never knowing who might be watching them, they would follow the prescribed line with openly expressed enthusiasm and zeal – whatever they really felt inside. Critics point to comparisons with Germany in the Third Reich, or the former Eastern European communist bloc.

This is an extreme portrayal, but this sort of indoctrination or conditioning has occurred in several alternative religions in the past, and perhaps still does in some. But it is very much the exception, not the rule.

There is, however, another form of conditioning, which is less aggressive, more subtle, and probably longer-lasting.

CONDITIONING, AND OVERCOMING IT

We are all conditioned by our parents, by our schools, by many other factors in our upbringing. It's called socialization; it's a perfectly normal parental and societal action, performed with love and care in order to help us grow up into responsible adults capable of functioning in society – but it's conditioning all the same.

Perhaps for the first time in years, a new recruit to a movement is with a bunch of really wonderful people who are sharing their beliefs, and their lives, with him. He grows to love them, and he knows they love him. And if he finds himself, in some dark moment, doubting what he's become involved in, he's got others to support him, to help him strengthen his faith. They are his friends; they pray together, and read the Bible or the Founder's teachings together, and worship together, and encourage each other.

This could be called conditioning; it's another form of socialization. It can make it difficult to leave, if a member begins to have doubts, because once you've been conditioned, you can't just turn it off like a switch.

Anyone from Britain who has spent a few weeks driving on the Continent, or in America, knows the problems of switching from driving on the left to driving on the right. For the first couple of days you're extremely careful, until driving on the right becomes a habit, and then there's little problem – until you return home. Then you have to remember to drive on the left again. Initially, you can't just throw away the conditioning of the last couple of weeks and go back to normal; you have to superimpose yet another new set of conditioning on top: 'I must remember to drive on the left. I *must* remember...'.

The new conditioning of someone who has joined a religious movement has overcome the previous 20 or 30 years of parental and other societal conditioning. Once it is in place, it can be very difficult to shake. The member not only has the new set of beliefs, which he has learnt in such a way that they are internally consistent and completely logical; he has also become bonded to a new set of friends; he has also had a powerful religious experience; he has also learnt to revere and love the prophet or founder of the religion and his (or more rarely her) teachings; he has also forged a strong new commitment to God.

All of this is very real. To expect him simply to be able to throw it all away and return to the 'normal' religion of his youth, without a titanic inner struggle, is unrealistic.

Cult-watching organizations, some of which offer various types of 'exit counselling' to people who are leaving a new religion, report that this can be one of the main difficulties they encounter, even with people who are happy to leave. Getting rid of new conditioning is not easy. Although the practice has now fallen into disfavour because of its coercive nature, professional 'deprogrammers' aimed to strip away the recently acquired conditioning through a form of 'reverse brainwashing', aggressively using exactly the same techniques that they accused the 'cults' of using.

There's a further factor. In the movement the member has been taught The Truth. How, knowing it, can he now turn his back on it? Like Christine in the example above, how can he risk losing his salvation and going to Hell? If you really believe it, this can be a genuine fear.

Some exit counsellors from Christian 'counter-cult' organizations (see Chapter 9) may seek to overcome a movement's conditioning by contrasting its 'spurious' teachings with the 'Biblical truth'. Often people with a strong religious belief will say 'I know this is true' rather than 'I believe this is true'. This applies to many Christians in mainstream Churches, especially born-again Evangelicals, just as much as to those in many of the alternative religions. It is a deep conviction of belief, a certainty. This is what makes it so difficult to argue someone out of their belief when trying to persuade them to leave their movement. Quite simply, they know that they are right. Whatever logical arguments anyone else might put up are irrelevant.

Paradoxically, this might explain why some former members of alternative religions have converted to Evangelical Christianity. They have met someone, perhaps an exit counsellor, whose conviction is even stronger than their own; they fight, with a great clashing of belief systems and a mighty battle of wills, and they are outclassed. Effectively, they exchange one set of certainties for another – and for one without the social stigma of belonging to a 'cult'.

What about the others, those who don't convert to another faith? An outsider, perhaps a concerned parent or friend, or a 'professional carer', is asking them to give up the absolute certainty they have, the safe, solid knowledge that they are right, and replace it with... what? With the doubts and uncertainties that most people have, who aren't committed believers.

It's hardly surprising that many people choose to stay with their movement, even if there are other things about it which might be less than ideal.

FELLOWSHIP, INSTITUTIONALIZATION & INVESTMENT

A member of any religious movement may feel a tremendous bond with other members. They share a common set of beliefs; and they have shared experiences.

They have worshipped, prayed and studied together; they have stood in the rain together, witnessing to passers-by, or (especially in the early days of the Moonies and ISKCON) selling flowers or candles or books 'for a donation'. This unites people, makes them one body, far more so than a crowd of fans at a football match or a rock festival. Even in the secular world people often find that if they join an organization – a charity, or a political or environmental group, for example – most of the people they then spend their time with are members of the same group. For someone in a religious movement, this is even more so; all their close friends, all the people they trust, are also members. Not only might they not have any friends outside the movement, they have learnt to mistrust anyone outside the movement. In addition, like the early Christians, they have faced persecution together – another strong bond.

All of this is even stronger if they live in a community, however large or small.

If they leave, they are not only giving up their beliefs, which is difficult enough; they are giving up their friends – their *family*. They are turning their back on everyone they know and love and trust. Both socially and spiritually, fellowship is an important part of belonging to a movement; to leave it behind is not easy.

In addition, if you have been a member of a movement, and again especially if you have lived in a community, you will have grown used to doing certain things at certain times. You get up and go to bed, you study and worship, you meditate and recite mantras, you eat, you do manual work, all at set times. In a very real sense, you can become institutionalized. When you leave the movement, you are suddenly thrust into a world of chaos, where *you* have to take decisions, seemingly every moment of the day, where *you* are responsible for filling every moment of the day with *your* choice of activity. In the same way, some ex-prisoners find this a problem. It's now accepted that people who have been made redundant, or even recently retired people, can find it difficult to cope with the loss of a framework in their lives. This can be a major problem for some people who leave a religious movement, having been a member for more than a few months. They can be bewildered by their new freedom.

Once a member does make the decision to leave, and carries it through, there is a further psychological problem they may have to cope with. Once they are outside, looking back at what they have done, what they have believed, how they have lived for the last several years, from the totally new viewpoint of an ex-member, they might be hit by the amount of time and effort and everything else – the amount of their *life* – that they have wasted, thrown away, given over to something which (with the blessèd view of somewhat bitter hindsight) was so full of contradictions and idiocies and awfulness. How could they have been so *stupid*?

The anticipation of such a realization can be part of what makes it so difficult for someone to leave, even if they are desperate to do so.

We saw in the example of Tony, above, how the anti-cultists can sometimes take this feeling of self-blame, self-anger, and turn it back on the movement: 'Don't blame yourself. You were deceived into it through a form of mind control. You should be angry with them. You were a victim.'

☼

In 1994 the BBC screened a powerful drama series, *Signs and Wonders*, written by Michael Eaton, which was very clearly based on the popular perception of the Moonies. A young woman, Claire, played by Jodhi May, is 'rescued against her will' from a cult headed by a Far Eastern 'Father', by a professional deprogrammer (James Earl Jones). What was particularly well portrayed was Claire's confusion at being torn away from the religion which had become her entire life, her terror at the damnation which must surely now be awaiting her, and her blazing anger at her concerned mother.

It was also interesting – and quite definitely true to life – that Claire was intelligent and artistic, and came from not just a 'good, middle-class home', but a home where she had had a traditional religious upbringing.

Signs and Wonders was (like the four fictional accounts in this book) just one example, one version of the story. It was powerful, but as a TV drama it was necessarily clichéd. It showed a little of the love and joy and wonder and responsibility that Claire felt while she was a member of the religion, but that wasn't the story the series was telling. It concentrated on the drama of the kidnapping and the horrors that Claire went through before she was 'of sound mind' enough to be able to cry in her mother's arms. It didn't say, 'Forget Claire's parents for a moment. Look at Claire. Is she happy where she is? Is she fulfilled? Is she at peace? Should we leave her be?'

The joy and peace which Claire experienced, and the austerity and discipline of her life in the movement, were probably very little different from those of a young nun in a convent. Yet, as was suggested at the end of Chapter 4, traditional Roman Catholic parents, though they might feel sad at losing their daughter, would feel pride that she had given herself to the Lord, rather than move heaven and earth to get her out.

SPIRITUAL CAREER PATH

Many religions have what could be called a 'spiritual career path': a gradual path of advancement through various levels, learning new truths and spiritual insights.

The cynical outsider might observe that if new recruits had any idea of what they would be expected to have to believe in a few years' time, they would never have joined the movement. The believing insider would observe that in all areas of life there are things you can't understand or appreciate until you've had a progressive grounding in the subject. There's no point in handing theoretical physics to someone who hasn't grasped basic algebra; you don't expect someone struggling with their first French irregular verbs to appreciate fully the great French novelists and poets. So, as knowledge increases, understanding increases, and as understanding increases, more knowledge can be revealed.

In many alternative religions such as Scientology, in the various occult schools, and in semi-esoteric organizations such as the Freemasons, there are clearly defined levels of attainment on the way up the career path, marked by levels of initiation following prescribed courses or grades. The completion of each level is the starting point for the next level up. There is always both an immediate goal to be aimed for, the next level, and an ultimate goal, the end of the path or the top of the ladder – the mountain peak. You start as one of countless millions, knowing nothing. Very quickly you become one of a few thousand, knowing something. As you progress through the levels you become more and more one of the select few.

Once a religion has been around for a while, the select few at the top of the ladder become a not-quite-so-select many. The solution to that is simple: when you eventually reach the aimed-for goal, you discover that it is in fact just another staging post, the bottom level on a new, higher, more esoteric path, the first rung of another ladder.

The outsider might say that this is a clever way of keeping people within the religion; otherwise, once they've reached the top, where else is there for them to go except out? The insider might say, quite reasonably, that there is always more to be learnt.

The spiritual career path is a further reason why some people may be reluctant to leave a religious movement. Over the years they have been a member, they may have invested a vast amount of their time and energy – a vast amount of their life – into it. Not to mention, in some cases, a vast amount of their money. They have been through all the early training exercises, the discipline, the lower levels necessary to prepare them spiritually, emotionally and intellectually for the higher levels of the inner group of members. They have very nearly reached the highest rungs of the ladder. They have put in a tremendous amount of study and effort and sweat and tears (and money) to get there. How can they possibly give it all up now, when they are so close to the final peak, the ultimate secrets which have yet to be revealed to them? Even if they have become disillusioned, and no longer care about reaching the highest peak, there can still be an understandable reluctance to throw this all away by leaving.

For all the reasons mentioned above, and more, 'breaking up is hard to do.' Leaving a movement is like ending a relationship: a lot of very confused emotions, a lot of contradictory motivations, a lot of trauma. Anyone who does want to leave a movement needs help, not harassment. Anyone wanting to stay in a movement would benefit more from love and support, than from arguments and antagonism. Staying or leaving: in the end, it *has to be* the decision of the member himself or herself, and no one else's.

CHAPTER SIX

After the Prophet Dies

How movements change

'The King is dead!' 'Long live the King!'

THE position of monarch continues, independent of the person. In practice there might be confusion over who the next incumbent should be; there might even be a war of succession between the followers of rival claimants. But the position remains.

'The pope is dead!' A few weeks later, after the conclave, there is an announcement: '*Habemus Papam.*'

There is always a pope. Again, the role is not dependent on the incumbent.

These are both institutions, with continuity built in. The same does not apply to the founder of a new religion. It cannot: the founder of a new religion, a prophet figure, is almost by definition outside the normal rules of society. And once he or she has died, the successor cannot also be founder, but must simply be leader.

In the last few years, the founders of several of the movements in this book have died; several others, at the time of writing, are quite old.

It could be argued that the most crucial point in the development of any religion isn't its foundation, or the initial revelation of its founder; it is the founder's death. In the months and years after the founder dies, many things can happen: at the two extremes, without its charismatic leader the movement could fizzle out and fade away completely, or it could mature from being a 'cult' (in either the tabloid or the classic sociological sense) into becoming a full-blown 'religion'; or it could fragment into a dozen competing sects; or it could consolidate and strengthen itself; or it could become something quite different from what its founder had ever intended.

The death of the founder precipitates the inevitable change, in the sociological terminology of Max Weber, from charismatic to rational/legal authority, from personal to organizational power, from a prophetic to a priestly type of leadership. What happens to cults after their founders die is to a large extent bound up with how successfully they manage this transition. (The word 'cult' is appropriate here because, while the founder remains alive, he or she is the focal point of the movement.)

Wise founders, aware of the inevitability of their death and desiring that their teachings should continue, may plan with their senior followers for how the movement will continue to function after their death. Sometimes this seems to work well; in other cases, it seems to add to the eventual confusion.

The model outlined in this chapter is an attempt to map the main directions a new religion can move in after the death of its founder.

	STASIS	CHANGE
STABILITY	**A Continuation** (Stays essentially the same)	**C Reform/Revolution** (New leader, new directions)
	Transition (Short-term confusion)	
INSTABILITY	**B Dissolution** (Fades and dies)	**D Schism** (Competing offshoots)

- Movements can change, or not (stasis). In either case, the outcome can be either stable or unstable. Stable stasis leads to continuation; unstable stasis to dissolution. Stable change leads to reform, perhaps after revolution; unstable change to schism.
- These four outcomes are not mutually exclusive. For example, schisms (D) may occur under the circumstances of (A), (B) or (C), or combinations of these.
- Category (A) accepts that *some* changes will be inevitable, such as an end to new teachings from the founder and changes in the hierarchy, and also allows for gradual change through evolution over the years.
- Category (B) may be relatively quick – a few months, or a year or two – or relatively slow – for example, until the death of the last member alive at the founder's death.
- It is possible for the original movement either to continue the same (A) or to fade and die (B) while a splinter group (D) under a powerful new leader (C) thrives.

A third dimension could be added to this model: convergence with or divergence from more mainstream society and religious beliefs and practices. Such convergence in Christian sects has been called 'denominationalization': 'the loosening rigour; the loss of the sense of dissent and protest; the reduction of distance from other

Christians; and the muting of claims that the sect's distinctive teachings are necessary for salvation.'[1] Another, more 'human' way of looking at this is that the movement might choose to downplay the person of their founder in favour of his teachings; there might be some embarrassment at some of the founder's excesses, and now that he is gone there is the opportunity for some of his more idiosyncratic teachings or practices to be quietly dropped. And once that has happened, it might turn out that the doctrines of the movement aren't so far removed from the mainstream after all.

In contrast, a movement might, at least in the short term, move further away from the mainstream after its founder's death. A new leader, or the members in general, in seeking to maintain their identity with the founder gone, might increase the emphasis on previously relatively minor aspects of his teachings.

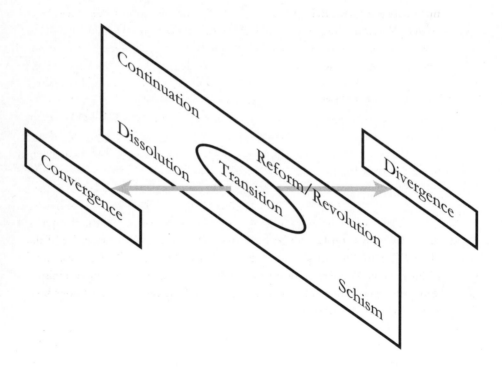

Social science models like this can be useful for both analysis and prediction. On the basis of this model, then, can we:

- find possible reasons why different movements react in different ways?
- project possible outcomes for movements whose founders are still alive?

First, then, although they are covered in more detail in their individual entries, let's look briefly at a range of movements which fit into each of these categories – and in some cases into more than one.

A. CONTINUATION

In several cases, the founder sought to set up a safe-continuation scheme. Sometimes it worked, sometimes it didn't.

The exact details of the ransition from L. Ron Hubbard to David Miscavige as the power behind the Church of Scientology may never be known. Miscavige was certainly a favourite of Hubbard, and was one of the very few to spend time with Hubbard during his last years, but we cannot know for sure how much Miscavige's takeover of the reins of power and subsequent purges of many senior Scientologists was planned between them. Before Hubbard's death, control of the Church had been passed to the All Clear Unit, whose ostensible purpose was to fill in for Hubbard while he was away and prepare for when he came back to prominence. Two organizations were set up, the Religious Technology Centre, to have control over the Church's doctrine to ensure its purity, and Author Services Incorporated, to control the publication of all of Hubbard's written works, fiction and non-fiction. With the structure set up, the changes began in 1982–3, three years before Hubbard's death, with the weeding-out of the Old Guard; Hubbard's assumed heir-apparent, David Mayo, was declared a Suppressive Person, and left the Church. By maintaining complete control over the purity of the 'Tech', the practical application of the teachings, those at the top can ensure that Scientology, as set up by its founder, doesn't change.

The School of Economic Science, in a way, has had three figureheads: Andrew MacLaren (d. 1975), his son Leon MacLaren (d. 1994), and the Shankaracharya of the North (d. 1997), whose teachings they follow. Because the Shankaracharya was their spiritual leader, Leon MacLaren's death caused little more than a shift in administration, already set up. The new administrative leader and the new spiritual leader both follow in the footsteps of their predecessors.

Long before David Berg, founder of the Family, died in 1994, his wife Maria had been accepted as the next prophet and leader. The running of the movement had also been democratised through the setting up of a Charter for all Family homes. A couple of co-leaders now share the practical leadership with Maria, so allowing the possibility of authority passing to them on her eventual death.

Richard Lawrence, British leader of the Aetherius Society, says that as their founder George King grew older they deliberately looked at other movements and how they had managed – or not. They already had an ecclesiastical structure in place, and so far as the Society's leadership and organisation is concerned, this has simply continued. Since King's death in 1997, the teachings and practice have continued much the same, with perhaps a slightly stronger emphasis on spiritual healing; as there will be no more Cosmic Transmissions from Ascended Masters, the balance between the Theosophical roots and the New Age aspects of the Aetherius Society is swinging more to the latter.

In the case of ISKCON, there was a hugely extended period of transition before things settled down in the form of reformed continuation. The founder of ISKCON, Prabhupada, appointed an International Management Group of teachers before his death in 1977. Immature and ambitious sanyassins took too much power, and the whole movement degenerated into chaos for several years before a reform group began, in 1984, to sort out the mess. The problem stemmed from a confusion and conflict between the charismatic authority of guru-like sanyassins, and a committee-led management structure – a modern version of Weber's 'rational/legal' authority type.

B. DISSOLUTION

After the prophetess Joanna Southcott's death in 1814, her followers continued to make claims about her for some years; but without her inspiration and prophecies there was no real substance to any of her successors, and eventually interest faded away – though not entirely. Even today, though as more of an historical curiosity than a religion, the Panacea Society in Bedford guards Joanna Southcott's box which contains, they believe, her prophecies and the secret of world peace.

The Catholic Apostolic Church failed less because of the death of its founder than because it set up a one-off system of 12 apostles in expectation of the return of Christ in 1855. The Church kept going, but when the last apostle died in 1901, no further priests could be ordained; the last active priest died in 1970. The German church broke away in 1863 (D. Schism), appointed new apostles, and today the New Apostolic Church claims to be the third largest church in Germany.

C. REFORM/REVOLUTION

Sometimes the change in a movement after the founder's death is such a revolution that, in a way, the successor might be the true founder of what follows, and the original founder is effectively relegated to the role of forerunner.

There was a huge power struggle within the Mormon Church after Joseph Smith was shot in 1844, partly because over the years he had named several people as his successor. There were at least half a dozen main leaders and groups, one under his son Joseph Smith III (one of his appointed successors), which is still the second biggest Mormon group; but the main battle, between Sidney Rigdon and Brigham Young, was won by the latter. Another problem was that different groups accepted Smith's teachings from different periods as the most authentic version of the religion; exactly the same is currently happening in the splinter groups from the Worldwide

Church of God (see Chapter 17). And a third problem is that the Mormon religion teaches continuous revelation, and several of the competing leaders claimed to have been told by God that they were the right one. Brigham Young emphasised certain doctrines and practices which other groups dropped (and perhaps Smith himself would have done); he was a fiery and charismatic leader who really remade the Mormon Church in his direction rather than Smith's.

The founder of the Jehovah's Witnesses, Charles Taze Russell, died in 1916. A very bitter power struggle was won by 'Judge' Rutherford, who de-emphasised Russell's role, so much so that around 4,000 members left to form another Church based firmly on Russell's teachings; the remaining Church under Rutherford for many years denied any connection with Russell.

And what of Christianity itself? It has been argued that Jesus did not found Christianity; the argument goes like this. Leaving to one side the question of whether he was God incarnate or not, as a man he was a Jew; he prayed and worshipped as a Jew. He preached, he taught, he healed, he gathered some disciples, and then he died. According to the New Testament accounts, the disciples fell apart for a while after their leader died; but then became fired up, so to speak, at the Feast of Pentecost. And then Paul came on the scene. Before Paul, Jesus' successor was his brother James, who was the leader of the believers in Jerusalem – i.e., those people, all Jews in both race and religion, who had actually known Jesus. But then the persecutor Paul, who had never met Jesus, had a religious experience, was converted, and began preaching. His teachings were considerably at variance with those of the Jerusalem believers; Paul fell out with them, and went off to take his own version of what was now becoming a new religious movement, to the Greek- and Latin-speaking peoples around the Mediterranean. It was Paul's version, not the version of Jesus' closest followers, which developed over the next few centuries into something approaching the Christianity we know today.

D. SCHISM

Social science models are not perfect. Like many others, the Seventh-day Adventist Church (SDA) is 'a special case', with the main schism occurring long *before* the founder's death. The SDA rose out of the ashes of the Great Disappointment of 1844 (see p.169), putting together explanations for the non-return of Christ along with other non-mainstream doctrines. As a Church it developed over several years, first as a loose federation of Sabbatarian Millennialists. It was when Ellen G. White held a major conference at Battle Creek, Michigan, in 1860, and forced through the new name of the Church, that some congregations splintered away as the Church of God (Seventh Day) and other variants. This century the SDA has moved closer to the mainstream (Convergence), while the schismatic offshoots have continued to schism. The tradition continues today, with one of these offshoots of offshoots, the

Worldwide Church of God, currently spawning over 200 offshoots of its own.

The religion of Islam split within a few years of the death of Mohammed (632 CE). As with Mormonism 1200 years later, some believed the leader should come from the Prophet's family. The first two caliphs had been close associates of Mohammed; the first nominated his successor, but the second was assassinated without doing the same. A six-man council (the *Shura*), choosing between two main candidates, offered the job to Mohammed's son-in-law Ali on condition he didn't declare a dynasty; Ali refused, and the other candidate was appointed. When he was killed, Ali became caliph and immediately declared a dynasty; he was briefly followed by his son, before a 'non-family' leader took control. Out of this very early conflict arose the two main divisions of Islam, Sunni and Shi'ite.

A COMPLEX COMBINATION OF TYPES

In a sense, every religion could be argued as a special case, because we're dealing with human beings and human institutions. But the Worldwide Church of God is an excellent case study of the problems of authority and legitimation of leadership. It will be considered in detail later in the book, but a very brief summary now will show how it fits several of the categories of the model on page 59.

Even when founder Herbert W. Armstrong was alive there were many internal problems: an authoritarian leadership and hierarchy; many hirings and firings and rehirings over the years; and a major conflict between Armstrong and his heir-apparent son Garner Ted, who was finally ejected from the movement in 1978, and went off to found his own Church.

Shortly before Armstrong's death in 1986 at the age of 94, he appointed Joseph W. Tkach as his successor; Tkach was almost unknown outside the church, and was not the most likely successor: he was not charismatic, not a great preacher, not a gifted theologian – but apparently he was an able administrator. Did Armstrong perhaps think that this would ensure a safer continuation of his church after his death, than if he appointed a charismatic leader, whose actions would not be foreseeable?

Very quickly Tkach instituted a full doctrinal review, and over the next few years many distinctive doctrines were first downplayed then completely dropped or reversed. In terms of the model above the Worldwide Church of God was now on a path of convergence with mainstream Christianity: a classic case of Bryan R. Wilson's 'denominationalization'. By 1994/5, so many core doctrines had been changed that vast numbers of ministers had left, taking many members with them. Briefly, the Worldwide Church of God itself has continued (A) in at least name, while having a reform/revolution (B) under a new leader, taking it into far closer convergence with the mainstream; meanwhile, many schisms (D) occurred, some following a path of greater divergence than before.

MOVEMENTS WITH LEADERS STILL ALIVE

Like the physical sciences, the social sciences aim to be predictive as well as descriptive. Can the model in this chapter help us predict what will happen in religions where the leader is still alive, when he or she does die? The simple answer is 'probably not', because there are so many unpredictable variables. But it's worth looking at a few religions to make, at the worst, some educated guesses.

Rev. Moon, founder of the Unification Church, was 80 at the time of writing this book. His wife is 23 years younger and in good health and, as the Perfect Wife of the Messiah, is spiritually an important person in her own right. She is expected to take over the leadership after Moon's death, with the support of senior members of the church hierarchy. The problem for the Unification Church is more likely to come after *her* death, because there appears to be no natural successor amongst the Moon offspring. A lot may depend on how Mrs Moon and her advisors decide Moon's memory should be revered after his death. In some respects she will be in an ideal position to use the transition period to establish a basis of authority which will outlive not just Moon but herself.

Raël, founder of the Raelian Movement, is still relatively young – 53 – and could live for several more decades. The Raelian Movement anticipate no problems when Raël eventually dies. The Raelian hierarchy is organised as levels of Guides, with the Guide of Guides (currently Raël) elected by the Guides every seven years; if anything happens to Raël, someone else would simply take the position. This might be helped by the fact that Raël has had no further extraterrestrial experiences since 1975; effectively they are already operating in a post-prophetic phase. On the other hand, because their mythology, teachings and practices stem wholly from the reported experiences of one man, when that man and his charismatic authority are gone, there may not be sufficient glue to hold the movement together.

The Guru Maharaji was only 13 when he sprang to prominence as leader of the Divine Light Mission, now Elan Vital, in 1971. As he became an adult, to quote the UK national organiser, Glenn Whittaker, he 'made it increasingly clear that the Knowledge was not an Indian teaching, but universal.'[2] Although he is still actively involved in the movement; he has changed the focus, has stepped back from the traditional Hindu position of guru, and has dropped many if not all of the Hindu trappings. To quote Whittaker again, 'he distances himself and his teaching strongly from the concept of religion. He regards himself as an educator.' Because the founder himself has made such sweeping changes, the movement is less strongly focussed on him than it previously was, and thus is perhaps more likely to continue relatively unchanged after his death.

Elizabeth Clare Prophet took over Summit Lighthouse after her husband's death in 1973, turning it into the publishing house of a new movement, Church Universal and Triumphant, with herself as the Messenger. Aged 61, she has recently retired from leadership because of ill health, appointing a president of the Church to handle the transition from charismatic prophetic leadership to rational/legal leadership, with the stated intention that the Church will move safely and smoothly into a new phase of its existence. No one will replace her as Messenger.

FACTORS AFFECTING CHANGE

J. Gordon Melton says that 'the problem of succession is not the determinative trauma it has often been considered to be.'[3] Sometimes, however, it is. The death of the founder is, at least potentially, a major crisis point. At the two extremes, the religion could fade and die, or it could mature from a 'cult' into a 'religion', with other options inbetween.

This is an area where further research might be profitable, but there is a strong case for suggesting that the *second* leader is crucial to the continuance of a movement; it is in his or her term of office that the NRM has to make the transition from charismatic to rational/legal authority. If the second leader also has charismatic authority, it is vital that he formalises the leadership procedure before he too dies.

To avoid confusion and chaos after his or her death, a founder needs to set up an unambiguous system for succession of leadership. Christian Science has been cited as 'a sociological model for routinisation of charisma'[4] Mary Baker Eddy spent 15 years working and reworking *The Manual of the Mother Church*, setting in absolute stone how the Church should be run. One result of this is that for the last 90 years Christian Science has been constitutionally unable to modify itself to adapt to changes in society.

Mrs Eddy would certainly not have accepted the alternative, to develop and announce an heir apparent. According to one writer, 'Mrs Eddy regularly sacked anyone who shined (sic) forth with the slightest glint of leadership ability.'[5] But some of the most successful new religions really only took off *after* the founder's death, under a strong new leader (e.g. the Mormons, the Jehovah's Witnesses). If Herbert W. Armstrong had appointed one of his more charismatic evangelists as his successor, instead of a supposedly safe administrator, things might have worked out very differently for the Worldwide Church of God. But for an ailing founder to appoint a charismatic successor is a huge personal risk: it sets up a potential rival, a leader-in-waiting while the founder is still alive; and it increases the likelihood that the movement will change after the founder's death, perhaps in ways he might not have approved.

There are many other factors affecting the continuation of a movement after the founder's death; it is worth looking briefly at a few of them.

One important element is the organisational structure that is already in place in a movement. If this is well-established, then the transition from personal to organisational authority is likely to be easier. Some founders, by the time of their deaths, have already delegated most of the running of their movement to others; the founder might still be the guru, the source of teaching, but he (or more rarely she) has become more of a figurehead than a leader. It is relatively easy for this situation to continue with only the slightest of modifications after the founder's death. So long as the organisation has a sound legal and financial basis – effectively, as an established business corporation – then it doesn't really need a living figurehead in order to continue its 'business'. It has a 'product' to 'sell' – the teachings, which might include books, tapes or videos of the founder, as well as ongoing and well-established magazines, radio and TV broadcasts featuring other leaders within the movement, evangelistic rallies, cultural events, in addition to the normal day-to-day aspects of a religion, such as regular and special services, study groups, nurturing existing members, recruiting new members, and so on – and it has the machinery and the momentum to continue doing so.

This is assuming that it has a positive attitude to proselytisation; some movements have an inward focus, seeing themselves as God's Elect, or as the 'Small Remnant' of Romans 11:5; they keep themselves withdrawn from the world, with a strong aversion to any possible corruption from contact with outsiders; in Roy Wallis's sociological term, these are extreme 'world-rejecting' groups.

There are also both doctrinal and demographic factors to consider, and the interaction between the two. The Catholic Apostolic Church, for example, had a doctrinal principle that no new apostles could ever be appointed. But without apostles to ordain them, there could be no new clergy; when the clergy grew old and died, no one replaced them, and the Church died too.

A movement which stresses celibacy must have a strong recruitment programme if it is to survive into another generation. (The Shaker community in America ran orphanages; some of the children grew up into the community, so maintaining the numbers. When the state took over such social provision, the Shakers began to decline in numbers.) A movement with a strong male or female bias in membership must also consider carefully how it will continue by natural growth without its charismatic founder drawing new members in. If at the founder's death most of the members are elderly, what inducements can they offer to recruit the young? If the membership is predominantly young, are there any older members in positions of authority, to offer teaching, guidance, continuity, stability? (This was one of the problems faced by ISKCON.) And how large is the membership? It is certainly possible for a movement only a few hundred strong to grow and prosper; but continuance is more assured if there are hundreds of thousands of members by the time the founder dies.

If a movement's focus is primarily on the figure of its founder, then his death will cause major problems; once the centre is removed, what is left? This is especially problematic if he had claimed some form of divinity. If the focus is on the founder's teachings, and these were from some form of revelation, is that an end to new teachings? Or can somebody else take on the prophetic mantle of the founder, stepping into his or her shoes as the channel for further revelations? The Mormons, for example, have continuing revelation, though this is reserved for the president of the Church.

Also, is the doctrine of the founder fixed in stone for ever, or may it be adapted to fit better with changing circumstances, or to avoid conflict with the civil authorities, or simply to drop possibly embarrassing beliefs or practices? If it is adapted, then by whose authority? This is one of the prime causes of splits in Churches after the death of the founder: the new leadership accommodates itself more to the world, causing doctrinal purists to leave and set up their own Church — 'Therefore, brethren, stand fast, and hold the traditions which ye have been taught' (2 Thessalonians 2:15).

And much depends on the doctrines themselves, whether concerning salvation, purity, the End Times, Church government, understanding of history, etc. How unusual are these? How close are they to the doctrines of mainstream Christianity, Islam, Hinduism, Buddhism? Are the differences great enough to invite condemnation from the 'establishment' of those religions? Are the similarities close enough that dialogue is possible, now that the (perhaps awkward and inflexible) founder is out of the way? Or are the teachings so precise, so tightly focussed, that members couldn't conceive of any change without risking their salvation?

The sociologists Rodney Stark and William Sims Bainbridge developed a theory of religion based on costs and rewards.[6] Sometimes the promised rewards are so great, and perhaps unique to a movement, that nothing, not even the death of the founder, will sway members from their chosen path. But in other cases the rewards are much the same as those found in many other movements, including mainstream Churches; if it turns out that the most significant difference was simply the personality or the idiosyncratic approach of the founder, then after his death members might seek the same rewards from a more conventional religion with fewer 'costs' attached; they may hold happy memories of their founder, but now that he or she has gone they'll go elsewhere, somewhere perhaps more socially acceptable, for their salvation; and so the movement will fade into memory with its founder.

The movement's relations with outside society are also important. Does it get on well with its neighbours, or is it at war with them? Some modern religions deliberately foster good relations with local schools, hospitals, social centres, charities; others constantly face their meetings being banned from community halls. Is the movement at all respected for its charitable works, or is it feared as a menace to decent, clean-living society? Is it well-integrated with its surrounding world nationally, even internationally? Some religious movements featured in this book sponsor international conferences on peace or on science; others have health, education, social work or emergency relief bodies which are recognised as United Nations Non-Governmental Organisations (NGOs).

Or is the movement an inward-looking, closed society? Does it actually live apart from the world, shut away in communities? Does it allow its members access to radio, TV, newspapers or the Internet?

The rapidly spreading availability of the Internet is potentially of major importance to alternative religions. Members of movements which had exercised strict control over sources of information, whether about themselves or about other movements, or about the outside world, may now have access to vast amounts of uncontrollable, uncensored material. Suddenly they might find that they are not, as they had been taught, the only ones who believe X and Y; or they could discover trenchant criticisms of their movement by ex-members, or by outsiders, providing them with information of which they were formerly quite unaware. Members with questions, doubts and problems now find that they can contact others with similar questions, perhaps anonymously; they are no longer isolated.

(The Internet is used by more established religions as well. But it is interesting to note that NRMs were among the first to set up their own websites, in many cases long before denominations of the established religions did so.)

There are clearly many factors which, singly or in combination with each other, can affect what happens to a movement after its founder dies. Trying to foretell what might happen in the case of any individual movement is likely to be no more accurate than any other prophecy. But as many of the new movements of the 1960s and 1970s either are already passing through this phase, or may do so in the next few years, an awareness of these factors can perhaps help us understand the sometimes traumatic changes which these movements may go through.

Notes

[1] 'How Sects Evolve' in Wilson 1990: 109.

[2] Glen Whittaker, former National Organiser of Elan Vital in the UK, in correspondence with the author, 28 February & 23 June 1995.

[3] Melton, J. Gordon, 'Introduction: When Prophets Die: The Succession Crisis in New Religions', Miller 1991: 11-12.

[4] John K. Simmons, 'Charisma and Covenant: The Christian Science Movement in its Initial Postcharismatic Phase', Miller 1991: 109.

[5] Ibid.: 113.

[6] Bainbridge 1997: 9-12.

CHAPTER 7

It's the End of the World as we know it

Apocalyptic beliefs

The first of January 2000 has passed, and we're all still here.

Why have a chapter on millennialism now that we're *in* the new millennium, and all the Pre-Millennial Tension of the late-1990s has come to nothing? There was even a website (www.olivetree.org) linked to a camera constantly filming the sealed Golden Gate in Jerusalem, through which the returning Christ was expected to enter the city. But Christ didn't return as scheduled – so isn't this a dead subject now?

The simple answer is 'no'.

In 1999 the Scripture Union conducted a survey of 687 children aged between 7 and 11, asking what they associated with the millennium. Among the answers, 16 per cent said the Millennium Dome, 9 per cent said the Millennium Bug, and 9 per cent said the hit song by Robbie Williams. Only 1 per cent connected the millennium with the Christian faith.

In one way those children were right. The Christian meaning of 'the millennium' is *not* the same as 'the year 2000' or 'the new millennium'. They are two completely different things – though, as we shall see later, there are reasons why people do connect them, beyond the fact that the same word is used for both.

A number of the movements covered in this book have millenarian beliefs, which are discussed in their individual entries. This chapter provides a background to these beliefs, explaining where they originally sprang from, and showing that millenarian expectation is nothing new.

THE CHRISTIAN MILLENNIUM

Within Christian theology since New Testament days there has been a belief that Christ will return to the Earth, though the precise details – how, why, when – have been open to a wide variety of interpretations. Within traditional, mainstream Christianity it hasn't often been a subject of major importance; it was a fairly undefined piece of doctrine which might, in any case, be allegorical or symbolic. But there have always been some who have seen the return of Christ as a real future event.

For centuries, many of these people have set dates; these were obtained from complex calculations based on their interpretation of passages in the biblical books of Daniel, Ezekiel and Revelation.

> And I saw an angel come down from heaven, having the key of the bottomless pit and a great chain in his hand.
>
> And he laid hold on the dragon, that old serpent, which is the Devil, and Satan, and bound him a thousand years,
>
> And cast him into the bottomless pit, and shut him up, and set a seal upon him, that he should deceive the nations no more, till the thousand years should be fulfilled: and after that he must be loosed a little season.
>
> And I saw thrones, and they sat upon them, and judgement was given unto them: and I saw the souls of them that were beheaded for the witness of Jesus, and for the word of God... and they lived and reigned with Christ a thousand years.
>
> But the rest of the dead lived not again until the thousand years were finished...
>
> And when the thousand years are expired, Satan shall be loosed out of his prison...
>
> And whoever was not found written in the book of life was cast into the lake of fire.
>
> *Revelation* 20:1–5, 7, 15

These books also provide possible clues to the exact timetable of events before and during the return of Christ. There have been many such timetables, most of them today owing something to the Dispensationalist teachings of John Nelson Darby, who was one of the founders of the Brethren in the 1830s. Central to most of them is the belief that the returned Christ will set up a thousand-year reign on Earth, and it is this that millennialist Christians mean by 'the millennium', rather than the new thousand-year calendraic period starting at 1 January 2000 (or, as some would argue, at 1 January 2001).

A TIMETABLE FOR THE END TIMES

There are many variations of the expected events surrounding the return of Christ, but this is a fairly standard version:

- 'The Signs of the Times': wars, rumours of wars, earthquakes, plagues, famines, false prophets etc.
- Seven-year rule of the Antichrist.
- For the first 3½ years he is thought to be a great leader, well respected, even loved; but then things begin to go wrong.

- The Rapture: believers are taken up into the skies to escape the Tribulation.
- At some point, the Christian dead will rise from their graves.
- Second 3½ years: awful Tribulation, then world war, probably with Russia attacking Israel, and culminating in...
- The Battle of Armageddon.
- Christ intervenes, and the Heavenly forces win.
- Christ sets up a world kingdom, physically here on Earth, which will last for 1,000 years: the millennium.
- Many millennialist groups believe that they, the true believers, will be rulers on Earth, under Christ.
- After 1,000 years, Satan is released from his chains, there's a final battle, Satan is thrown into the eternal pit, all believers go to heaven, and all non-believers to hell.

APOCALYPTIC WRITINGS

To understand the background to such millenarian thinking, it is necessary to look at its origins in Jewish apocalyptic writing. For those who believe in Christ's literal return, the following analysis might seem heretical, but it's straightforward biblical scholarship; in fact, most of these ideas were debated at great length in the third and fourth centuries CE by such well-respected Christian scholars as Hippolytus, Origen, Jerome and even the fourth-century Augustine of Hippo. The basic question is: should prophetic visions in the Bible be interpreted literally or allegorically? These Church Fathers all said allegorically; today's millennialist Christians say literally. It makes a huge difference.

There have been predictions of Christ's return, and of the subsequent end of the world or the beginning of the new world order, since New Testament times. The early disciples certainly expected the Messiah to come in all his power within their lifetimes. But we must be careful about this. The Messiah of Jewish thinking around the time of Jesus was not the same concept at all as the Christ whose return Christians look forward to.

The whole idea of the coming Messiah must be seen in its historical context, within the terms of Jewish apocalyptic thinking of two thousand or more years ago, related to their hopes and fears of release from foreign rule. The Messiah was the 'Anointed One', a priest-king,[1] a godly man sent by God, but most certainly not God himself; that very idea would have been unthinkable to every Jew of the time. The Messiah was a liberator, as much a military and political figure as a spiritual one. The Jews were an oppressed people; they were looking for a saviour, a Messiah, to free them from their oppression.

Although the Greek *christos* originally meant the same as the Hebrew *mashiah* ('anointed'), St Paul, followed by the Church Fathers of the first four centuries CE, changed its meaning dramatically. In Christian theology the Messiah, or Christ, is God incarnate, the God-man Jesus, whose purpose is not to save an oppressed race from their foreign rulers, but to save all of mankind from the penalty for their sins. Christians believe that he accomplished that through his life, death and resurrection two thousand years ago. If he has already accomplished this, then why do Christians believe he will return again?

Christianity, which began as a radical Jewish sect, very quickly absorbed and adapted ideas and influences taken from both Judaism and elsewhere; in the process, the Jewish messianic concept as understood by Jesus' contemporaries was changed into something quite different after his death.

Jewish scriptures contain, as well as history, law and poetry, a large amount of prophecy. Prophecy is usually thought of as foretelling the future, but for most of the Old Testament prophets it meant speaking out, giving God's message for their own times. Even when prophecies were about the future, they were usually spoken in the context of oppression or captivity – as, for example, when the Israelite people were taken as captives to Babylon in the sixth century BCE. Many biblical scholars believe that much of the Old Testament – the Jewish scriptures – was written down during, or strongly influenced by, this period of captivity. Certainly this applies to the books of the prophets found at the end of the Old Testament.

Most Christian apocalyptic thinking is based on two books of the Bible: Daniel and Revelation. Daniel is set in Babylon during the captivity, though the prophetic second half of the book was most likely written in the second century BCE – when, again, the Jews were oppressed.

The purpose of Jewish apocalyptic writing was to answer what would otherwise have had to be seen as a broken promise by God. God had promised King David, 'thine house and thy kingdom shall be established for ever before thee; thy throne shall be established forever' (2 Samuel 7:16). Yet 400 years later, Judah was conquered and the Israelites were in captivity, exiles from their own land. Had God lied to them? Had he broken his promise? Had he let them down? Perhaps he was less powerful than the gods of those who had conquered them. Maybe they should turn to those gods instead.

The prophets had an explanation. God was punishing his people for their unfaithfulness to him. If they returned to him, God would surely deliver his people from their bondage. According to Marina Benjamin in her book *Living at the End of the World*:

[A]t the very moment when God seemed to have abandoned history, prophecy took to imagining his grand re-entry into history. He would deliver his people, punish their enemies and bring the world to an end.

Thus was prophetic eschatology, the precursor of apocalypse, born. It was a theology tailor-made for an abandoned diaspora, and in it the Jews found a means of accounting for the catastrophic disparity between their votive expectations of national glory and the harsh truth of their miserable history. Henceforth, whenever reality seemed to stray from the path of destiny, as it did with the Selucid occupation, Hellenization, Roman invasion and the destruction of the Second Temple, apocalypse brought the pressure of an end to bear on everyday experience. It allowed the Jews to make sense of a present which otherwise defied comprehension, to transcend its disappointments and to feel the nearness of their future vindication. Its effect was one of reassurance.[2]

Revelation, the last book of the New Testament, was also written in a time of crisis. The Temple in Jerusalem had been destroyed, and both Jews and the fledgling Christian communities faced persecution from their Roman rulers. Had God forsaken them?

The writer of Revelation, which was one of many apocalyptic books written around that time, used the familiar imagery of the Jewish prophets like Ezekiel and Daniel – spectacular visions, complex symbols, esoterically meaningful numbers – to give hope to his readers; whatever troubles they were going through now, they should look to the glorious future when God would step into history and bring them peace and justice, and freedom from their oppressors.[3]

Apocalyptic writing was a particular literary genre, with its own rules and conventions, and a specific purpose. Most millenarian interpretations of Revelation, Daniel and other apocalyptic writings in the Bible seem to miss the context in which they were written.

For Fundamentalist Evangelicals, the Bible is the infallible Word of God, and through it God is speaking directly to them, today. And of ancient religious literature, *only* the Bible is of any importance; anything else, not being God's word, is not worth looking at. The fact that there were dozens of Jewish apocalyptic writings between 200 BCE and 100 CE, is irrelevant. From the standpoint of Biblical criticism, the Revelation to John is simply the one that happened to make its way into the Bible, albeit rather late in the day,[4] but from the standpoint of Evangelicals, Revelation is God's Holy Word, speaking to them, now, about the imminent End Times.

But just how imminent *are* the End Times?

'THE END OF THE WORLD IS NIGH!'

Those who, for the last few decades, have prophesied the imminent return of Christ tend not to mention that this has been a preoccupation of certain Christians for centuries. They all believed that they were living in the End Times, that Christ's glorious return was just around the corner – and every single one of them who set a date was wrong. Although the end of the world is certainly more nigh today than it was yesterday, or last year, or last century, there is no reason to suppose that today's prophets of the Second Coming should be any more accurate than their forebears. It is instructive to look at a small selection of millennialist prophecies through history, noting how often dates have been set.

As mentioned earlier, the very first Christians, who wrote the New Testament, believed that the Messiah – the Jewish Messiah – would come in their lifetimes.

In the second century a prophet called Montanus believed that the New Jerusalem would very shortly descend from heaven near a town in Phrygia (now Turkey). In preparation for this, Christians should lead ascetic lives and cut themselves off from the corrupt world.

The sixth-century Bishop Gregory of Tours, unlike many of today's prophets, set the date for the Second Coming long after his own death, which if nothing else avoids embarrassment. He believed the End would come some time between 799 and 806 CE, about two hundred years after he died. But in 589 CE, only five years after Gregory's death, a great earthquake was followed by devastating floods, and then by a plague; tens of thousands died. His namesake, Pope Gregory I, took these natural events as a sign that the end was actually much closer. This was the pope who sent the sixth-century Augustine (of Canterbury) to evangelize Britain while there was still time.

What about the year 1000, the first millennium? The idea that people went around in sackcloth and ashes, and in terror, believing that Christ's Second Coming would be a thousand years after his first, is 'a romantic invention, dating back no further than the sixteenth century'.[5] Apart from a few well-educated monks, hardly anyone even knew that it was the year 1000. The general populace certainly didn't; the two dating systems most in use were 'The sixth year of so-and-so's reign' and 'The third year since the Great Storm that blew down all the trees at the end of the village.'

But there were some indicators that it might be around then. Halley's Comet, always a good harbinger of doom, was visible in 989. It was also thought by some that the End would come when the Feast of the Annunciation coincided with Good Friday – which happened in 992; but even then they thought the Great Day would be within three years, not the year 1000. In fact, the year 1033 was thought by some monks to be a much more significant anniversary: 1,000 years since Christ's atoning death.

The most significant figure of the Middle Ages, so far as millennialism is concerned, was Joachim of Fiore (1135–1202). Like many others before and since, he focused on numbers, especially the two most sacred numbers, seven and three. He believed that there were three great Ages: the Age of the Father, the Old Testament and Law; the Age of the Son, the New Testament and Grace; and the Age of the Spirit, in which the religious Orders would convert the world. Like Gregory of Tours 600 years earlier, Joachim set the date just far enough ahead to avoid embarrassment. The Third Age would begin around 1260; a brief reign of the Antichrist would be followed by a new Adam or a new Christ. Joachim influenced, among many others, the great poet Dante, and the Spiritual Franciscans, followers of Francis of Assisi.

Pass on a little further in history, and in the middle of the Hundred Years' War there was the Great Schism in the Catholic Church (1378–1414), when rival popes excommunicated each other. Surely, with the civilized world (i.e. Europe) so devastated by war, and with the Church in such disarray at the very highest level, the

Antichrist must already be here? In fact, John Wycliffe wrote in 1379 that the pope was 'Antichrist heere in earth, for he is agens crist both in lif and in lore.'[6]

In the sixteenth century there were prophecies that the Day of Judgement would be in 1533, 1534, 1556 and 1593. Exactly half-way through that century Michel de Nostradame published the first of his annual almanacs; one of his obscure quatrains foretold the end of the world for a long way ahead, July 1999; but even dates so far in the future eventually come and go. Another set of prophecies, ostensibly dating from four centuries earlier, came to light in the sixteenth century. A Benedictine historian, Dom Arnold Wion, 'discovered' a set of 112 mottoes of popes by St Malachy of Armagh (1094–1148), and published them in his book *Lignum Vitae* in 1559. (The ease of fitting the mottoes to the popes drops off somewhat after the sixteenth century; judicious backdating of prophecies can be a useful trick.) Malachy's prophecies are perhaps very relevant to us today: there will be only two more popes after John Paul II, 'after which the seven-hilled city will be destroyed and the dreadful Judge will judge the people.'[7]

The seventeenth century saw a surge of prophets; it was also a great period for new religious movements – the 'sects and cults' of their day, many of them with social or political agendas as well as spiritual. There were Anabaptists, Levellers, Diggers, Socinians (early Unitarians), Ranters, Quakers, Muggletonians and Fifth Monarchy Men. These last took their name from a prophecy in Daniel that four great world empires would be followed by a Fifth Monarchy in which Christ would reign for 1,000 years. They supported Cromwell against the king, then changed their mind and saw Cromwell himself as the Great Beast; there were pitched battles in London, until the last of the Fifth Monarchy Men were either killed fighting, or arrested and executed.

By now, Protestantism was well established in much of Europe, and it had become standard practice to identify the Roman Church with the Whore of Babylon of Revelation. The pope, of course, was the Antichrist; among others, John Milton, George Fox, John Bunyan and Isaac Newton all proclaimed this. Some Protestant Fundamentalists even today still believe that the Church of Rome is the Whore of Babylon.

For those who see a great gulf between science and religion, it is worth noting that Newton – one of the greatest scientific thinkers of the last few centuries – spent much of his time studying biblical prophecy, and wrote a vast amount on it. He was not the only such combination of brilliant scientist and scholar of prophetic religion; about a hundred years earlier John Napier (1550–1617), who devised logarithms and an early version of the slide rule, worked out that the Last Judgement would be in 1688, going from Revelation, or in 1700, going by Daniel.

Several millenarian movements formed in the eighteenth century are still with us today. Emmanuel Swedenborg (1688–1772) believed that the New Jerusalem descended to Earth in 1757. As he lived a further 15 years after this, he came up with the explanation that this had happened on the spiritual plane; variants of this have been used since then by, among others, the Seventh-day Adventists and the

Jehovah's Witnesses. The New Church which developed from his teachings, although small, still exists today.

Joanna Southcott (1750–1814) was, for the time, a rare woman prophet. She believed that the millennium would start in her lifetime; she began prophesying in 1792, 'sealing' those who would form the 144,000 who would reign with Christ, and gathered quite a large movement. She is perhaps best remembered today for declaring herself to be pregnant with 'a man child, who was to rule all nations with a rod of iron' (Revelation 12:5); this was clearly a miracle, as she was not only 64 at the time but also a virgin. She died still believing that she was carrying the new Christ Child. Three days after her death surgeons cut her body open (having kept it warm); 'Damn me,' a doctor supposedly exclaimed, 'if the child is not *gone.*' Some of her followers continued their support for her for several decades after her death, one declaring that she had been carrying a spiritual rather than a carnal child. There is still an organization today, the Panacea Society, that guards Joanna Southcott's box which contains, they believe, her prophecies and the key to world peace; the box may only be opened in the presence of 24 bishops of the Church of England.

Moving on to the nineteenth century, we encounter some more familiar names. John Nelson Darby, one of the founders of the Exclusive Brethren or Plymouth Brethren (see page 162), a fairly small Christian sect formed around 1830, had a far greater influence on millennial thinking today than almost anyone else. Darby explored the idea of Dispensationalism. There are seven dispensations, or ages of man: first, the Age of Innocence, before the Fall; then the Ages of Conscience, Human Government, Promise, Law and then Grace, which was established by Christ. The last age, or dispensation, will be the millennial reign of Christ. Darby also clarified the fine detail of the End Times: the timetable, so to speak.

Darby's Dispensationalism was so well worked out that it caught the imagination of many Evangelicals in the nineteenth century, including the great American preacher Dwight L. Moody, and was taught at the Moody Bible Institute, perhaps the most influential Bible School in America. Even more importantly, it was incorporated into one of the most significant Protestant books of the twentieth century, the *Scofield Reference Bible*, and so has been accepted as straightforward biblical fact by millions of Christians.

So far this has been a European story. In America, the Church of Jesus Christ of Latter-day Saints, more usually known as the Mormons, was founded by Joseph Smith in 1830. The *Book of Mormon*, transcribed from golden plates, contains the story of the Lost Tribes of Israel going to America around 600 BC, and also tells of Jesus appearing in America after his resurrection. When he returns, Mormons believe, this will be in America as well; Joseph Smith designated a site in Independence, Missouri, where the returned Christ will establish his new Zion.

William Miller was an American Baptist minister. Like a lot of others before and since, he based his calculations on obscure verses in Daniel and Revelation, coming up with the answer that Christ would return in 1843. When nothing happened, he went back to his figures, and realized he hadn't taken account of the fact that there isn't a Year Zero between 1 BCE and 1 CE. Christ would now definitely return in 1844, specifically on October 22. Even having got it wrong the previous year, Miller attracted a lot of followers. Many sold their homes and businesses in anticipation of the great event, though the stories of them sitting on their rooftops in 'ascension robes' are apocryphal. October 1844 is known as the Great Disappointment – but out of it came a church which is still strong today, the Seventh-day Adventists. Miller himself, who died five years later, never followed any of their ideas – but the Adventists, like Swedenborg nearly a hundred years earlier, came up with a rationalization for Christ not appearing on schedule. Rather than returning to Earth, he had entered his heavenly sanctuary to start preparing it for Judgement Day, sorting out the sheep from the goats.

Probably the best-known End of the World preachers today are the Jehovah's Witnesses, who have several times made the mistake of setting the date. Although the Jehovah's Witnesses' theology is quite different from mainstream Christianity, their beliefs on the End Times, the return of Christ and the millennium are surprisingly similar, in the main, to those of most millennialist Christians. It was their second leader, Joseph Franklin 'Judge' Rutherford (1869–1942) who came up with one of the most effective religious slogans ever: 'Millions now living will never die'. He started using this as early as 1920; although millions of people alive in 1920 are still alive today, time is running out for Rutherford's prophecy.

The Worldwide Church of God (see Case Study, page 479) was an offshoot of some of the Sabbatarian Adventists who didn't join the Seventh-day Adventist Church when it was founded in 1860. Founded by Herbert W. Armstrong in 1937, its theology was an eclectic mix from several sources, but at the heart of it all was biblical prophecy. Current world events were clearly fulfilling biblical prophecy, claimed its many articles and booklets, including one entitled *1975 in Prophecy*.

Until very recently the Worldwide Church of God held a particular belief called British-Israelism, that whenever the Bible talks about the future of God's Chosen People, Israel, it is actually talking about Britain and America, which are specifically identified as the two tribes of Ephraim and Manasseh.[8] This is a relatively benign version of the beliefs of much more disturbing movements such as Christian Identity or Aryan Nations, which are openly white-supremacist and in some cases virulently anti-Semitic and, politically, extremely right-wing. Some of these are known as Survivalists, living in communities out in the woods and mountains, with a Bible in one hand and a gun in the other. Timothy McVeigh, who on 19 April 1995 killed 168 people in the Oklahoma bombing on the second anniversary of the Waco tragedy, had connections with such groups.

WHEN PROPHECIES ARE UNFULFILLED

As was said above, the one thing which every single one of these movements has in common is that their predictions were wrong. How do religious movements cope when their often very specific prophecies are unfulfilled?[9] As might be expected, there is sometimes a loss of membership; both the Jehovah's Witnesses and the Worldwide Church of God suffered in this way. But for both of these, as for most other movements in this position, frustration of expectation is overcome in one way or another, with quickly drawn-up explanations ranging from 'It occurred, but on an invisible plane,' or 'The Lord was merciful and stayed his hand,' or 'Our faith wasn't strong enough,' to 'We were mistaken in our calculations,' or 'We never actually claimed that anyway.' These are some of the ways of dealing with what sociologist Leon Festinger called cognitive dissonance, 'contradictory beliefs that cause mental distress when a person believes them both.'[10] Such rationalizations are a clear example of how movements, as one Victorian writer put it beautifully,

> are forced by the stern logic of life to turn their backs upon their past history, and to make their doctrines square with facts when facts absolutely refuse to square with doctrines.[11]

Or they could just set another date.

WHY THE YEAR 2000?

The months leading up to 1 January 2000 saw a great deal of interest in unusual religious groups, and forecasts of street riots, mass suicides, mass murders and much else, all linked either to the expected return of Christ on or around that date, or to the Millennium Bug, or to a combination of both. We were told that Y2K would cause our washing machines and video recorders to break down, traffic lights to go haywire, aeroplanes to fall out of the sky, and the world banking system to collapse. There would be chaos and devastation upon the face of the Earth – and (according to some millennialist groups) into this devastation, this man-made tribulation, would step the returning Christ to save all true believers.

The authorities in Jerusalem were particularly concerned with an expected influx of Fundamentalist Jews, Christians and Muslims; fortunately, the doomsayers were shown to be overly pessimistic[12].

Earlier in this chapter we saw that the calendraic millennium, about which so much fuss was made, and the Christian millennium are two quite different things. But for some people, they do tie neatly together.

A survey conducted by Scripps Howard News Service in the USA in 1999 found that 72 per cent of Americans believed the world will come to a sudden end some day, as the Bible predicts – but not soon. Only 15 per cent – *only* 15 per cent! – said that it was 'very likely' or 'somewhat likely' that the arrival of the (calendar) millennium would mean the world would come to an end.

From the 1960s onwards, particularly with the publication of books such as Hal Lindsay's *The Late, Great Planet Earth*, there has been an increased expectation of Christ's imminent return, and a strong belief that we are living in the End Times. Wars, earthquakes, famines, climatic changes, the multiplicity of 'false prophets' – all are used as evidence that these are the End Times. Not only Hal Lindsay, but former presidential candidate Pat Robertson, founder of the Moral Majority Jerry Falwell, and many other influential American preachers teach versions of the Dispensationalism which John Nelson Darby came up with over a century ago.

Some Christians, following Bishop Ussher of Armagh (1581–1656), believe from the internal chronology of the Bible that the world was created in 4004 BCE (on Sunday 23 October); there were therefore four millennia before Christ, and there have been two after Christ. Taking a literalist interpretation of the verse 'One day is with the Lord as a thousand years, and a thousand years as one day' (2 Peter 3:8) and linking it to the six days of Creation, they believe that we are on the eve of the seventh day; the year 2000 (or thereabouts) is the beginning of the seventh millennium, the Sabbath day when God rested. The new calendar millennium will therefore also be the spiritual millennium, the literal thousand years of Christ's reign on Earth – and Christ will return at the beginning of this millennium, in or around 2000 or 2001.

Such a specific belief is held by very few Christians, but those who do believe it tend to be members of strongly Fundamentalist Evangelical sects, and this is what causes concern among some religion-watchers. Most Evangelicals have a rather more down-to-Earth attitude. One radical Evangelical movement, the Family, has preached the imminent return of Christ ever since they began as the Children of God in the 1960s. As one senior member said some 18 months before the millennium, 'Most scholars think that Jesus was actually born in 4 BC, so if he was going to come back exactly 2,000 years later, it would have been in 1996 – and I think we'd have known about it.'[13]

It has been reported that the former leader of the world's most militarily powerful nation, President Ronald Reagan, read Hal Lindsay's *The Late, Great Planet Earth* in 1971, and was so impressed with it that when he became president in 1981 'he had Lindsay give a talk about "theological" plans for a nuclear war to the chief planners in the Pentagon.' Reagan also had Jerry Falwell attend a National Security Council meeting 'and speak about the relevance of the Bible for nuclear war.' People who worked with Reagan have said that his foreign and military policies stemmed from his apocalyptic beliefs. One of his closest colleagues reported that even Reagan's fiscal policies were in harmony with a literal interpretation of Biblical prophecies. There is no reason to get wrought up about the national debt if God is soon going to foreclose on the whole world.[14]

Millions of people, and many of the Christian movements in this book, believe that we are approaching, or are already in, the Last Days. A few are still setting dates,[15] but most take to heart Jesus' words, that 'ye know neither the day nor the hour wherein the Son of Man cometh' (Matthew 25:13). Without belittling their beliefs, it is helpful to have some understanding of the background to millenarian thinking; the passing of the year 2000 is unlikely to reduce the fervour of those who sincerely believe that Christ is going to return soon.

Notes

[1]Some recent scholarship, based on the Nag Hammadi texts and the Dead Sea Scrolls, sees evidence for belief in two *separate* Messiah-figures, one spiritual and one royal; a third, prophetic, figure is perhaps closer to the role played by John the Baptist.

[2]Benjamin 1998: 56.

[3]See Alexander 1999: 763, 768.

[4]Revelation was one of the last books to be accepted into the New Testament; until Athanasius set out the 'definitive' canon in 367 CE it was often not included, sometimes being replaced by The Shepherd of Hermas.

[5]Thompson 1996: 37.

[6]Quoted in Weber 1999: 57.

[7]Bander 1969/1979: 99.

[8]Most of the Worldwide Church of God's 200 or more offshoots still hold this belief.

[9] This question does not only refer to setting dates for the Second Coming of Christ. Several movements have set dates for the arrival of spaceships; the classic case of non-arrival is described in Festinger, Riecken and Schachter 1956.

[10]Bainbridge, 1997: 135. Festinger's book is *A Theory of Cognitive Dissonance*, Stanford CA: Stanford University Press, 1957.

[11]Edward Miller, 'Irvingism: The Catholic Apostolic Church', in *Religious Systems of the World*, 1908: 598.

[12]But in Uganda, in March 2000, the horrific killing of over 900 people showed that the fears were not groundless. See page 94.

[13]In conversation with the author.

[14]Katz and Popkin 1999: 211–16.

[15]Useful checklists of prophesied dates, both past and still to come, can be found in Mann 1992, and on 'The Doomsday List' at http://www.primenet.com/~heuvelc/skeptic/predictions.htm.

CHAPTER 8

Cults that Kill

How, why, and can it happen again?

T HE death of 913 members of the Peoples Temple in 1978 brought 'killer cults' to public attention. The tragic events in Jonestown, Guyana, were all the confirmation that was needed that cults are dangerous. Worried parents and concerned clergy banded together to brand several new religions as cults, and cults as killers.

It was to be some time before their fears were confirmed.

In 1993, after a well-publicized siege lasting seven weeks, millions of people watched the headquarters of a small Christian sect in Waco, Texas, explode into flames. Some 80 people died there, including 15 children.

Even if there had been no further deaths, the message was clear: cults kill. But there were further deaths.

In 1994 bodies were discovered in burnt-out buildings in Canada and Switzerland. This time it was an obscure occult group, the Order of the Solar Temple.

So far, apart from a number of ATF (Bureau of Alcohol, Tobacco and Firearms) and FBI men at Waco, those who had died had been members of movements. But in March 1995 there was a terrifying development: a cult that turned its deadly attentions outwards rather than inwards. Twelve members of the public were killed on the Tokyo subway in a poison-gas attack by Aum Shinrikyo.

And then, in March 1997, another previously unknown group hit the headlines, as 39 members of Heaven's Gate committed suicide.

All these events have two things in common: non-mainstream religions, and death. But when we start to look at the individual cases a little more closely, we see that drawing generalizations – 'Cults kill!' – is at best not helpful, and at worst potentially very dangerous.

The first point to note is so obvious that it shouldn't need saying. There are many thousands of murders every year that have nothing to do with religion. Causes include common theft, drugs, gangland feuds, *crimes passionnels*, mental instability, personal ambition, separatist politics and so on. Similarly, there are thousands of suicides, again for many different reasons, including (among others) relationship break-up, loss of job, exam pressure, and a general inability to cope in today's fast-paced world. Sometimes a suicide is a member of a new religion, so we might read 'Scientologist commits suicide' – but how often do we read 'Methodist commits suicide' which, simply because of the relative numbers of Scientologists and Methodists, probably happens far more often?

Secondly, we never, of course, see headlines saying 'Moonie doesn't commit suicide' or 'Cult member not murdered'. The absence of news isn't news. There can be 999,999 cases of something *not* happening, and the one case that does happen is reported. This is perfectly natural, because it's the unusual that makes news. But the point that is very easily missed is that it is the unreported non-event which is the norm; the reason that the event is reported is that it is unusual, not normal, exceptional.

In both cases, in scientific terms it depends on the set from which an event is selected; in everyday terms, it means applying a little common sense instead of getting carried away by tabloid headlines. Yes, there have been terrible tragedies in which members of modern alternative religions have committed suicide, or been murdered, or have murdered others – but these are exceptional cases. Such tragedies are actually extremely rare, in comparison to the number of religious movements, and their followers, in the world. To leap to the conclusion that all alternative religions are dangerous is fallacious reasoning.

Despite the similarity of event – members of religious movements dying *en masse* – and some other similarities, the headline stories listed at the beginning of this chapter had quite different circumstances, and different paths to tragedy. In most cases, the following accounts concentrate mainly on the events leading up to the tragedies, rather than being full accounts of the movements. The Branch Davidians are examined in more detail, as an extreme case of a Fundamentalist millennialist group under a powerful charismatic leader.

PEOPLES TEMPLE

One point of similarity between some of the movements was the strength of their leadership. Peoples Temple leader Jim Jones, Branch Davidian leader David Koresh, and Heaven's Gate leader Marshall Herff Applewhite were all charismatic leaders, both in the everyday sense and in the specialist usage of sociology.

According to psychiatrist Anthony Storr, Jones was, from his youth, seriously psychologically disturbed, with an obsessional personality and 'a strong wish to bring everything under his own control, including those around him.'[1] His faked healings and clairvoyance, the humiliations and beatings to which he subjected those of his followers who displeased him, and his sexual relations with some of his members all illustrate this need to control. Eventually he exercised the ultimate control, over not only the lives but the deaths of his followers.

The Peoples Temple was a gift to anti-cultists; because of the unchecked power exercised by one powerful leader, over 900 people died. It was also a gift to sensationalist writing in tabloid newspapers, and merited inclusion in books with titles such as *Killer Cults* and *Brotherhoods of Fear*.[2] But though lessons can and should be drawn from it, the tragedy at Jonestown ought not to be seen as representative of all NRMs. The Peoples Temple had not been labelled as a cult before the tragedy occurred. Indeed, most authorities agree that Jones performed genuine and very worthwhile social work through the Peoples Temple, particularly among blacks and the very poor; members have testified that belonging to his movement gave them a sense of dignity.

Sociologist James Richardson has drawn up an eight-point list of differences between the Peoples Temple and other new religious movements.[3] One of these is 'theology or ideology'. One writer has described the Peoples Temple as 'an adventurous experiment in Marxist philosophy masquerading as apocalyptic Christianity',[4] another makes the point that 'unusual violence' or 'wanton killing' has been far more common in Marxist groups than in religious groups, and even says that 'it seems unfair to religious movements to call the Peoples Temple a church'.[5]

Jones moved the Peoples Temple from California to Guyana partly because of disquiet about his 'healings', partly because of the risk of investigation of financial irregularities, and partly because he was attracted by the Marxist regime in Guyana, and believed he could establish a socialist utopia there. Perhaps there was a further reason: that it was part of an effort 'to overcome the inherent precariousness of charismatic leadership'.[6] Having built up his community of followers, it appears that Jones became more and more paranoid about losing control over them, about any signs of weakness in their dedication, and about members leaving. When US Congressman Leo Ryan and some journalists and concerned relatives visited Jonestown to investigate allegations that people were being held there against their will, Ryan questioned Jones about his armed guards; then several members asked if Ryan could take them back to the USA. It may be that Jones or his guards realized that if word got back to the USA about the true conditions in Jonestown, there would be trouble; Jones' control over his community would be threatened. Ryan and the journalists were shot, and the following day almost the entire community died, by their own hands or others'.

Most accounts have some version of Jones' words, 'It is better to die than to be harrassed from continent to continent.'[7] The tension between the movement and wider society had reached breaking point. Jones had rehearsed the mass suicide with his followers; he said that it was better that the community die together, rather than be split up, and that their mass death 'would vividly demonstrate to the world the evil nature of the US government.'[8] Jones' ideal of a socialist utopia was under threat; so was his control. Psychologically, says Storr, he was paranoid and psychotic, and the vast amount of drugs he took furthered his mental deterioration. If Storr and other commentators are correct, it appears that in the case of the Peoples Temple, more than the other tragedies, the mass suicide/murder was essentially the fault of one deeply disturbed man.

BRANCH DAVIDIANS

The history of the Branch Davidians is presented here to illustrate how a small Church can become, in the sense of devotion to its leader, a cult; to indicate how a religious movement can go seriously awry; and to suggest that the horrifying outcome was (despite the official verdict) easily as much the fault of mainstream society as of the movement itself.

The Branch Davidians were a splinter of a splinter of the Seventh-day Adventist Church; as with their distant cousins the Worldwide Church of God, the more fissioning took place, the further the drift from mainstream Christian beliefs. They were Sabbatarians – worshipping on the Saturday Sabbath – and believers in the imminent return of Christ. Their founder, Victor Houteff (1886–1955), taught at a Sabbath School until his apocalyptic interpretations of Daniel and Revelation caused the Church to expel him. With a dozen or so families he set up a movement called the Shepherd's Rod; in 1935 they moved from Los Angeles to set up a small community near Waco; in 1942 they were renamed the Davidian Seventh-day Adventists, after the Kingdom of David.

Houteff was succeeded by his wife, Florence, who announced that the Second Coming would be in 1959. The movement fragmented when Christ didn't return; many members left, but several formed different groups. One of these was led by Benjamin Roden, who told his followers, 'Get off the dead Rod and move on to a living Branch,'[9] and called his group the Branch Davidians. He died in 1978, and was succeeded by his wife, Lois.

David Koresh was born Vernon Howell in 1959; he joined the Branch Davidians in 1983, and quickly fell out with the Rodens' son George, who had announced himself to be the Messiah. George Roden was already clashing with his mother, and Howell took Lois' side; according to some reports, he also took to her bed in the hope of producing a new Messiah. He was rapidly working himself into a position of influence; in 1984 he married the 14-year-old daughter of a senior Church elder. Lois died in 1986, and George Roden forced Howell out of the community at gunpoint.

The following year Roden tried to establish his own position as leader by raising a 20-years-deceased member of the Church from the dead. Howell tipped off the police, and turned up to confront Roden. After a gun battle, Roden was eventually jailed, and Howell eventually freed. He moved his own followers back to Mount Carmel, near Waco, took over the movement, and in 1990 changed his name legally to David Koresh – David after the king, and Koresh after the Persian king Cyrus; Koresh was also said to be God's surname, and to mean 'death' or 'destroyer'.

Koresh increased the already strong emphasis on End-Time teaching. Over time, sustained by the belief of his followers, he claimed that he understood the seven seals described in Revelation (chapters 5 and 6), and had the power to break the seventh seal (Revelation 8:1); his belief that he was the End-Time messenger of the key to the seven seals led him to call himself the Lamb; though contrary to popular reports, he never claimed to be God.[10]

Koresh was a charismatic leader, and there is no doubt that most of his followers adored him. He was handsome, he was sexy, he played rock guitar; he also had a brilliant mind, knew the Bible inside out, and could preach for hours without notes. When he announced that he had the right to sleep with any woman in the movement in order to spread his holy seed, some members disapproved, but most accepted it. He is said to have slept with at least 15 of the women and girls, some mature and married to other members, and some very young, including the 12-year-old sister of his one legal wife.

Koresh was clearly a powerful and unscrupulous leader looking for a following. But he was also at least partly the creation of the supercharged apocalyptic atmosphere of the movement he had joined in 1983: his followers were looking for a leader. The more power he assumed, the more devotion they gave him; his claim to be the Lamb of God was bolstered by their belief and support.[11]

Life in the Waco community was not easy. Rising at six, the members spent their days building halls and dormitories, a swimming pool, a gym and an underground storm shelter. They spent their evenings listening to Koresh's Bible expositions, which often went on till the early hours. All this on a diet which was often only cornflakes, popcorn and fruit. Male and female members, even married couples, were segregated. The movement had taken on many of the classic features of a religious cult. Over the next year or two, several members gave up and moved out.

It seems that Koresh, like Jones, half-expected an apocalyptic showdown. As his teachings became more extreme, the group became more inward-looking, more separated from the world; the Us–Them mentality grew ever stronger. Mount Carmel was not unique: there are other isolated apocalyptic Christian groups, some of them, like the Branch Davidians, heavily armed and well stocked with military food supplies in anticipation of the final conflict. But because isolation from the corrupt world is one of the things they seek, they actively prefer to be left to themselves. Over time they might fade away, or fission into smaller groups, or continue to exist, either accommodating more to the world, or remaining separated. Although the Branch Davidians were certainly extreme in their beliefs and their isolation, there is no evidence to suggest that they would have committed mass suicide/murder if the ATF, and then the FBI, had not used heavy-handed tactics.

In February 1993, members of the ATF staged a raid on Waco, looking for illegal stockpiles of weapons and ammunition. According to members, although the movement did have weapons of its own, most of the weapons Koresh had purchased in the months before the ATF raid were for other people; Koresh was a registered arms dealer, and made much of the income for the community from legal trading in weapons. The ATF initially claimed that Koresh had been 'holed up' inside the compound, and that their raid was the only way they could arrest him; members – and local shopkeepers – say that he went into town at least once a week, and could have been picked up peacefully at any time.

Opinions differ as to who fired the first shots, but in the ensuing gunfight four ATF agents died, and over a dozen were injured. It is thought that six Branch Davidians were killed, and many were injured, including Koresh, who was shot in the wrist and the waist.

The FBI were called in, and laid siege to the compound. Fifty-one days later, after several surrender deals were unfulfilled by Koresh, they ended the siege by firing CS gas into the compound and ramming the buildings with tanks. The stockpiled weapons and ammunition exploded, and the entire compound became a fireball. The FBI did not allow fire trucks to approach the burning compound for 40 minutes.

Nine members of the movement escaped; around 80 died, a third of them British. At least 15 children were killed. The few survivors claim that they were strip-searched, had their clothes taken away and destroyed, were manacled and paraded in flimsy orange overalls, and were kept in prison for up to 200 days without any trial.

Survivors claimed from the start that the conflagration was sparked by the FBI's attack. The FBI denied this, saying that the members set fire to the compound themselves. In August 1995, the federal authorities were cleared of any culpability. But after years of denial, in court and before Congress, in August 1999 a former senior FBI official admitted that they had fired at least two 'US military pyrotechnic tear gas grenades' into the compound.[12] In view of the overwhelming evidence, US Attorney General Janet Reno appointed former senator John C. Danforth to head a new independent enquiry. Some of the evidence, including ATF and FBI videotapes, photographs and documentation, has apparently gone missing. Claims both by survivors and by independent experts that FBI agents machine-gunned the complex when members of the movement were trying to escape from the fire[13] have been denied by the FBI. An independent British firm has concluded that flashes seen on videotapes were probably caused by sunlight and not by gunfire. In July 2000 a five-member jury in a wrongful death trial advised the judge that the FBI were not responsible for the fire. At the time of writing Danforth's enquiry is still proceeding.[14]

There are many opinions about what went wrong at Waco. Some critics claim that anti-cultists and disaffected former members fed biased information to the authorities. For example, the accusations of child abuse which were widely reported by the media in justification of the FBI tactics rest on the findings of one psychiatrist at a Texas medical school, who found some physical marks but reported that the children he examined were 'friendly, happy and likable... bright and above average'.[15]

There is little doubt that there was a massive lack of understanding by the authorities of what they were dealing with. They consulted some biblical scholars, to analyse Koresh's teachings, and psychiatrists, to analyse his state of mind, but apparently they ignored attempts by sociologists of religion, specialists in new religious movements, to offer their help.[16] Dr Phillip Arnold, both an academic and a Sabbatarian who understood Koresh's strong emphasis on the seven seals of Revelation, went to Waco and offered to intervene.

> I implored the FBI to listen to David Koresh: 'I can help you interpret what he's saying so we can resolve this crisis peacefully,' I told them... But the FBI expressed no real interest in what I was saying to them.[17]

He did manage to speak on a local radio station that Koresh listened to. According to Arnold, Koresh had decided to surrender, and had started writing 'the message of the seven seals' late into the night of 18 April. On the morning of the 19th the FBI moved in. Arnold points to what he sees as the crucial difference in attitude:

> The FBI refused to believe David Koresh was a victim of messianic delusions of grandeur... They wrongly concluded that he was a lying con man. But I thought he was a religious figure. I don't use the categories a psychologist does. 'Delusional' doesn't really capture it as well as 'charismatic religious figure'.[18]

Conciliation rather than confrontation, and a waiting game rather than a frontal attack, might well have avoided the final conflagration which claimed 80 lives. Cutting off the water supply, refusing to allow parcels of baby food to get through, and bombarding the ranch with over-amplified rock music and the death screams of rabbits day and night were tactics more likely to strengthen than weaken the resolve of Koresh and his followers to stand firm against what they regarded as the forces of Satan.[19] The final attack, using tanks to punch holes through the walls, and flooding the ranch with CS gas (which is proscribed for military use because of its harmful effects), might appear almost calculated to precipitate catastrophe.

One leading academic has suggested that American public support for the FBI action at Waco 'reflects a real and possibly growing hostility toward minority religions rooted in the need of American society to have an enemy.'[20] James R. Lewis writes of 'the perpetuation of the cult stereotype' by the media, so that 'Once effectively demonized, the enforcement agencies of the state are free to undertake otherwise unthinkably repressive actions against the target group.'[21]

ORDER OF THE SOLAR TEMPLE

Over 70 members of the Order of the Solar Temple died in Switzerland, France and Canada in 1994, 1995 and 1997. The Solar Temple was an offshoot of the Renewed

Order of the Temple, an esoteric group that combined Rosicrucian and Neo-Templar ideas.[22] It was formed in 1984 by Joseph Di Mambro (1924–1994), with Luc Jouret (1947–1994), a homeopathic practitioner, as its charismatic public figurehead. Jouret gave lectures and workshops, called Amenta; these could lead to an Outer Order, the Archédia Clubs, and then to an Inner Order, the International Order of Chivalry Solar Tradition, which became known as the Order of the Solar Temple.

Several things began to go wrong for Di Mambro at the beginning of the 1990s. His own son revealed that Di Mambro faked the esoteric special effects at Solar Temple ceremonies; members began to doubt the reality of the Masters from whom Di Mambro claimed authority (cf. the origins of the Hermetic Order of the Golden Dawn on page 359); and membership (and thus revenue) began to fall from two or three hundred down to about a hundred. (Unlike the Peoples Temple and the Branch Davidians, whose members were typically unskilled working class, Solar Temple members included businessmen, senior civil servants, local politicians, journalists and other high-prestige occupations.) Di Mambro was also beginning to fall out with Jouret.

One authority on the movement, a Swiss historian, says that Di Mambro had become cut off from the real world, and had created 'his own virtual reality':

His was a world with secret masters, miraculous phenomena during impressively staged nightly ceremonies, an elite of Knights Templar gathered around him in order [to] fulfil a cosmic mission.[23]

Several former members began to speak out publicly against the movement. Then two members who were arrested in Canada for attempting to buy illegal guns implicated Jouret, which resulted in further unfavourable publicity. Things came to a head when a former member, Antonio Dutoit, and his wife Nicky named their baby Christopher Emmanuel. Di Mambro had a daughter called Emmanuelle, whom he claimed had been divinely conceived and was the 'cosmic child', spiritually important to the group. By using the name Emmanuel the Dutoits had created the Antichrist. The Dutoits, with their three-month-old baby, were brutally murdered.

The Solar Temple was an apocalyptic group, believing that the end of the world would be in 1994. Their teachings and imagery had a strong emphasis on fire and death. They also believed that they were only temporarily of this world, and that they were destined to reunite with the Source, which was connected with the star Sirius. By leaving their human bodies they would 'immediately receive new invisible, glorious and "solar" ones.'[24] It appears that their suicides (and in some cases murders) in burning houses were aimed at achieving this end.

Contrary to early rumours, the bodies of both Di Mambro and Jouret were identified among the dead. Contrary to more recent stories, Princess Grace of Monaco was never connected to the Order of the Solar Temple (she died two years before it was founded), though she and Prince Rainier apparently did know the Grand Master of a similarly named group, the Sovereign Order of the Solar Temple, which was established in Monaco in 1967.[25]

AUM SHINRIKYO

Aum Shinrikyo is different from the other movements in this chapter in that it turned its violence outwards, in an act of random killing.

Shoko Asahara was born Chizuo Matsumoto in 1955. After attending a school for the blind he began to study acupuncture and other forms of traditional healing, and also began teaching yoga. Following a spiritual experience he changed his name to Shoko Asahara in 1987, and renamed his growing group of followers Aum Shinrikyo, usually translated as 'Supreme Truth Society'.

In its beliefs Aum Shinrikyo stemmed from a school of Buddhism, with an added emphasis on yoga and a focus on Shiva, the Hindu god of creation and destruction. As the group developed, Asahara also included elements from apocalyptic Christianity, taken from the book of Revelation and from the writings of Nostradamus. The aim was to avoid the apocalypse by changing negative energy into positive energy, through his followers achieving enlightenment.

Right from the beginning there was conflict with society; Asahara wanted to register his movement, ensuring tax and other advantages, but was met with opposition from the families of some members, because he insisted that members separate themselves from their families. Asahara made the dispute into a *cause célèbre* with public demonstrations and legal action, eventually winning his case. Investigative newspaper articles about Aum Shinrikyo were also met with lawsuits.

In the West we are familiar with the sarin attack on the Tokyo subway, but this was actually the culmination of a series of killings. A lawyer, Sakamato Tsutsumi, had been investigating Aum Shinrikyo. He, his wife and young child disappeared in November 1989; their bodies were not found until six years later. In the same year Aum Shinrikyo tried moving into politics, but failed miserably. This very public failure, on top of the increasing attacks on Aum Shinrikyo, caused Asahara to change the emphasis of his teaching. The apocalypse was now inevitable, and Aum Shinrikyo must defend itself against it; it built nuclear fallout shelters, and increased its isolation from the evil world. It is claimed that Asahara used drugs to dominate and subdue some members.

On Asahara's instructions, scientists in Aum Shinrikyo began to develop chemical weapons, specifically sarin gas, for the defence of the group. This was first used offensively in June 1994 in the city of Matsumoto, near the homes of three judges who were involved in a case against Aum Shinrikyo. Seven people died in the attack, and hundreds, including the judges, were injured.

The Tokyo subway attack occurred in March 1995. Ten members of the group punctured bags containing sarin gas when trains were stopped at stations, one of which was near major government and police offices. Twelve people died; thousands were injured.

In the next two months many Aum Shinrikyo members were arrested including, eventually, Shoko Asahara. Some members confessed, and some of the trials have been concluded, with the members being found guilty. At the time of writing Asahara himself is still charged with murder for the three incidents described here, and faces several other charges, including kidnapping.

For several years Aum Shinrikyo steadfastly proclaimed its innocence, but in November 1999 it accepted responsibility for the sarin attacks, issuing a public apology to the victims and their families, and promising to pay compensation. Two months earlier it had said that it would suspend all its external activities, close its branches, stop recruiting new members, and provisionally stop using the name Aum Shinrikyo. In January 2000 Aum Shinrikyo dissociated itself from Shoko Asahara; he would no longer be their leader, or even their guru, though they would still follow his teachings. A new code of conduct would ensure that members did not break the law. There are believed to be around 2,000 members in Japan of what is now known as Aleph, perhaps 500 of them full-time devotees.

HEAVEN'S GATE

In the case of the Peoples Temple, Branch Davidians and, to some extent, Aum Shinrikyo, the deaths were, in one way or another, in direct response to probing from the outside world. The death of 39 members of Heaven's Gate in San Diego was a completely different story. Although Marshall Herff Applewhite had strong influence over his followers, to the extent that some of the men accepted castration because of his teachings, they were a small, tightly knit group with a high degree of consensus. They followed Applewhite's leadership because they were attracted by his teachings; their beliefs were a complex mixture of New Age, Theosophy and science fiction. One of their main beliefs, a version of Gnostic dualism, was that they were divine spirits trapped in human shells. At some point they would be able to cast off their physical shells and progress to the Next Level of development. Like End-Time Christian groups, they eagerly awaited the culmination of their belief system: not the return of Christ, but a sign that they could move on, in their own equivalent of the Rapture.

When Comet Hale-Bopp approached the Earth in March 1997, one photograph was thought to show a small dot in its wake; as a hoax, someone suggested that an alien spacecraft was following behind the comet. Through so-called 'Scientific Remote Viewing', two separate people claimed to have contacted the aliens on board the spacecraft, and reported that they were benevolent.

The members of Heaven's Gate made video recordings expressing their joy that the spacecraft had come to collect them, and that they would be able to leave their human shells behind. There is no indication in the videos of worry, fear or sadness that they were about to die. Unlike the Peoples Temple, there appears to have been a complete consensus, with no coercion from the leader. Thirty-nine men and women, working in three teams, helped each other to die, laid out each other's bodies, each under a purple shroud, and cleared up after each other. Again unlike Jonestown and Waco, which were crisis situations, this was all premeditated and carefully planned; the group posted a letter to a former associate, along with the video, shortly before killing themselves. Members who did not take part in the suicide later said that they approved of the action, though they didn't have the courage to do it themselves.[24]

The social structure of Heaven's Gate was quite different from that of the Peoples Temple and the Branch Davidians. Many of those who died in 1997 were aged around 40 and had been members from the beginning, in 1975. They were educated and intelligent; at the time of their deaths they made their living as a company called Higher Source, designing webpages for the Internet. No children were involved; all those who died were adults who had apparently made their own decision to die. They did not think of it as suicide; the movement's teachings and mythology, developing slowly over 20 years, culminated in Applewhite's warning in October 1996 that *for them to stay on Earth would be suicide*; their only salvation was to escape from the Earth. Six months later they were provided with the excuse to do so.

WHAT CAN WE LEARN FROM THESE TRAGEDIES?

All five of these movements had strong, charismatic leaders. All had a singular understanding of what 'salvation' means, and how and why they would attain it. All had a 'social reality' – beliefs, motivations and preferred lifestyle – distinctively different from those evident in mainstream society. All moved towards an increasing alienation from the world, though in different ways. The two esoteric groups, the Solar Temple and Heaven's Gate, were alienated more by their novel beliefs than by their physical situation: their members interacted with the outside world professionally and socially; it was their unusual beliefs which separated them from mainstream society. Although the Branch Davidians became more isolated towards the end, some members (including Koresh) visited the town of Waco regularly, and some members were able to leave. The Peoples Temple, once they had moved to Jonestown, were the most cut off from the world, with Jones not just a guru and prophet but effectively the dictator of a small 'nation'; the members were completely isolated from outside society, and incapable of leaving.

Whether any of these tragedies could have been avoided is impossible to say. If Waco had been handled differently by the authorities, the Branch Davidians might even now be just one more small, isolated, End-Time Christian sect. The Peoples Temple tragedy was triggered by Congressman Ryan's visit, but the very fact that this happened suggests that the movement was already imploding by that point; in contrast with Rajneeshpuram, a very troubled and well-armed religious community which came to an end relatively peacefully (see page 290), Jonestown seems to have carried the seeds of its own destruction in the disturbed personality of its founder. As for Heaven's Gate, although the mass suicide had an external cause, it was very much an internally motivated culmination of the movement's beliefs; if it had not been Hale-Bopp and the stories of a spacecraft travelling behind it, some other sign might have triggered the same outcome. The 'virtual world' of the leader of the Solar Temple was being exposed, and Di Mambro felt under attack from several angles. Aum Shinrikyo's Shoko Asahara saw persecution, opposition and threat everywhere.

Is there any threat of similar tragedies from other groups? It has been suggested that in the USA there is a possible danger from some white-supremacist ultra-Fundamentalist Christians, in part because they claim a religious justification for their political motivations. It must be stressed that there are millions of millenarian Fundamentalists, especially in the USA, and that the overwhelming majority of these, though fervent believers, have no violent intentions. However, the history of the last century shows that it need only take one finger to press a trigger, or one hand, like Timothy McVeigh's in Oklahoma, to plant a bomb. The risk is very small, but it would be irresponsible to pretend that it does not exist.

However, it would be equally irresponsible to name groups which might possibly have the potential for dangerous actions. Publicly identifying a group as potentially dangerous could actually cause such a group to feel stigmatized, 'demonized', threatened by the authorities; it becomes more inward-looking; the boundaries between 'Us' (the group) and 'Them' (the rest of the world) become more sharply defined; the outside world is seen as evil, corrupt, and worthy of destruction; and an act of violence might occur.

Religious beliefs can be very deeply held, and the more extreme the beliefs, the more different from everyone else's, the more important they are to their believers. As with any religious believers, it is important that we are careful not to cause offence by mocking or trivializing what are sincerely held beliefs. This is even more important in the case of groups which might have the potential for violence. Wider society, including perhaps most of all the media, does need to show some responsibility.

To take the obvious example, whoever was ultimately responsible for the tragedy at Waco in 1993, it is undeniable that there was a huge breakdown in communication and a huge gulf in understanding between the Branch Davidian community and the authorities. In the 'negotiations', David Koresh wanted to talk about his End-Time theology, which to him was the most important thing in the world. The FBI wanted to talk about the weapons he had at Mount Carmel. Once the movement began to feel threatened the gulf became even wider, the boundaries between 'Us' and 'Them' became more fixed, and the eventual horrific outcome became more likely. Because the FBI didn't understand – and apparently made no real attempt to understand – Koresh's millennialist theology, and actually refused to take advice from people who had spent years studying millenarian Churches, around 80 members of the group died, including at least 15 young children. Phillip Arnold, who was at Waco, says:

> The Waco situation cried out for an expert to think and then communicate in terms that the Davidians could comprehend. The expert would have helped control the situation by talking David Koresh's language and understanding his world view.[27]

It is vital that we avoid doing anything which might risk triggering such an outcome again. The gulf in communication, in understanding, between the two sides was not just a negative value, a lack of understanding. It was something much more dangerous: what sociologists call 'deviance amplification', in which both sides increasingly demonize the other in a self-sustaining vicious circle.

Demonizing your opponent is nothing new, and is not restricted to religion. It happens in war, where unpleasant epithets are used to make the enemy seem less than human; it's then easier to justify killing them. It's seen in the ritual exchange of insults between politicians of opposing parties. It's seen in the xenophobic and other campaigns of the worst of the tabloid newspapers. Historically, such demonization has been seen in very obvious ways in mainstream religion – literally, in the treatment of witches and heretics.

The danger with demonizing a heterodox religious movement is that of a self-fulfilling prophecy. Any teacher or youth worker knows that once a child has been branded a troublemaker, he *becomes* a troublemaker, even if he wasn't one before. If a new religion is publicly labelled dangerous, there is far more chance that it will become dangerous, even if it wasn't to start with.

These were movements that 'went bad', with horrifying consequences. There is no doubt that they themselves, and especially their leaders, are largely responsible for the deaths that occurred. But if we want there to be no more 'killer cults', it is we, mainstream society, who bear some of the responsibility for ensuring that something like Waco never happens again – not by banning movements, not by demonizing them as dangerous cults, but by seeking to understand their world view, by observing them carefully but not intrusively, and by seeking to defuse situations which might otherwise get horrendously out of control.

As this book was being completed in March 2000, the news broke of the deaths of at least 330 members (including 78 children) of the Movement for the Restoration of the Ten Commandments of God in the small town of Kanungu, in southwest Uganda. It appears that the windows and doors of their church had been boarded up, and the church then set on fire. At the time of writing little is known about the group except that its leaders were former Roman Catholics, who had preached that the world would end in the year 2000.

Initial reports spoke of mass suicide. It was thought that in the previous few days at least some of the Church members had begun 'to prepare for their deliverance at the hands of the Virgin Mary',[28] some are said to have sold their property, and Church members slaughtered cattle and purchased large amounts of Coca Cola to have a final meal together two nights before the fire. But reports in the following days that over 900 bodies, many of children, had been found in several mass graves on Church property point clearly to murder rather than suicide.

This tragedy exemplifies Massimo Introvigne's words: 'The most dangerous movements are often those we do not know enough about.'[29]

Notes

[1]Storr 1996: 6.

[2] Lane 1996, Elliott 1998.

[3]'People's Temple and Jonestown: A Corrective Comparison and Critique', *Journal for the Scientific Study of Religion*, 19/3, 1980: 239–55, quoted in Barker 1989/1992: 15.

[4]Elliot 1998: 215.

[5]Bainbridge 1997: 359.

[6]McGuire 1997: 165.

[7]Harrison 1990: 7.

[8]Storr 1996: 12.

[9]"And there shall come forth a rod out of the stem of Jesse, and a Branch shall grow out of his roots." Isiah 11:1.

[10]Wilson 2000: 18.

[11]Psychiatrist Anthony Storr finds great similarities between Jim Jones and David Koresh as charismatic leaders. His book is a psychological study of 'what makes a guru'; common factors include childhood intelligence and loneliness, and a physical or mental crisis – a 'creative illness' – in adulthood. But he barely touches on perhaps the most important factor which distinguishes a guru, or 'cult' leader, from all those with a similar psychological profile who never become a guru: the followers. A powerful potential leader looking for a following requires a group of people individually or collectively looking for a leader.

[12]*The Dallas Morning News*, 24 August 1999.

[13]*The Dallas Morning News/ Waco Tribune-Herald*, 2 February 2000.

[14]Danforth's Interim Report, published in July 2000, concluded that "the United States government is not responsible for the tragedy at Waco," but was highly critical of the FBI for its subsequent behaviour. See http://unquietmind.com/wacoreport.pdf

[15]Quoted in James R. Lewis, 'Child Abuse at Waco', in Lewis and Melton, 1994: 162.

[16]Bainbridge 1997: 112–15.

[17]*The Journal: News of the Churches of God*, no. 22, 30 November 1998: 10.

[18]Ibid.

[19]'Any group under siege is likely to turn inward, and pressure from the outside can strengthen the bonds between a leader and followers.' Nancy T. Ammerman, from *Recommendations of Experts for Improvement in Federal Law Enforcement After Waco*, 1993, quoted in Bainbridge 1997: 117.

[20]James R. Lewis, quoted in Bainbridge 1997: 115.

[21]Lewis and Melton 1994: 163–4.

[22]The history, interrelationship and structure of Neo-Templar groups are extremely complex. It should be noted that there are many different types: some are masonic, some charitable organizations, some esoteric Christian, some practise sex-magick, some are linked with secret services, and some are the religious wing of extreme right-wing political organizations. As with so many areas of religious and semi-religious movements, it is a mistake to generalize about them.

For further information on the Knights Templar and Neo-Templar groups, see Barrett 1997: 51–8, 161–2, 181–2.

[23]Jean-François Mayer, 'The Case of the Solar Temple', lecture at the University of Virginia, 13 November 1998, page 15, quoted on Religious Movements Homepage: Order of the Solar Temple at http://cti.itc.virginia.edu/~jkh8x/soc257/nrms/solartemp.html.

[24]Massimo Introvigne, 'Ordeal by Fire: The Tragedy of the Solar Temple', Turin: CESNUR 1995: 15.

[25]Massimo Introvigne, 'Hoaxes and Misunderstandings on the Order of the Solar Temple', CESNUR 1998, http://www.cesnur.org/testi/Grace.htm.

[26]J. Gordon Melton, 'NRMs & Violence', INFORM seminar, 3 May 1997.

[27]*The Journal: News of the Churches of God*, no. 22, 30 November 1998: 11.

[28]J. Gordon Melton, 'Was It Mass Murder or Suicide?' on http://www.beliefnet.com/story/16//story_1640_1.html.

[29]Massimo Introvigne, director of CESNUR, in correspondence with the author, 4 February 2000.

CHAPTER 9

Watching the watchers

The variety of cult experts

I N the same way that it is easy, but misleading, to generalize about 'cults', so it is to lump all 'cult watchers' together. There are several different types of cult expert, with different aims, different motivations, different methods. This chapter looks at some of the major players, in Britain, Europe and the USA, and asks them to define their own role.[1]

Briefly, one might identify three main types of cult-watcher, while noting that there can be overlap between them: observers such as sociologists of religion, the anti-cult movement and the counter-cult movement.

Academic observers study new religious movements in the same sort of way as biologists study fruit flies or cacti, and historians study the English or American Civil Wars: as interesting phenomena in their own right from which, more importantly, we can learn more about religion and society in general (or biology, or history).

The anti-cult movement actively try to discourage people from joining what they label 'cults' (see Chapter 2), encourage people to leave them, and sometimes seek to restrict the freedom of such movements. They emphasize the negative, anti-social, abusive, 'cultish' aspects of movements.

The counter-cult movement use words such as 'cult' and 'sect' to emphasize that such movements are false religions in comparison with their own beliefs, which are usually Evangelical Christian. They emphasize doctrinal aberrations from the Truth, and they seek to rescue people from darkness and help them turn to the Light.

All three types of cult-watcher try to help people who are having problems with religious movements, and families and friends of members, and also provide information about movements to enquirers including students, government bodies and the media.

It is worth making the point here that each of these broad groups is sincere in its aims – especially as there is often friction between them, and sometimes mutual misrepresentation of their aims and work.

ORIGINS OF CULT-WATCHING ORGANIZATIONS

The origins and history of the various cult-watching organizations, particularly in the USA and UK, have been well documented,[2] only a brief summary will be given here.

It is important to see both the upsurge of alternative religions of the last few decades and the consequent development of cult-watchers within their socio-historical context. It is too simplistic to ascribe the growth of new religions solely to the counter-culture of the 1960s, but undoubtedly some of the same factors which 'caused' the Sixties also contributed to the appeal of new religions. In the USA in particular, the post-war baby-boomer generation was coming of age. In comparison with previous generations they were well educated; they had grown up with more material prosperity than their parents' generation had known; they expected life to be good; but as they graduated from school, college and university there were far more of them than there were jobs available for them. Suddenly there was a whole generation of bright, educated, middle-class kids with time on their hands.

With a few notable exceptions, it was precisely this group – white, middle-class late-teens and twenties – who were attracted to new religious movements. Space precludes examination here of the urban poor, racial minorities and other socially disadvantaged groups who, in classic sociological theory, were the type historically attracted to religious sects.

In 1965, in order to gain the support of Southeast Asian countries for its war in Vietnam, the USA relaxed its previously highly discriminatory immigration laws against Asians. The doors to the land of opportunity were open, and an assortment of gurus arrived on America's shores, in some cases with little more than the clothes they stood up in and a begging bowl. Their message of Eastern enlightenment appealed to youngsters who had become jaded with a high-prosperity, consumerist society which delivered less (to them) than it promised.

Haight-Ashbury, Greenwich Village, poets and folk singers, college dropouts, hippies, long hair, draft-dodging: there was a spirit of revolt and revolution, of protest, of searching for meaning. Supply and demand came together.

In real terms, of course, the numbers who followed their spiritual quest into alternative religions were very few. But middle-class America is (in European terms) inherently conservative, and the sight of saffron-robed youngsters or bestickered Jesus People on their streets was as shocking as the burning of the American flag. Their kids were throwing everything away – their education, their future careers, their social position, their money – in order to live rough in communes, enthused by strange gurus and gods.

It was a Christian movement which sparked the first organized resistance to this disturbing new religious enthusiasm. In 1972 a group of concerned parents in America formed FREECOG, originally with the cumbersome title 'Parents Committee to Free Our Sons and Daughters from the Children of God'. The publicity they generated, from their newspaper advertisements and well-reported court cases, brought in parents of youngsters in other movements. In 1973 FREECOG briefly became Volunteer Parents of America, and then the Citizens Freedom Foundation (CFF) was set up, along with a number of small regional organizations.

CFF was in favour of deprogramming:

> ...the process of releasing victims from the control of individuals and organizations who exploit other individuals through the use of mind control techniques. Once released, the victims, rid of the fear that held them in bondage, are encouraged to again think for themselves and to take their rightful place in society, free from further threats to their peace and security.[3]

In the wake of Jonestown, anti-cult feelings understandably ran high, and the CFF was strengthened. But in the late 1970s there began to be a public reaction against deprogramming, and the CFF publicly dissociated itself from kidnapping cult members or holding them against their will; instead, it moved towards the more voluntary 'exit counselling'. In 1984, emphasizing its aims and activities, the CFF became the Cult Awareness Network of the Citizens Freedom Foundation, and then simply the Cult Awareness Network (CAN).

The American Family Foundation (AFF) was founded in 1979 as a 'research centre and educational organization... AFF's mission is to study psychological manipulation, especially as it manifests in cultic and related groups.'[4] It operates a cult information phone line, and publishes *Cult Observer, Cultic Studies Journal* and *Cults and Psychological Manipulation: An Internet Journal*. It also organizes annual conferences attended by a variety of cult-watchers.

> People who seek information or assistance from AFF are typically concerned about groups that appear to be disturbingly manipulative and/or exploitative. Many people use the term 'cult' to describe such groups...
>
> Most inquirers want information on a specific group that troubles them... AFF has developed resources that help inquirers understand how groups can manipulate, exploit, and harm individuals and families and what individuals and families can do to address this harm.[5]

Although CAN and AFF were quite separate organizations with different functions, during the 1980s they 'developed interlocking boards and several joint programmes which had made it ever more difficult to distinguish them.'[6]

To some, the ongoing American parents' campaign against new religions might appear something of an over-reaction; after all, their kids could have been sleeping around, taking drugs, getting involved in crime. In many cases, recruits to NRMs had been doing all these things and more, and had been 'saved' from such behaviour by their commitment to their new-found faith. But for middle-aged, middle-class American parents, it was as much a case of culture shock as anything else; it was not just the religious enthusiasm, but the rejecting of everything they themselves stood for (and had devotedly raised their children to stand for) – it was something outside their experience, something alien, something they simply couldn't comprehend. It was, in a very deep way, un-American. They'd thought that McCarthyism had seen off the menace of communism, but now their own children were living in communes, living without money, begging on the streets for pity's sake. After the careful, loving way they'd been brought up to appreciate American values, they must surely have been brainwashed. Robert Lifton's report on the 'brainwashing' of American soldiers captured by Chinese communists in the Korean War (see page 29) suddenly had a new relevance.

Unfortunately, as is often the way when there is a clash of cultures, some of the parents over-reacted. Some went to court to have their children (who were legally adults) declared mentally incompetent, on the straightforward grounds that no one in their right mind would ever join such a religion. (The same 'justification' gave credence to the brainwashing hypothesis.) With the benefit of hindsight and a much greater awareness now than existed then of what these religions are all about, one might wonder how the parents could ever have imagined such action would bring their children back into the loving family fold.

Some went further, and employed deprogrammers, despite the fact that such people charged high fees for their services with no guarantee of success. Sometimes the 'child' would be persuaded to come home on a pretext, or to meet their mother in a supposedly safe neutral place; sometimes they would literally be snatched on the street, bundled into a car, and driven away. They would then be locked up, held against their will, for as long as the process might take.

The idea was that as the errant son or daughter had been brainwashed, deviously programmed into believing a set of nonsense, a similar process could be employed in reverse. In the worst cases, deprogrammers would harangue the cult member for days and nights on end, attacking the cult leader, ridiculing the beliefs, stressing over and over again how evil and deceptive the cult was, that it had tricked the person into becoming a member, that it had turned them into a zombie, taking away their free will... and so on. Eventually the member would break down under this assault, the brainwashing would be stripped away, and all the beliefs and habits which had been programmed into them would be deprogrammed.

It hardly needs pointing out that such an approach was not only illegal – kidnapping, forcible imprisonment, etc. – but highly dangerous in its psychological effects. It was also, in the main, ineffective. Sometimes the parents, seeing their son or daughter attacked and humiliated in this way, would break down first and stop the proceedings. Sometimes the 'child' would pretend to be weakening, to lull their tormentors into a false sense of security, and then manage to get to a telephone to call for help, or even escape from wherever they were being held. In many cases, after the parents intervened or the deprogrammers gave up, the member would still be strong in their beliefs. After all, they had found love, peace and security in the movement they had joined; outside, they had been subjected to physical, verbal and mental abuse at the instigation of their parents. It simply confirmed and reinforced what they already believed about 'the System', the evil outside world.

To be fair, most cult-watching organizations condemned the activities of deprogrammers, some perhaps on the basis that the cure was worse than the disease, others because of the illegality of the whole process. But evidence has been presented to courts indicating that the Cult Awareness Network, while decrying the activity publicly, used to refer distressed parents of young members to deprogrammers, and collected a referral fee for doing so.

In 1996 the Cult Awareness Network was successfully sued, along with deprogrammer Rick Ross, over the deprogramming of a member of an American Pentecostal Chuch; the million-dollar judgement forced CAN into bankruptcy. The name, phone number and assets of CAN were purchased at auction by a group which included Scientologists; the Church of Scientology had bitterly opposed CAN for many years, even publishing a 145-page book entitled *The Cult Awareness Network: Anatomy of a Hate Group*, with the sub-title 'An Analysis of Violence and Crime Incited by the Cult Awareness Network'. The new Cult Awareness Network claims to promote freedom of religion and to offer unbiased information about new religious movements. It has been called 'an anti-anti-cult group'.[7]

BRITISH ANTI-CULT GROUPS

In Britain there are several cult-watching groups, with several different approaches.

FAIR (Family Action Information and Resource [formerly Rescue]) was founded in 1976 by Paul Rose MP, 'in response to requests for help and information from distressed relatives and friends of young adults who had joined various extremist cults.'[8]

'FAIR offers advice and support to families as well as individuals who have been adversely affected by cult involvement.' It appears to be concerned mainly about the separation of cult members from their families. In addition to supplying speakers and publishing fact sheets, it 'issues warning leaflets to put young people on their guard.' The word 'rescue' in their former name didn't mean kidnapping and deprogramming:

FAIR provides resource material and advice for cult members, but an individual's decision to leave a cult must remain his/her own. FAIR does not seek to convert cult members to any other belief. It merely aims to restore them to that state of mind in which rational judgement can be made.

'To me this is not a religious problem,' says Audrey Chaytor, chairman of FAIR.

It is a problem of influence and manipulation and can be one of harrassment. The main problems that I see with 'cults' are those. The number of people who go out searching for something to join is so small that one can almost ignore this aspect...

The main problems with 'cults' as I see them, is that cult membership is something which is promoted by those 'employed' to recruit, and is never simply for the good of the 'recruited'.[9]

FAIR publishes a quarterly magazine, *FAIR News*, containing articles about people's experiences in movements, and reprints of press stories about a wide range of groups.

The Cult Information Centre (CIC) was founded in 1987 by Ian Haworth, who had once briefly been caught up in a 'self-improvement' or therapy group in Canada. CIC is not concerned about the spiritual beliefs of movements so much as the human rights abuses it believes they commit, particularly in recruitment.

CIC is concerned about the use of deceptive and manipulative methods used by cults to recruit and indoctrinate unsuspecting members of society. CIC believes that these cult methods present a threat to the well-being of the individual and the family. Consequently CIC sees the need for gathering and disseminating accurate information on cultism and aims to meet that need.[10]

Rather than the term 'brainwashing', it uses the terms 'psychological coercion' and 'mind control'; it lists 26 'manipulative techniques'

(often combined with deception) that groups or individuals can use, which will impair a person's critical ability and restrict their freedom of choice... Because of our position on mind control we would not normally describe a person as 'joining' a cult but rather as 'being recruited'. Joining implies that a person has made the decision freely, without pressure or coercion, having had the opportunity to reflect on the level of commitment they are making and its consequences.[11]

CIC is careful to distinguish between cult groups, as they define them (see page 20), and

the many hundreds of new religious movements, alternative spiritualities etc. in existence. We would not define a group as a cult or see it as an object of concern simply because it is new or alternative (either in its framework of beliefs or lifestyle).

Catalyst was founded in 1993 by former university chaplain Graham Baldwin, 'who found that the availability of cult-related counselling was in short supply and heavily outweighed by those who needed help.'

When Catalyst is first approached for help, the initial step involves providing the victim and family with an introduction to cults... Secondly, a plan is prepared that gives support to the family and is tailored to the best interests of the victim. The third stage involves counselling the victim, if possible, and providing on-going support for the whole family.

Its use of the word 'victim' gives an indication of how it views new religious movements:

> The influence of cults and the devastating effects on the lives of victims and their families is a growing problem in Britain. It is estimated that since the end of WWII more than 1,500 new religious and cultic groups have been established in the UK, with a frightening explosive increase occurring in just the last 25 years...
>
> No one is immune to the influences of a cult. Dependence can be brought about in a fearfully short time, sometimes within a single encounter. The victim is often suffering emotional, marital, sexual or spiritual problems and is seeking help. Cult recruiters exploit these circumstances using well-documented psychological techniques to break down and re-mould the victim's personality, securing total dependence. Hypnosis, ego destruction and environmental and diet manipulation are often utilized to change the victim's perception of life and the truth.
> *The Victim is frequently estranged from their family by the cult – often for pure financial gain... Many suffer emotional and sexual abuse, and some attempt suicide.*[12] (Italics in original.)

Catalyst has no specific religious position; its trustees and its staff are multi-faith. 'Some of our work is about reconciling people with different beliefs,' says Baldwin. 'We specialize in helping people with religious problems, whether they are cultic or just a difference of cultural backgrounds.'[13]

COUNTER-CULT GROUPS

Counter-cult groups are also against alternative religions, but for different reasons from those of CIC, FAIR and Catalyst. Doug Harris, leader of the Reachout Trust, which was originally established to target Jehovah's Witnesses, says:

> We are an Evangelical Christian group and deal with many that are counterfeit Christian groups – that is those that claim to be Christian but their message is shown to be different to the original Christian message...
>
> The main test for counterfeit Christian cults would be to compare fundamental doctrines of the group with the original. Tests for other cults would include the way that people are treated especially if they are dominated. We do not use the term cult in a derogatory way.[14]

Reachout, then, on doctrinal grounds, would class the Mormons, Christadelphians,

Jehovah's Witnesses and other Christian-type movements as cults, while these might be ignored by anti-cult organizations because they rarely exhibit abusive 'cultic' characteristics.[15] Reachout was formed, says Harris, because:

> No one was seeking to show the original truth to these groups and we gave those in the groups the opportunity to compare the copy message they had with the original.

The main problems that he sees with cults also involve spiritual truth:

> There is a potential for causing unnecessary grief and pain to individuals and families in this life. Where the group also offers 'eternal life' there could be major problems for the future too if the way is not actually leading to the destination they promised...
>
> ...all offering a 'ticket to heaven' that is a dud will be harmful in the final analysis.

The Reachout Trust gained national prominence in the late 1980s and early 1990s when one of its founders, Maureen Davies, played an active part in the Satanic Ritual Abuse scare: 'The Reachout Trust is aware of 30 satanic ritual abuse rings operating in Britain.'[16] She also claimed that 'teenagers are prepared to be murdered and to commit suicide for their belief system in reincarnation,' and attacked the Duke of Edinburgh Award Scheme because its curriculum included the game 'Dungeons and Dragons' which, she said, 'is really witchcraft or Satanism dressed up and called fantasy' and is 'actually just a way of promoting witchcraft.'[17]

The Reachout Trust appears to have modified its stance on Satanic Ritual Abuse since then. Harris says: 'Are there instances of abuse that are wrapped up in satanic ritual – yes. But if you mean that every witches' coven sacrifices children – no.'

Evangelical counter-cult groups are also prominent in the USA. The promotional flier for the *Christian Research Journal* is headed, 'So many errors. So little time.' It goes on:

> Your younger *sister* is swayed by missionaries at her doorstep who advance a counterfeit – though persuasive – version of the gospel. Your *co-worker* openly promotes his New Age philosophy, claiming that Jesus was just someone who had attained a 'higher consciousness'. Your next-door *neighbour* dismisses the Bible saying, 'Darwin proved that we are a product of evolution.' BECAUSE YOU CARE ABOUT THEM, you have to get involved. Just think, you may be the only voice of biblical wisdom they ever hear. Souls are at stake. You owe it to them to be prepared.[18] (Emphases in original.)

This is published by the California-based Christian Research Institute (CRI), whose mission is:

> to provide Christians worldwide with carefully researched information and well-reasoned answers that encourage them in their faith and equip them to intelligently represent it to people influenced by ideas and teachings that assault or undermine othodox, biblical Christianity.[19]

The CRI was founded in 1960 by Walter Martin, author of the influential book *The Kingdom of the Cults*. 'He understood – when others would not – that biblical Christianity was under attack from the outside and inside – from liberalism and cultism and heresy.'[20] The CRI is concerned with 'equipping people like you with answers and training you to *use those answers* in the great eternal battle for the souls of people all around you.' It is openly Evangelical and evangelistic; indeed, the emphasis of its bi-monthly *Report*, a four- or six-page A4 leaflet, appears to be as much on scriptural exegesis and on promoting books by its current president Hank Hanegraaff (who runs a question-and-answer radio broadcast called *Bible Answer Man*), as on giving information on cults. The CRI offers over 130 books, tapes and videos, of which around 35 focus on Mormonism, Jehovah's Witnesses, Freemasonry, Roman Catholicism, the New Age and other movements.

There is a similar organization in Australia, Concerned Christians Growth Ministries (CCGM), founded by Churches of Christ minister Adrian van Leen in 1979, the year after the Jonestown tragedy. Their magazine *Take a Closer Look*, in its first issue, said that its aim was 'to make you aware of the constant and growing threat of pseudo-Christian and non-Christian cults.'[21] It is, however, aware of the disinformation which is sometimes spread, deliberately or unwittingly, by anti-cultists and Churches; in one issue it exposes the recurring hoax about Proctor & Gamble's trademark supposedly having Satanic connections:

> Our Ministry has further material available on this – and other hoaxes. Before accepting something new, dramatic, different – regardless of the source – stop and check it out before passing it on... And when you discover the truth about a hoax... let your pastor or priest know, stop hoaxes from spreading.[22]

OTHER GROUPS

There is a third broad category of cult-watchers, in addition to anti-cult and counter-cult organizations. Some of these are sociologists of religion; others have links with sociologists or other scholars of religion.

In Britain, INFORM (Information Network Focus on Religious Movements) was set up in 1988 by Eileen Barker, professor of sociology at the London School of Economics, with support from the Home Office and the mainstream Churches.

INFORM collects, analyses and provides information 'about the diverse beliefs, practices, membership, organization and whereabouts of new religious movements, and about the consequences of their existence.'[23] It also acts as the hub of an international network of useful contacts for those with an interest in or concern about NRMs; this includes both current and ex-members, friends and relatives of members, clergy, counsellors, and scholars and other researchers.

'Members of staff provide enquirers with objective information and practical suggestions on how best to deal with what can be extremely difficult situations,' says Rachel Storm, acting director of INFORM.[24] 'They can also provide a much-needed listening ear.' INFORM doesn't provide counselling itself, but can put enquirers, such as concerned parents, or people who are leaving or have just left a movement, in touch with trained counsellors. It also organizes twice-yearly public seminars, and gives talks to clergy, schools and colleges.

Barker set up INFORM 'because some of the information provided by both the movements themselves and some of the other cult-watching groups was inaccurate, and most of them provided only selective or biased information.'[25] She believes that 'the results of scholarly research should be made more accessible to the general public.'

INFORM stresses that it is neither anti-cult nor pro-cult. The leaflet it distributes to universities, colleges and schools points out many of the same problems emphasized by the anti-cult groups:

There are some new religious movements that promise solutions to life's difficulties but can land you with more problems that you started with!
Some are dishonest or secretive about who they really are.
Some demand much more of your time than you might have bargained for.
Some could cost you a lot of money and get you into serious debt.
Some might lead you into an emotional dependence, and you could find it harder to leave than to join.[26]

Many of the enquiries which come into INFORM are from family and friends of people who have become involved in movements; a considerable number also come from the media. 'We think it's important that balanced, accurate, up-to-date information should get out into the public domain, not least so that people aren't worried by sensationalist misinformation,' says Storm.

Based in Turin, Italy, CESNUR (the Centre for Studies on New Religions) was set up in 1988 by a group of religious scholars from European and American universities. 'Our idea was that although many academic organizations did deal with NRMs there was no academic organization devoted only to NRMs,' says Massimo

Introvigne, CESNUR's director.[27]

CESNUR's original aim was to offer a professional association to scholars specialized in religious minorities, new religious movements, contemporary esoteric, spiritual and gnostic schools, and the new religious consciousness in general. In the 1990s it became apparent that inaccurate information was being disseminated to the media and the public powers by activists associated with the international anti-cult movement. Some new religious movements also disseminated unreliable or partisan information. CESNUR became more pro-active and started supplying information on a regular basis, opening public centres and organizing conferences and seminars for the general public in a variety of countries.

Today CESNUR is a network of independent but related organizations of scholars in various countries, devoted to promote scholarly research in the field of new religious consciousness, to spread reliable and responsible information, and to expose the very real problems associated with some movements, while at the same time defending everywhere the principles of religious liberty.[28]

CESNUR's scholarly research does have practical applications; for example, 'We try to help law enforcement to distinguish between mere bizarre or fringe groups and others engaging in violent and other illegal activities,' says Introvigne. About the importance of research he says: 'The most dangerous movements are often those we do not know enough about.' In 1997 CESNUR organized a conference on new religions for the European Parliament at Strasbourg.

CESNUR does not believe that all religious movements are benign. The fact that a movement is religious does not mean that it could not become dangerous. To the contrary, our experience shows that dangerous or even criminal religious movements do exist... [C]ourts of law... could and should intervene when real crimes are perpetrated. Consumers of spiritual goods should not enjoy less protection than consumers in other fields... On the other hand 'cults' in general should not suffer for the crimes of a minority of them. We are against special legislation against 'cults'... Any minority happening to be unpopular could be easily accused [of using] the invisible and non-existing weapon of 'brainwashing', and special legislation would reduce religious liberty to an empty shell.

In the USA, CESNUR is independently represented at the Institute for the Study of American Religion, based in Santa Barbara, California. The Institute's director is J. Gordon Melton, who is also Specialist in Religion at the University of California, Santa Barbara, and author and editor of numerous major reference books on religious movements (see Bibliography). Melton, James R. Lewis and other scholars associated with the Institute have produced several book-length studies on individual movements, including the Family and the Church Universal and Triumphant.

◯

Over the last two decades unfriendly rivalry between the different types of cult-watching organizations has often surfaced. Scholars in new religions have accused anti-cult groups of believing uncritically the anecdotal stories of disgruntled ex-members, of encouraging ex-members to believe that they are victims of manipulation, deceit and abuse, and of irresponsible scare-mongering. Anti-cultists have accused the scholars of believing uncritically whatever cults tell them, of being pro-cult, and of ignoring the very real problems revealed by ex-members of movements. One of the most contentious issues has been the concept of brainwashing or mind control, in which most anti-cultists believe and most scholars don't (see page 29). On several occasions different types of cult-watchers have acted as opposed expert witnesses in court cases, leading to further antagonism and mutual mistrust.

Although these different types of groups have different motivations, they do share some similar aims – to provide information about new religions, and to help those who have difficulties with them. It might be hoped that the antagonism between them might diminish, and that they might find some areas of mutual tolerance and appropriate co-operation.

Notes

[1] While researching this chapter, I wrote to over a dozen 'cult-watching' organizations spanning the whole spectrum, for the same reason that I contacted religious movements: to seek their direct input in their own words. Because at the time of writing this book I was working one day a week for INFORM, and so might be thought not to be impartial, I sent the same list of questions which I sent to all the other cult-watching organizations, to the acting director of INFORM for her comments rather than my own.

[2] See, for example, J. Gordon Melton, 'Anti-cultists in the United States: An Historical Perspective'; Frank Usarski, 'The Response to New Religious Movements in East Germany after Reunification'; George D. Chryssides, 'Britain's Anti-cult Movement', all in Wilson and Cresswell 1999: 211–33, 235–54, 255–73; Bainbridge 1997: 234–7; etc.

I have drawn from these and other sources for the background information in this chapter; I also wish to thank Jane M. Cooper for the loan of *From Thought Reform to Mind Control: The Cultivation of the 'Brainwashing' Model*, her BA dissertation at the School of Oriental and African Studies, University of London, 1999 (unpublished), which contained some useful material.

The Religious Movements website of the University of Virginia contains a useful summary of the differences between the anti-cult and counter-cult movements, along with website addresses for several (mainly American) examples of each:

http://cti.itc.virginia.edu/~jkh8x/soc257/nrms/anticulttemp.html.

3'What is Deprogramming?', *Citizens Freedom Foundation News*, 1 (1), November 1974: 1, quoted in Wilson and Cresswell 1999: 218.

4Leaflet: *AFF: Family Education Service*, n.d.

5Ibid.

6Melton, in Wilson and Cresswell 1999: 223.

7'Anti-Cult, Counter-Cult, Analytical Links' on http://cti.itc.virginia.edu/~jkh8x/soc257/nrms/anticulttemp.html.

8FAIR leaflet, n.d.

9Audrey Chaytor, chairman of FAIR, in correspondence with the author, 11 December 1999.

10CIC leaflet, 1993.

11This and the next quotation are from correspondence from CIC to the author, December 1999.

12'The Growing Problem of Cults', Catalyst website: wysiwyg://1/http://www.catalyst-uk.freeserve.co.uk/home.htm.

13Graham Baldwin, founder of Catalyst, in conversation with the author, 17 March 2000.

14Doug Harris, Reachout Trust, in correspondence with the author, 9 December 1999.

15The counter-cult emphasis on spiritual truth is nothing new. The 1962 edition of a 1948 book, *Heresies and Cults*, by the then general director of the China Inland Mission of the Overseas Missionary Fellowship, includes Roman Catholicism:

> We place Roman Catholicism at the head of the list of heresies, since it is the largest and most influential of them all. Its emissaries circle the globe, claiming that their Church alone has universal sovereignty over the souls of men, and having as their avowed objective the bringing of every creature into subjection to the Roman Pontiff. (Sanders 1962: 20)

It works both ways; *A Handful of Heresies*, a book bearing the Catholic *Nihil obstat* and *Imprimatur*, includes Protestantism. (Cozens 1974: 66–72)

16Maureen Davies in the *Western Mail*, 14 August 1989, quoted in Gilbert 1993: 153.

17Maureen Davies in a public lecture, 'Report on American Trip', in Gilbert 1993: 108, 87.

18*Christian Research Journal* promotional flier, 1999.

19*Christian Research Report*, vol. 13, no. 1, January 2000: 6.

20Ibid.

21*Take a Closer Look*, vol. 20, no. 5, September 1999: 2.

22Ibid.: 6.

23INFORM leaflet, n.d.

24Rachel Storm, acting director of INFORM, in conversation with the author, 13 March 2000.

25Eileen Barker in conversation with the author, 1995.

26INFORM leaflet: *Searching?*, n.d.

27Massimo Introvigne, director of CESNUR, in correspondence with the author, 4 February 2000.

28'About CESNUR', CESNUR website at http://www.cesnur.org/about.htm.

CHAPTER 10

Historical Diversity

A brief summary of world religions

OST of the new religions described in this book stem from well-established mainstream religions. This chapter provides a very brief introduction to the major religious traditions of the world, to supply a context for the entries on modern movements. For a selection of the many excellent books giving far more detail on the major world religions, see the Bibliography.

EARLY RELIGION

Religion appears to have been with mankind ever since we were able to consider such things as the mysteries of birth and death, and where people go to, if anywhere, in their dreams and after death. Many volumes have been written on the origins of religion, on why it is that mankind has seemingly needed to have belief in God or gods or spirits since grunts became words, since *homo* became *sapiens*.

Christian Creationists, following the Genesis account literally, see religion as revealed by God to man, and seemingly to man created out of whole cloth (or at least out of the dust of the ground, and woman out of a rib), complete with speech and some glimmerings of civilization. Millions of people, particularly in the USA, believe some version of this. Others prefer to accept one version or another of evolution: evolution of plants and animals, of man, of civilization — and of religion.

We do not know how and why religion developed.[1] The nineteenth- and early twentieth-century theories of, for example, Sir James Frazer, in an evolution from magic to religion to science, and of Edward Tylor, in animism, a primitive belief in unseen spirits, have fallen into academic disfavour. Today's social anthropologists have a variety of theories, and it may be that some elements of all of them are correct — in other words, that we cannot generalize one single theory to account for the development of religion in many differing societies.

For early man to survive, animals had to be hunted and crops had to be grown; physical strength and the weather were all-important. At one time perhaps every tribe had its own gods and goddesses, who protected the people, helped them in war, and helped their crops to grow. It was accepted that other tribes had their own gods; if another tribe defeated your own, their gods were probably stronger than yours. As tribes fought each other, traded with each other, migrated and intermarried and intermingled, gods and the worship of gods also intermingled, and more complex religious beliefs and practices developed.

One theory suggests that there was often a multiplicity of gods or powerful spirits (the distinction is now not always clear), all of whom had their own responsibilities and, as religious ideas developed, their own personalities, and each of whom had to be persuaded or appeased in an individual, appropriate way. Sometimes there was one or more deity who was so big, so powerful and so distant that he or she could not be approached directly. The lesser gods were more approachable, more immediate; they could understand the need for rain, or sun, or healing from an injury, and might be persuaded to do something about it.

Another theory sees it a different way around: that early societies believed in one Supreme Being, the Source of All Life, the Oneness of the Otherworld, of the world of Nature, and of Man himself; and so the spirit of a tree, or a river, or thunder, was not God or even a god, but was *an aspect* of the Source. But there is often a disparity between the formal belief system of the spiritual leaders, the shamans and priests, and the actual beliefs of the common man – who, in this case, was perhaps more likely to have perceived these aspects as individual gods.

The idea of the distant, all-powerful God being approached through intermediaries is common to many major religions even today: for many Hindus, their multiplicity of gods are an attainable way of approaching the unapproachable Brahma, while Roman Catholics have for centuries asked Mary and the saints to intercede for them.

Sometimes gods would work together; at other times they would seem to be working against each other. As the gods developed personalities, they developed relationships and family hierarchies; they became humans writ large, with all the virtues and faults of humans magnified. Greek, Roman, Norse and other mythologies are full of stories of such gods. At times it is difficult to distinguish between the exaggerated stories of human heroes and the exploits of the gods; the latter were often based on the former, but also, to add to the prestige of a hero, he would often assume attributes of one of the gods – or be declared a god after his death.

Man-like gods and god-like men are common in mythology and early history. In some societies the king was the living embodiment of God. In early crop fertility religions, the king might symbolically (perhaps, sometimes, literally) be sacrificed to represent the death of crops and of the sun in winter, and be brought back to life to symbolize the rebirth of green shoots in the new year. The echoes in Christianity are obvious. (So are the differences. In nature, a plant dies in winter, then comes back again the following spring; it is possible that this simple observation could be the origin of belief in reincarnation.)

Various pantheons, neglected for centuries, are resurfacing in the Celtic revival in Britain, the interest in Native American shamanism in America, and in the Northern Tradition in central and northern Europe.

HINDUISM

Hinduism is the oldest of the major established religions, though it might more fairly be called a group of interrelated religions. The word Hindu actually refers to the people and culture of the Indus Valley region, now on the border between Pakistan and India – so, effectively, it means 'the religion(s) of the Indian peoples'. The earliest of the beliefs now incorporated in Hinduism dates back to maybe 3000 BCE, though the sacred book of 1,028 hymns, the *Rig Veda*, was composed around 1400–1200 BCE.

For the Westerner, Hinduism has a bewildering variety of gods and goddesses, and an equal variety of ways of worshipping and serving them. As Hinduism spread geographically, its inherent flexibility enabled it both to absorb and to adapt to local religious ideas. Of the almost countless gods and demi-gods (actually 33 million minor gods), most of them unique to individual villages, the best known are the 'trinity' of Brahma the Creator, Vishnu the Sustainer and Shiva the Destroyer – and also, today, Krishna, an avatar (the visible descent to Earth of a deity) of Vishnu.

Given the number of gods, and the age of the religion, it is hardly surprising that there are many quite different varieties of Hinduism; or that modern movements with Hindu origins can be quite different from each other, as we shall see later. Some focus in a traditional way on one of the gods, such as Krishna; others are more deeply philosophical.

Hindus believe in reincarnation, the idea that after death the soul is reborn into another body; the quality of the next life you live depends on what you do and what you learn in your current life: *karma*. Reincarnation is central not only to many present day Eastern-inspired religions, but also to many esoteric and Neo-Pagan movements.

BUDDHISM

The word 'Buddha' means 'Enlightened One' or 'One Who Is Awake', and there have been a number of Buddhas over the centuries, the best known (and founder of Buddhism) being Siddhartha Gautama (c. 560–480 BCE; some sources say 623–543 BCE), a prince who renounced his privileged life to seek understanding. In the traditional story, he achieved enlightenment while sitting under a bo tree, aged 35. His teachings are known as the *dharma*.

By practising morality and meditation and gaining wisdom, Buddhists aim to escape from *samsara*, the cycle of birth, death and rebirth, and attain *nirvana* (literally 'no-being'), the ultimate, peaceful, transformed consciousness.

The two main schools of traditional Buddhism are Theravada and Mahayana. The earlier of the two, Theravada Buddhism, is found mainly in Burma, Sri Lanka and Thailand, while different forms of Mahayana Buddhism are found mainly in China, Japan, Korea and Tibet, though Tibetan Buddhism is often considered to be a separate school. Within each school there are many different traditions.

Theravada Buddhism lays great stress on an individual's own self-improvement and salvation, though this can only be attained by living a strict monastic life. The Mahayana lifestyle is less strictly ascetic, depending more on faith and devotion. Mahayana Buddhism lays more emphasis on the possibility of anyone eventually becoming a *bodhisattva*, someone who has attained enlightenment, but delays his or her passage to nirvana in order to help others along the same path. Celestial bodhisattvas, or *mahasattvas*, are effectively equivalent to gods, which helped Buddhism take hold in Indian villages with their individual Hindu beliefs.

A third strand, Tantric Buddhism, is more text-based and ritualistic, with much recital of mantras, though it is often associated today with spiritual sexual exercises.

Zen Buddhism, very fashionable in the Western world since the 1960s, is a fusion of Mahayana and Chinese Taoist beliefs. Its aim is the direct experience of enlightenment (*satori*). Teaching, texts and worship can be useful unless they become important in themselves, and so get in the way of satori. All ordinary aspects of life, from cooking a meal to driving a car, are seen as a form of meditation. As there are no set doctrines or ceremonies, Zen particularly lends itself to blending with other religious traditions.

Most forms of Buddhism emphasize the basic teachings of the Four Noble Truths and the Noble Eightfold Path. The Four Noble Truths state that life is inherently full of suffering; at the heart of suffering lies craving; suffering can be removed by the cessation of craving through the attainment of liberation, or nirvana; and that the way to do this is to follow the Eightfold Path.

This emphasizes right knowledge, understanding or views, right thought or intentions, right speech, right action, right livelihood, right effort, right mindfulness and right composure or concentration. These eight are grouped in the Threefold Discipline: the first two are associated with *pajna* (insight), the next three with *vinaya* (morality), and the last three with *dhyana* (spiritual discipline and meditation). The essence of Buddhist living is: 'Not to do any evil; to cultivate good; to purify one's mind' (*Dhammapada* 183).

Buddhism came to both Britain and America at the very end of the nineteenth century; in Britain, the Buddhist Society was established by Christmas Humphries in 1924. Interest in Buddhism in America was rekindled after the Vietnam War.

ZOROASTRIANISM

Zoroaster, or Zarathustra, was probably the son of a pagan priest, living in Persia from c. 660 to 583 BCE – or perhaps earlier, c. 1200 or even 1400 BCE. At the age of 30 he had a religious experience in which the one god, Ahura Mazda (the Wise

Lord), told him to reform the polytheistic beliefs and sacrificial practices of his land. In a practical move, the earlier gods were absorbed into the new religion as assistants to the one god (compare the adaptation of local gods such as Brighid or Brigit into the well-loved Irish Saint Brigid). Although monotheistic, Zoroastrianism is responsible for the idea of a good spirit of god and an evil spirit of god, light and darkness, two equal but opposite beings; this dualist belief has informed much of later religion whether overtly, in some of the Gnostic religions, or covertly in the Christian counterparts of God and the Devil. The Zoroastrian evil force is Angra Mainyu, or Ohriman. Zoroastrianism has also had profound effects on Jewish, Christian and Islamic beliefs in the afterlife, including resurrection, heaven and hell.

The sacred texts are the *Avesta*; especially revered are the 17 hymns written by Zarathustra, the *Gathas*. Fire is central to Zoroastrian worship, symbolizing Truth, and God's power and purity – but contrary to popular misconception, it is not worshipped in itself. Zoroastrianism has high moral ideals, teaching a threefold path of good thoughts, good words and good deeds. Charitable work and civic duty are valued. Zoroastrianism has no equivalent of monasticism, asceticism, celibacy or fasting.

When Islam took hold in Persia in the eighth century CE, many Zoroastrians moved to India, where three-quarters of the roughly 150,000 total live today, known as Parsis. There are around 3,000 Parsis in Britain, and perhaps as many in northern America. Traditionalist Zoroastrians discourage marriages outside the religion; also, as in Judaism, proselytization is rare. There is a small liberal element in the USA which believes that Zoroastrianism should be a universal religion rather than being an ethnic Persian religion, and thus encourages conversion to the religion.

JUDAISM

Judaism is a landmark in the history of world religions. It is the last of the major religions to be associated almost entirely with one people: the Jewish race and the Jewish religion are inseparable. When an African tribe was found to have a religion very similar to Judaism, it caused tremendous debate on whether it was possible to be a Jew by religion if you were not a Jew by blood. It is, of course, possible for the opposite to occur, for a Jew by birth to join another religion. In the last few decades there has been a very strong missionary campaign by some Christian groups to convert Jews to Christ. One remarkable statistic put out by some of the 'cult-watching' organizations is that in the USA one-quarter of recruits to the more recent new religious movements are Jewish by birth. Judaism is unusual in that it does not actively seek to recruit new members from other religions.

Judaism was one of the first major monotheistic religions. Although initially Yahweh was seen as a tribal god – 'I am the God of thy father, the God of Abraham, the God of Isaac, and the God of Jacob' (Exodus 3:6) – and greater than any other gods – 'Thou shalt have no other gods before me' (Exodus 20:3) – as the religion developed he became the only true God, all others being false rather than lesser.

At the time of Jesus there were several factions in Judaism, the four most prominent being the class-based and conservative Sadducees, with their emphasis on the Temple; the Pharisees, who taught rigorous observance of the Law, and from whom today's rabbinical Judaism developed; the radical purist Essenes; and the freedom-fighting Zealots.

The exoteric and esoteric influences of Judaism on Christianity and Islam – particularly the idea of the Creator God having a personal relationship with his people – cannot be over-estimated. The Christian God-the-Father and the Muslim Allah are the same as the Jewish Yahweh; the great prophets and leaders of Judaism are also recognized in the two later religions, as are many of the Jewish scriptures.

The Kabbala (variously spelt with an initial C or Q, with one or two b's, and with or without a concluding h)[2] is a mystical philosophical system based on the esoteric interpretation of the Jewish scriptures, especially the Torah, the first five books of the Bible. Its deepest roots are unknown, but it developed into a formulated system in eighth-century Spain, and was further developed in the *Zohar*, a mystical work written in the late thirteenth century. The Kabbala's diagrammatic Tree of Life is used symbolically to represent the relationship between God and Man. The Kabbala has been called 'the foundation of the Western Mystery Tradition', and its study lies at the heart of many esoteric religious movements, including esoteric Christianity.

CHRISTIANITY

The essence of Christianity is that God came to Earth as a man, to pay the necessary sacrifice for the sins of mankind, so that God and man might be reconciled.

Christianity originated as just one of many Jewish sects of the time. The Pharisees, Sadducees, Zealots and Essenes have just been mentioned. There were prophets everywhere. For example, John the Baptist was already a well-established teacher, preacher or prophet when Jesus started his ministry. Part of his message was 'He that cometh after me is preferred before me' (John 1:15), paving the way for the new teacher, Jesus.

Christianity might have died with the death of Jesus, except for one thing which distinguished it from most other Jewish sects: the instruction to believers, 'Go thou and preach the kingdom of God' (Luke 9:60). But if it hadn't been for Paul, Christianity would probably have remained a fairly minor Jewish sect; Peter, one of the main leaders after Jesus' death, had seen no need to spread the faith to non-Jews, until God gave him a vision (Acts 10:9–29). But it was Paul who took the small reformist Jewish sect and transformed it into something more universal. (See page 72 for a discussion of the change from Messiah to Christ.)

Christianity spread, developing and becoming theologically more complex. Paul, and others, took the message to Rome, the hub of the empire. Again, it could easily have died out in those first few years. But the early Christians seemed to thrive on persecution, and kept preaching, and the movement grew. In the year 312 CE, the emperor Constantine invoked the Christian God for help in a war, and won; it is arguable whether his was a personal or a purely political conversion, but it is inarguable that Constantine allowed Christianity to transform from one relatively minor cult among many into a state religion.

Over the next few centuries Christianity was taken to most of Europe, including the British Isles. By around the year 1000, even the Norse were letting the new 'nailed god' supplant Odin, Thor, Balder and the other gods.

By around the fifteenth century, there were three great seafaring peoples, the British, the Spanish/Portuguese and the Dutch, and all three were Christian. Everywhere they went, from the New World (North and South) to Africa, to the East, they took their religion – and, for better or worse, imposed it on the native peoples of those lands. The fledgling USA, colonized by Christian Europeans, imported slaves from Africa, and they became Christian too.

Christianity had long left behind its origins as a minor sect of one of many Middle Eastern tribal religions. Now it was the 'establishment' religion of the 'civilized' world.

ISLAM

Muslims rightly object to being called Muhammadans; Muhammad (570–632 CE) was the Prophet, not God. In 611 CE Muhammad began to have meetings with the angel Gabriel. The teachings he received were written down in the Koran (or Qur'an), which for all Muslims is a far more sacred work than the Bible is to most Christians. Although the Koran may be 'interpreted' in other languages, it can never properly be translated, because its expression in Arabic is an integral part of its holiness. It was written in Arabic and is still read in Arabic by all Muslims, thus simultaneously maintaining the purity of that language, and identifying Islam largely with Arabic-speaking peoples.

'Islam' means 'submission' or 'surrender' to the will of God. The essence of Muslim belief is 'There is no God but God (Allah), and Muhammad is His Prophet.' There is only one God, but there have been several prophets, including Adam, Abraham and Jesus; Muhammad was the last of the prophets, with the final revelation.

Because of the Middle Eastern origins, Allah is the same God as the Jewish Yahweh and the Christian God-the-Father; these three great monotheistic religions (and, more recently, the Bahá'í Faith) are known as the Religions of the Book.

In 622 CE Muhammad, encountering religious opposition to his teachings of the unity of God and the denunciation of idolatry, moved north from his birthplace Mecca to Medina, both in Saudi Arabia. This *hejira* marks the start of the Muslim calendar. All Muslims should attempt to make a pilgrimage (*hajj*) to Mecca and Medina at least once in their lives; this is one of the five Pillars of Islam, the others being belief, prayer, fasting and alms-giving.

Like most religions, Islam has suffered schisms over the centuries. The main one occurred within a few years of the death of the founder. As with Mormonism 1200 years later, there were some who believed that the leader should come from the Prophet's own family, leading to the split between Sunni and Shi'ite Muslims. Muhammad's successor nominated his own successor, but he was assassinated without doing the same. A six-man council (the *Shura*), choosing between two main candidates, offered the position of Caliph to Muhammad's son-in-law Ali on condition that he didn't declare a dynasty; Ali refused, and the other candidate was appointed. When he was killed, Ali became Caliph, and declared a dynasty; he was briefly followed by his son, and some of Ali's followers decreed that all future Caliphs must come from the line of Ali; they also denounced the first three Caliphs, who had all been close associates but not relatives of Muhammad. The party of Ali (*shi'at al Ali*), known as Shi'a, or Shi'ite Muslims, became more hardline than the majority Sunni Muslims (*sunna* means 'the rule or custom'), and today are found mainly in their original Iraq, Iran and Pakistan. Shi'ites were led by twelve Imams, descended from Ali; the twelfth disappeared, and is expected to return one day as the Mahdi ('guided one') to restore pure Islam to the world. Around 80 per cent of the world's Muslims are Sunni. Other Muslim sects include the Ismaelis, who split from the Shi'ites around 765 CE.

Historically, most Muslims were actually more tolerant of other religions than were Christians. Like Christian countries, Muslim nations took their religion into the countries they conquered, but generally they allowed Christians and Jews to retain their faith and practices, albeit as second-class citizens. The Crusades, being both territorial and religious military campaigns, created a tension and distrust between Muslims and Christians, the repercussions of which are still with us today. Another cause of potential tension is that Islam has always been both religious and political in nature; an Islamic nation is ruled by an Islamic government with Islamic laws, which do not sit happily with the more relaxed laws and customs of Western liberal democracy – which, in turn, Muslims see as being degenerate.

Islam initially spread in the West as Indians and Pakistanis emigrated to Britain and the USA. In the last few decades there has been a growth in two areas: a more militant expression of Islam among Asian, Middle Eastern and North African Muslims in both Muslim countries and the West; and the rapid development of 'Black Muslims'. The latter began among African-Americans in the USA in the 1930s as the Nation of Islam, and have since split into various factions, some returning to Sunni Muslim orthodoxy, and others being more politically motivated, upholding black rights against both whites and Jews. Some Blacks saw Christianity as the religion of the oppressor, and were attracted by the greater racial equality they saw in Islam.

The majority of the 1.2 million British Muslims are Sunni rather than Shi'ite (around 25,000), and the majority of these belong to the Barelwi sect, which has Sufi influences, and gives very high status to Muhammad.

SUFISM

Sufism is a mystical branch of Islam, probably dating as far back as the first century of Islam. The word *sufi* is Arabic for 'wool-clad', referring to the traditional coarse robe of the ascetic believer; it might also have links with the Arabic word *safa*, meaning 'purity', the Hebrew term *en sof*, used for the Divine in Jewish mysticism, and maybe with the Greek *sophia*, meaning 'wisdom'. Sufism is rich with poetic literature, music and ecstatic dance; the famous whirling dervishes belong to the Mevlevis, a Sufi order (or *tariqa*, meaning 'way') founded by the poet Rumi (1207–1273).

Perhaps partly because it puts the believer's personal relationship with God before the strict outward observance of religious practices, Sufism has been regarded with suspicion by Islam itself since the very beginning – while at the same time being highly respected for its spiritual and intellectual worth. A further reason for suspicion is that Sufis have always had a close relationship with mystics and philosophers of other religious traditions, including Neo-Platonism, Greek Orthodoxy and Hinduism; a personal communion with and experience of God is valued, whatever the religion. In the Middle Ages Sufis and Kabbalists exchanged knowledge freely; the Knights Templar had links with Sufis; and it has been argued by Richard Burton and by Robert Graves, among others,[3] that Sufi symbolism influenced early Freemasonry. For influence in the other direction, there are elements of both Christian mysticism and Gnosticism in Sufism.

In the first few centuries of Islam Sufis were persecuted; some were executed. In the twelfth and thirteenth centuries CE a rapprochement took place, particularly with Sunni Islam, but there is still sometimes an uneasy tension between Sufis and orthodox Muslims. Shi'ite Muslims are particularly antagonistic towards Sufis; in Pakistan the Ahmadi order of Sufis is currently facing tremendous persecution from fundamentalist Muslims.

Among the twentieth-century Sufi writers influential in Britain and America were Hazrat Inayat Khan, who brought Sufism to the West, and Idries Shah. Sufism has influenced several of the more esoteric and mystical New Age movements in the West, where it is less strongly linked with its Muslim origins, claiming rather to be a universal religion; the emphasis is on dance, chanting the names of God, and healing; the aim is a loving union with God. Gurdjieff (see page 350) was also probably influenced by Sufism.

SIKHISM

Although the Sikh religion (*sikh* means 'disciple') is sometimes seen as a fusion between Hinduism and Islam, its founder Guru Nanak (1469–1539) wrote 'There is neither Hindu nor Muslim, so whose path shall I follow? I shall follow God's path. God is neither Hindu nor Muslim and the path which I follow is God's.' In this

Nanak followed the teachings of the mystic Kabir (1440–1518), some of whose words are contained, along with Nanak's and several other Sikh gurus, and some Hindu and Muslim writings, in their scriptures *Granth* ('the Book'). Because of its geographical origins and the beliefs of both Nanak and Kabir, however, Sikhism inevitably contains elements of both religions, specifically Bhakti Hinduism (devotion to God rather than religious ceremonial and idol worship), Advaita (founded by Samkara or Shankara – see pages 267, 270), and elements of (Muslim) Sufism.

The Sikhs, largely originating from the Punjab on the borders of India and Pakistan, have often been caught between Hindus and Muslims. The Moguls in particular were hostile towards them, and the Sikhs developed into a warrior people; their common male surname Singh means 'lion' (the female surname Kaur means 'princess'), and a devout Sikh wears not just a turban but a symbolic sword at all times. (This is part of the five Ks: *kesh*, unshorn hair; *kangha*, comb; *kirpan*, sword; *kara*, steel bracelet; and *kachch*, short trousers for ease in fighting.) During this century they have fought more through politics than the sword; their political party is the Akali Dal. But in recent years there has been armed conflict between Sikhs and Hindus, intensified by the Indian troops' storming of the Golden Temple at Amritsar, and the retaliatory assassination of prime minister Indira Gandhi by Sikh extremists. There is also traditional hostility between Sikhs and Muslims.

Although for historical reasons Sikhism is often seen as a militant religion, at its heart it is deeply democratic and egalitarian, with keen social awareness and a spirit of reconciliation. Sikhism is monotheistic, with God seen as the supreme Guru; each of the ten gurus from Nanak to Gobind Singh (1666–1708) is deeply revered. The *Granth*, containing their teachings, is seen as the immortal guru.

Of the perhaps 20 million Sikhs worldwide, around half a million live in Britain. In America, Sikh revivalist movements have taken hold throughout this century. One in particular, Sikh Dharma, is better known by its educational wing 3HO (the Healthy, Happy, Holy Organization). *Kundalini* yoga, which through breathing regulation and being 'centred' helps one to meditate on God's name, is also widely taught by Western Sikhs.

Although many of the movements in this book come from one particular religious tradition – the Christadelphians from Christianity, New Kadampa Tradition from Buddhism, and so on – a number draw their teachings from several different traditions. Both the Aetherius Society and the Church Universal and Triumphant, for example, have roots in Theosophy, which embraces both Eastern ideas and esoteric Christianity. Many movements founded in the last few decades, including those which have New Age elements, are deliberately eclectic: they will happily draw on teachings from several different traditions, on the premise that individual religions are man-made, while spirituality is universal.

Rudolf Otto's classic work *The Idea of the Holy* coined the term 'numinous' to describe the sacred, the divine, the holy; he also uses the expression *mysterium tremendum* when discussing the very deepest religious experience:

The feeling of it may at times come sweeping like a gentle tide, pervading the mind with a tranquil mood of deepest worship. It may pass over into a more set and lasting attitude of the soul, continuing, as it were, thrillingly vibrant and resonant, until at last it dies away and the soul resumes its 'profane', non-religious mood of everyday experience. It may burst in sudden eruption up from the depths of the soul with spasms and convulsions, or lead to the strangest excitements, to intoxicated frenzy, to transport, and to ecstasy. It has its wild and demonic forms and can sink to an almost grisly horror and shuddering. It has its crude, barbaric antecedents and early manifestations, and again it may be developed into something beautiful and pure and glorious. It may become the hushed, trembling, and speechless humility of the creature in the presence of – whom or what? In the presence of that which is a *mystery* inexpressible and above all creatures.[4]

For those brought up in any mainstream religious tradition, the beliefs and practices, even the terminology, of many of the movements in this book may seem strange, even off-putting. It could be the Toronto Blessing of Evangelical Christianity or the *latihan* of Subud; the 'vibrations' of *kundalini* energy in Sahaja Yoga or the Enlightenment or Realization in Adidam; the Light and Sound of God in Eckankar or the Knowledge in Elan Vital; the invoking of the Violet Flame in the Church Universal and Triumphant or surrender to the divine energy or Substance in the Emissaries. Whether it be earthquake, wind or fire, or 'a still small voice' (1 Kings 19:11–12), believers from many of these movements, in one way or another, seek this numinous experience, the presence of this *mystery*, a personal awareness of or union with the divine.

Notes

[1] 'It is impossible to discuss the religion of the earliest men except in terms of speculative theories.' (Smart 1969: 46)

[2] In quotations in this book, the spelling follows the source.

[3] Shah 1964: xix–xx.

[4] Otto 1923: 12–13.

alternative religions
and other groups

CHAPTER 11

The Complexity of Christianity

C HRISTIANS, generally, know that they have the truth, mainly because of Jesus' words 'No man cometh unto the Father, but by me' (John 14:6), and possibly, to a certain degree, because of historical imperialism.

Sometimes committed members of individual Christian denominations know that *they* have the truth. Talk to a dedicated Roman Catholic. He is right; he has history and the pope behind him. Talk to an Anglican or an Episcopalian. He is right; he has history but he's rejected the spurious authority of the Bishop of Rome. Talk to a Baptist. He is right; he has thrown aside the man-made accretions of history and gone back to the one legitimate source: the Bible. But then, so have the Exclusive Brethren. And the Pentecostals. And the Seventh-day Adventists. And the Christadelphians.

These all share the same sacred text, the Bible, they all believe in the same God, and they all preach the words of the same young Jewish man who was executed nearly 20 centuries ago.

Yet each of these Churches knows that it is right. Many of them will say that the others are wrong.

There are exceptions, of course. The ecumenical movement draws mainstream Christian denominations together to share the 99 per cent they have in common, rather than argue about the 1 per cent that separates them. In Britain, most of the Presbyterians and the Congregationalists merged to become the United Reformed Church. In Canada and in India, the major Protestant denominations merged to form national Churches. The Church of England claims as both its greatest strength and its greatest weakness the fact that it is a broad Church, ranging from 'high church' Anglo-Catholics to 'low church' Fundamentalist Evangelicals, with a troublesome left wing of outspoken liberals, including the Bishop of Woolwich who declared in the 1960s that God was dead, and the Bishop of Durham who in the 1990s said that it wasn't necessary to believe in the virgin birth and the literal resurrection of Jesus.

But still there are many denominations, many different Churches, each one believing that it is right.

THE 'EXPLOSION' OF SECTS?

The newspapers and the cult-watching organizations often give the impression that the profusion of cults, sects and other new religious movements in recent years is something new. It could be, they say, a reaction against materialist philosophy, which was in turn (at least in part) a reaction against dogmatic Christianity; or it could be a repeat of the millenarianism supposedly witnessed shortly before 1000 CE;[1] or it could be a sign of the Last Days before the return of Christ – 'For there shall arise false Christs, and false prophets, and shall shew great signs and wonders; insomuch that, if it were possible, they shall deceive the very elect' (Matthew 24:24).

It could be any or all of these things, and a host of others. Some of the reasons people join new religious movements are examined in Chapter 3.

But has there really been an 'explosion' of sects in the last few decades? True, many of the organizations covered in this book sprang up in the twentieth century, but several of them are nineteenth century in origin, and some are much older, and are simply reappearing in a slightly different guise.

The proliferation of Christian sects is no new phenomenon.

In 1827 the fifteenth edition of *A Sketch of the Denominations of the Christian World* was published, shortly after the death of its author, John Evans. After running through 'Christian Sects, According to the Person of Christ' (eight), 'According to the Means and Measure of God's Favour' (five), and 'According to the Mode of Church Government' (nineteen), Evans lists a further 'Twenty-four Miscellaneous Sects, not reducible to the above three-fold Division'.

This last list is fascinating. A few have continued to the present day, in the main as respected denominations; but for most we can only ask, 'Where are they now?' – and smile at some of the names.

These are Evans' 'Twenty-four Miscellaneous Sects':

Quakers; Methodists (plus *Lady Anne Erskine, Character of*); New Methodists; Primitive Methodists, or Ranters; Bryanites; Jumpers; Universalists; Destructionists; Sabbatarians; Moravians; Sandemanians; Hutchinsonians; Shakers; Dunkers; New American Sect; Mystics; Swedenborgians; Haldanites; Freethinking Christians; Joanna Southcott, Muggletonians, and Fifth Monarchy Men; Seceders from the Church of England; Sauds, or Saadhs; Jerkers and Barkers; and Millenarians.

These were all Christian sects, each worshipping in its own way and recruiting new members early in the nineteenth century. There were no doubt others as well.

It has often been pointed out that in America one can find a different Church on every street corner: a 'storefront church', or a converted cinema or car showroom. A lot of these originate when one member of a 'Free Church' congregation disagrees with his pastor over a perhaps minor doctrinal or organizational detail; or sometimes there is a battle of succession after the death of the founder; or sometimes just a clash of personalities. The member walks out, taking a few supporters with him, and starts his own Church. (See Case Study, page 479, for an example of this process taken to extremes.) Few of these Churches last much beyond the lifetime of their last founder member. Some do, and spawn daughter congregations. A very few grow into national or international denominations or Churches.

PROBLEMS IN INTERPRETATION

At least so far as membership is concerned, the majority of alternative religions encountered in Britain, Europe and the USA are offshoots, in one way or another, of Christianity; the word 'sect' is accurate, not insulting. Christianity has always been a many-hued creature; from its very beginnings it sprouted in different directions, as different groups emphasized different aspects of it, or formulated its developing theology in different ways. If the twelve Apostles could have travelled forward in time just a couple of hundred years, they would have found some difficulty in identifying the religion with the Jesus they had known; 1,000, 1,500, 2,000 years, and they would have been astounded – and at times horrified – at what professed to be Christianity, at its beliefs, its rituals, and the way it treated other people.

Many of the variants of Christianity today began as honest attempts to return to the simplicity of the original message. So why are there so many of them, with so many major differences? If they are all trying to get back to the original, why can't they agree on what the original is?

Part of the problem is that the New Testament (let alone the whole Bible) is not a manual of doctrine. It contains four overlapping but different accounts of the life and teachings of Jesus, each angled in a different way for a different audience; an account of the lives of some of the disciples after Jesus' death; 21 letters; and a vision. The Old Testament contains, among other things, history, law, poetry and prophecy. The whole assemblage was written by several dozen people over several hundred years, and the package which we now call the canonical Scriptures was only listed as we now have it in 367 CE, by which time the people who made the choice of which books to include and which to leave out had their own doctrinal agenda. There isn't such a thing as a statement of belief, a creed, in the Bible. If you want one, you have to study, search, analyse and interpret the Bible, and write your own.

Many do. A further problem is that everyone is convinced that his or her own interpretation is the only correct one. Ask a dozen well-educated people to state the main points of Marxism in a few hundred words, or to say what Plato's *Republic* or Shakespeare's *Tempest* or Dickens' *Hard Times* or Wordsworth's *Prelude* is about, and in each case there will be a dozen different replies. This is even more the case when spiritual matters are involved. The Evangelical Christian says 'My beliefs come solely from the Bible,' and will point out exactly where every Christian sect strays from the

Biblical truth. But most Christian sects also say 'My beliefs come solely from the Bible,' and will also point to their proof texts. Talk to the Evangelical or talk to the sect member, and each will say, 'This is the true interpretation; anyone else's interpretation is man-made and devil-inspired; God's word speaks clearly.' It doesn't, of course, or we wouldn't have all this diversity of interpretation in the first place.

A third problem is that the events of the New Testament took place in a particular geographical, historical, social and religious setting. There is no reason why the truths at the heart of Christianity should not be relevant for everyone, everywhere, at all points in history; but individual sectarian interpretations sometimes focus in on specific points which were relevant to a Jew living in a Mediterranean country occupied by the Roman Empire 2,000 years ago, but which might have been stated somewhat differently if Jesus had been talking or Paul had been writing in fifteenth-century Venice or twentieth-century Chicago. This can easily be forgotten by present-day literalist Christian sects.

And this is the fourth problem: deciding which parts of the Bible are to be taken at their literal face value, and which are metaphorical. Most Evangelicals will say that the whole Bible should be taken literally, but even they will accept that 'The mountains skipped like rams, and the little hills like lambs' (Psalm 114:4) is not a factual description of a major earthquake; it's a poetic metaphor. But where do you draw the line? Were the five thousand actually fed by five loaves and two small fishes? What about the four thousand, who had a slightly better deal with seven loaves and 'a few small fishes' between them (Matthew 15:32–39, 16:6–10), and who only had seven baskets of leftovers, whereas the five thousand had twelve. If we accept the miracle, are we to take each of these numbers as literal fact? Or do they simply mean 'a little food and a lot of people'? If so, what other small details in the Bible are not really significant? Or are the two stories different versions of one event? Or are they both metaphors (Matthew 16:11–12), and not factual at all?

Where do you draw the line? When Jesus said 'Be ye therefore perfect, even as your Father which is in heaven is perfect' (Matthew 5:48), did he mean that it is possible for people to achieve perfection in this life? The Holiness churches would say so, but most other Christians would say that this is blasphemy, because only God can be perfect; what it really means, they say, is that we should strive to be perfect, we should aim for it, even though we can never achieve it. But that's not what Jesus said; he said 'be'. So who is right? Who is interpreting the Bible correctly?

If there are such differences of opinion on such familiar texts, it is not surprising that questions such as the nature of heaven and hell, and the exact timetable for the 'End Times', should divide Christian sects as they do. Does the word 'perish' mean to become non-existent, or to suffer in hell forever? When believers die, do they go to be with God immediately, or are they put on hold until the Last Judgement? Will there be a literal battle at Armageddon, and a literal thousand-year direct rule of God on earth?

These are the very questions that separate most Christian sects from mainstream Christianity (which contains enough doctrinal differences of its own). There are no straightforward answers in the Bible to any of these questions. There are plenty of clues, but piecing them together in different ways leads to quite different solutions – which is why there are so many varieties of Christianity, and why so many of them contradict each other on fundamental points of doctrine, and why 'mainstream' Christianity regards most of the Christian sects as heretical.

A HANDFUL OF DOCTRINAL DIFFERENCES

Before we look at 'heresies', let us consider briefly just a few of the differences in points of doctrine (including both belief and practice) within 'mainstream' Christianity itself. In some cases these are more fundamental than those separating some of the small offshoots of the Christian religion from the mainstream.

SATURDAY OR SUNDAY

Today, Seventh-day Adventists are accepted by many as a denomination rather than a sect. Their main difference from mainstream doctrine (as with their close cousins the Worldwide Church of God and the Branch Davidians) is that the Christian holy day should be Saturday, not Sunday. They point to Exodus 31:15–16:

> Six days may work be done; but in the seventh is the sabbath of rest, holy to the Lord... Wherefore the children of Israel shall keep the sabbath, to observe the sabbath throughout their generations, for a perpetual covenant.

Present-day Jews still stick to this; it's one of the Ten Commandments; but mainstream Christianity changed it.

The reason given for the change is that Jesus rose from the dead on the first day of the week. (One or two of the new Churches have argued, albeit rather tortuously, that from the Gospel accounts even this standard belief isn't absolutely clear; he first appeared to someone on the first day of the week, they say, but he might have risen on the Sabbath, the day before.) Also, the disciples met on a Sunday. In Acts 20:7 we read that 'upon the first day of the week, when the disciples came together to break bread, Paul preached unto them'. However, this doesn't say that the Sabbath should be shifted from Saturday to Sunday, any more than the common habit of a Wednesday night prayer meeting or Bible study makes Wednesday the new day of rest and worship.

Within the first two centuries, though, Sunday became accepted as the Christian day of worship; to take just one of several examples from the Church Fathers, Justin Martyr (100–165) wrote, 'Sunday is the day on which we all hold our common assembly because... Jesus Christ our Saviour on the same day rose from the dead.' But if one looks solely for *biblical* evidence the theological argument is probably stronger for maintaining Saturday as the day of rest. Throughout mainstream Christianity, then, a major change rests more on tradition than on Scripture.

TRANSUBSTANTIATION OR REMEMBRANCE

The Roman Catholic Church believes that the bread or wafer at the Eucharist actually becomes, in its true nature, the body of Christ. The Protestant Churches say it represents the body of Christ – 'This do in remembrance of me' (Luke 22:19) – and that the Catholics are sacrificing Christ anew at every mass, which is biblically unsound; they cite 'after he had offered one sacrifice for sins for ever' (Hebrews 10:12). The Catholics, in return, simply point to the description of the Last Supper: 'And he took bread, and gave thanks, and brake it, and gave it unto them, saying, This is my body which is given for you' (Luke 22:19). 'This is', not 'This represents'.

Millions of words must have been written on this one point of doctrine alone; two paragraphs here cannot possibly approach the complexity of the problem, or the brilliant exegesis of attempts to reconcile the issue. The fact remains that it is a major point of doctrine at the very heart of Christian worship, and that there are fundamental and essentially irreconcilable differences of belief about it within the main strands of established Christianity.

PRIESTS OR THE PRIESTHOOD OF ALL BELIEVERS

The Roman Catholic, Orthodox and Anglican Churches have between them the pope, patriarchs, cardinals, archbishops, bishops, priests and deacons. The Methodist Church has ordained ministers and a wide network of lay preachers; the Baptist Church has pastors; the Presbyterian and Congregationalist Churches, now largely joined as the United Reformed Church, appoint leaders from the church members; some other Free Churches have no equivalent to ordained ministers at all.

Two main theological points divide all of these. Evangelicals believe in the universal priesthood of all believers; if you are a Christian, you don't need any other intermediary between yourself and Christ. Although some people clearly have a teaching or preaching vocation, they are not separate from other Church members.

At the other extreme is the authority of continuous Apostolic Succession. The Roman Catholic Church believes in an unbroken line of laying-on-of-hands from Christ, through Peter ('the first pope'), through all the bishops of the last 20 centuries, to every bishop today. A new bishop is consecrated by several other bishops. A priest at ordination, or a child at confirmation, is touched on the head by the hands of a bishop, and this touch goes right back to, and represents, Christ himself.

The Anglican Churches claim Apostolic Succession in that their first bishops were originally consecrated as Roman Catholic bishops, so the line is unbroken. Methodist ministers don't have Apostolic Succession, because John Wesley was a Church of England priest, not a bishop, so his ordination of ministers was technically invalid.

To non-Christians and to members of many Free Churches, Apostolic Succession might seem a somewhat esoteric if not trivial point of difference, and at worst pure superstition; but those churches which have it value its authority, and it has been a major sticking point in ecumenical negotiations.

For the Roman Catholic Church, any consecrations or ordinations in secessionist Churches, though valid, are illegal, even if they do have apostolic succession, because the original seceding bishops had turned their backs on the Church of Rome, wherein lies the only authority. By rejecting that authority they had become heretics, and so had no legitimacy. (See pages 192–196 for more on apostolic succession, and so-called 'Wandering Bishops'.)

PREDESTINATION OR FREE WILL

This is another extremely complex issue, which can only be touched on very briefly here. If transubstantiation and apostolic succession are among the issues dividing Roman Catholicism from Protestantism, predestination splits Protestantism, including the Free Churches, into two distinct groups, Arminian and Calvinist.

To put it at its simplest, Arminian theology states that Christ died for the sins of everyone; we can all be saved, but it is up to each individual to accept or reject salvation. Calvinist theology, summarized equally simply, states that God, knowing everything, already knows who is going to be saved and who isn't; as the future is foreknown, it is therefore fore-ordained, or predestined. It's a small step from knowing to choosing. God has chosen some to be saved, and some to be damned. We cannot therefore know that we are saved, as Arminian Christians believe.

DEVOTIONAL ART OR IDOLATRY

Roman Catholic churches are full of paintings and sculptures; Eastern Orthodox churches have icons; Anglican churches have a cross on the altar; most nonconformist 'low' churches don't even have that. In the older established denominations the priests wear richly patterned vestments; a Baptist minister will usually wear a suit. At a sung Eucharist the choir will sing anthems, perhaps in Latin; in a house fellowship someone might strum a guitar. Evangelicals claim that they are returning to the simplicity of worship of the Early Church, and accuse the Catholics in particular (and any priest who even bobs his head at the cross) of idolatry – 'Thou shalt not make unto thee any graven image' (Exodus 20:4). Anglicans, Orthodox and Catholics point out the difference between worship and veneration, and stress the important teaching and meditational value of stained-glass windows, paintings, and carvings of the Stations of the Cross. As the eighth-century John of Damascus said, they are 'books for the illiterate'.

On one level these are simply two different viewpoints, matters of taste: Evangelicals prefer to have a lack of clutter around them when worshipping God, traditionalists find that beautiful visual aids help them to get closer to God. If that were all, there should be room for both viewpoints, and each should be able to accept the other. But Evangelicals, in inveighing against Catholic idolatry, can very easily swing too far the other way. The presence or absence of paintings in a church can become symbolic of indulgence in the pleasures of the flesh on the one hand, and of a hard, moral puritanism on the other.

Evangelicalism has created little great art. Not just churches and cathedrals, but art galleries, public buildings and concert halls throughout the Western world are full of beautiful paintings, statues and music. Much of the artistic culture of the Western world stems from traditional Christianity. A few guitars and tambourines, and a couple of Day-glo posters on the walls of a Free Church somehow don't have quite the same resonance. This is a sadness for many Free Church Christians who, while wanting to keep their theology, would actually like to have some of the grandeur of a Bach oratorio, or some of the beauty of a Michelangelo painting, as part of their worship.

As one ten-year-old girl chorister said, 'Latin is lovely to sing in once you know it well. I would hate to sing *Ave Verum* in English.'[2]

It has been argued that by stripping the gospel message of all its later accretions, Evangelicalism has removed both mystery and mysticism from worship. Raising your arms in the air and shouting 'Hallelujah' with five hundred other people is one way of feeling God's presence; but so is silent, individual contemplation of a statue of Mary holding her baby.

There has been at least one attempt to bring Evangelical beliefs and traditionalist practice together: the Catholic Apostolic Church, founded in 1833 (see page 166). Its doctrine was Evangelical; its liturgy and ceremonial were as complex and artistically fulfilling as anything in the Orthodox, Catholic or Anglican Churches, from which they were largely borrowed. The Church also believed in speaking in tongues and prophecy, and in the imminent return of Christ, thus simultaneously taking on aspects of the New Testament Church and of many present-day new Christian movements. Detractors would see it as one of the first modern Christian sects.

It should be said that, particularly with the growing influence of African and West Indian Christianity, some Evangelical churches in the West are now integrating costume, dance and drama into their worship.

NON-CHRISTIAN ELEMENTS IN CHRISTIANITY

To step back to the early days again, schismatic storefront churches have had their equivalents since the first Christians picked themselves up after their teacher was killed and asked, 'What do we do now?' Even in the New Testament we see individual churches being put right when they strayed from what the early leaders had decided was the party line. The problem was that no one had yet set down a statement of beliefs and practices. The message of the first Christians was simply 'We preach Christ crucified' (I Corinthians 1:23), but what exactly did this mean?

This problem was compounded by the various elements which went into Christianity. There was its background in Judaism, of course. The Christian God the Father was the same as the Jewish Yahweh or Adonai; Jesus said 'I am not come to destroy, but to fulfil [the Law]' (Matthew 5:17); the main Jewish scriptures became the Christian Old Testament. But how much of Judaism should be carried forward into Christianity? There was a group of specifically Hebraic Christians up to the fifth century, and today there is a small but highly active movement of Jews who have converted to Christianity without giving up their Jewish religion.

But the developing Christian religion also absorbed other elements, from neo-Platonism, from Gnosticism, from the various Mystery religions around at the time, from the Roman Mithraism, and elsewhere. Even in the Bible itself, Paul quotes from Pagan writers in his letters, and makes no apology for it. The idea of a god dying for his people and coming back to life again is by no means unique to Christianity; it is one of the oldest religious ideas of all, and was at the very centre of the earliest solar religions and crop-fertility religions. The concept of the Eucharist or communion service, central to the beliefs of traditionalist Christians, was borrowed from Mithraism, which at the time of Jesus was the religion followed by many Roman soldiers. The idea of the virgin birth was widespread long before the Blessed Virgin Mary was visited by an angel; indeed, if you wanted to be taken seriously as a prophet – or even as a military leader – it was almost compulsory for you to have had a non-human father. As a later example, the Norse god Odin, the All-Father, was reknowned for fathering children on mortal women.

For small, individual churches in the early days of Christianity the difficulty lay in knowing which bits of other religions it was all right to borrow, and which bits were unacceptable. One clever solution, proposed by the second-century Justin Martyr, was that God had allowed some of the truths of Christianity to be made known to earlier thinkers, and so 'whatever things were rightly said by any man, belong to us Christians'.

Even the writers of the gospels and epistles had their differences in emphasis, if not in doctrine. Peter, Paul and the writer of John's gospel held widely differing views on the substance of their belief; it's partly because of this lack of cohesiveness in the New Testament that so many 'heretical' movements over the centuries have been able to claim that the Bible supports their beliefs.

HERESIES

It is useful to look briefly at Christian 'heresies' through the centuries; many of their beliefs resurface again and again, particularly in today's new religious movements. From the many books listed in the Bibliography, five will demonstrate the point.

Sects and cults are nothing new. David Christie-Murray's excellent *A History of Heresy* (1976) spends 243 pages covering 'heresies' from New Testament times to the present day. Leonard George's *The Encyclopedia of Heresies and Heretics* (1995) has over 600 entries. The Catholic *A Handbook of Heresies* by M.L. Cozens was first published in 1928. The 16 brief chapters of its 1974 edition include Protestantism among the 25 heresies covered; for traditional Roman Catholics, any other variant of Christianity is a heresy. From the opposite end of the theological spectrum, the 1962 edition of

Heresies and Cults, by the evangelical preacher J. Oswald Sanders, describes 21 heresies – including Roman Catholicism. Finally, *The Lion Concise Book of Christian Thought*
by Tony Lane, and from an Evangelical publisher, covers the development of
Christian teaching over the centuries; its index lists 24 'heresies and schisms', only 9
of which overlap with Cozens' list.

Christianity has been riven with disagreements since its very beginning. The Pagan
writer Celsus, around 178 CE, said:

> At the start of their movement they were very few in numbers, and unified in
> purpose. Since that time, they have spread all around and now number in the
> thousands. It is not surprising, therefore, that there are divisions among them
> – factions of all sorts, each wanting to have its own territory. Nor is it surprising
> that as these divisions have become so numerous, the various parties have taken
> to condemning each other, so that today they have only one thing – if that –
> in common: the name 'Christian'.[3]

Part of the problem is the basic simplicity of the Christian message, perhaps most
perfectly set out in John 3:16 – 'For God so loved the world, that he gave his only-
begotten Son, that whosoever believeth in him should not perish, but have everlasting
life.'

The message of the New Testament Christians, 'We preach Christ crucified', is
only rendered slightly more complicated by today's Evangelicals: 'You are a sinner
bound for hell; God loved you and sent his son Jesus to take your punishment on
himself; believe and be saved.' A simple message.

Unfortunately, it's not that simple. What do we mean by sinner, hell, God, son, Jesus,
take, punishment, believe, saved? To take just one example, why are we sinners? Is it
actually possible for a human being not to be a sinner? No, because 'All have sinned,
and come short of the glory of God' (Romans 3:23). So is this our fault, because of free
will, or God's, for creating us that way? If God knows everything, he already knows (in
fact, he knew before he created Adam) who will be saved and who will be damned. But
is this foreknowledge, or predestination? Are we condemned because of Adam's sin, or
our own? Does 'original sin' mean that because birth results from sexual intercourse, the
parents' sinfulness passes into the baby – and does that mean that sex is sinful?

Similar questions can be asked – and discussed endlessly – about every single term
in Christian theology. The basic message may be simple... until you start defining what
the words actually mean.

Most of the 'heresies' which the mainstream Christian Churches condemn in
today's sects were hotly debated 17 or 18 centuries ago, and very often it was the
precise usage and definition of words which was in dispute. One of the fundamental
questions concerned the nature of Jesus: how much was he God, and how much
man? This makes an enormous difference to every other point of Christian theology.

It's like a complex series of mathematical equations; if you change one value early on, it affects everything else.

If, for example, the virgin birth didn't occur, then Joseph was Jesus' father, and Jesus was born a normal man. Did he remain 'just a man', or did he take on the nature of God at some point, perhaps at birth, or perhaps when the dove came down upon him when John the Baptist baptized him? But this is man-become-God, rather than the God-become-man of what is now standard Christian belief; it takes away Christianity's uniqueness, and makes it more possible to view it alongside Islam and the Bahá'í Faith.

The dove represents the Spirit of God, the Holy Spirit – another bone of contention since the earliest days. Is the Holy Spirit, as standard Trinitarian Christians believe, an equal third person of the Trinity?[4] Or is the Holy Spirit God-in-action? A person or a process? He or it? Or is the Holy Spirit the missing female portion of the Judæo-Christian deity, Sophia, the Wisdom of God?

Brilliant theologians have spent hundreds of years and millions of words discussing these problems. Whatever varied conclusions they arrived at, the very amount of work proves, if proof were needed, that these are very real, complex issues; there are no simple solutions. Those who say they are returning to the beliefs of the Early Church, of the disciples, are deluding themselves; the theology they proclaim as the Truth wasn't worked out until centuries later, and would have been completely unfamiliar to those who actually knew Jesus. Those who claim that there is one straightforward outline of Christian beliefs ignore the centuries of dispute and discussion that formulated the particular set of beliefs which they now hold to be true – and refuse to allow the validity of the hundreds of variant sets of belief held true by others.

There *is* no such single thing as 'the Christian belief statement'.

THE EARLY CHURCH – AND EARLY HERESIES

Even at the time the books of the New Testament were written, there were different versions of the story of Jesus circulating. Paul writes of 'another Jesus, whom we have not preached' (II Corinthians 11:4), and rebukes those who preach 'another gospel' (Galatians 1:6–9). During this first century or so, there were some who believed in Jesus the man, who may or may not have attained some measure of godhood, and others who believed in the Christ, either as a Jewish messianic (revolutionary) figure or as God. And there were some who believed that Jesus the man was also Christ the God, which became the prevailing view of what we now know as Christianity. (See page 72 for further discussion on the Messiah and Christ.)

Fundamentalist Christians believe as an article of faith that every word of the Bible is divinely inspired. Bible scholars tend to hold the more liberal view that, for example, the gospels of Matthew and Luke were based on Mark, with large sections of a 'Sayings of Jesus' known as Q, plus material from other sources; and that both the gospels and the epistles were much edited, rewritten and added to over the years, by people other than their original writers, to highlight particular points. They also look at the large number of gospels and epistles which didn't make it into the New Testament, for a deeper understanding of the varieties of belief that existed at that time.

Even if the Fundamentalists are correct, and the books of the New Testament are divinely inspired and true and accurate in every word, the evidence of the non-canonical works shows that there never was one original gospel message which was accepted by all of the Christians of the first couple of hundred years. Christianity, right from the start, came in many varieties. Different Churches and their leaders had different beliefs – many of which which would soon be judged heretical.

Christianity did not exist in a spiritual vacuum. In the earliest days a Jewish Christian, or one preaching to Jews, would describe Christ and the new faith in terms relevant to Judaism. Similarly, someone educated in the Greek philosophers would naturally find points of comparison between their teachings and Christian beliefs. Neo-Platonist and Gnostic beliefs found their way into different versions of Christian theology.

Many of the great Church Fathers who have for over 1,500 years been revered for formulating the finer points of Christian doctrine, were at one time or another judged to be heretics.

Justin Martyr (c. 100–165 CE), for example, wrote 'Next to God we love and worship the Word', implying that the Word, Logos, or Christ was not actually God.

Tertullian (c. 160–220 CE), probably the first Christian theologian to write in Latin, and one of the first to make the Holy Spirit equal to the Father and the Son in the godhead, fought against Gnosticism, but embraced one of the very earliest Christian offshoots, Montanism.

Founded in 156 CE, **Montanism** was remarkable for many things, and was the forerunner of many more recent Christian movements. It must have been the earliest sect to demand a return to the beliefs and practices of the original Christian church, less than a century and a quarter after the death of Jesus. It practised speaking in tongues and prophecy (it had two main women prophets), both features of the nineteenth- and twentieth-century Pentecostal Churches and the Charismatic movement in both Protestant and Catholic Churches today. It preached the imminent return of Christ and end of the world, a common feature of many later movements; as with them, many of its adherents sold all their property in anticipation; and as with them, the failure of the world to come to an end on schedule apparently didn't affect membership too much. Montanists longed for martyrdom to prove their faith, and were highly critical of anyone who fled from it. They were also extremely ascetic, with long periods of fasting, and with complete celibacy. Amazingly, the movement lasted until the fifth century.

Clement of Alexandria (late second-century CE) believed that although Jesus ate and drank like a man, he didn't actually need to for bodily sustenance.

Origen (c. 185–250 CE) was the first major Christian theologian, who systematically set out the principles of Christian faith. Several of his beliefs were 'heretical'. He treated parts of the Old Testament as allegorical rather than literal. He accepted the Trinity, but he taught that the Father was greater than the Son, and the Son greater than the Holy Spirit; they were all eternal, but so were the next level of the hierarchy, 'rational beings', including angels and men. He also believed in a sort of two-stream Christianity; the basic message of salvation through faith was fine for the uneducated, but for the more intellectual and spiritual, salvation came through contemplation. He was officially branded a heretic in the sixth century.

Cyprian (d. 258 CE), bishop of Carthage, insisted on the authority and indivisibility of the Church, condemning all schismatics; it was not possible for someone to have divergent views of any kind and remain in the Church. Conversion and baptism by a schismatic Church was not only worthless but evil – 'it makes sons not for God but for the Devil'. Ironically, even the Bishop of Rome was more lenient to schismatics; it was Cyprian who created the authoritarian and unforgiving stance of the Christian Church throughout the centuries towards anyone with differing beliefs.

Eusebius (c. 260–340 CE), bishop of Caesarea, was the great historian of the Early Church. He was a strong supporter of the emperor Constantine, who first called on the Christian God in the middle of a war in 312 CE – an event with enormous consequences for the Church, both for good (the spread of Christianity throughout the Roman Empire) and for bad (the combination of Church and State). Eusebius, among many other bishops, accepted the beliefs of Arius, the most influential heretic of the early centuries.

Arius (d. 342 CE) taught that only the Father is God; although through the Son he had created the universe, he had first created the Son out of nothing, and there had been a time, however far back, when the Son had not existed. The Son, then, is not God in the same way as the Father is, though he became divine because of his moral purity. Arianism has resurfaced many times through the centuries, including in the present day Jehovah's Witnesses. In the early fourth century it was splitting the Church, with many bishops and their churches accepting it. Roman Christians and Arian Christians might sometimes live side by side or fight in the same army, but neither regarded the other as true Christians; although they preached from the same Scriptures, they were further apart theologically than Catholics and Calvinists centuries later.

The Emperor Constantine was unhappy about the divisions in the Church, and called the Council of Nicea in 325 CE to resolve them. The Council of Nicea (like the later Synod of Whitby in 664 CE, when Celtic Christianity was defeated by Roman Christianity) was an example of what happens when politics gets involved in religious debate. Several of the bishops signed up to its outcome more to please (or not to displease) the Emperor than because they actually accepted it.

The Council of Nicea finally agreed a creed (*not* the Nicene creed, which came out of the Council of Constantinople in 381 CE) that condemned Arianism:

But the holy catholic and apostolic church anathematizes those who say: 'There was once when he [Christ] was not' and 'He was not, before he was begotten' and 'He was made out of nothing' and those who assert that he is from some being or substance other than the Father or that he is mutable or liable to change.

One of the main opponents of Arius was **Athanasius** (299–373 CE), the Bishop of Alexandria, who was, incidentally, the first to set out the canon of the New Testament as we know it today, as late as 367 CE. (Several other authorities dropped some of the epistles, some added the Epistle of Barnabas, and the Book of Revelation was often not included, sometimes being replaced by The Shepherd of Hermas.)

Athanasius devoted much of his life to fighting Arianism and defining the correct balance of manhood and godhood in Jesus. For Athanasius, if Jesus was not fully God as well as fully man, the whole of Christianity fell apart. He also argued for the full equality of the Holy Spirit within the Trinity. The Athanasian Creed, though dating from around 500 CE, was ascribed to him because of his detailed work on the Trinity.

Such as the Father is, such is the Son, and such is the Holy Ghost.
The Father uncreate, the Son uncreate, and the Holy Ghost uncreate.
The Father incomprehensible, the Son incomprehensible, and the Holy Ghost incomprehensible.
The Father eternal, the Son eternal, and the Holy Ghost eternal.
And yet they are not three eternals, but one eternal.
And also there are not three incomprehensibles, nor three uncreated; but one uncreated, and one incomprehensible...
The Father is made of none, neither created, nor begotten.
The Son is of the Father alone: not made, nor created, but begotten.
The Holy Ghost is of the Father and of the Son: neither made, nor created, nor begotten, but proceeding...
And in this Trinity none is afore, or after other: none is greater, or less than another;
But the whole three Persons are are co-eternal together, and co-equal...

Well over half of this creed concerns itself with the Trinity; a further quarter with the nature of Christ; with the remaining few verses rushing through a brief synopsis of the passion and purpose of Christ. This degree of definition, which might seem astonishing today, was necessary to pinpoint the 'errors' of the 'heretics'.

Arianism was not the only heresy to cause dissension in the early centuries.

Monarchianism (sometimes known as Sabellianism), which began before 200 CE, held that there is only one God, not three-in-one; it saw Trinitarian belief as Tritheism. The Father, the Son and the Holy Spirit are all one being, simply performing three different roles, like an actor playing several parts. This version of the heresy was sometimes called Patripassian, because it implied that the Father suffered on the cross. A variant belief, Dynamic Monarchianism, held that Jesus was a normal man with divine power in him, a belief held by many alternative religions today. At least one bishop of Rome and a bishop at Antioch, among many others, believed in a version of Monarchianism.

Even the great theologian Augustine, Bishop of Hippo – **Saint Augustine** (354–430 CE) – is said to have been inclined to Monarchianism. Also, for 12 years earlier in his life, before he turned to more-or-less conventional Christianity, Augustine was a follower of **Manicheism**, a Gnostic Christian religion much influenced by Zoroastrianism. Two deities, of Light and Darkness, are in perpetual conflict; the god of Light is the creator of the soul, but we live in an evil world of matter created by the god of Darkness. Manicheism later resurfaced as the background to the Cathars of thirteenth-century France.

Perhaps because of his earlier beliefs, Augustine devoted much of his time to fighting heresy. His major battle was against **Pelagianism**, which held (among other things) that it was possible for a man, albeit with a great deal of effort, to avoid sin and attain salvation. Not so! thundered Augustine, and went on to clarify the Church's teaching on Original Sin. Everyone was a sinner, including newborn babies, because of Adam and because of the sin of the parents (not least of which was the sexual intercourse which had created the baby). Pelagius denied the doctrine of Original Sin.

Pelagianism was in some ways a very British heresy.[5] It was not so much 'salvation by works' as a striving towards holiness, and a belief that neither man nor nature was inherently evil; this struck a chord with Celtic Christians, who found the natural world an expression of God's goodness.[6] This belief has resurfaced within British Christianity in recent years (see page 215).

(see page 215)

The debate between Augustine and Pelagius, who was a Scots or Irish monk, occupied educated Christians throughout Europe for decades; eventually, and inevitably because of his power base, Augustine won, defining a central plank of mainstream Christianity against which many schismatic Churches are still rebelling.

The doctrine of Original Sin resulted in two other doctrinal innovations: infant baptism, so that babies who died need not go to hell; and (much later) the belief in the Immaculate Conception of Mary, on the grounds that Jesus was by definition sinless, so he could not have been born of a sinful woman, so if Mary had been without sin she herself must have been conceived without sin. (This, which only became official doctrine in 1854, is a rare example of a Roman Catholic belief which is judged heretical by the entire Protestant world, on the grounds that it puts Mary on a fairly equal footing with Jesus; in the words of a Catholic archbishop of the time, it made her 'above all our co-redemptress'. There was actually a minor pressure group in the nineteenth-century Roman Catholic Church wanting to make Mary 'the fourth member of the Trinity'.)

Augustine was responsible for various other teachings which were to affect the Church for centuries to come:

- He taught that the sacraments are valid even if administered by an unholy priest, which allowed for many of the clerical excesses of later years.
- He taught that it was permissible to coerce people into belief – or out of heresy – by force if necessary; this provided theological justification for the Church's treatment of heretics in medieval and renaissance times.
- He also taught that many people nominally within the Church were not really Christians; only God knows who the true believers are. This led him to a belief remarkably similar to Calvinism, a thousand years later: God not only knows who will be saved, he *chooses* to whom he will give the grace to accept him. (Pelagius was also opposed to predestination.)

Taking these last two teachings of Augustine together explains (though it cannot condone) the reputed words of the papal legate Arnaud-Amaury, Abbot of Cîteaux, at the French city of Béziers in 1209, when a soldier asked him how they should distinguish between true believers and heretics, Catholics and Cathars: 'Kill them all; God will know his own.' More than 15,000 men, women and children were massacred at Béziers, many of them while claiming sanctuary in the church.

Three other heresies to split the Church during the third to fifth centuries were **Apollinarianism**, which stated that Jesus was the Word in a human body, but did not have a human mind or soul; **Nestorianism**, which painted a clear distinction between God the Word and Jesus the man (Nestorius was bishop of Constantinople in c. 429 CE); and **Macedonianism**, which said, once again, that the Holy Spirit was not an equal member of the godhead.

A further brief mention must be made of **Gnosticism**, which resurfaces in many of the present-day esoteric movements. Gnosticism, like Christianity, existed in many varieties – some were extremely ascetic, others extremely libertarian – but in all of them the emphasis was on direct knowledge (Greek *gnosis*) of God. In general, Gnosticism follows Zoroastrianism in its concentration on the opposing forces of Good and Evil, Light and Dark, Spirit and Matter. The Gnostics of the first few centuries were rooted in Christianity, and concentrated on the *secret* teachings of Jesus;

this made them even more dangerous to the established Church, which systematically destroyed both them and their writings – many of which were lost until 1945, when a large number of texts were found at Nag Hammadi in northern Egypt.

Gnostic Christianity bears much the same uneasy relationship to mainstream Christianity as scholars of the Kabbala do to Judaism, or as Sufism does to Islam. Indeed, these three often get on better with each other than they do with their own 'parent' religions – mysticism, personal devotion and individual scholarship cannot readily be brought under the control of Church authority.

☼

Of the many heresies which occurred in medieval times – including the Paulicians, the Bogomils, the Waldenses and others – only one will be briefly mentioned here: the **Cathars**, or **Albigensians**. Their beliefs came from Manichæan Gnosticism, and sprang up in southern France – the Languedoc – in the late eleventh century. They believed that spirit is good and matter is evil; the material world was created by the evil demiurge. For the extreme *parfaits* or *perfecti* this meant abstaining from food and from sex, because the one sustains the flesh and the other sustains the race.

The Cathars (meaning 'pure ones'), with their own distinctive theology and their lack of respect for priestly authority, were a threat to the Church. Pope Innocent III launched the Albigensian Crusade under Simon de Montfort,[7] which culminated in the massacres at Béziers in 1209 and at the Cathar's last stronghold, the fortress of Montségur, in 1244.[8]

SIXTEENTH AND SEVENTEENTH CENTURIES
The sixteenth and seventeenth centuries rival the nineteenth and twentieth centuries for new Christian ideas; they saw many revolutionary movements within Christianity, with Germany and Switzerland as the main breeding grounds. **Martin Luther** nailed his famous Ninety-five Theses to the church door at Wittenburg Castle in 1517. **Huldreich Zwingli** began to proclaim his Protestant ideas in the 1520s, and **John Calvin** started off what became known as Reformed theology in the 1530s. From this **John Knox** founded Presbyterianism as a Scottish church system around 1560. The idea of small, independent, self-governing Congregationalist churches began to spread in England during the reign of Elizabeth I.

The **Anabaptists**, who believed in adult baptism for believers, grew up in the early sixteenth century. The beginnings of formal **Unitarianism** can be traced to Laelius Socinus (1525–1562) and his nephew Faustus (1539–1604), though its ideas had been around in central Europe for some years previously.

There were many other varieties of belief, stemming from individual scholars who had formerly been members of other Churches – some of them Catholic priests; many of these independents were considerably more tolerant than the Churches they had left.

It should not be assumed that each separate type of belief was self-contained; there was some overlap between them, and great division within them. The different groups of Anabaptists, for example, kept trying to work out a common creed, but had so many differences of belief that this proved impossible.

Neither should it be thought, because of the profusion of beliefs, that this was an age of religious toleration. Everybody condemned everybody else as a heretic. The Anabaptists in particular were hated; Catholics, Lutherans and Calvinists actually united to try to destroy them. Today we tend to think of the burning of heretics as the special province of the Roman Catholic Inquisition, but this was by no means the case: Calvin had the Spanish scholar Michael Servetus burnt at the stake in 1553 for being both an Anabaptist and a Unitarian.

In England, the first **Baptist** church was founded in 1611. **George Fox** started off the Religious Society of Friends, soon known as the Quakers, around 1650. In 1689, a year after William of Orange came to the British throne, a Toleration Act allowed freedom of worship for Presbyterians, Congregationalists, Baptists and Quakers – but not for Unitarians, and certainly not for Catholics.

It is a common misperception that the early English settlers of what would become the USA were Puritans and Quakers looking for religious freedom. The term Puritan is too loose; the Pilgrim Fathers of 1620 were Congregationalists, and that was the religion which took hold in New England. They were anything but tolerant to other religions, initially outlawing any other, though by the end of the century some areas reluctantly allowed Baptists and Episcopalians. Congregationalist Massachusetts imprisoned and whipped Quakers, even executing three in 1659. Despite this persecution, the Quaker William Penn's Pennsylvania was always tolerant of other varieties of Christianity.

The Quakers are today perhaps the most widely respected 'heretics' of all. Their basic belief is that each person should worship God in his or her own way; the authority of the Church – any Church – is rejected; priests and sacraments, including baptism and the Eucharist, are irrelevant. There is no creed, and not really any theology; the only authority is the Inner Light of Christ, or 'that of God', in the heart of each individual believer. Like the Unitarians and the Salvation Army, the Quakers are perhaps respected by outsiders more for their commitment to social issues – including prison reform and the abolition of slavery – than for their spiritual beliefs, though this social commitment stems from their inner spirituality.

EIGHTEENTH CENTURY

In terms of new religious movements, the eighteenth century was fairly active, as witness John Evans' *Sketch of the Denominations of the Christian World* (fifteenth edition, 1827; see page 123). Only a few will be mentioned briefly here.

Probably most significant, in mainstream terms, was the founding of the **Methodists** by John Wesley and George Whitefield in the 1740s. Like every other religious movement, this had a wide range of splinter groups – even Wesley and

Whitefield fell out with each other very bitterly over doctrinal differences – though most of these were reunited by the early twentieth century.

The eighteenth century is often called the Age of Enlightenment, and the intellectual rigour of its rationalist or scientific materialist ideas had an effect on religious thinking. Atheism became intellectually acceptable, and the application of reason to faith aided the growth of **Unitarianism** – the convoluted conundrum of the Athanasian creed being felt unreasonable and so unnecessary – and also of **Universalism**, the belief that the loving God would save everyone eventually.

Emmanuel Swedenborg (1688–1772) brought a mystical intellectual rigour to Christian doctrine. By taking everything back to first principles and approaching it from a different angle, he redefined everything from the Trinity and the nature of Christ to the nature of man's relationship with God.

Finally, the **Shakers** were a fairly small British sect who, because of persecution, moved to America in 1774. Their teaching was millennialist, and there is no doubt that many of the new American religions which sprang up in the nineteenth century owe a debt, directly or indirectly, to them.

NINETEENTH CENTURY

The nineteenth century was also a fertile period for new religious movements, especially in America. Particularly for struggling frontiersmen, the Mormon promise that Americans were God's chosen people was a revelation too powerful to be ignored. Add to this the millenarian message, that Christ would shortly return and set up his Earthly kingdom for a thousand years, and people flocked to join. The **Seventh-day Adventists**, **Christadelphians** and **Jehovah's Witnesses** are but three of many millennialist religions which sprang from that same fruitful ground. **Christian Science** came from a different angle: making a rational 'scientific religion' out of the formerly rather hit-and-miss nature of faith healing.

Not all the new religious movements were born in the USA. In 1831 the Presbyterian minister Edward Irving started the **Catholic Apostolic Church** in London (see page 166); although this eventually died out, it spawned the New Apostolic Church, a thriving denomination in many countries other than Britain. The **Exclusive Brethren** was also British in origin; it began in 1840 when John Nelson Darby led a schism in the recently formed Brethren movement. Although small today, it has had an immeasurable effect on current millennialist beliefs (see pages 77 and 162).

The **Salvation Army** was founded by William Booth in 1877. It grew out of his Christian Mission in the East End of London, where he was appalled by both the social and the spiritual deprivation. As with the Quakers, mainstream Christianity is more tolerant of the Salvation Army than of many other Christian offshoots because of its inarguable good works. Its theology is straightforwardly Evangelical, though it does not practise the sacraments.

TWENTIETH CENTURY

Some of the new Christian-based movements founded in the twentieth century have their roots in earlier Churches. Both the **Worldwide Church of God** and the **Branch Davidians** grew out of the Seventh-day Adventist movement, for example, and the many radical Evangelical Churches are little different in their main beliefs from the Evangelicals of the eighteenth and nineteenth centuries. Others, although their founders may have started off in a mainstream denomination, have branched out at quite unusual angles – the **Unification Church** and the **Family**, for example.

From all of these fairly recent Christian offshoots we shall look in more detail at a selection, in roughly historical order. Some have become well-established Churches, but have beliefs substantially different from mainstream Christianity. Others have fairly orthodox beliefs, but some of their practices cause concern to outsiders. And some, such as **Opus Dei** and the **Alpha Course**, are movements within mainstream denominations.

Each one sees itself as a legitimate form of Christianity (in some cases, as the only legitimate form of Christianity), but mainstream Christians might regard them all with some suspicion, for one reason or another.

It should be remembered that there are many, many other Christian offshoots, with a wide variety of beliefs and practices, not only in Britain, Europe and the USA, but throughout the world.

Notes

[1] Most modern authorities agree this did not actually occur; see page 75.

[2] Quoted in Graham, 1993: 224.

[3] R. Joseph Hoffmann (trans.), *Celsus on the True Doctrine: A Discourse Against the Christians*, Oxford: OUP, 1987: 70.

[4] The main proof text of the Trinity, I John 5:7, is not in the earliest manuscripts; most scholars accept that it was inserted after the doctrine of the Trinity was formulated, in order to substantiate it from Scripture.

[5] Barrett 1997: 43, 130–1.

[6] See Robinson 2000: 103–17.

[7] Father of the Simon de Montfort who was responsible for the institution of the British representative parliament in 1265.

[8] For more detail on the far-reaching effects of both Gnosticism and the Cathars, see the author's *Secret Societies* (Blandford, 1997).

CHAPTER 12

Christian Origins

UNITARIANS

Historically, the main point of division between Unitarian Christianity and mainstream Christianity is their rejection of the doctrine of the Trinity and their denial that Jesus is God. Some Unitarians, like many other Christian offshoots, claim to be more faithful to the original truths of Christianity, which they believe were lost in the many Councils of the early Church. In terms of early 'heresies' they are closest to Arianism; in present-day theological terms they would be called liberal. For others, the Christian theology of their historical roots is less important than living a good life and serving others.

HISTORY

Unitarian Christianity is essentially Arian in its rejection of the deity of Christ – though pure Arianism actually states that the Son, albeit divine, is subordinate to the Father. Despite the Councils and creeds of Nicea, versions of Arianism lasted from the time of Arius himself up to at least the end of the sixth century. It was particularly strong in the Germanic lands, among the Goths and Huns who, when they gave up their belief in the Norse/Germanic gods in favour of the new religion, were not prepared to accept the Roman version of Christianity. The fifth-century warlord Attila the Hun, though not normally thought of as a religious exemplar, was way ahead of his times in allowing members of his warband to follow whichever gods they wished, so long as they didn't interfere in each other's freedom of worship or, more importantly, disrupt the warband. Arians lived and fought alongside Pagans with no difficulty; the more authoritarian Roman Christians were both less tolerant, and less tolerated. The Roman Church, however, had greater secular power, and Arianism (if it continued to exist at all) went underground for nearly a thousand years.

The most widely quoted 'proof text' of Trinitarianism is I John 5:7, 'For there are three that bear record in heaven, the Father, the Word and the Holy Ghost: and these three are one.' In theological terms, Unitarianism owes much to Desiderius Erasmus (1466–1536), who discovered that this verse does not appear in the oldest and most reliable manuscripts of the New Testament, and is almost certainly a late interpolation to give scriptural support to the doctrine of the Trinity.

The beginnings of formal Unitarianism – in its early years sometimes known as Socinianism – can be traced to Laelius Socinus (1525–1562) and his nephew Faustus (1539–1604), though non-Trinitarian ideas had been around in central Europe for some years previously. For example, the Spanish scholar Michael Servetus (1511–1553), despite his possessing a safe-conduct, was burnt at the stake by Calvin's supporters in Geneva; his beliefs included a rejection both of Calvinism's predestination and of the Trinity. Laelius Socinus, who also rejected the Trinity, was appalled at the death of Servetus. His own life would be in danger if he remained in Italy; like other non-Trinitarians, he spent some years travelling around central Europe spreading his beliefs.

In Transylvania (in modern Romania), the Reformed Bishop Francis (or Ferenc) David was first an Antitrinitarian, then a full-blown Unitarian. Through him King John II Sigismund of Transylvania accepted this belief, becoming the only openly Unitarian king in history. In the Declaration of Torda in 1568 he made Unitarianism one of four officially recognized versions of Christianity in his country – the first such declaration of religious tolerance in Europe in modern times.

Faustus Socinus was first a Catholic, and then a Calvinist, before eventually following his uncle in rejecting the Trinity. He spent some years in Transylvania, where Unitarians first took that name around 1600 – it had been used against them by their opponents since 1569 – and ended his life in Poland, where Socinianism took a strong hold. When Socinians were first persecuted and then expelled from Poland by its Catholic rulers in the middle of the seventeenth century, they went to Transylvania, Germany and the Netherlands.

In England, the Act of Uniformity in 1662 imposed severe limitations on who could preach, and what they were allowed to preach; ministers had to have received episcopal ordination (see page 127), to conform to the Book of Common Prayer, and to take their services in accordance with the rites of the Church of England. Some 2,000 ministers refused these restrictions and went off to do exactly what they had been told not to, and their followers built churches and chapels for them. Relatively few of these dissenters were Unitarian in theology at this stage, but among them were a sizeable group who pursued a rational interpretation of scripture, seeking to reconcile the Bible with the newly emerging scientific outlook; many of these had moved to a Unitarian position by the end of the eighteenth century under the influence of figures such as the radical Unitarian minister and scientist, the Reverend Dr Joseph Priestley. These dissident congregations, with others of different Nonconformist beliefs, came to be known as Free Churches; this is still reflected today in the name of the Church's co-ordinating body, the General Assembly of Unitarian and Free Christian Churches.

The Act of Toleration in 1689 allowed freedom of worship for Congregationalists, Presbyterians, Baptists and Quakers – but not for Roman Catholics or Unitarians. But despite the prohibitions of the law, Arianist doctrines continued to be preached in the early eighteenth century, sometimes by Anglican priests.

Unitarians share some common ground with the Deists or Freethinkers of the early eighteenth century, the Universalists of later that century, the more secular Utilitarianism of the nineteenth century, Modernism from the nineteenth century onwards, and the demythologizing work of (particularly German) Biblical criticism. The Age of Enlightenment, of scientific rationalism and enquiry, and of educated egalitarianism, lies behind all of these. Whatever their individual beliefs might be, the twentieth-century Bishops of Woolwich and Durham (see page 122) follow in the same tradition which, in a phrase, could be summed up as not being afraid to question taught truths.

Such free thinking always brings condemnation. Evangelicals seem to view Unitarians with particular abhorrence, seeing them not just as a sect or cult (bad enough in themselves) but as a wickedly heretical movement:

> All too many fill the pulpits of professedly evangelical churches. It appears to be a matter of policy for a fifth-column of ministers with Unitarian leanings to infiltrate the churches, with a view to future conquest.[1]

This writer, J. Oswald Sanders, although specifically attacking Unitarians, is really expressing the widespread Evangelical distaste for liberal theology. What seemed to worry Sanders the most was that, particularly in America, Unitarianism was adopted by a large number of intelligent, well-respected and highly influential writers, teachers, and leaders of society.

Indeed, in America Unitarianism was both intellectually and socially acceptable; it had become 'the thinking man's religion'. Critics saw it more as humanism with a spiritual basis, or a religion for the religious sceptic.

Unitarianism took particularly strong hold in New England, especially in Boston. The writer and minister William Ellery Channing embraced it, and became instrumental in splitting the Congregationalist Church in America on Trinitarian–Unitarian lines. The essayist Ralph Waldo Emerson was for a short time a Unitarian minister, and his views were taken up by others, becoming very influential in Unitarianism.

> A key text is Emerson's *Divinity School Address* where he calls on preachers to speak from their own experience rather than relying on the Bible. This emphasis on the validity of the religious truth to be found in nature and in everyday experience, rather than solely through the Bible, remains a key and distinguishing feature of the Unitarian movement today,[2]

says Matthew F. Smith, information officer for the General Assembly of Unitarian and Free Christian Churches.

As education, morality and social activism were central to Unitarianism, Harvard College became a centre for Unitarian teachers. At least five US presidents, including Thomas Jefferson and John Quincey Adams, held Unitarian beliefs.

Another free-thinking movement, Universalism, arose in the USA around 1770 under the influence of a Scottish emigrant, John Middleton Murray; they believed that all would be saved, and also rejected the doctrine of the Trinity. In the USA the Universalist Church merged with the American Unitarian Association in 1961, forming the Unitarian Universalist Association, with a current membership of around 150,000.

In Britain, well-known Unitarians of the past included Joseph Priestley, Charles Dickens, Elizabeth Gaskell, Mary Wollstonecraft and Josiah Wedgwood.

BELIEFS AND PRACTICES

Perhaps the most important point to note about the Unitarian creed is that there is no creed. Individual Unitarians may tend to accept much the same set of beliefs, but among these is the belief that no one has the right to impose a set of beliefs on them. As with the Quakers, freedom of belief and freedom of worship are paramount. According to Smith,

> The main point of division between Unitarians and mainstream Christianity is our welcome acceptance of religious pluralism encompassing a broad spectrum of views such that some members think of themselves more as religious human-ists, for example, rather than Christians.

Historically, the main plank of the 'liberal-Christian' wing of Unitarianism is that there is one God, not three, or even three-in-one. They are Unitarian as opposed to Trinitarian. The Father is God, Jesus was a man, and the Holy Spirit is God's influence. But there is no formal belief statement on Jesus. 'What do Unitarians believe about Jesus? The interested enquirer will find no single answer to this question.'[3]

Many reject the dogmatism so carefully worked out by the early Church Councils. They believe that the (human) Jesus of the Gospels was transformed into the God-man Jesus Christ by the Church Fathers, and that the simple Christian truths were confused and obscured by Graeco-Roman influences.

Unitarians would generally be careful to distinguish between Jesus' deity and his divinity. Deity would mean that he was, and always had been, God, in the Trinitarian Christian sense. Divinity could mean that God indwelt him; although he was but a man, he was a good man, a holy man, a perfect man, and an example to be followed. Smith comments:

> If we speak of the 'divinity of Jesus' we are saying that he had a particular quality of 'holiness'; some Unitarians see Jesus as the pre-eminent spiritual

teacher while others do not. This quality of 'divinity' is an attribute that arguably every person can find within themselves and act upon.

The idea of Jesus as an exemplar is central to Unitarian Christians. As one Unitarian has said, 'For me, the supreme affirmation of Christian discipleship is not "I believe" but "I follow".'[4]

Jesus' death on the cross was nothing to do with atonement, with God dying for the sake of sinful man; it was an example of love and sacrifice. Unitarians are Universalists doctrinally, believing that there is no everlasting suffering in hell for non-believers. Opinion is divided on whether or not there is a heaven in its traditional sense; it is, in any case, more important to establish heaven on earth through right living and, for example, supporting the underprivileged. Although undeniably there is wickedness in the world, human beings are essentially good, rather than sinful, and it is up to all individuals to lead good lives in the service of others.

Smith stresses that doctrine is really not of paramount importance to Unitarians:

Unitarians today are not so much interested in refuting orthodox Christian theology as with exploring the religious values that should shape our lives... We are not seeking to undermine the faith of orthodox believers but rather to provide a relevant way of being religious for those who have already decided that they cannot go along with the creeds and dogmas of the mainstream Church.

Historically, Unitarianism has always been essentially a rationalist belief system; Unitarians place reason before revelation. The Bible is worth reading and studying, but it is not in any way the inspired and infallible word of God; it was written by a number of fallible men in particular places, times and circumstances, has been copied and edited and altered, and should therefore be interpreted in the light of reason. Parts of it are clearly allegorical, and parts are the opinions of the individual human writers.

The rationalist stance has changed a little over the last few years.

Unitarians continue to take reason seriously, but increasingly we are coming to value the intuitive and the exploration of feelings and emotions as steps towards spiritual growth. This shift of emphasis can be seen from the growing popularity of Adult RE programmes with a personal development focus and also through an increasing interest in New Age thought and Green Spirituality among our membership.

Although most Unitarians would call themselves Christians, some feel that this label is too restrictive; as with the Quakers, many Unitarians see no reason why they should not find just as much truth in the sacred texts of the other world religions as they do in the Bible. The term 'universalism' today, Smith says, has developed the meaning that:

spiritual truth is obtainable from diverse sources: other faith traditions, psychology, science, art, the natural world, personal experience. This is where many Unitarians are at today.

Indeed, Unitarianism itself has changed.

I would tend to say that we have evolved away from the mainstream churches over the last fifty years because we have become religious pluralists. We have become less Bible-based and Christocentric and more concerned with each person being the authority for their own beliefs, drawing on whatever sources of inspiration they personally find helpful.

In addition to Unitarianism's primarily Christian roots, Smith says,

we also respect the tradition of critical thought and reason going back to classical thinkers such as Socrates which flowered once again in the Age of Enlightenment. Some Unitarians look more towards Nature-based religion and Green Spirituality. Some regard Ralph Waldo Emerson and the Transcendentalists as precursors of the New Age movement.

Stressing the Unitarian commitment to 'unity in diversity', Smith quotes from Andrew Hill's book *The Unitarian Path* (1994):

The Unitarian path is a liberal religious movement rooted in the Jewish and Christian traditions but open to insights from world faiths, reason and science; and with a spectrum extending from liberal Christianity through to religious humanism.

Unitarians are strongly against discrimination or prejudice of any kind, racial, sexual or religious. The Church was the first denomination in Britain to appoint professional women ministers, in 1904, and several women have been president of their General Assembly. It actively welcomes gays, lesbians and bisexuals, and fights for their legal rights and social equality.

Because of their Nonconformist roots and their historical congregational polity, every Unitarian congregation is independent and self-governing; in Britain the General Assembly of Unitarian and Free Christian Churches is a co-ordinating and representative body. Power is decentralized and lies with the congregations, rather than being centralized at Unitarian Headquarters.

It is ironic that a Church which believes strongly that 'people of faith can and should seek to learn from one another through inter-religious dialogue and interfaith activity', and which was a founder member in 1900 of the world's oldest surviving international inter-faith organization, the International Association for Religious Freedom, 'has not found a place in the World Council of Churches because we are in conscience unable to accept the "Christ as God" formula. Although the Unitarian General Assembly was a founder member of the British Council of Churches, the Unitarian application for Observer status in the new Churches Together in Britain and Ireland (CTBI) has attracted insufficient support among the mainstream member Churches to be accepted,' says Smith.

There are around 8,000 Unitarians in 180 congregations in Britain. Worldwide there are around 300,000, about half of those in the USA; Unitarianism is still strong in Romania (80,000) and Hungary (25,000).

THE NEW CHURCH AND SWEDENBORGIANISM

Emanuel Swedenborg (1688–1772) was a Swedish nobleman, the son of a Lutheran bishop. He showed intellectual brilliance at an early age; he was a doctor of philosophy by the age of 21. Although his work was in metallurgy and mining engineering, he spent his early life in the pursuit of scientific knowledge, particularly in human physiology and in astronomy, and he wrote a number of well-respected scientific works. In 1736 he began recording his dreams, in 1743 he began having visions of angels and spirits, and of heaven and hell, and in 1747 he resigned his job as assessor-extraordinary with the Swedish Bureau of Mines, to devote the rest of his life to researching and writing about his spiritual discoveries. These spiritual writings, particularly *Heaven and Hell*, attracted a large following.

He wrote his many books in Latin. The titles of two of them – *On the New Jerusalem and its Heavenly Doctrine* and *The True Christian Religion Containing the Universal Theology of the New Church* – led to the two most well-known names of Swedenborgian organizations, the Church of the New Jerusalem, and the New Church. In addition to these Churches, which apparently work well together, there is the Swedenborg Society in London. Founded in 1810, its purpose is to translate and publish Swedenborg's works; it has a library and a bookshop, and also arranges lectures. There is also an independent New Church College in Manchester, which promotes study and training.

Swedenborg did not himself found a Church, or even a movement; this was done by people who had read his books. In Britain one of his earliest proponents was an Anglican priest, John Clowes, the rector of St John's Church, Manchester, for 62 years; he was the first to translate any of Swedenborg's works into English, and though he remained within the Anglican Church he was probably initially responsible for the movement's strength in the northwest of England. Swedenborg's ideas were taken up by a number of Methodist ministers, and members of other denominations; a group of these, including a Methodist, Robert Hindmarsh, founded the New Jerusalem Church in 1787.

John Wesley was impressed by Swedenborg's obvious intelligence and spirituality, and studied some of his books. He wrote in his diary on 28 February 1770:

> I began with huge prejudice in his favour, knowing him to be a pious man, one of a strong understanding, of much learning, and one who thoroughly believed himself. But I could not hold out long. Any one of his visions puts his real character out of doubt. He is one of the most ingenious, lively, entertaining madmen that ever set pen to paper. But his waking dreams are so wild, so far remote both from Scripture and common sense, that one might as easily swallow the stories of 'Tom Thumb' or 'Jack the Giant-Killer'.[5]

Wesley's conclusions were not shared by all ministers; over the last two hundred years clergy and laity in the mainstream Churches have often joined Swedenborgian study groups and drawn inspiration from his teachings without leaving their own Church. Among the many who were influenced by Swedenborg's work were the French Symbolists, the New Thought movement, William Blake, Dostoyevsky, Robert and Elizabeth Browning, W.B. Yeats, Ralph Waldo Emerson, Immanuel Kant, Goethe, and Helen Keller.

Swedenborg taught that there is only one God, and that as Jesus he came to Earth; this is a resurgence of Monarchianism (see page 135). The three parts of the Trinity are God's love, wisdom and energy – 'the universal creative love, the personal revelation of that love as human, and its activity in all people and things,' says the Reverend Ian Johnson, Minister of the General Conference of the New Church.[6]

Swedenborg saw the Second Coming as something happening in his lifetime – he saw visions of it in 1757 – but on an inner spiritual dimension, beginning a new dispensation: hence 'the New Church'.

He developed a long list of correspondences between things in the physical world and their spiritual equivalents, and applied this to study of the Bible. The Bible is to be understood chiefly for its spiritual teachings, and is generally not to be taken on a literal basis. Only certain books of the Bible are divinely inspired; in the New Testament these only include the Gospels and Revelation, though in his later writings Swedenborg did use the Epistles (especially I John) as a source.

Swedenborg taught that the soul is immortal; after death we go to a spirit world and eventually to heaven or hell. We can choose to go to heaven by putting our faith in Jesus' way of love, friendship, forgiveness, helpfulness, honesty, courage and self-denial. Believing them must obviously involve practising them, obeying the Ten Commandments in the way that Jesus showed.[7]

If instead we 'delight in pride, scorn, greed, revenge and deception' we will go to hell, but this is our own choice; 'the Lord is for ever eager to save us from such a fate, but this can only happen through our change of heart.' When our physical bodies die,

and the pressures and limitations of earthly life are removed, then our inner character will become clear to us and to everyone around us in the spiritual world. There we can continue for ever seeking our particular kind of happiness.

To summarize the beliefs on man's relationship with God:

God is love. The whole purpose of the universe is to share heavenly joy with as many people as possible. This creating love is revealed in Jesus Christ as Divine Humanity, to show us what his love and joy are like, to make his power easier for us to share. God is wisdom. He knows what is needed for us to share his joy. He shares that knowledge with us so far as he can, through the laws, stories and poetry of many religions, and in everyday situations of life. God's love and wisdom are the life in all things, and each thing in the world represents something of his heavenly kingdom.

Such teachings, and Swedenborg's clairvoyant powers, have led to his being a major influence on some New Age movements. He is generally respected as a deeply spiritual mystic, even by those who don't accept all his theological teachings. Johnson comments:

He was quite clear both that spirit-contact is possible, and that it sometimes carries great danger. Most of his followers think it important to realize:
a that we are all continually affected by spirits unconsciously,
b also that conscious contact can sometimes be genuine and useful, but
c that seeking it for gain or from mere curiosity will attract only bad spirits, and so is asking for trouble.

Swedenborgians have sometimes been criticized for being too intellectual. Johnson takes the point, but explains that:

the muddle of Christian tradition has needed thorough unravelling; also the idea of inner meaning requires considerable explanation and illustration for people used to literalism; but, once these barriers have been cleared away, our belief is beautifully simple.

The heyday of the Church in Britain was around 1900, when it had about a hundred churches. There are far fewer now, and the Church concentrates more on study groups, residential courses and dispersed learning schemes, offered by the College, and involving Church ministers and others. Committed membership in Britain has fallen from around 1,900 ten years ago to 1,500 today, but Johnson suggests that informal interest is increasing. There are around 7,000 members of the two main Swedenborgian Churches in America, and a further 10,000 with some connection to the Churches. According to Johnson there are steadily growing movements in Africa and Asia, with 20,000–30,000 members altogether (mainly in south and west Africa), and some groups in former Communist countries have been 'enthusiastically revived'.

MORMONS

The Church of Jesus Christ of Latter-day Saints – usually known as the Mormon religion – was founded in America, but now has a presence in over a hundred countries around the world; it has become a major religion very distinct from, but with its roots firmly in, mainstream Christianity. From its beginnings in the 1820s it has grown to a current world membership of nearly 11 million, 180,000 of those in the UK. Non-Mormons may find it difficult to credit their beliefs, yet Mormons everywhere are well-respected pillars of society. In America they have long held major government positions as senators and ambassadors; a former President of the Church, Ezra Taft Benson, served as the Secretary of Agriculture in the Eisenhower administration. In the UK the first Mormon MP, Terry Rooney (Labour: Bradford North), was elected in 1990, and a Mormon has also been elected to the new Scottish Assembly.

Unless otherwise stated, references to the Mormons apply either to the common history of all varieties of Mormons, or specifically to the main, Utah-based Church.

HISTORY

More than with any other 'new' Christian-based religion, the early history of the Mormons really is part of history-book history. More than many others, also, the founding story is a powerful myth, in the sense defined on page 17. We are not concerned with establishing the factual truth of this myth, only with accepting it as the basis of the religion.

Because the story of the origin of the Mormons is so well known, and so well documented, it will only be briefly outlined here. It should be remembered also that all history books are selective with their facts and interpretations. Pro- and anti-Mormon histories put very different slants on the same series of historical events; the 'historical truth' probably lies somewhere in between.

Joseph Smith (1805–1844) came from a farming family in western New York State, an area which was known as the 'burned-over district' because so many revivalist evangelists had 'set fire' to people's hearts in the early nineteenth century.[8] In 1820, at the age of 14, Smith asked God which of the many available varieties of Christianity was the true one; the main choice was between a host of different versions of Congregationalists, Baptists, Quakers and Methodists. God the Father and Jesus appeared to him in a vision, telling him that he should join none of these, because they were all wrong, but that he should wait a few years. In 1823 Smith had another vision, of the angel Moroni, who told him about some golden plates buried in a nearby hillside. In 1827 he was allowed to dig them up and begin the work of translating them, using a huge pair of eye-pieces called the Urim and Thummim which enabled him to understand the text, written in 'reformed Egyptian hieroglyphs'. Smith sat behind a curtain and dictated the English text initially to his wife Emma and a neighbour Martin Harris, and mainly to a young schoolteacher, Oliver Cowdery. Most of the work with Cowdery was done between April and June 1829.

When the translation was finished, the angel took the golden plates away. Martin Harris mortgaged his farm to pay for the printing, and the first edition of the *Book of Mormon* was published in 1830.

The *Book of Mormon: Another Testament of Jesus Christ* tells of two migrations to the American continents, the first of the Jaredite people to central America after the fall of the Tower of Babel (c. 2250 BCE), and the second of a group of righteous Jews whose leader was called Lehi (c. 600 BCE). Two of Lehi's sons were Nephi and Laman; in years to come the Nephites were godly, but the Lamanites were evil, and were cursed by God so that their skin turned dark, and they became the ancestors of the Native Americans. After his resurrection, Jesus Christ visited America and preached to the Nephites. The Lamanites wiped out the Nephites around 428 CE on the hill Cumorah near Palmyra in New York State – the hill where Smith found the golden plates in 1827. The golden plates, a history of the migrations and the American settlements, were collated by the prophet Mormon and his son Moroni, who were the last of the Nephites.

The *Book of Mormon* also records in detail the appearance of Jesus in America, after his resurrection.

Because the validity of Mormonism rests so much on both Joseph Smith and the *Book of Mormon*, critics of the religion attack the credibility of both. They quote Smith's contemporaries describing him as 'a notorious liar... utterly destitute of conscience', who was vulgar and lewd. The Smith family, they say, were known as treasure hunters; Joseph Smith hired himself out searching for buried treasure by peering into a magical stone, or 'peepstone'. The Mormons accept that in 1826 he was arrested as a 'glass looker' under a New York State law which made it illegal 'to tell fortunes, or where lost or stolen goods may be found'. This, critics say, is the origin of the magic eye-pieces and golden plates.

Such evidence, it must be said, is largely circumstantial; it is always easy to damn someone from the mouth of his enemies.

The *Book of Mormon* presents more substantial problems. For a start, scholars of the Middle East have never heard of 'reformed Egyptian hieroglyphics'. Among the other Mormon scriptures is a small book called *The Pearl of Great Price*. In one section, 'Extracts from the History of Joseph Smith, the Prophet', Smith tells of his friend Martin Harris taking a copy of some of the characters, and Smith's translation of them, to Professor Charles Anthon in New York.

> Professor Anthon stated that the translation was correct, more so than any he had before seen translated from the Egyptian. I then showed him those which were not then translated, and he said that they were Egyptian, Chaldaic, Assyriac and Arabic; and he said they were true characters.[9]

However, the *Book of Mormon* itself says, 'But the Lord knoweth the things which we have written, and also that none other people knoweth our language; therefore he hath prepared means for the interpretation thereof.'[10] If no one knew the language, critics ask, how could Professor Anthon have known that it was a correct translation?

Moreover, Professor Anthon has written:

> The whole story about my having pronounced the Mormonite inscription to be 'reformed Egyptian hieroglyphics' is perfectly false... Upon examining the paper in question, I soon came to the conclusion that it was all a trick, perhaps a hoax... It existed of crooked characters disposed in columns and had evidently been prepared by some person who had before him at the time a book containing various alphabets. Greek and Hebrew letters, crosses and flourishes, Roman letters inverted or placed sideways, were arranged in perpendicular columns, and the whole ended in a rude delineation of a circle, divided into various compartments, decked with various strange marks...[11]

On this incident, the Church today comments, 'There is some confusion about what happened in these interviews, but Martin Harris was unequivocally satisfied.'[12]

Critics also point not just to the large number of verses from the Bible in the *Book of Mormon* (over 27,000 words), but to the fact that they are taken from the King James version, and ask why an 1829 translation of a 428 CE text should be in 1611 English. The *Book of Mormon* apparently also contains quotations from the seventeenth-century *Westminster Confession of Faith* and an excerpt from a Methodist book of discipline.

In addition, Mormons say that Smith's 'translation' was inspired by God, and was perfect – Joseph Smith called it the 'most correct of any book on earth';[13] yet critics say there have been over 100 editions of the *Book of Mormon*, with a total of well over

3,000 revisions to the text. The Church points out that the vast majority of these are corrections of typographical errors, or rationalization of spelling, grammar and punctuation; for example, the 3,000 revisions include 891 changes of 'which' to 'who'.

If the *Book of Mormon* wasn't a miraculous translation from golden plates revealed by an angel, where did it come from? The theory most often proferred by critics in the past is that the historical portions were based on the manuscript of an unpublished novel called *Manuscript Found* written by a retired Presbyterian minister, Solomon Spaulding, which had been left at a local printers at which Joseph Smith's right-hand man in the early days of the Church, Sidney Rigdon, was (depending on sources) a regular visitor or even a compositor. Spaulding's widow, and others, claimed to recognize her husband's work when the *Book of Mormon* was published.

The Church points out that when a manuscript by Spaulding entitled *Manuscript Story* was eventually discovered, in 1884, it bore no resemblance to the *Book of Mormon*. Also, it says, Rigdon did not actually meet Smith until December 1830 – after the *Book of Mormon* was published. According to the authoritative *Encyclopedia of Mormonism*, 'Since 1946, no serious student of Mormonism has given the Spaulding Manuscript theory much credibility.'[14]

Some of the original papyri from which Joseph Smith translated the 'Book of Abraham' in *The Pearl of Great Price* were discovered in 1966. When translated by scholars, they were found to be standard funerary documents, bearing no resemblance to Smith's 'translation' of 'the writings of Abraham while he was in Egypt'. This discovery does not appear to have dented the faith of Mormons: 'the papyrus purchased by the Church in 1966/67 is just one of a whole bunch of papyri and, as such, neither proves nor disproves Joseph's assertions,' says Bryan J. Grant, the Church's Director of Public Affairs in the UK.[15]

There are two further arguments against the *Book of Mormon* which should be mentioned. First, there is no archaeological evidence at all of the settlements in America recorded in the *Book of Mormon*, and no genetic evidence for the Semitic origin of the Native American peoples. On a related, but wider, issue, Grant comments:

> One of the most remarkable aspects of *The Book of Mormon: Another Testament of Jesus Christ* is its assertion that great civilizations existed in the Americas, before Columbus. This was certainly not common knowledge, during the 1820s–30s.
>
> *The Book of Mormon* is not a history book, however, and our belief in it comes through spiritual, not academic means – in just the same way that the validity of the Bible does not depend on archaeological evidences and support.

Second, the three witnesses quoted at the beginning of the book as having 'seen the engravings which are upon the plates', including Harris and Cowdery, all later left the Church. One of them said, 'I saw them with the eye of faith', rather than as material objects.

Whatever the critics may say, millions of intelligent, well-educated Mormons believe absolutely in the miraculous origins of the *Book of Mormon*. One of the most important distinguishing tenets of their faith is that God's revelation continues in the present day; for them, the *Book of Mormon* is firm evidence of this.

As well as the *Book of Mormon* and the Bible, Mormons have two further books of scripture, often bound in with the *Book of Mormon*. *Doctrine and Covenants* is a compilation of revelations given to Joseph Smith and a few of his successors; new sections are occasionally added. *The Pearl of Great Price* contains two further inspired translations by Joseph Smith, a brief extract from Matthew's Gospel out of Smith's own partial translation of the Bible, and an extract from *The History of Joseph Smith, the Prophet*, in which he tells of the origins of the *Book of Mormon*.

In 1829 John the Baptist appeared to Smith and Cowdery and conferred the Aaronic Priesthood on them, after which the two baptized each other. Later, the apostles Peter, James and John appeared to the two of them, and conferred the Melchizedek Priesthood on them. These two priesthoods are still fundamental to the Church.

In April 1830 the Church, originally called simply the Church of Jesus Christ, was established, with Smith as First Elder and Cowdery as Second Elder. During the year Smith was twice tried, and twice acquitted, of being 'a disorderly person'.

Smith sensibly solved one potential problem very early on: although continuous revelation was an important plank of doctrine, and God could speak to anyone in the Church, commandments and revelations for the entire Church could only come through one man; initially this was Smith, and then his successor Brigham Young, and then each successive President of the Church.

The Church grew, with a number of converts from the Campbellite Movement, which later became the Disciples of Christ; one of these was Sidney Rigdon. Over the next few years, as membership grew, so did opposition, and the Church was forced to move from New York State to Ohio, Missouri, Illinois, and finally to Utah, in the famous great trek of 1846–7.

Even as early as the mid-1830s there was dissension in the Church over the fact that its doctrines and organization were becoming increasingly complicated (Campbellites aimed for the simplicity of the New Testament Church), and over the increased involvement of Smith in temporal affairs. There was continuous friction with non-Mormon neighbours, which often led to bloodshed and death on both sides. In 1839 10,000 members moved to Nauvoo in Illinois.

Meanwhile, nine senior members led a mission to England in 1840; thousands were converted, and during the next six years nearly 5, 000 Britons emigrated to America to join the Mormons at Nauvoo. The mission was based in Preston, Lancashire, which was for a long time the centre of British Mormonism – and which is, in fact, the oldest continuous branch of the Church anywhere in the world. (In June 1998 a second British Mormon temple was completed and dedicated at Chorley, near Preston.)

Things were not going well in Nauvoo. Non-Mormons were unhappy about the amount of power that Smith wielded, as editor of the local newspaper, commanding general of the local militia, and mayor of the town. (In 1844 he also made a bid for the Presidency of the USA.) In the spring of 1844 a number of former members of the Church set up a rival newspaper, the *Nauvoo Expositor*, which attacked both Smith and the Church. Smith, via the city council, ordered the *Expositor*'s press to be smashed and every copy of the paper to be burnt. In the ensuing furore, Smith and others were put in jail. While they were awaiting trial, Joseph Smith and his brother Hyrum were murdered on 27 June when a mob attacked the jail.

There followed a brief struggle for leadership between Sidney Rigdon and Brigham Young, each of whom was in a powerful position in the Church hierarchy. Young won, leading to an eventual split in the Church; many members were already concerned at the changes to the Church in their time at Nauvoo, particularly relating to the Temple and to polygamy, and Young's leadership laid even greater stress on these. The main breakaway Church eventually became the Reorganized Church of Jesus Christ of Latter-day Saints.

Local hostility continued, and in February 1846 members of the Church began their westward journey, breaking for the following winter in Nebraska and Iowa. In July 1847 Brigham Young arrived at the Great Salt Lake valley in what is now Utah.

Once they were safely established in effectively their own city and their own state, the Church sent out missionaries, particularly to Britain and Scandinavia. By the end of the century nearly 90,000 converts had moved to Utah.

Their troubles were not yet over. In 1862 Congress passed an Anti-bigamy Act, and in 1879 the Supreme Court upheld this as constitutional. Mormons held to their belief in the practice of polygamy. In 1882 the Edmunds Act allowed up to five years' imprisonment and a $500 fine for polygamy, with lesser penalties for unlawful cohabitation. This was enforced by federal marshalls searching for evidence of polygamy or cohabitation. Many Mormons, including their leaders, went underground for several years. Between 1884 and 1893, over 900 Mormons were imprisoned for polygamy-related offences. In 1887 the Edmunds-Tucker Act dissolved the Church as a legal corporation and required the forfeiture of any property worth over $50,000.

Mormons were being imprisoned, and Mormon property was being confiscated by the government. Faced with the options of the complete destruction of the Church they had fought so long and endured so much to protect, or the maintenance of a practice which had caused even internal dissension, the Church made the only realistic choice. Grant comments:

Two commandments were in conflict: the need to sustain the law of the land, and the need to follow what God had ordained. The prophet took it to the

Lord, and the directive was that the principle [of plural marriage] should be suspended.

In 1890 Church President Wilford Woodruff issued a proclamation, later added to *Doctrine and Covenants*, which concluded, 'And I now publicly declare that my advice to the Latter-day Saints is to refrain from contracting any marriage forbidden by the law of the land.'

BELIEFS AND PRACTICES

Although the majority of Christian denominations would disagree, the Church insists that it is Christian – in fact, 'a restoration of the Church Christ organized when upon the Earth,' says Grant. He continues:

Indeed, the name of our Church bears His name and as members we are encouraged to make Him and His teachings the centre of our lives. This should permeate our relationships with our personal families, our Church family, those that we work with, our neighbours and those in our community. In fact, everyone!

On the surface, the Articles of Faith of the Church are, with a couple of exceptions, little different from those of many other Christian Churches. The two main exceptions are Article 8, 'We believe the Bible to be the word of God, as far as it is translated correctly; we also believe the Book of Mormon to be the word of God'; and Article 10, 'We believe in the literal gathering of Israel and in the restoration of the Ten Tribes; that Zion will be built on the American continent, that Christ will reign personally upon the earth; and that the earth will be renewed and receive its paradisiacal glory.'

As will be seen with other Christian-offshoot religions, statements like Article 1, 'We believe in God, the Eternal Father, and in His Son, Jesus Christ, and in the Holy Ghost,' can mean quite different things. For Mormons, according to Grant, 'the Godhead is made up of three distinct, separate personages. God the Father and Jesus Christ have bodies of flesh and bones, while the Holy Ghost, the third member of the Godhead, is a personage of spirit.'

There has been some doctrinal confusion over the years as to whether Adam was God the Father, which critics say Brigham Young taught at one point; the Church itself has never actually taught this, regarding it as 'speculation' on Young's part.

Many anti-Mormon books take such early theological speculations as part of Mormon doctrine. Part of the problem is that Mormons were so busy surviving in their first few decades that it took them a while to work out their doctrine in detail; it should be remembered, though, that many of the fundamental doctrines of mainstream Christianity were not properly formulated until three or four hundred years after Jesus' death.

Behind many of the Mormon beliefs which are different from mainstream Christianity lies the doctrine that our souls exist before we are born. On a planet near the star Kolob, God and his many wives have children; these are spiritual beings without bodies. When a child is about to be born on Earth, one of these spiritual beings inhabits the child, the spirit and the body becoming 'a living soul'.

Lucifer, who was Jesus' brother, wanted everyone on Earth to be saved, without any choice; Jesus wanted us to have free will. By his death Jesus unconditionally paid the penalty we had inherited from the fall of Adam and Eve ('original sin'); his death will also redeem us from our own sins if we believe in him and keep his commandments.

Protestant Christians believe that salvation comes through faith, and that we have faith through the grace of God; they generally condemn the idea of salvation through works, though theologically this is something of a hot potato. Mormons believe that salvation requires both grace and works – 'a revealed yet common-sense reconciliation of these contradictory positions'.[16]

For Mormons, salvation actually depends on five things: belief in Christ; repentance of sins; baptism in water; receiving the Holy Ghost; and enduring to the end, by which they mean 'the member must press forward in faith, and continue in obedience to all the commandments of God.'[17]

'Receiving the Holy Ghost' is the same as the 'baptism in the Holy Spirit' found in Pentecostalist and Charismatic Evangelical Churches; it bestows the gifts of the Spirit including prophecy, speaking in tongues, interpretation of tongues, etc.

Despite – or perhaps because of – the persecution they received through most of the nineteenth century, Mormons are very strong on religious tolerance. Article 11 states, 'We claim the privilege of worshipping Almighty God according to the dictates of our own conscience, and allow all men the same privilege, let them worship how, where or what they may.' But this doesn't mean that they believe that other religions lead to salvation.

'We believe that our Church has all the truth whereas other religions have some of the truth,' says Grant, acknowledging that there are holy people in other religions. But salvation can only come through 'the Gospel of Jesus Christ in its fullness', and that is only found in the Mormon Church. 'We believe that before the gospel was restored to the earth in 1830, man did not have the authority of God to provide the ordinances necessary for salvation.'

These ordinances include the two orders of priesthood given to Joseph Smith and Oliver Cowdery, which validate Mormon baptism and all other ordinances.

The fact that baptism is essential for salvation accounts for one of the more unusual elements of Mormon doctrine, baptism for the dead. A Mormon can be baptized *on behalf of someone* who is dead; it is up to the dead person whether or not to repent and thus be saved. Because Mormons quite naturally want as many as possible to be saved, each member researches his or her family history at least four generations back, so that their parents, grandparents, great-grandparents and so on may be baptized in proxy by name. The Mormon genealogical database in Salt Lake City is the largest in the world. The Church makes the information available to anyone who wishes to trace their ancestors; in May 1999 it launched a free website for public use.[18]

Mormons are encouraged to have children, whether to increase the number of saved or to provide more bodies for the spirit children born on Kolob. Obviously with polygamy a man may have many more children within marriage; Brigham Young is said to have had 56 by his 17 wives. For its own survival the main Church very reluctantly had to drop the practice of polygamy; whether it would reintroduce it if the federal government were to change its mind is unknown. The Reorganized Church was against polygamy from the very start; but several of the more minor offshoots of the Church still practise it.

The Mormon Church is millennial, in that it believes that Christ will return and rule on Earth; Joseph Smith designated a site in Independence, Missouri, where Christ would establish his new Zion.

There is much speculation among non-Mormons as to what they do in their Temples. Joseph Smith, and most of the early Mormons, were Freemasons, and much of the ritual within the Temple is said to be similar to Masonic rites and symbolism. Normal services are held in normal churches, and the Temples are reserved for special rites. Non-members can be allowed in before a Temple is consecrated; in the case of the London Temple, 55,000 viewed it on Open Days in 1992 after it had been refurbished, and over 123,000 viewed the Preston Temple prior to its dedication in 1998. But otherwise, the Temples are reserved for members 'in good standing' – about a half of all active adult members, and only about 6 per cent on a regular basis. The restricted access 'is not a matter of secrecy; it is a matter of sacredness and sanctity.'[19]

In the temples, members of the Church who make themselves eligible can participate in the most exalted of the redeeming ordinances that have been revealed to mankind. There, in a sacred ceremony, an individual may be washed and anointed and instructed and endowed and sealed.[20]

The rites include solemnization of marriage for eternity, baptism for the dead, and other ordinances. Special white clothing is worn within the Temple to symbolize purity, cleanliness and setting aside the things of the world. Although the Church is reluctant to speak of it, Mormons 'in good standing' wear a white under-garment like a long tee-shirt all the time, under their normal clothing.

Having made covenants of righteousness, the members wear the garment under their regular clothing for the rest of their lives, day and night, to remind them of the sacred covenants they have made with God.[21]

The Mormon religion lays great stress on morality and 'worthy' behaviour. Sex before marriage and infidelity within marriage are condemned, as are homosexual practices.

Tobacco, alcohol and other drugs are banned for members, as are tea, coffee and cola drinks because of the stimulants they contain. Mormons do not have to be vegetarians, but meat should be eaten sparingly. These restrictions are known as the 'Word of Wisdom', a revelation given to Joseph Smith in 1833.[22] The Church claims that by following the Word of Wisdom, Mormon white males in California live eight years longer than non-Mormons, while in Utah Mormons have one-third less cancer than non-Mormons.

The Church was often accused in the past of being racist; its early leaders made a number of statements about non-White people being lower than Whites. Although the First Presidency of the Church urged Mormons to work for civil rights for Blacks in the 1960s, Blacks were not allowed to become priests or participate in Temple ordinances until 1978. Today, says Grant,

> the priesthood is open to worthy men of all races. The fastest-growing areas are South America and Africa, and 70% of all new converts are now being made *outside* of North America. The predominant language in the Church will soon be Spanish!

The Mormon Church was in the forefront of the fight for female emancipation, but only men may belong to either of the orders of priesthood. Boys are ordained into the Aaronic Priesthood at 12; this has levels of deacon, teacher, priest and bishop. At 18 they can receive the Melchizedek Priesthood, with levels of elder, high priest, patriarch, member of a seventy, and apostle. The majority of active adult male Mormons, including those who do missionary work on doorsteps around the world, are elders. At the top of the hierarchy is the President, who with his two counsellors makes up the First Presidency of the Church. Next comes the Quorum of the Twelve Apostles, who collectively and latently hold the same authority as the President, and appoint a new President on the death of the old one. The Quorums of the Seventy and the Presiding Bishopric are senior administrative levels.

The Church is organized in 'wards' – congregations of 200–600 members – led by a bishop; stakes (equivalent to dioceses), of up to ten wards, led by a stake president; regions; and areas. Missionary areas have missions, made up of districts, made up of branches, with fewer than 200 members; a branch is the equivalent of a small ward. In the UK at the end of 1998 there were more than 180,000 members in 44 stakes and 264 wards, plus 8 missions and 106 branches; there are two Temples, one near London and the other near Preston.

OFFSHOOTS

The Church has been plagued with schisms since it began; there are currently more than 25 offshoots, each claiming to be the only true version of the Church set up by Joseph Smith. And from the days of Joseph Smith, dissenting members have been swiftly excommunicated.

Several of the earliest breakaway groups – one headed by Joseph's brother William when Brigham Young was appointed President, and another headed by Joseph's former right-hand man, Sidney Rigdon – joined together in 1860 to form the Reorganized Church of Jesus Christ of Latter-day Saints (RLDS), based in Independence, Missouri, which is by far the largest and most significant offshoot. Until 1996, when Wallace B. Smith retired, their Presidents have always been descendants of Joseph Smith, starting with his own son, Joseph Smith III (the prophet Joseph's father was also called Joseph). RLDS see themselves as remaining true to Joseph Smith's original message and Church practices, which were altered by Brigham Young. Their theology is closer than the main Church's to mainstream Christianity; they have always been anti-polygamy; and they use Joseph Smith's *Inspired Version* of the Bible (the main, Utah-based Church prefers to use the King James version). Unlike the main Mormon Church, their priesthood has always been open to all races – and, since 1984, to women. They have always refused to be known as Mormons, insisting on the full name of their Church, or RLDS; however, in April 2000, because of the continuing problem of confusion between themselves and the main Mormon Church, they decided on a new name, the Community of Christ, though the original name will remain their legal name. There are around 250,000 members worldwide, in 40 countries. The Church has been in Britain since 1863, and has around 1,600 baptized members in 20 churches.

Another offshoot of interest is the Church of Christ (Temple Lot), founded as far back as 1852, largely in protest – again – against Brigham Young and the growing practices of polygamy and baptism for the dead. Based in Independence, Missouri, they still own the Temple Lot, which Joseph Smith had said would be the site of New Zion when Christ returns.

A very fundamentalist polygamist offshoot began in the 1930s in Short Creek, a small town in northwest Arizona. This split in 1951, over the usual issue of disputed leadership succession. One wing, the United Order Effort, is still based around Short Creek, now renamed Colorado City. The other wing, the Apostolic United Brethren, led by Rulon Allred, led to at least three other Churches. The Church of the First Born of the Fulness of Times in 1955 was led by Joel LeBaron. Joel's brother Ervil left this Church to form the Church of the Lamb of God; he had Joel killed in 1972, and Allred in 1977, among several other murders including his own daughter. Another offshoot of the Apostolic United Brethren was the Church of Jesus Christ in Solemn Assembly, now known as the Confederate Nations of Israel, founded in 1974.

With regard to the quite frequent media publicity given to polygamous 'Fundamentalist Mormons', Grant, speaking for the mainstream Mormon Church, makes the point that 'these polygamous groups have *nothing* to do with the Church. They are not members; most never were; and we disapprove of their activities unreservedly.'

There is currently a movement of theological liberals who want to stay within the Mormon Church, while taking a more relaxed attitude towards the historicity of the origins of the Church.

EXCLUSIVE BRETHREN

The Exclusive Brethren, albeit a small Protestant denomination with fairly straight-forward Evangelical Christian beliefs, are significant for two main reasons: their exclusivity, and Dispensationalism. Often known as the Plymouth Brethren, they should not be confused with the Open Brethren (or Christian Brethren), or with the much larger Church of the Brethren denomination in the USA. The term 'Brethren' used on its own below refers to both the Exclusive and the Open Brethren; 'the Church' refers only to the Exclusive Brethren. The Exclusive Brethren have no central administrative body; their central tract depot in the UK is the Bible and Gospel Trust.

※

The Brethren originated when four men – a doctor, a lawyer, an ordained minister and a 'gentleman' – started meeting together in Dublin in the winter of 1827–8 to celebrate the Lord's Supper. They believed in simplicity of worship, with no ritual, no set prayers and no set form of service – just a group of brothers meeting together in God's name; like many other Churches, they wanted to return to the basic princi-ples of the Early Church, as they found them in the Bible. They were opposed to the complexities of all the Christian denominations, and believed that an ordained ministry was not needed; one of the founders, John Nelson Darby, later wrote a tract entitled 'The Notion of a Clergyman: Dispensationally the Sin against the Holy Ghost'. And they believed, as did so many other new Churches in the nineteenth century, in the imminent return of Christ.

John Nelson Darby (1800–1882), had been a curate in the Episcopalian Church of Ireland. He left the Church, moved to Plymouth in 1830 and set up meetings there. Most of the early tracts were published in Plymouth, hence the name Plymouth Brethren, which is still commonly used, and which the Church dislikes. At this time the movement was largely composed of professional and upper-class people, though apparently Darby wrote to another leader telling him not to neglect the poor members in the Plymouth assembly.

Darby was an effective evangelist, and took his message to Switzerland, Germany, France, Italy, the USA, the West Indies, Australia and New Zealand; the Exclusive Brethren say that meetings are still to be found in each of these countries.

The Church says that Darby's main contribution to Christian theology was 'his translation of the Scriptures from the original Greek and Hebrew texts, which is widely recognized as the most accurate and dependable translation available.'[23] It is not, however, a translation with any wide use outside the Church.

In fact, Darby's most enduring contribution to wider Christian theology was his teaching on Dispensationalism, though the Church says 'This does not appear to be a term coined by Mr Darby, nor is it in common use amongst brethren'. This teaches that there are seven Ages of man, starting with the Age of Innocence, before the Fall, and progressing through the Ages of Conscience, Human Government, Promise, Law, and Grace, this last established through Christ; the seventh Age, still to come, is the Millennial reign of Christ. Darby was one of the first to work out the 'timetable' of the Last Things, and taught that the saved will be caught up in the Rapture before Christ's return, and so will be spared the great tribulation.

Dispensationalism in one form or another has been preached by many Evangelical Churches since then, right up to the present day (see page 71). The influential American evangelist of the late nineteenth century, Dwight L. Moody, was convinced of the idea by Darby, and one of the most significant Protestant reference books of the early twentieth century, the *Scofield Reference Bible*, followed the teaching, and so introduced it to even more Christians. Although the Brethren at one time saw belief in the Rapture as a hallmark of the true believer, so many diverse Churches now teach it that it can no longer be seen as the unique touchstone of the Brethren.

Theologically, all Brethren are conservative Evangelical; they believe implicitly in the Bible as the inspired word of God, they are orthodox Trinitarian, and they believe in the assurance of salvation by faith in Christ alone. They do not formally hold to any of the creeds, believing that the Bible is the sole source of authority for their teaching.

The Exclusive Brethren also believe in an absolutely upright moral standard of behaviour, and in keeping completely apart from the world. Darby's strictness on this was too much for many in the movement – there were also some minor but very bitter doctrinal disputes – and in 1848 it split into two, the larger portion calling themselves the Christian Brethren or the Open Brethren to distinguish themselves from Darby's minority group, the Exclusive Brethren, also known for a while as Darbyites. The Open Brethren are now effectively indistinguishable from any other Free Evangelical Church. They welcome Christians from other Evangelical Churches to their services, though it depends on the individual church whether they allow outsiders to join in the Lord's Supper, the communion service.

The Exclusive Brethren are another matter. They keep apart from every other Church. They hold their exclusivity, or 'separation from evil', as a primary virtue 'in view of maintaining suitable conditions for partaking of the Lord's Supper.' They will include in their fellowship any believers who 'wash their robes', or keep themselves free of every wrong association. They will exclude from their fellowship not just anyone who doesn't share their beliefs, but any of their members who fall from the true path of absolute purity. It is the duty of every member to point out the failings of any other member, 'in a spirit of loving correction'. If the erring member does not repent and reform 'the other members would, with sorrow, withdraw from him'. This even applies to the spouse of an errant member; it is forbidden, for example, to eat at the same table, because this is regarded as fellowship; they 'will only eat with those with whom they partake of the Lord's Supper.' If a member of the Church, however otherwise godly, 'should persistently and wilfully refuse to separate from someone thus disciplined, they would prove themselves also unfit for fellowship.'

It is vital that they 'abstain from all appearance of evil' or in Darby's own translation of the Bible, 'hold aloof from every form of wickedness' (I Thessalonians 5:22). In their own words:

> Manifest errant behaviour in a member would call for sympathetic investigation. If this fails to gain their ear, the member may be 'shut up', i.e. shrunk from (2 Thessalonians 3:6) until the situation is clarified.

In effect, this means that the member is not admitted into church services and meetings.

The Exclusive Brethren were led through much of the twentieth century by father and son James Taylor Senior (1870–1953) and Junior (1899–1970). The latter

> served in post-war years to liberate the brethren from increased worldliness and relaxing of standards that threatened to engulf the fellowship. It became clear to many that membership of professional associations (as with Trade Unions), social eating with business associates and unconverted natural relatives etc., were all incompatible with their participation at the Lord's Supper.

But all was not well in the Church. Taylor wanted increasing separation from the world, but some of the members

> [held] the terms of the truth without the corresponding moral practice. This culminated in meetings at Aberdeen in 1970 in which Taylor provoked a reaction by ambush exposing in a number of prominent leading men spiritual pride and hidden moral corruption.

This precipitated a crisis in the Church:

> Pure persons saw what was at stake and rallied to the truth (Titus 1:15). Others wanting an easier way of life... abandoned the path and no longer formed part of the universal fellowship in which Taylor was a respected leader.

Something like 28 per cent of the membership left the Church after Aberdeen.

Today the Exclusive Brethren are scrupulous about keeping themselves separate from the corruption of the world, including what they feel are depraving influences such as TV, computers and the Internet.

> The devil is using the computer to prepare people in their very homes to receive the 'man of sin'...
> Should computers be part of our young people's education? I would say unhesitatingly, 'NO!' No enlightened Christian would embrace computerization for himself or for his children...
> Will the priceless experience of parents and elders be discounted in favour of information independently obtained on the screen?
> Will experiences *with* parents and loved ones be lost through computer obsession?
> Will morals be even further eroded?
> Will the devil and the 'man of sin' gain further direct access to households?
> What will happen when a dreadfully immoral 'Computer Generation' comes to power and influence in government, indistry and education?[24]

The Church's younger children are in the main educated in normal State schools, but do not take part in competitive sports or any extra-curricular activities, and they are strongly discouraged from making any friends outside the Church. Because they believe that student life is full of wickedness and temptation and also that 'an over-trained faculty is inimical to spiritual progress', young people are not encouraged to go to university, with the result that there are now very few professional people in the movement. Learning practical skills, however, is encouraged.

There is a curiously old-fashioned feel to the Church; for example, few of its tracts make any concession to the 1990s, many of them still referring to World War II. They accept that they practise 'a way of life which makes no concession to the world with its latest fashions and advances in communications technology.' They make the point, however, that they are not completely isolated from the wider world; they 'preach in most towns each weekday and employ and work alongside persons both Christian and others in their everyday life.'

As with the Quakers, all services are extempore, with all prayers, preaching and choice of (unaccompanied) hymns inspired by the Holy Spirit. Preachers have no formal training at all. Unlike the Quakers, women are not allowed to pray, teach or preach during services, in accordance with I Corinthians 14:34–35.

There are some recruits to the Church through their outdoor preaching, but the majority of members have been brought up in it. Family life is important to the Exclusive Brethren; they devote a lot of care and attention to their children, who are brought up within a consistently sound moral code. Because they have been taught almost from the cradle to keep themselves apart, and so have few if any friends outside the Church, it is reckoned to be difficult for members to leave the Church. Some do, of course, and the impression to non-members is that overall numbers are falling, though the Church disputes this, saying that there is an increase 'as the young marry and have families'. Accurate figures are not available, but there are thought to be something in the region of 35,000 members worldwide, with maybe 14,000 in the UK. (The Open or Christian Brethren have around 60,000 members in the UK.)

For those outside the movement it might seem a harsh and unforgiving Church; for those inside, the Church is like an extended family, with members supporting each other in their desire to stay close to God and serve him unreservedly.

THE NEW APOSTOLIC CHURCH

The New Apostolic Church is fairly small in Britain, but is a significant denomination in other countries. Its roots lie in the Catholic Apostolic Church, founded by Edward Irving and others in London and Albury, Surrey, in the early 1830s. This was in some ways an attempt to bring Evangelical beliefs and traditionalist practice together. Its doctrine was Evangelical; its liturgy and ceremonial were as complex and artistically fulfilling as anything in the Orthodox, Catholic or Anglican churches, from which they were largely borrowed. The Church also believed in speaking in tongues and prophecy, and in the imminent return of Christ, thus simultaneously taking on aspects of the New Testament church and of many present-day new Christian movements.

Irving, formerly a Presbyterian minister of the Caledonian Church in London, was one of the main leaders of the movement until his death in 1834 at the age of 42; members were sometimes known as Irvingites. The most prominent figure in the Church was Sir Henry Drummond (1786–1860), a banker and Member of Parliament (not to be confused with Henry Drummond (1851–1897), a scientist and also an evangelist). It was Drummond who built the Apostles' Chapel on his family estates at Albury Park, near Guildford, Surrey, where some of the Church's apostles are buried; his position in society, and consequential influence, can be gauged by the fact that his daughter married the Duke of Northumberland. Another of the apostles was the son of Spencer Perceval, Britain's only assassinated Prime Minister.

The Catholic Apostolic Church had two related problems. Believing themselves to be in the End Times, they consciously mirrored the organization of the Early Church, appointing twelve apostles who were responsible for taking what was called the Great Testimony, 'couched in lofty language, for presentation to the Potentates of the world and the bishops of the Church universal' in an effort 'to seek to unite the entire Christian Church in preparation for the Lord's arrival.'[25] They came to the belief that Christ would return between 1838 and 1855, and when this failed to happen, and they also failed to excite the rest of Christendom with their message, they lost some of their impetus.

This is a difficulty which has faced every Church which has named a date for the Second Coming, and most of them have managed to deal with it in one way or another (see Chapter 7). But because the Catholic Apostolic Church had expected their twelve apostles to be *in situ* when the Lord returned, they never made any provision for appointing new apostles when any of the original twelve, appointed in 1835, died – and without apostles to appoint them the entire Church hierarchy of bishops, elders, shepherds, evangelists, priests and deacons would ultimately dwindle away.

When the last English apostle, Francis Valentine Woodhouse, died in 1901, aged 95, the Church knew it was the end of the road.

This pattern of the house has been before the eyes of Christendom for five and sixty years. And Christendom as a whole has given no heed to it. And now the tabernacle is being taken down. The taking down commenced almost as soon as the pattern had been set up.[26]

Over the decades, co-adjutors, archangels and angels (levels of bishop) died. According to one writer in 1960, because of this 'ultimate difficulty' of the Church, 'at the present time it is being gradually absorbed into the Church of England.'[27] The last active priest died in 1970; if any members still remain, they can be no more than a handful.

Long before this situation had reached its inevitable conclusion, in 1863 the Catholic Apostolic Church in Germany split from the UK parent Church in the 'Hamburg Schism', over precisely this issue. The German Church, now called the New Apostolic Church, believed that new apostles *could* be 'called'. With apostles there could be the whole Church hierarchy. The New Apostolic Church grew and thrived. Today it has around 10 million members worldwide, in almost 50 congregations in some 170 countries. It claims to be the third-largest Christian Church in Germany, after the Catholics and the Lutherans. It is also strong in the Indian sub-continent and parts of Africa, and has a significant presence in North and South America and France, 'with great activity in Russia and the surrounding countries'.[28] Although its parent Church was established in Britain, the New Apostolic Church has never been strong there; it has maybe 2,000 members in about 40 congregations.

The New Apostolic Church is generally Evangelical in its beliefs, with a strong emphasis on the imminence of the Second Coming. Its one unusual point of doctrine is its 'Services for the Departed'; according to Raymond A. Thomas, UK Office Manager of the Church:

> These services are specifically to invite those who have died without grace to come to the altar of grace, where an Apostle of Christ can administer the sacraments of Holy Baptism, Holy Sealing [equivalent to confirmation] and Holy Communion. This is done by two Priestly office holders receiving the sacraments as proxy for those who are invited from the realms of eternity.

This is a similar 'second chance for the dead' as the Baptism for the Dead performed by the Mormon Church.

SEVENTH-DAY ADVENTISTS

The name Seventh-day Adventist expresses two of the main distinguishing features of this Church: they worship on the seventh day of the week, and they await the second advent, the Second Coming of Jesus. Although there is one main denomination with the name, in some ways Seventh-day Adventism *per se* is less a Church than a movement; there have been dozens of offshoots, some little more than a handful of congregations, others considerably larger, like the Worldwide Church of God, and some it would prefer not to be associated with, like David Koresh's ill-fated Branch Davidians. To attempt to draw a family tree of all the offshoots of offshoots would be a fascinating but well-nigh impossible exercise.

HISTORY

Seventh-day Adventists grew out of the Adventist movement of the early nineteenth century – though in fact anyone who believed Christ's return was imminent could be called Adventist, including the Shakers (the United Society of Believers in Christ's Second Coming) in the 1760s. A German Lutheran minister, J.G. Bengel, taught the doctrine in the mid-eighteenth century, setting the date of the Second Coming at 1836. William Miller, an American Baptist minister, attracted thousands of followers with his message, based on prophecies in Daniel and Revelation, that Christ would return in 1843. When nothing happened, he reworked his calculations, taking account of the calendraic fact that there isn't a year 0 between 1 BCE and 1 CE, and announced that the event would take place in 1844, specifically, on 22 October. Some believers sold their properties and possessions in readiness, though apparently the oft-quoted story of them sitting on their rooftops in 'ascension robes' is without foundation; once again, nothing happened, and the great event became known as the Great Disappointment.

Adventists, or Millerites, divided into a number of Churches and movements, each coping with the Great Disappointment in its own way. Miller himself died in 1849, not endorsing any of these groups.

The Seventh-day Adventist Church was founded on three main doctrines put forward by different Adventists in the immediately ensuing years. One, revealed to Hiram Edson the day after the Great Disappointment, was that Christ had not returned to Earth in 1844, but had entered his heavenly sanctuary to cleanse it and sort out the sheep from the goats in preparation for the Judgement. Another, a teaching put forward by Joseph Bates in 1846, was that Christians must obey God's law, as set out in the Ten Commandments, which include the observance of the Sabbath. (There had in fact been a few Seventh-day Baptist Churches in the USA for nearly 200 years.) The third was that in these last days the gift of Prophecy would come on the Church; Seventh-day Adventists believe that the visions and teachings of Ellen G. White are a fulfilment of the Biblical gifts of the Spirit.

Ellen G. White (1827–1915), then Ellen Gould Harmon, was brought up a Methodist, and joined the Millerites when she was 17. She had illness and injury as a child, and some critics believe that her visions were a continuation of these conditions. Her first vision, in December 1844, convinced her that belief in the October 1844 date was not an error or delusion, despite the Great Disappointment of only a couple of months before.

Her visions, and her interpretations of them, are the basis of her several books, including *The Great Controversy* and *The Desire of Ages*. In her books she expanded on the teachings of the Church, particularly on keeping the Sabbath and on Christ cleansing the sanctuary. She also taught healthy living, instituting several dietary regulations. Her writings were regarded as prophetic and inspired, but not as replacing or even adding to the Bible.

She later married James White (1821–1861), a very prominent Adventist minister. After his death she became the acknowledged leader of the movement.

This movement, initially almost a federation of independent congregations, set up its headquarters in Battle Creek, Michigan, in 1855; it didn't take the name Seventh-day Adventist until a conference there in 1860 (see page 482), and was formally organized as a Church in 1863. In 1903 it moved its centre to Takoma Park, Washington DC.

The theology of the Church mellowed a little over the years, as Mrs White grew older, and became closer to mainstream Christian doctrine during the twentieth century. Realizing, perhaps somewhat belatedly, that some of their earlier and more extreme writings were still being quoted against them, the Church produced in 1957 a 700-page work entitled *Seventh-day Adventists Answer Questions on Doctrine*, which clarified many contentious issues. This was followed in 1988 by *Seventh-day Adventists Believe... A Biblical Exposition of 27 Fundamental Doctrines*.

Over the years the Seventh-day Adventist Church has met with a lot of opposition, partly because of some of its more over-enthusiastic claims of sole correctness, which have now been toned down considerably. To avoid alienating potential enquirers, for many years it deliberately adopted a policy of anonymity, presenting its books, magazines and meetings simply as Christian rather than Seventh-day Adventist. This practice attracted claims of deception, and was eventually dropped.

The Church today stresses its roots among the European reformers of Christianity in the sixteenth and seventeenth centuries as much as its American origins as a denomination, 'most teachings having been held formerly by European believers prior to the organization of the Seventh-day Adventist Church.'[29]

Fewer than 10 per cent of the Church's current membership of over 10 million live in North America. It is still strong throughout Europe; in Britain, where there are around 20,000 members in 250 congregations, around 15,000 are African-Caribbean in origin.

BELIEFS AND PRACTICES

Evangelical counter-cult writers are divided on how close Seventh-day Adventist beliefs are to mainstream Christian doctrine. Seventh-day Adventists quite naturally become annoyed at being branded a cult when they believe in the Trinity, the full divinity of Christ, his incarnation and resurrection, the need for salvation, the indwelling of the Holy Spirit, and so on. Unlike many other Christian offshoots, they have not redefined these terms in their own way; their theology, on the whole, is straightforward mainstream Christian. In one publication they say that 52 per cent of their Statement of Fundamental Beliefs is 'the same as that held by all conservative Christians'; 39 per cent of their beliefs fall into the 'denominational-difference' category, each being held in common with at least one other denomination; and the other 9 per cent are distinct from normal Protestant theology.[30]

One of these distinctive doctrines is that:

Christ was inaugurated as our great High Priest and began His intercessory ministry at the time of His ascension. In 1844, at the end of the prophetic periood of 2,300 days, He entered the second and last phase of His atoning ministry. It is a work of investigative judgement which is part of the ultimate disposition of all sin, typified by the cleansing of the ancient Hebrew sanctuary on the Day of Atonement.[31]

Critics of Seventh-day Adventism tend to quote from the works of Ellen G. White, and from other books and articles by the Church's early writers, to prove that they are heretical. They sometimes ignore the fact the Church itself now accepts that some of these early writings were perhaps over-enthusiastic and at the very least badly phrased, and has tidied up its doctrinal statements in the last few decades.

Seventh-day Adventists attach some weight to Ellen G. White's books, but do not in any way regard them as scriptural, or even as infallible. Any revelations in the 'Spirit of Prophecy' are to be tested against the Bible, which is the sole authority. 'Seventh-day Adventists accept the Bible as their only creed and hold certain fundamental beliefs to be the teaching of the Holy Scriptures.'[32] In any case, Mrs White's visions and writings are only relevant for this Church, not for all of Christendom. There is little public emphasis on her today; the 1995 pamphlet quoted in this entry does not even mention her.

Seventh-day Adventists believe that they are 'the remnant' of true believers, but they do not believe that they are the *only* true believers:

> We fully recognize the heartening fact that the host of the true followers of Christ are scattered all through the various churches of Christendom, including the Roman Catholic communion. These God clearly recognizes as His own.[33]

They observe the Saturday Sabbath as one of the Ten Commandments, but they do not condemn as unbelievers those who worship God on Sunday – and they do not, as critics often claim, say that Sunday worship is the Mark of the Beast.

> The majority of those in Christian churches still conscientiously observe Sunday. We ourselves cannot do so, for we believe that God is calling for a reformation in this matter. But we respect and love those of our fellow Christians who do not interpret God's word just as we do.[34]

Although they teach obedience to the law, and are more legalistic than many other branches of Christianity, they stress that salvation does not come through keeping the law – 'by works' – but by the grace of God, through faith in Christ's atoning death.

They do have two unusual teachings about the fate of believers and non-believers. First, they believe that after death we remain in our graves, rather than going straight to heaven; when Christ returns to establish his millennial kingdom, the saved will be resurrected to everlasting life. Secondly, they do not believe in everlasting punishment for non-believers; eternal death means just that: final destruction. These two doctrines, of 'soul sleep' and the annihilation of the wicked, are not standard Christian doctrines, though they are held by a number of theologians, preachers and laity within mainstream Christianity.

The Seventh-day Adventists have been attacked for teaching that Christ possessed a sinful human nature; this, they say, is a misinterpretation (based on some admittedly clumsily written early statements) of what they actually believe, which is that Christ, being human as well as divine, had a fully human body and could be tempted in all ways. They stress that he was, however, completely sinless.

> He clothed His divinity with humanity, He was made in the 'likeness of sinful flesh,' or 'sinful human nature,' or 'fallen human nature,' (cf. Romans 8:3). This in no way indicates that Jesus Christ was sinful, or participated in sinful acts or thoughts. Though made in the form or likeness of sinful flesh, He was sinless and His sinlessness is beyond questioning.[35]

It should be remembered that the Early Church argued for centuries about the full implications of the God-man nature of Christ, and that mainstream Christianity has had more than one interpretation.

Since the days of Ellen G. White the Church has emphasized healthy living. As well as campaigning against smoking, discouraging the drinking of alcohol and encouraging a balanced vegetarian diet, the Church also runs many hospitals and health centres offering both conventional and alternative medicine.

The Church also believes in 'a broad education in a Christian context',[36] and in Britain runs nine primary schools, two secondary schools, and a higher education college, Newbold College in Bracknell, Berkshire, affiliated to the Open University.

OFFSHOOTS

The Seventh-day Adventist Church, and the Sabbatarian movement in general, are responsible for a large number of schismatic Churches; most of these offshoots have also splintered in various directions, and their beliefs and practices may be quite different from those of the Seventh-day Adventist Church.

The Church of God (Seventh Day) originated from those individual congregations which, though both Seventh-day and Adventist, didn't join the Seventh-day Adventist Church associated with Ellen G. White; apparently each sees the other as the offshoot. Its two main divisions are the General Conference of the Church of God (Seventh Day) and the General Council of the Churches of God.

The Worldwide Church of God (see Case Study, page 479) has been described as 'an offshoot of an offshoot of an offshoot of the Seventh-day Adventist Church.'

Note that a movement with 'Church of God' in its name might be an offshoot of the Seventh-day Adventist Church or of the Worldwide Church of God, or might be quite separate from either.

There are also a large number of African-American Churches with origins in the Seventh-day Adventist movement.

The Branch Davidians (see page 85) also have roots in the Adventist movement. According to John C. Surridge, Communication Director of the Church:

It was their knowledge of the Seventh-day Adventist Church which led them to target Adventist members in their recruitment drives of the early 1990s, though their teachings and code of practice were totally alien to that of ours.[37]

CHRISTADELPHIANS

The Christadelphians were one of the several new Christian offshoots to spring up in America in the mid-nineteenth century. They are millennialist and Bible-believing, but their interpretation of Christian doctrine is markedly different from mainstream beliefs.

HISTORY

The Christadelphians, or Brothers of Christ, were founded in 1848 by an English doctor, John Thomas (1805–1871), who had emigrated to America in 1832. He was involved in a shipwreck *en route* to America, and vowed that if his life were saved he would devote it to religion. Although brought up a Congregationalist, he joined the newly formed Campbellites, later the Disciples of Christ, in Brooklyn, New York, in the 1830s. This was a Puritan group, with similarities to both the Baptists and the Congregationalists, but with no fixed creed. After much study of the Bible, Thomas worked out his own beliefs, and left the Campbellites to form his own distinct brand of Christianity, which he believed was a return to the original New Testament beliefs.

In 1849 Thomas published a book called *Elpis Israel* (Hope of Israel), in which he wrote that the Latter Days had begun; before Christ's return, Israel would be restored. An early companion book to this was *Christendom Astray* by Robert Roberts, who took over the leadership after Thomas' death in 1871. Michael Ashton, current editor of *The Christadelphian* magazine, describes *Elpis Israel* as 'a seminal work', but stresses that 'our main text remains, and always will remain, the Bible itself.'[38]

On several trips back to Britain Thomas preached widely and converted many, so unusually the American and British Churches both stem from the founder himself. Although historically Christadelphianism was found mainly in the UK, USA, Australia and New Zealand, today it is probably stronger in Britain than in the USA, with somewhere between 10,000 and 20,000 members in the UK in 337 *ecclesias* or congregations. The Church spread to most English-speaking countries by the end of the nineteenth century, and is now found in most countries of the world, particularly Africa, Asia and the Pacific Rim. 'There are probably more members in Malawi today than in North America,' says Ashton. They don't count their membership, but he says the worldwide total is between 50,000 and 100,000.

With his Congregationalist background, Thomas set up no central authority. 'Each separate congregation is responsible for its own members,' says Ashton. 'Fellowship between the congregations is on the basis of a shared Biblical faith. There are no leaders as such, either over local congregations, over areas, countries or worldwide.'

The Christadelphian magazine has been published monthly since 1864 and is, says Ashton, 'the recognized mouthpiece of our organization worldwide.'

BELIEFS AND PRACTICES

Christadelphians are ardent students of the Bible, which they believe to be the absolute word of God. Their reading plan, the *Bible Companion*, takes them through the entire Old Testament once a year, and the New Testament twice a year. All their teaching comes from the Bible, and not from the teachings and creeds of the Church Fathers.

'We do not claim to be the only group with a correct understanding of the scriptures,' says Ashton, 'nor do we deny that other individuals not associated with us hold true Bible teaching.' On the other hand, they recognize that their interpretation of the Bible is a minority viewpoint: 'We disapprove of those churches and organizations which claim to base their beliefs on the Bible, and yet preach a false gospel. In our opinion, all the mainstream churches in Christendom fall into that category.'

They disagree with traditional Christian belief on the nature of Christ, whom they see as 'the Son of God not God the Son'[39] They are not Trinitarians – but they are also not, they say firmly, Unitarians.

> They [i.e. Christadelphians] really do believe that Jesus was, and is, *literally* the Son of God. They are *not* Unitarians, who think of Jesus as just a very superior man; nor are they 'adoptionists', holding that God 'adopted' Jesus as His spiritual Son. They believe that Jesus was God's 'only begotten Son' in the way the Scriptures describe.[40]

The Christadelphian doctrine of the atonement is fairly similar to that of mainstream Christianity – 'being himself sinless, was able to be offered as a sacrifice for sin'[41] – with one major difference: he could not have done this if he himself had been God.

> It was the vital atonement for sin which makes it possible for us sinners to have hope. It is a tragedy that in popular Christianity this understanding has been perverted by the doctrine of the Trinity, which arose 300 years after the ascension of Jesus as a result of disputes within the Church. The creeds expressing the Trinity were decisions of Catholic Church Councils in the 4th and 5th centuries. Their teaching is not found in the Bible.[42]

Most Christadelphians probably have a better understanding of the Trinity than most mainstream Christians do; they have to, in order for them to argue against it. They are quite correct in saying that the Bible nowhere teaches the doctrine of the Trinity; the Bible, as mentioned earlier (see page 124) is not a book of doctrine. The concept of the Trinity was formulated by the Church Fathers in an attempt to codify the God-man nature of Christ, and the relationship of the Father, Son and Holy Spirit. It is precisely because this is still a live issue today, with the Christadelphians, Unitarians, Jehovah's Witnesses and others each having their own understanding of the problem, that the section on Early Church 'heresies' is included in this book.

The Holy Spirit is seen as 'the power and influence by which God achieves His ends'[43] – or, in more detail:

God's own radiant power, ever outflowing from Him, by which his 'every-whereness' is achieved. The Spirit is personal in that it is of God Himself: it is not personal in the sense of being some other person within the Godhead.[44]

Christadelphians do not believe in Satan as a personal devil; such words

represent only the evil tendencies of human nature. It is significant that throughout the Bible sinners are never encouraged to blame something or someone else for their failings, but only themselves.[45]

Christadelphians do not believe in the immortality of the soul, or in hell, which is simply the grave, or in heaven; eternal life for the saved and resurrected (Christadelphians, and perhaps others who have found the truth) will be on Earth after Christ's return. The unsaved will simply not be resurrected; as with the Jehovah's Witnesses, the reason for wanting to be saved is more of a carrot than a stick.

The millennialist teachings of the Christadelphians are broadly similar to those of most other Churches, whether 'mainstream' or 'alternative'. In their booklets there is perhaps more emphasis than usual on the importance of the Jews, whom Christadelphians see very much as the Chosen People and the key to the coming Millennium. They believe that we are currently in the End Times, comparing two Biblical verses with current events: 'He that scattered Israel will gather him, and keep him, as a shepherd doth his flock' (Jeremiah 31:10) refers to the establishment of the state of Israel in 1948; while 'Jerusalem shall be trodden down of the Gentiles, *until the times of the Gentiles be fulfilled*' (Luke 21:24) refers to the Jews retaking Jerusalem at the end of the Six Day War in 1967. We are thus at the end of the era of Gentile times.

The Jewish return to their homeland has occurred at a time when world statesmen vainly seek a formula for peace. The mushroom growth of Israel has coincided with the mushroom cloud of the nuclear age. Is this a mere coincidence? Or does it portend greater things? It means but one thing: Christ is coming back to the earth.[46]

Abraham, they believe, will be raised from the dead so that he will see the Holy Land with his own eyes and inherit it as promised (Genesis 13:15–17).[47]

Long before the establishment of the state of Israel was even a possibility, an 1866 publication said 'It is pretty certain that Jesus will return within the lifetime of the present generation.'[48] The Second Coming was forecast for 1868, then for 1910. In a somewhat more honest response than most millennialist Churches give, Ashton now comments:

> Our eager anticipation of the establishment on earth of God's kingdom has led us in the past to some inaccurate predicting of dates. The scriptures explain clearly that no one knows the day of the Lord Jesus' return to the earth.

Christadelphians do not believe in a priesthood; 'each congregation elects members from its own number to act on its behalf for a set term of office (one, two or three years),' says Ashton. They will not take up arms in war, and they do not vote or take part in political affairs, but otherwise their social behaviour is standard; on morality, 'we seek to uphold the Bible standards of sexual behaviour, i.e. only in heterosexual marriage,' says Ashton. Friendly relationships with non-members are not discouraged.

It is a common criticism of the Christadelphians that they put more effort into explaining themselves to mainstream Christians than in preaching the gospel to non-Christians. But for Christadelphians, mainstream Christians, through their acceptance of centuries of 'false' teaching, have got the message wrong; in any case, because the terminology is identical but the meaning so different, it is essential for them to explain what they mean, to show how their beliefs are different.

CHRISTIAN SCIENCE

Christian Science is best known for its Reading Rooms in many towns, for its well-respected newspaper *The Christian Science Monitor*, and for its belief in healing physical illnesses by spiritual rather than medical means. It sees itself as a Christian denomination in much the same way as the Methodist and Baptist Churches. In fact, its theology is markedly different from established Christianity in many respects, hence – in addition to its origins in the late nineteenth century and its emphasis on spiritual healing – its inclusion here as an 'alternative religion'.

HISTORY

Mary Baker Eddy (1821–1910), known by Christian Scientists as 'the Discoverer and Founder', was born in the village of Bow in New Hampshire, USA. Her parents were

Congregationalists, and she grew up in a strict Calvinist household. She was a sickly child, and remained in ill-health for her first few decades. Her first husband died of yellow fever a few months after they married in 1843. Her second husband, whom she married in 1853, treated her badly and eventually deserted her; she divorced him in 1873. She married her third husband, Asa Eddy, in 1877; although she was then 55, her age is given on her marriage licence as 40. Although critics have cited this as dishonesty on her part, David Vaughan, of the Christian Science Committee on Publication, suggests that the real reason is that she 'was not present when her husband procured the marriage certificate';[49] Asa Eddy apparently refused to give either of their ages. This marriage was some years after she had founded Christian Science, and in the five years until his death Asa Eddy helped her promote her new religion.

To avoid confusion 'the Founder' will be referred to throughout by her final married name.

Her second husband unwittingly started the process which resulted in the new religion, by introducing her to Phineas P. Quimby (1802–1866), a watchmaker who had set up as a mesmerist (hypnotist) and faith healer. In 1862 Quimby, who taught that all disease is caused by faulty reasoning on the part of the sufferer, healed her of a crippling spinal disease. Quimby ascribed his healing powers to correct thinking rather than to God, but Mrs Eddy thought otherwise – though she spent two years lecturing on his work.

In February 1866, one month after Quimby's death, she slipped on ice and fell badly. A few days later she was reading her Bible and noticed the passage where Christ heals 'a man sick of the palsy' (Matthew 9:2–8). 'The healing Truth dawned upon my sense,' she wrote; 'and the result was that I rose, dressed myself, and ever after was in better health than I had before enjoyed.'[50]

This, for Christian Scientists, was the true start of it all.

'In the year 1866 I discovered the Christ Science, or divine laws of Life, Truth, and Love, and named my discovery Christian Science.'[51] She studied the Bible for three years and formulated her doctrine, then began to teach it to others. In 1875 she published the first edition of *Science and Health with Key to the Scriptures*, which Christian Scientists read alongside the Bible in their Sunday services.

Christian Scientists today try to distance both their Founder and their religion as much as possible from Quimby.

'Her original ideas are misrepresented as coming from other sources, notably Phineas Quimby, a mesmerist with whom she had some contact before her discovery of Christian Science,' says Alan Grayson, former District Manager of the Christian Science Committees on Publication for Great Britain and Ireland. [52] 'In contrast to Quimby's method, which was based on the action of the human mind and wholly divorced from any Bible basis, Mrs Eddy's system relies wholly on the divine Mind, God, and is rooted squarely in the Scriptures, particularly Christ Jesus' example.'

However, there is no doubt that her thinking was at least initially very much influenced by Quimby. Even after his death, when she was teaching from 1867 to 1870, she apparently used as her text Quimby's manuscript, with her own hand-written annotations.

Critics have pointed out that Quimby referred to his own healing system in 1863 as 'Christian Science', and at other times as 'the Science of Christ', 'the Science of Man' and 'Science and Health', and that he called disease 'an error', which is a term often used by Mary Baker Eddy.

It has been suggested that portions of at least the early editions of *Science and Health* are based both on Quimby's own manuscripts (eventually published in 1921), and also on a work by Francis Lieber, an authority on Hegel. Lieber had apparently sent a copy of his manuscript to his friend Hiram S. Krafts, who was one of Mary Baker Eddy's first students, and in whose home she lived for over a year. The Church disputes both claims, emphasizing the differences between Quimby's teachings and Mrs Eddy's rather than the similarities, and arguing that the Lieber document was actually a later forgery produced with the intent of discrediting Christian Science. Mrs Eddy's recent biographer, Gillian Gill, says there is 'overwhelming documentary evidence'[53] to refute the charges of plagiarism.

According to Mrs Eddy, 'No human pen nor tongue taught me the Science contained in this book, *Science and Health*'.[54] She also said, 'It was not myself but the divine power of truth and love infinitely above me, which dictated *Science and Health*'.[55] However, the book underwent several substantial revisions over the years, largely by the hand of a retired Unitarian minister, the Reverend J.H. Wiggin, who edited the text, rearranged the contents, and corrected Mrs Eddy's grammar. He is quoted as saying later that Mrs Eddy was no scholar, and that 'Christian Science, on its theological side, is an ignorant revival of one form of ancient Gnosticism.'[55A] The current edition, with standardized page numbering, inset subheadings and numbered lines for easy reference, dates from 1907; it has been alleged that the Church has attempted to destroy copies of all earlier editions.

The Church of Christ, Scientist, was founded in 1879; in 1894 Mrs Eddy reorganized it in the form it still has today, with the Mother Church in Boston, Massachusetts, and branches around the world.

Mrs Eddy opened the Massachusetts Metaphysical College in Boston, where she taught students from 1881 to 1889, charging $300 for a 12-lesson course and also selling *Science and Health* at $3 a copy – substantial sums for a course and a book in the 1890s, though Vaughan points out that clergymen weren't charged, and there were reductions in the fees for those of modest means.

Over the next few years her churches multiplied rapidly. In 1897 she ordered

Christian Scientists to refrain from teaching students for a year; instead they should sell them copies of her book *Miscellaneous Writings* and her other books.

> The Bible, *Science and Health, With Key to the Scriptures* and my other published works are the only proper instructors for this hour. It shall be the duty of all Christian Scientists to circulate and to sell as many of these books as they can.
>
> If a member of the First Church of Christ, Scientist shall fail to obey this injunction it will render him liable to lose his membership in this church.[56]

In Christian Science services from 1894 to today, the readings are from both the Bible and *Science and Health*. 'In order to move away from personal preaching, Mrs Eddy ordained these two books to be the pastor of her Church.'[57]

The compulsory purchase of reading material is also still part of Church practice. Christian Scientists today are required by a Church by-law to subscribe to the daily newspaper *Christian Science Monitor*, the weekly *Christian Science Sentinel*, the monthly *Christian Science Journal* and the *Christian Science Quarterly*, unless they would find it a financial burden to do so.

Christian Science, in common with many other new religions, does well out of its publications; Mary Baker Eddy left over $3,000,000 at her death in 1910, aged 89. Vaughan points out, however, that 'for some years the Church has heavily subsidized the publication of the *Christian Science Monitor*.'

Although, like several other movements, the Church claims to have had no splinter groups, there have been a number, right from the very beginning.

A close associate of Mary Baker Eddy and a former editor of the *Journal of Christian Science*, Emma Curtis Hopkins, split away in 1885 to found the Emma Hopkins College of Metaphysical Science. Hopkins, through a number of her students, was instrumental in the creation of the influential New Thought movement which combined the ideas of Phineas Quimby and Mrs Eddy. Not a religious organization itself, New Thought is the basis of a wide range of other religions, of which probably the two most significant are the Unity School of Christianity, founded in 1903 by Charles and Myrtle Fillmore, and the Church of Religious Science, founded in 1948 by Ernest Holmes and based on his 1926 book *Science of Mind*. Both have themselves produced a number of offshoots.

Mrs Eddy set up a Board of Directors to run Christian Science after her death, though according to several documentary sources she expected a successor to appear within 50 years, 'the man that God has equipped to lift aloft His standard of Christian Science'.[58] However, she later modified this:

I did say that a man would be my future successor... By this I did not mean [any man] on earth today... What remains to lead on the centuries and reveal my successor, is man in the full image and likeness of the Father-Mother God, man the generic term for mankind.[59]

There was a bitter battle of succession in the years after her death. When the Board of Directors gained legal authority from the Massachusetts Supreme Court for their directorship to be self-perpetuating, a splinter group broke away from the Church. One of the directors, John V. Dittemore, left the Board and joined forces with Annie C. Bill, an English Christian Scientist, to proclaim her the successor and to set up the Christian Science Parent Church, which published *The Christian Science Watchman*.

There have also been more recent splinter groups. The Christian Science Parent Church may long have faded away, but the Board of Directors, which still runs the Church in the absence of an accepted successor to Mrs Eddy, is still accused of being too authoritarian. The International Metaphysical Association promotes Mrs Eddy's teachings for 'independent' Christian Scientists who have broken away from the main Church. Another group, the United Christian Scientists, broke away in 1975 in protest against the strict rule of the Church leaders.

Part of the problem appears to be the *Church Manual*, in which Mrs Eddy laid down in immense detail, back in 1895, exactly how the Church should be administered, including the order of service which is still followed to the letter today. Many of the by-laws mention Mrs Eddy by name. For example:

Unless Mrs Eddy requests otherwise, the First Reader of the Mother Church shall occupy, during his term of Readership, the house of the Pastor Emeritus, No 385 Commonwealth Avenue, Boston. (Article II)

There shall be a Board of Education, under the auspices of Mary Baker Eddy, President of the Massachusetts Metaphysical College... (Article XXVIII)

Loyal students who have been taught in a Primary class by Mrs Eddy... are eligible to receive the degree of CSD. (Article XXIX)

Mrs Eddy faced a lot of opposition, not all of it from people outside her Church, and the *Church Manual* includes procedures for dealing with this. The section on Discipline, Article XI, Complaints, contains Section 8, 'No Unchristian Conduct':

If a member of this Church were to treat the author of our textbook disrespectfully and cruelly, upon her complaint that member should be excommunicated. If a member, without her having requested the information, shall trouble her on subjects unnecessarily and without her consent, it shall be considered an offence.

In the same section, Article VIII, 'Guidance of Members', contains Section 27, 'The Golden Rule':

A member of The Mother Church shall not haunt Mrs Eddy's drive when she goes out, continually stroll by her house, or make a summer resort near her for such a purpose.

This rule book is still in use, unaltered in a single word, nearly a century after Mrs Eddy's death, and it seems that she intended this. In a letter to the Board of Directors on 27 February 1903 she wrote:

Never abandon the By-laws nor the denominational government of the Mother Church. If I am not personally with you, the Word of God, and my instructions in the By-laws have led you hitherto and will remain to guide you safely on.[60]

BELIEFS AND PRACTICES

The Tenets of Christian Science are:

1 As adherents of Truth, we take the inspired word of the Bible as our sufficient guide to eternal Life.

2 We acknowledge and adore one supreme and infinite God. We acknowledge His Son, one Christ; the Holy Ghost or divine Comforter; and man in God's image and likeness.

3 We acknowledge God's forgiveness of sin in the destruction of sin and the spiritual understanding that casts out evil as unreal. But the belief in sin is punished so long as the belief lasts.

4 We acknowledge Jesus' atonement as the evidence of divine, efficacious Love, unfolding man's unity with God through Christ Jesus the Way-shower; and we acknowledge that man is saved through Christ, through Truth, Life and Love as demonstrated through the Galilean Prophet in healing the sick and overcoming sin and death.

5 We acknowledge that the crucifixion of Jesus and his resurrection served to uplift faith to understand eternal Life, even the allness of Soul, Spirit, and the nothingness of matter.

6 And we solemnly promise to watch, and pray for that Mind to be in us which was also in Christ Jesus; to do unto others as we would have them do unto us; and to be merciful, just, and pure.[61]

Like many new variants on Christianity, Christian Science claims to have returned to what Christianity was originally all about: it is 'a church designed to commemorate the word and works of our Master, which should reinstate primitive Christianity and its lost element of healing.'[62] The Church reckons, however, that even the apostles misunderstood the message:

> Jesus' students, not sufficiently advanced fully to understand their Master's triumph, did not perform many wonderful works until they saw Him after His crucifixion, and learned that he had not died.[63]

Unlike some other new religions, Christian Science doesn't claim that it alone has the truth. Grayson says:

> Although we feel we have the clearest possible idea of this infinite spiritual truth in divine Science, we don't feel we have a monopoly on inspired insights into God's nature, His love, and spiritual reality. Clearly then we accept – and expect! – to find holy people in many ways of life. We sincerely see the ultimate fate of members and non-members alike to be their complete salvation as a result of their realization of God's healing and redeeming love. This comes not through affiliation with our, or any, organization. It comes through the relinquishment of all within oneself which is ungodlike.

At the heart of Christian Science is its emphasis on spiritual healing. Grayson explains:

> The real history of our movement is the recent restoration and continuation of the Christian record of healing and reformation inaugurated by Christ Jesus and demonstrated by his immediate followers, as recorded with great gusto in the Bible's book of Acts. This healing element of Christianity – lost sight of in the early centuries after the crucifixion of Jesus – was rediscovered by Mary Baker Eddy towards the end of the last century, and has been responsible for countless physical and moral healings since then.

What distinguishes the Church from others, says Grayson, is:

> the commitment to Christian healing and to the direct communion of individual members with God through their own prayers and spiritual understanding. We don't, however, consider we have a monopoly on either of these things, just that the current devotion of Christian Science to both these points is at present unique.

There is no doubt that Christian Science has over the last century brought a strong new emphasis on spiritual healing, or that through it many thousands of people believe they have been healed, but day-to-day spiritual healing within a Church is by no means as unique to Christian Science as the Church claims. Healings have taken place through the work of evangelists such as John Wesley in past centuries, and it only takes a glance at American TV to show that many present-day evangelists also have a healing ministry. Particularly in the last few decades, with the growth of the Charismatic movement within the established Christian Churches, it has become commonplace for an individual, or a small group of Evangelical Christians, or a church leader during a service, to pray for the healing of someone, and often with apparent success. Over the same period, the Neo-Pagan movement has also laid great emphasis on healing, with equal apparent success.

The difference with Christian Science is that healing is accomplished not by asking God to heal someone of an illness, but by believing that the illness does not exist. We only *think* that we have toothache or flu or cancer. It is an error, a lie, an illusion. Once we accept that it is an illusion, we will be healed.

The basis of the teachings of the Church is simply: God is Spirit and Truth and Love; anything which is not of spirit and truth and love is therefore not of God, and so is not real.

> If God, or good, is real, then evil, the unlikeness of God, is unreal. And evil can only seem to be real by giving reality to the unreal...
> The only reality of sin, sickness, or death is the awful fact that unrealities seem real to human, erring belief, until God strips off their disguise. They are not true, because they are not of God.[64]

To counter the obvious objection that the material world, rocks, trees, tables and chairs and our own physical human bodies are demonstrably real, Christian Scientists say that:

> matter is a limited, temporal, and incorrect view of present reality, as the apostle Paul described when he wrote, 'For now we see through a glass, darkly' (I Corinthians 13:12)[65]

– a belief which is closer to Buddhism than to Christianity. Illness is clearly not of God; by ceasing to hold our erroneous belief in it, we can accept its unreality, and realize that it isn't actually there.

But Christian Science doesn't 'blithely dismiss the evils that afflict humanity,' says Vaughan:

> Far from ignoring evil, Christian Scientists endeavour to challenge both sin and suffering through prayer based on an understanding of God.
> Eddy opens the first chapter of *Science and Health* with a statement which is of fundamental importance in understanding our approach to healing. 'The prayer that reforms the sinner and heals the sick is an absolute faith that all things are possible to God, a spiritual understanding of Him, an unselfed love.'[66]

To the Christian Scientist, healing is a deeply religious, profoundly spiritual experience, in which moral regeneration goes hand in hand with physical restoration. Healing involves much more than an intellectual exercise or mechanical adjustment of thought. It occurs when human thought yields to the awareness of the presence and power of God's infinite love... Every healing, we feel, brings a progressive understanding of the basic unreality of evil and matter – *in the sense that they are neither ordained nor sustained by God.*

The Church doesn't only concentrate on healing physical illnesses. 'Christian Science healing involves more than mending sick bodies. It heals broken hearts and minds as well as broken homes, and is directly applicable to all of society's ills.'[67] Healing has a much wider sense: 'The word 'healing' as used in Christian Science extends to the healing of family and business problems, of social injustices, intellectual limitations, psychological tensions, and moral confusions.'[68] Indeed, according to one book, "Christian Scientists are not primarily concerned with bodily health; in fact they undoubtedly give far less attention to their bodies than do most people.'[69] And Mrs Eddy herself wrote:

Healing physical sickness is the smallest part of Christian Science. It is only the bugle call to thought and action... The emphatic purpose of Christian Science is the healing of sin.[70]

Yet spiritual healing of physical illness is still the distinctive hallmark of Christian Science. Healing is clearly important; and so are general health and morality. 'When members join the Christian Science church,' says Grayson, 'they make a commitment to refrain from smoking, drinking alcohol, taking drugs, and from sexual relationships outside of a legal marriage partnership.' Like Mormons, strict members also refrain from drinking tea and coffee.

Christian Scientists

feel a spiritual fellowship with all who worship a supreme and righteous Deity... Wherever the law of God has been glimpsed and demonstrated in any degree by men of any faith, there is evidence of the essential unity of good. While this is true of non-Christian as well as of Christian religions, it should be noted that Christian Science is rooted wholly in Christianity.[71]

There are, however, some major differences between the theology of mainstream Christianity and that of Christian Science. For example:

Distinguishing between the human Jesus and his eternal, spiritual selfhood as the Christ, or Son of God, they recognize that the Christ has been expressed in varying degree by good men and women throughout the ages and that Christianity has always reflected a generous portion of the Christ-spirit.[72]

Jesus was man; the Christ was God's indwelling of him: 'Jesus is the human man, and Christ is the divine idea; hence the duality of Jesus the Christ'.[73] God is Spirit, so the Holy Spirit is not a distinct personage. The Trinity is therefore not a belief of Christian Science. Man is not a sinner: 'The real man is not a suffering, sinning mortal, incomplete or imperfect.'[74] Sin is not real. Hell, like sin and evil and the Devil, is non-existent.

Some of these beliefs were seen in Chapter 11, on the diversity of early Christian beliefs.

The Christian Science Church does not aggressively recruit new members, in the way that some alternative religions do. It doesn't make it difficult for members to leave, if they wish to. It teaches high moral standards and a very genuine devotion to God, and its healing ministry can only be highly respected.

In common with some of the other religions which began in the nineteenth century, Christian Science has had a declining membership for the last few decades (in the UK it is down to around 10,000). This is probably due in part to the alleged authoritarian nature of its leadership, and in part to its continued use of nineteenth-century rules; but it is probably also because the Church has lost its monopoly on spiritual healing.

JEHOVAH'S WITNESSES

Most people meet Jehovah's Witnesses on their own doorsteps; door-to-door witnessing is an essential part of the religion. Their magazines *Awake!* and *The Watchtower* are also well known, as is some idea of their belief in the saving of the 144,000.

The Jehovah's Witnesses are very open about their beliefs, but until quite recently have been rather less forthcoming about their history. However, in 1993 they published the 750-page book *Jehovah's Witnesses: Proclaimers of God's Kingdom*, which is a detailed account of their religion, covering its origins, history, beliefs, and present scope.

BELIEFS AND PRACTICES

Like many of the new religions which began in the nineteenth century, the Jehovah's Witnesses are a millennialist Church, believing strongly in the literal return of Christ and the setting up of his heavenly kingdom over the Earth. Originally they seemed to believe, with most millennialists, that Christ would come openly, but from early on this became a belief that he would return invisibly; initially they believed this would start happening in 1874, and then in 1914. Now they say that 1914 'marked the end of the Gentile Times and the beginning of the transition period from human rule to the Thousand Year (Millennial) Reign of Christ.'[75]

Other attempts to set dates – specifically 1925 and 1975 – resulted in disappointment and sometimes loss of members on the one hand, and rapid back-peddling of the Church leaders and, it is claimed, subtle altering of Watchtower books on the other.

Much is made of the 'little flock' of 144,000 who will go to heaven and rule with Christ, while the 'great crowd' of 'other sheep' will remain on Earth and be ruled. Critics of the religion have suggested that this careful distinction between two groups of believers (all of them Jehovah's Witnesses) only came about when the total number of Jehovah's Witnesses began to reach 144,000; all the places in heaven would now be filled – depending on the source, by 1931 or 1935. This, it is said, caused some dissension in the Church when members from the 1930s onwards realized that they stood no chance of becoming one of the chosen few. However, the Church points out that in 1935 they only had 56,153 members.

On the doorstep, Jehovah's Witnesses often give the impression that they are the only variety of Christianity to emphasize the End Times and Christ's Return; in fact, the broad picture of what they (and most other millennialist Churches) believe is not too dissimilar to what most Evangelical Christians believe about the Second Coming. Some of the details and the exact order of events may be a little different, but not much more so than between any two groups of Evangelicals. It is their unwavering emphasis on God's coming Kingdom to the apparent exclusion of most other doctrine, and their repeated attempts in the past to set the date, that set them apart from most Christian Churches on this subject.

But it is actually on other major points of doctrine that they are at odds with traditional Christian beliefs.

Jehovah's Witnesses, like most other Christian offshoots, turn to the Bible to support their beliefs. 'It is of vital importance to them that their beliefs be based on the Bible and not on mere human speculations or religious creeds,' they say.[76] As often happens, their interpretation of the Bible is quite different from traditional Christian teaching. Unlike most other Christian offshoots, the Jehovah's Witnesses have produced their own translation of the Bible, the *New World Translation*, which tends to support them in their doctrinal differences.

> One of the outstanding features of this translation is its restoration of the divine name, the personal name of God, Jehovah, 237 times in the Christian Greek Scriptures. This was not the first translation to restore the name. But it may

have been the first to do it consistently in the main text from Matthew through Revelation.[77]

Jehovah's Witnesses take their name from Isaiah 43:10–12, which twice says 'Ye are my witnesses, saith the LORD,' or 'Ye are my witnesses, saith Jehovah', in the *American Standard Version*. The word translated as 'Lord', usually shown as 'LORD' in the King James version, is actually the main Jewish name for God, YHWH (written Hebrew did not use vowels), which is usually expanded as 'Yahweh' and in some translations appears as 'Jehovah'. The Jews, both in the centuries immediately before Christ and at the time of Christ, were unwilling to pronounce the sacred name of God, and substituted the phrase 'the Lord' instead. When the tetragrammaton YHWH appeared in the Scriptures, a Jew would have read out 'Adonai', meaning 'my Lord'. (Even today, following the same sort of idea, many Jews print the word 'God' as 'G-d.')

Jehovah's Witnesses claim that Jesus, showing his new relationship with God, named him aloud as 'Jehovah'; most Biblical scholars dispute this. In any case, the rendering of the name as Jehovah is 'a medieval coinage';[78] it was unknown before the fourteenth century CE, according to some authorities, while others (including the *Jewish Encyclopedia*) say it was not formulated until c. 1520 CE. The pronunciation Jehovah comes from imposing the vowels of Adonai on the consonants YHWH, with Y shifting to J, W shifting to V, and the initial (unvoiced) A of Adonai becoming an E.[79]

Jehovah is the true name of God the Father, Jehovah's Witnesses believe, but Jesus Christ isn't God the Son; he is the first of God's creations, and he is God's son, but he is inferior to God. This is similar to the fourth-century Arian heresy; Jehovah's Witnesses reject the carefully formulated Trinitarian Nicene and Athanasian creeds as false, man-made doctrine not supported by the Bible. Similarly, the Holy Spirit is not a person of the godhead, but simply a term for God-in-action.

Until the 1930s, Jehovah's Witnesses taught that Jesus died on a cross. In 1936 they rejected this, and insisted he had died on a stake. The Greek word *stauros* does have the main meaning of 'stake', but it has subsidiary meanings including 'cross'; the Latin word *crux*, meaning 'cross', can also be translated as 'stake', depending on the context. Since taking up this issue Jehovah's Witnesses have always said that archaeology will eventually back them up; in fact, recent archaeological findings tend to support the usual concept of a cross for executions at the time of Jesus.

As well as their millennialist doctrine and their doorstepping evangelism, Jehovah's Witnesses are known for one other aspect of their beliefs: their refusal to accept blood transfusions. This is on the basis that Jewish law in the Old Testament forbids the eating of blood from living creatures, and on James' words in Acts 15:20, 28–29, 'That ye abstain from meats offered to idols, and from blood, and from things strangled, and from fornication.' Jehovah's Witnesses believe that they should uphold this law. (On the other hand, 'Sabbath observance was given only to the Jews and ended with Mosaic Law.'[80]) The Church's view on vaccinations and organ transplants has changed several times over the last few decades, but seems to have stabilized – officially – at being a matter for a member's individual conscience. In March 2000 a British man received a kidney transplanted from his wife; both were Jehovah's Witnesses, and the operations were performed successfully without any blood transfusions.

Less well known is their refusal to fight in war, apparently on the grounds of not taking up arms for an earthly government, rather than on the moral ground that killing people is wrong. Whatever one's own stance on this subject, their steadfastness of belief in the face of legal persecution has to be admired. But again, their literature implies that they are the only ones to be prosecuted and imprisoned for their beliefs:

> Persecution for preaching has never equalled that visited upon Jehovah's Witnesses. Many hundreds of them were executed in Hitler's concentration camps. To this day Jehovah's Witnesses are under ban in many countries, and in others they are arrested, imprisoned, tortured, and killed. This is all part of the sign Jesus gave.[81]

One might think that this 'sign' must apply equally to everyone else who has ever been persecuted for their religious beliefs – and that includes members of many other religions over the centuries – but this is not the case. To Jehovah's Witnesses, all traditional Christian Churches, of whatever denomination, are wrong. The Church's second President, 'Judge' Rutherford, followed founder Charles Taze Russell in regarding anyone who is not a loyal Jehovah's Witness as an 'evil slave':

> The ecclesiastical systems, Catholic and Protestant, are under supervision and control of the Devil, and form a part of his visible organization, and therefore constitute the anti-Christ.[82]

HISTORY

Charles Taze Russell (1852–1916) was brought up in a Congregationalist household in Pittsburgh, Pennsylvania. Like many another Christian teenager, he found difficulty with the idea of a God of love condemning countless millions to an everlasting hell of punishment and torment. Studying his Bible, he came to the conclusion that when it speaks of eternal death, that is exactly what it means: Gehenna, Hades and Sheol are simply words for the grave. After death there is nothing – until, for believers, the Second Coming.

Much of the teaching of Jehovah's Witnesses can be found in other movements. Millenarianism was rife in the USA in the second half of the nineteenth century, and Russell was strongly influenced in his beliefs on the Last Things by Jonas Wendell, among others.

Wendell dated the return of Christ at 1874. When nothing much happened in that year, Russell said that God's *presence* had returned to Earth; his *physical* return would be in 1914. (This is similar to the line taken by Ellen G. White, founder of the Seventh-day Adventists, when William Miller's dates of 1843 and 1844 passed uneventfully: the date was right, but it referred to the 'cleansing of the divine sanctuary' rather than to the physical return of Christ, which would be a little later.)

Russell's theory on the invisible return of Christ, a booklet entitled *The Object and Manner of the Lord's Return*, was first published in 1877, though later editions 'backdate' it to 1873 so that Russell could be seen to have avoided Wendell's error in advance. In 1877 he co-wrote a booklet saying that living believers would be 'caught away bodily' in 1878, in what is usually called the Rapture. When that didn't happen either, it was changed to refer to believers who died after 1878 going straight to God, rather than lingering in the grave, as they would have previously.

In 1879 the first issue of *Zion's Watch Tower and Herald of Christ's Presence* was published, and in 1881 the Watch Tower Bible and Tract Society was formed; this is still the official name of the huge publishing operation at the heart of the Jehovah's Witnesses organization.

Over the next 30 years Russell wrote six volumes of *Studies in the Scriptures*, which underlie the theology of the Jehovah's Witnesses. Christian critics of the religion make much of Russell's claim that true understanding of the Bible can only come through these volumes, and not through unassisted study of the Bible itself.

> ...people cannot see the divine plan by studying the Bible by itself... if anyone lays the *Scripture Studies* aside... and goes to the Bible alone, though he has understood his Bible for ten years, our experience shows that within two years he goes into darkness. On the other hand, if he had merely read the *Scripture Studies* with their references, and had not read a page of the Bible, as such, he would be in the light at the end of two years, because he would have the light of the Scriptures.[83]

Although they still insist on 'directed' Bible study rather than individual reading, Jehovah's Witnesses today tend to play down such claims of Russell. They have also had to answer attacks on his personal conduct by critics; as with the Mormons' Joseph Smith, criticisms of the founder, whether justified or not, are a common weapon against religious movements.

There is also some embarrassment over failed prophecies. 1874 was forgotten before too long, to be replaced by 1914, when, initially, Christ was supposed to return.

For the origins of prophecy, Russell looked not just to the Bible but also to the measurements of the Great Pyramid at Giza, though these were altered in different editions of *Studies in the Scriptures* to reflect the change in emphasis from 1874 to 1914.

In the 1901 edition of volume 3, the length of the entrance passage is given as 3,416 inches, 'symbolizing 3,416 years from the above date, BC 1542. This calculation shows 1874 as marking the beginning of the period of trouble.' In the 1923 edition of the same volume the length of the passage is given as 3,457 inches, and 1874 is changed to 1915.[84]

The problem with setting dates, as millennialist Churches have frequently discovered to their cost, is that eventually the year arrives, and the event doesn't. Now Jehovah's Witnesses admit, 'Not all that was expected to happen in 1914 did happen, but it did mark the end of the Gentile Times and was a year of special significance.'[85] In a carefully worded admission that they made mistakes, they say:

> Jehovah's Witnesses, in their eagerness for Jesus' second coming, have suggested dates that turned out to be incorrect. Because of this, some have called them false prophets. Never in these instances, however, did they presume to originate predictions 'in the name of Jehovah'.[86]

Russell died in 1916, and was succeeded in 1917 by Joseph Franklin 'Judge' Rutherford (1869–1942). His election as President and some of his behaviour soon afterwards caused a very bitter fight within the movement. Part of the reason for the dissension was the posthumous publication of *The Finished Mystery*, the seventh volume of Russell's *Studies in the Scriptures*, which overturned some of the previous prophecies. It also contained such harsh language about the clergy of Christendom that it was banned in Canada. Around 4,000 members left the religion because of Rutherford, going off to become the Pastoral Bible Institute and the Laymen's Home Missionary Movement, and maintaining Russell's teachings; this left the remaining Church for many years almost denying any connection at all with Russell.

Rutherford added greatly to the doctrinal writings of the Church. He also coined the famous saying, 'Millions now living will never die', still used today by Jehovah's Witnesses. This is a highly effective advertising slogan, until one realizes that it was first used in 1920; although millions of people alive then *are* still alive today, the years, as always, are moving steadily on.

The return of Christ was strongly expected in 1925. In 1920 Rutherford wrote that Abraham, Isaac and Jacob would return physically to Earth in 1925. A luxurious house was prepared for them, 'Beth-Sarim' in San Diego; in the meantime, Rutherford lived there. The name 'Jehovah's Witnesses' was adopted in 1931.

Rutherford was succeeded in 1942 by Nathan Homer Knorr (1905–1977), the former manager of the printing works. Although, unlike his predecessors, Knorr was not a charismatic preacher, he was a tremendous administrator, and was responsible for the more systematic door-to-door evangelism which has resulted in the growth of the religion over the last few decades. He set up a training school for Jehovah's Witness missionaries, and was also responsible for initiating the movement's own *New*

World Translation of the Bible. One of the team of translators is thought to have been Frederick Franz (1893–1992), who became president at the age of 83 after Knorr's death.

The *New World Translation* (the whole Bible was published in English in 1961) is often worded in such a way as to give Scriptural support to Jehovah's Witness doctrines; for example, John 1:1, '...and the Word was God' (AV) reads '... and the Word was a god' (NWT). Despite Jehovah's Witness claims that it is 'not only readable but scrupulously accurate', few respected Bible scholars have given it their support, and it is rarely seen outside the movement itself.

By the time of Knorr's death, the organization's Governing Body had become much more powerful, taking power away from the President. Franz was succeeded in 1992 by Milton G. Henschel.

After the world didn't come to an end in 1975, a large number of members, including some senior leaders, left the Church. Former members who have since written books about the Church describe it as authoritarian, and often uncaring; a recurrent theme is the lack of compassion and support shown to any Witnesses with problems, whether spiritual, emotional or financial. The movement finds this an unfair criticism, and teaches that elders should be careful and gentle with members:

Elders know it would be wrong to denounce a fellow believer in a haughty, holier-than-thou manner!...

As a mild-tempered undershepherd, an elder will be encouraging and upbuilding in speech, not intimidating...

Instead of magnifying matters, then, elders should deal with contrite fellow believers in a mild manner, like our compassionate and merciful God, Jehovah.[87]

On the Second Coming, the official position of the Church now is to quote Jesus' warning that no one knows when he will return. A 1995 issue of *Awake!* says, 'When someone goes beyond what Jesus said... there will be false, or inaccurate, predictions...'[88] They now admit that they made a mistake in setting the date for 1914, 1925 or 1975. 'The wrong conclusions were due, not to malice or to unfaithfulness to Christ, but to a fervent desire to realize the fulfilment of God's promises in their own time.'[89] This does not, however, mean any change of emphasis for Jehovah's Witnesses. The next few pages of the same magazine list the usual Signs of the Times: great wars, food shortages, great earthquakes, disease and crime.

There can be no question about it. All the things that the Bible foretold would happen during 'the final age', or 'the conclusion of the system of things', are occurring right now. We are seeing true prophecy in the course of fulfilment, and it is vital that we give heed to it... There are many who belittle the evidence that Bible prophecies are in the course of fulfilment... But today's ridiculors are mistaken. The fact is, *things have changed*. Bible prophecies *are* being fulfilled. The evidence that the end is near is overwhelming.[90]

Jehovah's Witnesses are enthusiastic and sincere missionaries for their faith. All their work is voluntary, and even elders of the Church and members of the Governing Body are unpaid. The loss of members after 1975 was soon countered; there are now around 6 million Jehovah's Witnesses in 234 countries around the world, including 126,000 'active publishers' (members who do door-to-door witnessing) and a further 215,000 interested but more occasional members in the UK, and 980,000 active and over 2 million occasional members in the USA.

LIBERAL CATHOLIC CHURCH AND WANDERING BISHOPS

The Liberal Catholic Church is usually thought of as a mystical-Christian spin-off from the Theosophical Society, but its roots go back much further than that. Founded in 1917, it can be seen as an offshoot of an offshoot of the Roman Catholic Church.

Today's Catholics see Vatican II, Pope John XXIII's great liberalizing conference in 1962, as a watershed in the history of the Church; a fresh breeze was being allowed to blow away some of the dust of centuries. However, the sweeping changes to the Church in the 1960s brought a reaction from traditionalists who believed they weakened the Church's authority.

Vatican I, held in 1869–70, also had those who were opposed to its innovations, but for the opposite reason. This was when Pope Pius IX announced the doctrine of papal infallibility; this was not actually something completely new, but more of a clarification of existing teaching that the Church is 'the Infallible Guardian of Christ's Revelation.'[91] The pope, as 'Supreme Pastor over the whole Flock', could now claim infallibility under certain circumstances.

According to one traditionalist Catholic source:

> This decision while it was received with joy by the vast majority of the Faithful was extremely unwelcome to a group of Liberal or minimizing Catholics, among whom certain German theologians were particularly prominent. About fourteen thousand met in Germany in the September following the definition and repudiated it... [I]n the following year all the malcontents gathered together to form what is known as the Old Catholic Church, which gained episcopal orders from a Dutch Jansenist bishop.[92]

The Jansenists had split away from Rome in the mid-seventeenth century, over Pope Innocent X's insistence that they condemn a treatise on St Augustine written by Cornelius Jansen, Bishop of Ypres, and published in 1640. The Jansenists were holding to older, and from the Roman point of view, less well-developed interpretations of the faith, and were in bitter conflict with the Jesuits, who loyally upheld the right of the pope and the Church to develop and adapt doctrine over the years. There were many Jansenists in France, but they were strongest in the Netherlands, a largely Protestant country; in effect, practically the entire Dutch Catholic Church became separated from Rome.

Whatever the doctrinal points at issue, the two important facts for future centuries were first, that the Jansenists believed they were maintaining a purer version of Catholicism (which the Catholic Church, of course, would dispute); and second, very importantly, that because they had consecrated bishops among their number, they could legitimately pass on the apostolic succession when consecrating new bishops and ordaining priests (see page 127). The Old Catholics who seceded in 1870 did not have any bishops; however, the Jansenists in the Netherlands did have, and

> were thus able to transmit the Apostolic Succession to the Old Catholic Churches of Germany and Switzerland when these became separate from the Roman Church... Thus, although the various Old Catholic Churches were excommunicated by the popes of the day, the validity of their sacred orders has never been seriously contested by theologians.[93]

In some ways the Old Catholics were very similar to Roman Catholicism, including in their ritual; in other ways, including priestly celibacy, or the use of Latin or the vernacular, they differed. The most important difference was their rejection of the ultimate authority of the pope.

Old Catholicism was brought to Britain in 1908 by Bishop Arnold Harris Mathew, under the misapprehension that there were a significant number of Roman Catholic clergy in Britain who would be willing to turn against papal authority. Mathew managed to antagonize almost everyone, including the Roman Catholic Church of which he had formerly been a priest, the Anglican Church (he wrote to the Archbishop of Canterbury offering to 'regularize' their holy orders), the Old Catholic Church in Utrecht which had made him a bishop, and his own auxiliary bishop and other leading members of his clergy in England.

Mathew found that he was out of sympathy with the Church he was running, many of whose clergy and members were, unlike him, interested in Theosophy (see page 344). He decided he wanted to return to the fold of Rome, and in 1914 consecrated Fredrick Samuel Willoughby (founder of what became St Chad's College, Durham University) to be his successor as bishop. The two men immediately fell out. Willoughby, despite his Theosophical leanings, also considered 'making his submission' to Rome, but feeling 'that he was morally obliged not to leave his friends in the Old Catholic Movement without the Apostolic Succession,'[94] in 1915 and 1916 consecrated three new bishops, including James Ingall Wedgwood, who was also a Theosophist, and who became the Presiding Bishop.

At a meeting in 1917 it was felt that because the London Church had moved some distance away from its parent Church in Utrecht, it would be fairer to take a new name, the Liberal Christian Church; this was changed to the Liberal Catholic Church the following year.

Wedgwood, who had been doing missionary work in India as a priest just before his consecration, now went out to Australia as Presiding Bishop of a new Church. There he met up with a leading Theosophist, Charles Webster Leadbeater, who had formerly been an Anglican priest. He ordained him as priest in the Liberal Catholic Church, and then consecrated him as bishop. Together they set about revising the mass and compiling the liturgy of the new Church. In 1922 Wedgwood resigned and Leadbeater succeeded him as Presiding Bishop of the Church. In 1926 the Church consecrated its cathedral in Caledonian Road, London. By this time it was beginning to spread around the world.

The Liberal Catholic Church currently has around 40 bishops, and several thousand members worldwide. It still sees itself as being part of the historical Catholic tradition, while also stressing its liberal nature:

> It aims at combining Catholic forms of worship, stately ritual, deep mysticism and witness to the reality of sacramental grace with the widest measure of intellectual liberty and respect for the individual conscience.[95]

It is entirely open about its Theosophical beliefs:

> Theosophy (Greek for 'divine wisdom') differs from theology in emphasizing the importance of each individual's quest for spiritual understanding based upon personal experience (*gnosis* or *sophia*) as opposed to dogmatic imposition of particular interpretations of scripture which may be limited by man's knowledge of the world at any one historical period...
>
> Christ surely intended his religion to be one of love and freedom, which should help people at their many different stages along the path of spiritual growth; he did not intend it to dictate in God's name formulas the acceptance of which is a condition of salvation.

The Church does not see the Bible as 'verbally or uniformly inspired, but only in a general sense.' It does not aim to proselytize members of other Christian Churches, and seeks friendly relations with them. Its priests are unpaid, usually with secular jobs; they are allowed to marry. It believes in reincarnation, and in mystical illumination; it welcomes study into such areas as extra-sensory perception and psychical research. An indication of the esoteric nature of its beliefs is that the founder of the esoteric school Servants of the Light (see page 367), W.E. Butler (1898–1978), was a priest in the Church.

The remaining Old Catholic Church in Britain came into communion with the Anglican Church in 1932. However, all was not to be well. In 1997 the *News of the World* revealed that several of its priests were engaged in paedophilia and child pornography; its titular leader, Monsignor Frederick Linale, was already serving a ten-year sentence for child sex offences. The Church had stripped Linale of his office in the 1970s when his offences first came to light, but he 'ignored the injunction and carried on as a bishop with his own group, still using the Old Catholic name.'[96] Other Old Catholic priests severed their formal connection with the Church because of the scandal.

In continental Europe Old Catholic Churches are quite substantial, well-established and respected denominations, which are in communion with the Anglican Church. In Britain and America the situation is different; there are several different strands of independent episcopacy. In most cases these trace their line of Apostolic Succession (see page 127) back to a legally consecrated bishop who rebelled against the Church hierarchy, sometimes as far back as Vatican I in 1870. In America there are as many as 17 different Old Catholic Churches, most with only a few hundred members, some with a thousand or more; some, though not all, can be traced back to the Dutch Church. Generally, they still seem to share most Roman Catholic doctrine, but differ on the authority of the pope, and on issues such as clerical marriage, accepting divorced members, and contraception.

Some of the independent bishops have established small denominations, consecrating further bishops and ordaining priests; others have merged with branches of the Orthodox Church; others are basically one-man bands, sometimes known as 'Wandering Bishops' – or more technically, *episcopi vagantes* or Bishops Irregular. Some of these head Churches, with priests, church buildings (or borrowed church buildings) and congregations whom they serve in much the same way (albeit on a smaller scale) as any other clergy. Others, however, just seem to enjoy collecting titles. Perhaps the most famous of these was Hugh George de Willmott Newman, who became interested in the Old Catholic movement in the 1920s.

From his first extremely questionable consecration as a bishop in 1944 he sought to unify in his own person as many lines of succession as he could. He gained consecration after consecration from all manner of alleged bishops, and consecrated them in turn into his own Church, the Catholicate of the West. There are numerous photographs of Mar Georgius, his principle but by no means only title (others include Patriarch of Glastonbury, Apostolic Pontiff of Celtica, Prince-Catholicos of the West, Exarch of the Order of Antioch for Britain, Ruling Prelate of the Order of Reunion, etc., etc., *ad nauseam*) in full regalia, but despite a few faithful followers, his umpteen bishoprics and dominions seemed to exist only on paper.[97]

The Catholicate of the West eventually became the Orthodox Church of the British Isles. Under the leadership of Newman's nephew, William Newman Norton, or Abba Seraphim, this Church finally achieved the legitimacy that Newman craved when in 1994 it was accepted into the Coptic Orthodox Church of Cairo, one of the genuinely ancient Patriarchates, Norton being made a Metropolitan of that Church. The British Church now has one bishop, seven priests, two deacons, and around 250 members. With the confused and chequered history of such small organizations, it might be wise not to attempt to see too far ahead into its future.

THE CHRISTIAN COMMUNITY AND ANTHROPOSOPHY

HISTORY

Rudolf Steiner (1861–1925) had an interest in both esoteric wisdom and social reform for some years before he joined the Theosophical Society (see page 344). His unusual intelligence was recognized quite early; he was only 22 when he was invited to edit the scientific works of Goethe for a standard edition. He joined the Theosophical Society around 1900, and became leader of the German organization in 1902.

His leaving stemmed from two causes. In 1912 he expelled a particularly troublesome member, only to have his decision overridden by the leader, Annie Besant. But he had been moving in his own direction away from the Society's particular combination of beliefs and practices for some time; Besant's championing of the coming World Teacher in Krishnamurti was the last straw, and in 1913 he broke away, setting up his own Anthroposophical Society, and taking many of the German Theosophists with him.

Steiner also belonged for a while to the Rite of Memphis and Misraim, a quasi-Masonic occult order, and probably also to the Ordo Templi Orientis (O∴T∴O), a quasi-Rosicrucian German occult society founded in 1906, which studied and perhaps practised sex-magic. It is probable that Steiner didn't join these so much to gain secret knowledge, as to find others who shared his own ideas. Indeed, on sex-magic, N.C.

Thomas, General Secretary of the Anthroposophical Society in Great Britain, says:

> A careful study of his work shows he would have had nothing to do with that, and indeed he warns us of the dangers of such developments for humankind and for esoteric students. His early association with the OTO and Masonic Orders had to do with the necessity for an esoteric researcher to know of the work of other such researchers in order to be free to conduct his own researches.[98]

In 1906 Steiner started giving a series of lectures in Paris, which drew many people interested in his teachings on clairvoyance. He delivered over 6,000 lectures in 25 years; most of his many books are effectively barely edited lecture notes, rather than cogently argued texts, which tends to make them rather difficult to understand. In the next few years he influenced education, agriculture, architecture, the arts and politics, among other areas of life.

BELIEFS AND PRACTICES

The Christian Community is a Church founded in Germany in 1922, with Steiner's help. As a movement it is quite separate from Anthroposophy, which is 'concerned with a development of spiritual research and understanding that is scientific as opposed to religious.'[99] Nevertheless, the Christian Community stems from Anthroposophical ideas.

Theosophy is God-wisdom; Anthroposophy is Man-wisdom. Rather than evolving forwards to become God-like Masters, as in Theosophy, Steiner taught that man used to have these powers but has lost them, and must strive to regain them. Buried deep within us are these lost secrets; through meditation and study we can find our lost nature and achieve spiritual growth on four levels: the senses, imagination, inspiration and intuition.

It should be noted that Steiner continued to use the word Theosophy, but his use of it is quite different from that of the Theosophical Society.

> Rudolf Steiner, however, uses the term independently and with different and much wider connotation... Ultimately it leads us back to St Paul who says (I Cor 2:6–7): '...We speak the wisdom of God (Greek *Theosophia*) in a mystery, even the hidden wisdom which God ordained before the world into our glory.'[100]

Anthroposophy is much closer to Christianity than is Theosophy; in itself it could be described as a form of esoteric Christianity. Steiner taught that Christ's life, death and resurrection were supremely important. Christ can help man ascend to the higher spiritual levels he once knew; but Lucifer and Ahriman are two evil powers holding man back, Lucifer through internal pride, and Ahriman through the external material world.

Like Theosophy, Anthroposophy seeks to unite science and religion. As Anthroposophy developed, its teachings spread into various areas of life, including education and agriculture; in the latter case, Steiner introduced a spiritual and scientific basis to what would now be called organic farming, with 'natural' times for sowing and harvesting, and with no chemical fertilizers. In the case of education, he was in the forefront of 'child-centred' education, Anthroposophical theories concentrating on 'awakening what is in a child' rather than forcing knowledge into a child. Over 500 Waldorf schools now teach according to Steiner's principles, and are very highly regarded. His methods, including the use of guided movement to music, are particularly effective with retarded children. In addition to this social legacy, Anthroposophy has influenced esoteric Christianity.

> [Steiner's] spiritual-scientific methods, unique in that he saw the Incarnation of Christ as the central event in human evolution, served to develop not only a spiritual theology and Christology, but a widened understanding of the Gospel and a basis for a new practice of pastoral care.[101]

The Christian Community does not have any fixed dogma; 'There is a basic freedom of teaching which accords with what is expressed in the sacraments. Would-be members are not asked to accept any official theology or articles of faith.'[102]

The central service of the Church is the Act of the Consecration of Man: the communion service, but with a different significance:

> With his death and resurrection the Last Supper was transformed into the Christian Eucharist...
>
> With Christ's resurrection a new creation began. In the first creation the visible world was brought forth. In this creation what is visible (and temporal) is being changed into what is eternal and invisible. In the Act of Consecration, in which the spirit penetrates the physical world, human beings participate in the working of the divine... Humanity, and in consequence nature, is thus united again with the eternal. This is a deed which enables humanity to develop further and with it the earth, transforming and re-enlivening it.[103]

The traditional sacraments, and their associated symbolism, are deeply important to the Christian Community. As in the Catholic, Orthodox and Anglican Churches, its priests (men and women since the founding of the Church) wear different-coloured vestments for the different festivals and seasons of the Christian year. The priesthood is hierarchically structured into priest, lenker, oberlenker and erzoberlenker; *lenker* meaning 'one who guides, directs, steers, leads.'[104] The lenker is equivalent to a bishop; they do not, however, have Apostolic Succession (see page 127).

The Christian Community began in Germany, Switzerland and Austria, then spread to the Netherlands, Scandinavia and Czechoslovakia. It came to Britain in 1929, but is still quite small; it currently has 18 churches, with some 1,000 members. It has around the same number of members in the USA, where it opened its first centre in 1948; there are also churches in Canada, South Africa, Australia, New Zealand, and South America. There are around 15,000 members worldwide, 10,000 of these in Germany.

OPUS DEI

The Roman Catholic Church is often thought of by non-members as an undivided, traditionalist religion. In fact, it is neither.

Throughout its history the Church has had liberal and traditionalist movements, the latter often formed to counteract the spreading influence of the former. The Society of Jesus (the Jesuits) was founded in 1534 precisely for this reason: to maintain orthodoxy against liberalism, though today it is seen as orthodox but progressive. Several organizations with similar aims have been founded this century.

Dissent is strong within the Roman Catholic Church today. Large numbers of priests and nuns are leaving the Church, while others are staying, to fight from within. Many of these rebels are more liberal than the official Church, but some are more traditional.

On the traditional side, the sweeping changes to the Church instituted by Pope John XXIII and Vatican II brought a reaction; Archbishop Lefevre in France was not the only one to refuse to abandon the Latin Tridentine mass in favour of the Novus Ordo, the new mass.

On the liberal side, many Roman Catholic bishops and priests in South America have embraced 'liberation theology', effectively left-wing, sometimes revolutionary politics. In Britain, as elsewhere, the Charismatic revival, with its emphasis on the individual experience of Spirit-led worship, has swept through the grass-roots level of the Roman Catholic Church almost as much as in any other denomination.

Hundreds of Catholic priests have gone against the pope's ruling and married, and not all of them have given up their calling; there are numerous splinter denominations, especially in the USA, with married priests. Many of these movements also deny the infallibility of the pope.

In both America and Europe there are several different strands of independent episcopacy, with their Apostolic Succession (see page 127) stemming originally from the Roman Catholic Church. In continental Europe Old Catholic Churches are quite substantial denominations, which are in communion with the Anglican Church; these should not be confused with Liberal Catholic Churches, which developed from them but are basically Christian-Theosophical (see page 192).

Within the official Roman Catholic Church several organizations have been formed to maintain the purity of the faith against both internal and external liberal influence. The best known of these, after the Jesuits, is Opus Dei ('The Work of God'), which 'was founded to spread the message that everyone is called to holiness,' says Andrew Soane, Director of its Information Office in the UK.[105] Opus Dei was founded in 1928 by a Spanish priest, Monsignor Josemaría Escrivá de Balaguer y Albas (1902–1975), who took the first step to becoming a saint when he was beatified in 1992.

Over the last 20 years there has been a great deal of controversy over Opus Dei; many articles and at least two books have described it in language typically used by anti-cultists. It is said to be politically right-wing (Escrivá supported Franco during and after the Spanish Civil War), to be authoritarian, and to encourage strict forms of behaviour, strict penances, such as wearing a *cilice* or spiked bracelet on the thigh, and strict mortifications, such as lashing oneself with a cat-o'-nine-tails. (Opus Dei says that such pracices are entirely voluntary, are traditional, and are symbolic of the sufferings of Christ.) It has rules and regulations for its members; it gives 'guidance' on what they may read and what they may do. It has been criticized for separating children from their parents, and men from women. It is dedicated to the holiness of its members, and is condemnatory of anything they do which it decides is wrong. It has been said that, like many other religious movements, it claims to have the only truth; some members have claimed to find it difficult to leave the organization for fear of losing their holiness or even their salvation. If former members had put any money into the organization, they are unable to reclaim any of it. Companies or associations linked with Opus Dei have been criticized for their business dealings and for the wealth of property they have accumulated. Opus Dei has been described by its critics as a secret society, a Church within a Church, with a disproportionate amount of power in the Vatican: it has been called 'the Holy Mafia' and 'Octopus Dei'.

These are the criticisms. The more than 80,000 members of Opus Dei – including three archbishops, at least ten bishops and 1,750 priests (plus a further 2,000 deacons and priests of the closely linked Priestly Society of the Holy Cross) – see it very differently. For them, Opus Dei is an organization which helps them in their daily commitment to Christ within the Roman Catholic Church. They study the Church's doctrines in more depth; they are encouraged to pray; they find ways to live a fully Christian life in their daily working life, rather than the two being kept separate; they do vital social work among the inner-city poor. Far from being any sort of cult, they point out, Opus Dei is fully a part of the Roman Catholic Church, and has the personal blessing of the pope himself.

It is a personal prelature of the Catholic Church which helps ordinary lay people seek holiness in and through their everyday activities and especially through sanctifying their work.

It helps ordinary people live up to their Christian calling in their day-to-day affairs by giving them the spiritual support and formation they need to achieve this. It promotes an awareness of the universal call to holiness – the radical idea that every single person is called by God to be a saint – especially holiness in and through one's ordinary work and daily routine.[106]

Pope John Paul II made Opus Dei the first (and so far only) 'personal prelature' in 1982. This means that it does not have the geographical boundaries of dioceses and parishes, but is defined by the persons within it, who are mainly lay people; it has its own prelate, Bishop Javier Echevarría, who is answerable to the Sacred Congregation of Bishops – in effect, directly to the Vatican, to the pope. One of the criticisms of Opus Dei is that members can become more loyal to the organization, and the hierarchy of it, than they are to the Church's hierarchy. Opus Dei do not accept this:

> The relationship of lay members of Opus Dei with their parish priest, bishop and the Pope is exactly the same as that of other Catholic citizens. Just like other Catholics they are bound by diocesan regulations and follow the teachings and guidelines of the bishop, and participate fully in the life of the parish according to their circumstances. Their commitments to Opus Dei are complementary commitments which begin where the authority of the bishop leaves off and relate to areas (for example, spiritual development and apostolic commitment) in which the faithful are free to follow whatever path to holiness they choose.[107]

About 30 per cent of Opus Dei members are 'numeraries', who live in strictly single-sex residences and take a commitment to celibacy. They tend to be graduates, and to be in professional careers – 'engineers, business people, lawyers, etc.'[108] Their income doesn't actually go to Opus Dei itself, as is often claimed; as Soane explains, after personal upkeep 'the excess goes to support the apostolic works (not the prelature) which are run autonomously by members of Opus Dei.' Around 20 per cent of members are 'associates'; they don't live in residences, but otherwise are much the same as numeraries, including the commitment to celibacy. The remaining half, known as 'supernumeraries', live in the wider community, and may be married with families.

Opus Dei is quite small in Britain, with only around 500 members. There are 1,500 in Africa, 4,500 in Asia and the Pacific, and around 5,000 in the USA, of 28,000 in North and South America. It is on continental Europe where, understandably, the organization is at its strongest, with around 47,000 members. The numbers of men and women members are roughly equal.

Opus Dei runs student hostels and other youth organizations, and has been criticized for high-pressure recruitment of young people, particularly in Catholic secondary schools and universities. The late Archbishop of Westminster, Cardinal Basil Hume, was concerned enough about this that he issued a statement in 1981:

For a considerable time I have studied carefully certain public criticisms made about the activities of Opus Dei in Britain...

...in so far as it is established within the diocese of Westminster, I have a responsibility, as bishop, to ensure the welfare of the whole local Church as well as the best interests of Opus Dei itself...

These recommendations must not be seen as a criticism of the integrity of the members of Opus Dei or of their zeal in promoting their apostolate. I am making them public in order to meet understandable anxieties and to encourage sound pastoral practice within the diocese...

1 No person under 18 years of age should be allowed to take any vow or long-term commitment in association with Opus Dei.

2 It is essential that young people who wish to join Opus Dei should first discuss the matter with their parents or legal guardians...

3 ...care must be taken to respect the freedom of the individual; first, the freedom of the individual to join or to leave the organization without undue pressure being exerted...

4 Initiatives and activities of Opus Dei, within the diocese of Westminster, should carry a clear indication of their sponsorship and management.[109]

While it is clear how careful he is being not to criticize Opus Dei, which has the personal approval of the present pope, the issues which he addresses show his deep concerns.

Opus Dei has also been criticized for the amount of attention paid to its founder, Josemaría Escrivá. It is highly unusual for anyone to be beatified so soon after their death: only 17 years. Opus Dei have poured a vast amount of effort into 'pushing' Escrivá towards sainthood, making sure that he is on the 'fast track'. Many Catholics who are not members find this haste unseemly, when people who are widely recognized as saintly, such as Pope John XXIII, have yet to be canonized. It has been said that the Jesuits (the Society of Jesus) are particularly critical of Opus Dei.

Opus Dei are very sensitive to criticisms that there may be anything at all worrying about them. Soane says that Opus Dei:

was founded to spread a message, and that message is the universal call to holiness. To achieve this requires study and formation, and therefore members of Opus Dei, having a grounding in theology, tend to be straight down the line in matters of doctrine – a further proof (if one is needed) that Opus Dei is not an alternative religion.

Opus Dei is not the only ultra-orthodox movement within Roman Catholicism. Three others which have caused concern in recent years are the Focolare, founded in 1943, Communion and Liberation, founded in 1954, and the Neocatechumenate, founded in 1964.[110] Each, like Opus Dei, is outside the normal diocesan structure of the Catholic Church, and has been criticized for being its own uncontrolled master, and for bringing division within individual congregations, its members sometimes being seen as the spiritual elite, outside the normal pastoral hierarchy of the Church. Each, from its own point of view, is promoting true spirituality, religious orthodoxy, and conservative morality.

THE UNIFICATION CHURCH

The Unification Church is part of a wider organization known officially, since the late 1990s, as the Family Federation for World Peace and Unification; before that it was the Holy Spirit Association for the Unification of World Christianity (HSA-UWC); while unofficially the Church is usually known as the Moonies (after their founder Sun Myung Moon), a term they dislike partly because of the bad 'cult' publicity associated with it in the late 1970s and early 1980s, and partly, no doubt, because it rhymes with 'loonies'. They are very anxious to play down such images, and to present themselves as a spiritually, morally, socially and culturally sound Christian movement.

HISTORY

The Reverend Sun Myung Moon was born as Yong Myung Moon in what is now North Korea in 1920. ('Reverend' is a term of respect for Moon; he has no formal theological training. Within the Church he is usually known as Father, and his wife, Hak Ja Han, as Mother.) When he was 10 or 11 his family converted from their native Confucianism to Presbyterianism. At the age of 16 he had a vision of Jesus Christ, who told him he must further the building of God's kingdom on Earth. He spent the next nine years in prayer and intensive study of the Bible, during which he came to a completely different understanding of Christian theology.

During World War II he studied electrical engineering in Japan. He began preaching in 1945, in South Korea. In 1948 he changed his name to Sun Myung Moon, meaning 'Shining, Bright, Word', and moved back to North Korea, where the communist authorities imprisoned him for two-and-a-half years; this probably cemented his fervent opposition to communism. He was liberated by United Nations troops in 1950, and resumed preaching. Apparently he had no intention of starting up a new Church, but his reinterpretation of Christianity was so radical that the mainstream Churches would not accept his teachings, so in 1954 he founded the HSA-UWC, usually known as the Unification Church.

There is sometimes confusion about how many times Moon has been married: two, three or even four times. According to George Robertson, spokesman for the Unification Church in the UK,[110A] Moon's first marriage ended in divorce, and a later engagement failed to work out; Hak Ja Han, whom he married in 1960, is thus his second wife. They have had 14 children, one of whom died as an infant, one died in a car accident, and one fell from a hotel balcony in October 1999 in an apparent suicide.

In 1966 Moon published the text *Discourse on the Principle*, which was translated into English in 1973 as *Divine Principle*. 'While this text doesn't contain the whole revelation given Reverend Moon, it is regarded as the official teaching of the Unification Church.'[111] It is unclear whether this means that some of the revelation is for the moment being withheld from the world, or whether there are further teachings not yet translated and published. There are 300 volumes of transcripts of Rev. Moon's speeches, which are considered to be an expression of his revelation.

Three missionaries were sent to the USA in 1959, and the first church was established in 1961 in Berkeley, California. The Church, then known as the Unified Family, grew slowly during the 1960s, despite several visits by Moon, and it was not until he moved to New York State in 1972 that it really began to pick up; in the next four years membership grew from a few hundred to around 6,000.

Progress was similarly slow in Britain; the Church was given charitable status in 1968, but it was not until 1978, when Moon sent 800 missionaries to Britain as the One World Crusade, that communities began to be set up all over the country, high streets began to see young flower-sellers in profusion (though flower-selling had been happening since 1973) – and the controversy began.

The Church became the prime focus of attention of anti-cultists, at times even more so than the Children of God, the Hare Krishna movement and the Scientologists; most of the usual charges against 'cults' were levelled against the 'Moonies'. (The powerful 1994 BBC drama series *Signs and Wonders*, in which a young woman is 'rescued against her will' from a cult headed by a Far Eastern 'Father', was very clearly based on this popular perception of the Church; see page 56.)

Young recruits were sent out on the streets selling flowers or candles, partly to bring in money for the Church, partly as a form of disciplinary training, and partly to find new recruits. According to the cult-watchers, it was common for them to spend many hours trying to reach the targets they had been set, then return to their communal homes often very late at night, and work out their accounts before stumbling to bed. In the morning they might rise at 5am to perform some 'condition', a form of penance or self-denial – sometimes praying for others for a set time, sometimes taking cold showers for a week – before going out on the streets again. And however they felt, they had to look happy and enthusiastic.

On the streets they often didn't tell people they were from the Unification Church, saying they were raising money for a charity – which was true, but not the whole truth; what the media labelled 'Heavenly Deception' was permissible in the service of the higher Truth. New recruits brought into a community would be 'love-bombed', hugged, surrounded by care and attention; for people in their late teens and early twenties, with all the usual personal and social problems, this in itself could be both wonderful and utterly disorientating.

For those living in the communities, lectures, study sessions and worship might go on for hours, late into the night and first thing in the morning; meanwhile, said the cult-watchers, their food was often minimal, and low-protein; and discipline was strict, with 'conditions' imposed for any infringements – such as failing to achieve their target, or failing to look happy and enthusiastic. This was the basis of the accusations of sleep deprivation, indoctrination, brainwashing and authoritarianism.

Such was the popular image of the Moonies, regularly bolstered by the media and the anti-cult organisations.

George Robertson accepts that some (though not all) of this went on, but puts it down to the youthful enthusiasm and zeal typical of any new convert, and to some extent to the immaturity of both the organization and the leaders of individual communities. 'We have learned that this is perhaps not the best way to present ourselves to the world. Now we're more careful; we've grown up.' In any case, he says, most members are now married with families and living in their own homes, so as there are very few communities of that sort any more, such criticisms are no longer relevant.

In 1980 the Church sued the *Daily Mail* for libel for describing it in such unfavourable terms. After a long and very expensive court case, the Church lost. Although Robertson can't brush that to one side, he points out that this was the only court case in Britain, and that when the Attorney General spent four years investigating the Church, he eventually concluded in 1988 that it should be allowed to continue as a registered charity. Court cases in the USA, he says, tend to be brought by individuals, usually ex-members, with a personal complaint.

However, not all of them. In 1982, Moon was prosecuted for non-payment of taxes on the interest on his personal bank account; he was fined $25,000, and imprisoned for 13 months. Moon had argued that although the money was in his personal account, it was actually the Church's money, and so tax-exempt. The prosecution was regarded as unfair by many other Christian Churches.

These are not the only charges which opponents have made against the Church. It has several times been criticized for its support of right-wing politicians, including General Garcia Mesa in Bolivia, General Gustavo Alvarez in the Honduras, and Jean-Marie le Pen in France. Robertson says that when the Church realized what such people actually stood for, it withdrew its support. To the outsider it seems that Moon's acknowledged hatred of communism has persistently led the Church, somewhat naïvely, to swing to the opposite extreme.

It has also been criticized for its numerous businesses, presumably on the grounds that God and mammon shouldn't be mixed. The Church owns companies in, among others, pharmaceuticals, ginseng, titanium, manufacturing and military equipment; the last is quite simply because in South Korea, under permanent threat from North Korea, all manufacturing companies must produce some weaponry. It also owns the *Washington Times*, 'a characteristically right-wing paper', according to Robertson; the editor and most of the staff are not Church members, and it has 'complete editorial freedom'. After several years of heavy subsidy it is now standing on its own financial feet. In 1996 the movement bought *Tiempos Del Mundo*, a major pan-Latin American newspaper based in Buenos Aires; it currently owns seven newspapers in all. It is also the majority shareholder in the University of Bridgeport, Connecticut.

The reason for all the business involvement is twofold: first, 'one should seek to bring Christian values into every aspect of life'; and second, it brings in useful money which finances the Church's evangelistic, humanitarian and cultural work.

Another criticism, similar to 'Heavenly Deception', is that the Church (or rather, the Unification Movement, which is wider than the Church) hides behind a large number of 'front' organizations which rarely state their origins openly. These include major international conferences and symposia in science, peace and religion, run by bodies such as the International Conference on the Unity of the Sciences, and the Professors' World Peace Academy ('which discusses strategies to create a harmonious, peaceful world'), both promoted by the Movement's International Cultural Foundation; and the New Ecumenical Research Association and the International Conferences for Clergy, both promoted by the Movement's International Religious Foundation. Robertson argues that all this is more a case of influence than subversion. 'We want to help transform the world,' he says, 'and you can't do that by sitting on your backside.' In any case, he says, most of the people at these conferences do know of the involvement of the Unification Church; there is nothing clandestine about it. 'We have learned that you do that at great cost; it doesn't accomplish anything except make people feel they've been duped, and make them angry.'

In addition to these, which tend to be academic or clergy-orientated, the Unification Movement is involved in cultural promotion. Probably the best-known outlet is the Little Angels of Korea dance troupe of 7- to 15-year-olds, which has performed worldwide, including before Queen Elizabeth II in 1972. The Movement is also responsible for the Universal Ballet Company in Korea and a ballet school in Washington DC; it is financially involved with the Kirov Ballet Company, owns a recording studio in Manhattan and sponsors the New York City Symphony Orchestra.

The Church also operates the International Relief Friendship Foundation, which has provided medical supplies, materials and help in more than 20 countries struck by war, natural disaster or famine, and which sponsors medical missionaries in Kenya and Zaire.

Robertson quotes General Booth, founder of the Salvation Army: 'Soup, Song and Salvation'. The welfare, cultural and academic activities of the Church are all a wider part of spreading the message, without ramming it down people's throats – 'to entertain, to serve, and for PR,' says Robertson; 'there's nothing covert about it.'

The Church runs the Unification Theological Seminary in Barrytown, in upstate New York. In keeping with the original 'unification of world Christianity' idea, both the teaching and the teachers are multi-faith, including a Greek Orthodox theologian and a Jesuit priest; only 20 per cent of the faculty are members of the Unification Church. Although the Church has no ordained priesthood, people who have been to the Seminary may call themselves Reverend if they wish.

The Church claims that, as of February 2000, there are 4.5 million fully committed members of the Church worldwide. The largest national Churches are in Nigeria, the Philippines and Brazil; there are 220,000 full members in South Korea and 50,000 in Japan. Astonishingly, there are only about 500 fully committed members in the UK, plus another 700 more peripherally involved in the Unification Movement. Why so few?

'It's a question we ask ourselves,' says Robertson. Over the years several thousand have been to Church seminars, and many people have joined the Church for a few months or years and then left, as in any Church. 'There's quite a turnover of membership. Living a seriously religious life is quite a difficult thing to do – a challenging lifestyle.' Even so, he seems to think the Church ought to be doing better in the UK. 'There are probably many lessons we have to learn as an organization.'

Sun Myung Moon is still actively involved in the Church he founded, and at 80 is still in good health. (His eightieth birthday celebration on 10 February 2000 included greetings from former British Prime Minister Sir Edward Heath and former US Vice-President Dan Quayle.) In the event of Moon's death it is expected that the leadership will pass to his wife, who is 23 years younger, with the support of the senior members of the Church, who are mostly Korean.

Rev and Mrs. Moon's third son, Hyun Jin Moon, and his wife, Jun Sook Kwak, are being groomed for longer-term leadership. Hyun Jin Moon, a Harvard MBA graduate, was inaugurated as the Vice President of the Family Federation for World Peace and Unification and the President of World CARP, a Unificationist student organization.

BELIEFS AND PRACTICES

Although it has moved a very considerable distance away from mainstream Christian beliefs, the Unification Church still calls itself Christian. 'A Christian is someone who believes in Jesus as the Messiah (Christ anointed), who is one with God, and who makes Jesus the absolute standard for one's own life of faith,' says Robertson. 'Unificationists are Christian and so is Reverend Moon. After all he was commissioned by Jesus Christ and has been striving to realize his will all of his life.'

However, the differences from traditional Christian beliefs are quite major.

The Church believes the Judaeo-Christian Bible to be inspired by God, though it does not regard it as word-for-word infallible; the Bible was written down by fallible men, and copied and edited by fallible men, each with his own motivations. Given equal weight to the Bible as 'a further revelation' is Moon's own book *Divine Principle*.

> Knowing that no one can find the ultimate truth to save mankind without going through the bitterest of trials, he fought alone against myriads of Satanic forces, both in the spiritual and physical worlds, and finally triumphed over them all. In this way, he came in contact with many saints in Paradise and with Jesus, and thus brought into light all the heavenly secrets through his communion with God.
>
> The Divine Principle revealed in this book is only part of the new truth. We have recorded here what Sun Myung Moon's disciples have hitherto heard and witnessed. We believe with happy expectation that, as time goes on, deeper parts of the truth will be continually revealed. It is our earnest prayer that the light of truth will quickly fill the earth.[112]

Divine Principle covers among much else the purpose of creation, the real meaning of the Fall of man, a discussion of the life, work and death of Jesus, a detailed study of the history of religion from the time of Adam and Eve right up to the present day, and an explanation of how, when and where Christ will return: as a physical man, born after World War I, in Korea.

For some years, although his followers believed him to be the Messiah, Moon himself avoided answering the question directly, much as Jesus did ('Whom do men say that I am?' [Mark 8:27]). In 1992, however, he made a formal declaration that he was indeed the Messiah. Moon is not, however, God – and neither was Jesus.

The doctrines of the Church can be summed up under the headings the Principles of Creation, the Fall of Man, and the Principles of Restoration. *Divine Principle* is 536 pages long, but it is possible to summarize its main teachings fairly briefly.

> God's original plan was for men and women to grow to maturity, developing a perfect relationship of love with God. Based on this spiritual maturity, all people would come to love one another as brothers and sisters... God-centred men and women would enter into the most intense give and take of love in the family... Children born to such families would experience the love of God directly from their own parents, and would themselves develop a mature love of God. The love generated in this kind of family would then be multiplied to the society, nation and world.[113]

That was the plan; it didn't happen, because of the Fall of Man.

The story of the Fall is at the centre of the theological differences between Unification belief and mainstream Christianity. The angel Lucifer, placed in the Garden of Eden to serve the first two people, falls in love with Eve; he tempts her, and they have sex together (the 'fruit' is a symbol of sexuality). Eve, repenting her sin, tells Adam what she has done – and then has sex with him to try to put things right when, at that stage in their relationship, they should still be living as brother and sister, not husband and wife. Adam and Eve had misused their love, and became separated from God. 'Due to the Fall, the bond between man and God was broken, resulting in a long history of grief to man and his Creator.'[114]

According to Robertson, the Church accepts the literal existence of the original couple, though whether their names were actually Adam and Eve (Hebrew for man and woman) is doubtful.

God sent prophets to guide his people back to him. The original, ideal trinity is redefined by the Church as God, Man and Woman united in perfect, unsullied love. This was lost because of what happened in the Garden of Eden, so that the fallen trinity is Satan, Man and Woman. Jesus did not come to the Earth to be crucified; he came as the Messiah to recreate the lost ideal. The plan was that he should marry and have children, re-establishing the ideal trinity through his ideal family, for all mankind. Again the plan was thwarted; instead of that happening, he was not recognized as who and what he was, and was crucified. His resurrection brought only partial salvation to mankind.

> After the crucifixion, God gave Jesus the Holy Spirit as a mother spirit, or feminine spirit, to work with the risen Christ in Eve's place. Making restitution for Eve's part in the Fall, the Holy Spirit inspires and comforts the human heart, leading us back to God. Reflecting her feminine essence, the Holy Spirit is traditionally known as the 'Comforter'. As children are born through the love of parents, so through the give and take of love Jesus and the Holy Spirit give spiritual rebirth to all those who follow them.[115]

But to complete the job Jesus was unable to finish, it is necessary for the Messiah to come again. 'The purpose of the Lord of the Second Coming is thus to marry and establish the trinity *both spiritually and physically*.'[116] This is what Sun Myung Moon has accomplished. Through the Messiah's perfect marriage, the fallen nature of mankind can be transformed to the ideal trinity of God, Man and Woman again. Moon is able to pass this on to believers through the well-known mass wedding ceremonies; each couple, blessed by God through Moon, is now in a right relationship with God (if they continue to live in the right way), and their children will be born untainted by the sin of Adam and Eve. The whole of mankind can be transformed in this way, and God's original plan can come to pass. This is the aim and the sacred duty of the Unification Church.

Moon's own "True Family" has had its problems. Several of his children have had marital problems, and one son had heroin and cocaine addiction, and was accused of physically abusing his wife. According to Robin Marsh, Public Affairs Director of the Unification Movement in the UK, he has now been reblessed and is trying to make a new start.

The mass weddings have come in for a lot of criticism. Their spiritual purpose can be understood, but how can so many people be prepared to have their spouse (nearly always of another nationality) chosen for them by someone who has never met most of them? Until recently Moon himself, even for the largest weddings, matched up the couples in most cases, praying over their photographs and being guided by God to put the right ones together. From 2000 'the process of matching couples is being increasingly delegated to elder members whom he has trained over many years.'[117] The largest weddings are *large*: the previous record of 6,516 people in 1988 was somewhat overtaken in 1992 when 30,000 couples were married in one huge ceremony – about 10,000 of them via satellite hook-up at eight locations on three continents.

Even this paled into insignificance with a ceremony at the second World Culture and Sports Festival in August 1995: 364,000 couples were blessed at 52 different locations around the world. Of these, 25,000 couples, members of the Church, were actually being married in a stadium at Seoul; the remainder were members of other religions – Christians, Moslems, Jews, Buddhists, Hindus – who were resanctifying their existing marriages. Although they weren't members of the Unification Church, and didn't necessarily believe the teachings of the Church, says Robertson, 'they felt there was a great value in demonstrating with us their belief in the potential sanctity of marriage.'

Blessings since then, in 1997, 1999 and 2000, are claimed to have raised the cumulative total to 360 million. However, the procedures have been relaxed considerably, with blessings being given by Moon on video, or by couples who have previously received the Blessing, instead of by Moon himself. The vast majority of people participating in these Blessings are already-married couples of other faiths.

Unificationist couples are given time to get to know each other before marrying, and have the option of declining their chosen partner. 'The majority of people don't, but it does happen and it's not considered anything more than their individual responsibility.' Robertson is emphatic that the Moon-type marriage is not imposed on members of the Church, 'it's a fundamental aspect of our understanding and belief.'

According to Robertson, this wedding is the ultimate sign of the believer's trust in Moon – and, of course, in God. Believers look at Moon as someone who 'has a profound relationship with God, and through his mediation they're going to get a partner that is very deeply appropriate to them.' It seems to work; Robertson claims that the divorce rate among members of the Church is only 3–5 per cent, way below that of the rest of Western society, where marriages are usually based on the often ephemeral emotion of falling in love.

Marriage, for members, is a vitally important part of God's work; the new couple are creating a new ideal family, and their children will be born without Original Sin. To symbolize the holiness of their marriage, and its place in God's plan, the newly married couple make a private and sacred ritual of their first three nights of love-making. On the first two nights the woman lies on top, symbolizing Eve's transgression and the victory over Satan; on the third night the man is on top, symbolizing the reversal of the process of the original 'Fall' and the re-establishment of God's plan. (After the first three nights they can make love however they wish, just like any other couple.)

To the outsider it seems bizarre; within the context of their beliefs, it makes sense. Sex is valued as an important part of a true loving relationship within marriage; having sex outside marriage is abusing it.

In this, as in other ways, the Church holds to traditional moral standards.

THE LATE TWENTIETH-CENTURY EVANGELICAL RESURGENCE

It can sometimes seem quite astonishing just how many Christian Churches and movements there are, beyond the established mainstream denominations – Roman Catholic, Eastern Orthodox, Anglican, Methodist, Baptist, United Reformed, etc. Scattered around Britain, America, Europe, Africa, the West Indies and elsewhere are thousands of independent Christian Churches, many of them Evangelical, some of them Fundamentalist, and most of them quite small – and some of these claiming to be the only true Church. Some of these have the word True in their name: the True Jesus Church in China, the True Followers of Christ, a faith-healing church in America, the Afro-American True Fellowship Pentecostal Church of God of America, among others.

When Herbert W. Armstrong was looking for a church to join in the 1920s, he insisted on it being called the Church of God, as he believed this was the only name ever given to the Church in the Bible (see page 482). There are several hundred of these to choose from in the USA, many adding qualifying words or phrases: the Church of God (Apostolic), the Church of God of Prophecy, the Church of God (Jesus Christ the Head), several varieties of the Church of God in Christ, as well as all the offshoots of Armstrong's own Church.

Why do all these Churches spring up? There are several reasons. Most are born in a schism from some other (often fairly small) independent Church. Either the founder of the new sect (in its true sense) disagrees with his current Church on, for example, the exact details of the return of Christ, or the nature of heaven and hell, or on the Trinity or the God-man nature of Christ; or else there is a power struggle between the leaders of the old and the new, often on the death of the previous leader. And many of them begin for the same reason as the more historical (and now mainstream) Christian sects, such as Methodism: because the founders don't feel that the existing Christian Churches are doing a good enough job of preaching the gospel.

Many of them claim to be returning to the teachings and practices of the New Testament Church; many are Fundamentalist in believing the Bible to be absolutely true in every detail; many are millennialist, believing in the imminent return of Christ and in his setting up of a literal thousand-year reign on earth; some of them are Charismatic, accepting the Gifts of the Spirit including speaking in tongues and prophecy; several have a doctrine of healing by faith alone. These differing emphases are discussed below or elsewhere in this book.

The word 'Fundamentalist' often has similar pejorative overtones to the words 'cult' and 'sect'; Fundamentalists are seen as extremists. Some – a few – of them are. These are the ones who are prepared in the name of Jesus (or for Muslim Fundamentalists, in the name of Allah) to commit acts of terrorism, or to murder abortion doctors. But the overwhelming majority of Christian Fundamentalists are simply Bible-believing Christians who believe deeply and absolutely in the fundamentals of their faith, and who love and serve God in their own way.

Some of the Christian movements in this book see themselves as the only ones who have the Truth, and consequently the only ones who will be saved. In many cases, the smaller the 'Small Remnant' the more they think they have an absolute monopoly on the correct interpretation of the Bible. The words of a nineteenth-century writer on the Catholic Apostolic Church apply equally to many other movements:

> For how few must they suppose that the salvation of mankind was intended! They blot out nearly eighteen centuries from the existence of the Church. They reck little of the growth of the Church, of the conversions, the endurance of persecutions, the noble martyrdoms, the earnest contentions for the faith. They are bound up in a world of their own, narrowed and becoming narrower, when around them religious hope is burning brighter and wider, and religious faith is becoming sounder and more inspiring.[118]

Whether or not the last few words of this quotation are still valid today is a matter of opinion, and of some dispute; while some sociologists of religion write lengthy papers on the increase in secularization (i.e. the decreasing influence of formalized religion in society), others write of a significant increase in the personal search for spirituality of one sort or another.

But for some small Christian sects, and some movements from other traditions, there is a very real danger that 'they are bound up in a world of their own, narrowed and becoming narrower'. Some of those whose world became so narrow that they imploded, are examined in Chapter 8.

Such groups tend to be inward-looking and, in the sociological term, world-rejecting. Unless something goes seriously wrong, they are unlikely to be noticed. How many people had heard of the Branch Davidians before the siege began at Waco? But there are numerous Christian movements which make a point of being seen; they go out into the world, because they want the world to be saved. Most of these are Evangelical, and many of them have sprung up in the years following the 'Sixties youth revolution'.

THE JESUS MOVEMENT

The late 1960s and early 1970s were exciting times for the many thousands of young Christians in the Jesus Movement. 'Jesus Freaks' wore Day-glo orange Jesus stickers, wrote 'Jesus' in studs on their leather jackets, strummed acoustic guitars and sang choruses in market squares and bus stations, and preached 'the permanent revolution' to their friends, or to anyone they met on the streets. 'Hey, peace and love, man. Are you saved? Do you know Jesus? He died for you, man.' The theology was a stripped-down version of basic Evangelical Christianity. One of the most popular tracts was a little grey leaflet called 'The Four Spiritual Laws'; you read it, you agreed (often under high-pressure encouragement) to its logic, you signed the back page, and you were a Christian.

House fellowships proliferated everywhere. The lack of any sort of central organization or authority was one of the attractions – but also, eventually, one of the problems. Although many of the house fellowships were loosely attached to a local Evangelical church, their leaders sometimes felt they had a private hotline to God which put them outside the authority of any ordained minister. 'God has given me a message' was a frequently heard phrase; but the theology was often shaky, and a surprising number of early Christian heresies began to resurface. The Second Coming was expected imminently.

Some of the Jesus Freaks eventually cut their hair and settled down to raise mortgages and children; if they stayed within Christianity it was as 'normal' members of 'normal' churches, and they perhaps looked back on their sticker-wearing days with a little embarrassment. Many, having dropped in to Jesus, dropped out again as soon as the initial enthusiasm waned. Others went on to join or to form other 'alternative' religious movements; among these were the Children of God (now the Family) and the Jesus Army, which began as just two Jesus Movements among many.

EVANGELICALISM

Once you are in a religion, or a denomination within a religion, you believe it's the right one; why else would you be in it? If it's a particular variety of Christianity, it's the most right version. For example, because Roman Catholicism is historically the oldest extant denomination, and because it has the pope at its head, and no doubt for many other reasons, for many Catholics it is synonymous with Christianity; anything else is a pale imitation, a johnny-come-lately, and by definition not *real* Christianity. Evangelical Christians believe the same of themselves, for different reasons. They'll fight among themselves about the finer points, but the basics are indisputable: 'All have sinned and come short of the glory of God' (Romans 3:23); 'God so loved the world, that he gave his only begotten Son, that whosoever believeth in him should not perish but have everlasting life' (John 3:16); 'Ye must be born again' (John 3:7). Salvation is by faith alone, through grace. Unless, personally and individually, you commit your life to Christ, you are damned. Any other variety of Christianity, for an Evangelical, is wrong, or misled, or confused. There is only one Truth, and Evangelicals have it.

For Christians of any other tradition, Evangelicals can sometimes come over as somewhat arrogant. When a recently converted 14-year-old tells a 60-year-old Anglican or Catholic priest that he must be born again to be saved (and it does happen), the priest might understandably feel a little put out.

Several of the Christian movements which have caused concern among 'cult-watchers' over the last few years are straightforwardly Evangelical in their beliefs. There's nothing in their theology that you won't find in the Evangelical C of E church down the road. But in some cases the application of their beliefs has been problematic, as in the heavy 'shepherding' of the International Church of Christ, and of some house churches in the 1980s and early 1990s, or the prosperity theology of groups such as the Universal Church of the Kingdom of God, or the deliverance ministry of Ellel Ministries and others. In many cases it's the expectation of a heavy commitment of time and energy – and, of course, money – which causes concern.

THE CHARISMATIC MOVEMENT

The Charismatic experience, or being 'baptized in the Spirit', once almost the sole possession of the Pentecostal denominations such as Elim and the Assemblies of God, started spreading as a grass-roots phenomenon into the Church of England and the Methodist, Baptist and other Churches in the late 1960s, leading to such strange nicknames as Anglicostal, Pente-Meth and Bapticostal.

Christians who are baptized in the Spirit manifest the gifts of the Spirit listed in I Corinthians 12:8–10:

> For to one is given by the Spirit the word of wisdom; to another the word of knowledge... to another faith... to another the gifts of healing... to another the working of miracles; to another prophecy; to another discerning of spirits; to

another divers kinds of tongues; to another the interpretation of tongues.

To the outsider, and often to the insider, the most obvious of these is 'speaking in tongues' or *glossolalia*, in which, often in a state of ecstasy, the believer speaks rapidly in what appear to be unknown languages. Sometimes this is part of prayer and worship, and is not interpreted; at other times it is a hidden prophecy, or message from God, which is then interpreted, usually by another believer.

There are many unverified stories of someone in a congregation identifying a tongue as Hebrew or Swahili or Croatian, or some other living language unknown to the speaker; there are other equally unverified cases in which the speaker is found to have been blaspheming in such a little-known language. But when linguistic experts have studied tape recordings of speaking in tongues, they have found the 'speech' to consist of repeated random syllables with no discernible language structure.

But whatever the 'scientific' rationale of speaking in tongues might be, there is no doubt that for the speaker it is a tremendously moving spiritual experience, while the more rare singing in tongues can be beautiful for listeners.

EMOTIONS AND ENTHUSIASM

In August 1995 a Church of England minister in Sheffield was suspended from duty for committing sexual indiscretions with female members of his flock. But those who criticized him were the first to praise him for the work he had been doing for five years in the field of experimental worship. His congregations had become too large for his church, so he used a local sports centre for his weekly 'Nine O'Clock Services', which were likened to Christian Rave parties. Rock music, laser lighting, videos, dancing, all were part of the service. Also, in common with a few other clergy in the 1990s (particularly some of the new women clergy) he introduced some elements which were very close to Neo-Paganism – a love, respect and near-worship of nature, almost of the planet itself. This acknowledgement of the goodness of God's Creation was, in some ways, a resurgence of early Celtic Christianity – and of the Pelagian heresy condemned by Augustine (see page 136).

He was also criticized, however, for becoming more of a personality than a priest: people came to *his* services to see *him*. The former manager of a rock band, he appeared to be attracting a cult following, in the pop-star sense of the word.

Criticisms aside, the sort of work he was doing has been actively encouraged by the present Archbishop of Canterbury, George Carey, an Evangelical, who is keen to find new forms of worship and new means of evangelism. These include the open expression of emotion – something which is very foreign to the traditional Anglican pew-sitter.

The Exclusive Brethren might not approve, but dancing in the aisles has become a legitimate part of worship for many thousands of Christians.

There's nothing new in expressing emotion in Christian worship – John Wesley was frequently criticized for encouraging 'enthusiasm'. Evangelists such as Billy Graham and Oral Roberts have for years skilfully manipulated the emotions of their congregations; it's one way of drawing people to Christ, and if only a few of those who 'get up out of their seats' remain committed six months later, that's still a success in evangelistic terms.

HEALING AND DELIVERANCE MINISTRY

It was noted earlier (see page 185) that one reason the Christian Science Church is waning could be that it no longer holds anything like a monopoly on Christian healing. Practically every town now has at least one perfectly standard Christian church, of whatever denomination, in which healing services are commonplace.

The rapid spread of Christian healing in mainstream churches in recent years could also diminish the attraction of mass-media healing evangelists such as Morris Cerullo.

> When Morris was fourteen and a half years of age through a unique witness and a tremendous spiritual visitation from God, the Messiah, in all his fulness was supernaturally revealed to him. At fifteen he was brought into the heavenlies and given a clear and unmistakable vision for his life... to minister God's Salvation and Healing Power.[119]

As with some other prominent healing evangelists, there has been criticism of Cerullo for the many non-medically verified 'miracles' which happen night after night at his rallies. Many of the illnesses they claim to heal people from had never actually been diagnosed, and some of the healings turn out to be rather short-lived.

Cerullo was also criticized for 'Heavenly Deception' in a poster advertising a 1990s UK campaign. The poster showed a woman holding a baby, and the caption read, 'I couldn't have a baby – Miracles can happen.' It turned out that the woman in the poster was already the mother of three children. The poster was withdrawn.

Cerullo, like many evangelists, 'binds' un-Godly powers.

> In travail I would in the name of Jesus bind these powers of the enemy – the spirits of sin, the spirits of sickness, the spirit of religion, the false cults, the spirit of idol worship, and the false prophets of Baal. I was binding these things for hours in the Spirit.[120]

The idea of sickness being caused by an evil spirit is biblical; Jesus several times 'cast out demons' from someone who was sick. Many Bible scholars, without in any way diminishing it, see this as equivalent in modern-day terminology to someone being cured of a psychosomatic illness: take away the psychological cause, and the physical symptoms will also go.

But today there is a new upsurge in what has become called 'deliverance ministry'.

Some preachers specialize in casting out demons – the demon of a recurrent migraine, the demon of cancer, the demon of impure sexual urges, even the demon of smoking. While accepting the power of God to heal, many traditional Christian leaders – in addition to many doctors and psychiatrists – are becoming increasingly concerned by the practice of deliverance ministry. Several TV documentaries on religious affairs have highlighted this concern. Sometimes the 'healer' will scream and shout at the person with a problem; sometimes he will take hold of him and shake him; and there have been many documented occasions when a sick or troubled person has been pinned to the floor by three or four Deliverance adherents while the leader has interpreted his struggles to get free, or to breathe freely, as the demons fighting to maintain their hold. There have been cases, for example, when the 'victim' has shouted 'Let me go, you bastards,' and the Deliverance 'healer' has said, 'The demon is crying out.'

The concern of both spiritual and medical critics is that deliverance ministry, in the name of Jesus, could do far more harm than good, and could itself create very serious psychiatric problems in those it is seeking to heal.

Two movements which practise deliverance ministry are discussed below.

The following entries include several movements which would be horrified at any suggestion that they might in any way be considered 'cults'; they are ordinary, Bible-believing Christians, doing what they see as God's work, spreading the message of the gospel. They are included here – this book not making any presumption of theological 'correctness' – because they are highly visible; while not all of them have given cause for concern, non-Evangelicals might see them as threatening simply because of the level of their enthusiasm and commitment. From the point of view of the person unwillingly being witnessed to, an Evangelical Christian is no different from a member of any other movement in this book.

The Evangelical Alliance is a British 'umbrella group' which is widely seen by Christians as bestowing a badge of respectability and doctrinal orthodoxy on its members, which include Churches, other organizations and individuals. In April 2000 it produced a book which described hell as a real place. One of many media comments on this described the Evangelical Alliance as 'the fastest-growing Christian movement in Britain – God, they're wacky'.[121] No one is immune against critical opinion.

THE FAMILY

Formerly the Children of God, and then the Family of Love, this movement has been one of the four or five new religious movements to receive the most attention, criticism and attacks, both in the press and from anti-cult organizations. The present-day Family, because of its roots, is still regularly attacked, and finds it difficult to shake off the popular perception. Their formal name is now simply the Family, and they describe themselves as the Fellowship of Independent Missionary Communities.

HISTORY

The first incarnation of the Family was as the Children of God, which was originally a nickname the press gave to a bunch of hippie-type Jesus people on a Californian beach in 1967–9. Other names for them – and for many similar groups in America and the UK – were Teens for Christ, Revolutionaries for Jesus, the Jesus Children, or (more broadly) the Jesus Movement. Their leader was David Brandt Berg (1919–1994), an evangelist from the Christian and Missionary Alliance Church with a powerful End-Time message: Jesus would be returning very soon, so as many people as possible must be converted before it was too late.

From 1964 to 1971 Berg regularly took part in Christian radio and TV programmes, in association with Pentecostal evangelist Fred Jordan; as the Children of God (COG) grew as a movement, they would join him on the broadcasts. In 1971 the Fleetwood Mac guitarist Jeremy Spencer left the band mid-tour to join the COG; he is still with the movement today.

In 1972 COG missionaries began taking their message to the UK and Europe. The Day-glo orange Jesus stickers which appeared everywhere around that time were representative of the tremendous appeal of the wider Jesus Movement among young people. Paperback editions of the New Testament were published as *The Jesus Book*, tracts became lively rather than solemn, and Christian comics began to appear. Guitars were everywhere. The Children of God were at first simply part of the same environment.

Within a year or two they were seen as something quite different. The COG encouraged communal living. David Berg became known as Father David, or Moses David, Mo, or simply 'Dad'; he was not merely an evangelist, but a prophet, and the Children of God were his followers. Wherever he was, he communicated with the COG by 'Mo Letters', often with comic-strip illustrations. But most disturbing of all, his former teaching of the value of celibacy was turned around 180 degrees. He took on a second wife, Maria (originally Karen). Jane, his first wife, was faced with accepting the new situation or leaving; largely due to her wish to pursue other interests, the Church says, including outside missionary work, she left Berg. Rachel Scott, formerly the Family's spokesperson in the UK, comments:

His first wife stayed within the Family quite happily for many years and is still positive about her time in the Family. David Berg continued to support her financially the rest of his life despite the fact that she has had a new husband for the last 20 years.[122]

Berg 'shared' the wives of some of the members of the movement. From 1976 he encouraged members to follow his example and practise sexual freedom. Some ex-members allege that at some stages he advocated lesbian and gay relationships, group sex, sexual involvement (if not actual intercourse) with children, and incest. Another spokesperson, Abi Freeman, explains the background to this controversy:

> David's letters (Mo Letters) were often written to provoke us to question things. He wanted to help us look at the standards of mainstream society, to look beyond face value, to view things through the perspective of our faith. What in society is really based on God-given principles, or what is a tradition of man?...
>
> Throughout his writings David questioned the political system, the world's religion of materialism, wars and other current events, mainstream education, the standards of modern entertainment, the traditions of the mainstream churches, etc., etc.
>
> One line of questioning was regarding society's sexual practices, particularly hypocrisy over sexual matters and lack of love. I'll give you one example regarding polygamy:
>
> '...Now the Bible was in favour of polygamy, but strictly against sequential polygamy [i.e. leaving one spouse to marry another]. And yet man has twisted the whole thing around & made sequential polygamy legal & Biblical polygamy illegal. Think of that! – Man's rules diametrically controverting the laws of God!... Under the polygamous society of the Old Testament, God forbade them to get rid of the first wives...'
>
> David was not saying that polygamy was right or not (and for the record, polygamy is not encouraged in our movement), but he was trying to help us see that the way the issue is being dealt with in the modern world is opposite to what God intended, as the basic principle that should govern all of our relationships is love, and to abandon one wife (or husband) for another would be breaking his laws of love.[123]

At the time that Berg wrote about the possibilities of non-marital sex among adults being permissible in the eyes of God, there were few children in the movement; in neglecting to make it clear that he was referring to adults, and in the explicit nature of some of the cartoons in his Mo Letters, he provided ammunition for his critics. 'It was naïve and unwise to publish such material without making it explicit that this was only supposed to involve adults, and in retrospect we realize it was a mistake,' says Freeman.

On homosexuality, Scott agrees that Berg 'speculated on the possibility that homosexuality could be covered by the Law of Love [see below] but it was quickly dropped because of the way God talks about homosexuality in the Bible. I doubt it was ever practised, and the Family has had a very strong stance against homosexuality ever since.'

In the years when some individual communities got out of control there were cases of group sex, says Scott, 'and then David Berg stopped this with a letter called 'Ban the Bomb' in 1983.' As for sex with children, she says, 'When it came to the attention of Family leadership that some children had been involved in sexual interaction with some adults, a message went out making sure that everyone understood that it was an excommunicable offence.'

The Family later realized just how controversial some of Berg's Mo Letters were, and what a mistake they had made in publishing them. Freeman comments:

> Some of David's questioning in this manner, particularly on sexual matters, should never have been put into print. It was simply unwise for this to be printed and naïve to expect that some people would not jump to conclusions and put into action what had only been meant as 'food for thought'. In later years we realized this and that is why our publications were sorted through and we destroyed the writings (of David and others) that we found objectionable.

Long before this point, though, around 1972, an organization, FREECOG, was set up specifically for parents to 'rescue' (i.e. kidnap) their teenagers back from the COG. This was probably the first 'anti-cult' organization to be formed (see page 98).

Some tabloid headline writers might be surprised to learn that the Children of God came to an end in 1978.

> In late 1977, Father David received reports that some regional leaders in the Church were misusing their authority and violating fundamental rules and principles upon which the movement had been founded. In an action that had the support of the grass-roots membership, he subsequently dismissed the entire leadership and formally dissolved the Children of God. He invited those who wished to remain in fellowship with him to form a new group, the Family of Love, with a new organizational structure. Several years later this name was shortened to the Family.

The sackings and reorganization occurred in February 1978. Over 300 leaders were dismissed, and 2,600 members, one-third of the world membership at the time, 'chose to return to secular lives or remain independent missionaries with no further ties to Father David.'[124] It was, understandably, not a happy time, and had repercussions which continue to this day. 'A number of its former leaders, who were resentful because of their dismissal, still actively campaign against our present-day fellowship.'[125]

These included one of Berg's own daughters, Deborah (originally Linda – members usually change their names on joining, to symbolize their new lives), who was dismissed along with her first husband 'for abusing their positions of leadership in South America'. The movement suspected that her book denouncing Berg and the Children of God was written by her second husband, who had also been dismissed, and by 'another ex-member called Bithia who has now retracted her writings.'

The new movement was far more loosely controlled. In an effort to avoid the authoritarian leadership which had characterized some COG communities – the leaders 'were sometimes hard and unloving and had lost the desire to be missionaries and were more interested in power than in spreading the gospel,' says Scott – each local Family of Love community was self-governed, electing its own leaders and confirming them by a re-vote every six months.

However, the controversy didn't come to an end with the change of name. Indeed, in one particular respect it grew. In 1973 David Berg's wife Maria had begun sleeping with some of the men she was witnessing to. In 1978 Berg introduced the practice to the new movement as Flirty Fishing, or FFing.

Jesus said, 'I will make you fishers of men' (Matthew 4:19). Fishers need bait. Family of Love women went out to bars and nightclubs to meet men, catch them, and draw them into the movement. Inevitably the press dubbed them 'Hookers for Jesus', and even Berg called them 'God's Whores' in one of his Mo Letters. To mainstream Churches the practice was outrageous, but Berg argued that Christians were called upon to make supreme sacrifices for God, even laying down their lives in martyrdom; if laying down their bodies in bed brought people to Christ, it was fully justified.

> Christians were therefore free through God's grace to go to great lengths to show the Love of God to others, even as far as meeting their sexual needs... sex could be used as an evidence to them that we loved them with the Lord's Love, and were willing to sacrificially meet their sexual needs in order to show them that love... Needless to say, linking the spiritual Love of God with the physical manifestation of that love in the form of sex, in this very intimate form of personal witnessing, was, to put it mildly, not very well received by mainstream Christianity, where sex and God are seldom, if ever, associated. In fact, one might even get the erroneous impression that sex is totally of the Devil and not God's idea or design at all.[126]

Commenting on the practice of FFing, Scott says, 'Sex was offered only if the girl felt it was necessary and it was not used as a recruitment method, although some men did join as a result because of their new-found faith in Jesus, and some later married the girls with whom they had fallen in love.' She also adds, 'it may be true to say that more women actually joined as a result of FFing by men.'

This new form of witnessing was fairly short-lived. The sexual freedom of members with each other started to be restricted in 1983; for various reasons, including the threat of AIDS, Flirty Fishing came to an end. 'FFing was officially banned as an outreach method in September 1987. All FFing abruptly stopped.'[127]

'Actually, some people still wish we would practise flirty fishing and are disappointed to find out that we don't!' says Freeman, wryly.

In any case, the Family say, relatively few members ever used FFing as their major form of outreach. The main methods were, and still are, creating and distributing literature, posters, and cassette tapes and videos of their own Christian music and evangelism. In some parts of the world they produce radio and TV programmes.

The Family now tend to live in small communities – effectively extended families – with their children, whom they educate at home wherever possible. There are around 10,000 members around the world, one-third of these adults. Around a quarter of their present adult membership were formerly members of the Children of God.

David Berg died in 1994; his wife Maria took over as prophetess and leader of the Family.

BELIEFS AND PRACTICES

The Family's beliefs, with two exceptions, are those of straightforward Evangelical Christianity. They believe that the Bible is the divinely inspired word of God; they believe in the Trinity; they believe that Jesus died on the cross to save mankind from its sins, and that salvation is by faith, through the grace of God. As Charismatic Christians they believe in the Baptism of the Holy Spirit, and the gifts of the Spirit, including healing, prophecy and speaking in tongues. Evangelism is an essential part of their lives; 'the born-again believer's primary purpose in life [should be] to make Christ's love known to the whole world, and to seek to win others into God's Heavenly Kingdom.'[128] They believe strongly that these are the Last Days, and that Christ will shortly return to establish the millennium. In common with many Fundamentalists they believe in the literal biblical account of Creation, not in Evolution.

Unlike many Christian alternative religious movements, they have no argument with other Christian Churches. 'Basically for us, any and all who love God and love their fellow man and are trying to make it a better world for them to live in, to us are doing good,' says Scott.

The two differences concern their founder, and the 'Law of Love'.

'Members of the Family hold our founder, David Berg, to be a prophet whom God has ordained to proclaim the Endtime message to this generation. With David Berg's passing in the latter part of 1994, we accept his wife, Maria, as his successor and prophetess and leader of the Family,' says Scott.

The Law of Love is based on Jesus' teaching,

Thou shalt love the Lord thy God with all thy heart, and with all thy soul, and with all thy mind. This is the first and great commandment. And the second is like unto it, Thou shalt love thy neighbour as thyself. (Matthew 22:37–39)

This, they teach (in common with most Christian Churches) has replaced the point-by-point rules of Mosaic Law.

'The Family holds Christ's Law of Love to be the supreme tenet upon which all Christian conduct and interpersonal relationships should be based, that all acts motivated by unselfish love for others are acceptable to God,' says Scott. (In both motivation and effect this could be seen as akin to the basic Pagan law: 'An it hurt no one, do as thou wilt shall be the whole of the Law.' Scott disagrees with the comparison: 'This is actually the opposite to the Law of Love [which] states that our actions should help someone; it is certainly not enough not to hurt someone.')

She emphasizes that the Law of Love does not mean licence. 'David Berg always stressed that this liberation is not a selfish, reckless freedom wherein you are free to disregard the rights or feelings of others or act unkindly, selfishly, lustfully or lawlessly towards them, for "love worketh no ill to his neighbour" (Romans 13:10).'

The controversial point is the application of this Law of Love to sexual relationships.

We believe heterosexual relationships between consenting adults are permissible in the eyes of God regardless of marital status, providing these relationships are motivated by unselfish love, are desired by all parties, are agreed upon and hurt no one.

Scott stresses that despite the persistent allegations, this applies to adults only.

We have been accused of sexually abusing our children. This is an excommunicable offence. Over 600 of our children have been taken in dawn raids from our communities and have been returned when no evidence of abuse was found.[129]

She also points out that 'in his writings on sexual relationships, David Berg emphasized that these should remain within the legal boundaries of society.'

Perhaps partly as a response to the allegations of sexual misconduct, but mainly because of the threat of AIDS, the Family now has very strict rules on sexual relationships, which may now only be between Family members. New members must belong to a community for six months before they are allowed to share in sexual relationships.

The whole application of the Law of Love to sexual relationships is misunderstood by outsiders, Scott says. It is 'primarily for the sake of single people within our communities who because of the fact that they cannot have relationships with people outside our communities would otherwise have to remain celibate. We do not believe this would be the loving thing to do. It is not an excuse for excess and it is carried out extremely discreetly with just two people involved.'

Freeman adds, 'We also believe that sexual sharing among adults in our communities, whether single or married, when carried out according to the principles of The Law of Love and within the guidelines of the Charter, helps bring about a greater strength of love and unity between us.'

The Family do not actively encourage people to join their communities. Anyone who wants to must first spend some months getting to know and understand the beliefs and lifestyle, and what their commitment would entail.

> If after a time they are firmly convinced they want to join, are of legal age and free from debts, legal or military obligations that would prevent them joining, we would allow them to live in for a three-week 'trial' period. The members of the Home would then vote on whether to accept them or not as a full-time member, in which case they would have another six-month probationary period before becoming a full member.

The communities or homes are where the fully committed Charter Members (formerly called Disciples Only, or DO) live; they can range in size from four voting members (aged over 16) up to a maximum of 35 people altogether. At 16 members can vote on anything except expenditure and financial matters, which are restricted to those over 18. Charter Members commit everything to their home, 'forsaking all'; this usually includes giving up their job to work full-time for the community.

This work is partly internal – cooking, cleaning, repairing the vehicles, teaching the children, secretarial work, and so on; and partly external – going out on an evangelization team. 'The Family ministers largely to the unchurched: individuals who cannot – or will not – be attracted to mainstream Christian denominations,' says Scott.

A community's income comes mainly from donations, both from supporters and for their posters, music cassettes and videos. From time to time a member of a community may take on a secular job to bring in more income if needed. The community itself gives 10 per cent of its income each month to World Services, the closest the Family has to a central HQ, which is responsible for publications and for funding new 'pioneer' homes in, for example, Eastern Europe. Part of the income is also put into an emergency fund for purposes such as supporting individual members who become ill.

'The Family does not seek to establish a denomination, own property or build lavish church buildings or in any way acquire power or excessive material wealth,' says Scott. 'It considers such activities unscriptural, and believes that if mainstream Christianity were to abandon such pursuits and dedicate all their material resources to winning others to Christ and being an example of true Christian love, the world would be a far better place.'

The total worldwide Charter Membership of the Family, as of June 1999, was 10,219 living in 840 homes, with a further 2,750 Fellow Members in 532 homes.

Adding all these together, 37 per cent are adults over 21, 8 per cent are young adults aged 18–21, and 55 per cent are children and teenagers under 18. These figures have remained fairly steady for some years, though members obviously come and go; apparently there are around 35,000 former members who, 'for the most part, remain on friendly terms'.

In the UK in 1999 there were 136 Charter Members living in 20 Family homes or communities, and a further 154 Fellow Members. This is a reduction from the 1993 figures of 373 Charter Members; many members have left Britain in the last few years to do missionary work elsewhere. In Europe, in June 1999, there were 1,067 Charter Members and 739 Fellow Members.

Members are free to leave their Home to join another one, or to set up a new one, or to leave community life and become Fellow Members (formerly called TRF supporters after their Tithing Report Forms), associate members who might still witness but not full-time. Anyone who wishes to leave the Family altogether may do so, and their community will usually help them out.

'In recent years,' says Freeman, 'as some of our young people who have been born and raised in The Family decide to leave, their parents have been helping them as much as they possibly can to make the adjustment to secular society, often helping them get relocated with relatives willing to take them in, get enrolled in college, finding an apartment etc. If it is a family or a single mother with children, likewise efforts are made to make the transition smoother.'

Scott stresses that 'for the most part all our communities are "open" to visitation by the public and anyone is free to visit.' This includes the families of members; contrary to popular belief members 'are encouraged to keep in contact with their relatives. In fact we like to visit the parents beforehand and encourage the new disciples to visit them whenever is reasonable, and we also encourage the parents to visit the homes.'

Although each Family home is autonomous and self-governing, the Family put together a 200-page governing charter early in 1995, which outlines the most important principles, goals and beliefs of the movement and provides a broad governing structure for the communities. The document includes a Charter of Responsibilities and Rights, and the Fundamental Family Rules. It was compiled in the year before his death by David Berg, with Maria and others, based on suggestions from grass-roots Family members; the draft Charter was then discussed in workshops around the world before being finalized. The Charter makes a major point of the rights and responsibilities of parents and children: 'The children's rights include having their spiritual, physical and emotional needs met, and to be free from any kind of abuse. They should also receive sufficient time, opportunity and materials to obtain an adequate education, including regular physical education.'

Scott also points out that 'our understanding of a nuclear family is the same as yours – Mum, Dad and the kids. Traditional family bonds are of prime importance. If there is a single mother or single father with children, we make sure that there is someone to help them with the children, and there is plenty of support from the whole community.'

As well as their evangelistic work, members of the Family help in the wider community, including giving humanitarian aid. In 1995 they set up soup kitchens for the survivors of the Kobe earthquake in Japan, and helped in the rescue after the bomb explosion in a federal building in Oklahoma City. Their community work also includes prison visiting, and working in homes for the elderly, and for delinquent children. Their more descriptive formal name reflects how they see themselves today, as independent missionaries.

The Family have probably been tarred more than any other new religious movement by their past excesses; newspaper stories still call them the Children of God and concentrate on selected events decades old, and anti-cultists in general resolutely ignore the very major changes in the movement over recent years.

'They just take whatever sounds the most scandalous to print in their paper, and if we talk to them and tell them things from our side, they usually go ahead and print whatever is sensational anyway,' says Scott.

A clear case of completely inaccurate reporting occurred in a 1996 book entitled *Cults: Prophecies, Practices & Personalities*. Commenting on a child custody case involving 'the Children of God' it says, 'On November 24, 1995, a British High Court judge issued a damning indictment of a cult... He found against the cult.'[130]

In fact, after criticizing certain past practices of the Family as 'revolting' and 'possibly blasphemous', the judge concluded (following his three-year study of the movement, culminating in a 340-page, 135,000-word judgement) that they had left such practices behind, and said there was 'compelling evidence that this is not a pernicious cult'.[131] Far from finding 'against the cult' he actually found in favour of the child's mother (a member of the Family), ruling that her three-year-old son should be allowed to live with his mother, despite his grandmother's protests. *Cults: Prophecies, Practices & Personalities*, which contained other similar errors, acknowledged by name the assistance of four British anti- or counter-cult leaders, who were presumably aware of the true facts of the case.

Scott comments on the judge's decision:

We are very gratified that this judgement endorses the findings of numerous other court cases around the world, that Family communities are safe and wholesome environments in which to bring up children. Hopefully this case provides a punctuation mark in our development, and that the Family can now proceed with its calling of telling others about Jesus.

The impression given by the Family today is that they are sincere and dedicated Evangelical Christians whose only real difference from any others is that they are honest about sleeping with each other. They appear to have put the excesses of the 1970s and early 1980s behind them; they are very conscious of their bad image, and now seem to make a deliberate effort to 'abstain from all appearance of evil' (I Thessalonians 5:22).

THE JESUS ARMY

The Jesus Army, or the Jesus Fellowship Church (its formal name), developed at around the same time as the hippie-style Jesus Movement of the late 1960s and early 1970s, but from related but different roots: 'more the impact of the charismatic movement on an old-established Baptist chapel,' says John Campbell, communications officer for the Jesus Army.[132] Its doctrine is straightforward Evangelical Christianity, with both a Reformed and a Charismatic element; it is included in this book because of its very visible style, and because of some concerns which have been raised about it over the years.

The Church seems particularly sensitive about being regarded as any form of new religious movement, stressing its theological orthodoxy. At the foot of its letterhead are the words, 'Jesus Fellowship Church upholds the full historic biblical faith, being Reformed, Evangelical and Charismatic. In particular, it upholds the doctrine of the Holy Trinity and the full divinity of the Lord Jesus Christ.'

'There is no sense in which we represent an "Alternative Religion",' says Campbell. 'Our beliefs are mainstream Christian, and we uphold the historic creeds of Christianity. We also recognize and respect the wide spread of "flavours" within the Christian Church at large.'

The origins of the Jesus Army can be traced back to 1969, when Baptist minister Noel Stanton and some members of his small church in Bugbrooke, Northamptonshire, were baptized in the Holy Spirit, and began speaking in tongues, healing, and preaching the gospel with new enthusiasm and effectiveness.

His church soon became too small for his rapidly increasing congregation; money was raised and donated to buy more buildings, including an old rectory and then a farm, which became the New Creation Farm. Stanton's congregation became a community. The Jesus Fellowship now numbers about 2,500 members.

The Jesus Fellowship Community Trust owns around 60 New Creation Christian Community houses in the UK; it also owns a health food company and health food shops, building and plumbing companies, and a clothes shop. Members of the Church may continue to live in their own homes, but about a quarter – some 700 – live in communities.

All members are on an equal footing, with no privileges or extra financial incentives being accorded to anyone, including any of the leaders.

The assets of the community consist solely of the houses we live in, the vehicles we drive, and the stock and goodwill of the businesses that we operate to provide employment for members. There are no other 'riches' of any kind.

Within the community, each house has a 'common purse' arrangement, with members pooling their income to meet all personal and household expenses.[133]

The way of life in Jesus Army communities has been described as austere. Everything is shared – their money, their possessions, even sometimes their clothes. TV and radio are banned; only Christian music is allowed. Children are allowed few toys, and are given strict discipline, including corporal punishment, though the slipper has replaced the rod because of external criticism.

The popular Christian festivals such as Christmas are not celebrated, on the quite accurate grounds that they have Pagan origins. (One of the reasons that Christianity took root throughout Europe during the Dark Ages was its habit of taking over local Pagan festivals and sacred sites, adapting the customs of the Winter Solstice into Christmas, and of the Spring festival into Easter, and building churches over ancient wells and springs.)

Non-members are most likely to be aware of the Jesus Army by its brightly painted double-decker buses and highly visible form of street evangelism. Their clothing is often military-style; the colours may be brighter, but their jackets appear to be based on camouflage combat jackets. Campbell stresses that 'our evangelism is based on friendship', and strongly disputes any suggestion of a militaristic, assertive form of evangelism, but the Church does have a public image of being 'macho', which some critics have found off-putting. The Jesus Army does a lot of work among homeless street-people, those involved in drug or alcohol abuse, and prisoners and ex-prisoners. Unlike most new religious movements, a large proportion of its predominantly young membership is working class and without higher education.

The Church teaches that celibacy is a holy calling; even long-married couples living in their communities sleep in separate beds. Romantic liaisons between community members have to be approved by the leadership.

The Jesus Army has been accused of being very male-orientated, not only in its thrusting approach to evangelism, but also in its treatment of women. It believes firmly in traditional gender roles in society. Men are the leaders; the women in the membership have very much a supporting role. They appear content to ignore the societal changes of the last few decades, giving up the rights and status women have fought to achieve in recent years.

The Church organizes occasional 'Men Alive for God' days, when hundreds of men meet together for fellowship and worship, and to help men re-establish their manhood. They have never had an equivalent day for their women members. 'We've never found that we've been able to do that, simply because we haven't had a woman who has the vision and the calibre to lead it,' says Ed Hunt, organizer of the event.[134]

✳

The Church has had problems with the wider Christian community; it was expelled from the Baptist Union, and it resigned from the interdenominational Evangelical Alliance in 1986 over its 'perceived isolationism'. However, it 'is part of the Multiply Christian Network, a partnership of independent churches and groups promoting living charismatic Christianity'[134] which it launched in 1992, and which is a member of the Evangelical Alliance; it rejoined the Alliance itself in 1999.

The Jesus Army is careful with both members and money. New members have to live in a community for a probationary period for two years, and must be over 21, before being allowed to commit themselves to full community membership. Community members donate all their money to the Community Trust Fund; if they later leave the Community, their capital is paid back, sometimes with interest. The Community keeps its running expenses and its capital completely separate, and has its accounts audited by the international firm PriceWaterhouseCoopers.

UNIVERSAL CHURCH OF THE KINGDOM OF GOD

The Universal Church of the Kingdom of God hit the headlines in Britain in 1995, when it purchased the Rainbow Theatre in London for £2.3 million. It is a Charismatic Evangelical Church with a strong emphasis on healing and deliverance ministry (see page 216), and also on prosperity theology.

The Church was founded in 1977 in Rio de Janeiro, Brazil, by Edir Macedo (b. 1945). Macedo moved to the USA in 1986, and churches were opened there. In the mid-1990s the Church began to have a presence in Britain. At a time when mainstream Churches face declining congregations, the Universal Church of the Kingdom of God often has thousands at its services.

The Church was involved in considerable friction in its native Brazil. Macedo declined to join the Brazilian Evangelical Organization, made up of the historical Protestant denominations, mainly Presbyterians and Methodists, Baptists and some Pentecostal Churches; instead he set up his own association, drawing in several other Pentecostal Churches. In addition to clashing with other Christian Churches, the

Church has been involved in what American newspapers have called a 'holy war' with the powerful Afro-Brazilian spiritist groups, such as 'the Umbanda and Candomble cults, accusing them of devil worship and offering to exorcise them of evil spirits.'[136]

Prosperity theology, which is taught by the Church, is the idea that the more you give to God, the more he will give back to you. (The well-known American evangelist Oral Roberts calls this 'seed-faith giving': you plant a seed in faith, and God will give you a harvest.) In its huge and lively services the Church also emphasizes faith-healing miracles and exorcism for persons 'possessed by malignant spirits' and the Devil. 'Though these are part of our message,' stresses Bishop Renato Cardoso, head of the Church in Britain, 'our main emphasis is on salvation.'[137]

The Church has also faced criticism from the British press. In 1995 *The Observer* newspaper ran a story headlined 'Sex, tithes and leaked videotape', with the strap-line 'Brazil's billion-dollar church has global ambitions, but has been exposed by a major scandal'.[138] According to *The Observer*, the videotapes showed 'the self-styled "Bishop" Edir Macedo, grinning from ear to ear as he counted piles of dollars, gambling with his preachers, whooping it up in luxury hotels and engaging in sexual horseplay.' Bishop Cardoso says only that these are 'unfounded allegations which have never been proven.' The Church has a policy of not responding to criticisms, and of not co-operating with journalists or researchers.

INTERNATIONAL CHURCH OF CHRIST

One Evangelical Church which is currently causing perhaps more concern than almost any other in the UK is the International Church of Christ (ICOC), which takes the name of whichever town it is in, such as the London Church of Christ or (the original congregation) the Boston Church of Christ. This entry focuses more than many others on criticisms of the Church (giving its responses where available), but it should be remembered that these are criticisms which are sometimes made by ex-members of many new religious movements (NRMs).

The Church of Christ is a well-established Evangelical denomination in the USA. In the late 1960s the Crossroads movement in a Florida Church of Christ had the mission of winning students to Christ, and ICOC grew out of this. Kip McKean was a member of the Crossroads movement evangelizing Eastern Illinois University, before moving to Boston in 1979, where he established the Boston Church of Christ, from which the movement developed. In 1982 ICOC 'planted' its first church outside the USA, in London. ICOC now has no connection with the older Church of Christ denomination, which seeks to distance itself from the controversies surrounding its offshoot. It is important to distinguish between the two.

ICOC's theology is strictly Evangelical, though with certain strong emphases. It is 'seeking to be the New Testament church,' says its British leader, John Partington.[139] Although it is careful not to say that salvation can only be found through ICOC, there is little doubt that this is what many of its members believe, and what, in practice, is more or less the case. 'Each Christian must be a committed disciple of Jesus. The gospel must be received by faith, and obedience, confession, repentance and baptism as our response to God's grace gift,' says Partington. Baptism is essential to salvation, and any new member who has previously been baptized in another Christian Church must be baptized again in ICOC.

The main criticisms of ICOC are about its recruitment techniques, its level of commitment, its 'discipling' or 'shepherding' practice, its 'sin lists', cutting members off from their former friends, and the difficulties faced by members who wish to leave. Following the practice of the Crossroads movement, ICOC specifically targets university and college students, as well as stopping people in the street or, particularly in London, drawing people into conversation on Underground trains and inviting them to a meeting or church service (usually without identifying the Church). A number of universities in the UK have banned ICOC from their campuses.

Along with many other new religious movements, ICOC has been accused of 'love-bombing', of showing a great deal of love, affection and attention to prospective members to draw them in. The criticism is that vulnerable or lonely people, and this includes many students, will be attracted by this. In response, Partington says,

> We believe in John 13:34–35, that Christians can be known for their love. We believe in showing great love to prospective members, both before membership and for the rest of their lives after they become Christians. Loving people is not a technique to attract people, it is a call to live like Jesus.

Because 'the mission of the church is to seek and save the lost', members are expected to devote a great amount of their time to evangelizing; the concern of universities is that this can have a negative impact on students' studies. New members are often encouraged to move into single-sex communal flats or houses with older members, which means that they spend more time within the context of the Church, and less time with former friends or family.

'Discipling' or 'shepherding' means that new members are put under the authority of an older member, who in turn has his or her 'discipler' or 'shepherd', up the hierarchy through lay-leaders and pastors, to the leader. Disciplers have a tremendous amount of influence and authority, not just in guiding their disciples in the faith, but on matters such as where they should live, who they should spend time with, and even who they should have relationships with. Clearly this is a practice which could lead to abuse. Partington comments:

The discipling we practise has been called 'controlling' at times. Certainly we advise people against sin. We are sure that some leaders in the church have at times been insensitive or overly demanding. This is not a flaw in the concept of discipling in the Bible, but rather a flaw in sinful men (our church consists 100% of reformed sinners each of whom still have [sic] temptations to sin).

ICOC's own website explains discipling in this way:

Being 'discipled' simply means getting input, advice and teaching from people we know and respect so that each one of us can become more like Jesus. Being 'discipled' does not mean that someone else makes our decisions for us nor does it mean blindly doing whatever we are told.[140]

But founder Kip McKean has been quoted as saying, 'The only time you don't obey [your pastor] is if he violates scripture or violates your conscience. But, other than that, in all opinion areas, you... obey!'[141]

Confessing sins is important to the Church, and confession is made to one's discipler or to other members. Partington explains this:

The church is distinguished from many churches by its family focus, where members are involved in each other's lives, where there is a loving commitment to each other's spiritual growth and an accountability to do right. Forgiveness for repentant sinners and church discipline for unrepentant sinners is practised.

There have apparently been occasions when a disciple's sins, which include those of an intimate nature, have without his knowledge been written down by his discipler, and the resulting 'sin list' passed on to other leaders in the Church.

As in many other NRMs there is a high turnover of members, many leaving after a few months because they find the discipline of life in the movement too demanding or oppressive. There are probably far more ex-members of ICOC than current members. Again like many other NRMs, ICOC tries to discourage people from leaving. The fact that many members live in communal homes, and have been encouraged to break off contact with non-member friends, can make it difficult to leave, simply because the member has to find somewhere else to live. Once they have left, the Church often visits or phones members for weeks, encouraging them to come back. This can include 'love-bombing', but can also include the implicit or explicit warning that the member could lose his salvation by leaving the Church. Some ex-members who still maintain their belief in the Christian message have found their main problem is accepting that salvation can be found in other Christian Churches, and that they will not face damnation by leaving ICOC. From ICOC's point of view, of course, they don't want to lose a member who has become a friend, whom they love, and whose moral and especially spiritual welfare is of great concern to them.

ICOC has grown considerably in the last decade. Ten years ago it had about 21,000 members worldwide, 15,000 of those in the USA, 1,080 in the UK, and only 250 in Europe outside the UK. Today it claims around 120,000 members worldwide, 50,000 of these in the USA, 2,700 in the UK, and 2,500 in Europe outside the UK. Its own statistics for September 1999 showed a Sunday attendance totalling 186,000 in 372 churches in 158 nations.

In the last decade ICOC has attracted a huge amount of criticism and hostility from anti-cultists; the organization Triumphing Over London Cults (TOLC) was founded by two former ICOC members. It has certainly been made aware of the concerns expressed above, but unlike some of the other movements founded in the 1970s, does not yet appear to have reached the point in its development where it becomes sensitive to the genuine distress some of its members and their families have experienced, and willing to modify some of its practices to reduce the possibility of causing such distress.

ELLEL MINISTRIES

Ellel Ministries is a Charismatic Evangelical organization focusing on healing, particularly on what is often called deliverance ministry.

It was founded in 1986 at Ellel Grange, in the village of Ellel, near Lancaster in northern England. Fortuitously, Ellel is a very apposite name for their work, as founder Peter Horrobin explains:

> On investigation the word Ellel was found to be a modern-day corruption of the old English name of the community, meaning 'All Hail'. In Hebrew the word El represents God and Ellel would mean God of God's (sic) or King of Kings and Lord of Lords. In ancient Cantonese a word that sounds like Ellel means 'love flowing outwards'. When the various meanings of the word Ellel are run together, they very effectively sum up the whole ministry – 'All hail Jesus, King of Kings and Lord of Lords, love flowing outwards.' It would be hard to improve on this as a descriptive name...[142]

Ellel's foundational scripture is Luke 9:11, 'Jesus welcomed the people, taught them about the Kingdom of God and healed those in need' (translation unknown). The emphasis is on teaching Christian leaders both how to be right with God themselves, and how to help others through Christian healing.

Since their beginning in 1986, Ellel Ministries have expanded rapidly, opening centres in Surrey and Sussex, and also in Hungary and Canada (there are close personal links with leaders of the Toronto Airport Vineyard Church); between 1987 and 1999 the full-time workers increased from 14 to 180, plus 350 voluntary Associate Counsellors.

Deliverance ministry means delivering people from evil spirits or demons. For Horrobin and the Ellel team, demons are literally real – an idea which meets quite a lot of opposition both within mainstream Christianity and elsewhere. Horrobin says:

> Whilst no one could deny the fact that in the Gospels Jesus is described as frequently casting evil spirits out of people, it seemed as though the idea of doing this today was more than some people wanted to acknowledge.
>
> There was, of course, opposition from the more liberal theologians who say Jesus only believed in demons because he was a man of his day... Now, they say, with the advances of medical science, we can see, as people of our day, that what Jesus and others formerly thought was demonic can be accounted for by more sensible scientific explanations. What such comments can't explain, however, is how it is that by casting out demons and bringing deep healing to the broken, people get healed![143]

In fact, many critics would explain this as a mixture of psychosomatic healing and the effects of TLC – tender loving care. Experiments have shown, for example, that the more patients are touched by nurses, the more rapidly they heal.

Deliverance healing has been criticized for some of its more extreme manifestations. TV programmes have shown six burly men holding down someone who is shouting and struggling, while a minister casts demons out of the person. If the person is protesting, perhaps swearing, this is seen as the voice of the demon. Critics have suggested that deep psychological damage can be done under these circumstances. Horrobin is emphatic in distancing Ellel from such practices, and says that his team work closely with psychiatrists and social workers when healing people who are seriously disturbed.[144]

Some see deliverance ministry – whether that of Ellel, or the more dramatic (and much more public) work of some American televangelists – as a resurgence of medieval superstition within fringe Christianity. Horrobin, though, points to the close links of Ellel with the mainstream denominations: at least two Anglican bishops have been closely associated with and very supportive of Ellel's ministry.

Ellel is not a new Church; its leaders and teachers come from a variety of denominations. As well as healing services and retreats, for which it does not charge, it offers a residential training school and a wide variety of short courses, including Healing Abused People, Healing for Women, Ministry to the Childless, and Steps to Healing from Addiction. It also runs a six-month training school for young Christians, with in-depth Bible teaching and training in evangelism and healing. In addition, it is frequently invited to teach in churches across Britain.

TORONTO BLESSING AND VINEYARD

In the last few years a new phenomenon has caught the Christian headlines: the Toronto Blessing. During services which combine worship, prayer and healing, some people spontaneously burst into tears, some into laughter, shouting, even animal noises – and some are pole-axed, 'slain in the Spirit', crumpling unconscious to the floor. Those who have witnessed it, even those who have experienced it, can find no explanation. In psychological and physiological terms it is probably a form of hysterical reaction – or, in a less loaded term, social compliance – but those involved claim that in spiritual terms it is a very real personal blessing.

The Toronto Blessing began in the Toronto Airport Vineyard church in January 1994 – and led ultimately to that church's expulsion from the Vineyard Church denomination. Vineyard itself was initially a daughter Church of the Calvary Chapel Movement, a non-denominational Church which began in the mid-1960s, focusing its ministry initially on hippies, whom it felt would not be attracted by conventional mainstream Churches. In 1982 two Calvary Chapel pastors, Kenn Gulliksen and John Wimber, felt that their churches' emphasis on speaking in tongues, prophecy and healing had moved sufficiently far away from Calvary Chapel that they should separate from their parent Church, forming the Vineyard Movement. Over the next few years, around 30 other Calvary Chapels joined Vineyard under Wimber's leadership. Shortly before his death in 1997, Wimber changed the structure of Vineyard from effectively a federation of independent churches to a denomination, currently with over 100,000 members in around 750 churches, 500 of these in the USA. Unusually, some 35 per cent of these congregations came over to Vineyard from other denominations or movements.[145]

Much of the attraction of Vineyard, it is generally agreed, is the style of worship, with a mixture of lively, upbeat songs and mellow, prayerful ones; the musical emphasis owes much to Wimber, who was formerly keyboardist for the 'blue-eyed soul' band the Righteous Brothers.

Enthusiastic, emotional, lively and informal Vineyard may be, but it drew the line at the Toronto Airport church's acceptance of animal noises, along with the (acceptable) uncontrollable laughter which supposedly showed a manifestation of the Holy Spirit. Toronto Airport was disfellowshipped from the Vineyard Movement.

However, literally hundreds of thousands of people have visited the Toronto Airport church since the first appearance of what became known as the Toronto Blessing – and they have taken the experience back to their own churches around the world. In some ways the Toronto Blessing can be compared with a highly contagious virus: it is nearly always 'caught' by someone in contact with others who already have it, and then 'transmitted' by the 'carrier' to others in their own environment – including many churches in Britain. (This is similar to the spiritual experience of Subud's *latihan*, which is also passed on by personal contact; the effects are also remarkably similar. See page 354.)

Many Christians are deeply uncomfortable with the Toronto Blessing, saying that it panders to emotionalism, and questioning how and why collapsing on the floor or barking like a dog are signs of God's presence filling a believer – and in any case, how can people possibly behave in such an outlandish way? In one sense this reveals the common human failing of decontextualizing a newly observed phenomenon; similar criticisms were made about the effects of the preaching of John Wesley and other early Methodist preachers 250 years ago. In the twentieth century social compliance, which can cause people to overcome their social conditioning and behave in ways they would not normally dream of, has been seen in everything from the Nuremberg Rallies to Beatlemania.

In 1999 there was an even stranger phenomenon at some churches with the Toronto Blessing: believers claiming that God had replaced the amalgam fillings in their teeth with gold fillings. The Toronto Airport church said:

> ...over 50 people were on the platform at Toronto Airport Christian Fellowship testifying to having received what appeared to be gold or bright silver fillings or crowns, which they believed had supernaturally appeared in their mouths after receiving prayer during the Intercession Conference. Many received one, two, three or more, and in some cases up to ten changed fillings!... By Sunday night, well over 300 people were testifying to this unusual sign.[146]

The Church asked, 'Why would God fill people's teeth with gold?', and gave some possible answers:

> Perhaps because He loves them and delights in blessing His children. Perhaps it is a sign and a wonder to expose the scepticism still in so many of us. Perhaps His glory and presence are drawing very near.

This supposed manifestation of God's power also came to Britain. A member of the Folly's End Christian Fellowship in Croydon, Surrey, was quoted as saying, 'I was amazed! I was absolutely stunned. I thought, Isn't God good? You feel humbled that He's purified your mouth.'[147]

Some have seen this phenomenon as a fulfilment of Psalm 81:10: 'Open thy mouth wide and I will fill it.' But the reaction outside the Toronto Blessing community was somewhat more sceptical. The editor of a British Christian online magazine,

Ship of Fools, said:

> Many will be thinking, why is God concerning himself with people's fillings, while there is such serious trauma in the world as Kosovo. They are bound to ask, hasn't God got anything better to do?

THE ALPHA COURSE

One of the liveliest Church of England churches in Britain is Holy Trinity, Brompton (HTB) in west London – a centre for both the Toronto Blessing and one of the most significant recent developments in mainstream denominational Christianity, the Alpha course.

The Toronto Blessing came to HTB when one of its leaders visited the Toronto Airport church, then returned to HTB; other leaders then experienced it, and it then passed to members of the church.

The Alpha course is 'a ten-week practical introduction to the Christian faith, designed primarily for non-churchgoers and those who have recently become Christians.'[148] It began in a small way in 1977, as a four-week course at HTB devised by Anglican clergyman Charles Marnham; over the following years different leaders extended it. It began to take off in 1991 under HTB curate Nicky Gumbell, who produced a book-length written version of the course, *Questions of Life*, in 1993, followed by *Telling Others* (1994), giving the practical details of how churches can run their own Alpha courses. From that point on it began to spread throughout Britain, in all mainstream denominations, and then around the world. In 1998 6,300 churches in Britain – around a quarter of all British mainstream Christian churches – were running Alpha courses. Alpha has grown from five courses given in 1992 to over 14,000 in 1999. To date, over a million people have attended the courses in churches, universities, prisons and private homes. Alpha courses are now given in just over 100 countries.

The course typically runs on a weekday evening over 11 weeks. After a supper or light meal, there is a talk for 40 minutes, either by a live speaker or by Nicky Gumbel on video or cassette. After coffee the participants split into groups of around 12 people to ask questions and discuss the topic of the evening; these include such subjects as 'Christianity: boring, untrue and irrelevant?', 'Who is Jesus?', 'How does God guide us?', and 'Does God heal today?'

The Alpha course has been phenomenally successful, turning many relatively uncommitted churchgoers into committed Christians. At a time when the ageing and dwindling congregations of the mainstream denominations are causing them to close churches across the country, HTB – an Anglican parish church – has pioneered a counter-flow, taking over moribund churches and filling them with enthusiastic believers, something that in recent years only radical independent Churches such as the Universal Church of the Kingdom of God have done. But such churches are often criticised for being too experiential, too shallow. HTB is performing a delicate balancing act, with lively Charismatic services in which healing and the Toronto Blessing are strongly evident, and also careful doctrinal teaching. Whether this success will continue indefinitely, or whether it will reach a natural plateau and then gradually decline, or whether for some reason the balance will tip too sharply one way or the other, cannot be foreseen.

There have been criticisms of the Alpha course.[149] Some are concerned that Nicky Gumbel, who wrote the books and presents the course in the videos and cassettes, could become too much of a personality; concern has also been expressed that (with rare exceptions to suit local conditions) the course must be run exactly as Gumbel's course guide dictates. Others criticize the content for being doctrinally simplistic; the phrase 'a McDonaldization of Christianity' has been used, particularly with regard to the slick presentation and the 'happy-clappy' type of worship which is encouraged. Some find the emphasis on being filled with the Holy Spirit at the climax of the course disturbing; as one person put it, 'Getting to know the Holy Spirit theologically and emotionally by Sunday lunchtime.'[150] Gumbel's – or Alpha's, or HTB's – belief in the Baptism in the Holy Spirit is not shared by all Christians; this can be a highly charged area, which has been known, when handled insensitively, to split Churches apart.

In contrast to the 'relaxed, non-threatening' atmosphere which is crucial to the course – 'It is low-key, friendly and fun'[151] – some find the content of the course too morally conservative, saying that there is too much of a focus on sexual morality and 'family values', and that it is too hardline against both gay and premarital sex. Gumbel quotes with approval – indeed, as an object lesson – a couple who were in a sexual relationship, became Christians, and decided they should stop sleeping together; for whatever reasons they were not able to marry for two-and-a-half years, and remained chaste for all that time.[152] At the start of the twenty-first century there are significant numbers of Christians, including born-again Christians, who are gay, and there are no doubt far more who are sleeping together in unmarried heterosexual relationships. Some of them might find Alpha's hard line on morality a problem.

Notes

1. Sanders 1962: 66.

2. Unless otherwise stated, all quotations are from Matthew F. Smith, information officer for the General Assembly of Unitarian and Free Christian Churches, in correspondence with the author, 13 June and 25 September 1995, and 2 November 1999.

3. Leaflet: *Unitarian Views of Jesus*, ed. Matthew Smith, n.d.

4. Betty Smith, quoted in ibid.

[5]*The Journal of John Wesley*, condensed version, Chicago: Moody Press, n.d.: 309.

[6]Unless otherwise stated, all quotations are from the Reverend Ian Johnson, Minister of the General Conference of the New Church, in correspondence with the author 24 June and 21 September 1995, and November 1999.

[7]These quotations are taken from the leaflet 'What is the New Church?', n.d.

[8]This widely accepted revivalism has recently been disputed by some historians of religion.

[9]*The Pearl of Great Price*, 'Writings of Joseph Smith', 2:64.

[10] Mormon 9:34.

[11]Letter to E.D. Howe, 17 February 1834, quoted in Martin 1967: 160.

[12]'History of the Church', *Encyclopedia of Mormonism*, Macmillan, 1992: 602.

[13]*History of the Church*, 4:461.

[14]'Spaulding Manuscript', *Encyclopedia of Mormonism*, Macmillan, 1992: 1403.

[15]Unless otherwise stated, all quotations from Bryan J. Grant are from correspondence with the author, 11 July 1995, and 17 June and 22 October 1999.

[16]'Grace', *Encyclopedia of Mormonism*, Macmillan 1992: 560.

[17]'Gospel of Jesus Christ', ibid.. 557.

[18]http://www.familysearch.org.

[19]Booklet: *History, Beliefs, Lifestyle*, 1994.

[20]Booklet: *Temples of the Church of Jesus Christ of Latter-day Saints*: 6.

[21]'Garments', *Encyclopedia of Mormonism*, Macmillan, 1992: 534.

[22]*Doctrine and Covenants*, Section 89.

[23]Unless otherwise stated, all quotations are from the secretary of the Bible and Gospel Trust in correspondence with the author, 23 June and 6 September 1995, 11 November 1999, and 3 March 2000.

[24]Tract: P.S. MacGregor, 'How the Spell was Broken', Hounslow: Bible and Gospel Trust, n.d.

[25]Edward Miller, 'Irvingism: The Catholic Apostolic Church', in *Religious Systems of the World*, 1889/1908: 596, 597.

[26]H.S. Hume, 'Letter to the Flock', 6 February 1901, quoted in Seraphim Newman-Norton, *The Time of Silence: A History of the Catholic Apostolic Church 1901–1971*, Studies in Charismatic Renewal, Privately published, 1974: 7.

[27]Routley 1960: 173.

[28]Raymond A. Thomas, Office Manager of the New Apostolic Church in the UK, in correspondence with the author, 15 August 1996.

[29]Pamphlet: *Adventists: A Caring, Sharing Church World-Wide*, 1995: 4.

[30]Mike Stickland, *An Inside Look at Seventh-day Adventists*, n.d.: 8–10.

[31]Ibid.: 31.

[32]*Seventh-day Adventists Believe...*, 1988: iv.

[33]*Questions on Doctrine*, 1957: 197.

[34]Ibid.: 193. (See also page 126.)

[35]*Seventh-day Adventists Believe...*, 1988: 46–7.

36*Adventists*: 14.

37John C. Surridge, Communication Director, Seventh-day Adventist Church, in correspondence with the author, 15 November 1999.

38Unless otherwise stated, quotations are from Michael Ashton in correspondence with the author, 28 April 1995 and 27 October 1999. All other quotations are taken from booklets from Christadelphian Publications, Birmingham, UK, undated.

39Fred Pearce, *Who are the Christadelphians?*: 8.

40Fred Pearce, *Jesus: God the Son or Son of God?*: 2.

41Ibid.: 12.

42Fred Pearce, *Who are the Christadelphians?*: 8.

43Fred Pearce, *Jesus: God the Son or Son of God?*: 13.

44Harry Tennant, *The Holy Spirit*: 3.

45Fred Pearce, *Who are the Christadelphians?*: 9.

46Harry Tennant, *Back to the Bible*, n.d.: 49.

47Ibid.: 42.

48*Ambassador of the Coming Age*, 1866: 2.

49Quotations from David Vaughan, of the Christian Science Committee on Publication, are from correspondence with the author, 11 January 2000.

50Mary Baker Eddy, *Miscellaneous Writings*, 1897, chapter 2: 24.

51Eddy 1906: 107.

52Quotations from Alan Grayson, then District Manager of the Christian Science Committees on Publication for Great Britain and Ireland, are from correspondence with the author, 2 March 1995, and a meeting with the author on 28 June 1995; Grayson died in January 1999.

53Gillian Gill, *Mary Baker Eddy*, Persus Books, 1998: 658.

54Eddy 1906: 110.

55*Christian Science Journal*, January 1901.

55AQuoted in Sanders 1962: 43.

56*Christian Science Journal*, March 1897.

57Media Guide to Christian Science, 1993: 2.

58*The Christian Science Watchman*, vol. 4, no. 5.

59Mary Baker Eddy, *The First Church of Christ, Scientist and Miscellany*: 347.

60Quoted in Robert Peel, *Mary Baker Eddy: The Years of Authority*, New York: Holt, Rinehart & Winston, 1977: 228.

61Eddy 1875: 497.

62Mary Baker Eddy, *Church Manual*, 1895: 17.

63Eddy 1875: 45.

64Ibid.: 470, 472.

65*Media Guide to Christian Science*, 1993: 19.

66Eddy 1875: 1.

67 *Media Guide to Christian Science*, 1993: 16.

[68] *Facts about Christian Science*, 1959: 6.

[69] *A Century of Christian Science Healing*, 1966: viii.

[70] Mary Baker Eddy, *Rudimental Divine Science*: 2.

[71] *Facts about Christian Science*, 1959: 19.

[72] Ibid.: 20.

[73] Eddy 1875: 473.

[74] *How Prayer Can Help You*, 1956: 7.

[75] Booklet: *Jehovah's Witnesses in the Twentieth Century*, 1979, 1989: 15.

[76] Ibid.: 3.

[77] *Jehovah's Witnesses: Proclaimers of God's Kingdom*, 1993: 609.

[78] 'The Nature of God' in Rowley, 1956: 53.

[79] For detailed discussion of the names of God, see Harris 1988: 54–72, 246–7; Rowley 1956: 53, footnote 2; and G.T. Manley, 'God, Names of' in J.D. Douglas (ed.), *The New Bible Dictionary*, London: Inter-Varsity Fellowship, 1962: 477–80.

[80] Booklet: *Jehovah's Witnesses in the Twentieth Century*, 1979, 1989: 13.

[81] Ibid.. 10.

[82] J.F. Rutherford, *Deliverance*: 222.

[83] *The Watch Tower*, 15 September 1910.

[84] Quoted in Harris 1988: 143–4.

[85] *Jehovah's Witnesses in the Twentieth Century*, 1989: 7.

[86] *Awake!* 22 March 1993: 4.

[87] 'Elders: Readjust Others in a Spirit of Mildness', *The Watchtower*, 15 November 1992: 26–9.

[88] *Awake!*, 22 June 1995: 8.

[89] Ibid.: 9.

[90] Ibid.: 11–12.

[91] Cozens 1928, 1974: 93.

[92] Ibid.: 94.

[93] Taylor 1987: 5.

[94] Ibid.: 7.

[95] This and the following quotations are from *The Liberal Catholic Church: Statement of Principles and Summary of Doctrine*, 1986: 5, 7, 9, 8.

[96] Danny O'Sullivan, 'Bishops on the Loose', *Magonia*, no. 65, November 1998: 12.

[97] Ibid.: 12.

[98] N.C. Thomas, General Secretary of the Anthroposophical Society in Great Britain, in correspondence with the author, 26 October 1999.

[99] Ibid.

[100] Steiner 1965: 5.

[101] Madsen 1995: 37.

[102]Ibid.: 34.

[103]Ibid.: 19.

[104] Ibid.: 35.

[105]Andrew Soane, Director of the Information Office of the Opus Dei Prelature in Britain, in correspondence with the author, 8 November 1999 and 24 March 2000.

[106]Leaflet: *Questions People Ask About Opus Dei*, London: Opus Dei Information Office, n.d.

[107]Ibid.

[108]Coverdale 1994: 63.

[109]Statement by Cardinal Basil Hume: 'Guidelines for "Opus Dei" in Westminster Diocese', 2 December 1981.

[110] See Urquhart 1995 for a detailed examination of these.

[110A]Unless otherwise stated, all quotations are from George Robertson, spokesman for the Unification Church in the UK, in conversation with the author, 23 June 1995.

[111]*The Divine Principle Home Study Course #1: The Principle of Creation*: vii.

[112]*Divine Principle*: 16.

[113]*Toward the Ideal: An Introduction to the Unification Movement*: 8.

[114]Ibid.: 9.

[115]*The Divine Principle Home Study Course #3: Mission of the Messiah*: 37.

[116]Ibid.: 39.

[117]Press release, 8 February 2000.

[118]Edward Miller, 'Irvingism: The Catholic Apostolic Church', in *Religious Systems of the World*, 1889/1908: 600–1.

[119]Morris Cerullo, *The New Anointing is Here: Handbook for the Harvest*, 1972: 4.

[120]Ibid.: 20.

[121]Newspaper reviewer speaking on *Broadcasting House*, BBC Radio 4, 2 April 2000.

[122]Unless otherwise stated, all quotations are from Rachel Scott, in correspondence with the author, 16 June, 21 September, 27 November and 14 December 1995.

[123]Abi Freeman, Family Information Department, in correspondence with the author, 8 November 1999.

[124]Pamphlet: *Our Family's Origins*, World Services, Zurich, 1992: 1.

[125]Ibid.: 1–2.

[126]Ibid.: 2.

[127]Ibid.: 3.

[128]*Our Statement of Belief*: 5.

[129]See Lewis and Melton, *Sex, Slander, and Salvation*, for considerable detail on this.

[130]Jordan 1996: 56, 57. This book is extremely unusual in that the publisher's name does not appear anywhere in it; the only indication is the ISBN.

[131]From the Judgement of Lord Justice Ward of the High Court in London, 19 October 1995.

[132]Quotations from John Campbell, communications officer for the Jesus Army, are from correspondence with the author, 31 January 1995, 5 June 1998 and 21 October 1999.

[133]Jesus Fellowship Church/Jesus Army information sheet.

[134]Interview on *PM*, BBC Radio 4, 25 September 1995.

[134]Jesus Fellowship Church/Jesus Army information sheet.

[136]*The Tampa Tribune*, 14 January 1989.

[137]Bishop Renato Cardoso, in correspondence with the author, 15 February 2000.

[138]*The Observer*, 3 December 1995.

[139]Unless otherwise stated, all quotations are from John Partington, in correspondence with the author, 9 November 1999.

[140]International Church of Christ website: http://www.icoc.org/html/whoweare/subpages/12.html.

[141]Quoted in 'International Churches of Christ' on the University of Virginia religions website, http://cti.itc.virginia.edu/~jkh8x/soc257/nrms/icc.html.

[142]Horrobin 1998: 71.

[143]Ibid.: 37

[144]Telephone conversation with the author, January 2000.

[145]Source: 'Vineyard Churches' on the University of Virginia religions website, http://cti.itc.virginia.edu/~jkh8x/soc257/nrms/Vineyard.html.

[146]Official Statement of the Toronto Airport Christian Fellowship, 17 March 1999, quoted on the CESNUR website, http://www.cesnur.org/testi/goXgold_01.htm.

[147]This and the following comment quoted on BBC News Online Network, 21 April 1999.

[148]Gumbel 1994: 15.

[149]See *Church Times*, 4 April 1997: 11-30.

[150]Personal conversation with the author.

[151]Booklet: *Alpha: An opportunity to explore the meaning of life.*

[152]Gumbel 1993: 258.

CHAPTER 13

Other 'Religions of the Book' Origins

T HE last section explored some of the huge diversity of movements with Christian origins, several of which would claim to be the only true version of Christianity. The other Religions of the Book, Judaism and particularly Islam, have also spawned numerous offshoots, old and new. This section will look briefly at a few of the new movements.

In some, though by no means all cases, these new religions are as much based on racial and political as on spiritual foundations, the most obvious example being the variety of Black Muslim movements. Unfortunately, despite repeated requests, the Nation of Islam, the Holy Tabernacle Ministries and the Rastafarians did not supply first-hand information about their history, beliefs and practices; unlike the rest of the book, therefore, there are no responses to any comments and criticisms.

The first entry is a world religion with no racial or national focus.

BAHA'I FAITH

In the last 30 years membership of the Bahá'í Faith has grown at an astonishing rate. By their own figures, in 1963 worldwide membership was 400,000, living in 11,000 localities, and organized into 56 national and regional communities. By 1994 membership had risen to five million, living in over 120,000 localities, and organized into 165 national communities. There are approximately 6,000 registered Bahá'ís – adults and children – in the UK.

Although this is a relatively new religion, and although it had its origins in Islam, the Bahá'í Faith claims to be no more a Muslim sect than Christianity today is a Jewish sect. It is a new worldwide religion, the next in order after Judaism, Christianity and Islam, worshipping the same one God as they do.

From time to time God sends his prophets or messengers to Earth; these have included Abraham, Krishna, Moses, Zoroaster, Buddha, Jesus, Muhammad – and now two others, the Báb and Bahá'u'lláh. Each has revealed God to the people of a particular time and place. The message of God which Bahá'u'lláh brings is for all the people of the world.

> The summons and message which We gave were never intended to reach or to benefit one land or one people only. Mankind in its entirety must firmly adhere to whatsoever hath been revealed and vouchsafed unto it. Then and only then will it attain unto true liberty. The whole earth is illuminated with the respendent glory of God's Revelation.[1]

HISTORY

The Bahá'í Faith began in Persia, now Iran, when a young Muslim merchant called Mirza Ali Muhammad (1819–1850) began in 1844 to preach that the Day of God was at hand. He proclaimed himself to be the Báb or Gate, and said, like John the Baptist, that he was the forerunner of one greater than himself, who would initiate a new age of peace and justice. Although initially within Islam, the Báb's teachings grew further away from that religion, and in 1848 he formally announced that Bábism was a new religion. He was executed by firing squad in 1850.

There are several versions of the Báb's martyrdom, but Bahá'ís believe that when the smoke cleared, the Báb was found to be back in his cell, unharmed, teaching one of his disciples. Only when he had finished did he say to his guards, 'Now you may proceed to fulfil your intention'; this time the bullets found their mark.

After the death of the Báb one of his closest followers, Mirza Husayn-Ali Nuri (known as Bahá'u'lláh, 'the Glory of God'), who was the son of a wealthy government minister, was arrested and flung into jail. On his release he was banished to Baghdad, then withdrew to the mountains of Kurdistan where he spent two years in solitary contemplation. Returning to Baghdad he took over the leadership of the Báb community, and in 1863 he announced that he was the one whom the Báb had foretold.

Bahá'u'lláh spent much of the rest of his life as a prisoner or in exile in various cities in the Ottoman Empire. From 1868 until his death in 1892 he lived in Acre, in present-day Israel.

He was succeeded by his son, Abdu'l-Bahá (1844–1921) and great-grandson Shoghi Effendi (1897–1957), each of whom played a key role in the development of the Bahá'í Faith.

The Báb wrote a sacred book, *al-Bayan*, and Bahá'u'lláh wrote vast numbers of books and letters including *The Hidden Words*, 'a distillation of the spiritual guidance contained in the successive revelations of God'; the *Kitáb-i-Íqán* or *Book of Certitude*, the principal exposition of his doctrinal message; *The Seven Valleys*, a small mystical work in poetic language, and the *Kitáb-i-Aqdas*, or *The Most Holy Book*, which contains the laws and institutions for the new world order. Unlike the Gospels, Bahá'ís say, these books are first-hand writings by God's messenger, rather than second-hand accounts *about* God's messenger; Bahá'u'lláh's writings are counted as equal to the Bible and the Koran. The original hand-written texts, in Bahá'u'lláh's handwriting, still exist, and are preserved in the International Archives building at the Bahá'í World Centre in Haifa, where they are available for inspection and study.

It is interesting that Bahá'ís claim 1844, the year when the Báb began to preach, as the beginning of their religion. Many millennarian Christians, including the forerunners of the Seventh-day Adventists, foretold the Second Coming for 1844, their calendraic calculations based on a particular interpretation of Biblical prophecies. The Bahá'ís, then, can point to their faith as being in line with Christian prophecy for the return of Christ.

Critics have suggested that the choice of this rather convenient date is somewhat arbitrary; it would be the same as beginning the Christian calendar from when John the Baptist began to preach, rather than from the supposed date of the birth of Christ. The Bahá'ís could have chosen 1817, when Bahá'u'lláh was born, or 1863, when he announced that he was the Promised One, or 1892, when he died; or 1819 or 1850, the years of the birth and death of the Báb. George Ballentyne, of the Bahá'í Publishing Trust, explains:

> The whole point of dating the origin of the new religion from the beginning of the Báb's teaching is in recognizing how he opened a new chapter in the religious history of the human race, showing his teachings to be a definite break with the past, as well as part of the fulfilment of ancient expectations. The revelation is given primacy, rather than the person (which is why the beginning of the Bahá'í era is not dated from the dates of birth or death of any of its central figures).[2]

There was dispute at the very start of the new religion. After the death of the Báb, Bahá'u'lláh's half brother Mirza Yahya was actually the Báb's appointed successor. When persecution of the Báb's followers began, he went into hiding; 'on several occasions he publically disavowed any association with the Báb,' says Ballentyne. In contrast, Bahá'u'lláh 'put himself in the way of harm by pleading the innocence of the martyr-prophet's followers,' and began to attract a following. Two factions developed, the majority accepting Bahá'u'lláh's claim to be the messenger of a new religion, the minority (Azali Babism) following his brother, who saw Babism as a movement within Shi'ite Islam; there are currently only a few thousand members of Azali Babism, living mainly in Iran.

There was also factionalism after Bahá'u'lláh's death, with Abdu'l-Bahá's half-brother Mirza Muhammad Ali claiming to be the legitimate successor.

Bahá'ís often say that unlike every other religion the Bahá'í Faith does not have any offshoots or sects. In fact, there have been several, though the Bahá'í Faith claims that none of them has survived. Dr Stephen Lambden, a leading Bahá'í scholar, does accept that 'Sectarianism has sporadically surfaced though no single group has become a significant threat to the larger community.'[3] Most of them came about, as often happens with new religions, over disputed leadership and contested successions.

The New History Society and the Bahá'í World Union (or the World Union of Universal Religion and Universal Peace), were founded in New York and in Germany respectively, in 1929 and 1930, in each case by close friends of Abdu'l-Bahá, Bahá'u'lláh's son; both were opposed to the rule of Bahá'u'lláh's great-grandson Shoghi Effendi as Guardian of the Faith, claiming among other things that he was turning Bahá'í from a movement into an organization. The Bahá'í Faith took the New History Society to court in an attempt to stop them calling themselves Bahá'ís, but lost the case. There was also the Bahá'í World Federation, founded in 1950 by Amin Effendi, the last surviving grandson of Bahá'u'lláh, which united several dissident groups opposed to the leadership of Shoghi Effendi.

The other secessionist groups were opposed to the changes that happened after Shoghi Effendi's death in 1957. Abdu'l Bahá had stipulated in his will that Shoghi Effendi should succeed him, and become the first Guardian, and that each Guardian should in turn appoint his successor. But Shoghi Effendi instead set up what was to become the Universal House of Justice, a governing council, with an American Bahá'í, Mason Remey, as its president; this first met after Shoghi Effendi died without issue, without naming his successor, and without leaving a will. Remey claimed that this effectively made him the second Guardian, but the other 'Hands of the Cause of God', nine people set up by Shoghi Effendi as spiritual advisors to the movement, did not accept him. Remey moved back to the USA and set up the Mother Bahá'í Council of the Orthodox Bahá'ís of the United States, and later the Orthodox Abha World Faith.

There were Bahá'ís who did accept Remey; after his death in 1974 several other groups were formed with competing 'third Guardians' claiming to have been appointed by Remey; these include the Orthodox Bahá'í Faith under the Regency, and the Remey Society.

Most of these movements, however, have had few members, and Ballentyne is very dismissive of them:

[T]hey are consumed in internecine squabbling over the leadership of a rump of followers. Their very behaviour towards each other exemplifies the destructive force of disunity, the antithesis of everything the Bahá'í Faith stands for.

The position of the main Bahá'í organization is that these groups, simply by being dissident, have gone against the World Order of Bahá'u'lláh and have violated the Covenant; they can no longer be considered anything to do with the Bahá'í Faith and are not, therefore, Bahá'í sects. Ballentyne explains:

What is different about the Bahá'í Faith is that it contains within its authoritative texts a mechanism (for want of a better word) that prevents any such disputes, or any attempt at factionalism from dividing the body of believers, and allowing disunity to sap the strength of the Faith itself. Normally referred to as 'the Covenant', this mechanism depends on the clear delineation of a line of successorship and authority, from Bahá'u'lláh to Abdu'l-Bahá to Shoghi Effendi to the Universal House of Justice... Consideration of the relative merits of alternative claimants to authority do not enter into it.

From an outsider's perspective, such insistence on preventing diversity of opinion – seen also in some other movements such as the Church of Scientology – might appear a little worrying.

BELIEFS AND PRACTICES

Although Lambden points out that this is 'highly generalized', it has been said that Judaism brought knowledge of God's law; Christianity brought grace, salvation, and a relationship with God; Islam brought submission to God's will; while the Bahá'í Faith brings unity of all peoples under God.

> Bahá'ís believe that in every age God sends a Messenger to mankind... Each Messenger builds upon the Messages of Those gone before, leading us to new spiritual heights and bringing social teachings designed for that particular age... Bahá'ís believe that, although the Messengers are all different individuals, it is the same spirit, the spirit of God, which animates them all... We believe that the same spirit which was in all the Messengers is in Bahá'u'lláh.[4]

Bahá'í beliefs about the afterlife are fairly similar to those of Christianity:

> When the human body dies, the soul is freed from ties with the physical body and the surrounding physical world and begins its progress through the spiritual world... Entry into the next life has the potential to bring great joy. Bahá'u'lláh likened death to the process of birth... The physical world provides the matrix for the development of the individual soul. Accordingly, Bahá'ís view life as a sort of workshop, where one can develop and perfect those qualities which will be needed in the next life... In the final analysis, heaven can be seen partly as a state of nearness to God; hell is a state of remoteness from God. Each state follows as a natural consequence of individual efforts, or the lack thereof, to develop spiritually.[5]

For a major world religion the Bahá'í Faith is unusual in having no priesthood and no set liturgy for services. The religion operates a 'grass roots'-up democracy by which representatives are elected at every level from local community to senior world-wide administration, in a process which not only forbids canvassing for votes, but also has no candidates; the electors, at whatever level, vote for anyone they wish 'who can best combine the necessary qualities of unquestioned loyalty, of selfless devotion, of a well-trained mind, of recognized ability and mature experience'.[6] After Shoghi Effendi's death, a new senior governing body, the Universal House of Justice, which is elected by national and local spiritual assemblies, came into operation.

The Bahá'í Faith has grown from nothing in 1863, when Bahá'u'lláh announced that he was the Expected One, to more than five million followers in over 200 countries today – the second most globally widespread religion after Christianity. There are several factors which have contributed to this phenomenal growth.

Much of its appeal to members of the other 'Religions of the Book' – Judaism, Christianity and Islam – is that the Bahá'í Faith is a continuation of the same theme: one God, the Creator, who cares enough for his people that he sends them a messenger. The familiar prophets of each of the religions are accepted and respected by Bahá'ís. For Jews, Bahá'u'lláh is seen as a descendant of Abraham and a fulfilment of Old Testament prophecy: 'And there shall come forth a rod out of the stem of Jesse, and a Branch shall grow out of his roots' (Isaiah 11:1). For Christians, the uniqueness of Jesus as *the* Son of God, and the uniqueness of his sacrifice – 'after he had offered one sacrifice for sins for ever' (Hebrews 10:12) – are necessarily lost, but because the Bahá'ís see Jesus as a prophet rather than as God himself, they can point to Bahá'u'lláh as the promised return of Christ. For Muslims, Bahá'u'lláh could be seen as fulfilling the promise in the Koran for the 'Day of God' and the 'Great Announcement' when God will come down to Earth; in addition, the Báb began his teaching within Islam, saying that he himself was the one promised in the Koran.

Because Bahá'ís accept a number of previous messengers of God, they can say to Hindus that Bahá'u'lláh is the new incarnation of Krishna, the 'Tenth Avatar', while for Buddhists he is the foretold Maitreya, the Buddha of universal fellowship.

There is, then, both a continuity and a familiarity in the Bahá'í Faith for members of many other religions, who might feel that their own religion is not as relevant as it might be in today's world.

The Bahá'í Faith also has an appeal to those interested in New Age ideas:

> The former age was dominated by male characteristics, leading to aggression and obsession with power, but the new age concept is based on a balance of male and female qualities, leading to a more complete and rounded human character and civilization.[7]

The New Age, from the 1960s onwards, has been characterized by seeking after truth, and peace, and the Bahá'í Faith might seem tailor-made:

> Truth is one in all religions, and by means of it the unity of the world can be realized... If only men would search out truth, they would find themselves united.[8]

The democratic nature of the Bahá'í Faith is also appealing. There are no priests or bishops, gurus, imams, ayatollahs or popes. All members are equal, all have a say in every decision at local level, and all can take part in electing their representative at national and international levels. Consultation and group decision-making is paramount in Bahá'í thought.

Bahá'í s are also very strong on the equality of all races, and the equality of the sexes. Women can hold any position in the religion, except membership of the nine-strong Universal House of Justice, the international governing council of the Bahá'í Faith.

Although the Bahá'í Faith has a strong spiritual aspect, it is perhaps at its strongest in the community. Education is very important to Bahá'ís, particularly at local level in Third World countries. Education should be:

> compulsory for all; be based on spiritual principles; be equally available to all children, but if any preference has to be given it is to the female child; and be based on the realization of the absolute oneness of all mankind, to be implemented by the teaching of world citizenship.[9]

Healthy living is important to Bahá'ís; alcohol and drugs are forbidden, smoking is discouraged, and vegetarianism is recommended as being healthier than eating meat, though 'most Bahá'ís today are not vegetarians and are not pressurized to become so,' says Lambden. Traditional family values are also central to Bahá'í teachings; 'Marriage and the family are advocated as the basis of social order,' says Ballentyne.

NATION OF ISLAM

The Nation of Islam is one of the most visible and controversial black religions; it came to public attention with the membership and later the murder of Malcolm X in the 1960s, but its roots go back much further.

HISTORY

The pre-origins of the Nation of Islam (NOI) can be traced back to Timothy Drew, or Noble Drew Ali (1886–1929), who taught that the black races originated in

Morocco, not Ethiopia, as was believed by some American blacks. He set up the Moorish Science Temple of America in 1926, teaching that America's black population can only be united through Islam.

In 1930 W.D. Fard, or Master Fard Muhammad, appeared on the scene in Detroit, claiming to have come from Mecca, and to be the reincarnation of Drew. His actual origins are unknown, and the one known photograph of him suggests that he was white in colour. Fard's mission was to bring freedom, justice and equality for America's blacks, in a world dominated by 'blue-eyed devils'. His message attracted large numbers of followers; Fard's organization was called the Lost-Found Nation of Islam, and included a Temple of Islam and a University of Islam (in fact an elementary and secondary school). Fard taught that blacks were not negroes, but members of the lost tribe of Shabazz; their religion must be Islam, their Holy Book the Koran, and their language Arabic. He gave his followers new names to replace their 'slave names'. The teachings included elements of Freemasonry, with an emphasis on astronomy and mathematics which would become significant later. The militaristic nature of the Nation of Islam was established early on by Fard; those who guarded the members were called the Fruit of Islam.

By 1934 Fard was gone, vanished back to wherever he had appeared from. One of his earliest followers, the Honourable Elijah Muhammad (born Elijah Poole in 1897), moved to Chicago, where he set up a new headquarters in the movement's temple there, quickly becoming established as the leader of the whole movement. He spent 1943–6 in prison for opposing America's war effort, but the movement continued to grow – and to expand dramatically after his release. By the time of his death in 1975 there were 76 temples, and between 50,000 and 100,000 members across the USA.

Elijah Muhammad did much to develop both the creation mythology and the End-Time beliefs of the Nation of Islam. These are hugely complicated, and only a few aspects will be summarized briefly later in this entry.[10]

Malcolm X was born Malcolm Little in 1925. He became a follower of Elijah Muhammad while serving a prison sentence for robbery; from his release in 1952 he became an important and highly visible figure in the Nation of Islam, establishing mosques and helping in the movement's expansion. In 1964 Malcolm X made the pilgrimage (*hajj*) to Mecca, during which, much influenced by the relative unimportance of race compared with religion among mainstream Muslims, he became convinced that the Nation of Islam was heading in the wrong direction, and committed himself to traditional Islam. This did not go down well in the Nation of Islam, and in February 1965 he was murdered; three members of NOI were found guilty of the murder, but there have been persistent (though unsubstantiated) rumours that the US government was also in some way involved.

The murder of Malcolm X following his dispute with NOI was an extreme symptom of underlying problems within the movement. When Elijah Muhammad died in 1975 his son Wallace D. Muhammad completely changed the direction of NOI, dropping much of his father's distinctive theology, and leading the movement into far closer harmony with traditional Islam[11] – indeed, changing its name to the American Muslim Mission. He dropped the racial policies, allowing whites into membership and advocating racial integration rather than black nationalism. In 1985 he disbanded this organization altogether, to allow local centres to be autonomous under imams, rather than led by the Chicago headquarters.

One of Elijah Muhammad's closest lieutenants was former nightclub singer Louis Farrakhan (born Louis Eugene Wolcott in 1933). Farrakhan, like a number of other early NOI members, had been brought up with the teachings of Marcus Garvey (1887–1940) (see page 259), the famous Jamaican advocate of black nationalism, and one of the forerunners of the Rastafarian Movement. Farrakhan was the official spokesman for Elijah Muhammad, and was tipped as his likely successor. Instead, Wallace D. Muhammad was appointed leader and began changing his father's movement; Farrakhan left in 1978, founding his own movement based on Elijah Muhammad's teachings, and taking back the name Nation of Islam when Wallace D. Muhammad dropped it.

Under Farrakhan the NOI became even more militant than before; he imposed a strict dress code for members, and re-formed the Fruit of Islam, NOI's own security force. Farrakhan and the new sharp-suited NOI came to public attention in 1984 when he gave very visible support to the Reverend Jesse Jackson's US presidential campaign.

In 1995 the NOI organized the 'Million Man March' in Washington DC. Although official estimates of the number attending this day of public unity are considerably less than a million, there is no doubt that it was a huge morale raiser and publicity success for the NOI.

In Britain the Nation of Islam, formerly a wholly American phenomenon, started becoming visible towards the end of the 1990s, with members selling their newspaper *The Final Call* in city high streets.

BELIEFS

Outsiders sometimes see the Nation of Islam as primarily a Black Power political movement with some religious trimmings. In religious terms it certainly has little, if anything, in common with Islam itself, but it does have a very distinct, and extremely detailed, theology.

Briefly, as in several other black religious movements, it is believed that the original people of the world were black. In NOI creation mythology, the white races were created by an evil scientist called Yakub, a dissident member of the tribe of Shabbaz and a skilled geneticist – and very much a devil figure. All white people today are therefore seen as children of the devil, 'who allowed his white offspring to rule the black man by means of lies and treachery'.[12] Believing this, it is unsurprising that Farrakhan could not accept the idea of white members of NOI, or of peace and progress through integration.

At the other end of time, NOI's theology is strongly based on Ezekiel's famous vision (Ezekiel 1: 4–28) of the glory of the Lord on the marvellous throne-chariot, known in Hebrew as the *merkabah*. This becomes, in NOI eschatology, the Mother Plane, effectively a massive UFO, which is vital to the ultimate victory of blacks over whites. Whites, Christians, Jews, all seen as oppressors of the black races,

> face ultimate obliteration through the workings of the Mother Plane as a vehicle both of destruction and salvation. In its annihilation of the enemy and its resuscitation of the faithful at the time of Armageddon, the Mother Plane will have fulfilled its true calling.[13]

Consciousness of race is thus at the very heart of the NOI's teaching from one end of time to the other. In a set of 'truths' revealed to Elijah Muhammad by W.D. Fard are the following:

> **8** It is true that the white race (the devils) had its beginnings 6,000 years ago and its time was limited to that period of time (6,000 years).
> **9** It is true that they have lived and ruled the darker people under evil, filth, indecency and deceit...
> **12** It is true that messenger Muhammad is now warning this government that Almighty God Allah has numbered America as being number one on His list for destruction because of the evil done to His people, the Lost-Found members of the original Divine People of the earth, with storms, rain, hail, snow, and earthquakes. These plagues of judgement are now going on over America.[14]

Armageddon is also very real to NOI. Like several other new religions, it borrows from other traditions when it fits in with the rest of the message. When he is seen coming in the clouds of heaven, Jesus 'has got a sword, and it's dripping with blood. No come back to teach nobody. He comes back to judge the wicked.'[15]

And there is no doubt who the wicked are. The Nation of Islam has often been accused of stirring up racial hatred, through its rhetoric, against whites; it has also been accused of being anti-Semitic, though it denies this.

There is also no doubt, however, that movements such as the Nation of Islam have given back pride to an oppressed people, Black Americans. In addition, in keeping with Marcus Garvey's earlier work, the NOI's huge welfare and education effort for Blacks must be noted.

HOLY TABERNACLE
MINISTRIES/
NUBIAN HEBREWS

As with the Nation of Islam, the development of Nubian Hebrew groups is complex and (certainly for outside observers) muddled.

Underlying such groups is the belief that the black races originated in Nubia, 'a region and ancient country of N. Africa extending along both sides of the Nile from Khartoum to Aswan.'[16] Modern Nubia includes the Nubian Desert, part of the Sahara in northeast Sudan between the Nile and the Red Sea. Present-day Nubians or Nubans are the original black inhabitants of central Sudan.

Nubian Hebrews believe that the black races (Nubians) were the original people, right back to Adam and Eve (Hawwah). After the Biblical Flood, Noah became drunk, and his son Ham saw his father's nakedness; Ham called his brothers Shem and Japheth to see, but they looked away while covering their father. Because Ham didn't look away, Noah cursed Ham's son Canaan (Genesis 9: 20–27). According to the Nubian Hebrews, the curse was leprosy; Canaan's skin turned pale, and he became the father of all the white races. Abraham (Ibrahiym), a descendant of Shem, had two sons, Jacob/Israel and Ishmael; the black peoples of today (including those in the USA) are descendants of Ishmael, and therefore Hebrews. The children of Israel were enslaved in Egypt for 430 years, and there was apparently a prophecy that the Ishmaelites would also be 'enslaved in a land not of their own for 400 years'.[17] The curse on Canaan is that 'a slave of slaves shall he be to his brothers'; for Black Americans, with their own history as slaves, the idea that the tables would be turned on the white races had a more than poetic appeal.

The Nubian Islaamic Hebrew Mission was founded in a small apartment building in Brooklyn, New York, in the late 1960s by As Sayyid Al Imaam Isa Al Haadi Al Mahdi (born 1945), apparently the great-grandson and third successor to Muhammed Ahmed Ibn Abdullah (1845–1885), a Sudanese leader believed to be the prophesied Mahdi, the returned Saviour of Islam.

In the 1960s and 1970s the Mission (also known as the Ansaaru Allah Community) published literature setting out its beliefs, which gained popularity across America and the Caribbean, spreading still further in the 1980s. In addition to its own original teachings, the movement uses the Old and New Testaments and the Koran.

The Nubian Islaamic Hebrew Mission appears to have changed its name to the Nuwaubian Moors or United Nuwaubian Nation of Moors, and then to the Holy Tabernacle Ministries (HTM), while its leader As Sayyid Al Imaam Isa Al Haadi Al Mahdi also used the name Ammunubi Rooakhptah *en route* to his present name, Supreme Grandmaster Maku Nayya: Malachi Zodok York-El, or the more common variant, Dr Malachi Z. York.

York's own version of the history (or 'ourstory') of HTM is just as complex. He originally started teaching under the name Imaam Isa in Brooklyn, New York, in 1967, with his mission called Ansaar Pure Sufi. In 1969 'the group metamorphized to the Nubian Islaamic Hebrews' and the following year opened the Pure Sufi Bookstore.

> I began publishing the pamphlets of peace. I wrote, typed, illustrated, reproduced and distributed them almost single handedly. I diligently treaded (*sic*) the streets of New York and the surrounding area as I propagated Sufi Islaam. I was blessed with the 'gift of gab' and combined with a sense of humour and charisma that draws people of all walks of life to me. People began to wonder who this man [was] that spoke so profoundly and so persistently on many subjects which were previously considered unmentionable.[18]

As the movement expanded it changed addresses several times; under its leader's direction it also changed its 'official garb' frequently, to the confusion of its critics in more mainstream Islam, to whom York responded:

> Our children were raised speaking fluent classical Arabic, reading the Qur'aan in Arabic, yet the Qur'aan is a fourteen hundred year old book, and Islam is a fourteen hundred year old religion the way they practised it. And was doing absolutely nothing to change the condition of the Nubian in the Western hemisphere.

Present-day practioners of traditional Islam, he said, had got it wrong:

> with all these teachers and saviours they were still in need of a Right Knowledge a Right Wisdom and a Right Overstanding. It is my job to reform all the false teachings that had been taught to Nubians in the west and restore Islaam to it's (*sic*) pristine purity. It is because of the false teachings of these so-called Arabs who deliberately mistranslated verses of the Qur'aan to confuse non-Arabic speaking Nubians in the west.

In several HTM publications, York provides his own translation of verses from the Koran or the Bible. York's message has developed over the years, and so has his own importance:

> The sun is truly coming out of the east unto the west and those who endure to the end are receiving the crown of life, in The Ancient Mystic Order of Melchizedek; Where this message is coming forth to you in order to restore your identity as Nubians. Behold the 'Sun of Righteousness' stands before you

with the Scroll of Malachi, that rebukes the liars for their transgressions, and who will prepare the way for the Messiah by turning the hearts of the fathers to the sons and the sons to the father, or else I, Malachi, will strike the Earth with utter destruction... You can't be fooled by religious doctrines of any kind. No not now a days! You have your first tool, this Holy Tablet, not someone else's interpretation. Your own scripture that will dispell (*sic*) all the lies causing all falsehood to perish. Making the truth come to light...

The Holy Tablet is a large book containing York's teachings. Among these are details of his origins:

I am a being from the 19th galaxy called ILLYUWN. We have been coming to this planet before it had your life form on it. I manifest into this body to speak through this body. I am an Entity an Etheric being... In order to get here I travelled by one of the smaller passenger crafts called SHAM out of a motherplane called MERKABAH or NIBIRU.[19]

The concept of the motherplane called Merkabah is also to be found in the beliefs of the Nation of Islam. York is highly critical of traditional religion –

Judaism, Christianity and Islaam... It is nothing more than a combination of mythological beliefs combined with paganistic practices... they are all based on man's insecurities and attempts to avoid his responsibility as one of the most intelligent creatures on this planet[20]

– and also of the teachings of other Black Muslim groups such as the Nation of Islam:

No more can these so-called black revolutionists or so-called Africans try to make you think that the Caucasians are the most devious devils... Nubian people tend to point the finger at what they call 'the white man', to gain the ears of deprived Nubians... thus they begin to hate the oppressors... They make up fictitious stories about the origin of the 'white race' and how they all must be the devil, which in turn would make you think that all Nubians are good, and that the only reason why they are not succeeding is because the Caucasians are holding them down... NO ONE WINS THE RACE IN RACISM.[21]

He is attacked with even stronger invective. A group called 'Citizens against Malachi York and the Nuwaubians' (though it gives no further information about itself) criticizes York's teaching that he is a being from another galaxy, incarnated on Earth to bring us right and true knowledge. The criticism is hardly of a high level:

▲ Emanuel Swedenborg (1688–1772), on whose teachings the New Church was founded. *(Reverend Ian Johnson)*

▲ Ellen G. White (1827–1915), one of the main founders of the Seventh-day Adventist Church. *(Stanborough Press Picture Library)*

◄ Mary Baker Eddy (1821–1910), founder of Christian Science. *(First Church of Christ, Scientist)*

▲The dome of the Mother Church, First Church of Christ, Scientist, Boston, Massachusetts, with the smaller original church. *(First Church of Christ, Scientist)*

▼ Magazines of the Jehovah's Witnesses.
(Watchtower Bible and Tract Society of New York, Inc.)

▲ The Temple at Independence, Missouri, of the Reorganized Church of Jesus Christ of Latter-day Saints.

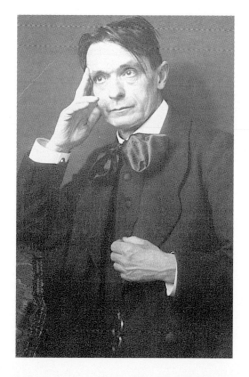

▲ The Temple at Preston, England, of the Church of Jesus Christ of Latter-day Saints.

◀ Rudolf Steiner (1861–1925), founder of Anthroposophy. *(Philosophisch-Anthroposophischer Verlag, Goetheanum)*

▲ 'The True Parents', Reverend Sun Myung Moon (b. 1920) and Mrs Hak Ja Han Moon (b. 1943). *(Family Federation for World Peace & Unification)*

◄ Monsignor Josemaría Escrivá de Balaguer y Albas (1902–1975), founder of Opus Dei, with Pope Paul VI. *(Andrew Soane, Opus Dei)*

▼ David Berg (1919–1994), founder of the Family (formerly the Children of God). *(© 1996 The Family, Zurich, Switzerland. Used by permission.)*

◀ A bronze relief of 'Philosophy' by sculptor Nathan David at the entrance to the School of Practical Philosophy, New York. This shows Marsilio Ficino's description of Philosophy as a Goddess welcoming everyone into the gardens of the Platonic Academy. *(Nathan David & School of Economic Science)*

▲ 'The Maharishi Mahesh Yogi (b. 1911 or 1918), founder of the Transcendental Meditation movement. *(Maharishi Foundation)*

▲ 'Yogic Flying, practised in Transcendental Meditation. (Nigel Kahn, Maharishi Foundation)

▲ 'Osho, formerly Bhagwan Shree Rajneesh (1931–1990), founder of Osho International. *(Osho International)*

▶ 'Their Lordships Sri Sri Radha Gokulananda, Bhaktivedanta Manor, Watford, England. *(ISKCON)*

▼ 'Universal Peace Hall, Mount Abu, Rajasthan, India. *(Brahma Kumaris World Spiritual University)*

▲ ISKCON World Headquarters, Sri Dam
Mayapur, West Bengal, India. *(ISKCON)*

► Avatar Adi Da Samraj (b. Franklin Albert Jones
1939), founder of Adidam. *(Adidam)*

▼ Sho Hondo at the foot of Mount Fuji, the
largest temple in Asia, built by Soka Gakkai for
the priests of Nichiren Shoshu and completely
destroyed by the priests in 1998 after the two
organizations separated. *(SGI UK Archive)*

◄ A Rupa (statue) of Amitabha, the Buddha of the West, at the London Buddhist Centre, England. This is an archetypal Buddha figure which emphasizes meditative absorption, and is associated with Sukhavati, the Land of Bliss. *(Friends of the Western Buddhist Order)*

► Geshe Kelsang Gyatso Rinpoche (b. 1931), founder of New Kadampa Tradition. (Jim Belitha, New Kadampa Tradition)

▼ Kadampa Buddhist Temple, Manjushri Mahayana Buddhist Centre, Ulverston, England. *(New Kadampa Tradition)*

▲ Andrew Cohen (b. 1955), founder of the Impersonal Enlightenment Fellowship. *(Impersonal Enlightenment Fellowship)*

▲ John-Roger (b. Roger Delano Hinkins 1934), founder of the Movement for Spiritual Inner Awareness, and of Insight. *(Mark Lurie, MSIA)*

▲ Peddar Zaskq, spiritual name of Paul Twitchell (?1909–1971), founder of Eckankar, with (clockwise from top left), impressions of Eck Masters Towart Managi (Abyssinia), Rebazar Tarzs (Tibet), Fubbi Quantz (India) and Lai Tsi (China). *(Eckankar)*

▲ Georgei Ivanovitch Gurdjieff (1866–1949), photographed on a trip with his students to Vichy, France, in the year of his death. *(Professor Tilo L.V. Ulbricht, the Gurdjieff Society)*

▲ Muhammad Subuh (1901–1987), founder of Subud, who spontaneously experienced the *latihan* in 1924, later realizing that he could pass this on to others. *(Subud)*

▲ The Maitreya appearing to 6,000 people in Nairobi, Kenya, 11 June 1988. *(Share International)*

▲ Benjamin Creme (b. 1922), artist and proclaimer of the Maitreya. *(Share International)*

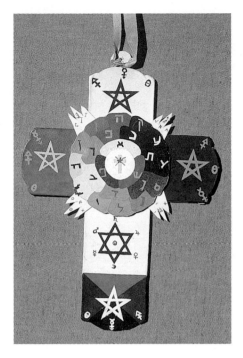

▲ Hermetic Order of the Golden Dawn: William Wynn Westcott's lamen. *(R.A. Gilbert)*

▲ The Kabbalistic Tree of Life, the pillars of Solomon's Temple, and other esoteric symbols. *(Builders of the Adytum)*

▼ Hermetic Order of the Golden Dawn: The Seal of the Second Order, Rosae, Rubeae et Aureae Crucis. *(R.A. Gilbert)*

▲ Dion Fortune (b. Violet Mary Firth, 1890–1946), esoteric author and founder of the Society of the Inner Light. *(Gareth Knight)*

◀ Martin Cecil (1909–1988) and Lloyd Meeker (1907–1954), founders of the Emissaries, photographed May 1950. *(The Emissaries)*

▲ The god Osiris, in an esoteric Egyptian ritual, 'The Judgement of Osiris', held by the Servants of the Light at Denderah, Egypt, 1993. *(Dolores Ashcroft-Nowicki)*

THE ASCENDED MASTER SAINT GERMAIN

▲ Mark L. Prophet (1918–1973) and Elizabeth Clare Prophet (b. 1939), founders of Summit Lighthouse and the Church Universal and Triumphant, with an impression of the Ascended Master Saint-Germain. *(Church Universal and Triumphant)*

◀ Chart of Your Real Self. From the top, the three figures represent the I AM presence, or God; the Holy Christ Self, or Higher Consciousness; and the soul evolving through the four planes of matter. *(Church Universal and Triumphant)*

▼ The Inauguration of Operation Prayer Power, Holdstonedown, England, 30 June 1973. George King (1919–1997) is standing second right of the prayer battery. *(Aetherius Society)*

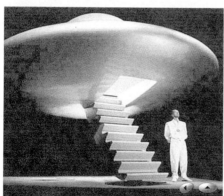

▲ Wiccans of the Alex Saunders coven (*Museum of Witchcraft, Cornwall*)

◄ Raël (b. Claude Vorilhon 1946) standing with a replica of the flying saucer in which he claimed to have travelled to the planet of the Elohim. *(Raelian Movement)*

▼ Eclipse ritual at Men-an-Tol, Cornwall, 11 August 1999. (*Su Jolly*)

▼ L. Ron Hubbard (1911–1986), creator of Dianetics and founder of Scientology. *(Church of Scientology)*

▲ *Astounding Science Fiction* magazine, May 1950, in which L. Ron Hubbard launched Dianetics in a 44-page article. John W. Campbell's two-page editorial, devoted to Hubbard's article, described Dianetics as 'a technique of mental therapy of such power that it will, I know, seem fantastic.' *(Street & Smith Publications; cover artist: Brush)*

▲ Saint Hill Manor, East Grinstead, UK headquarters of Scientology. *(Church of Scientology)*

▲ The legacy of Herbert W. Armstrong: the *Plain Truth* magazine and some of its successors. *(Worldwide Church of God, United Church of God, Global Church of God, Living Church of God, Philadelphia Church of God)*

◀ Herbert W. Armstrong (1892–1986), founder of the Worldwide Church of God. *(Worldwide Church of God)*

He has never incarnated at any time... This man is insane... This is made up by york (*sic*)... RIGHT KNOWLEDGE: Malachi York is DEMON-POSSESSED, not angel-possessed. This accounts for his success in deceiving so many people. He does indeed have a power. This power comes from Satan, not from the righteous God.[22]

The same group issued an open challenge to York to 'admit to being both a great liar and deceiver' if 'before, during or after the year 2003... your so-called spaceships do not come to earth to pick up 144,000 or any number of the nuwaubians'; if the spaceships don't come, they challenge York to commit himself in advance to hand over all his property to their group. If York will not meet their challenge, 'Your refusal shall imply to all the nuwaubians that your teachings are not worth listening to...' – a tactic which is unlikely to be successful.

MESSIAH/H'AL MAHSHIYACH

One of the groups criticizing Malachi Z. York's Holy Tabernacle Ministry, along with some other religious movements, is a small organization called Messiah or H'al mahshiyach, whose output is astonishingly disproportionate to its size.

Messiah's beginnings stem from a 'theophany' which an American Jew now known as Rabbi Ulen Khora had, with his wife, in 1978: 'a conscious one-on-one communication with the Creator, the wonderful loving God.'[23] Khora teamed up with Jeffrey B. Parker, and together they set about their research into the *New Torah*. Twenty-two years on, the two of them have produced around 7,000 pages of material, available on their website.[24]

One of the main revelations of Messiah is that Judaism abandoned its original God, El, for Jahweh. 'El is a wise, loving, wonderful, creative, learning, non-destructive God,' says Khora. Abandoning El was a huge mistake for Judaism – and hence for Christianity and Islam. 'We are how we model ourselves after our God,' says Khora. Jahweh is a God who encourages fighting, wars and destruction; controversially, Khora sees him as 'the epitome of evil – a real power, given energy by believers, and by speaking about him.' Khora and Parker's mission, through Messiah, is to issue 'an open challenge to all religions and belief systems' by spreading the knowledge of the true God, El.

Their website, and their work of the last 22 years, is a painstaking study of the Torah, the Old Testament, word by word, even letter by letter, in its original Hebrew. Each Hebrew letter can be pronounced as a word, and so spelt out, and each letter of that spelling out can then be analysed. 'Every letter opens up,' says Khora. 'It's a wonderful discovery; it's so uplifting. When it opens up it's so mind-expanding; it increases your perception and enhances what you're doing.' He sees this study as deeper and more complex than more traditional Kabbalistic analysis of the Biblical text. A modern equivalent could be the 1990s book *The Bible Code*, which Khora doesn't dismiss entirely: '*The Bible Code* shows that there's something there, but doesn't provide a teaching.' It is also, he says, very dark and negative in its revelations, whereas Messiah's *New Torah* is positive: 'It's methodical, mathematical, rational, not mystical,' he says; 'it all comes out of the language.'

In a phrase, Messiah's teaching is that Love is the answer to all the world's problems.

> The problems that face us today are immense, complex, nevertheless approachable. Resolution of these problems, the achievement of a precise objective, goal or aim, will require the best minds (technical and specialized genius, along with the genius exuding from a supportive population), guided through a spiritual leadership that this organization, Organization Messiah, will provide and mandate by implementation of a comprehensive global system promoting and assuring full planetary restoration. This mandate must and will include the necessary closure on prior and problematic religious understandings and their practices, unfortunate misadventures conclusively replaced by a consistent and constant standard of spirituality, LOVE.
>
> The Messianic Standard is this:
>
> 'LOVE is the highest standard by which everything is to be measured, determined, built, and understood.' Anything less as Spiritual teaching and nurture is inexcusable and frustrates human potentiality and definition, threatens the verity of planetary worth and stability.[25]

Messiah's teaching that 'The religions of this world are Satanic!' will clearly offend believing members of other religions; the relevant chapter of the on-line book looks briefly and critically at Judaism, Christianity, Islam, Buddhism, New Age beliefs, Satanism and occultism, religious racists – 'the Select of God, the Chosen Ones, chosen of a racially preferential God' – and Pluralists, who 'mix and meld together in some universal cauldron all spiritual falsehoods to effectively summon forth a Truth'.

Messiah is unusual in that it used to have members, but disbanded itself as a religious organization in the 1980s in order for its founders to concentrate more fully on their work. They have since re-registered in Illinois as an organization; it appears that when their work is completed around 2002 or 2003, they will set up as a religion again.

RASTAFARIAN MOVEMENT

For many observers, Rastafarianism appears to be more of a lifestyle than a religion: the hair, the music, the ganja. For some who follow the Rastafarian culture, this may indeed be so; but underlying the visible 'trappings' are very distinct religious – and political – beliefs.

Rastafarians are named after Ras Tafari Makonnen, the birth name of the Emperor Haile Selassie of Ethiopia, whom they regard as divine. The pre-origins of the religion can be traced back some years before he became emperor.

The Jamaican-born political activist Marcus Garvey (1887–1940) founded the Back to Africa movement. A powerful campaigner for the dignity and rights of black people in America (he founded the Universal Negro Improvement Association in 1914), he saw Ethiopia as the birthplace of the black races; his aim was to help blacks who were held in captivity in 'Babylon' (i.e. the descendants of slaves in America) to return to their homeland and establish a black-governed country there. In 1927 he prophesied that when a black king was crowned in Africa, this would be a sign that the day of liberation was near.

In 1930 Haile Selassie (1892–1975) succeeded to the throne of Ethiopia on the death of the Empress Zauditu, taking the traditional titles of King of Kings, Lord of Lords, His Imperial Majesty the Conquering Lion of the Tribe of Judah, Elect of God. He was a Christian monarch; Haile Selassie means Power of the Holy Trinity. For those in America who had followed Garvey's teachings, this was the sign they had been looking for. Four Jamaican ministers independently came to this conclusion and began to teach that Selassie was the saviour of the black people; Leonard Howell, Joseph Hibbert, Archibald Dunkley and Robert Hinds can be seen as the true founders of Rastafarianism.

Rastafarians see in Haile Selassie a fulfilment of biblical prophecy – 'He hath on his vesture and on his thigh a name written, King of kings and Lord of lords' (Revelation 19:16) – and believe that he is the incarnation of God (Jah); many Rastafarians put 'Jah' before their name. They believe that black people are the true Hebrews, that white people are inferior to them, that Jamaica is hell and Ethiopia heaven, that Haile Selassie would enable them to return to Ethiopia, and that black people will be the future rulers of the world. Since Selassie's death, some believe that, as God, he is still alive, though not in his physical body; others believe that he is still physically alive.

Selassie is often shown, in poster-sized photographs, sitting on the Lion Throne of Judah; the distinctive Rastafarian dreadlocks, as well as following an Old Testament injunction against cutting the hair, represent the lion's mane. Strict believers emphasize a moral life, and maintain a diet with no pork, shellfish, salt, milk or coffee; medicines are made from natural herbs; their smoking of ganja (marijuana) is seen as a sacrament, a mystical experience. The Rastafarian colours often seen in their head coverings are symbolic: red symbolizes the martyrs in their history, black their skin colour, green natural vegetation, and gold the Jamaican flag.

As with most religions, there are variant beliefs and factions. On Selassie himself, some now see him as more of a human prophet than as divine; they accept Jesus as the Son of God, but in the context of a 'black Christ' rather than the 'white Christ' in whose name so much harm was done to black people. The Twelve Tribes of Israel have developed from this group.

Some Rastafarians still focus on the original idea of repatriation to Africa and the setting up of a black kingdom; others focus more on improving the social conditions of blacks where they currently are, in Jamaica, the USA, Britain or elsewhere (including New Zealand, where Rastafarianism has a certain popularity among Maoris). The two ideals are not mutually incompatible; Marcus Garvey was a social reformer as well as a visionary. For most Rastafarians it is a religion of peace, but there are some who advocate violence. However, the violent image which white society has sometimes formed of Rastafarians over the last couple of decades probably owes more to disaffected Jamaican youth who have adopted the physical appearance of Rastafarianism, rather than to actual believers. Reggae music, popularized by Bob Marley, has become symbolic of both Rastafarian and Jamaican identity. Its popularity among white youth has probably helped to break down some racial barriers, and perhaps to assist in the gradual integration of blacks in predominantly white society.

Unlike followers of the Nation of Islam, some young Rastafarians actively favour closer integration between races, seeing no reason why there shouldn't be white Rastafarians. They see themselves as the true Hebrews, but are not anti-Semitic; as one young Rastafarian said of the tension between black Muslims and Jews, 'Ishmael and Israel were brothers; it's a family squabble, man.'[26]

Notes

[1] *Gleanings from the Writings of Bahá'u'lláh*: 96.

[2] Unless otherwise stated, quotations are from George Ballentyne, of the Bahá'í Publishing Trust, in correspondence with the author, 15 February 2000.

[3] Stephen Lambden, in correspondence with the author, 22 August 1995.

[4] Leaflet: *Bahá'u'lláh: The Promised One*: 2–3.

[5] *The Bahá'ís: A profile of the Bahá'í Faith and its worldwide community*: 35.

[6] Ibid.: 42.

[7] Leaflet: *The New Age*: 2.

[8] Ibid.: 4.

[9] Hugh Adamson, former Secretary General of the National Spiritual Assembly of the Bahá'ís of the United Kingdom, in correspondence with the author, 27 January 1995.

¹⁰Numerous books, both from the Nation of Islam itself, and by scholars, explain the beliefs of the movement in detail. The second half of Michael Lieb's *Children of Ezekiel* focuses particularly on the eschatology of the Nation of Islam; it is one of the main sources for this entry.

¹¹Cf. the 'denominationalization' of the Worldwide Church of God; see Case Study, page 479.

¹²Lieb 1998: 143.

¹³Ibid.: 7.

¹⁴*Muhammad Speaks*, 1 April 1966: 1–2, quoted on University of Virginia Religious Movements Homepage: The Nation of Islam, http://cti.itc.virginia.edu/~jkh8x/soc257/nrms/Nofislam.html.

¹⁵Mattias Gardell, *Countdown to Armageddon*, New York 1995: 131, quoted in Weber 1999: 213.

¹⁶*The New Lexicon Webster's Dictionary of the English Language, Encyclopedic Edition*, New York: Lexicon Publications, 1988 edn: 687.

¹⁷Melton 1993: 892.

¹⁸This and the following quotations are taken from an Internet extract from *The Holy Tablets*, chapter 19: 'Al Khidr, Murdoq Tablet 6-Zodoq:Melchisedek', 1643–8, found at http://www.geocities.com/Area51/Corridor/4978/ourstory.html.

¹⁹Extract from Malachi Z. York, *'Man from Planet Rizq' Study Book One: Supreme Mathematics Class A for the Students of The Holy Tabernacle,*:23, quoted on http://www.geocities.com/Area51/Corridor/4978/york.html.

²⁰HTM leaflet: *Who are the Holy Tabernacle Ministries of the world?*, n.d.

²¹Extract from Malachi Z. York, *Are there Black Devils?*, quoted on http://home.sprynet.com/interserv/mulatto/blkdevil.htm.

²²'The Deception of Malachi York', cumulative website formerly at http://www.geocities.com/Athens/Atlantis/9381/index.htm.

²³Quotations by Rabbi Ulen Khora are from a telephone conversation with the author, 11 January 2000.

²⁴http://www.messiah.org.

²⁵'Declaration', on http://www.messiah.org/p8610.htm

²⁶In conversation with the author at the UK headquarters of the Rastafarian movement, December 1999.

CHAPTER 14

Eastern Movements in the West

ENTION Eastern-inspired new religions, and many people will think of saffron-robed young men and women banging drums and chanting 'Hare Krishna' in the High Street, or the Beatles sitting down with the Maharishi Mahesh Yogi among heaps of flowers. In fact, most of the Eastern religions which were so prominent in the 1970s have changed considerably in the last few years; in some cases the founder has died, and without his presence the followers have reformed themselves in a different style; in other cases the Eastern origins have become all but forgotten. Some of the movements in this section are several decades old; others were founded in the 1980s and 1990s.

This section also examines several movements which are partly esoteric, but which are included here because they are inspired, at least in part, by the East.

THE APPEAL OF THE EAST

What is the appeal of Eastern-inspired religions to Westerners? On the surface, they often involve strict discipline and obedience to a teacher and a tradition, hardship, renouncing everything, completely changing your way of life including your diet, sometimes wearing very noticeable clothing, rising hours before dawn, and meditating or chanting mantras for hours on end.

Perhaps this in itself is the appeal for some of the devotees: the traditional Eastern guru–disciple relationship. They want to give up control of their own lives; they want someone else to tell them what to do, to make decisions for them. There's an element in many people which longs to let go and give it all away; as the world becomes ever more complicated and decisions ever more difficult, it can be a tremendous relief to hand it all over to someone else. There is a parallel in the mundane world: many, on leaving the army, or prison, find it very difficult to adapt to a world where they now have to make all the decisions, where there is no fixed structure for them to live within.

And the discipline, the clothing and the way of life of an initiate in an Eastern religion are actually not too dissimilar to those of monks and nuns through two thousand years of Christian history. When Pope John XXIII's Vatican 2 initiated sweeping changes in the Roman Catholic church, including considerable freedom of choice, many monks and nuns found it difficult to adapt. Some people like to know exactly where they stand; Hare Krishna devotees and Christian monks and nuns alike find peace in submission.

Many would say that it is through this submission that they learn who they really are, or that they come to a realization of the Divine within themselves, and so become fulfilled.

Another factor is the antiquity of the Eastern message. The East is old, and old is original, and original is true. The logical gaps in that sentence are easily ignored. Many members of new religions are searching for Truth with a capital T. They find it in the religions of the East. After all, you can't get much older than Hinduism, and therefore more original, and therefore more true. Holy men traditionally come from the East, and Hinduism has had a lot of holy men in its five-thousand-year history. An elderly man, sitting in the lotus position, draped in a blanket, uttering gnomic statements in an ancient language, must be holy. He has seen through the complexity and falseness of modern life, has found an inner core of stillness deep within himself, and is in tune with God, or the gods, or the immutable laws of the cosmos.

That is, of course, a highly simplistic account of the spiritual fascination of the East for the intelligent Western seeker, but it probably contains an element of truth. Look into the depth of peace in an Eastern guru's eyes; there is something there that many people want. Few Western religions can offer it. For those disenchanted with the faith of their fathers, the apparently deep spirituality of Eastern religions can be very attractive. For people brought up in Western culture, there is something very different about religions with Eastern roots.

The movements in this section come from Hindu, Buddhist and Hindu/Sikh Sant Mat roots. (The entries are in rough chronological order within these three groups.) Some are quite traditional; others are conscious attempts to take the spiritual ideas of the East and adapt them to Western culture; some were founded by Eastern gurus, bringing their beliefs to the West; others are 'home-grown', with British or American founders. As with all new religious movements, it's a mistake to generalize; there is probably more variation between the movements in this section than between those in the Christian section.

BRAHMA KUMARIS

The Brahma Kumaris World Spiritual University (BKWSU) is a meditation movement catering mainly for women – *kumari* means 'unmarried woman'. However, they also offer courses specifically for men, and their founder was a man.

Dada Lekh Raj (1876–1969) is unusual for the founder of an Eastern movement which has spread to the West, in that his name is almost unknown, compared to such gurus as the Maharishi Mahesh Yogi, Osho/Rajneesh, Maharaji, or ISKCON's Prabhupada. Born Lekhraj Khubchand Kirpalani into a poor Indian family, he became a jeweller and eventually a wealthy diamond merchant. A devout Hindu, he had a profound spiritual experience at the age of 60.

> [O]ne day, while in a meditative state, he felt a warm flow of energy surrounding him, filling him with light and exposing him to a series of powerful visions. These visions continued periodically over several months, giving new insights into the innate qualities of the human soul, revealing the mysterious entity of God and explaining the process of world transformation.[1]

His visions appeared to be of heaven, and of hell – or rather, of a human-created hell-on-Earth, with cities which had been destroyed by bombs, and countries destroyed by pollution. He began to hold *satsangs*, religious meetings, under the name Om Mandli (the gathering of Om), which were attended mainly by women. In 1930s Hindu society, women were often treated as property, with no rights, and Dada Lekh Raj felt strongly about their poor conditions.

Within a short time the obvious dedication of the women to the meetings was so strong that Dada Lekh Raj put them in charge of Om Mandli.

> Gradually the mainly young female members of the Mandli felt themselves imbued with unprecedented strength and resolve. They began to be self-determining, to lose their fear and terror of men, and to have genuine self-esteem. In fact, the Om Mandli gave assertiveness and consciousness-raising training to young women long before these concepts even existed in the West.[2]

The women began to replace their brightly coloured clothes, which symbolized their husbands' or fathers' wealth, with simple white cotton robes. They also began to take vows of celibacy. In a society where women had no choice over their marriage, and where their husbands could beat them with impunity, this caused ructions. Amid a flurry of legal action from opponents, Om Mandli moved from Hyderabad to Karachi; here, in 1936, it changed its name, and the Brahma Kumaris World Spiritual University (BKWSU) was established. After the partition of India in 1947 it was decided to move from what was now (Muslim) Pakistan to Mount Abu in Rajasthan, India, in 1951. This is still the headquarters of the movement.

Centres were set up initially in Delhi and Bombay, and the BK movement grew; by the time of Dada Lekh Raj's death in 1969 there were around 250 centres in India. Two women from the original group 30 years before were chosen to be the administrative and spiritual leaders; one of these, Dadi Prakashmani, is still the administrative head of the BKs. The other leader today, responsible for all BK work outside India, is Dadi Janki. The title 'Dadi' means elder sister.

☼

Like most movements which originated in Hinduism, BKs believe in the law of karma, that the eternal soul goes through many births, each life reaping the harvest sown in the previous life. Unlike traditional forms of Hinduism, their teachings come not so much from the ancient scriptures, as from revelations given in trance states. They believe that there is one God, 'seen as eternal, non-physical, non-material and as One, as the Supreme Soul.'[3] Time is cyclical, with each 5,000-year cycle consisting of a perfect Golden Age, a slightly degenerate Silver Age, a decadent Copper Age, and an Iron Age which is characterized by violence, greed and lust; each of these lasts for exactly 1,250 years. Our current Iron Age will shortly come to an end, after which the cycle will begin again, eternally.

When the BKWSU came to Britain in 1974 it was initially known as Raja (meaning Royal) Yoga. For Brahma Kumaris this doesn't involve any of the physical postures and exercises usually associated with yoga; nor does their meditation involve the chanting of mantras. They sit comfortably, eyes open, fixing their attention on the 'third eye' of another person, and focusing their minds on peace and tranquility.

Many of the Brahma Kumari courses are concerned with the practical issues of living in the real world; they offer courses on positive thinking, stress-free living, self-management for improved quality of life, building self-esteem, and so on. Although it is very much a movement run by women for women, men are not ignored; there are courses, for example, on men and spirituality. Brahma Kumaris teach that there are five vices – anger, greed, ego, lust and attachment – and that there are ways of overcoming all of these.

[W]e could, with practice, actually choose not to feel anger. If we felt insulted by something someone had said, that was our problem rather than theirs. We should try to feel nothing but benevolence towards others...

Through regular meditation and turning inwards... we would learn to distinguish and discriminate between good and bad actions in ourselves. We should never judge others, but should always be the harshest critics of ourselves.[4]

One of the primary teachings of the BKWSU is 'When we change, the world changes.' By becoming better people themselves, members aim to make the world a better place. They are involved in education, health, prisons, youth, and other community work. Like several other religious movements, they are linked to United Nations organizations such as UNICEF and UNESCO as Non-Governmental Organizations (NGOs), and, more unusually, they participate in the UN Economic and

Social Council; in 1987 they were given Peace Messenger Awards by the Secretary-General of the UN for their work during the International Year of Peace. In 2000 they took a major part in Manifesto 2000, a UNESCO initiative for a culture of peace in one's personal life and in the world.

For dedicated members, the Brahma Kumaris teach an ascetic lifestyle. Where possible, the women meet at BKWSU centres at 6am to meditate together, they wear white robes to symbolize their purity, and they abstain from meat and sex. Perhaps inevitably, some of the criticisms of the movement come from disgruntled husbands. The very strong emphasis on celibacy, that sex is an expression of body-consciousness and leads to the other 'vices', probably stems in part from the origins of the movement in the social conditions of 1930s India, when women had to submit to their husbands.

BK has a reputation for being a very wealthy religion, drawing its income from its predominantly middle-class members. But a low income is no bar to joining; it makes no charges for any of its retreats or courses.

In 1996 the Brahma Kumaris claimed exactly 467,759 members, or 'regular (daily) students', worldwide, with 452,250 of these in Asia, 5,100 in North and South America, 4,867 in Europe, and 2,000 in the UK.[5]

SCHOOL OF ECONOMIC SCIENCE

The perhaps misleadingly named School of Economic Science (SES) is not a religion *per se*, but at the heart of its teachings is a very distinctive religious philosophy which, although it has both elements of Christianity and some esoteric origins and beliefs, is largely Eastern. The School is included in this book partly because of its spiritual teachings, and partly because it has been branded as a 'cult'; it is a particularly good example of how tabloid sensationalism can create considerable amounts of smoke from not very much fire.

HISTORY

When founded by Andrew MacLaren, the School was for the teaching and study of economic and political theory. MacLaren, who was a Labour MP for most of the years from 1922 to 1945, held deeply rooted beliefs on taxation reform, on the basis of taxing land rather than income. He began the School of Economic Science (SES) in London in 1937. Over the years his son Leon, a barrister who had also tried, unsuccessfully, to enter parliament, took over the running of the school. Andrew MacLaren died in 1975, aged 91. (All further references to MacLaren are to the son.)

Leon MacLaren (1910–1994) shared his father's zeal for social justice, but 'realized that the laws governing human nature needed to be discovered before meaningful change could occur for the well-being of society,' according to David Boddy, spokesman for the School.[6] This led him into a study of philosophy (which literally means 'the love of wisdom'), and this deepened into a search for spiritual wisdom, with study of Plato and his successors, the Bible and Christianity, the wisdom of the great poets such as Shakespeare, and the Upanishads, part of the Hindu scriptures.

Then, as now, the School taught orally in small groups, following the Socratic tradition of dialogue between teacher and students, rather than establishing a set course with a curriculum, textbooks and examinations.

In the 1950s MacLaren joined the Study Society (formerly the Society for the Study of Normal Psychology), which had been founded in London by Dr Francis Roles on the basis of P.D. Ouspensky's teachings (see page 351). Ouspensky and Gurdjieff had taught, along with much else, that the study of religious or esoteric philosophy should be on the basis of a teacher and his disciples. Although MacLaren was a teacher in his own School, he was looking for someone who could effectively become his, and the School's, guru.

In 1960 the Maharishi Mahesh Yogi came to Britain, and members of the Study Society, including MacLaren, went to hear him and were introduced to Transcendental Meditation. Both the Society and the School realized the value of this, and began to teach it. In 1961 MacLaren organized a major meeting for the Maharishi in the Royal Albert Hall.

Dr Roles and other members of the Study Society returned to India with the Maharishi, and there met Sri Shantanand Saraswati, the Shankaracharya of the North in India. Shantanand Saraswati and the Maharishi had been fellow students of the previous Shankaracharya, Guru Dev (1869–1953).

Shankara (sometimes spelt Samkara) was a Hindu philosopher who is generally thought to have lived from 788 to 820 CE, though many scholars place him a century earlier. He was the founder of Advaita Vedanta, one of the most important Hindu philosophical systems.

He established four monasteries – or perhaps four schools of learning – of Advaita in the North, South, East and West of India, in Badrinath, Srngeri, Puri and Dwarka respectively; some believe he established a fifth at Kanchi or Conjeeveram. The schools of thought have been passed on through the centuries by each teacher, or *acharya*, to his successor, up to the present day.

Roles returned from India fired with enthusiasm, and shortly afterwards Leon MacLaren went to India to meet the Shankaracharya. On his return, the Society and the School jointly set up the School of Meditation, specifically to study and teach the principles and practical use of meditation. MacLaren, having found the teacher he was looking for, began to pass on the Shankaracharya's teachings in the SES.

Every two years from 1965 MacLaren went to India to talk with the

Shankaracharya through an interpreter, for a couple of hours a day for a week. The conversations, taped and transcribed, form the material for the senior students at the School, as well as the basis of the more introductory teaching.

Throughout the 1960s and 1970s the School grew steadily, acquiring thousands of students, and through bequests acquiring some very desirable properties, and establishing daughter Schools around England and abroad. There are currently branches in Bath, Colchester, Stourbridge near Birmingham, Leeds, Manchester and Edinburgh, and courses are held in nearly 50 towns and cities. Associated Schools around the world, under a variety of similar names such as School of Philosophy and School of Practical Philosophy, are based in seven European countries, the USA, Canada, Australia, New Zealand, South Africa, Trinidad and Venezuela. These are separately financed and separately governed by their own constitutions, though they are supplied with the Shankaracharya's teachings by the SES. There are currently around 20,000 students worldwide, 4,000 of those in Britain, of whom 750–800 are in London.

Controversy hit the School in 1984, with the publication of a book called *Secret Cult* by Peter Hounam and Andrew Hogg. Hounam and Hogg were journalists on London's right-wing *Evening Standard* newspaper, and according to Boddy their original story in the paper, in 1983, was largely politically motivated. They had discovered that the chairman of the Liberal Party and several Liberal parliamentary candidates were involved with SES, and splashed this in their story, with a lot of pejorative information about the 'cult'. This was on the day before the 1983 general election, which resulted in a landslide victory for the Conservative Party under Margaret Thatcher. What Hounam and Hogg hadn't realized at the time of their original political exposé was that David Boddy (who has now been with SES for 27 years) was, until 1983, Director of Press and Public Relations at the Conservative Party's Central Office, and a close advisor to Margaret Thatcher. 'That really upset them, when they found that out,' he says; 'it blew their whole story.'

Boddy is still angry about Hounam and Hogg's book, and about the 'severe misunderstanding, and in some cases libel and slander' which have occurred since its publication. The book has, however, had one beneficial result. Hounam and Hogg wrote, 'In many ways the SES is its own worst enemy, for without the secrecy that surrounds the cult, there would be no need for an exposé such as this.'[7] Boddy tacitly accepts that they had a point.

In retrospect, we may well have been mistaken in not describing fully enough our activities, the things we stand for and the way we work. This led to the accusation of secrecy... At the time Hounam and Hogg published their book, we took guidance from Shankaracharya. Among the advice given was to examine whether there was a need for change. What was quite clear was the need for new openness.

Part of the problem, he says, is the difficulty of 'explaining subtle and spiritual matters to people whose interest is more centred on materialism and sensationalism.' Any mystical religion or philosophy requires progressive understanding, step by step; but people want to 'know the end of the philosophy without working from the beginning. That is not possible. It is rather like an O-level physics student expecting to sit in on a couple of advanced classes and coming out with a PhD.'

Athough the School also teaches Economics, Art, Music and Languages, among other subjects, it now makes it clear to all students from the first lesson that its principles are based on a particular spiritual philosophy, and its introductory booklet, *The School*, openly states that MacLaren

sought guidance from the Shankaracharya of the North, one of the great spiritual leaders of India and successor to the first Shankara who wrote the famous commentaries on the Gita and other Vedic masterpieces. From the first contact to this day the Shankaracharya has poured wisdom and guidance on the School.[8]

Leon MacLaren died in 1994, aged 84, having appointed 38-year-old Donald Lambie, also a barrister, to succeed him as senior tutor; this succession was approved by the 200-strong Fellowship of senior members of the School.

When the Shankaracharya of the North, Sri Shantanand Saraswati, stepped into an honoured semi-retirement some years ago, appointing his successor, he retained his own existing followers. He died in December 1997, and his successor died shortly afterwards; the new Shankaracharya of the North is Sri Vasudevananda Saraswati. Lambie has already been out to India to meet the new Shankaracharya and learn from him. Boddy notes that the School has a new leader and a new guru at about the same time, and that as both are quite young the relationship between them should provide continuity and stability. Vasudevananda Saraswati, according to Boddy, is following the same course as Shantanand Saraswati; he gives answers that are both philosophical and practical, and relevant to the modern world, 'valuable to everybody'.

BELIEFS AND PRACTICES

The spiritual philosophy underlying the SES stems from a form of mystical Hinduism. The main Hindu scriptures are the Vedas, some 8,000 poems, hymns and stories – 'in a sense, embodying the knowledge of how things work,' says Boddy. Advaita, or Unity, the Shankaracharya's philosophy taught by the SES, comes from the end of the Vedas, hence Vedanta (*anta* meaning 'end'). According to Boddy, though, the Shankaracharya speaks of Advaita Vedanta not in any religious form, but as a philosophy of unity in which all religions can unite. He has stressed the philosophic, as distinct from the religious, nature of Advaita Vedanta. To put it another way, the philosophy of unity is no more Hindu than the teaching of Jesus Christ is Middle Eastern.

The basic belief of Advaita Vedanta can be expressed very simply: the Atman (individual Self) is identical to the Brahman (universal Self) – or, in Christian terms, 'I and my Father are one' (John 10:30).

> The essence of his teaching is that there is a Self in everyone, which is the same Self: Atman, or Param-Atman, or Absolute. The essence of any true religion is its acknowledgement of the God, or the Absolute, or the Atman. Shankaracharya would say that the philosophy transcends any particular or narrow religious view, and is really talking about the nature of the human race and the nature of Creation, and above all, the all-pervasive nature of this consciousness. So if you said to him, 'Are you a Hindu?' he would say, 'No, I am myself.'

The description of the single unified Self or consciousness is best embodied in the Upanishads, which are studied by the School.

> People will come to know the truth about themselves, which is what we mean by 'the Knowledge'; and that truth about themselves is that there is a single Self, and there is an identity between everyone. They will come to it either through their hearts, in a sort of devotional way, or through their minds, or through their actions. The School adopts a composite approach, coming at it differently according to people's natures.

Boddy stresses that neither MacLaren nor the Shankaracharya were anything other than men; MacLaren never even called himself a teacher, while

> the Shankaracharya is the same as you or me, but has developed this clarity of mind and purity of heart which enables him to recognize this true expansiveness of God, or Absolute, whereas you and I probably have further to go.

The School regards the Shankaracharya as 'a Realized Man, of high consciousness'; they follow his teachings because, they say, 'his wisdom, which we've followed, works.'

Like most varieties of Eastern religion, the SES holds the doctrine of reincarnation. 'The way you spend this life is very important as to the way you will spend any future lives. The completion of your journey through humanity would be to reach the supreme unity with God, the actual Realization that you are not different from your Self.'

Unlike some Eastern religions, the School does not teach the unreality of the material world; it does, however, stress the reality of the Self or Absolute, of pure consciousness.

> This consciousness permeates all. The material world is totally supported by pure consciousness, and we teach the value of discriminating the pure consciousness, which does not change, from that which always changes. For example, the human body is born, grows, decays and departs, and throughout this whole process the consciousness remains the same. However, it is very important that people do not negate the value of the material world, but instead come to see it for what it really is, namely a passing show in a glorious play, all within the vision of the Absolute. Shankaracharya encourages full participation in the world whilst continuing to recognize and acknowledge the single consciousness which is not affected by the drama.

Strangely, the School takes no interest in the other three Shankaracharyas, and is unaware of whether they have any Western schools equivalent to the SES. They all teach Advaita philosophy, and the essence of their teaching will be broadly the same, says Boddy, because it comes from the same source, the Shankara, but the style of the teaching may be different. Each Shankaracharya presents the teachings in his own way; the current Shankaracharya of the West, for example, has a great interest in medicine, while the former Shankaracharya of the South was particularly interested in mathematics. But whatever their personal interests, their work is the education of people in Vedanta. Boddy sees no merit in examining and comparing their teachings; once a disciple has chosen a teacher, he should stick with him. 'You find a teacher, you trust that teacher because his wisdom works, and you follow him through. It saves an enormous amount of anxiety.'

The School teaches a variety of ten-week courses beginning each January, May and September. Foundation courses in Philosophy and Economics are taught each term, but the third course varies; recently it has been on Metaphysics, Ethics, Socrates and Plato, Marsilio Ficino, Reason, Aesthetics, Globalization and Education. The Philosophy course aims to be practical, rather than an academic course in philosophy. The introductory booklet, *The School*, states:

> The Philosophy of the School is one of 'Advaita'. That means 'not two, not many' in ancient Sanskrit. The aim is to discover and realize the unity that lies

behind the creation and everyone and everything in it. Understanding this unity releases you from the pressures and stresses of life. Even the memory of it helps. The Self is the same as the unity. The Self does not recognize differences.

The School's doors are open to all, regardless of creed or race. The teaching is based on traditions that have been handed down for thousands of years. Man's search for truth is not new. It is as old as mankind. The quest and the truth are in all of us. Exercises and meditation can help discover your Self.

Who am I? is a profound and effective question. It shows up the limits and limitations which you are not, and leads to the limitless, which you are.[9]

After the introductory Philosophy course, taken by more than 80,000 students over the years, and the following two terms, those who continue at the School normally take a course in meditation, and are encouraged to practise meditation to a simple mantra every morning and evening. 'The process of meditation takes you from an agitated mind to a state of stillness, and that which takes you there is the mantra,' says Boddy. Everyone uses the same mantra, though if anyone comes to the School from Transcendental Meditation, they are allowed to keep their own mantra.

Vegetarianism is encouraged on health grounds: a healthy body, a healthy mind and a healthy spirit. The Shankaracharya's teaching is 'they should eat that which does not produce clouds of heaviness in the mind or body, and they should only eat as much as the body requires.'

This is part of the teaching known in the School as Measure. The same applies to sleep; students are encouraged to get up when they first naturally wake up, rather than drowsing in bed, which is not considered to be healthy.

> Measure simply means knowing when to stop. The idea is that you stop eating before your stomach fills up; that you stop working before the body is exhausted... The idea of measure is to learn to take on some degree of self-discipline so that the body and mind do not get over-used, and so that you can come to rest in the innermost part of your being, which is known as the Self or Absolute. The essence of a measured life is to start each day at rest in meditation, and to bring each day to a conclusion with another period of rest and meditation.

They accept that not everybody can live up to this ideal; although it would be difficult to progress very far in the School's teaching without regular practice of meditation, a few minutes instead of the recommended half hour, or once a day instead of twice, is considered better than none at all. Similarly, vegetarianism is not compulsory; quite a few students have progressed through the School without becoming vegetarians. 'The wise have said, "Don't eat meat," but they're not going to jump up and down with a meat-axe if you do!' says Boddy.

He suggests that it is a fairly typical outsider's misunderstanding of the application of Measure which has led to some of the criticisms of the SES. For example, the School's teaching that most healthy adults do best on around five hours of deep sleep can give rise to the usual anti-cultist accusations of sleep-deprivation.

The accusation in Hounam and Hogg that they discourage the eating of cooked food seems to stem from the fact that at their weekend and week-long residential courses, the meals tend to be bread, cheese, salad and fruit. This, Boddy points out, is simply because it is a lot easier, and cheaper, to prepare this for a hundred people than a four-course banquet would be. Any special dietary requirements for cooked food are provided for.

Hounam and Hogg also accuse the SES of putting pressure on people who have signed up for a course one night a week, to come in on extra nights as 'volunteers' for menial work such as serving coffee and sweeping up the rooms. According to Boddy, it is not a case of pressure, but

> encouragement is given to people to work with and for fellow students, and with and for the communities in which they live, without seeking any personal reward or gain. This aspect of service to fellow human beings is an important one for a man or woman seeking the truth about themseves and their fellow humanity.

In fact, apart from two office staff, all the School's work is done on a voluntary basis, including the teaching, and also including Boddy's work as media spokesman, and Lambie's as senior tutor. 'So far as the tutors are concerned, there is a very important principle here: nobody gets paid for imparting knowledge.' The standard courses are put on in the evenings not just to enable students to attend after work, but also because the tutors all have full-time day jobs, many of them as teachers, doctors or lawyers, or running their own businesses; both teachers and students tend to be professional people. 'In addition, nobody is allowed to profit commercially or financially from any association that they have in the School.'

Most of the tutors teach one night a week, and attend their own group another night; before being invited to be a tutor people have usually been in the organization for 15 to 20 years, and will have contributed to the work of the School in one way or another during those years.

According to Boddy, people give their time to the School because they believe in what it's doing – and on matters like sleep, and vegetarianism, and meditation, if students accept the teachings, they are prepared to accept the changes to their way of life. 'People throughout the ages have always taken to a discipline, to meet this inner development,' he says. 'At the end of the day, people have got to take a look at themselves and ask, "Is my life more fulfilled, is it happier?"'

As well as the adult courses, the SES runs separate junior and secondary schools, the St James Independent Schools for girls and boys. Around half of the 600 pupils come from homes with no connection with the SES, but the parents are now made fully aware of the association of the schools with the School – all the teachers, apart from a few specialists, are SES members. In the past, Boddy admits, this might not always have been made clear. The pupils come from a variety of religious backgrounds, and the schools have a close relationship with the local Anglican Church, where the children worship.

'In many ways St James is very traditional,' says Boddy, 'but in other ways it is highly innovative.' In addition to normal academic courses up to A-level, the schools teach Latin, Greek, Sanskrit, calligraphy and philosophy from a very early age. Each lesson starts and ends with a few moments of silence, to dedicate the lesson to the Absolute and focus the minds of teachers and pupils. From the age of ten, with parental consent, pupils may be taught meditation. There is also a strong emphasis on sport through team games. 'The children are given the finest material to develop body, mind and spirit. They sing, they learn their tables by heart, and they are taught the virtues of politeness, courtesy, truthfulness and honesty.'

These traditional moral values are a feature of the School as well as the schools. The family unit is seen as vitally important to society. Sex outside marriage is regarded as wrong, as is homosexuality. Women members are referred to as 'ladies', and are encouraged to dress decorously, in long skirts. Boddy stresses that this is not a case of treating women as second-class citizens; rather, 'the first responsibility of the men is to regard the lady with great honour and as a Goddess.' Generally, woman is seen as the nourisher, and man as the protector.

> The word 'lady' seems to embody the qualities which Shankaracharya has indicated that we as men should see, to move away from seeing them as sex-objects. There is a tremendous equity between man and woman; and a husband and wife, the two of them together are an individual unit.

But although women are treated with the greatest respect, the School's teaching is the same as St Paul's, that 'the head of every man is Christ, and the head of the woman is the man' (I Corinthians 11:3).

Within the School, slightly more than half the tutors, and around half the students, are women. In the early groups for the first few years, both men and women tutors take mixed-sex groups; the more senior and more specialist groups tend to be single sex, with a tutor of their own sex, though 'of course [they] come together from time to time,' says Boddy. Around 30 per cent of the Fellowship are female.

Both the SES and the children's schools teach the basics of Sanskrit: the concepts, grammar and common terms. Some of the members are able to translate from Sanskrit, and a very few are able to speak the language. The point is that

Sanskrit is one of the oldest languages, and underlies most Western languages. 'It is a fantastic foundation to grammar; if you can crack Sanskrit grammar, which is very simple and very beautiful, you can then move through to Greek, Latin and English with a great deal of facility'; also, it is the language of the Vedas and Upanishads.

The spiritual study in the SES is not restricted to the East. In a recent several-year project, members prepared a new translation from Latin, in five volumes,[10] of the letters of Marsilio Ficino (1433–1499), the founder of Renaissance Neo-Platonism and leader of the Platonic Academy in Florence. Ficino is most significant for his own translations of the works of Plato, Plotinus and Hermes Trismegistus, after whom Hermetic Philosophy, a version of Western esoteric spirituality, is named. Greek scholars of the School are currently working on a new translation of Plato. In 1999 senior students and teachers of the School published a fresh translation of some of the works of Hermes Trismegistus,[11] which were probably penned by a number of Greek and Egyptian esoteric philosophers between 300 BCE and 300 CE.

Unlike the esoteric schools of the Western Mystery Tradition, however, the SES has no interest in 'occult science'. The Shankaracharya, when asked, said that 'those who are interested in self realization don't get diverted by such mystical powers, but keep their attention on discovering the unity of consciousness alone.' Marsilio Ficino and Hermes Trismegistus are studied 'solely for what they have to say – which is a lot – about the philosophy of unity,' Boddy stresses.

The teaching from both Eastern and Western traditions, he says, is because 'if you strip away the coverings you'll come to the same essential truth in them all; and where that essential truth is proclaimed, or thought to be proclaimed, we will go and study it.'

In line with the practical application of philosophy, the teachings are applied to all aspects of life. For example, the School is very keen on the Arts, teaching fine art, music and literature. People have different talents but 'everybody is here to express their full personality and self' – or to learn to be excellent at whatever it is they can be excellent at. The SES organizes the annual Art in Action Festival at Waterperry House in Oxfordshire.

The Shankaracharya puts it like this. You participate completely in your life in the world, with your family, and your job, but you come to an inner stillness which lets you meet your true happiness, and at the same time will allow you to be more efficient and more effective in what it is you do. To play this full role in the world you need to have your intellect fed, your emotions fed, and engage in service.

The 'spiritual career path' in the SES is a case of personal development, rather than attaining knowledge. According to Boddy, students in the SES are encouraged to realize their true natures, and to ask the question 'Who am I?' They are encouraged to connect more fully as their studies progress, with the power of consciousness through attention and efficiency in all actions. They are discouraged from acquiring 'bodies of knowledge'.

As students progress through the School, Boddy says, they don't so much learn deeper truths, as gain a deeper appreciation of the same truth, which they were presented with on the first night.

The SES does not claim to have a monopoly on the truth. 'There are some for whom this is entirely appropriate, and there'll be some for whom another way is entirely appropriate. The important thing is that people go to it in the way which is most natural to them.'

TRANSCENDENTAL MEDITATION

Transcendental Meditation says firmly that it is not a religion, but a scientific technique. It aims to help develop the full potential of the individual. The movement emphasizes that it is practised by people of all religions, and enhances the experience of their own religion. It is included in this section because of its very clear Eastern origins.

The abbreviation TM is used here to mean both the type of meditation and the organization which teaches and promotes it, also called the Maharishi Foundation.

HISTORY

The Maharishi Mahesh Yogi was born Mahesh Prasad Varma (or possibly J.N. Srivastava) in 1911 or 1918; it is traditional for Indian gurus to put their early life behind them as no longer important, which accounts for the common difficulty in pinning down such factual details. He trained as a physicist at Allahabad University, gaining his degree in 1940, then went to study for 13 years under Guru Dev, then the Shankaracharya of the North (see page 267), at Jyotir Monastery, Badarinath. Guru Dev died in 1953, and according to some sources there was a power struggle between two or three of his disciples, including Mahesh, before Sri Shantanand Saraswati became the new Shankaracharya of the North; the TM movement refutes this on the grounds that Mahesh was not a Brahmin by birth, so could not have become Shankaracharya. They also say that he has continued to honour the Shankaracharyas after Guru Dev.

Mahesh went into seclusion for two years before emerging in 1956, then set out on his mission to bring to the world the ancient mystical Hindu techniques of

Transcendental Meditation taught to him by Guru Dev. Taking the title Maharishi (Sanskrit for 'Great Seer'), he established the Spiritual Regeneration Movement in Madras on 1 January 1958, in Los Angeles in 1959, and in Britain in 1960.

At the beginning of 1960 he gave some lectures at Caxton Hall in London. Several members of the Study Society (a Gurdjieff/Ouspensky group), including its leader Dr Francis Roles, and Leon MacLaren of the School of Economic Science, went to hear him and were introduced to TM; both the Society and the School realized its value, and began to teach a version of it. In 1961 MacLaren organized a meeting for the Maharishi in the Albert Hall, and later that year the Society and the School jointly set up the School of Meditation, specifically to study and teach the principles and practical applications of meditation.

It has been suggested that the Maharishi fell out with the School of Meditation soon afterwards, probably because its teaching of TM was 'polluted' by association with GO teachings. According to the TM movement, Roles never completed the teacher training course of TM. They say that 'the techniques involved in the School of Meditation are not the same as Transcendental Meditation, despite some superficial similarities. For example, a vital and distinctive feature about TM is that no attempt is made to control the mind.'[12]

Determined to spread his teachings around the world, the Maharishi started training people to teach the techniques of TM, and set up a number of organizations including the International Meditation Society in 1961, the Students International Meditation Society in 1965, and the Academy of Meditation in Rishikesh, India, in 1966.

In early 1968, through George Harrison's encouragement, the Beatles went to India to sit at the Maharishi's feet, which brought him a vast amount of publicity. Reports that the Beatles also gave the movement a great deal of money have been denied, though the publicity of their brief discipleship certainly brought large numbers of recruits to TM, along with their fees.

The Maharishi International University was established in Iowa in 1971, followed by what is now the International Association for the Advancement of the Science of Creative Intelligence. In 1972 the Maharishi announced his World Plan, to create one teaching centre per million people in the world, with the eventual target of one TM teacher per thousand people in the world. In 1976 he began teaching the TM-Sidhi Programme, which included Yogic Flying, and the idea of simultaneous meditation by many people beneficially affecting the world.

For some years TM was taught in schools and colleges in the USA, until this was challenged by Evangelical Christians who saw in it the insidious encroachment of Hinduism. Court cases in 1977 and 1979 ruled that TM was in fact a religious activity, which meant that under the American Constitution it could not be taught in State schools. Although the TM organization disagreed with the ruling, they gave up the legal battle for the time being.

Even with these problems, nearly a million people had taken the basic TM course by 1980 – one of the most impressive results of any new religious movement. The figure today, say TM, is around four million. In Britain 180,000 people have learned TM, 3,000 of those going on to the TM-Sidhi programme.

In 1982 TM set up the Maharishi University of Natural Law at Mentmore Towers in Buckinghamshire, which it had bought in 1978 for its UK headquarters. In 1985 the movement started promoting Ayur-Veda, an ancient Indian method of natural medicine. Then came the Maharishi's World Plan for Perfect Health in 1985, and Maharishi's Programme to Create World Peace in 1986. In 1980 TM established an Ideal Village in Skelmersdale, Lancashire, with a Golden Dome, completed in 1988, in which members meditate morning and evening.

The title of the TM organization, from 1994 the Maharishi Foundation, was formerly the World Government of the Age of Enlightenment. Although this 'never aspired to political government,' according to Kahn – 'its sovereignty is in the domain of consciousness, which is the unseen governor of life everywhere' – it had established ten government ministers, in charge of the Ministry for the Development of Consciousness, the Ministry of Cultural Integrity, the Ministry of Celebrations and Fulfilment, the Ministry of All Possibilities, and six others. According to Kahn in 2000, 'its concepts and positions are not being used any more.'

The 1990s saw a move into British politics with the Natural Law Party, which puts up candidates in local, parliamentary and European elections. Unlike the World Government, the Natural Law Party's political manifestos clearly speak of it becoming the government of Britain and implementing a wide range of political policies. Kahn stresses that the Natural Law Party 'is a separate entity from Maharishi Foundation... legally and organizationally the two organizations are separate.'

A plan to purchase the 1,000-acre former US air base at Bentwaters in Suffolk for a full-scale University of Natural Law offering accredited degree courses to 4,000 students, fell through in 1995. In 1999 TM sold Mentmore Towers, and moved the headquarters of the Maharishi Foundation to Roydon Hall, near Tonbridge, Kent, which it has owned since 1974. According to Kahn, the move was to enable them to start putting a new programme into operation, with purpose-built premises designed on the principles of Maharishi Sthapatya Veda, a style of architecture developed by the Maharishi to take account of, among other things, the physical orientation of buildings.

BELIEFS AND PRACTICES

Transcendental Meditation is described as 'a technology of consciousness' and 'the Science of Creative Intelligence', with the aim of developing the full potential of the individual. It is both a psychological and a spiritual process; it fulfils some of the same self-improvement functions as certain religious, semi-religious and personal development movements, and its techniques, or something like them, are used in several other movements. But Kahn comments:

> Although some elements of the technique (of Transcendental Meditation) can be found in other practices (for example, some other techniques also use a mantra), the practice of Transcendental Meditation remains unique. Any extra element that might be added would automatically interfere with the naturalness and effortlessness of Transcendental Meditation and would compromise its effectiveness. Transcendental Meditation is taught only by instructors trained by Maharishi.

After basic training, costing £490, people are given a mantra, which is claimed to be specially chosen for each individual; ex-members say, however, that the mantra is selected on the basis of sex and age from a list of only around 16 mantras altogether. Those who wish can go on to study more advanced techniques, including Yogic Flying. Other programmes include different areas of Vedic Science such as 'Maharishi Sthapatya-Veda, the science of Vedic architecture and town and home planning in accord with Natural Law; Maharishi Gandharva-Veda, the science of creating balance in individual and collective consciousness through music; Maharishi Jyotish, the Vedic Science of astrological prediction; and Yagya, the programmes for removal of obstacles resulting from cosmic influences.'

Every morning and evening users of TM meditate for 20 minutes. There are three major differences from most forms of meditation with mantras. First, the TM mantra has no meaning (in Eckankar, for example, the mantra 'HU' is supposed to be a sacred name of God); it is the sound itself which is sacred. Second, it isn't chanted, either aloud or mentally; instead, the meditator thinks the sound. Third, says Kahn, 'the technique of TM is completely natural and effortless, involving no concentration or effort, and also not involving 'thinking about' something, as is found in contemplation techniques.'

The TM movement makes tremendous claims for the benefits of TM. It brings you in touch with your own inner Self; regular use increases your creative intelligence; you will be healthier in mind and body, and will live longer. The organization quotes figures which indicate that TM practitioners spend less time in hospital, have a much lower incidence of heart disease, are more resistant to infections, and are less likely to suffer mental illness. Critics argue, first, that any form of meditation, or yoga, or conscious relaxation, has similar beneficial effects; and second, that TM's figures are not statistically sound for various reasons, including the way that the non-TM control groups are selected. The movement strongly disagrees with this, citing:

> over 500 scientific research studies conducted on Transcendental Meditation, of which nearly 200 have been published in independent, peer-reviewed scientific

or professional journals... The benefits of TM, backed by that huge weight of scientific research, are not merely matters of opinion. They are established scientific facts... All the authors of studies on Transcendental Meditation took pains to ensure that their research did not suffer from bias.

The other major claim of TM is rather more startling. If a large group of people are practising TM at the same time, it will have a peaceful effect on the immediate area. So, for example, they claim that as a result of the practice of TM and Yogic Flying in the Golden Dome in Skelmersdale, reported crime in nearby Merseyside reduced by 60 per cent between 1987 and 1992 – relative to national crime trends, a phrase it is easy to miss; on questioning, they say that crime went down by 15 per cent in Merseyside while increasing by 45 per cent nationwide. The reduction occurred, they say, because in March 1988 'participation in the Transcendental Meditation and TM-Sidhi programme passed the critical threshold of the square root of one per cent of the population.'[13]

So for a population of one million, 100 people practising TM and Yogic Flying together in a group will have a noticeable effect; for ten million it's 316, while for the 56 million in the UK you would need 748 meditators. Less than ten times that, 7,000 people meditating together are enough to cause significant changes for the entire population of the world. TM claim that this was done in 1983 and 1984, and that crime, accidents and illnesses worldwide were reduced for a three-week period. On several occasions TM claim to have reduced international tension.

There are now over 40 research studies on the effects of TM on society, several of them published in important peer-reviewed scientific journals. One study, published in the international *Journal of Conflict Resolution* in 1987, showed reduced war intensity in Lebanon and improved quality of life in Israel. The study on Merseyside crime was published in 1996 in the British journal *Psychology, Crime and Law*. Most recently, a study was published in 1999 in *Social Indicators Research* showing dramatic (more than 20 per cent) reductions in violent crime in Washington DC over an eight-week period in 1993 when a specially convened group of 4,000 Yogic Fliers were in the city.

Figures supplied by Merseyside Police, however, do not seem to support TM claims. Figures were not made available for 1987 and 1988, but total recorded crime in the whole Merseyside area in fact rose year by year between 1989 and 1992. Recorded crimes did reduce in 1993 and again in 1994, perhaps due to 'many policing initiatives which have all helped to either prevent or detect crime.' Unfortunately this does not seem to be a continuing trend. 'Regrettably there has been a recent increase in crime on Merseyside; the reasons for this are complex and numerous.'[14]

Guy Hatchard, author of the TM study on crime reduction, however, insists that the statistics 'substantiate a sustained fall in Merseyside crime when compared to national crime trends between 1988 and 1993.'[15]

Even if there was a reduction in crime, can TM claim the credit? 'My study carefully examined nine other possible causes of reduced crime and found no evidence that they had had any significant impact on crime. These included economic factors, population movements and police practice,' says Hatchard. His study used 'Time Series Analysis – the most sophisticated statistical technique available to analyse complex social data. Using this technique our conclusion that reduced crime was due to Transcendental Meditation participation was found to be accurate to 9,996 parts in 10,000.'

It is not known how localized the effects are, or how much they are dissipated by distance, though Hatchard adds, 'My study also examined crime trends in Skelmersdale and found a consistent trend of falling crime relative to other police districts in Lancashire very comparable to that reported in Merseyside.'

It would be interesting to know whether there have been any 'blind' tests of the claims of TM, designed and analysed by non-TM statisticians.

Also controversial is another aspect of the TM-Sidhi Programme, started in 1976: Yogic Flying. Early photographs showing smiling young people sitting cross-legged in mid-air didn't show the mattress 12 inches beneath their knees, but in recent years there have been Yogic Flying competitions open to the press. In physical terms, Yogic Flying is usually accomplished by sitting cross-legged, and first rocking, and then bouncing, until one is able to bounce a foot or more into the air. To the outsider it might appear ludicrous, and a far way from true levitation; but TM say it is the moment of maximum spiritual awareness.

> Yogic Flying is accomplished by first bringing the mind to a state of restful alertness through the practice of Transcendental Meditation. Yogic Flying is a phenomenon created by a specific thought projected from Transcendental Consciousness, the Unified Field of Natural Law, the field of all possibilities. Yogic Flying demonstrates perfect mind-body co-ordination and is correlated with maximun coherence, indicating maximum orderliness and integration of brain functioning, as has been measured by EEG research. Even in the first stage of Yogic Flying, where the body lifts up in a series of short hops, this practice gives the experience of bubbling bliss for the individual, and it generates coherence, positivity, and harmony for the environment.

The TM organization says that TM isn't a religion; however, there are many aspects of its beliefs and practices which are spiritual. At the *puja* ceremony, for example, when a new member is instructed and given his or her mantra, the Maharishi's spiritual lineage back through Guru Dev is recited, there is a typical Hindu offering of fruit and flowers, and a song of gratitude to Guru Dev is sung. The TM movement, however, stresses that this is not a religious ceremony.

TM, the World Plan, and the Natural Law Party are inextricably linked. The basis and the ideals of the Natural Law Party are clearly spiritual:

> Natural Law is the intelligence and infinite organizing power that silently maintains and guides the evolution of everything in the universe.
> ...a new principle... by which human life can be raised to the same level of perfection with which Natural Law eternally governs the entire universe.[16]

TM itself might not be a religion, but such spiritually cosmological principles behind a political party very clearly underlie the basis of all religion – though Kahn sees it differently. The Natural Law Party, he says,

> was founded to bring the light of science into politics. It offers conflict-free politics and problem-free government. It is the only party offering programmes that are scientifically proven (other parties offer something that they *think* and *hope* will work), and it is the only party to put man and his happiness at the centre of politics.

There is some concern among non-members about the political aspirations of the TM movement; history suggests, they point out, that however laudable their aims, and however godly their religion, we should beware of theocratic governments. Any religious movement hopes to improve society in one way or another; but the Natural Law Party, in addition to:

> Stimulating the economy and eliminating unemployment... Lower taxation for all... Creating a healthy nation... Energy and environment creating a pollution-free nation,

and other inarguably attractive manifesto headings, also promises:

> We will educate the population in Natural Law...
> The first action of the Natural Law Party will be to implement programmes to eliminate negativity in collective consciousness.[17]

ISKCON

ISKCON, the International Society for Krishna Consciousness, is better known as the Hare Krishna movement; the popular image of the movement is of groups of young people dressed in saffron robes, dancing in the streets, playing cymbals, and chanting 'Hare Krishna, Hare Krishna, Krishna Krishna, Hare Hare; Hare Rama, Hare Rama, Rama Rama, Hare Hare.' After the death of its founder in 1977 the organization went through several years of turmoil, from which it now appears to have emerged.

HISTORY

ISKCON was founded by A.C. Bhaktivedanta Swami Prabhupada (1896–1977), who was born Abhay Charan De, in Calcutta. He became a follower of the Gaudiya Mission, a Hindu revivalist group, and in 1933 was charged by the leader Bhakti Siddhanta to take Krishna Consciousness to the West. He spent the next 30 years working as a sales executive for a pharmaceutical company, and translating Hindu scriptures into English; the movement uses his translation of the *Bhagavad-Gita*, with his commentary, believing all other translations to be badly flawed, 'motivated', while his is pure. He became a sannyasin in 1959, renouncing his earlier life, possessions and family for his new spiritual life. For various reasons, including immigration laws and lack of funding, he was unable to go to America until 1965; when he did, with his robe and sandals, begging bowl, and little else, he quickly found acceptance among the hippies of the Bowery district of New York, and shortly after in the Haight-Ashbury district of San Francisco. He founded ISKCON in 1966.

In 1968 six American ISKCON members came to Britain, and the following year, fresh from the Maharishi Mahesh Yogi's Transcendental Meditation, the Beatles' lead guitarist George Harrison helped in the recording of the song 'Hare Krishna Mantra', based on the Hare Krishna chant; performed by Radha Krishna Temple, the American 'missionaries', and reaching Number 12 in the charts in October that year, the song brought the fledgling movement tremendous publicity. Harrison bought a country mansion in Letchmore Heath, Hertfordshire for the movement's use, and later sold it to them for a token £1; Bhaktivedanta Manor is still the UK headquarters of ISKCON.

Over the next few years the movement spread rapidly, in America, England, and elsewhere. At that time it particularly attracted ex-hippies, ex-dropouts, and ex-drug-takers, all of whom seemed to find fulfilment in the vastly different lifestyle. Bhativedanta Manor, meanwhile, became both a Hindu temple and a theological college, training priests in the movement.

Before his death, at the age of 82, Prabhupada set up the international Governing Body Commission (GBC) to run ISKCON; the idea was that there would be no one successor stepping into his shoes. It had 29 members, 11 of whom were gurus, with both spiritual and administrative control over different territorial zones around the world. The gurus were all sannyasin, who had taken final and irrevocable vows of chastity and renunciation. They were able to initiate new disciples on Prabhupada's behalf, effectively acting as him; very quickly they became higher in status and authority than the other members of the GBC.

'That was really an error, to do that,' says Bhagavat Dharma, former Communications Manager for ISKCON in the UK.[18] 'Looking back, we can see now that Prabhupada wanted the governing body to have authority, without anyone above them.' But instead, the gurus had absolute power.

At one point there was nearly a 90 per cent failure rate of those who had taken sannyasa vows.

'The gurus found themselves in impossible situations, really; they had thousands of disciples; the elevation they received in some cases went to their heads. They were unable to carry the responsibility that Prabhupada carried, basically. Some of them deviated, in various different ways.'

A German devotee, Hansadutta, began stockpiling guns, in Berkeley, California; in 1980 he started shooting out the windows of liquor stores. 'This got him, and the movement, into an awful lot of trouble. He was the first one to really go off the rails. According to our scriptures, the guru should be worshipped as being as good as God, and here was this man breaking the law. No one really knew what to do, so we just patched it up.'

In 1982 the guru for England, Jayatirtha (originally named James Immel), began taking LSD and having sex with some of his female disciples – both strictly forbidden for any devotee, let alone a guru. His dancing was particularly ecstatic, and for a long time his followers believed him to be tremendously spiritual. He left ISKCON, taking some of his followers with him. In 1987 he was killed by one of his devotees, who was psychologically disturbed.

Jayatirtha's successor as guru in Britain, Bhagavan, had been a very early follower of Prabhupada. He had previously been in charge of central and southern Europe, particularly Italy, and had been extremely successful; he was apparently very intelligent, and an extremely good organizer and manager, and printed and distributed millions of Prabhupada's books. After Jayatirtha's downfall in 1982, Bhagavan was asked to take over Britain and South Africa. A lot of the older devotees didn't like his style, which tended to be autocratic, and left to go to the USA. Under Jayatirtha and especially under Bhagavan, some 30 million books were distributed in Britain alone.

Bhagavan also fell from the straight and narrow; he began having an affair with his secretary which, for a sanyassin, was not acceptable behaviour. When this was discovered, the two of them left the movement, in 1986.

'It was too much for one man, what he was trying to do,' says Bhagavat Dharma. The same applies to the others who went awry, he says.

'In one sense it was the system rather than the individuals. Of course you can't condone criminal activities, but the sexual relationships, the drug-taking – the system put too great demands on individuals.'

Ravindra Svarupa, who joined ISKCON in 1971, and is now both a guru and current chairman of the executive committe of ISKCON's international GBC, puts the blame on the immaturity of both the individuals and the organization.

[Prabhupada's] early followers were young, immature, untrained and inexperienced. Many of them had suffered mental, moral and spiritual disorders as a result of their sojourn in the counterculture... The movement's early explosive growth created a further problem. New people, without much material or spiritual maturity or even training, had to assume positions of leadership and responsibility.[19]

Within ten years of Prabhupada's death, six of the original 11 gurus (including both gurus responsible for Britain) had left or been expelled.

ISKCON has had to do a lot of soul-searching in recent years. 'We're going through the process of admitting to ourselves that we've made mistakes,' says Bhagavat Dharma. Since 1984 a 'reform movement' within the organization has been analysing what went wrong and finding ways to stop it happening again.

The basic problem was that:

the conception of guru was implicitly based on a traditional model of an inspired, charismatic spiritual autocrat, an absolutely and autonomously decisive authority, around whom an institution takes shape as the natural extension and embodiment of his charisma.[20]

How could this be squared with a modern committee-led management structure?

Members saw the guru more as an *acharya* – a pure devotee, God's direct representative, a model to be followed, literally, 'one who teaches by example'. Traditionally, as in the Shankaracharya of the North (see page 267), the acharya was the appointed successor to the originating leader of a movement and his successors; it was a position of great honour, great responsibility and great power. The 11 territorial gurus saw themselves in the same light.

But Prabhupada's intention had been that there should be no spiritual successor to him, no acharya; the gurus should teach, and initiate new devotees, but otherwise should be responsible to the GBC. The reform movement eventually managed to bring this about: the territorial zone system was scrapped, and the number of gurus was increased. There are currently around 70, and devotees anywhere in the world can now choose to be a disciple of any one of them. In the Soho Street temple in London, for example, there are disciples of maybe ten different gurus.

In addition, one senior member of ISKCON is a trained management consultant; his job in the movement is to help them with management techniques.

While all of this internal confusion and reform was going on, ISKCON was facing a quite different problem in the UK. Bhaktivedanta Manor had become a major temple, and Hindus from all over Britain – most of them not ISKCON members – were coming to it for the main spiritual festivals. On two days a year, at the Janmastami festival celebrating Krishna's birth, the roads in the small village would be clogged with cars and coaches bringing thousands of believers, disrupting the lives of local people. ISKCON was eventually able to build a relief road leading directly to the Manor and bypassing the village. Since the road opened in 1996, attendance at the festival has increased from 30,000 to 60,000, and relations with local people have improved markedly.

BELIEFS AND PRACTICES

Unlike some of the other forms of Hinduism, Krishna Consciousness teaches a relationship between individuals and a personal God, Krishna, who was the eighth incarnation or avatar of Vishnu – though ISKCON sees Krishna as the original form of Vishnu. Rama was another avatar of Vishnu – as was the Buddha.

There is Truth in all the great scriptures, but the oldest surviving scripture, the Vedic Hindu *Bhagavad-Gita*, is the literal words of Krishna. This is a small section of the vast *Mahabharata*, and records the conversation between Krishna and a young warrior, Arjuna, just before a major battle 5,000 years ago.

Krishna is regarded as the Supreme Godhead; this is effectively a monotheistic form of Hinduism, known as Vaishnavism. Krishna is all-knowing, eternal, omnipresent, all-powerful, and the sustaining energy of all creation. But he is also personal, rather than unknowable, as the more mystical Hindu movements teach; he cares individually about every *jiva*, every living entity. Unlike the teaching of Shankara, for example, which is that the *atman*, or higher soul of every person is the same, ISKCON teaches that every person is an individual.

The last incarnation, or avatar, of Krishna was as a Bengali saint, Chaitanya Mahaprabhu (1486–1533). There was a long-established tradition of Vaishnavism (worship of Vishnu) in both the north and the south of India; Chaitanya began a reformed branch of this known as Gaudiya Vaishnavism, or Vaishnava Bhakti (loving devotion and complete surrender to Krishna), specifically related to Krishna as a young man. Chaitanya's devotion and worship consisted of singing the names of Krishna, and ecstatic dance; one of several stories of his death is that he danced into the sea and was drowned; another, a little more prosaic, is that he injured his foot dancing, and died of the subsequent infection. ISKCON believe he was absorbed back into the Deity form in the temple.

Bhakti Hinduism has been a widely respected form of the religion since Chaitanya's death. Krishna Consciousness, far from being a new religious movement, is simply a modern version of a 500-year-old tradition, concentrating its attention more on the West than the East.

ISKCON devotees believe that by living a life of deep spirituality they can achieve pure, blissful consciousness in this current life. The ultimate purpose of man, in this or any other world, is serving God – and chanting the Hare Krishna mantra, repeating the names of God, helps them to attain a deep love of God. All the souls in the original spiritual world are in love with Krishna, says Bhagavat Dharma. 'Krishna is eternally enjoying Himself, with His cow-herd boyfriends and His cow-herd girlfriends, in His spiritual world; He is always happy, He is always having fun, in the spiritual world.'

Devotees don't have such an easy time. Those who choose to live in the temples – now a very small minority – chant the Hare Krishna mantra 1,728 times a day – once per bead, for 16 rounds of 108 beads – to purify their consciousness. This is known as *japa*, and takes about two hours a day, first thing in the morning. Prabhupada's guru used to chant 64 rounds; cutting it to 16 was Prabhupada's concession to the West, says Bhagavat Dharma. That is one of the few concessions, however.

At their initiation, when they take their vows, devotees are given Indian names. Their appearance is quite conspicuous. Some shave their heads, though this is no longer very common among those not living in a community, or ashram. All wear the *sikha*, a small plait or pigtail, to show that they are an individual – they haven't shaved *everything* off, as a Buddhist might. They usually wear a *tilaka*, a white stripe of clay from a sacred lake in India, on their forehead, and on seven other points on their body; this is sometimes called 'the footprint of Lord Vishnu', and marks the body as the Temple of God. And they wear a *dhoti*, a robe – saffron for celibate men, white for married men – or saris for women. They see this as spiritual clothing, not as Indian cultural trappings – and in any case, says Bhagavat Dharma, in the spiritual world, people wear *dhotis*; India is the closest to the original spiritual culture.

Those living in an ashram – far fewer than in the 1970s – have to get up at 4am for worship. All members have to give up meat, fish and eggs; alcohol, tobacco, drugs, tea and coffee; gambling, sports, games and novels; and sex except for procreation within marriage – which means only on the two or three days a month when the woman is fertile, and not while she is pregnant or lactating.

'The scriptures teach that the pleasure to be obtained by spiritual activity, compared to the pleasures of the material world, of which sex is the highest pleasure, without a doubt, is like an ocean compared to the water in a calf's footprint,' says Bhagavat Dharma.

☼

It's a demanding lifestyle. Outsiders might wonder why people join. In ISKCON's heyday as a distinctive movement, in the late 1960s and early 1970s, many members were ex-hippies. The new spiritual awareness and identity gained from ISKCON, underlined by the strict asceticism of the lifestyle, came as a welcome clarity after their search for something similar through 'sex and drugs and rock'n'roll'. But it was this very background which contributed to the disastrous events in the years following Prabhupada's death. In his article, Ravindra Svarupa explains:

> The difficulty for ISKCON was exacerbated from the beginning, however, by the marginal social position of most of the early recruits. They were very young and very alienated, and in joining ISKCON they became double dropouts – from mainstream society into the counterculture, from the counterculture into ISKCON.[21]

The public image of ISKCON has modified considerably over the years. Devotees may still sell books on the streets, but they haven't sold records since Jayatirtha's time as UK leader, and much of the fund-raising necessary to support the temples now comes from the Hindu community. The money doesn't only support the temples. ISKCON runs a charity, Food for Life, claimed to be 'the biggest vegetarian free food distribution charity in the world – they give out a meal every two seconds,' according to Shaunaka Rishi Das, editor of the *ISKCON Communications Journal*, an academic-style journal which examines the role of ISKCON today.[22] Food for Life distributes free food wherever there is need: to the homeless in London, to earthquake victims, to war refugees around the world.

Chanting in the streets continues much as it has done, weekly in cities like Manchester and Liverpool, while the Soho Street temple in London still chants on Oxford Street most lunchtimes.

The chanting with drums and cymbals – *sankirtan* – is an essential part of their teaching. As Bhagavat Dharma says:

> Just by chanting the name of God you can realize God; ISKCON is a movement for spreading that teaching. If a person chants sincerely, their heart becomes purified. In this material world we are trying to find enjoyment, just as we see Krishna enjoying himself.

The reason mankind is in such a mess is that 'each one of us trying to be a Lord of the Material World breeds conflict and hypocrisy because of the identification of the *jiva* with something material.' But unlike Buddhism, which seeks to negate such desires, Krishna Consciousness transforms them. 'The only permanent, non-conflicting identity is as a servant of the Living God; the desires become purified, and find an attachment to God.'

Over the last decade the movement has matured and developed; it is now far more orientated towards study than in the past, and the temples aim to educate the devotees about Vaishnavism, rather than simply teach them by rote.

Like many religious movements, ISKCON has been criticized for its treatment of women; but in fact, it was some years ahead of the Church of England in having women priests – another of Prabhupada's few concessions to the West. Some of the temple presidents in Germany and in Northern Ireland, and a vice-president in London, are women, and there is a woman on the international GBC. There are no women gurus yet, but internationally there is now no bar on women taking any priestly or managerial function in ISKCON.

It's difficult to say exactly how many members ISKCON has now. As with many movements, there is a high attrition rate of members – but there are also many still around from 30 years ago, and many others, no longer active members of ISKCON itself, who still keep in touch and attend reunions.

Many members are now in their forties and fifties, living with their families in their own homes as part of the wider community, 'indistinguishable from anyone else,' says Shaunaka Rishi Das. Only about 4 per cent of members now live in temples, and only about 1 per cent live there permanently. In Britain many of the 300 or so devotees living in temples are students doing one-, two- or three-year courses at Bhativedanta Manor.

'The temples are developing an identity as places of community worship and places of education,' he says.

This fits in with other changes in the movement over the last few years. 'People are learning the process of integration, without losing the principles and values that they learned through ISKCON,' says Shaunaka Rishi Das. This integration is with both the wider Hindu community and the outside world. In Britain, he says, 'The second generation of Hindus have been brought up with ISKCON as part of the scene.' Rather than being a very separate and identifiable movement, ISKCON is becoming accepted as part of Hinduism in Britain. The same applies, though sometimes in different ways, in other countries: again, a process of integration into society. ISKCON is also taking part in inter-religious dialogue, and learning to relate better to other religious traditions.

Shaunaka Rishi Das sees these changes in ISKCON as 'developing in a way that is totally consistent with Gaudiya Vaishnava community perception.' Conversion is now seen as 'not joining a society (head-counting), but an individual choice.'

OSHO INTERNATIONAL

Osho International used to be known as the Rajneesh Movement; its guru Bhagwan Shree Rajneesh changed his name to Osho shortly before he died. Since the troubled times of the mid-1980s, and since Osho's death in 1990, the movement has seemed to become more relaxed, but it was dogged by controversy through the 1970s and 1980s.

HISTORY

Rajneesh (1931–1990), born Rajneesh Chandra Mohan, studied philosophy at university in Jabalpur, India, going on to teach philosophy there. Finding the university too restrictive, in 1966 he began lecturing and preaching around India, promoting meditation and free love. In 1969 he settled in Bombay, then moved to Poona in 1974, attracting large numbers of followers to his ashram, including hippies, spiritual seekers, 'rebels, drop-outs and jaded intellectuals',[23] partly through his contentious style and his discourses on such unusual subjects, for an Indian guru, as politics and sex.

Therapists and followers of the 'human potential movement', personal development or self-help groups, who had already been using meditation to assist inner growth, also came to Poona. They were attracted by Rajneesh's Dynamic Meditation, an active meditation featuring breathing.

> The rationale for this departure from static, silent meditations such as *vipassana* was that these were devised at a time when life and the human mind were much simpler. The complexity and stress of contemporary life, with its frenzied activity and emotional repression made it hard for Westerners to sit in meditation for long periods.[24]

Among other visitors to Poona was the British journalist Bernard Levin, who wrote in 1980 that Rajneesh was 'one of the most remarkable orators I have ever heard', and said that the disciples seemed more content and serene than any other group of people he had seen.'[25]

But Rajneesh upset the local authorities in both Bombay and Poona. He left Poona in 1981 and moved to the USA, setting up a large community in a 325sq km (126sq mile) ranch in Oregon, where his followers or sannyasins built the 'city' of Rajneeshpuram.

Rajneesh was criticized for a wide range of things over the years. Perhaps the most obvious was his ostentatious wealth. He was said to preach his message only to the well-off; the poor have enough to do simply surviving to have any time or energy left for spiritual development. The well-off, in contrast, have the time – and the money – to go to spiritual retreats, meditation classes and so on. His followers brought money with them, and were encouraged to bring more – living in the ashrams was never cheap – and the money was openly spent on gold, jewellery, at least 11 Rolls Royces (some say 85), and 4 aeroplanes. It also got him into trouble with the tax authorities, first in India and then in the USA.

Rajneeshpuram initially attracted praise for 'greening the desert' through its agricultural and environmental projects. Soon, however, it became a centre of controversy. Intended to be a centre for meditation and love, it had become regimented and authoritarian. There were accusations of effectively slave labour, as Rajneesh's devoted followers built the city for little or no pay. Many suffered from exhaustion and illness, and sexually transmitted diseases were rife. Hugh Milne, for several years the head of Rajneesh's personal bodyguard, comments:

> What had begun as the dawn of a new age, a glorious spiritual movement, already had the makings of a fascist nightmare. All my dreams of showing people how to live in love and harmony seemed to be vanishing... We were being used as slaves under the guise of spiritual surrender.[26]

There was conflict over land use with the local towns of Antelope and The Dalles, whose residents objected to the influx of Rajneesh's followers, especially when they began to buy up more property and allegedly tried to rig local elections by bussing in homeless people to vote, and by planning to give local people food poisoning on election day. Everywhere in Rajneeshpuram was electronically bugged, including 'every table in the dining commons', and 'hotel and guest rooms, public meeting places, and inside Rajneesh's own chair.'[27] The 'city' became an armed camp, with watchtowers and its own security guards. 'Deceit, deception and distrust finally characterized the movement,' says Milne. 'I left when I saw it was degenerating, and was not the utopia we had desired.'[28]

The focus of hatred for both the local people and the authorities was not so much Rajneesh himself as Ma Anand Sheela, an Indian woman who had been Rajneesh's secretary and who was now the leader of both the religion and the community, supposedly acting as Rajneesh's spokesman – he made no public pronouncements for several years – but actually taking complete control. When matters came to a head in 1985, Sheela fled to Germany. Rajneesh denounced her: 'She turned the ranch into a concentration camp... She was a dictator.'[29] Sheela was extradited from Germany and, with other senior members, faced a number of charges including attempted murder, firearms offences, burglary, immigration offences and financial irregularities. She eventually served two-and-a-half years in prison.

Kate Strelley, a follower for nine years, who had worked closely with Sheela, accepts that things went badly wrong, and that Sheela 'seemed more and more concerned with paranoia and politics' and had become 'hard, withdrawn, nervous, a black, dead monotone'. Sheela was certainly the driving force: 'She knew just what she had done to seize control of the Ashram, and she was careful to make sure nobody turned the tables on her.' But so far as the corruption which eventually destroyed Rajneeshpuram is concerned, Strelley disagrees with most members: 'If the term "evil" means anything, Bhagwan certainly played the major part – not Sheela.'[30]

Rajneesh tried to repair the damage among his followers, with the local community, and with the authorities, but things had gone too far. In September 1985 he declared the end of Rajneeshism as a religion, and in October he too tried to leave the country. He was arrested when his plane stopped to refuel. Rajneesh was fined $400,000 for immigration offences, given a suspended jail sentence, and expelled from the USA.

Rajneeshpuram was closed down in 1986, with its physical stock, from an aeroplane to caravans to kitchen equipment, being sold off – some of it to other movements, including the Church Universal and Triumphant.

Two British women were senior in the organization: Sally-Anne Croft was in charge of finance, and Susan Hagan ran the Rajneesh Investment Corporation, which included overall responsibility for the construction of Rajneeshpuram. Both were charged, with others, with conspiracy to murder a local federal attorney. They managed to return to Britain, and spent several years fighting extradition back to the USA, claiming that they were innocent but would probably be found guilty simply through association. In July 1995 their fears were proved correct; in October they received prison sentences of five years, though they were both released and returned to Britain part-way through their sentences. The evidence for their guilt had rested largely on the testimonies of other senior members, who had used plea-bargaining to reduce their own sentences.

In failing health, Rajneesh himself eventually returned to India, where he died in Poona in 1990. He claimed he had been poisoned by the American authorities; rumours that he died from AIDS are refuted by his doctor for over 12 years, Swami Amrito, who 'arranged that the head of HIV in Pune [Poona]... personally test Osho's blood for this disease', with a negative result.[31]

Since his death, Osho International has re-established itself in Rajneesh's original commune in Poona, India, setting up a 'multiversity' and continuing to pass on Rajneesh/Osho's teachings.

BELIEFS AND PRACTICES

The name Bhagwan is variously translated as 'the Blessed One', 'god-man', and 'master of the vagina'; according to Rajneesh himself, it was coined from words for the female and male genitalia. Rajneesh used the name as a 'challenge', but at the end of 1988 he announced that he had tired of the joke. For a few days he was called Gautama the Buddha, and then Shree Rajneesh Zorba the Buddha, but when both names brought complaints he dropped them, and eventually took the name Osho (pronounced O-sho rather than Osh-o), meaning 'friend', by which the whole movement is now known. If nothing else, the new name separates the present-day movement from the tarnished image of the last days of the earlier Rajneesh organization.

As a youth and as a student Rajneesh was argumentative and disruptive; he challenged and questioned everything he was taught. The philosophy he later taught sprang from this: one must challenge everything traditionally taught by religions from both the East and the West.

It is intentionally difficult to pinpoint the beliefs of Rajneesh/Osho. There was a book, *Rajneeshism: An Introduction to Bhagwan Shree Rajneesh and His Religion*, but it was withdrawn only two years after its publication in 1983. Rajneesh's teachings often appear contradictory, but he explained:

> this is one of my basic insights: that in life there are no contradictions. All contradictions are complementaries. Night is complementary to day, so is summer to winter, so is death to life. They are not against each other. There is nothing against, because there is only one energy, it is one God... Opposites are just like wings of a bird, two wings – they look opposite to each other but they support each other. The bird cannot fly with one wing.[32]

His teachings are a mixture of homespun philosophy and deep spiritual insights. His followers tend to be intelligent, middle-class people; it has been said that although he preached a non-intellectual message, his followers needed to be intelligent in order to understand the message that they must lay their intellect to one side.

> My message is very simple. That's why it is difficult to understand. I teach the obvious; it is not complex at all. Because it is not complex there is nothing much to understand in it. It has to be lived, experienced. My message is not verbal, logical, rational. It is existential, so those who want to understand it intellectually will only misunderstand it.

For Rajneesh, God is not 'somewhere out there'; he is everywhere, in everything; every part of life can be communion with God.

> My trust is total. I trust the outer, I trust the inner – because outer and inner are both together. They cannot be separated. There is no God without this world; there is no world without God. God is the innermost core of this world. The juice flowing in the trees is God, the blood circulating in your body is God, the consciousness residing in you is God. God and the world are mixed together just like a dancer and his dance; they cannot be separated, they are inseparable...
>
> I teach the whole man. I am not a materialist or a spiritualist. My approach is wholistic – and the whole man can only be holy.

(As a philosopher Rajneesh may well have known that the English words whole, holy, health and hale – as in 'hale and hearty' – all come from the Old English root *hal*, *halig*, meaning 'whole', while the word 'holistic' comes from the Greek root *holos*, also meaning 'whole'.)

Through all his teachings Rajneesh was opposed to doctrine and indoctrination. Spirituality may be learnt, but it cannot be taught, at least not as a set of rules.

> The people who are with me are not my followers. They are my lovers, but not my followers. They are my friends, but not my followers. They are my disciples, but not my followers. And what is the difference between a disciple and a follower? A follower believes; whatever is said, he makes a dogma out of it. The disciple learns, experiments, and unless he finds the truth himself he remains open. I am not giving any dogma to my friends here, to my sannyasins. All that I am doing here is helping them to understand themselves. All I am doing here is helping them to be themselves...
>
> ... man has not to follow anybody. Understand certainly, learn certainly, listen certainly, remain open. But follow your own inner spontaneity, follow your own being...
>
> I am not the leader and they are not the followers. And I am not creating a cult, I am not creating a church. The sannyasins are just a commune of friends, not a church. We don't have any dogma that everybody has to believe in.

That was certainly the theory, though the practice under Ma Anand Sheela may have been somewhat different.

Although there is no argument that things fell apart seriously in the early and mid-1980s under Ma Anand Sheela, and that at various times in his career Rajneesh was chased by tax authorities for non-payment, most of the other usual criticisms of the movement by ex-members and anti-cultists could be seen more as a matter of perception than anything else. Briefly, they can be listed as sexual orgies, violence, mind-control, authoritarianism, and deliberate reduction of self-dignity. There may have been some truth behind some of these on some occasions, but a lot also depends on viewpoint and interpretation.

From the critics' point of view, guided meditation could perhaps be seen as mind-control; submerging oneself in God might lead to a reduced sense of the importance of self; while there is a fine perceptual line between the necessary discipline of living in a religious commune, and authoritarianism.

At one point Rajneesh did encourage people to scream and shout, to flail around themselves, to express their anger and frustrations. Sometimes this became uncontrolled violence, causing physical injuries, but Rajneesh put a stop to this as early as 1979.

Within the ashram he also promoted free love, encouraging people to view sex as a powerful affirmation of spirituality. Although this spiritual belief is common to both Tantric Buddhism and some areas of Neo-Paganism, it was viewed with a mixture of horror, disgust and prurience by mainstream religious society in both the West and the East. With sexual liberation perhaps more than anything else, it is a truism that what seemed a good idea at the time can change its appearance markedly when portrayed by a disaffected ex-member, and then hyped up in the tabloid press. But according to Swami Amrito, speaking now of the Osho commune in Poona, 'This may be the only place on the planet where there are no rapes.'

Western religions, Rajneesh said, taught that sex was sinful, while most Eastern religions insisted on celibacy for their gurus. Both condemned him for his teaching on 'energy-giving sessions'.

In return, Rajneesh roundly condemned both Western and Eastern religions:

The East is against love. That's why Eastern spirituality is sad, dull, dead. No juice flows through the Eastern saint. He is afraid of any flow, any vibration, any streaming of his energy. He is constantly controlling himself, repressing himself. He is sitting upon himself, on guard. He is against himself and against the world. He is simply waiting to die, he is committing a slow suicide...

The Western man has lost all idea of who he is. He has lost track of consciousness, he is not aware. He has become more and more mechanical because he denies the inner. So laughter is there but laughter cannot go deep, because there is no depth. The depth is not accepted. So the West lives in a shallow laughter and the East lives in a deep sadness. This is the misery, the agony that has happened to man.

At the same time he absorbed into his own teachings much of both Western and Eastern spiritual teaching.

We are experimenting in a multi-dimensional way. We are experimenting with Tao, we are experimenting with Sufism, we are experimenting with Jainism, Hinduism, Islam, Christianity. We are experimenting with Tantra, Yoga, alchemy; we are experimenting with all the possibilities that can make the human consciousness rich and a human being whole...

I am not against anything, I am for all. I am utterly for all, I claim the whole human heritage, and whatsoever is good in any tradition is mine[33] and whatsoever can make man richer is mine. I don't belong to any tradition, all traditions belong to me.

So this is a new experiment. It has never been done before in such a way. This is the synthesis of all the paths.

This synthesis is seen most clearly in two aspects of Osho International: meditation and courses.

One of the central meditational practices of the movement is the Mystic Rose. This involves laughing for three hours a day for the first week, crying for three hours a day for the second, and sitting in silence for three hours a day for the third week. Another, usually done first thing in the morning, is Dynamic Meditation,

> Osho's basic and most popular meditation, consisting of five phases including breathing, catharsis and jumping up and down on one's heels shouting the Sufi mantra 'Hoo', 'Hoo', 'Hoo'. In the Dynamic Meditation a Gurdjieff 'stop' exercise is followed by the deep relaxation needed to be a witness of oneself, watching whatever is happening within and without.[34]

Many other forms of meditation are taught, but the primary principle is that meditation should be a part of every aspect of life: 'work and relaxation are not contradictory but integral to the transformative process.'[35]

The commune, or multiversity, in Poona offers courses in meditation, dance, mysticism, tantra, and a wide variety of spiritual, psychological and alternative healing practices. It also publishes hundreds of pamphlets and books, mostly transcribed from Osho's spoken teaching.

The commune discourages visitors bringing children with them; those under 12 are only allowed in during the lunch hour, and must be accompanied by an adult; those between 12 and 18 are told that 'the commune exists for people who want to meditate,'[36] and have to participate in meditation themselves.

It also discourages anyone who is physically or psychologically unfit, sensibly warning that for such people 'coming here can be unsettling and may aggravate the condition.'[37]

There is one other requirement of interest. The commune is 'an AIDS-free zone'; the brochure insists that 'all visitors who wish to participate in its activities' take an AIDS test on arrival.

SAHAJA YOGA

Sahaja Yoga was founded in 1970 by Shri Mataji Nirmala Devi. Born in 1923 into a wealthy Christian family in Chindawara in the central Indian state of Maharashtra, she claims that she 'knew from a very young age that she had a unique gift which had to be made available to all mankind.'[38] She married Sir Chandrika Prasad Srivastava, a senior civil servant who was Joint Secretary to the Indian Prime Minister's office in 1964–6, and was later Secretary General of the United Nations International Maritime Organization for 16 years until 1989.

According to the movement, in 1970 Shri Mataji was sitting under a bilva tree on a lonely beach when she had a transforming spiritual experience. She felt the *kundalini* power from the sacrum, the base of the spine, rise up through her seven *chakras* to emerge from the crown *chakra*, the fontanel area at the top of her head, as a gentle fountain of coolness, bringing her Self-Realization. This movement of *kundalini* energy she called 'vibrations', an approximate translation of the Sanskrit *chaitanya*. She realized that she could pass this experience on to other people, and founded Sahaja Yoga; *sahaja* means 'spontaneous' or 'easy', and *yoga* is translated as 'Union with the Self'. The movement claims 20,000 followers in India, and 100,000 in 75 countries outside India.

Self-Realization, say Sahaja Yoga, has been the goal of many religions, but has always been difficult to achieve, and restricted to a select few.

> In these modern times, Shri Mataji has made this knowledge available to everyone, and spontaneous *en-masse* Self Realization has become a reality experienced by hundreds of thousands...
>
> Through Sahaja Yoga meditation, our awareness gains a new dimension where absolute truth can be felt tangibly – on our central nervous system. As a result of this happening, spiritual growth takes place effortlessly, like the sprouting of a seed into a big tree. Physical, mental and emotional balance are achieved as a byproduct of our spiritual ascent.

From this comes the awareness that we are not mere body, mind or emotions, but that our true eternal being is Self or Spirit.

> The Spirit is the source of true knowledge, peace and joy. Self Realization (second birth, Satori, enlightenment) is the actualisation of this connection with our Spirit, and, as Shri Mataji says, it is the birthright of every human being to have it.

Sahaja Yoga, like many other new religious movements, is involved in charitable social work, including a hospital and a cancer research centre – both using Sahaja Yoga methods for healing – a classical music school, and a shelter for the poor in Delhi.

Sahaja Yoga makes a big point of its teaching being free:

> Amazingly, without any financial support from any person, Shri Mataji neither charges for Her lectures nor for Her ability to give Self Realization, nor does one have to become a member of this organization. She insists that you cannot pay for your enlightenment and to-date she continues to denounce the false, self-proclaimed 'gurus' who are more interested in the seekers' purse than their spiritual ascent.

But in fact this is one of the major criticisms of the movement, that the often middle-class members are encouraged to make regular donations to pay for Shri Mataji's trips around the world, and to buy expensive properties such as Shudy Camps Park House near Cambridge, England, in 1986, and an Italian castle in 1991. There also seems to be a strong emphasis on Shri Mataji herself, her background (growing up in Gandhi's ashram), her accomplishments (honorary doctorates, and other awards and honours made to her), and on how she is welcomed by high-ranking dignitaries in cities around the world (cf. Herbert W. Armstrong's 'world's most expensive autograph hunt', page 488) – rather than on her message. Devoted members refer to her as the Divine Mother, and she has called herself Adi Shakh, Primal Mother of All; many take her advice on child-rearing, and some ask her to choose their marriage partners. This amount of influence over her followers' lives has caused concern in several countries. Some former members have said that they were expelled from the movement because they resisted Shri Mataji's influence over their lives. Apparently, neither her husband nor her two daughters are followers of Sahaja Yoga.

ADIDAM

There can be great confusion when reading or hearing about this movement, because both it and its founder have gone through numerous name changes over the last 30 years.[39] Franklin Albert Jones was born in 1939 near New York City.

> Very early in life, He noticed that no one else enjoyed the same freedom, humour and true delight that He did. Noticing this, He consciously sacrificed His 'Bright' Divine Awareness in order to discover the way by which others could be drawn to realize the great Happiness he had known since birth.[40]

Following a 'crisis of despair' Jones tried out various religions, before beginning to study with Swami Rudrananda (Rudi), an American disciple of Muktananda, who was a disciple of Nityananda. These gurus taught a form of yoga in which energy is drawn up from the base of the spine to the crown of the head, causing one to become spiritually enlightened; this is usually known as *kundalini* yoga. Jones studied under Rudi, then went to India to study under Muktananda. He states that he achieved yogic liberation in 1968, and Transcendent Being Consciousness in 1970. He returned to the USA and set up his own movement, initially known as Dawn Horse Communion, in 1972.

Over the years the movement has changed its name several times; it has been the Crazy Wisdom Fellowship, the Free Primitive Church of Divine Communion, the Johannine Daist Community and the Free Daist Communion, settling on Adidam (The Way of the Heart) in 1996. Its founder has been known as (among many other names) Bubba Free John (*Bubba* meaning 'brother'), Da Free John (*Da* meaning, according to one source, 'giver'), Da Love-Ananda, Da Avabhasa and Adi Da; his title and name at the time of writing, Ruchira Avatar Adi Da Samraj, is an expansion of this.[41] For simplicity the movement will be referred to as Adidam, and the founder as Adi Da (or in some quotations, Da Avabhasa).

Adi Da now does little teaching, but spends most of his time at his retreat at the Adi Da Purnashram on the island of Naitauba in Fiji, working with his closest disciples. Two other 'sanctuaries' are in northern California, the headquarters of the movement, and the island of Kauai in Hawaii. In Britain the main centre is in London, but a new centre was opened in Leeds in 1999.

☼

Adi Da teaches that one does not need to attain Enlightenment, because it already exists; it does, however, have to be realized. For this to happen, the follower must first deny the illusion of the separateness of his individual existence, and recognize that the ego is the cause of all suffering.

Sri Da Avabhasa does not perceive our apparent reality as we do. He is constantly undermining our presumption that each one of us is an 'I' – a separate entity – and He calls us to really consider that presumption. Consider it now – where is this 'I' that we refer to all the time? Can you locate it?[42]

According to the movement's teachings, Adi Da himself is the presence of the Divine in bodily form on Earth, making it possible for followers to have a personal relationship with God.

The Ruchira Avatar, Adi Da Samraj, has always lived his Life as the most profound Submission to humankind. He did not come on mythic clouds of glory, recognized by all. He appeared 'incognito', in a humble circumstance. As an American child growing up in the 1940s and 50s, He totally surrendered His 'Bright' Awareness to the un-Illumined condition of those around Him, in order to find the way whereby human beings might Awaken to His Condition, the Self-Existing and Self-Radiant Divine State of everything and everyone.[43]

He is, they believe, the only one who has reached the seventh stage of life, Divine Enlightenment. The earlier stages are Individuation, Socialization, Integration (all normal stages in growing up), Spiritualization, Higher Spiritual Evolution, and Awakening to the Transcendental Self.

The 'Brightness' which is frequently mentioned refers to 'the condition of all-pervading radiance, joy and love: blissful divine consciousness'; Adi Da himself shows this brightness, and it can be transmitted to devotees when they meditate on photographs of him. The principle is that 'you become what you meditate on'.

> And so when you see Adi Da Samraj, or see His photograph, or hear His voice, or read His words, or hear others speak about Him, you may feel directly Touched by God, or the Divine Spirit.[44]

Most members live in communities, and meditation with other devotees is an important part of the movement's practices. Members also study Adi Da's many books, known as the 'Wisdom Teaching'. An important part of their communal activity is the telling of sacred personal stories or 'leelas', which consist of either inspiring stories about incidents in the life of Adi Da, or followers' testimonies about the transformations in their lives which devotion to Adi Da has brought.

One of the criticisms levelled at Adidam, as at many other movements, is of hypocrisy; the members are expected to follow strict dietary requirements – no meat, dairy products, eggs, sugar, salt, caffeine, alcohol or tobacco – but several former members have claimed that Adi Da himself has been known to indulge in some of these. Adi Da teaches a form of the traditional Eastern religious sexual practice, whereby orgasmic energy is not wasted, but is used positively for spiritual enhancement; almost inevitably, there have been allegations of sexual misconduct and abuse at high levels in the movement. One Adidam practice, Crazy Wisdom, is reminiscent of Gurdjieff's techniques (see page 350): leaders sometimes behave in unpredictable, arbitrary, even bizarre ways in order to shock devotees out of their complacency; again, this could easily lead to potentially abusive situations, and has brought some criticism.

Adidam has around 1,200 members around the world.

THE IMPERSONAL ENLIGHTENMENT FELLOWSHIP

Andrew Cohen is an American guru within an Eastern-style tradition. Born in New York City in 1955, he experienced a spiritual awakening in 1986. His followers founded Friends of Andrew Cohen Everywhere[45] (FACE) in London in 1991. The movement changed its name to the Impersonal Enlightenment Fellowship in 1999.

Cohen's message of Impersonal Enlightenment is that through individual spiritual transformation (*moksha*) the whole world can be changed: 'spiritual liberation's true significance is its potential to completely transform not only the individual, but the entire way that human beings, as a race, live together.'[46] Many teachers offer

Enlightenment, he says, but few really know what it is or how to attain it. Enlightenment is already in us. The harder we strive towards it, the more we put barriers in the way – and the main barrier is self-centredness: the ego.

Cohen recalls his first spiritual insight when he was 16, when he realized that:

> there was no such thing as death and that life itself had no beginning and no end. I saw that all life was intimately connected and inseparable. It became clear that there was no such thing as individuality separate from that one Self that was all of life.[47]

At 22, having tried the Greenwich Village scene, including playing drums in a band, he decided to devote his life to further study of this discovery. He spent ten years with a succession of teachers, exploring Sufism, Zen, yoga and *kundalini* experiences. In 1986 he became a disciple of an Advaita Vedanta teacher (see page 269), Poonjaji, who told him that what stands in the way of Realization is not knowing that one is already Realized. For Cohen this Zen-like revelation was what he had been searching for. Within weeks he began teaching, first in India, then in England and America, and soon began to attract a following. In 1991, says Peter Bampton of the Impersonal Enlightenment Fellowship, 'the relationship between Cohen and Poonjaji fell apart as a result of a fundamental difference in their understanding of the meaning and significance of Enlightenment.'[48]

Cohen teaches that Enlightenment, Realization of the Self, is only the beginning; one must manifest this in one's everyday life.

> Can human beings trust each other, and in that trust abide together harmoniously? History would tell us that mankind has not done that well. The point of all spiritual experience is to bring a human being to the point where he or she can be a social creature who is able to live with other human beings in a non-aggressive manner. Looking very objectively, the spiritual journey is more practical than esoteric.[49]

Cohen's uncompromising stand and his continual questioning of popular paradigms in the modern spiritual world have made him a controversial figure. 'In particular, his insistence on personal integrity as a prerequisite for genuine spiritual evolution has created significant tension in the spiritual world, and has elicited at times strong opposition,' says Bampton.

The Impersonal Enlightenment Fellowship currently has nine centres in seven countries, with some 350–400 students living in communities worldwide, and a further 200–300 followers who regard Cohen as their teacher and attend his retreats, while not living in communities.

SOKA GAKKAI INTERNATIONAL

Soka Gakkai International (SGI) is a lay organization which developed from the Japanese Buddhist sect Nichiren Shoshu, although they now have no organizational connection.

HISTORY

Nichiren Buddhism owes its origins to the Japanese Buddhist monk Nichiren Daishonin (1222–1282). Like many another before and since (cf. Joseph Smith, founder of the Mormons), he was confused and unsettled by the large number of varieties of religion available to him. Instead of opting for any one of them, he devoted several years to careful study of the writings of Gautama, the Buddha, and eventually came to the conclusion that not only were all the current variants of Buddhism both wrong and corrupt, but also he had rediscovered the true essence of Buddhism.

Buddha's purest teachings, Nichiren found, were summed up in the Lotus Sutra, which he wrote six years before his death. All of Gautama Buddha's other teachings, which led up to and underpinned this, were 'provisional', and were superseded by the Lotus Sutra. Nichiren taught his followers that by chanting just the title of this Sutra they would implicitly be chanting the whole Lotus Sutra, and thus would attain enlightenment.

Nichiren persistently warned that Japan would suffer both internal strife and invasion by the Mongol leader Kubla Khan, because it had turned from the true way. He was branded as a heretic for his denunciation of all the traditional forms of Buddhism, was persecuted by the authorities, beaten up, and very nearly executed. After a dozen years of persecution he was eventually pardoned in 1274, and settled down to write doctrinal theses.

Since the ruling authorities seemed determined to continue to rely on adhering to provisional teachings, and convinced that he had done all he could to warn the nation's leaders, Nichiren Daishonin now turned his efforts towards ensuring the correct transmission of his teachings to the future. In keeping with an old Chinese maxim that a sage who warns his sovereign three times and is not heeded should retire to a mountain forest, he left Kamakura for good and went to live in a remote hermitage in the wilderness of Mount Minobu. Here he gave lectures on the Lotus Sutra and devoted himself to writing and training his disciples.[50]

Over the centuries Nichiren's version of Buddhism split in many directions; by the twentieth century there were around 40 different Nichiren sects. One of these was founded by Nikko Shonin, who had left Nichiren's temple at Minobu after falling out with other disciples, and had built a temple at Kitayama. Eventually, in 1913, Nikko's version of Nichiren's version of Buddhism, which was battling against not only all the rest of Buddhism but against the other Nichiren sects as well, set itself up firmly as the Orthodox Nichiren Sect, or Nichiren Shoshu.

In 1930, two devotees of Nichiren Shoshu, Tsunesaburo Makiguchi (1871–1944) and Josei Toda (1900–1958), founded a lay movement, Soka Kyoiku Gakkai, the Value-Creating Education Society. During World War II the Japanese government demanded religious unity, and insisted that every home should have a Shinto shrine for the worship of the Emperor. Although the Nichiren Shoshu priests acceded to these demands, the Soka Gakkai refused to, and Makiguchi and Toda, among other leaders, were imprisoned. Makiguchi died in prison, but Toda, on his release, put all his energies into reviving the lay movement. Seeing its purpose as more universal than just education, he dropped 'Kyoiku' from the name. In 1951 he announced his goal of 750,000 new members in the next seven years; he just lived to see this accomplished.

Under his successor as president of Soka Gokkai, Daisaku Ikeda (born 1928), the movement continued to spread around the world. American servicemen stationed in Japan – particularly those who had married local women – took it back to America with them. Soka Gakkai International (SGI) was founded in 1975, with Ikeda as president, and is affiliated to the United Nations as a Non-Governmental Organization.

A British businessman, Richard Causton, who had worked in Japan, became chairman of the then Nichiren Shoshu UK, now SGI-UK, in 1974. The headquarters of the UK organization are at Taplow Court, a Tudor stately home in Berkshire, purchased with a £6 million interest-free loan from the Japanese headquarters. Taplow Court also houses the European Centre of the Institute of Oriental Philosophy, which conducts independent research into Buddhism and comparative religion. There are currently around 5,000 British members, about 20,000 in the rest of Europe, some 300,000 in the USA, and 10 million in Japan; world membership is around 11.3 million.

BELIEFS AND PRACTICES

Traditional forms of Buddhism turn their back on the world, describing its pleasures and pains as illusory. SGI believe in a living, working faith which affects every part of our everyday lives in a contemporary world. They spell out the difference from other forms of Buddhism very clearly:

Early forms of Buddhism taught that everything in the universe is impermanent, and that suffering results from first desiring, and then trying to cling to, what is essentially unstable and transient. As nothing can last forever, one should try to eradicate this suffering by eliminating one's desires and illusions and so achieve a state of total selflessness, or *nirvana*. Indeed, *nirvana* was often viewed as being a state of life achieved beyond this world, after death.

Later Buddhist teachings pointed out the limitations of this view of suffering and desire. Not only is wanting to achieve the state of *nirvana* a strong desire in itself, but to totally eradicate desire ultimately means to eliminate life, as a fundamental desire of all living things is to carry on living.[51]

Nichiren Daishonin taught that 'earthly desires are enlightenment (*nirvana*)'; his followers believe they can attain Buddhahood

by transforming illusions and earthly desires into enlightened wisdom rather than extinguishing them; *nirvana* is, therefore, nowhere else but in this world. Thus earthly desires and enlightenment are not different in their fundamental essence. It follows that enlightenment is not the eradication of desire but a state which the entity of life can experience by transforming innate desires from influences which are negative to desires which are positive.[52]

The main religious practice of SGI members is the chanting, every morning and evening, of the phrase 'Nam Myoho Renge Kyo'. *Nam* is a Sanskrit word meaning 'devotion', and the remainder of the phrase is the title of the Chinese translation of the Lotus Sutra. *Myoho* means 'the enlightenment of the law', *Renge* means 'lotus', and *Kyo* means 'sutra', or the teaching of a Buddha. The whole phrase, then, means 'devotion to the enlightenment of the law of the Lotus Sutra'.

This is chanted in front of the Gohonzon, a 25 x 50cm (10 x 20in) scroll given to each new devotee. On the Gohonzon, which means 'object worthy of honour and fundamental respect', is written 'Nam Myoho Renge Kyo Nichiren', along with characters representing all aspects of life. The original Dai-Gohonzon, inscribed by Nichiren in 1279, is in a shrine at the head temple at the foot of Mount Fuji. As well as chanting the phrase a member will also recite part of the second and all of the sixteenth chapter of the Lotus Sutra. The entire ritual is known as Gongyo, or 'assiduous practice'.

In sociological terms, SGI teaches a world-affirming, rather than a world-denying, Buddhism. Its practice is accessible to all types of people, though in Britain its membership tends to be middle class, with many members from the creative arts.

The movement has been criticized for its materialistic philosophy, summed up as

'Chant "Nam Myoho Renge Kyo" and ask for a new car'. They stress, however, that although you might get a new car, you might not, but instead could receive an inner peace and understanding of why you don't actually need a new car.

According to the movement, there are nine consciousnesses or levels of perception. The first five are the five senses; the sixth integrates the information received from these so that we can make physical judgements; the seventh makes moral and value judgements; the eighth stores our karma, everything from past lives and our present life that makes us who we are. The ninth and deepest level is the very essence of life.

> Because this level of consciousness might be described as pure life force, and is unaffected by cause and effect, tapping it by chanting Nam Myoho Renge Kyo enables one to purify all of the other eight consciousnesses. In other words, when one chants Nam Myoho Renge Kyo, the pure life-force of the ninth, or Buddha, consciousness permeates our entire being. Therefore one sees, hears, smells and tastes more clearly; one's sense of touch becomes more sensitive; one begins to perceive and make judgements about both the physical and the abstract world with greater clarity. One also begins to become aware of, and cleanse, those aspects of one's karma which cause unhappiness and which are therefore detrimental to the functioning of the pure Law of life, since they are a hindrance to developing one's full potential or purpose in life.[53]

Soka Gokkai is a lay movement: members remain in the outside world, in normal jobs, rather than, for example, training for the priesthood. It describes itself as 'a movement for culture, education and peace: its activities both on a local and global level always aim to "create value" through the active support of these three pillars of civilization.'[54]

Members live in society, and it is their duty to work within society – in part, simply by being who they are.

> The ultimate purpose of those who practise the Buddhism of Nichiren Daishonin is to reveal the creative potential of their lives for the benefit not only of their personal fulfilment but also, and equally, of the development of society.[55]

And to change society, they first must change themselves.

> Buddhism teaches that if you want to change your life, it is no use blaming your circumstances. On the contrary, you must change that aspect of yourself which has given rise to the circumstances in which you find yourself. When you change, your environment will automatically change with you.[56]

The motto of SGI-UK is 'Trust through Friendship, Peace through Trust'; the entire movement is dedicated to world peace. The aims of SGI are:

1 To contribute to peace, culture and education throughout the world based upon Nichiren Daishonin's Buddhism.

2 To contribute to world peace, specifically through deepening the links between the ordinary citizens of different countries of the world.

3 To further the study and practice of Nichiren Daishonin's Buddhism, which declares absolute pacifism, and, upon this basis, to contribute to the above fundamental aims as excellent citizens in accordance with the culture and laws of the individual countries.[57]

Soka Gakkai has at times been criticized for its recruiting techniques, which have been known to be somewhat heavy-handed, particularly in Japan. Evangelism is known as *shakubuku*, meaning 'break through and overcome'. Members are encouraged to apply whatever pressure they can on their family and friends to join; the movement gained a bad reputation in Japan for what they admit as 'over-enthusiastic propagation', but which some critics have alleged to be violent behaviour – a strange attribute for a pacifist religion.

Other Buddhist movements criticize SGI because, just like Fundamentalist Evangelicals in Christianity, it claims to be the only legitimate version of Buddhism; all the others are wrong, and must be shown to be wrong. From the viewpoint of mainstream Buddhism, it is Nichiren Shoshu which is heretical.

There is now a major rift between Nichiren Shoshu and Soka Gakkai. The priesthood in Japan was inherently conservative, inward-looking, hierarchical and to some extent hereditary; the lay movement was radical, modern and expansive. Each saw the other's attributes as faults. In 1992, after a long-running power struggle between them, the High Priest of Nichiren Shoshu excommunicated Daisaku Ikeda and every Soka Gakkai member for 'refusing to change their ways'. Although they paid for its construction, Soka Gakkai members were refused access to the huge temple complex at the foot of Mount Fuji – the largest temple in Asia, and possibly in the world. In 1998 the Nichiren Shoshu priests destroyed the temple.

The Soka Gakkai movement is extremely wealthy, owning large amounts of property in Japan. Former members have claimed that they felt under tremendous pressure to contribute to its funds. Further criticism is raised by Soka Gakkai International's close links with the Mitsubishi Bank.

Daisaku Ikeda founded the Soka University in Japan in 1971; the movement's money has made it a highly successful and influential establishment. In the USA, which has 300,000 Soka Gakkai members, there is a campus in California. As founder of the university Ikeda often awards honorary degrees to royalty and politicians, including among many others Nelson Mandela and Mikhail Gorbachev. Critics claim that he uses these hand-shaking occasions for photo opportunities to show that he is on familiar terms with great world leaders, so increasing his own standing (cf. Herbert W. Armstrong's 'world's most expensive autograph hunt', page 488) – but SGI point out that Ikeda has published dialogues with over 20 world figures, including Gorbachev, Arnold Toynbee and Henry Kissinger.

In its efforts for world peace and cultural reformation Soka Gakkai in Japan also seeks political influence. Just as the Christian religious right (the 'Moral Majority') exerts a strong influence on the Republican Party in the USA, Soka Gakkai, although legally separate, has strong links with the third main political party in Japan, Komeito (Clean Government Party). Komeito currently has three members in the government, including one cabinet member. Critics claim that Soka Gakkai, through its power over its members, controls six million votes – 10 per cent of the Japanese electorate.

FRIENDS OF THE WESTERN BUDDHIST ORDER

The Friends of the Western Buddhist Order (FWBO) was founded in 1967 by an English Buddhist monk, Sangharakshita (born Dennis Lingwood in 1925). Growing up in South London, Lingwood became a Buddhist at the age of 16, and travelled to India during World War II. An FWBO profile speaks of 'the years as a wandering truth-seeker and hermitage-dweller, the hippie days in sixties Britain' as 'the stuff of FWBO legend'.[58]

The 'legend' tells of Lingwood going AWOL from the British army in India in 1946,

> donning the yellow robes of a wandering ascetic and taking to the dusty roads. After two years he settles in Kalimpong to begin his life's work – a synthesis of the three major vehicles of Buddhism: Theravada, Mahayana, and Vajrayana. For almost twenty years he studies under various teachers such as Yogi Chen, Dhardo Rinpoche, and Jagdish Kashyap, who respectively expose him to the east Asian, Tibetan, and Theravadin tradition. He also receives initiations from Tibetan lamas, is ordained in the Theravada tradition, and is subsequently called Sangharakshita.[59]

The details of this account, such as the validity of Sangharakshita's initiations, have been questioned; as is the case with several movements in this book, the early life of the founder takes on its own mythology.

After 20 years in India practising, studying and teaching Buddhism, Sangharakshita returned to England in 1964, initially to run the English Sangha Trust, a Buddhist organization founded by the well-known Buddhist writer Christmas Humphreys.

> On returning to the West, dissatisfied with the contemporary Buddhist scene, he decided to found a movement (and the following year an order, the Western Buddhist Order) to transmit the essentials of Buddhism in a manner relevant to the modern west.[60]

After 30 years as head of the Order, Sangharakshita retired from active leadership in 1995, though he remains influential in the movement.

> The forms in which Buddhist truths are expressed always adapt according to the circumstances. But the essence of Buddhism transcends culture and conditions.
> In the West today we are heirs to the whole of the Buddhist tradition. We need not be restricted to Theravada Buddhism, to Zen, or to Tibetan Buddhism, but can draw from them all. The FWBO's attitude is not one of eclecticism, however. We take what is useful according to our actual spiritual needs. We take whatever will help us to grow under the conditions of Western life.[61]

The various centres of the FWBO offer training in two types of meditation, the Mindfulness of Breathing, 'which unifies and focuses our scattered mental energies and gives profound peace of mind', and *Metta Bhavana*, 'the development of unlimited friendliness, which brings about a gentle but radical transformation in our emotional state',[62] changing negative feelings to positive. They also offer courses and talks on many aspects of Buddhism, and retreats where members can devote themselves to meditation or study in peaceful surroundings. FWBO also encourage members to work in 'Right Livelihood Businesses' run on ethical lines; these include wholefood shops, vegetarian restaurants, bookshops, gardening businesses and so on. Like many other movements in this book, FWBO engages in social work; its charitable arm funds healthcare and education in poor areas of India. The Western Buddhist Order itself has nearly 400 ordained men and women in Britain, who have taken the ceremony of 'Going for Refuge to the Three Jewels'; the 'jewels' are the Buddha, the Dharma (his teachings) and the Sangha (the community of committed Buddhists).

☼ .

FWBO appears to be more relaxed about some contemporary social issues than some other Eastern-originating movements. For example, in 1995 it held its first retreat for lesbian members of the Order, with talks on areas such as 'coming out' and the relationship between a lesbian identity and practising the Dharma, and on feminism, gender and the Dharma. But sexual issues have also caused some of the controversy about the FWBO in recent years. One ex-member said that the leader of his FWBO centre had coerced him into sex with him. That centre, in Croydon, Surrey, is now acknowledged to have been authoritarian, with a charismatic leader: a potent and dangerous combination. (The leader in question was later expelled from the Order.) In 1997 *The Guardian* newspaper published an article detailing the allegations of several ex-members; one of these said that in the 1970s a leader had had homosexual relations with him in order to help him 'to get over his anti-homosexual conditioning, which was blocking him from devoting his energies to the spiritual life.'[63] The FWBO accept that mistakes were made in the past, and that in some of its single-sex communities there was sexual experimentation. According to one FWBO leader, at Padmaloka, a retreat centre in Norfolk,

you had a lot of people who were gay. It did get a bit out of hand and it got disbanded in 1989. But I've never heard of anything unethical going on there. It was just a rather tangled sexual mess.[64]

As for the authority problems that occurred in FWBO centres, another FWBO member, Ananda, says:

In the early days, we weren't big on practice; we were just Buddhists hanging out, going to lectures, doing yoga. We were naïve. People who had been ordained by Sangharakshita tended to develop their own little castles of which they were the unchallenged masters.[65]

Similar problems occurred in ISKCON (see page 284), but that was after their founder Prabhupada died, leaving that organization in the hands of people without sufficient maturity to lead wisely. In FWBO, they occurred while the founder was still in charge.

A related problem seems to stem from Sangharakshita's teaching that men are inherently more spiritually advanced than women, which has apparently caused some of the male leaders to behave in a misogynistic manner. Everything in FWBO is organized on a single-sex basis; women have their own retreats, and women ordain women. It could be that this very separation, by causing the men to remain in ignorance of the women, creates an attitude of superiority in some men. But so far as the FWBO as an organization is concerned, women may be different but they are equal; when Sangharakshita retired from actively running the FWBO in 1995, three of the seven Public Preceptors appointed to head the movement were women.

Another problem, as the FWBO passes through its fourth decade, is how to square the ideal of single-sex communal living with the increasing numbers of members who are married with families.

The FWBO, like other Buddhist (and Hindu) orders in the West, faces a genuine conundrum.

If one simply transplants a Buddhist tradition from Asia, it will come encased in Asian cultural forms that are liable to hinder the Dharma from meeting the real spiritual needs of Westerners. Then again, if one just picks those bits of Buddhism that seem appealing and relevant, the Dharma will be filtered through one's pre-existing concerns (say, those of psychotherapy) and its distinctive message will be obscured.[66]

Critics allege that not only does Sangharakshita not have a valid lineage, but he doesn't maintain contact with other Buddhist teachers. However, the FWBO has sought, at least in theory, to go back to the common principles underlying the many different schools of Buddhism, and to apply those principles in the quite different social context of the Western world. The public revelations of the problems it has faced over authority and sexuality, while clearly distressing for the members involved, and unpleasant and embarrassing for the Order, have at least had the positive effect of forcing these matters into the open, where they have to be faced squarely.

In addition to 850 members of the Order itself worldwide, there are around 2,500 members known as *Mitva* (Sanskrit for 'friend'), who have made a formal commitment to FWBO. There is also 'an indeterminate number' of those who may attend centres regularly, but have made no formal commitment. Taking all three levels together, there are around 4,000 people associated with FWBO in the UK, with around 700 living in 90 residential spiritual communities. The FWBO has 30 teaching centres in the UK and 5 in the USA, out of around 80 centres worldwide.[67]

NEW KADAMPA TRADITION

The New Kadampa Tradition (NKT) is one of the newest and most controversial Buddhist movements in the UK. It derives from the Tibetan Buddhist tradition, but has attracted publicity by its opposition to the best-known Tibetan Buddhist leader, the Dalai Lama.

NKT began in the UK. Its founder, Geshe Kelsang Gyatso (born 1931), was the spiritual director of an existing Mahayana Buddhist centre at Conishead Priory, near Ulverston, Cumbria. Relations between Gyatso and the Foundation for the Preservation of the Mahayana Tradition (FPMT), which had set up the centre, became strained, and in 1982, five years after he took over there, the centre severed its links with the FPMT. The New Kadampa Tradition was formally established in 1991.

The NKT shares many of the same roots as the Dalai Lama; both belong to the Gelugpa tradition, the most influential of four main schools of Tibetan Buddhism. The NKTs name goes back to a well-respected eleventh-century Buddhist school called the Kadampa, founded by the Indian teacher Atisha; his teachings inspired the forming of the Gelugpa tradition by the fourteenth-century Je Tsongkhapa. The name 'Kadampa' comes from *ka*, meaning 'word', or the Buddha's teachings, *dam*, referring to Atisha's special Lamrin instructions, known as the 'Stages of the Path', and *pa*, a school or tradition.

By integrating their knowledge of all Buddha's teachings into the practice of Lamrin, and by applying this to their everyday lives, Kadampa Buddhists are encouraged to use all Buddha's teachings as practical methods for transforming daily activities into the path of enlightenment.[68]

The NKT was established:

to preserve and make available Kadampa Buddhism throughout the world in a form that is suited to the modern world and way of life... The word 'New' is used not to imply that the tradition is newly created, but to show that it is a fresh presentation of Buddhadharma in a form and manner appropriate to the needs and conditions of the modern world... By using the title 'Kadampa', Geshe Kelsang Gyatso encourages his disciples to follow the perfect example of simplicity and purity as shown by the ancient Kadampas.[69]

Geshe Kelsang has written many books, which form the main focus for the study programmes of the members. This in itself has raised criticism from some other Tibetan Buddhists, who feel that NKT is a sectarian movement.

While the Dalai Lama has drawn together teachings and practices from all four Tibetan schools, the NKT focuses on what it sees as the pure teachings of the Kadampa tradition. It does not accept the Dalai Lama's authority 'simply because there is no political or ecclesiastical reason for doing so,' says Jim Belither, NKT secretary.[70]

There is a major theological dispute between the NKT and the Dalai Lama. The NKT worship a protector deity, Dorje Shugdän, 'an emanation of the Wisdom Buddha Manjushri'; many Tibetan Buddhists regard Dorje Shugdän as unpredictable, even dangerous. The dispute came to a head when the Dalai Lama declared that public worship of the god caused harm both to himself and to the Tibetan Buddhist cause. In 1996 NKT followers staged several public demonstrations against the Dalai Lama, accusing him of 'a policy of discrimination against Dorje Shugdän practitioners within the exile Tibetan community'.

NKT is a very new movement, but has grown strongly; it is estimated that there are between 3,000 and 6,000 followers in its 300 centres and groups in Britain and other European countries, Asia (Malaysia and Hong Kong), Australia, North, Central and South America, and recently South Africa.

ECKANKAR

Eckankar[71] claims to be the root religion: 'ECK is the ancient teaching that is the source from which all religions and philosophies spring.'[72] This and the next two entries could easily be called esoteric movements; they are included in this section because of their Hindu/Sikh Sant Mat roots.

ECKists experience ECK through light and sound in their 'spiritual exercises, dreams and everyday life.' They also explore heavenly worlds through 'Soul Travel', in which they meet the Masters and learn from them. There is always a Living ECK Master, currently Harold Klemp, who speaks on Eckankar at seminars around the world, and whose inner being, the Mahanta, meets and guides other ECKists on the other planes.

HISTORY

Born in Kentucky, Paul Twitchell (?1909–1971) claims to have learnt the technique of Soul Travel at the age of three from his elder sister, who had been taught it by their father, who had learnt it from an Indian guru, Sudar Singh. Twitchell first met Sudar Singh in Paris when he was quite young.

Twitchell's family do not confirm this version of the story.

It is significant that Twitchell was adopted. Writing of an eighteenth-century ECK Master, he says, 'He came into this world... in the usual manner of the ECK Masters – very mysteriously. Few know how they are given birth, but always some family adopts them during their infancy and while raising them, one member of the family who is adept at Soul Travel teaches them at an early age.'[73]

In 1944, Twitchell says, he met a Tibetan Master, Rebazar Tarzs, in his soul body, who taught him about Eckankar. Twitchell was at that time in the US Navy; later, like L. Ron Hubbard, the founder of Scientology, he 'made his living by writing for pulp magazines.'[74]

Before founding Eckankar Twitchell was, from 1950 to 1955, a member of the Self-Revelation Church of Absolute Monism, a Hindu movement led by Swami Premananda. He was apparently required to leave the Church because of misconduct, and in 1955 he joined Scientology, becoming one of the very first to go Clear. Also in 1955 he joined Ruhani Satsang, a Sant Mat movement founded by Kirpal Singh (see page 320). Twitchell's second wife Gail was initiated in 1963, but then he fell out with Kirpal and they left the movement the same year.

The Eckankar explanation of Twitchell's religious background is that he met Rebazar Tarzs and other Masters of the Vairagi; then, 'while they trained Paul to become the Living ECK Master, he explored a wide range of spiritual traditions under different teachers.'[75]

Twitchell founded Eckankar in the USA in 1965, at the same time declaring himself to be the 971st in an unbroken line of Living ECK Masters stretching back many thousands of years. His lectures and books on self-realization and God-realization – particularly *The Tiger's Fang* and *The Spiritual Notebook* – publicized the new movement, which grew rapidly. It was registered as a non-profit religious organization in 1970.

After Twitchell's death from a heart attack in 1971, leadership passed to his appointed successor, Darwin Gross (Living Master No. 972), despite some dissension among senior members of the movement, several of whom left. Gross later married Gail Twitchell, who had supported his succession, though they were divorced in 1978. Gross moved the Church's HQ to California, and membership continued to rise, despite adverse publicity about much of Eckankar's teachings having been 'borrowed' from Ruhani Satsang and other Sant Mat movements.

Gross's leadership was apparently controversial, and in 1981 he handed the Living Master's 'rod of power' to Harold Klemp (No. 973). Gross remained as president of the Eckankar corporation until 1983, but in 1984 Klemp declared that Gross was no longer to be recognized as an ECK Master, and his books on Eckankar were banished from the movement. Despite this, Eve Illing, the regional Eckankar spiritual aide for the UK, says, 'I regard Darwin Gross's ten years with gratitude for the learnings it gave.'[76] Gross, a former musician from Oregon, returned there to set up a new movement, Sounds of Soul, with other ex-ECKists; this later became known as Ancient Teachings of the Masters (ATOM).

Klemp moved the HQ to Minneapolis in the 1980s. He has gone on to write the overwhelming majority of the inspirational and teaching books of the movement, leading to the suggestion by some critics that he is the St Paul to Twitchell's Jesus. Illing, who joined Eckankar only two months after Twitchell's death, disagrees with this interpretation. 'Eckankar is a living, evolving religion in which the message of a past ECK Master is always secondary to that of the current Living ECK Master.' She outlines their different roles:

It was Paul Twitchell's mission to put spiritual truths that had always been handed down from Master to pupil into book form for the growing number of seekers. Harold Klemp has continued this but part of his mission has been to establish a seat of power in the building of the ECK Temple at Chanhassan, MN, USA. Also he has established the RESA (Regional ECK Spiritual Aide) structure which puts a regional representative of the Living ECK Master in each area. Sri Harold has also done much to show how the spiritual principles can be applied in everyday life through divine love and service to all.

Klemp's pre-eminence is emphasized in talks transcribed in one of his books.

We must be careful that we in ECK don't create gods out of past Masters, no matter how much we love and revere them, no matter how important they have been to the history of ECK. As soon as we start to look to a past ECK Master for our present guidance, we become no different from an orthodox religion...

The Living Word refers to the Mahanta, the Living ECK Master of the times. Whenever we look to a past master for our present spiritual guidance, we take a detour.[77]

Although Twitchell's founding role and his teachings are of immense importance to the movement, the man himself now seems to be down-played. 'To say he had a checkered life is an understatement. In many ways he was quite a rascal.'[78]

Eckankar claim 'tens of thousands of ECKists in over a hundred countries', mainly in the USA and Africa; there are around 650 members in Britain.

BELIEFS AND PRACTICES

In *The Spiritual Notebook* Twitchell defines Eckankar as 'the ancient science of Soul Travel'.

The term 'bilocation', which is the ability to be in two places at the same time, is no longer in the vocabulary of ECK. This word has been dropped from our terminology because it sounds too much like astral projection. The expression 'Soul Travel' is used instead, as it gives more depth and breadth to the teachings of ECK.[79]

Soul Travel, ECKists explain, is the ability to expand one's consciousness, which may include the inner self travelling independently of the body, on the Astral and higher spiritual planes. Some of these travels are experienced during sleep, and one of the earliest parts of ECK training is in recalling and recording one's dreams.

On these planes one can meet both the Living ECK Master, and other Masters. Both Gross and Klemp had been practising soul travel before they encountered Eckankar; both claim to have recognized Twitchell's photograph on the back of his books as someone they had met on the other planes.

According to one source, Jesus and St Paul became ECK Masters. Twitchell wrote that the Living ECK Master at the time of Christ was Zadok, who worked with a group who had broken away from the Essenes – 'a secret, mystical organization which exists to this day in the Middle East'. Jesus apparently

studied for some time under the great Zadok. The ECK Master gave Jesus the basic fundamentals of Eckankar, who (*sic*) used them in His own teachings. Out of His knowledge of ECK came what we know today as Christianity.[80]

There are a dozen known planes between the Physical and Sugmad, 'the Ocean of Love and Mercy'. Each has its temple, its Guardian and its unique sound. Above the Physical plane is the Astral plane; according to Eckankar this is as far as most occultists ever reach. Its Guardian is Gopal Das, and its sound is the roar of the sea. Next comes the Causal plane, where the memories of all our past lives are stored; this plane can be recognized by the sound of tinkling bells. Beyond that is the Mental plane, which is the source of all religions and philosophies; its sound is running water.

Although Eckankar does not have a dualist belief, it teaches that the Mental plane

is the home of the Kal Niranjan, the God of the lower worlds and ruler of the negative forces. He is known by many names, including Satan, the Devil, Asmodeus, Beelzebub and Ahriman, to name a few. The negative power is often known as the Universal Mind, which many sects and religions worship as the true God power.[81]

The illusions of the physical world include religions, philosophies and the ideas of social reformers. The entire material universe is really a prison in which mankind is trapped. According to Twitchell, the ECK Masters

come from outside this prison to liberate all souls from Kal's possession forever. It is with the help and grace of these Masters that we leave this dark land of illusion and begin the journey homeward again.[82]

The top level of the Mental plane is the Etheric plane, which is the source of unconscious, primitive thought.

We now step out of the lower planes into the pure spiritual worlds: the Soul plane, Alakh Lok (plane), Alaya Lok, Hukikat Lok, Agam Lok, Anami Lok and the Sugmad World. There are apparently other, un-named planes before reaching Sugmad itself.

The *chela*, or student of Eckankar, rises through various levels of initiation, becoming able to access successively higher planes. After the second initiation, to the Astral plane, the ECKist has avoided the necessity for any further physical incarnations; he can also teach Eckankar classes. Higher initiates, those who have reached the Soul Plane and above and who have had additional training, are the clergy of Eckankar.

'The function of ECK clergy is much the same as in other religions, e.g. ECK wedding ceremonies, memorial services, worship services etc.,' says Illing. Clergy can be male or female. However, 'Living ECK Masters up to this moment in time have always been male. This is because the male body is stronger to withstand the great energy flowing through it.'

As with other esoteric religions, or any movement with a series of initiations, there is a clear 'spiritual career path' with many levels.

The goal of every ECKist is to experience life to the fullest. That is spiritual mastery. Some of us may eventually serve on earth as 'guardian angel' ECK Masters, while others will pursue specialized interests in the spiritual worlds.[83]

Twitchell was given the ECK rod of power by the Tibetan Master Rebazar Tarzs, and this has since been handed on, first to Gross and then to Klemp.

The departing Master always leaves on... October 22nd, and in turn his successor always accepts the Rod of ECK Power on the same day, at midnight, at the full of the moon in the valley of Shangta, in northern Tibet, near the Katsupari Monastery. The ritual takes place at the site of the ancient Oracle of Tirmer under the direction of the ancient sage Yaubl Sacabi, whose age is beyond the imagination of the normal senses. The Adepts of the ancient Order of the Vairagi meet at the time of the handing of the mantle of spiritual power from the departing Master to his successor.[84]

These meetings are not in the physical, material world – i.e. Twitchell did not physically go to Tibet when he became Living Master, and again when he handed the Rod on to Gross – but on a higher plane, through Soul Travel.

It is not always clear whether the Vairagi ECK Masters whom Twitchell met early in his spiritual career were earthly people or purely on the spiritual planes. According to Eve Illing, most of the Vairagi Masters 'exist in the various levels of heaven.' It appears that Twitchell may have met Rebazar Tarzs, who was over 500 years old, in physical form, but he met Fubbi Quantz (over 1,000 years old) and Yaubl Sacabi (possibly over 2,000 years old) at Golden Wisdom Temples (see below).

Twitchell writes:

All ECK Masters, like Rebazar Tarzs, Fubbi Quantz and Yaubl Sacabi, may live on for years in their physical bodies, far exceeding the normal lifetime of man. Then they will retire and give up their duties to another. However, they will still stand in the background, watching and helping the world unfold spiritually toward its higher destination.[85]

It might seem strange, then, that Twitchell died when he was only around 60, especially as he says,

Usually the ECK Master does not die, in the same way we know human death, but merely moves out of this arena of action into another. The living ECK Master turns over the Rod of Power to his successor at a particular time and then withdraws into the other worlds. Sometimes he stays around, like Rebazar Tarzs, Fubbi Quantz and Yaubl Sacabi.[86]

Rebazar Tarzs was apparently born in 1461 in Tibet. 'He stayed on earth for seventy-five years teaching ECK, then he retired in the same body to the mountainous vast-ness of the Himalayas.'[87]

Twitchell is apparently now working in the heavenly worlds. 'I have no scientific proof myself of this, nor do I know what work he is doing, but I have met him briefly in the inner worlds,' says Illing.

The Adepts of the ancient Order of the Vairagi are 'ECK Masters who are the guardians of the Shariyat-Ki-Sugmad in the Temples of Golden Wisdom.'[86] These Temples include

> the Katsupari Monastery in Tibet (Fubbi Quantz, guardian); the Gare-Hira Temple at Agam Des in the Himalayas (Yaubl Sacabi, guardian); the Faqiti Monastery in the Gobi Desert (Banjani, guardian); and the Temple of ECK, in Chanhassen, Minnesota (Harold Klemp, guardian).[89]

An earlier version of this list of temples included 'the House of Moksha, the Temple on Retz, Venus (Rami Nuri, guardian)'[90] in place of the Faqiti Monastery. According to Illing, these Guardians 'once served as Living ECK Masters on Earth.' There are also

> nine secret ECK Masters who are responsible for the hidden knowledge of the spiritual worlds... These Masters are responsible for the collection of the secret knowledge and its placement into the greatest of sacred books, the *Shariyat-Ki-Sugmad*.[91]

There are 12 volumes of the *Shariyat* on the higher planes, of which the first two have been transcribed by Twitchell and published by Eckankar.

ECK, the power or Spirit of God, can be experienced directly through Light and Sound. This experience is the focal point of the religion, the proof to its members that it works.

> The Light and Sound of God – the Holy Spirit. The two aspects through which God appears in the lower worlds. The Holy Spirit can appear to us as Light, which is a reflection of the atoms of God moving in space, or as Sound, which is the Audible Life Current that carries Soul back home to God. The spiritual exercises of ECK show people how to look and listen within themselves for these qualities of Divine Spirit for uplift and guidance.[92]

The Light and Sound may be seen or heard with the physical eyes and ears, but are usually experienced in a different way. Eckankar, like many of the esoteric religious movements, trains its members in the techniques of visualization, sometimes known as guided meditation; in sleep it is known as lucid dreaming, in which the dreamer takes control of the dream. 'Dreams play an important role in spiritual unfoldment. They are a look into the heavenly worlds. In many cases, the dream becomes a teaching tool.' In fact, 'The ultimate purpose of dreams is to bring the individual closer to the Light and Sound of God'.[93]

This is how visualization works:

> Begin to visualize a growing, golden light surrounding you. It may be very subtle at first. It embraces you, flows with you.
> Soon you are riding currents of light into the vastness of the cosmic sea...
> Ever so lightly, you sense a breeze. You hear the sound of a wind from deep within. It creates tiny ripples on the surface of the sea. Suddenly you realize you're experiencing the Light and Sound of God. You can stay here for a while if you choose, basking in this radiant, soothing ocean of Light and love.
> When you're ready, slowly come back...[94]

Eckankar often borrows the phraseology of other religions (though ECKists see it the other away around) to describe the spiritual benefits of their own.

> Rami Nuri, the great ECK Master in charge of the third section of the *Shariyat-Ki-Sugmad*, at the Temple of Golden Wisdom on Venus, said, 'He who drinks of the stream of ECK can never thirst, but in him is a well of water springing up into life everlasting.'[95] (cf. John 4:14)

The ECK Master Gopal Das is quoted in the *Shariyat-Ki-Sugmad* as saying,

> Those who follow the ECK take nothing for granted, for they must prove it themselves. Only then will they know that God so loved them that He sent a Living ECK Master to bring Souls home to Him.[96] (cf. John 3:16)

Much of the criticism of Eckankar focuses on whether their beliefs are original, truly revealed to Twitchell by Tibetan Vairagi Masters, or whether, to put it bluntly, he cobbled them together from bits of other religions. But in one way, it could be asked, does this really matter? Many of the esoteric and Neo-Pagan religions are openly eclectic, with the philosophy 'If it works, use it.'

For its members, Eckankar works.

'I have been studying the ancient teachings of Eckankar for 28 years and for me they have fulfilled my dreams and answered my questions about Life,' says Illing. 'I am truly grateful for having been shown how to live a balanced life and how to find my own answers.'

The point only becomes important if the religion claims uniqueness in its origins, its vision and its teachings, beliefs and practices, which was certainly the case in the early days of Eckankar.

> But each of those who leave the path of ECK, or refuse to accept the living ECK Master, will come to grief upon the rocks as surely as a captain wrecks his ship on the reef by not listening to the pilot.
>
> Again and again I have pointed out that there is no other path than ECK... anyone who tries another path is trying to start on a lower rung...
>
> The Order of the Vairagi is the only pure line of spiritual Masters in the world.[97]

(Paradoxically, despite this belief that it is the only true path, 'There is no desire to convert people to Eckankar.'[98]) Emphasizing that only Eckankar had the truth, Twitchell also wrote:

> Only by the use of ECK can we take the straight road to this absolute kingdom. All other practices leave us in the lower worlds, because the vehicle they use is not purely spiritual.
>
> The ECK makes use of a true spiritual entity, and consequently gets us access into the pure spiritual regions. Whoever is properly initiated into the mysteries of ECK by a perfect Adept may easily scale spiritual heights that are inaccessible to those who follow any other path to God.[99]

More recently the current ECK Master, Harold Klemp, has taken a different line, accepting that Eckankar is by no means unique, as Twitchell had claimed.

> There are many routes we can take to heaven. God has established so many different paths and means for us that there is a way for everyone... If you are ready, the spiritual exercises of ECK will help you to find your own custom-made approach to the Kingdom of God.[100]

Implicitly accepting that Eckankar is not the only religion of its kind, the Church's website says, 'Of all religions on earth today, Eckankar offers the most direct teachings on the Light and Sound of God.'[101]

For several years, though, Eckankar simply ignored the mounting evidence that Twitchell had borrowed from other sources, even directly plagiarizing other people's books (including Sant Mat teacher Julian Johnson) in his own. This was revealed by researcher David Lane, and later published in his book *The Making of a Spiritual Movement: The Untold Story of Paul Twitchell and Eckankar*.[102] The official explanation since the mid-1980s is that fragments of the Truth are to be found, often distorted, in all the world's religions, and that Twitchell had drawn these together. Nevertheless, Lane showed that in some of his books on Eckankar Twitchell ascribes quotations to various named Masters which, in earlier articles, he had ascribed to L. Ron Hubbard, Kirpal Singh, and the leader of the Self-Revelation Church of Absolute Monism, Swami Premananda.

In reality, Eckankar (like MSIA, page 321) is one of many modern Western versions of the Hindu/Sikh-inspired Sant Mat tradition of Northern India. Of the three religions Twitchell was involved in before founding Eckankar, Ruhani Satsang is the most significant; the teachings of Eckankar are generally similar to those of Kirpal Singh, and several of the teachings Twitchell ascribed to Rebazar Tarzs (a name not recognized by other Sant Mat movements, which also do not recognize Eckankar's lineage of Masters) were actually taken from Kirpal Singh.

There is a large range of esoteric movements in the Western world stemming from the Sant Mat tradition. In the West, these are constantly splintering to form new movements, each one claiming to be the true successor to one of the others; for example, Radhasoami Satsang Beas, Kirpal Singh's previous movement, was itself one of several splinter groups from Radhasoami Satsang, which was founded in 1861 by Soamiji Maharaj. When Kirpal Singh lost the leadership succession in Radhasoami Satsang Beas in 1951 he founded Ruhani Satsang, which itself has spawned at least four other movements – one of them Eckankar.

From an outsider's point of view, such constant splits in this type of religion are almost inevitable because of the essentially subjective nature of the spiritual experience; when the leader of a movement dies, it is quite possible that more than one senior member of the movement, in their individual Soul Travels, will be 'told' by the Masters that they have been appointed to take over.

Quotations from three of the other offshoots of Ruhani Satsang will illustrate the similarities to Eckankar.

- Sawan Kirpal Ruhani Mission: 'We can attain self-knowledge and God-realization through mystic experiences on the path of the Masters.'
- Sant Bani Ashram: '...initiation into the path of Surat Shabd Yoga [i.e. the yoga of the celestial sound], a path of love and discipline that embraces the essence of the teachings of all True Masters.'
- Kirpal Ruhani Satsang, founded by Kirpal's disciple 'the present Living Master, Sant Thakar Singh Ji', is 'devoted to communicating the truth about human existence, its nature and purpose as expressed by the Masters of the Yoga of Inner Light and Sound.'[103]

In response to this, Eve Illing says, 'I can only say my truth is that the teachings of the Light and Sound of God are the root religion, the source of all teachings. There was no one name for this path before 1965 when Paul Twitchell was given the word Eckankar by the Vairagi Masters to be able to identify these ancient teachings by name.'

Eckankar itself has produced at least one offshoot, in addition to Darwin Gross's movement: the Divine Science of Light and Sound, founded by a former Eckankar leader, Jerry Mulvin, in California in 1980.

MOVEMENT OF SPIRITUAL INNER AWARENESS

The Church of the Movement of Inner Spiritual Awareness (MSIA) shares common origins with the personal development movement Insight (see page 434), but both organizations stress that they are completely separate. According to a senior staff member, Mark Lurie, most members pronounce MSIA as separate initials, rather than as 'Messiah', as is often stated.[104]

MSIA was founded in 1971 by John-Roger, who was born Roger Delano Hinkins in 1934, into a Mormon family in Utah. He left the Mormons in the 1950s and tried out a number of religious movements. He took courses from the Rosicrucian organization AMORC (see page 356), and was involved for a while with Eckankar (see page 312), though he says he was never an initiate. There are similarities between the beliefs of MSIA and those of Eckankar, which was founded by Paul Twitchell in 1965, and which has roots in Kirpal Singh's esoteric Hindu/Sikh Sant Mat teachings. John-Roger explains:

> I had a private interview with Twitchell, and he said, 'You have the sound [and] the names of the Gods on every realm.' I said, 'They're all the same God, it's just a different vibration.' He said, 'You know them?' I said, 'Sure I know them.' And we discussed the initiation words, and he told me a sampling of his. And I said, 'I don't use those, I use the five names.'[105]

Much of the spiritual teaching of MSIA is broadly the same as that of Eckankar, though some of the terminology is different (in contrast with some Christian offshoots, which might keep the same terminology but change its meaning).

In 1963 Roger Hinkins, then a high-school English teacher, fell into a nine-day coma after an operation to remove a kidney stone. He became aware of a new spiritual personality called John, who had merged with his existing personality; and so he became John-Roger (often known within the movement as J-R). He met 'John the Beloved' on the spiritual plane, though apparently he was confused for some years about who it was he had met, thinking initially that it was Rebazar Tarzs, the ECK

Master, and then that it was Sawan Singh, the Radhasoami Satsang Beas master who died in 1948. Twitchell was endowed with Mystical Traveller Consciousness, which appears to be similar to being Eckankar's Living ECK Master.

John-Roger started to give 'Light Studies' seminars in 1968, in Santa Barbara, California, and when these developed, set up MSIA in 1971. There was a period, as with many movements of the day, when communal living was encouraged at MSIA's Prana centre in Los Angeles, but the building soon became MSIA's headquarters and home to the Peace Theological Seminary. MSIA students receive monthly 'Soul Awareness Discourses', a series of 144 lessons based on transcripts of John-Roger's talks. Of the roughly 5,000 MSIA members, over half are in the USA, and around 40 per cent of those are in California.

As the Mystical Traveller, John-Roger claims to have total awareness on all levels of consciousness; MSIA aims to teach this same awareness to others. Its various linked organizations include the University of Santa Monica, which offers Masters degrees in subjects such as Spiritual Psychology and Counselling Psychology; the Peace Theological Seminary and College of Philosophy, which gives classes, work-shops, retreats, a Master of Theology degree in Practical Spirituality, and a Doctor of Spiritual Science degree; the Heartfelt Foundation, a volunteer service to the sick, terminally ill, lonely, and at-risk families; the Institute for Individual and World Peace, which seeks to promote peace through workshops and seminars; and Insight, a personal self-improvement seminar. MSIA also lays strong emphasis on alternative health therapies.

In 1988 John-Roger passed the mantle of Mystical Traveller on to John Morton, who had been working with him since 1977, and who is now the spiritual director of MSIA. John-Roger is still very much involved with MSIA and its associated organi-zations, as a teacher and source of inspiration, but is not regarded in any way as a 'guru'; MSIA is emphatic that it focuses on Soul Transcendence, not on its founder or leader. (In his study of the movement, academic James Lewis describes John-Roger as 'one of the least charismatic people I had ever met.'[106])

MSIA's beliefs stem from the Sant Mat tradition, which developed out of Hinduism and Sikhism, and spawned numerous movements in the USA (see page 320). It teaches that by meditating under a teacher's guidance, one's inner eyes and ears will be opened to the sight and sound of God. Unlike other Sant Mat offshoots, including Eckankar, MSIA holds Christ to be important.

Jesus Christ is the head of the Church of the Movement of Spiritual Inner Awareness, and the Traveller's work through MSIA (Soul Transcendence) is based on Jesus' work. Jesus was a Mystical Traveller, and he made it possible for all people to enter the Soul realm; before that time, this was available to only a few people.[107]

On a casual reading of MSIA's magazine *The New Day Herald*, with its many references to Jesus, Christ and the Holy Spirit, one might think that MSIA is a Christian religion. In fact, their understanding of Jesus, and of Christ, is quite different from those of most Christian Churches, though they have something in common with the more esoteric interpretations of Christianity:

> The Christ Consciousness is a universal consciousness of love and pure Spirit, which exists through each person through the Soul, and it is the spiritual line of energy on which MSIA is based.

As in Eckankar, there is an acceptance of several different realms; these are the physical; the astral, which is imagination, fears and fantasies; the causal, relating to feelings and emotions; the mental, or processes of the mind; the etheric, which equates to the subconscious; and the Soul realm, 'which equates to the Soul, which is your beingness. The Soul is your truest reality.' All the other realms are lower levels, and are illusory and transient. The central idea of MSIA is that by experiencing the transcendence of the Soul one can move one's consciousness into the Soul. This has practical consequences:

> When you are in the Soul, you can more easily see the pitfalls and the obstacles of your life on the lower levels. You can experience a love for and a oneness with other people that is beyond anything you have ever experienced before.

By moving one's consciousness into higher levels of awareness, it becomes possible to deal with the ordinary problems of life more easily and effectively, and to take more responsibility for oneself.

> More people are learning to take responsibility for their own actions. It becomes more and more difficult to lay your troubles at someone else's doorstep and say, 'My misery is your fault.' No, your misery is only your choice. Your joy is also your choice. Those choices and all the variables between are available to you at any moment. Too often, you allow the temporary feeling state of the body to misrepresent who you are inside.[108]

MSIA doesn't have a 'creed'; John-Roger's books and courses stress that people should apply the teachings of MSIA where they work:

> If it's not practical, if you can't work it, why bother with it. If it works for you, use it; if it doesn't, have the wit to let it go... If you said, 'What's your definition of God?' I'd have to say, 'God is God.' I have no more definition than

that. I can tell you more about the experiences of God. God loves all Its creation, out of God come all things, and not one Soul will be lost. I can tell you how that works down here. Take care of yourself, so you can help take care of others. Don't hurt yourself, and don't hurt others. And use everything for your advancement, upliftment and growing.... Those are the guidelines, not the rules.[109]

John Morton, now the spiritual director of MSIA, also emphasizes the importance of personal responsibility:

The reality is that there is a dynamic in MSIA that I haven't experienced elsewhere. The responsibility is clearly placed on each person to check things out and validate them for themself. We often say that MSIA is a group of non-joiners, people who backed into one another because they were backing away from all these other forms that are out there. We find ourselves in a quadrant of people who are independent and have done a lot of self-processing, looking and considering. MSIA is not usually their initial effort in adapting something religiously or spiritually. I like that.[110]

Although study of the monthly Discourses continues for 12 years, members may apply for initiation after two years. In the first initiation they are given the sacred names of God for the astral and causal levels, to be chanted in their daily meditations or spiritual exercises. Further initiations – mental, etheric and Soul – may follow at roughly two-year intervals, or when the member is ready for them. After the first initiation into the Sound Current, the initiate may apply to be ordained as an MSIA minister.

Like many new religions, MSIA has had its share of controversy. David Christopher Lane, an American academic who was a Radhasoami initiate (a Sant Mat group which long preceded both Eckankar and MSIA), accused John-Roger of plagiarizing Sant Mat teachings. (Similar accusations have been made about Eckankar.) He also alleged that some ex-members had claimed that John-Roger had sexually manipulated them. These criticisms hit the headlines in the USA in 1994 when the *Los Angeles Times* and *Time* magazine revealed that Arianna Stassinopoulos Huffington, wife of the US multi-millionaire and Senate candidate Michael Huffington, was a member. Two court cases resulting from these allegations went in MSIA's favour. There have also been allegations that Insight Transformational Seminars are a front, a recruiting device, for MSIA (see page 436). However, over 500,000 people have taken Insight seminars, and MSIA has around 5,000 members; as one of MSIA's leaders, Mark Lurie has said, 'If Insight was a recruiting arm for MSIA, it was a poor one.'

ELAN VITAL

Like several of the other religious movements which were popular in the heady days of the 1960s and 1970s, Elan Vital has moved on from its origins. Originally the flamboyant and definitely Eastern-inspired Divine Light Mission, it has matured into something new, changing its name to reflect its current emphasis and approach and, presumably, to distance itself from the past. It might now be thought of as a 'spiritual personal development movement' teaching meditation techniques; it is included in this section because of its origins, rather than its current teachings.

HISTORY

There were several popular Eastern gurus in the late 1960s, including the Maharishi Mahesh Yogi, Bhagwan Shree Rajneesh, and Guru Maharaj Ji. The first two, with their long flowing beards, fitted the Western conception of an Eastern guru; the third was, when he sprang to prominence in 1971, a 13-year-old boy.

Maharaji (the version of his name used from the 1980s) was born in 1957. He was the son of Shri Hans Ji Maharaj, who in 1960 founded a mission in Delhi, later known as the Divine Light Mission. This was based on the Sikh/Hindu Sant Mat teachings of his own guru, Sarupanand Ji, of enlightenment through knowledge.

When his father died in 1966, the eight-year-old Prem Pal Singh Rawat stood up, announced that he was the new guru, and started teaching. As Guru Maharaj Ji he embarked on a world tour in 1971, and quickly established a large following in Britain and America. In 1973 he held what should have been a huge event in the Houston Astrodome; Millennium '73 was intended to launch the spiritual millennium, but the event was a washout in its effects and in attendance, and was a financial disaster. In 1974, at 16, Maharaji married his 24-year-old secretary Marolyn Johnson.

At about this time he fell out with his mother, Mata Ji, who had until then really been running the organization along with one of Maharaji's three older brothers, Bal Bhagwan Ji, who (after legal battles) still heads the Divine Light Mission in India. Press reports at the time said that she disapproved of Maharaji's lifestyle, which was described as luxurious.

According to Glen Whittaker, former National Organizer of Elan Vital in the UK,[111] 'he married an American woman he loved (rather than taking an Indian bride), and behind this was the subtext of her declining influence over the way the teaching was promoted as Maharaji became adult and made it increasingly clear that the Knowledge was not an Indian teaching, but universal.'

Maharaji had seen that the Indian influences on his Western followers were 'unnecessary and in fact a hindrance to the wider acceptance of his teaching.' Over the next few years the style of the teachings changed, dropping the Eastern terminology and ideas and focusing entirely on the Knowledge.

In 1983 the movement's name was changed to Elan Vital to reflect the change in emphasis. Maharaji agreed with the closing of ashrams, or communal homes, which had become a feature of the movement by the early 1980s. He also renounced his almost-divine status as guru; his followers began referring to him as a humanitarian leader rather than Lord of the Universe. (One member has suggested that some of the criticisms of the movement come from members from the early days 'who wanted to make Maharaji into a god, and now resent him for not being one.'[112]) The teachers of the Knowledge, formerly called mahatmas, became simply instructors. In 1987 Maharaji took over all the teaching and giving of the Knowledge himself, 'for the sake of clarity, simplicity and effectiveness,' says Heather Evans, UK spokesperson of Elan Vital.[113]

The move from the Divine Light Mission to Elan Vital was much more than simply a name change, she says; it was a different conception:

> Divine Light Mission had become a movement with all the trappings of a new religion. This was dismantled. There are now various organizations called Elan Vital which organize themselves according to their own cultural, national and legal customs. These are run by a mixture of volunteers and paid staff.

She stresses that Maharaji himself did not set up either the Divine Light Mission or its successor, Elan Vital, 'the registered charity that promotes Maharaji's teachings. He has never had an official or formal role in the Elan Vital organizations established around the world.'

The British organization Elan Vital was founded in 1991, 20 years after Maharaji first took Britain by storm; it was registered as an educational charity in 1992.

BELIEFS AND PRACTICES

Elan Vital has now dropped all of its original Eastern religious practices. According to Whittaker,

> although Maharaji is originally from India, there is no connection between what he teaches and the religions or religious background of that country. In particular, the teaching does not concern itself with such concepts as reincarnation, heaven or life after death. Maharaji only encourages people to experience the present reality of life now.

Unusually, the fact that Maharaji came from a line of 'Perfect Masters' is no longer relevant to the reformed movement. 'This is not where the authority comes from, nor the recognition of Maharaji as the master by his student; this comes rather from the nature of the teaching and its benefit to the individual.'

Maharaji himself has put his early life behind him.

In a simple metaphor explaining his position, he will... say although the service history and list of previous owners of a car is useful to have, what is more important is does it work and is it in good enough condition for you and what you need it for now.

The Divine Light movement used to be criticized for the devotion given to Maharaji, who was thought to live a life of luxury on the donations of his followers; Whittaker, clearly conscious of past criticisms, is emphatic that Maharaji has never earned anything from Elan Vital or any other movement promoting his teachings.

'He lives as a private individual in the United States with his wife and four children and spends most of his year on teaching tours in various parts of the world.' He speaks at around 250 meetings a year,

on his own experience of life, its nature and purpose, often with humour and perception. He speaks essentially of an experience of stillness, peace and contentment it is possible to achieve within, and his Knowledge consists of techniques to go within for this purpose.

At the heart of Elan Vital is this Knowledge – loosely, the joy of true self-knowledge. Whittaker explains:

In brief, his view is that each individual should seek to know his or her true self. In his talks, he explains the rationale for the need to know oneself and to explore the clues which point to that within us which is worthy of our knowledge, and which, when experienced, brings with it a feeling of well-being, of happiness, of being in harmony with one's own source...

For those who wish to pursue his teaching in a practical way he is able to direct them in certain simple techniques of inner stillness, which when practised allow the sense of well-being, of inner satisfaction, to be experienced; this teaching is given the name 'knowledge'.

The Knowledge includes four meditation techniques; these have some similarity to techniques in other Sant Mat-derived movements, and may derive originally from *surat shabd yoga* (see page 320). 'That which we seek is already within us,' says Whittaker; 'the process of reaching it is one of learning to experience what is already there. It is one the individual has to perform for him- or herself, with the guidance and help of the teacher.'

The emphasis is on individual, subjective experience rather than on a body of dogma, and in its Divine Light days the movement was sometimes criticized for this stressing of emotional experience over intellect.

The teachings could perhaps best be described as practical mysticism.

It is important to understand that his teaching is practical and pragmatic; he will speak of the great value of trust in that power which gives life, and orders life most perfectly, but only in terms of a real experience. He does not refer to 'God', but to the god within you, or the divinity within, as the power that gives existence. He has sometimes referred to the existence of two gods – the one created by humankind and the one which creates humankind. But though such references obviously infer an acceptance of a creative, loving power, he distances himself and his teaching strongly from the concept of religion. He regards himself as an educator.

In the UK Elan Vital is a very small operation, with only three or four full-time staff, depending very much on volunteer help and funding. As a charity it 'provides the legal framework and support structure for the personal teaching between master and student to take place.' It presents video screenings and satellite broadcasts of Maharaji's talks around Britain, and arranges for his teaching tours.

'When visiting Britain in person, Maharaji is also able to instruct people who wish in the techniques of Knowledge. This process is sometimes called receiving Knowledge,' says Whittaker. Evans explains further:

People aspiring to learn the techniques are asked to study, listening to Maharaji's addresses for at least five months before asking to be shown the techniques. I would also like to make it clear that the instruction sessions in which Maharaji teaches the techniques are not secretive, but private, between master and student.

At present around 35,000 people in India are 'waiting to receive Knowledge'; in Europe around 800, and in the USA around 300. As Elan Vital is not a 'membership organization', the numbers of those who 'practise the techniques of Knowledge' are not certain, but there are thought to be around 75,000 outside India, including perhaps as many as 10,000 in the UK; there are a further 250,000 in India. Over 305,000 people attended Maharaji's lectures in 1998, including 233,000 in India, 28,000 in Europe, and 25,000 in North America.

Followers in the West do not see themselves as members of a religion. Whittaker explains:

We are simply people who appreciate and practise the teaching of a unique individual, who asks nothing of us other than that we enjoy our life to the full... Beyond the intrinsic merit of the teaching, it differs from many other teachings which might seem similar from the outside by being free of charge at every stage.

The aim of Elan Vital, says Evans, is 'to promote an inner experience of peace and an understanding of what it means to be alive.' She quotes Maharaji:

> My efforts have always been to help people understand and feel the feeling within. People through the years have tried to place me in a mould, and from the very early years I have not been able to oblige them. When I was very young, people were looking for the 'old silver-haired Guru with flowing white robes.' I was only eight. When people were flocking to India for their search, I was in the West. When people were looking for sophisticated discourses, I spoke of simple things. When people wanted *nirvana*, I said, 'You need peace.' When people said, 'Tell us of the scriptures,' I said, 'Look within you.' When people asked, 'What is your qualification?' I said, 'Judge me by what I offer.'

Notes

[1] Booklet: *Brahma Kumaris: A University for the World*, London: Brahma Kumaris Information Services Ltd, 1998: 26.

[2] Hodgkinson 1999: 22.

[3] Ibid.: 49.

[4] Ibid.: 85.

[5] Membership figures from Maureen Goodman, Programme Co-ordinator, Brahma Kumaris World Spiritual University (UK), in correspondence with the author, 29 December 1999.

[6] Unless otherwise stated, all quotations are from David Boddy, in correspondence and conversation with the author, 28 June and 21 July 1995, and 21 February 2000.

[7] Hounam and Hogg 1984: 83.

[8] Booklet: *The School*, London: School of Economic Science, n.d.

[9] Ibid.

[10] Published by Shepheard-Walwyn.

[11] *The Way of Hermes*, London: Duckworth, 1999.

[12] Unless otherwise stated, all quotations are from Nigel Kahn of the UK press office of the Maharishi Foundation, in correspondence with the author, 6 and 28 October and 10, 17, 18 and 22 November 1995, and 18 February 2000.

[13] Natural Law Party European Election Communication, 1994: 6.

[14] Merseyside Police Press Office, in correspondence with the author, 13 September 1995.

[15] Quotations from Guy Hatchard taken from his letter (28 October 1995) to Nigel Kahn in response to a query by the author.

[16] Natural Law Party European Election Communication, 1994: 4, 7.

[17] Ibid.: 4, 4–5, 6.

[18] Unless otherwise stated, all quotations are by Bhagavat Dharma, former Communications Manager for ISKCON in the UK, in conversation with the author, 19 June 1995.

[19]'Cleaning House and Cleaning Hearts: Reform and Renewal in ISKCON', Part 1, *ISKCON Communications Journal*, no. 3, January–June 1994: 47.

[20]Ibid., Part 2, *ISKCON Communications Journal*, no. 4, July–December 1994: 25.

[21]Ibid., Part 1: 44.

[22] Shaunaka Rishi Das, editor of the *ISKCON Communications Journal*, in conversation with the author, 21 and 22 March 2000.

[23]Puttick 1997: 28.

[24]Ibid.: 18.

[25]Milne 1986: 21.

[26]Ibid.: 201.

[27]Strelley 1987: 360, Milne 1986: 314.

[28]Milne 1986: 24.

[29]Quoted in Milne 1986: 295.

[30]Strelley 1987: 348, 361–2, 364.

[31]Swami Amrito in correspondence with the author, 18 March 2000.

[32]Unless otherwise stated, all quotations are taken from an Osho International document entitled 'Can you give me a message to take to the world so that people there might understand you and your followers?', n.d.

[33]Cf. the similar words of Justin Martyr (see page 130).

[34]Osho International booklet: *The World of Meditation*, n.d.

[35]Brochure: *Osho Commune International: An Invitation/Osho Multiversity*, n.d.

[36]Ibid.

[37]Ibid.

[38]All quotations are taken from the Sahaja Yoga website at http://www.sahajayoga.org.

[39]Although they are not quoted in this entry, I would like to thank Charlotte Bie for providing copies of her unpublished BA thesis *God is not a Gentleman and I Am That One: An analysis of the charismatic authority of Avatara Adi Da*, SOAS, 1997, and her unpublished MSc dissertation *The Sacred Stories of Adidam*, London School of Economics, 1998, which have provided very useful background information.

[40]Adidam flier: *Da Avabhasa (The Bright)*, 1994.

[41]*Ruchira* means 'radiant' or 'bright'; he is an *Avatar*, or God in physical form; *Adi* means 'first'; *Da*, according to another source, means 'real God', and *Samraj* means 'universal ruler' or 'supreme lord'.

[42]Ibid.

[43]Lee 1998: 721.

[4]Booklet: *The Ruchira Avatar: An Introduction to Adi Da Love-Ananda Samraj*, 1997.

[45]Originally Friends of Andrew Cohen in England, then Friends of Andrew Cohen in Europe.

[46]FACE press release.

[47]Andrew Cohen, *Autobiography of an Awakening*, Corte Madera: Moksha Foundation, 1992: 5–6, quoted in Rawlinson 1997: 213.

[48]Peter Bampton of the Impersonal Enlightenment Fellowship, in correspondence with the author, 1 March 2000.

[49]Andrew Cohen, FACE press release.

[50] Booklet: *The Art of Living: an Introduction to the Buddhism of Nichiren Daishonin*, 1993: 30–1.

[51]Ibid.: 19.

[52]Ibid.: 20.

[53]Ibid.: 22.

[54]Booklet: *Introducing SGI-UK*, n.d.: 2.

[55]Ibid.: 3.

[56]*The Art of Living*: 23.

[57]Ibid.: 32.

[58]*Golden Drum: A Magazine for Western Buddhists*, Aug/Oct 1995: 1.

[59]*Tricycle: The Buddhist Review*, Summer 1999: 68.

[60]Letter to the author from Dh. Karmabandhu, London Buddhist Centre manager, 8 March 1996.

[61]Booklet: *Buddhism for the West: A short introduction to the Friends of the Western Buddhist Order*, n.d.

[62]Ibid.

[64]*The Guardian*, 27 October 1997.

[65]Vishvapani, head of the FWBO Communications Office at the London Buddhist Centre, quoted in *Tricycle: The Buddhist Review*, Summer 1999: 114.

[66]Ananda, quoted in Ibid.: 114.

[67]Vishvapani, 'Face to Faith: Buddhism Distorted', *The Guardian*, 11 November 1997.

[68]Figures supplied to the author by Vishvapani, FWBO Communications Office, 30 March 2000.

[68]New Kadampa Tradition website at http://www.users.dircon.co.uk/~kadampa.

[69]New Kadampa Tradition page at http://www.charasambara.org/nkt.htm.

[70]This and the following quotation are from Jim Belither, NKT secretary, in correspondence with the author, 1 March 2000.

[71]Eckankar, ECK, Soul Travel and Mahanta are trademarks of Eckankar.

[72]Twitchell 1971: 198.

[73]Ibid.: 194.

[74]Klemp 1988: 139.

[75]Cramer and Munson 1995: 5.

[76]Quotations from Eve Illing are from correspondence with the author, 25 February, 18 July , 8 August 1995 and 14 November 1999.

[77]Klemp 1991: 1, 15.

[78]Klemp 1988: 139.

[79]Twitchell 1971: 57–8.

[80]Ibid.: 192.

[81]Ibid.: 104.

[82]Ibid.: 43.

[83]Cramer and Munson 1995: 110.

[84]Twitchell 1971: 152.

[85]Ibid.: 80.

[86]Ibid.: 131.

[87]Ibid.: 193–4.

[88]Ibid.: 152.

[89]Cramer and Munson 1995: 60.

[90]Cramer and Munson 1993: 60.

[91]Twitchell 1971: 153.

[92]Cramer and Munson 1995: 10.

[93]Ibid.: 30, 34–5.

[94]Ibid: 70–1.

[95]Twitchell 1971: 118.

[96]Ibid.: 112.

[97]Ibid.: 195–6.

[98]Cramer and Munson 1995: 8.

[99]Twitchell 1971: 42–3.

[100]Sri Harold Klemp, *The Golden Heart Mahanta Transcripts*, Book 4, quoted in Cramer and Munson 1995: 1, though not in the 1993 edition.

[101]http://www.eckankar.org/light.html.

[102]Del Mar, CA: Del Mar Publishing, 1978.

[103]Beit Hallahmi 1993: 256, 254, 160.

[104]Quotations from Mark Lurie are from a conversation with the author, 12 November 1999.

[105]Quoted in Lewis 1998: 21.

[106]Lewis 1998: 7.

[107]Unless otherwise stated, quotations are taken from the booklet *Soul Transcendence: An Introduction to the Movement of Spiritual Inner Awareness*, Los Angeles: Peace Theological Seminary & College of Philosophy, 1999.

[108]John-Roger 1986: 126.

[109]*Interviews with John-Roger and John Morton*, 1999: 70–1.

[110]Ibid.: 83–4.

[111]Unless otherwise stated, all quotations are from Glen Whittaker, former National Organizer of Elan Vital in the UK, in correspondence with the author, 28 February and 23 June 1995.

[112]Correspondence with the author.

[113]Heather Evans, UK spokesperson of Elan Vital, in correspondence with the author, 15 March 2000.

CHAPTER 15

Esoteric and Neo-Pagan Movements

THERE are some overlaps between Neo-Pagan beliefs, witchcraft or Wicca, Druidry, esoteric and occult beliefs, magical groups, and Satanism, but there are also many differences. Headline-hungry journalists who lump them all together and equate, for example, Tarot-reading with witches with black magic with Satanists, haven't done their homework; or if they have, why let the facts get in the way of a good story? Fundamentalist Christians who do the same have other motives: any belief which isn't of Christ must necessarily be of the Devil – 'He that is not with me is against me' (Matthew 12:30) – so all Neo-Pagans are by definition Satanists, whether they think they are or not.

Christians in particular shy away from the word 'occult', as though it must have devilish connotations. In fact, the word simply means 'hidden' or 'secret', and since many of the traditional occult teachings are now widely available – indeed, many of the esoteric or 'occult' schools now have websites explaining their purpose – the term no longer really applies.

This section begins with a brief look at 'Satanic Ritual Abuse' and Satanism, then examines a number of esoteric movements and Neo-Pagan movements. There is sometimes considerable crossover between these two broad categories. For example, although the esoteric movements are usually either Eastern-based or Judaeo-Christian in origin, some of them are closer to Goddess-worship, which is essentially Pagan. Similarly, although the Neo-Pagan movements are mainly based on Celtic, Norse or Native American traditions, many also use Tarot, and some the Kabbala, which are essentially esoteric. Especially since the development of Chaos Magic in recent years, there is an increasing convergence, not necessarily of beliefs, but of shared interests. The fortnightly Talking Stick meeting (now known as the Secret Chiefs) in a central London pub, for example, is usually attended by Wiccans, Druids, Odinists, shamans, workers of Crowleyan-type magick, esoteric Christians, Chaos magicians, and at least two or three PhD researchers doing participant observation.

In addition to the specific groups considered in this section, there are millions of individual people who belong to no movement, but who have some interest in what are loosely called 'New Age' ideas. A glance at the 'Mind-Body-Spirit' shelves in a general bookshop, or at the contents of a specialist esoteric bookshop, will reveal books on healing, spiritual environmentalism, crystals, channelling, Tarot, astrology, mythology, the Goddess, reincarnation, hermetic philosophy, Rosicrucianism, the Hermetic Order of the Golden Dawn and esoteric Christianity – to name but a few subjects – stacked side by side. Some book buyers may only be interested in one particular subject; but probably most will have an interest in several, which will overlap in different ways for different people.

There are also many today who use aromatherapy, reflexology, acupuncture, homeopathy, herbal remedies, yoga, meditation and a host of other alternative medical or psychological methods. The New Age (or Aquarian) ideology which encompasses all of these interests, ideas and therapies, and which has now almost entered the mainstream, overlaps strongly with the development of Neo-Pagan religious movements over the last three or four decades.

ESOTERIC GROUPS

The wide range of esoteric groups which have grown up over the last century or so have many differences, but also have a number of things in common. Some are a synthesis of Western (Judaeo-Christian) and Eastern (Hindu, Buddhist or Sufi) thought; others could be described as mystical, magical, Judaeo-Christianity. Many believe in Secret Masters (sometimes called the Great White Brotherhood) who have tremendous powers and who have guarded the true religious teaching, the origin of all world religions, for thousands of years. Some are, in one way or another, Gnostic, in that they emphasize secret knowledge, restricted to a select few (their own members). Their originators were often both brilliant and highly unorthodox in both their thought and their lifestyles.

Their beliefs and practices can be described as occult (hidden), esoteric (within, i.e. only for the initiated) or hermetic (after Hermes Trismegistus, but also implying 'sealed', as in an hermetic seal); they also usually include both magic and mysticism. They are highly complex, and progressive, in that the teachings build up on each other in steps.

Most present-day esoteric movements are eclectic: they borrow from several traditions, and from movements slightly earlier than themselves. Schisms and offshoots are frequent, partly perhaps because of the unorthodox nature of both the beliefs and the believers. The entries on esoteric groups – a small but probably representative selection – can only be brief summaries, giving a broad indication of those beliefs and practices which are known to outsiders.

NEO-PAGAN GROUPS

The word 'Pagan' originally meant 'country-dweller'; the sophisticated, cosmopolitan, educated Romans applied the term to anyone (usually on the fringes of the Empire) who held to strange, primitive beliefs – the uneducated barbarians. Stripping off the pejorative overtones, Pagan simply means someone who follows the old native religion of their land, rather than an imported religion; usually, but not always, this includes worship either of the Earth Mother Goddess with or without her consort, or of a pantheon of gods – or both. (Hinduism has sometimes been called a Pagan religion because of its multiplicity of gods, but polytheism is not synonymous with Paganism. Overlaps with Hindu ideas, such as reincarnation and meditation, can be found in Western Neo-Paganism, but there are also many differences. For the purposes of this book Hinduism and its offshoots are treated only as Eastern religions, and Paganism refers only to Western Paganism.)

'Heathen', similarly, meant 'people who live on the heath', again in distinction from sophisticated city-dwellers.

'Neo-Paganism', to quote Oberon Zell, founder of Church of All Worlds, who is said to have coined the term, is 'a revival and reconstruction of ancient Nature religions adapted for the modern world.'[1]

Probably the largest area of Neo-Paganism encountered in Britain and Europe is one form or another of Wicca, though there are also, among others, Druidry, Shamanism and Norse religion. In North America the revival of ancient cultural traditions, including those of Native Americans, was well under way before Wicca started to make inroads there in the 1970s. Also, as we shall see, Wicca is largely the legacy of one British man in the 1950s, whereas North American Neo-Paganism, to quote Zell, 'emerged in the 1960s, and was strongly affected by the whole Hippie consciousness – sex, drugs, rock'n'roll, communes, hair etc.'

Most followers (and self-acknowledged recreators) of the Norse religion prefer the term Heathen to distinguish them from the more Goddess-based Wicca-type Neo-Paganism.

Because nearly everything that can be called Neo-Pagan is eclectic, borrowing from several sources, there are overlaps between the various forms of Neo-Paganism. There are links between some forms of Wicca and Druidry, and between both of these and Shamanism. In Britain, several leading Druids are also Wiccan priests.

There is a wide variety of books available on all aspects of Paganism and related subjects. On the Celtic, Arthurian and Western Mystery Traditions, prominent writers include Caitlín and John Matthews and R.J. Stewart, among many others; on Wicca, writers include Janet and Stuart Farrar and Marian Green; on the Northern (Norse/Germanic) Traditions, Kveldulfr Gundarsson/Stephan Grundy, Nigel Pennick and Freya Aswynn; on Druidry, Ross Nichols, Philip Carr-Gomm and Philip Shallcrass; and on Shamanism Joan Halifax and Kenneth Meadows. This is by no means an exclusive list of authors, but includes some of those whom the present author has found useful, sound, and readable.

One of the most important facets of Neo-Paganism for the non-Pagan to understand is its diversity.

> The trouble with general Paganism and Wicca, from the point of view of an encyclopedia, is that they are non-hierarchical and do not have organizations that are religion-based beyond their own small groups; it is therefore advisable to talk to as many people as possible... Beware of those who claim to speak for all witches![2]

Oberon Zell says much the same:

> We have met dogmatic and non-dogmatic Christians from the same church. The same goes for Pagans. Some may be dogmatic about the form of their practice, while others are not. Some people believe that magic is stronger when actions are repeated the same way each time. Others make their rituals completely new each time. The general structure of Neo-Paganism, however, is so varied as to be impossible to dictate to any large number of people. As the saying goes, ask two Pagans a question and get three different answers.
>
> We generally believe the world is to be discovered, not dictated. We are not arrogant enough to think we have all the answers, and believe flexibility is essential in reflecting an organic, Nature-based religion. Dogmatism stagnates. Only flexibility allows evolution to occur.

This seems to be a fairly general view in the Neo-Pagan world – though, as he says, not everyone will agree...

The entries on Neo-Pagan movements are necessarily a small handful of the many hundreds of different groups, but they should give some idea of both the diversity and the commonality of Neo-Paganism today.

It should be stressed that the individuals quoted in these entries are speaking for themselves and their own movements, and not on behalf of Neo-Paganism as a whole. Even those who offer introductory courses to the whole movement are speaking from their own perspective.

MAGIC

One term which both esoteric movements and Neo-Pagan movements have in common is 'magic', a word which immediately summons up Dennis Wheatley-type images, giving opponents an easy rod with which to beat both types of movement. Speaking very broadly, esoteric groups with a Judaeo-Christian lineage tend to practise what might be called high ritual magic, while Neo-Pagans generally practise a more Nature-centred magic, though this also usually involves ritual. Generalizing again, perhaps esoteric magic tends to be more cerebral, and Neo-Pagan magic more emotional. But what do they actually mean by 'magic'? (see page 404)

Magic in the sense of casting spells to harm people, or to make people do things against their will, simply is not part of any Neo-Pagan or esoteric religion. For a Neo-Pagan, magic might mean healing someone of a headache by drawing power into them; or it might mean encouraging plants to grow healthily. Blessing a new child, or a home, or any positive activity, perhaps by dedicating it to the Goddess and/or God, might also be called magic. But Neo-Paganism also shares with esoteric religion the main purpose of magic: that it is more a reworking of the inner person than of the outer world. The alchemical transformation of base metals to gold was always an analogy for the transformation of the soul.

All magic involves the will and the imagination, or controlled visualization; a person pictures what he desires to occur, realistically or symbolically, and wills it to be. Part of the work of most esoteric schools is training in visualization techniques, and in concentration of the will.

Does magic actually work? The short answer has to be 'Yes', *so far as those who use it are concerned.* Whether a sceptical observer could be persuaded is another matter, and is perhaps irrelevant. If someone believes that magic works, then magic does work, at least for that person. (Magic has been beautifully described as 'a creative and potentially valuable self-delusion.'³) So far as some of the examples of magic just mentioned are concerned, there can be little doubt that healing often appears to work, and whether it is through a Christian's prayers and the Holy Spirit's work, or through a Neo-Pagan asking the Goddess, or through a channelling of natural power, the headache is still gone. So far as encouraging plants to grow healthily is concerned, some people naturally have 'green fingers', which could be seen as a form of magic – certainly by those people who can't keep a plant alive for more than a week.

As for the transformation of the soul, so that someone becomes more spiritual and a better person, and so has a positive effect on the world around them: prayer, devotion, meditation, mysticism, miracles and magic could all be seen as different names for much the same interrelated causes, processes and effects. Too much concentration on the precise definition of separate labels isn't really all that useful.

In general, the groups in this section were extremely helpful, and were far more forthcoming about their beliefs and practices than several of the better-known Christian movements. Because of past media distortion, and because of deceptive practices employed by some previous 'investigators', some of the schools of magic were initially understandably wary; most of these were eventually far more open than might be expected.

I acknowledged the help, in the first edition of this book, of Stewart Farrar, for providing several pre-publication chapters of his excellent book *The Pagan Path* (Phoenix Publishing, USA); Stewart, one of the most visible of Britain's witches, sadly died in February 2000, while the current book was being written.

Few of the groups, organizations, movements or schools in this section go out actively recruiting new members. Some do advertise in New Age magazines or book-shops, or take a stand at Mind-Body-Spirit fairs, but the high-pressure sales tech-niques often employed by 'sects and cults' are alien to the entire philosophy of most esoteric and Neo-Pagan groups.

People who are interested in joining them, one way or another track them down, and ask (usually very politely) if they might be allowed to find out more about them. In the case of what might be called the Eco-Pagans, they are generally welcomed with open arms; in the case of the schools of occult science, they might be required to prove their sincerity over the first few months, and to spend their first year or more on an intro-ductory, probationary course, before being invited to go on to deeper study – or not.

All the organizations listed here have given permission for their addresses to be quoted. Several of them have post boxes, and these often, in the UK, have BM names. British Monomark (BM for personal and BCM for business post boxes) is a long-established London company which offers secure post boxes to anyone who needs one. Many Neo-Pagan and esoteric organizations use them, not particularly through any desire for secrecy, but because in a world of religious intolerance, they want to protect themselves against possible physical attack – including, occasionally, from Fundamentalist Christians.

This threat can be all too real. One Neo-Pagan healer, not even a practising witch, who is known personally to the author, was publicly denounced by name as an enemy of Christ, by a minister who had never met her, in a Church of England service at which she was not present; she learnt of this through some of her workmates ostra-cizing her. Neo-Pagans have received death-threats from Christians. Esoteric book-shops have been set on fire.

The overwhelming majority of Fundamentalist Evangelical Christians, whatever their views of Neo-Pagan and esoteric faiths, would be horrified at this. But with the rise in Fundamentalism, some present-day witches genuinely fear the return of 'the burning times', the literal witch hunts which lit up Europe only a few centuries ago. There have been recent cases where schools have notified social services when they have discovered that a child's parents are Wiccans. There is still a great deal of prej-udice in society against all forms of Neo-Paganism and esoteric religion.

As mentioned above, for Fundamentalist Christians anyone with any form of esoteric or Neo-Pagan belief is by definition Satanically inspired. (This only has any logic if one first redefines 'Satanist' to mean 'anything which isn't Evangelical Christianity' – which would then include Hinduism, Buddhism, Judaism, Islam and, for the hardcore Fundamentalists, Roman Catholicism.)

But witchcraft is not the same thing as Satanism; they are quite different religions. The original Paganism was pre-Christian; Wicca, though actually a new religion created in the 1950s, makes use of pre-Christian mythologies; high ritual magic is a mixture of Judaeo-Christian, Greek and Egyptian esoteric beliefs, via medieval alchemy; while Satanism, where it actually does exist, is not just a perversion but an inversion of Christianity.

In the late 1980s and early 1990s Wiccans came in for a lot of misrepresentation when Britain was hit by the 'moral panic' of Satanic Ritual Abuse. It was hardly surprising that Fundamentalist Christians leapt on the bandwagon; what is less well known is that the bandwagon was the creation of Fundamentalist Christians in the first place.

Before examining esoteric and Neo-Pagan movements, then, we shall first take a brief look at 'Satanic Ritual Abuse', and at Satanism itself.

SATANIC RITUAL ABUSE

In February 1995 eight children were returned to their families in Ayrshire, Scotland. They had been 'taken into care' by social workers five years earlier, after some of the parents had been accused of ritually abusing them. The parents were innocent of any such behaviour.

In the early 1990s Britain was shaken by case after case of so-called Satanic Ritual Abuse (SRA). Around the country, children were taken away from protesting families. Apparently when one home was raided by police and social workers, the Satanic evidence included an inverted cross, a full-length black cloak, and a recording of disturbing, obviously occult music. The inverted cross was later revealed to be a wooden kite, the cloak a normal clerical cloak belonging to the local priest, and the disturbing music was Holst's *The Planets*. No evidence was ever found of any Satanic Ritual Abuse.

A vast amount of distress was caused to the children and their parents. Some discomfort was also caused to thousands of practising Neo-Pagans who, in the headline-conscious eyes of journalists, were synonymous with witches who were synonymous with Satanists. Some claimed that it was hardly possible for them to brew a pot of herbal tea without people believing that they sacrificed babies. The air was thick with accusations, Christian spokespeople and social workers monopolized radio interviews – but almost no one was actually prosecuted.

Suddenly it all faded away. Even the then Chief Constable of Manchester, James Anderton, widely referred to at the time as 'God's spokesman', said there wasn't enough evidence to sustain a prosecution. Some social workers were reprimanded for being over-zealous, and the children were eventually returned home.

The entire concept of Satanic Ritual Abuse was based originally on the unsubstantiated claims of first one, then several women to have been 'teenage brood mares' of babies for sacrifice by Satanic cults.[4] The usual pattern was that, under counselling or therapy, the woman would come out with more and more detailed accounts of horrific tales which had lain buried in her subconscious for years.

(In later cases in the USA, stories obtained under therapy, sometimes including hypnotic regression, have led to the prosecution of quite a large number of adults for sexual offences. In many of these cases there was no evidence apart from the 'victims'' formerly repressed memories; in some cases there was actually evidence counter to the 'memories', such as one case of a woman who claimed to have been raped many times, but was later found still to be a virgin. Psychiatrists, doctors, social workers and the police are now becoming a little more wary of the dangers of 'False Memory Syndrome', whereby an already disturbed person can be led, through hypnosis or 'counselling', to remember in graphic detail events which never occurred. The American anthropologist Sherril Mulhern, who is based in France, has produced disturbing evidence suggesting that certain therapists first draw out their patients' fantasies, and then encourage them to believe them.[5] It could be argued that these are the real abusers. In passing, False Memory Syndrome also throws considerable doubt on accounts gained through therapy of both past lives and alien abduction.)

In the 1980s stories of Satanic Abuse were believed by a few child-care specialists, and in 1987 a small group of Fundamentalist Christians in America passed the idea of Satanic Ritual Abuse across the Atlantic to Britain. It was taken up by a few British social workers and some Christian counter-cultists, leading to the distressing accusations and seizing of supposedly abused children described above.

An extremely detailed British government report in 1994, by social anthropologist Professor Jean La Fontaine, concluded that there was no evidence whatsoever for Satanic Ritual Abuse.[6] Some paedophiles, for their own perverted fun, might on a few occasions have cloaked what they did with some form of ritual trappings, but this is not the same thing as genuine believing Satanists abusing children as part of their religious rites.

Satanic Ritual Abuse scares have occurred in other countries: Canada in 1985, the Netherlands in 1986, and in Scandinavia, Australia and New Zealand. In each case, it seems, the scares followed in the wake of SRA 'experts', social workers or Fundamentalist Evangelicals, visiting these countries. The stories, whether taken from adults recovering 'repressed memories' during therapy or from children interviewed by SRA-believing counsellors, contain many recurring features, leading anthropologists and religious scholars to identify the 'transmission of the mythology from place to place.'[7] Effectively, they are a modern equivalent of medieval Christian belief that Jews ate babies, and of the sixteenth- and seventeenth-century witch hunts. Massimo Introvigne, an Italian scholar on religious movements, comments:

Although some Satanists have been guilty of real crimes, Satanic Ritual Abuse is largely an urban legend perpetuated by a fraction of social workers and child psychologists who have done a lot of damage.[8]

But the story continues to recur. In February 2000 the BBC reported allegations by London psychotherapist Valerie Sinason that 'children are being bred for sacrifice and sexual abuse, kept in cages, forced to eat human flesh and excrement, and made to watch abortions and murders. Today. In Britain.'[9] Sinason's revelations come from her patients' stories; she specializes in treating 'multiple personality disorder'. No other evidence was provided.

There is no doubt that Satanic Ritual Abuse, as such, is a modern myth. The danger is that the lurid publicity which accompanies each new resurgence of the scare could blind us to the very real cases of non-Satanic, non-Ritual child abuse which do occur.

SATANISM

Satanism is effectively an offshoot of Christianity; it has nothing whatsoever to do with Neo-Paganism. Satan, or the Devil, is part of the Christian religion – though as many of the Christian sects point out, the biblical evidence for him as a personal being, though it is there, is slight. The Devil is a carry-over from Gnostic Dualism, which has some of its roots in Zoroastrianism; this gave us the neat contradiction, still present in Christianity, that although there is only one God – monotheism – he has an evil opponent: not quite, but almost ditheism, the difference being that Christianity has changed the Devil from an evil God into a powerful but limited fallen angel.

Most good Bible dictionaries[10] reveal that there is no simple identification in the Bible of the Devil equals Satan equals Lucifer; instead there is talk of demons and devils, and also of 'the satan' meaning 'the adversary or accuser' as in a court of law. The terms sometimes seem interchangeable. One Christian authority accepts the lack of clear identification: 'We can only conjecture, therefore, that Satan is a fallen angel.'[11] The identification of Lucifer with the Devil is thought to be a mistake made by St Jerome in the fourth century CE, which is still with us; Lucifer, far from being a proper name, is simply Latin for 'light-bearer' or 'light-bringer', a term sometimes applied to the morning star, the planet Venus. (In Victorian times matches were known as lucifers, without any demonic inferences being drawn.) The 'name' only appears once in the Bible, in Isaiah 14:12. Allegorically, according to the Evangelical *New Bible Dictionary*, 'the true claimant to this title is shown in Revelation 22:16 to be the Lord Jesus Christ in His ascended glory,'[12] and not the Devil at all.

Whatever hellfire-and-damnation preachers might want us to believe, the concept of the Devil with horns, a tail and cloven hooves is entirely medieval in origin, and not biblical at all. The medieval mind was intensely superstitious, and the medieval imagination intensely fertile; Hieronymous Bosch's painting *The Garden of Earthly Delights*, astonishing as it is, was a product of its age. And while the Renaissance brought great changes in art, culture, and much else, the effects of the medieval mind-set were slow to fade away. Arguably they are still with us today, in Christian 'deliverance ministry' and in some extreme Fundamentalist attitudes.

As for Satanism, with its Black Masses, rituals and incantations, this is almost entirely the bastard child of nineteenth-century occultism and the darker side of the Romanticism of the period, Gothic and decadent. J. Gordon Melton, a conservative evangelical Methodist minister, and one of America's most respected authorities on alternative religions, points out that practically everything we know about 'Satanism' and Black Magic actually comes from the pens of Christian writers:

> Though none had ever seen a Satanist ritual or met a real Satanist, these Christian writers described their practices in great detail. That is to say, the Satanist tradition was created and sustained by generation after generation of anti-Satanist writers.[13]

'Satanic Ritual Abuse' was simply a recent version of the same process.

Present-day 'Satanists', few as they are, fall into several categories. Some are groups of teenagers who, inspired by the lyrics and stage trappings of heavy metal bands, have read Aleister Crowley, or more likely, have read about Crowley, because his own works are rather difficult to read; then, borrowing from Dennis Wheatley novels and horror films, they have tried their own recreation of Black Magic rituals. If they are particularly unpleasant youths, they might sacrifice a cockerel or a cat; few are likely to go as far as attempting sex magick, though they might talk about it. (If they were to attempt it with an unwilling participant – i.e. rape – the laws of magic state that any magical effects would rebound negatively on them.)

Some supposed Satanists, as mentioned above, are the very small minority of paedophiles who dress up their perversion with pseudo-Gothic religious trappings, either to instil more fear in their victims, or to increase their own sense of 'fun', or perhaps, in some warped psychological reasoning, to excuse to themselves their own actions. Such people are not Satanists, though they almost certainly practise more genuine evil than those who really are.

There is apparently a small subset of people interested in esoteric studies who use the word Satanism as a synonym for their seeking after hidden knowledge. Although this might seem a strange definition, it fits in with the Garden of Eden story of the tree from which the serpent persuaded Eve to eat the fruit: 'For God doth know that in the day ye eat thereof, then your eyes shall be opened, and ye shall be as gods, knowing good and evil... the woman saw that the tree was... a tree to be desired to make one wise' (Genesis 3:5–6). But they are not truly Satanists either, in the sense of worshipping the force of evil.

There are, however, a few who proudly and openly take the name of Satanists, and who have created their own Satanist religion – though most of these are basically anti-Christian rather than being actual worshippers of Satan. Probably the best-known recent Satanist of this type was Anton LaVey, author of *The Satanic Bible*, and founder of the Church of Satan in San Francisco, in 1966. His aim was to make carnal desires a proper object of celebration. 'Satanism is a blatantly selfish, brutal religion,' says Burton H. Wolfe in his Introduction to LaVey's book. LaVey lists nine Satanic statements, including:

1 Satan represents indulgence, instead of abstinence!
4 Satan represents kindness to those who deserve it, instead of love wasted on ingrates!
5 Satan represents vengeance, instead of turning the other cheek!
8 Satan represents all of the so-called sins, as they all lead to physical, mental or emotional gratification![14]

As one anthropologist has said of LaVey's writing, 'Here Satan clearly represents an idealized, empowered self rather than an external evil.'[15]

LaVey courted publicity, and was often photographed performing rituals over a 'living altar' – a naked woman.

In the mid-1970s the Church of Satan became less centralized and more low-key. It was still in existence at the time of LaVey's death in October 1997. A breakaway group, the Temple of Set, was founded by Michael Aquino in 1975. The number of members of either group is difficult to ascertain, but it is certainly nowhere near as high as either tabloid scare stories or the groups themselves claim. According to one British academic, in all there are fewer than 100 Satanists in Britain, in six organized groups;[16] another reckons that:

the figures for those committed to, or seriously interested in, Satanism in Britain are likely to be between 100 and 250 – certainly no more than 400, which is negligible in a population of about 60 million.[17]

This entry should not be read as a whitewash of Satanists or Satanism. There is no doubt that there are people who call themselves Satanists, some of whom genuinely worship Satan, and some of whom (perhaps) practise evil. But there are many more people who practise evil without taking the name of Satanists.

THEOSOPHY

The Theosophical Society is associated with two names in particular, Madame Blavatsky (1831–1891) and Annie Besant (1847–1933). Important in its own right in its day, it is more significant now for other movements which owe it a debt, and for two of the most important esoteric teachers of this century, Rudolf Steiner (1861–1925) and Krishnamurti (1895–1986), both of whom had links with Theosophy.

Madame Helena Petrovna Blavatsky (usually known as HPB) claimed psychic abilities even as a small child in her native Russia. The surname Blavatsky came from her husband, whom she married at the age of 17; he was 40. The marriage was never consummated, and she left her husband after a few months, though they never divorced and she kept his name.

Like several other modern founders of movements (e.g. Gurdjieff, Hubbard, etc.) she travelled to the Far East, and claimed to have studied with the Secret Masters in Tibet for a while. The years 1848–58, when she was travelling and studying, she called 'the veiled time' of her life. She went to Cairo, and founded the Société Spirite. She was well practised in the usual late-nineteenth-century arts of table-tapping, clairvoyance and levitation. Both then and later in her life she was accused of fraudulent mediumship.

In 1873 she emigrated to New York, and the following year met Colonel Henry Steel Olcott, who had similar esoteric interests. In 1875 they founded the Theosophical Society, along with William Q. Judge, and in 1877 HPB published her first book, *Isis Unveiled*, which told of the Masters and their secrets. By 1878 the Society was faltering, and HPB and Olcott travelled to India in the hope that the source of Hinduism and Buddhism might revive it. The Society's headquarters were moved to Adyar, near Madras, where HPB continued to receive communications from the Masters on the spirit level. In 1885 she moved to Germany, where she wrote her second book, *The Secret Doctrine*. This set out the Theosophical beliefs on the evolution of the universe and mankind, and on reincarnation, and attempted to build bridges between religion and science, and between the occult traditions of the East and the West. She wrote two more books, *The Key to Theosophy* and *The Voice of the Silence*, before her death in 1891; *The Theosophical Glossary* was published posthumously in 1892. She claimed that parts of her books were 'dictated' by the Masters, though critics have accused her of plagiarizing other people's books.

The second major name associated with Theosophy is Annie Wood Besant. She was a freethinker and a radical, a colleague of the freethinker Charles Bradlaugh and a member of the Fabian Society. She was a feminist campaigner, and was once unsuccessfully prosecuted for selling a leaflet on birth control. She wrote a review of *The Secret Doctrine*, met HPB in 1889, and became a supporter of Theosophy, turning her London home into the UK headquarters. After HPB's death, Besant and Judge took joint control of the Theosophical Society, until they fell out in 1894. By this time, even though Judge had been there since the beginning, Besant had established a power base, and took over the British, Indian and some of the American organizations. Judge died in 1896, and Olcott in 1907.

HPB had been a mystic and probably something of a fraud, though some believe she had genuine psychic powers. Besant had no great psychic abilities, but was a great intellect, and was responsible both for the continued growth and influence of the Theosophical Society, and for something of an improvement in the respect given to it. She herself was held in great esteem in India, and was heavily involved in education and politics, founding several schools (one of which is now the University of Benares), founding the Indian Home Rule League, and becoming president of the Indian National Congress. Olcott also founded a number of schools in India and Ceylon (now Sri Lanka). Besant was also heavily involved in the Boy Scout movement, and in Co-Masonry, a version of Freemasonry which admitted women as equal to men.

Besant became closely associated with a former Anglican clergyman, the Reverend Charles W. Leadbeater; together they changed the emphasis of the Theosophical Society more towards esoteric Christianity than esoteric Buddhism.

Annie Besant wrote many influential books, including *Esoteric Christianity*, *Introduction to Yoga*, and a translation of the Buddhist scripture the *Bhagavad Gita*; she also co-wrote several books with Leadbeater. She died in 1933.

Leadbeater wrote a number of significant books of his own, and in 1916 became one of the earliest members and a bishop of the Liberal Catholic Church (see page 192), which split off from the Old Catholic Church when the latter's bishop, Arnold Harris Mathew, announced that Theosophy was incompatible with it.

It was Leadbeater who in 1908 first discovered the 14-year-old Jiddu Krishnamurti (1895–1986; Jiddu is the surname). The boy apparently had a remarkable aura; Leadbeater announced that he would become the Maitreya, the long-prophesied fifth Buddha (Gautama was the fourth), the living incarnation of a Master, and the new World Teacher. Besant and Leadbeater promoted Krishnamurti, initiating him into the Great White Brotherhood in 1910, and founding a separate organization for him to head, the Order of the Star in the East, in 1911. Krishnamurti wrote of his acceptance by the other Masters of the Great White Brotherhood in his book *At the Feet of the Master*, though some critics believe the book was actually 'ghosted' by Leadbeater.

Krishnamurti became increasingly uncomfortable with the role which had been thrust upon him, and in 1929 he disbanded the Order of the Star of the East, resigning from the Theosophical Society the following year. He continued teaching throughout his long life, but insisted that the Truth could not be apprehended through any religion or organization; it must always be an individual, personal discovery through complete self-knowledge. Despite this, and the fact that he never wanted any followers, there are now several schools around the world presenting his teachings.

The word Theosophy comes from the Greek *theos*, God, and *sophia*, wisdom. Many of the concepts of Theosophy have been around for well over 2,000 years, since Pythagoras and others. The German mystic Jakob Boehme (1575–1624) gave them a wider audience. The word is generally used to describe mystical philosophies which seek to explore the relationship between mankind and the Universe or God.

From the start the threefold aim of the Theosophical Society was to form a universal brotherhood of man, irrespective of race, religion or social class; to study the ancient religions, philosophies and sciences; and by investigating the laws of nature to reveal and develop the divine psychic powers latent in man.

To understand the strong appeal that Theosophy had to intellectuals in its heyday, it is necessary to see it in its historical setting. In 1859 Charles Darwin's *The Origin of Species* had introduced Western society to the theory of evolution, and had driven an apparently immovable wedge between science and religion (the reverberations are still echoing through American courts, where Fundamentalists have successfully fought for rulings that evolution cannot be taught in schools unless Creationism be taught alongside). Science had stripped God of his role as Creator; intellectuals were torn between being godless scientists or irrational believers.

Theosophy neatly took the concept of evolution and projected it forwards instead of backwards. Not only was the human race still evolving, but each individual person, progressing from life to life through reincarnation, was evolving to a far higher state. The Masters had long held secret knowledge, which was now available to all, to help us progress more rapidly until we too could become Masters.

Add to this the lure of the mysterious East, the thrill of HPB's spiritualist manifestations, and the ideas of social reform, and the whole package became a powerful and very attractive mixture at the turn of the last century.

The diversity of ideas which the Theosophical Society encompassed were both its strength and its weakness. There were many who disliked Madame Blavatsky's showmanship, though her demonstration of psychic or spiritualist abilities, genuine or not, undoubtedly attracted many others. Later there were some, including Rudolf Steiner, who were put off by Annie Besant's championing of the young Krishnamurti as the coming World Teacher – but again, the publicity brought Theosophy to a wider audience. And then there were many, including Colonel Olcott, who thought the most important parts of Theosophy were its social and educational work, and its scholarly work in bringing Eastern texts to the attention of the West.

With the exit of Krishnamurti, the Theosophical Society lost its impetus. There are still Theosophical Societies in Britain, America and around the world, but the fire has gone out of the movement; they appear to be little more than study groups, custodians of interesting libraries. What is far more important, though, is the legacy of the Theosophical Society, in both individual people and later movements. Krishnamurti became a widely respected mystic and teacher. Rudolf Steiner, once head of the German Theosophical Society, went off to found Anthroposophy (see page 196). P.D. Ouspensky (see page 351) was influenced by Theosophical teachings. The poet and mystic W.B. Yeats was a member for a few years, before moving on to the Hermetic Order of the Golden Dawn (see page 359). There were many others.

Beyond that, many of the esoteric movements which are thriving today, including the Church Universal and Triumphant (see page 373), have borrowed liberally from Theosophical teachings, particularly in respect of the Great White Brotherhood. (The word 'white' does not refer to race, but to the aura of white light which apparently surrounds these Ascended Masters.) The idea of the Secret Masters was not original to the Theosophical Society, but it greatly fleshed out and popularized the concept. The Master Koot Hoomi in particular not only gave HPB much of the content of her books, but later inspired Alice Bailey (founder of the Arcane School) in the writing of her own books of mystical teaching, and also Robert and Earlyne Chaney, who founded the Astara Foundation in California in 1951; this was a school of the ancient mysteries and a centre for psychic research, and perhaps one of the closest of all the Theosophical Society's successors to the original.

BENJAMIN CREME AND MAITREYA

Christ is alive and well and living among the Pakistani community around Brick Lane, London, according to Benjamin Creme. This was Creme's message in 1982, as perceived by Evangelical Christians, who were greatly offended by it. In fact, Creme was speaking of Maitreya, the most senior of the Masters, or the Great White Brotherhood, who have usually been based in the Himalayas. Maitreya had 'overshadowed' Jesus, making him the Christ; now he would be returning in his own right.

Creme's teachings are based on Alice Bailey's developments from Theosophy. Bailey (1880–1949), born in Manchester, joined the Theosophical Society in California, where in 1919 she met the American secretary of the Society, Foster Bailey, whom she later married. Alice Bailey claimed she was contacted by several Masters, including Koot Hoomi and Djwhal Khul; she began 'channelling' messages from them, and writing books from their messages. She fell out with Annie Besant, H.P. Blavatsky's successor in the Theosophy Society, who clearly saw her as a threat; eventually she and Foster Bailey left the Society.

In 1922 they founded the Lucis Trust to publish her books (she wrote 20 in all), and in 1923 they founded the Arcane School to teach their followers. Bailey's teachings were basically Theosophical, with an emphasis on the imminent coming of the Maitreya Buddha, which could be seen as the second coming of Christ, or as another avatar of Krishna, or as the Jewish Messiah, or as the Muslim Imam Mahdi. Maitreya is all of these.

After Alice Bailey's death her movement splintered into several offshoots; the Arcane School itself continued under her husband until his death in 1977. Bailey has had a tremendous influence, often unrecognized, on New Age philosophy; she is responsible for the Great Invocation, to be spoken, usually by groups of three people, while visualizing the movement of spiritual energy.

> From the point of Light within the Mind of God
> Let light stream forth into the minds of men.
> Let Light descend on Earth.
>
> From the point of Love within the Heart of God
> Let love stream forth into the hearts of men.
> May Christ return to Earth.
>
> From the centre where the Will of God is known
> Let purpose guide the little wills of men –
> The purpose which the Masters know and serve.
>
> From the centre which we call the race of men
> Let the Plan of Love and Light work out.
> And may it seal the door where evil dwells.
>
> Let Light and Love and Power restore the Plan on Earth.

Benjamin Creme (b. 1922) studied the works of Blavatsky, Leadbeater and Bailey, among many others, in his youth. In 1957 he joined the Aetherius Society (see page 385), but left them in 1959 after disagreements.

He was contacted by a Master in 1959, and told of the Maitreya's imminent return, and of his own importance in spreading the word. Nothing much seems to have happened until 1972, when he received further messages. In 1974 he began to set up an organization of followers; with them he learnt to transmit spiritual energy. Later that year, Maitreya himself spoke through him. Creme began to publish books containing messages from Maitreya. He is the editor of *Share International* magazine, which contains information about Maitreya, and teachings which are partly Theosophical and partly New Age.

In 1982 Creme announced that Maitreya was living anonymously in the Asian community in East London, and would reveal himself to the world shortly; the media must be ready. Sensing a good offbeat story, a number of journalists searched the Brick Lane area, but no one could point them at the returned Christ. Creme lost both credibility and supporters, and gained some serious enemies among Evangelical Christians. An Evangelical book, *The Hidden Dangers of the Rainbow* (1983), attacked all New Age and esoteric movements – especially Creme and the Maitreya – as a Satanic conspiracy; it was one of the first of several such books in which conservative Evangelicals attacked the New Age, and did much to promote the illogical belief that members of New Age movements, Neo-Paganism, Wicca and esoteric religious movements are all Satanists (see page 338).

According to Creme:

On 31 July 1985, largely through the efforts of one freelance journalist who had actually seen Maitreya in His local area in 1984 and who was convinced of the truth of Creme's information, an internationally representative group of 22 influential journalists met in an Indian restaurant in London's East End, hoping that Maitreya or an envoy would approach them there.[18]

They were to be disappointed.

In an unusual twist on the urban myth about the vanishing hitch-hiker, Creme claims that Maitreya has hitched lifts with Evangelical Christians, told them they would shortly see Christ, then vanished from their cars.

His most publicized appearance, however, was at a healing meeting in Nairobi, Kenya. He was seen by 6,000 people, photographed, and reported in the *Kenya Times* and on CNN and BBC news. Since 1992, says Creme, Maitreya has appeared – and disappeared – in front of many groups of Christians, Jews, Muslims, Hindus and Buddhists 'from Mexico City to Moscow, from Geneva to Johannesberg; in North Africa and the Middle East, India and Pakistan.'[19] At several of these meetings he spoke to the assembled people for 15–20 minutes before vanishing again. In July 1994 he finally turned up in London, addressing a group of 300–400 Christians for 17 minutes.

These appearances are all a prelude to the Day of Declaration, when Maitreya will appear on radio and TV all over the world, and speak to everyone, simultaneously, in his or her own language.

Maitreya's message (as with the Aetherius Society, the Raelian Movement and others) is simple: 'Share and save the world... Take your brother's need as the measure for your action and solve the problems of the world. There is no other course.'[20]

GURDJIEFF

HISTORY

Georgei Ivanovitch Gurdjieff (c. 1866–1949) was one of the most colourful and controversial gurus of the last century. Gurdjieff was a powerfully charismatic teacher, a clever businessman (some called him a shyster), and an unpredictable, even volatile personality (he has also been called a charlatan and a showman). Born of a Greek father and Armenian mother in Alexandropol near the Russian–Turkish border, he spent some years wandering in the East. 'Gurdjieff spent most of his time with the Seekers of Truth in the Caucasus and Central Asia, though he also went to Egypt and Tibet,' says Professor Tilo L.V. Ulbricht of the Gurdjieff Society.[21] In Tibet he claimed to have studied under Masters of ancient wisdom, learning, among much else, the techniques of hypnotism and yoga.

It should be noted that a number of authorities present Gurdjieff's early travels more as myth than as history. His biographer, James Moore, who has been an active Gurdjieff follower since 1956, comments wryly, '[W]e are chasteningly reliant on Gurdjieff's own four impressionistic accounts, which – in the nature of myth – are innocent of consistency, Aristotelian logic and chronological discipline.'[22] (Madame Blavatsky and L. Ron Hubbard, among others, share similarly mythological early life stories.)

'Unlike Blavatsky,' says Ulbricht, 'he never spoke of "Masters". He did find a monastery, whose whereabouts he had to vow not to reveal, where the tradition of sacred dances had been preserved. It may have been in Afghanistan.'

On his travels, at times working for a railroad company, Gurdjieff set up stores, restaurants and cinemas, and traded in expensive carpets, making a small fortune; at the same time he was seeking after deep philosophical and religious wisdom, and gathering a band of like-minded seekers around him. By the time he had moved to Moscow, and later to St Petersburg, he was lecturing on what he had learnt. But Russia, being in the middle of a revolution, was not the safest place for a wheeler-dealer and unorthodox philosopher, and he moved to France, where in 1922 he bought an estate, the Prieuré des Basses Loges near Fontainebleu, setting up his Institute for the Harmonious Development of Man. He moved to Paris in 1933.

One of his earliest followers, whom he met in Moscow in 1922, was the Russian mathematician Piotr D. Ouspensky (1878–1947), who had earlier been greatly influenced by Theosophy. Ouspensky established the largest Gurdjieff-derived school, in Surrey, England. He later wrote a book, *In Search of the Miraculous: Fragments of an Unknown Teaching*,[23] to some extent clarifying Gurdjieff's teachings. What made for a powerful synthesis between the two is that Gurdjieff was intuitive and unpredictable, encouraging the unexpected and the out-of-balance, while Ouspensky was rational, logical, methodical, and looked for a systematic approach. Outside observers suggest that Ouspensky's contribution lay in codifying Gurdjieff's seemingly disconnected teachings into a cohesive spiritual system. Many movements today with some sort of background in Gurdjieff's teachings are actually Gurdjieff-Ouspensky (G-O) inspired. This rankles with the Gurdjieff Society:

> The teaching, including the ideas, came from Gurdjieff... Groups who couple the names Gurdjieff and Ouspensky base themselves on the ideas presented by Ouspensky in his book, and his lectures after he left Gurdjieff, and actually have no direct connection with Gurdjieff's teaching at all. Ouspensky was only with Gurdjieff for a few years.

In fact, Gurdjieff treated Ouspensky so badly in 1922 that the latter forbad his students even to mention Gurdjieff's name; they were never reconciled.

Gurdjieff's own books are *Beelzebub's Tales to his Grandson*, *Meetings with Remarkable Men* and *Life is Only Real when 'I Am'*.

Among many other things, Gurdjieff has been criticized for imposing quite unsuitable exercises – most of them exhausting and some actually dangerous – on his followers. The writer Katherine Mansfield, for example, went to Fontainebleu suffering from tuberculosis; critics allege that he ordered her to ignore her illness, and made her sleep above the cowshed; she died shortly afterwards, aged only 35. The Gurdjieff Society paints a different picture:

> It was known that Katherine Mansfield was dying of TB when she asked to come to the institute. Although foreseeing unfavourable publicity, Gurdjieff was impressed by her sincerity and allowed her to come. He did not order her to ignore her illness. He suggested that she sleep above the cowshed because he believed the atmosphere would relieve her pain. Alexander de Salzmann painted the ceiling and walls of her room with beautiful murals. In the letters she wrote before her death... she says how kindly she was cared for, and allowed to participate to the extent that she wished, and how there, for the first time in her life, she had found inner peace.

After his death Gurdjieff's teachings were continued by one of his closest followers,

Madame Jeanne de Salzmann, who died in 1990 aged 101, having established or consolidated Gurdjieff Foundations or Societies in London, Paris, New York, California, Caracas and Sydney.

BELIEFS AND PRACTICES

Gurdjieff's teachings could be described as a sort of esoteric Christianity, or as a blending of the West and the East, or as a combination of religious thought and philosophical psychology (or perhaps psychological philosophy). They are a hugely complex mixture of almost science-fictional cosmological mythology, esoteric number theory, sacred dance, and spiritual development from sleep to wakefulness.

The two main states of consciousness are to be either awake or asleep; though most people, Gurdjieff said, more or less sleep-walk their way through their waking life. He put forward two other states of being, self-consciousness and objective consciousness. Like some of the personal development movements covered later in this book, Gurdjieff's philosophy points out that most of us are not really in touch with ourselves, with the entirety of our inner being, our 'I', and so are cut off from anything approaching full use of our abilities. Ouspensky likened this to people living in the basement of a house, without ever realizing there are other floors upstairs. Life passes us by, and we are mere observers of it, like an audience at a play, rather than being up there on the stage, a combination of participants, script-writers and directors. Even if one changes the analogy to make us the actors, we are confined to a script, having grown into roles imposed on us by upbringing and strengthened by unthinking habit. Our several 'brains', our Instinctive, Moving, Emotional and Intellectual Centres, are out of kilter with each other.

We can only be woken up by performing arduous physical exercises, which break our deeply ingrained habits. Gurdjieff made his followers perform tasks well below their intellectual or social level; part of his teaching on esoteric development was unquestioning submission to a teacher – a Man Who Knows.

One of the most important practical aspects of Gurdjieff's teachings was sacred dance.

The sacred dances... express the laws of the universe, they demand such a fine attention from those who practise them that all their faculties need to work together in harmony. Being able to execute well the postures required, in their correct sequence, rhythm and tempo, is very hard, but still only a stage: then, how to be so calm and collected inside, that the body, meant to be a temple for the spirit, serves as an instrument for a higher force. This is an extraordinary call to obey and submit consciously, and in that akin to the deepest religious experience.

His methods also included rhythmic exercises to music, and breathing exercises. The emphasis on music came from a new interpretation of Pythagoras' esoteric teaching on the music of the spheres and the numerical or numerological significance of rhythm and the functions of parts of the body.

By performing these exercises one can reach a higher level of consciousness, become truly self-aware, and tap one's reserves of spiritual and psychic power. Perhaps from Pythagoras, Gurdjieff developed a Law of Seven to do with music, and a Law of Three to do with the working of the universe (active, passive and neutral), the human body (carnal, emotional and spiritual), and food. He devised a symbol called the enneagram, a circle divided by nine points, which join up to illustrate his teachings.

Many of his followers, including Ouspensky, deserted him, but most of these continued to follow what he taught: the message without the man. Today's movements which follow Gurdjieff's teachings – sometimes called the Fourth Way School or the Way of the Sly Man, combining and moving on from the three old ways of the fakir (physical), the monk (emotional) and the yogi (intellectual) – tend to concentrate more on their mystical aspects rather than on the punishing physical exercises he required. Gurdjieff's Fourth Way of spirituality has also influenced much New Age thinking, though his biographer is utterly dismissive of these 'thousand contemptible modern parodies'.[24]

SUBUD

HISTORY

Subud began in Java, Indonesia, in 1924, when Muhammad Subuh Sumohadiwidjojo (1901–1987), a clerk in a local treasurer's office, unexpectedly had a series of powerful religious experiences, in which he experienced the inner power of God. By the 1930s he had realized that he should pass on this experience to others, and in 1933 he set up Subud, which is not related to his name but is an abbreviation of the Sanskrit words *Susila*, *Buddhi* and *Dharma*, meaning 'to follow the Will of God, with the help of the Divine Power that works both within us and without.'[25]

Over the next 20 years Subuh worked quietly, spreading Subud slowly in Indonesia. Eventually some Europeans came into contact with Subud.

Gurdjieff, in common with other esoteric teachers, had spoken of One who is to come; for some it was the Maitreya; for Gurdjieff it was the Prophet of Consciousness, the Ashiata Shiemash. A group of Gurdjieff's followers invited Subuh to England in 1956, believing him to be the Prophet foretold by Gurdjieff. First in

Britain, then in America and Australia, Subud spread rapidly; recently there has been 'significant growth' in Eastern Europe, the former Soviet Union, parts of Africa and South America.

Muhammad Subuh, known to his followers as Bapak (an affectionate and respectful Indonesian term for 'father'), died in 1987.

BELIEFS AND PRACTICES

Subuh discovered not only that he could enable others to receive the spiritual energy he had first encountered in 1924, but that those who had received it from him could pass it on to others. (This is similar to the Toronto Blessing in Evangelical Christianity, which also seems to be passed on by personal contact; the effects are also remarkably similar. See page 235.) The basis of Subud is the *latihan kejiwaan*, Indonesian for 'spiritual exercise', usually just known as the latihan, or exercise 'in which one surrenders to, opens up one's inner feeling to and comes into contact with the power of God'.[26] Some three months after first attending Subud meetings, a new member stands in a group with several others, including some experienced 'Helpers', and the latihan occurs. The first time is known as the Opening.

The experience is different for different people; this is part of the basis of Subud. Some will experience joy, others peace; some will laugh, others cry; some feel an inner vibration, others a quiet simplicity; some will dance, others will pray. Every one of these is equally valid.

The latihan lasts for about 30 minutes, and is usually done twice a week with the group. Once members are experienced, they can do an additional latihan once a week on their own, at home.

> The effects of the latihan vary greatly. People usually have a feeling of well-being and relaxation after doing latihan. In the longer term, the process for some may bring a peaceful, gradual development in their acceptance of themselves and others and their experience of constant inward wholeness. For others it may initiate dramatic changes in their lives.

The experience of latihan is apparently not always pleasant; the power of God is acting directly on the inner person, and may well be purging out the dross within. 'Often people experience suffering and difficulties at some stage as the purification begun by the latihan takes its course.'

Subud says firmly that it is not a religion in its own right; it has no priests, no rituals, no dogmas or doctrines. 'Subud is not foreign. It did not "originate" in the East and it did not "come" to the West... It comes from the Spirit of God, which is nowhere a stranger,' said Subuh.[27] Members are actively encouraged to continue to belong to the religion they came from. Because they are directly in touch with the

Power of God, or the Holy Spirit, or the Great Life Force, they become brothers and sisters together, irrespective of whether they are Christians, Muslims, Buddhists, Hindus or anything else.

> Therefore, in the latihan of Subud we do not have a teaching; there is nothing we have to learn or do, because all that is required of us is complete surrender...
> So this divine power, which works in us during the latihan, will bring to each person what is already in himself... the latihan of two people can never be the same, because everyone is different from everyone else. It is clear, then, that there cannot be a theory or spiritual teaching in Subud because each person is different. Whatever he needs and whatever he receives will differ from what somebody else needs and receives...
> Every person will find for himself the right way towards God, and what may be the right way for one may be completely wrong for another. You must become your own self and you must develop your inner self if you want to find the way to God. You must not follow or imitate anyone else, because you must find your own way to God... it is God who will lead you towards himself and what really happens in the latihan is that you will be introduced to your real inner self – to the real I.[28]

Like a number of other movements from the Quakers to the Bahá'ís, and from Soka Gokkai to the Theosophists and Anthroposophists, Subud is very strong on the brotherhood of all mankind. It has a number of subsidiary organizations working in welfare, education and community work. Susila Dharma International, the charitable arm of Subud, is accredited as a Non-Governmental Organization (NGO) to the United Nations Economic and Social Council (ECOSOC) and UNICEF. It is currently involved in nearly 100 projects, including health and education, in 35 countries. Most Subud members donate a portion of their income (usually 3 per cent) to the movement, and they are actively encouraged to set up businesses which will donate a portion of their profits to support Subud, particularly in its charitable work.

Subud does not evangelize or actively recruit new members. People might read about it, or know someone who is a member, and so decide to find out more about it. There are 13,000–15,000 members worldwide in 385 groups in about 80 countries; the UK has the largest membership at around 1,300.

ROSICRUCIANS

There are many different Rosicrucian organizations in Britain, Europe, the USA and around the world, with widely differing teachings. Some are quite secretive; others advertise widely. Some reserve their membership to Freemasons of the highest grades; others have a more open membership, but paradoxically are perhaps more difficult to join. Some trace their lineage back – legitimately or not – to the earliest 'history' of the Rosicrucians; others are clearly far more recent.[29]

☼

In the early seventeenth century three mysterious works were published in Germany: *Fama Fraternitas* or *The Praiseworthy Order of the Rosy Cross* (1614); *Confessio Fraternitas* or *The Confession of the Rosicrucian Fraternity* (1615); and *Chymische Hochzeit* or *The Chymical Marriage of Christian Rosenkreutz* (1616). These told the life story of Christian Rosenkreutz, who was born in 1378, travelled in the Middle East, and died aged 106 in 1484. When his tomb was discovered in 1604 his body had not corrupted. Rosenkreutz set up a fraternity, the Spiritus Sanctum or House of the Holy Spirit, dedicated to the well-being of mankind, social reform, and healing the sick; this reformation of the whole world was to be accomplished by men of secret, magical learning.

The documents are now thought to have been written by a Lutheran priest, Johann Valentin Andreae (1586–1654), who created the symbolic myth of Christian Rosenkreutz in an attempt to stimulate others to take up Rosicrucian ideals.

Within a couple of years other Rosicrucian writings appeared, including one by the influential physician, alchemist and Hermetic philosopher Robert Fludd (1574–1637), and Rosicrucian societies began to spring up around Europe. There was a resurgence of interest in the nineteenth century, particularly in Britain and America; new societies included the Fraternitas Rosae Crucis (1858), the Societas Rosicruciana in Anglia (1865), the Rosicrucian Fellowship (1907), the Societas Rosicruciana in America (1907), the Ancient and Mystical Order of the Rosy Cross (1915), and Lectorium Rosicrucianum (1924); the last two will be looked at briefly as examples of, respectively, personal development based on revived esoteric Egyptian, Greek and other ancient beliefs, and Gnostic Christianity.

The Ancient and Mystical Order of the Rosy Cross (AMORC) was founded in 1915 by H. Spencer Lewis (1883–1939). Lewis claimed esoteric legitimacy from his membership of Aleister Crowley's Ordo Templi Orientis (see page 361); he was initiated into the International Rosicrucian Council in France in 1909, and authorized to begin a new order in the USA. AMORC moved to its present headquarters in San Jose, California, in 1927. The following year an earlier Rosicrucian Order, the Fraternitas Rosae Crucis, took Lewis to court over the right to call his order Rosicrucian; the courts eventually decided that no organization can own the name. Lewis was succeeded as Grand Imperator by his son Ralph M. Lewis (d. 1987). His successor, Gary L. Stewart, was removed from office in 1990 following charges of attempting to embezzle $3 million of AMORC's funds. The money was returned to AMORC by court order, and Stewart founded his own group called the Order Militia Crucifera Evangelica.

Like several other Rosicrucian Orders, AMORC runs correspondence courses on its teachings, which it advertises in ordinary newspapers and magazines. It is generally said to have around 250,000 members, though it is uncertain whether this figure includes everyone who has ever taken any of its courses.

As a 'mystical fraternity', AMORC claims to teach its students to function 'in accordance with the Cosmic and its laws of nature', to bring about 'a harmonious level of interaction within your body' and to make it possible that, 'through the experiments in the Rosicrucian teachings, your psychic faculties can be one of the greatest powers within you.'[30]

AMORC traces its traditional roots to:

the mystery traditions, philosophy and myths of ancient Egypt from approximately 1500 BC. However, the Rosicrucian movement is eclectic and uniquely draws upon the diverse mystical traditions of ancient Greece, China, India and Persia. The result is a consolidation of mystical principles which focus on a purposeful direction for the future. That being the enlightenment of humanity by way of establishing a mystical study of knowledge.

AMORC is non-sectarian, and members are encouraged to continue in the religion of their choice. It claims to offer:

the world's foremost system of instruction and guidance for exploring the inner self and discovering the universal laws that govern all human endeavour.[31]

Lectorium Rosicrucianum was originally founded in the Netherlands in 1924 under the name Rozekruisers Genootschap (Rosicrucian Fellowship) by two brothers, Zwier Wilhelm Leene (1892–1938) and Jan Leene (1896–1968); the latter used the *nom de plume* J. van Rijckenborgh. It was linked for a while to the Rosicrucian Fellowship in America, but broke this connection in 1935. After World War II, when it was banned by the Nazis, it re-formed as Lectorium Rosicrucianum, the International School of the Golden Rosycross. It has centres in Britain, America and over three dozen other countries, and its magazine *Pentagram* is published in ten languages. It has 12,500 full members (known as pupils) worldwide, 7,700 of these in Europe, though only 50 in Britain and 200 in the USA. It also has around 2,500 probationary members, 2,100 of these in Europe.

More than most Rosicrucian Orders, its teachings are a version of Gnostic Christianity (see page 137), stressing 'the living spiritual core in the original revelations of all the great world religions and mystery schools' and imparting 'the inner knowledge which points the way to soul-rebirth and ultimately the re-establishment of the link with the Spirit of God.'[32]

Gnosticism generally teaches the contrast between the spiritual world (good) and the material world (evil). Lectorium Rosicrucianum, which in its doctrines is close to the twelfth- and thirteenth-century Cathar religion of southern France,[33] teaches that there are two nature-orders, 'the familiar one containing both the living and the dead... characterized by pairs of opposites and by perishability' – which it calls 'dialectics' – and 'the original divine nature-order. Although this interpenetrates our nature-order completely, it is not perceptible to dialectical sense organs because it is separated from our nature-order by an enormous difference in vibration.' The divine nature-order is also known as the Kingdom of Heaven, and the human heart contains a remnant of it, a Divine Spark (cf. Church Universal and Triumphant, page 376) or Rose of the Heart, which causes us 'to seek out the original state of being 'with the Father', the state of being immortally at one with God.'

Following insight into the difference between the two nature-orders, and the desire for salvation, one can achieve the rebirth of transfiguration through self-mortification, the 'total self-surrender of the I-personality to the actualization of this salvation.' This is followed by a new mode of life, 'under the direction of the aroused spirit-spark-atom, the newly born soul,' and fulfilment, 'the resurrection in the original field of light'.

In common with other Rosicrucian movements, Lectorium Rosicrucianum places a great deal of emphasis on symbols, including the golden rose on a golden cross, the circle containing a square and an equilateral triangle – 'the Circle of Eternal Love containing the Trigonum Igneum or Fiery Triangle and the Square of Construction', and the Pentagram, 'ever the symbol of the reborn, new Human Being'.

There are strict behavioural standards; the full members, or pupils, abstain from meat, alcohol, tobacco and TV.

In addition to *Pentagram* Lectorium Rosicrucianum, like many other esoteric schools, provides a wide range of books on its beliefs in English and other languages, including *Elementary Philosophy of the Modern Rosycross*, *The Universal Gnosis*, *The Egyptian Arch-Gnosis* and *The Secrets of the Brotherhood of the Rosycross*, all by J. van Rijckenborgh.

Although Rosicrucianism is not, in itself, a religion, we can see from these two examples that it contains very powerful religious ideas. There are clear links and cross-influences between the Rosicrucians, the mystical side of Freemasonry, alchemy, Hermetic Philosophy, the Western Mystery Tradition, Theosophy, and esoteric Christianity.

HERMETIC ORDER OF THE GOLDEN DAWN

Like Theosophy, the Hermetic Order of the Golden Dawn (HOGD) is important for the people associated with it during its relatively short existence, and for its continuing effect on later movements.

It is now generally accepted that, from a critic's viewpoint, the HOGD was founded on a lie – in fact, a series of lies. An apologist might say that, like most esoteric organizations, it was eclectic – it borrowed some of its teachings and rituals from various places, and created others out of whole cloth. As for the invention of a German 'predecessor', it was necessary for it to be able to claim authority. In any case, such a practice is hardly new; the Early Christian Church was littered with gospels and epistles supposedly written by the apostles; the Athanasian Creed was certainly not written by Athanasius, but it reflected his beliefs, and giving it his name ensured that people would take notice of it. Much the same applies with esoteric societies.

The Hermetic Order of the Golden Dawn was the creation of Dr William Wynn Westcott, Dr William Robert Woodman, and Samuel Liddell 'MacGregor' Mathers. All three were Freemasons, and leading members of the masonic Societas Rosicruciana in Anglia (SRIA). It was the brainchild of Westcott, who in 1887 was given a manuscript of around 60 pages, containing (in an artificial language) fragments of 'Golden Dawn' rituals which clearly owed much to Freemasonry, with large elements of the Kabbala, astrology, alchemy and related subjects. Westcott asked Mathers to flesh out the fragments into full working rituals, and recruited Woodman, who was then Supreme Magus of the SRIA, to be the third leader of the new organization.

The lie came in with Westcott's invention of Fräulein Sprengel, Chief Adept of a non-existent German occult order, the Goldene Dämmerung, who granted a Charter to the HOGD. The HOGD thus became the British branch of an ancient continental order, whose teachings went back into the mists of antiquity. It had a provenance; it therefore had authority.

By 1888 the HOGD was up and running: a secret society very like the Freemasons and the Rosicrucians in that it awarded 'degrees' as members progressed up the ladder, but with its main emphasis being the study of magical theory and ritual. There was plenty of material they could study; French writers such as Éliphas Lévi, Papus and Etteilla had produced books on the mystical meanings of Tarot and the Kabbala, and much else; and there were Mathers' 'ancient' rituals to be learnt.

The main degrees of the HOGD were Neophyte 0=0, Zelator 1=10, Theoricus 2=9, Practicus 3=8, and Philosophus 4=7. But for a few (and unknown to the rest) there was an inner circle, the Ordo Rosae, Rubeae et Aureae Crucis, 'the Rose of Ruby and the Cross of Gold', based on the Rosicrucian symbolism of Christian Rosenkreutz; this had three degrees, Adeptus Minor 5=6, Adeptus Major 6=5, and

Adeptus Exemptus 7=4. The outer order only studied the theory of magic; the RR et AC taught practical ritual magic, and was almost certainly the most intensive and all-embracing esoteric school of its time.

Beyond this was an even higher order, the Mysterious Third Order of the Silver Star, or Argentium Astrum (A∴A∴); this had three more degrees, Magister Templi 8=3, Magus 9=2 and Ipsissimus 10=1. The adepts of this order were beyond mere humanity, existing purely as spirits on the astral plane.

The HOGD was open to non-masons and also, unusually for its day, to women. It attracted Freemasons, Theosophists, Rosicrucians, and people interested in magic and mythology, alchemy and astrology, the Kabbala, Tarot, numerology and much else. Members included the poet W.B. Yeats, the influential esoteric historian A.E. Waite, the tea heiress Annie Horniman, the actress Florence Farr and briefly, to the dismay of many of these, Aleister Crowley.

In 1891 Dr Woodman died suddenly. From 1892, when the RR et AC was introduced, to around 1896, the HOGD flourished under Mathers and Westcott. Then things started going wrong.

Annie Horniman fell out with Mathers and resigned in 1896. The following year Dr Westcott was told that his membership of a secret society which practised magic did not look good for a man in his position as a senior London coroner. He resigned from the HOGD, leaving it entirely in Mathers' hands.

Aleister Crowley joined the HOGD in 1898; by the next year he had risen to Philosophus, the highest degree in the outer order. He demanded entry to the inner circle, but was turned down on the grounds of unsuitability. Mathers had moved to Paris, setting up a temple there. Crowley went to Paris, where Mathers initiated him in the first grade of the RR et AC, but when he returned to London in 1900 the other members refused him access to papers he said he was entitled to have. Crowley tried to take possession of the London temple. Around the same time Mathers revealed the truth about the non-existent Fräulein Sprengel, which understandably created a storm throughout the HOGD. Both Mathers and Crowley were expelled.

W.B. Yeats took over the Order, Annie Horniman returned, and together they tried to sort out the mess. The HOGD as a major force was finished, though remnants of it continued. A.E. Waite took over the London temple, changed the name from Hermetic to Holy Order of the Golden Dawn, and changed the emphasis from ritual magic to a more spiritual – and more Christian – 'mystical path'. This faded out in 1914, to be replaced by the Fellowship of the Rosy Cross, whose members included the Christian occult novelist Charles Williams, and the mystic, poet and academic Evelyn Underhill.

There were two other spin-off Orders, from which came two people who were to become extremely important in the continuing British esoteric tradition. Those who wanted the original HOGD emphasis on magic formed Stella Matutina, the Order of the Morning Star; these included Yeats, and Israel Regardie – who later published a four-volume work containing the teachings of the HOGD.[34] Some followers of Mathers formed the Alpha et Omega Temple, though Mathers himself stayed in Paris; Dion Fortune (see page 364) joined this group in 1919.

The HOGD's reputation often suffers from its brief association with Crowley. Because he is known to have been heavily into sex-magick, it is wrongly assumed that the same applied to the HOGD. Although the *theory* of sex-magick might have been studied, it never formed part of HOGD practice; in fact, both Mathers and his wife were revolted by the very idea of physical sex – they never consumated their marriage. Annie Horniman has been described as a prude; in contrast, Florence Farr had liaisons with, among others, W.B. Yeats and George Bernard Shaw.

Aleister Crowley (1875–1947) also fell out with Mathers, and went off to form his own Order called Argenteum Astrum (A∴A∴), the Order of the Silver Star, and to become reknowned for his sex-magick exploits and his outrageous behaviour. He later became British leader of the Ordo Templi Orientis (OTO).

Crowley is often credited with what has become the Wiccan rede, 'Do what thou wilt shall be the whole of the law' (now usually prefixed by 'An it hurt none...'). In fact it originated from François Rabelais, nearly four centuries earlier, in his famous scurrilous satire *The Histories of Gargantua and Pantagruel,* first published in 1532. In that book, for the monks and nuns of the Abbey of Thélème:

> In all their rule, and strictest tie of their order, there was but this one clause to be observed,
>
> ### DO WHAT THOU WILT.
>
> Because men that are free, well born, well bred, and conversant in honest companies, have naturally an instinct and spur that prompteth them unto virtuous actions, and withdraws them from vice, which is called honour.[35]

Crowley used the phrase in his *Liber Legis* or *Book of the Law* (dictated to him by Aiwass, a spirit speaking for the Egyptian god Horus, in 1904). Largely, it must be said, because of Crowley's own hedonism, the maxim has been much misinterpreted. It never meant 'You're free to do whatever you like,' a recipe for self-indulgence. The point of the precept is that for the esoteric adept one's will should be totally in line with the will of God, so that one acts always within the will of God. It was also intended by Crowley to be half of a greeting; the response should be 'Love is the law, love under will', which fills out the meaning considerably.

Although few would dispute Crowley's unpleasant, at times disgusting, character and behaviour, many serious esotericists say that his written work, particularly *Magick in Theory and Practice* (1929), contains much of value.

SCHOOLS OF OCCULT SCIENCE

The Hermetic Order of the Golden Dawn may have self-destructed, but numerous groups have continued its legacy, calling themselves Hermetic Tradition Mystery Schools, or Schools of Occult Science. Because of the concern many people feel over 'occult' movements, four of these are described here. For their correspondence courses these schools generally charge enough to cover the printing and administration; although this can mount up over several years, it is usually considerably cheaper than most personal development movements, which take a different approach to self-knowledge and self-improvement.

BUILDERS OF THE ADYTUM

The Builders of the Adytum (BOTA) is an American offshoot of the HOGD. It was founded, originally as the School of Ageless Wisdom, by Paul Foster Case (1884–1954), who had been interested in the esoteric since his childhood. Case joined the New York branch of the HOGD, rose through the ranks, and then took the teachings into his own school in the early 1920s. After his death he was succeeded by Dr Anne Davies, who further extended his teachings until her own death in 1975.

Most of the books supplied by BOTA are by Case or Davies, but they also recommend Dion Fortune's *The Mystical Qabalah*. The School offers correspondence courses in Tarot, the Kabbala, alchemy and other related subjects.

> Hitherto, the great practical secrets have been guarded carefully from spiritual dilettantes and have only been given to duly initiated men and women under the strictest pledges of secrecy. In the past, this secrecy has been necessary because of the ecclesiastic and legal restrictions upon freedom of thought and worship. Today such close secrecy is no longer necessary. Much may now be given out openly which formerly could be imparted only in private and by word of mouth.[36]

After 'associate members' have taken the introductory courses, they may be admitted into a group known as a Pronaos; the Pronaos Ritual is a healing ritual.

As with similar schools, the philosophy is practical; the aim is that as the member 'continues with the process of self-unfolding, he gradually increases mastery of himself, first in small things, then in greater.' Progress can only be made if there is sincerity, desire and willingness to work.

For you to be successful in our Work, your personal goals must correspond to those of the Order: personal enlightenment, self-transmutation, and service to Life. To only desire healing and wealth is not enough and will surely result in failure... BOTA does not offer to remake your world for you. It does offer you the keys to knowledge that will enable you to do it for yourself, with the inner help that linkage with a true Mystery School confers.

'Adytum' is Greek for 'the innermost part of the Temple, the *Holy of Holies, that which is not made with hands*' (italics in original). The name Builders of the Adytum 'indicates that we propose to help you build the *Inner Temple* wherein conscious contact with the Higher Self may be made and your true spiritual heritage may be realized.'

There may well also be physical improvements in a member's life, such as health and wealth, as a result of their studies, but these should not be the reason for joining. However, if they are as powerful as BOTA indicate, they should certainly not be dismissed:

The practical work of BOTA, which includes study, meditation, imagery and ritual, initiates a series of subtle but important changes in your inner world, not the least of which is an expansion of your conscious awareness. Even a slight increase in this area has a remarkable effect on your mental/emotional capacities. Your intelligence increases and you become more aware of your motivations. You become more observant, which improves your memory. Your ability to anticipate future effects of present causes is enhanced, improving your discrimination in making choices. Objectivity is increased, aiding the ability to think more logically and clearly, which increases control over your environment and helps you define your goals...

The list is remarkably similar to L. Ron Hubbard's claims about a 'Clear' (see pages 449-450), except that his techniques are psychological in nature, while those of BOTA and other mystery schools are spiritual. Their expression here is also akin to many of the goals of the 'self-improvement' courses and seminars, which have always had a great appeal in America (see page 426).

But the main aim is to enable the initiate to be raised to a higher state of consciousness; other terms used include 'an awakening' and 'illumination', or an awareness of the God within.

BOTA's teachings are not tied to a particular national mythos, nor its members to a particular nationality; the School is international, with centres in Europe, South and Central America, New Zealand, Canada and throughout the USA. Unusually, it also doesn't require members to relinquish membership of any other Orders. There are around 4,000 members worldwide; members are usually over 18.

TAROT

BOTA, like most esoteric groups, teaches both the Kabbala and Tarot. The Kabbala's Tree of Life is used symbolically to represent the relationship between God and Man; as Tarot expert Rachel Pollack has said, 'Tarot has come into being as a lively pictorial version of the inner knowledge found on the Tree.'[37] BOTA say of Tarot,

> The particular potency of this system lies in its use of symbols, which are a universal language that directly instructs subconsciousness with its pictorial wisdom, regardless of language differences... It was originally devised as a means of conveying universal principles regarding Man's structure, place and purpose in the Cosmos, through the use of symbols.

In common with most esoteric schools, BOTA uses Tarot for study, meditation, imagery and ritual, rather than for fortune-telling or divination.

Like several other HOGD offshoots, BOTA has published its own design of Tarot, the images symbolizing the deep esoteric truths taught by the movement. The cards are black and white, and members are encouraged to colour them to bring out their personal interpretation of the symbolism and the member's own relationship with them.

There are now several esoteric Tarot packs claiming to stem from the teachings of the HOGD. These include the well-known Rider-Waite Tarot designed by Pamela Colman Smith to the instructions of A.E. Waite, Aleister Crowley's Book of Thoth, Robert Wang's Golden Dawn Tarot (based on Israel Regardie's pack, which was based on a pack painted by Mathers' wife to his instructions), Godfrey Dowson's Hermetic Tarot, and the Morgan-Greer Tarot, which is based on the interpretations of Waite and Paul Foster Case. Considering that these all stem from the same root, their images and symbolism are often markedly different from each other, though the BOTA pack, drawn to the instructions of Case, is very similar to the Rider-Waite, and is presumably a copy of Mathers' pack.

The HOGD and some of its offshoots were closely linked with Freemasonry and Rosicrucianism; much of the symbolism is similar between all of them. Interestingly, the Masonic Tarot, a French pack, is quite different from any of the HOGD-offshoot packs.

SOCIETY OF THE INNER LIGHT

Dion Fortune (1890–1946) was born into a Christian Science family as Violet Mary Firth; she took her pseudonym from her family motto, *Deo, non Fortuna* – By God, not by chance. She had visions from her childhood, and joined the Theosophy movement briefly; from them she took the idea of the Masters, but saw them as spiritual rather than physical beings.

In an early job, when she was 20, she felt that she was under psychic attack from a female superior, and set out to discover how she could defend herself; one of her most significant works is *Psychic Self-Defence* (1930). She studied psychology, particularly the works of Freud and Jung, and worked as a lay psychoanalyst.

Fortune's visions continued. In one she met Jesus and the Comte de Saint-Germain, and learnt about her past lives. She joined the HOGD offshoot Alpha et Omega, run by the novelist Brodie Innes, in 1919, and began doing trance work in 1922. She then transferred to Stella Matutina, which was run by Moina MacGregor Mathers. With some like-minded friends she joined the Christian Mystic Lodge of the Theosophical Society in 1925, 'as a means of counteracting the Theosophical Society's Star of the East movement [see page 345] to promote Krishnamurti as the new World Teacher,' says Gareth Knight, Fortune's biographer.[38] They resigned from this in 1927 and founded the Community (soon renamed the Fraternity, and later the Society) of the Inner Light. In the same year she was ejected from Stella Matutina by Mathers' wife.

From 1927 to 1938 she worked with her husband, a Welsh doctor, Thomas Penry Evans. With Evans as her priest she developed her study and practice of magic, a blend of esoteric Christianity, Kabbalism and Tarot, with some strong Pagan elements; her 24 books, including 6 occult novels, are read and recommended today by both esoteric and Neo-Pagan movements, though the Society of the Inner Light stresses that she was never a witch, and down-plays the Pagan aspects of her work.

When Evans left her in 1938 (they were divorced in 1945) Fortune took a lower profile, partly because her publishing activities were curtailed by wartime paper rationing. She continued her researches into Arthurian and Grail material; she was also instrumental in mounting a magical defence of Britain during World War II.

[O]ver the years [she] produced teaching on a wide range of metaphysical subjects, including masculine and feminine relationships, the esoteric orders and their work, the training and work of an initiate, the Arthurian legends, principles of esoteric healing, and much else besides.[39]

It is claimed that, through spirit-contact with certain members, Fortune continued to run the Society of the Inner Light for several years after her death from leukaemia.

The Society has changed some of the emphasis of its teachings over the years. It was strongly influenced for a while by Alice Bailey's teachings on the Secret Masters; it picked up on the Alexander Technique for improving physical posture; it even dabbled briefly, 'for purely practical reasons', with Scientology's E-meters. However, its founder's teachings continued to be of prime importance.

For public consumption the Society of the Inner Light is 'a registered charity based on the Christian religion,'[40] and indeed, from 1961 to 1991 the Christian side was given greater emphasis, says Knight. But in fact it is a school within the Western Mystery Tradition.

> The principle aim of the Western Esoteric Tradition is expansion of consciousness. It deals with the 'ground of all being', unmanifest, beyond time and space, which differentiates countless modes of being in evolving through a manifest universe. The purpose of these modes of being is to realize the Divine Intention... [which] is concerned with the true purpose and destiny of each one of us. To achieve this we train our members in the Qabalah, Bible and with ritual, as well as daily usages, including meditation.[41]

Its main source books are Dion Fortune's *The Mystical Qabalah* and *Cosmic Doctrine*. As with other British esoteric schools, there is a great emphasis on mythology, particularly Celtic and Arthurian mythology; Fortune herself was closely linked with Glastonbury.

Following initial training the Society teaches three different paths, the Mystic, the Hermetic and the Path of the Green Way.

> On the Mystic Path the ego casts everything aside that separates it from God. It seeks to know even as it is known; and as the mind cannot know God, it even casts away the mind to enter into the Divine Union. All that is not God to it is dross; and it purges and repurges the soul until nothing remaineth but pure spirit. This is a steep and narrow way, though swift and sure.

The Path of the Green Ray seeks God in Nature, in his works.

> For the god within, being lifted up and exalted to ecstasy with a divine inebriation, perceives the God Without in hill and herb and elemental force... it is an inebriation of the soul, not of the flesh. An inebriation of colour, sound and motion that lift the senses out of the flesh into a wider vision, for Dionysius is a Messiah as well as the Christ, and the soul can transcend the mind by sublimating the senses as well as by renouncing, and some find God on this Path as truly as by the Way of the Cross.

The Hermetic Path is a middle way between the other two.

> Use the mind God gave you to reach up and realize the things of the spirit upon the one hand, and reach down and control the things of the senses on the other, and thus you shall stand equilibrated between them, as the Initiated Adept.

Like most other esoteric schools the Society stresses the difficulty of the work, almost to the point of actively discouraging people from becoming members. It also lays great stress on moral living, courteousness, good citizenship, self-discipline, responsibility and other similar virtues.

Two former members of the Society of the Inner Light, who have produced very significant books in the esoteric tradition, are W.E. Butler and Gareth Knight. When the Society dropped to only a couple of dozen members in the late 1990s, Knight was asked back to help get it on its feet again, which meant having to leave his own esoteric movement, the Gareth Knight Group (now renamed the Avalon Group). With access to her manuscripts, he has co-authored or edited two 'new' Dion Fortune books,[42] as well as writing her biography.

The Society is quite specifically British in emphasis, though it does have an overseas membership. After a one-year correspondence course 'designed to give an adequate knowledge of the Tree of Life of the Qabalah', members progress through three degrees, the 'Lesser Mysteries',

which are broadly based upon traditional Masonic symbolism. These are designed to develop and strengthen character, to give experience of ceremonial working, and to develop the visionary powers of the mind as a means toward attaining higher consciousness...

Those who successfully pass through this process... may elect to move on to the 'Greater Mysteries', which are concerned with developing consciousness at the level of the Evolutionary Personality and ultimately the Spirit. This is the level of the Adept as a natural progression from that of the Lesser Mystery initiate. Here specialized work may be undertaken under the direction of the inner plane hierarchy.[43]

SERVANTS OF THE LIGHT

The Servants of the Light (SOL) was founded in 1973 by W.E. Butler (1898–1978) and is based in Jersey; the Helios Course, which led up to its formation, was founded by Butler and Gareth Knight (b. 1930) in 1964. Both were former members of Dion Fortune's Society of the Inner Light; Butler was an ordained priest in the Liberal Catholic Church, founded by the Reverend Charles W. Leadbeater, who helped turn the Theosophical Movement more towards esoteric Christianity (see pages 194-195, 345). Butler has written a number of significant works on the Western Mystery Tradition. His successor as SOL's Director of Studies is Dolores Ashcroft-Nowicki.

Servants of the Light is organized on standard lines of progression from Novice upwards. The Entered Novice takes a 50-lesson main course over four or five years; the first six lessons are based on *The Art of True Healing* by Israel Regardie, a former member of Stella Matutina, and Lessons 7–50 on *Practical Guide to Qabalistic Symbolism* by Gareth Knight. By the tenth or twelfth lesson, if progress is satisfactory, the Novice becomes a Fellow within the Fellowship of the SOL; this is the First Degree.

If a Fellow wishes to progress to the Second Degree, he or she must attend three practical (i.e. ritual) workshops, at Beginners, Intermediate and Advanced level. The correspondence course takes 44 weeks. At some point during this time the Fellow may be offered initiation, and at the end of the main course may enter the Second Degree, becoming a Frater or Soror of the Fraternity of the SOL. Fraters and Sorors help to teach Novices and lead Fellows in their ritual work.

Beyond this is a Third Degree, by invitation only. 'The work involves worldwide communications with other Schools and Orders,... much of the work is of an advanced Inner-Plane nature, and... Third Degree members are known as Councillors.'

Servants of the Light, like most mystery schools, has outer and inner levels; the outer level (i.e. visible to the outside world) is the First and Second Degrees. From these are drawn the members of the Inner Court. SOL is a 'contacted' school:

> by contacted, we mean those schools that are in close psychic touch with the overshadowing Hierarchy on the Inner Planes. It is in this Inner Group that the real power resides; and from there it is mediated in various ways to its counterpart on the physical level. The SOL is so contacted, and its inner powers are slowly becoming available to those who come within its sphere of influence.[44]

It sees the esoteric sciences as:

> the Western equivalent of the Eastern Yoga systems. The Western system is just as effective and noble as the Eastern systems, and they both lead to the same ultimate goal: integration of the psyche and soul and a direct knowledge of the spiritual realities which underlie manifestation.[45]

The main emphasis of the teaching for Novices and Fellows is on the Kabbala, whose Tree of Life

> has been described as 'the Mighty, All-Embracing Glyph of the Soul of Man and the Universe.' Without this composite system, it is probable that the Western Tradition would have been entirely destroyed. Owing to its simplicity, however, the glyph is easily committed to memory; and because of its profundity, from this sparse simplicity can be derived a complete and satisfying philosophy and knowledge of life in both its inner and outer aspects.

SOL see the Kabbala as

the foundation of the Western Mystery Tradition... the great body of philosophy to be found in the religion texts of the Jews, including the Old Testament of the Bible, particularly the Pentateuch. It can also be seen in the vast complex of astrological, alchemical and occult symbology that has come down to us, as well as in the Rosicrucian and Masonic myth – including the Tarot, which is indigenous to the West.

The Western Mystery Tradition, sometimes called the Hermetic Tradition, also has clear links with Egyptian and Greek thought from around the time of Christ – the Gnostics and Neo-Platonists. SOL's 'contact' is from the ancient esoteric School of Alexandria, from the Temple of On, or Heliopolis. The Third Degree is also known as the House of the Amethyst.

> The *House of the Amethyst* is one of the outer names of the great Alexandrian Fraternity, the *Fraternitas Alexandrae*, which has its existence on the Inner Planes, and of which the SOL is an earth-level expression. The *Fraternitas Alexandrae* is the inner fountainhead from which all our teaching ultimately stems. It is a withdrawn Order under whose authority the whole school works, teaches and has its existence.[46]

SOL also encourages its members to become familiar with mythology, particularly but not solely Celtic mythology and the Arthurian cycle – the Matter of Britain. 'Any mythological knowledge you acquire will not be wasted. The ability to cross-index the legends and god forms can be of immense value in the understanding of the ancient past.' During the course students must make a detailed study of at least two pantheons in addition to their native tradition.

The School sees

> an urgent need for seekers of all ages to resume the Quest of the Grail. The need for sound esoteric training is more urgent than it has ever been. We do not claim, as others do, that the occult way holds all the answers to the world's ills; but we do claim that it has a part to play in the eventual victory over them. We believe, sincerely, that the ancient traditions hold a timeless key which may be applied to modern life and its problems. We aim to train dedicated men and women who will help others to achieve the inner serenity that is their birthright.

The SOL have added to the number of esoteric Tarot packs with their own Servants of the Light Tarot. For once this doesn't claim to be a copy of Mathers' pack, or even to contain the true symbolism of the HOGD; instead, Dolores Ashcroft-Nowicki has worked together with two artists to produce a pack which reflects the esoteric teachings of the School. Her book, *Inner Landscapes*, uses the SOL Major

Arcana for 'pathworking', or guided meditational journeys.

SOL has around 2,600 members in 23 countries, making it one of the largest and most influential esoteric movements.

THE LONDON GROUP

Like the Servants of the Light, the London Group was founded by a former senior member of the Society of the Inner Light, in 1975. It is also, in its initial training programme, or Outer Court, a correspondence school, and despite its name, is not limited to London.

The London Group offers two introductory courses, to be taken consecutively: first, basic occult tenets and introduction to the Kabbala; and second, introduction to the modern mysteries, particularly the practical use of symbols and ritual; the second part also outlines the structure and methods of a modern occult group.

The Group stresses the practical nature of its work.

> Our keynote is 'action'. We have no room for arm-chair philosophers. We welcome innovation and use many techniques to help individuals become truly 'themselves'.[47]

The primary goal is personal regeneration, with the clear understanding that this will benefit others:

> [T]he principles learnt are lived out in the daily life of its members... like yeast working in a mass of dough, right thinking and a right ethic based on Cosmic Law, are set to work in the national life. And it is surprising just how much even a single such archetypal 'pattern' can help to redress the chaos so prevalent in the world today... There has never been a greater need for sane, well-balanced men and women than there is today.

The London Group, like its forerunners, is based firmly in the Western Mystery Tradition.

> A notable feature of all the religions of the past is that each had an inner and an outer aspect. The outer form became the Race religion, whilst the inner form contained deeper teachings which offered a direct path to personal experience of the inner realities and an opportunity to help in the spiritual evolution of the Race.

Some Mystery Schools appear to the outsider to be rather conservative, even a little old-fashioned in their transmission of what are, after all, very traditional teachings. The London Group emphasizes that it 'passes on that tradition in a modern form suitable for the use of 20th century men and women' – and now, presumably, twenty-first century. It also gives the impression of being a little more flexible than some of the other Schools:

> We welcome enquirers of all denominations and beliefs – the New Age is the Age of synthesis. There is room for many viewpoints... There are many ways of service and many groups seeking to put New Age ideals into action... [I]f this group is not what you are seeking, then at least we have helped you to know more clearly what it is that you *do* seek! There is no 'one way'; but there *is* a best way for each one of us.

The leader of the London Group, Alan Adams, who wrote as Charles Fielding, died in 1998, and the group says that 'there have been a few changes in the last two years.'[48] From its literature, its aims and objectives appear to be the same as they were, but the criteria for full membership and the structure of the more advanced courses may have changed.

CHAOS MAGIC

Chaos magic (sometimes spelt magick) is a fairly new development in 'occult science'. Its name springs from Chaos Theory in quantum physics, and also from what might seem to outsiders to be the chaotic approach to practising it, in comparison with the careful application of tried and tested magical ritual from existing traditions.

Many of those interested in esoteric religion, perhaps especially the more 'occult' areas, and also Neo-Paganism, are well educated and well read. Just as most Wiccans have now come to accept that theirs is actually a new religion, very largely created about half a century ago (see page 398-399), so those interested in ritual magic(k) have come to accept that even the most traditional magical rituals were 'invented' at some point. Much of today's occult science can be traced back to the Hermetic Order of the Golden Dawn, and much of its ritual, rather than being carved in ancient stone, was created by MacGregor Mathers (see page 359) little more than a century ago.

Chaos magicians, accepting that, as one says, 'It's all made up anyway,' are happy to experiment, and to make things up themselves, more relevant to their own lives, circumstances and interests – and to the present day. Instead of invoking the angels who guard the four cardinal points by their Hebrew names, then, they might call on John, Paul, George and Ringo. Instead of the traditional elements of Air, Water, Fire and Earth, why not have a spicier alternative and call on Posh, Sporty, Scary and Baby? (For those who recognize the invisible fifth element of Spirit, they could add Ginger.)[49]

As Chaos magicians often say, 'Nothing is True. Everything is Permitted.'[50] One prominent Chaos magician, Pete Carroll, puts it this way: 'Chaoists usually accept the meta-belief that belief is a tool for achieving effects; it is not an end in itself.'[51]

There is clearly a playfulness in the attitude of Chaos magicians, but (like all esotericists and Neo-Pagans) their study and ritual work has a serious purpose: to know oneself, and to develop spiritually. The attraction of Chaos magic is summed up by Carroll: 'Chaos Magic for me means a handful of basic techniques which must be adhered to strictly to get results, but beyond that it offers a freedom of expression and intent undreamt of in all previous forms of magic.'

Chaos magicians come from many backgrounds, from ritual sex-magick groups such as Ordo Templi Orientis to Wiccans and Druids exploring different paths.

THE I AM MOVEMENT

The I AM movement, with its various offshoots, has its roots in Theosophy; it was founded in 1931 by Guy and Edna Ballard. The previous year Guy Ballard (1878–1939), who had read widely in Theosophy and other esoteric religion, was on a walking holiday on Mount Shasta in California, looking for a supposed esoteric Brotherhood of Mount Shasta, when he met the Ascended Master the Comte de Saint-Germain, a historical eighteenth-century alchemist who features in a number of esoteric movements. Saint-Germain had apparently been scouring Europe for centuries looking for someone to whom he could give the Great Laws of Life; finding no one worthy, he had turned his attentions to the USA.

The Ballards began to make regular contact with Saint-Germain and other Masters. They set up the Saint Germain Press to publish their books on I AM, including *Unveiled Mysteries* (1934) and *The Magic Presence* (1935) under the pseudonym Godfre Ray King, and *I AM Adorations and Affirmations* (1936). They began teaching classes and training other teachers of their message across America. By 1938 it was estimated that they had had up to a million students. After experiencing problems with hecklers at their open meetings, they started to hold membership-only classes.

After Guy Ballard's unexpected death in 1939 the movement ran into a series of difficulties. Apparently he had taught mastery over death, and many members felt cheated. As with many religious leaders, the Ballards had become wealthy through their movement; some ex-members accused them of using the US postal service for fraudulent purposes – obtaining money for a false religion. Unusually, the validity of the teachings of a religion were tested in court. From 1942 to 1954 the movement was unable to use the normal mail, and had to distribute its books and magazines by Railway Express. In 1957 it was finally granted tax-exempt status as a religion. Edna Ballard died in 1971, leaving the leadership in the hands of a Board of Directors.

The movement teaches that the omnipotent, omniscient and omnipresent creator God ('I AM' – Exodus 3:14) is in all of us as a spark from the Divine Flame, and that we can experience this presence, love, power and light – the power of the Violet Consuming Flame of Divine Love – through quiet contemplation and by repeating 'affirmations' and 'decrees'. By 'affirming' something one desires, one can cause it to happen; in a sense the I AM movement overlaps with the Personal Development or Human Potential movements, because of this 'positive thinking' aspect of its teachings.

The Ascended Masters are religious adepts who have (like Buddhist *bodhisattvas*) stepped off the wheel of reincarnation and now devote themselves to the guidance of mankind; they are the same as the Great White Brotherhood. Because Jesus is one of the Ascended Masters, the movement calls itself Christian. The Ballards and their son Donald (who left the movement in 1957) were the only Accredited Messengers of the Ascended Masters – they received over 3,000 messages between them – though all believers may experience the Christ Self within them. It is the duty of believers to use the divine power wisely, for harmony and purity; its misuse has been the cause of discord and death throughout the centuries.

The teachings of the Ballards were not new, but the publicity they gave to them encouraged their spread through the developing New Age movements, many of which have taken up the idea of the Masters.

CHURCH UNIVERSAL AND TRIUMPHANT

The Church Universal and Triumphant, and its publishing wing Summit Lighthouse, have much in common with the I AM movement – they even recognize Guy Ballard as an Ascended Master – though they are quite independent; they are also one of the most prominent modern versions of Gnostic Christianity. In recent years they have come in for much criticism from the anti-cult organizations, particularly the Cult Awareness Network (pre-1996; see page 101), which ran public lectures against the Church in America.

HISTORY

Mark L. Prophet (1918–1973) had been involved in an I AM offshoot, the Bridge to Freedom (later the New Age Church of the Christ, and now the Bridge to Spiritual Freedom), for some time before he founded Summit Lighthouse in Washington DC in 1958 to publish the teachings he had received from the Ascended Masters. Prophet, incidentally, was genuinely his family surname. In 1961 he met Elizabeth Clare Wulf (b. 1939), who had been raised a Lutheran, had joined Christian Science in her early teens, and started reading I AM literature when she was 18. She was trained by Mark Prophet and by the Ascended Master who had appointed him a Messenger, El Morya, who had been King Arthur, Thomas à Becket and Sir Thomas More in three of his incarnations. She married Mark in 1963, and a year later she too became a Messenger. The Ascended Master Saint-Germain instructed them to form the Keepers of the Flame Fraternity to teach others about the Masters.

On Mark's sudden death from a stroke, Elizabeth Clare Prophet took over the organization; the following year she set up the Church Universal and Triumphant (CUT), and Summit Lighthouse became its publishing house. She has grown in importance as the Church has grown; within the movement she is known formally as Guru Ma and usually as Mother, though not as Ma Prophet, her popular name in the US press.[52]

Over the years CUT has been based in several areas, outgrowing each one and moving on to the next. Mark Prophet was living in Washington DC when he founded Summit Lighthouse. In 1962 they moved to Fairfax, Virginia, and in 1965 to Vienna, Virginia. In 1966 they moved to a mansion in Colorado Springs, which became the world HQ of Summit Lighthouse. During these years the two Messengers travelled around America and Europe spreading their teachings. They also set up 'the Motherhouse' in Santa Barbara, which housed Summit University for a few years; other centres were set up around America. CUT leased a Church of the Nazarene college campus in Pasadena, California in 1976, then moved yet again the following year, buying from the Claretian Fathers an estate in the Santa Monica Mountains near Malibu; this they renamed Camelot.

In 1981 the Church bought its present home, the Royal Teton Ranch in Paradise Valley, near Livingston, Montana; it is next to the famous Yellowstone National Park. Along with many other organizations it bought up caravans and kitchen equipment from the Rajneesh community when that broke up in 1985. CUT moved its HQ to the Royal Teton Ranch, a 10,000ha (24,000-acre) site, in 1986.

The Church was at the centre of controversy for some years. Misunderstandings had first developed because the Church bought up large areas of land, which local people found worrying, especially after the political takeover attempt at Rajneeshpuram (see page 291); then because it built fallout shelters against the threat of nuclear disaster; and then when two members, including Mrs Prophet's then husband, Edward Francis, illegally attempted to buy otherwise legal weapons without Church knowledge. Francis was jailed for a short time for his involvement – which the authorities determined was not linked to the Church – and the Church suffered for a while from negative public perception. Relations with neighbours, and with both state and federal government, have improved markedly in recent years.

(Francis was Mrs Prophet's fourth husband, whom she married in 1981; her first, before Mark Prophet, didn't join in her belief in the Ascended Masters; she also had a brief third marriage after Mark's death. She was divorced from Francis in 1996, but he continued as executive vice president of the Church until 1998, and is still an active member of the Church.)

Elizabeth Clare Prophet continued to receive messages from the Ascended Masters, particularly Saint-Germain, 'the Knight Commander of the Keepers of the Flame Fraternity,'[53] and Lanello, the Ascended Master name of her late husband. The weekly *Pearls of Wisdom* magazine contains messages from the Ascended Masters. Her many books, incorporating these teachings (and the teachings given earlier to Mark Prophet), have gained a much wider circulation than the Church itself, becoming influential in more general New Age circles.

Elizabeth Clare Prophet was trained by Mark Prophet and by El Morya, and had been a Messenger for ten years when Mark died. No one has been trained as a Messenger to succeed her; the Church expects the Holy Spirit to direct them on this when the time comes, but currently has no plans to elect a new spiritual leader. (It will not stay 'in the family'; two of her four children by Mark Prophet have now left the Church. At the age of 54 Mrs Prophet had a fifth child, Seth, in 1994, before separating from Edward Francis.) The Board of Directors actually run the Church, and will continue to do so after Mrs Prophet's eventual death. In 1996, management consultant Gilbert Cleirbaut was elected Church president, with the remit to make major changes in the Church's management structure and culture. The Church is clearly preparing for its stable continuation once Mrs Prophet is no longer with it; it is reducing its focus on her, and aiming to be less authoritarian and more decentralized. In sociological terms, it is in the process of changing from charismatic leadership to rational/legal leadership (see pages 65-66).

In the late 1990s Elizabeth Clare Prophet was diagnosed with Alzheimer's Disease and revealed a lifelong condition of epilepsy, and stepped down from her administrative positions in the Church. In 1998 Prophet asked Murray Steinman, a long-time friend, to apply legally for a limited guardianship on her behalf, to assist her with legal, financial and medical matters. 'While I can carry on my spiritual functions and the Executive Board is doing an excellent job remoulding the Church's organizational structure, there are areas of my personal life where I need additional support,' Prophet wrote.[54]

BELIEFS AND PRACTICES

The Church Universal and Triumphant teaches that people are born with an innate spark of divinity and can realize their full potential of oneness with God – the same mystical message which they say is embedded at the heart of all the world's major religions. It also teaches that many people have mastered life, realized their full potential and ascended back to God; these enlightened spiritual beings, or Ascended Masters, now assist humanity from spiritual realms.

Although some of its teachings derive from the I AM movement, and ultimately from Theosophy (though 'Theosophy has a far more intellectual approach,' says Murray Steinman, formerly the Church's director of media relations[55]), CUT has its own distinctive theology which in recent years has embraced large elements of Gnostic Christianity. It identifies itself as a Church firmly based in the Judaeo-Christian tradition.

> Jesus Christ and Saint-Germain – together with all of the heavenly hosts: Ascended Masters, Elohim, archangels, angels and servant-sons of God, who comprise the Spirit of the Great White Brotherhood (the multitude of saints robed in white witnessed by Saint John) – have come forth from the inner Mystery School at the end of Pisces and the beginning of Aquarius to teach us how to call upon this name of the Lord, alchemical formulas whereby we may put on our individual Christhood even while we overcome personified evil and the *energy veil* of our negative karma, the so-called sins of our past lives.[56]

In common with the I AM movement, CUT teaches that there is an element of the Christ, a divine spark of the God flame, within each of us.

> The fundamental principle of the teachings of the Ascended Masters is that all sons and daughters of God have a divine spark which is their potential to become, or realize, the Christ within and ascend to God as Jesus did. This concept is at the heart of the major religions, East and West. And it was part of Jesus' original teachings to his disciples which were either destroyed or obscured by Church Fathers.[57]

His teachings were also corrupted by the New Testament writers. Jesus studied in India and Tibet between the ages of 12 and 30; two of CUT's publications are *The Lost Years of Jesus* and the four-volume *The Lost Teachings of Jesus*. The first is based on old Buddhist stories of Saint Issa, who travelled to the East and studied under Masters there before returning to Palestine to take up his ministry.

> Then it was that Issa left the parental house in secret, departed from Jerusalem, and with the merchants set out towards Sind, with the object of perfecting himself in the Divine Word and of studying the laws of the great Buddhas.[58]

Jesus is here given the same sort of 'early-life mythology' as Madame Blavatsky, G.I. Gurdjieff, L. Ron Hubbard and other founders of modern religions.

The Lost Teachings incorporates some of the ideas of such non-canonical works as the Secret Book of James and the Gnostic Gospels of Philip, Thomas and Mary Magdalene, but is actually 'a reconstitution of Jesus' basic message through the Messengership of Mark and Elizabeth Prophet, which they have written down,' says Steinman. CUT emphasizes particularly the Book of Enoch, another of the many books which never made it into the Bible.

The Church does not accept all the Gnostic teachings, says Steinman, but 'a lot of the things we totally agree with, like where Jesus is saying in the Gospel of Thomas, "If you drink from the same stream that I have, you will be just like me, we'll be twins";[59] that's essentially our core teaching, that you can become like Jesus. If you miss that point, then you're missing the point of his message.'

While the Church believes that Jesus was God the Son, their beliefs differ from traditional Christianity; Jesus was a man in complete touch with the Christ-consciousness within him, and says that we are all Sons and Daughters of God who can do the same. He ascended to God immediately after leaving his human body, and is now one of the Ascended Masters. Mary Magdalene, who was Jesus' twin flame, is now the Ascended Master Magda. The Virgin Mary is venerated as the perfect expression of the Mother aspect of God. The Statue of Liberty is symbolic of the Goddess of Liberty. In this Aquarian Age the Church places equal emphasis on the masculine and feminine aspects of both God and individual people, whether they are female or male.

Saint-Germain is a very significant figure in the Church's teachings. He is an Ascended Master who sponsors projects that promote soul freedom, including the founding of the USA where he inspired the American Constitution and the Declaration of Independence. Before becoming an Ascended Master he lived on Earth as the prophet Samuel, Mary's husband Joseph, Merlin, Roger Bacon, Christopher Columbus and Francis Bacon. The nineteenth-century writer Voltaire mentioned him as 'the Wonderman of Europe.'

Saint Germain also introduced at large a high frequency spiritual energy long known to mystics as the violet flame, which can be invoked through spoken prayer and visualization for healing of body, mind and spirit.[60]

Central to the Church's teachings – and its art – is 'the violet flame':

When invoked and visualized in the giving of dynamic decrees, this seventh-ray aspect of the sacred fire transmutes the cause, effect, record and memory of negative karma and misqualified energy that result in discord, disease and death. Those who correctly call forth the violet flame daily, experience transformation, soul liberation, and spiritual upliftment.[61]

The Church teaches that we can step off the wheel of reincarnation – in ascension – by becoming united with our Christ-consciousness through study and prayer and, as in I AM, through affirmations and decrees. Affirmations affirm the person's relationship with God; decrees use the name of God (I AM) to make statements of power such as 'I AM the light of the heart, shining in the darkness of being, changing all into the infinite mind of Christ,' or 'I AM a being of violet fire, I AM the purity God desires.' Ascension is not physical, but 'a spiritual acceleration of consciousness which takes place at the natural conclusion of one's lifetime when the soul returns to the Father and is freed from the round of karma and rebirth.'[62]

But CUT does not claim to be an easy short-cut to God.

> The path to the summit of being is steep. With fellow seekers and with the Ascended Masters who have gone before us we can make our way through these hitherto uncharted paths, and reach the summit of being.[63]

CUT believes that it is 'a very valuable path for some people,' says Steinman, but it does not believe that it is the only path. Neither is the Church dogmatic in its teachings: members are not required to believe every aspect. It also believes that it is more important to look for the similarities between religions than to emphasize the differences. In keeping with this philosophy, the Church's doctrines are still developing, as it explores the mystical paths of all the world's religions; it has already examined Hinduism, Buddhism and others, and is currently looking into the Kabbala.

'The Ascended Masters present a path and a teaching whereby every individual on earth can find his way back to God,' says Prophet.

> I do not claim to be a Master but only their instrument. Nor do I claim to be perfect in my human self. I am the servant of the Light in all students of the Ascended Masters and in all people. My books and writings are intended to give people the opportunity to know the Truth that can make them free – so they can find God without me. My goal is to take true seekers, in the tradition of the Masters of the Far East, as far as they can go and need to go to meet their true Teachers face to face.[64]

Elizabeth Clare Prophet, like her late husband, is a Messenger of the Ascended Masters. The Church sees this as similar to the prophets of the Old Testament, who delivered messages from God.

> She is fully conscious and in possession of her faculties, yet in an exalted state, while delivering the words of the heavenly host as 'dictations'. Her work is not a form of psychism or spiritualism in which a discarnate entity from the spirit world takes over the body of a channeller. Rather it is a conveyance by the Holy Spirit of the sacred fire and the teaching of immortal beings who with Jesus have returned to the heart of the Father.[65]

There have been many criticisms of the Church, both by some of their neighbours in Montana and by anti-cultists. Deprogrammers kidnapped one member of the Church in Belgium; she managed to get away after a few days, and the police eventually arrested her mother, brother and the deprogrammers.

The Church has been accused of being right-wing. Steinman accepts that they espouse conservative morality, and that they think that 'civil defence and strategic defence are a good thing,' but he points out that on other topics, particularly environmental issues and their stand against pesticides, they tend to be conservationist, and that in their criticism of nuclear power plants they are positively liberal. They follow what the Ascended Masters tell them on different issues, so their stance is more spiritual than political, he says.

He also suggests that middle-class Americans in general tend to be more patriotic and more conservative than their British counterparts.

It is often said that Mrs Prophet forecast the end of the world – or at least a cataclysmic disaster – for April 1990. This is, says Christopher Kelley, spokesman for CUT, an exaggeration of Prophet's prediction of 12 years of increased negative karma as the age of Pisces ends and the Age of Aquarius begins. In fact, says Steinman, she had been told by Saint-Germain to have the underground shelters ready by then – not just for sheltering members of the Church, but also for protecting all the world's spiritual teachings in the event of a major attack. Nevertheless, the Church estimates that membership dropped by about 50 per cent during the 'shelter phase'; by 2000 it had only regained around 30 per cent of these.

On the firearms story, which brought the Church a lot of bad publicity, the facts – as established in court – are that the Church itself owns no weapons; individual members may own whatever weapons they want for sporting purposes or for self-defence. Edward Francis, Mrs Prophet's then husband, with another Church member, tried to buy guns to defend the Church's fallout shelter if necessary against local right-wing extremists. The weapons would have been quite legal if Francis hadn't made the mistake of trying to buy them under a false name – ironically to avoid publicity. 'Obviously we screwed up. It was a huge mistake and it was ill-conceived,' says Francis,[66] who was at the time vice-president and business manager of the Church. Mrs Prophet had not known of the firearms purchase in advance.

Mrs Prophet has also been criticized for her love of expensive clothes and jewellery; her response is that the clothes were a gift, and the jewellery is a focus of spiritual power, and belongs to the Church, not to her.

Like many other alternative religious movements, the Church has been accused of brainwashing its members, a charge which it calls absurd. An independent study of the Church, sponsored by the Association of World Academics for Religious Education (AWARE), concluded that there was no evidence of anything approaching brainwashing. The members are predominantly white middle-class adults; three-quarters are between 30 and 60; a quarter have an advanced degree. They are generally of above-average intelligence. Politically they do tend to be right of centre; a half describe themselves as conservative, and a further 8 per cent as very conservative; a quarter say they are moderate, and only 4 per cent say they are liberal. But as for CUT being another Waco-in-the-making, as some anti-cultists have asserted, the study found that adult members 'scored lower than the normed population on the Aggression subscale.' Using a number of different indicators, the study concludes that CUT has the characteristics of a denomination rather than those of a cult; as with mainstream denominations, for example, it is quite possible to be a 'nominal' member. Part of the study concentrates on the children in the Royal Teton Ranch; 'contrary to the claims of critics, they found the children bright, well taken care of, loved, and well educated.'[67]

In common with its spiritual great-grandparent, the Theosophical Society, CUT places great value on education, and has run a Montessori school to offer quality education to children from pre-school to high school age.

Although the Church makes use of music, it is opposed to rock music. 'We don't think that rock music is all that healthy for you,' says Steinman. 'Rhythm and music are extremely important as an expression of sound, and we see sound as the creative power of the universe – 'In the beginning was the Word'. Where the rhythm becomes destructive, that's where we draw the line.'

Communicants of the Church pledge to abstain from alcohol, tobacco and drugs; other members might smoke or drink, though 'We don't think it's a good idea for them to do it,' says Steinman. The Church recommends a macrobiotic diet without much red meat, but Steinman suggests the most important thing in diet is balance and common sense.

Like many other religious movements, the Church doesn't give membership figures. There are practical reasons for this. It has a core membership of communicants, who have committed themselves completely to the Church, pledging acceptance of the Tenets, and tithing their income to the Church; Keepers of the Flame are 'signed-up members', but are not necessarily deeply committed; and in addition there are thousands of people around the world who, having read Mrs Prophet's books, accept much of the teaching, but are not actually members of the Church. CUT has around 120 groups in the USA, and a further 120 groups in about 40 other countries, as well as individual members in another 20 countries. Some communicants live in communities, like the Royal Teton Ranch, but the majority live and work in the outside world. In the UK, there are groups in London, Leeds, Litchfield and Solihull.

THE EMISSARIES

The Emissaries could be called one of the earliest 'New Age' movements. They live in a dozen small communities – from 20 to 150 people – in the USA, Canada, the UK and elsewhere, with a further 150 centres for meetings. The UK community at Mickleton House, near Stratford-upon-Avon, calls itself a 'centre for personal renewal and honouring the sacred in all things'.

The Emissaries were founded in Tennessee in 1932 by Lloyd Arthur Meeker (1907–1954), the son of a farmer and minister. He had searched through philosophies and religions for a purpose to his life, and had found nothing to satisfy him.

> He finally looked to himself and came to the profound realization that he was completely responsible for the state of his world and the quality of his experience in it. He knew he could not continue like the mass of humanity, victim or victor in the world of circumstance. He now and experienced a life of peace and value.[68]

Meeker wrote widely under the name Uranda; his ideas began to spread. In 1940 he met Martin Cecil, later the seventh Marquess of Exeter (1909–1988), who took Meeker's mass of ideas and developed them into a more systematic and comprehensible system. Their writings and the transcripts of their talks are now collected in a set of volumes called *The Third Sacred School*.

By 1948 the Canadian headquarters of the movement was at Cecil's cattle ranch, 100 Mile House, in British Columbia, which eventually became a thriving Emissary community. The international headquarters, established by Meeker in 1945, is Sunrise Ranch in Colorado.

When Meeker died in a plane crash in 1954, Cecil took over the organization which was then known as the Emissaries of Divine Light, later shortened to their current name, the Emissaries. Other early names for the movement included the Foundation of Universal Unity, the Ontological Society and the Integrity Society.

It is difficult to pin down the Emissaries on exactly what they believe: it's been described as a combination of Gurdjieffian self-awareness and the Christian ideal of loving one another. This might sound vague, but

> the philosophy was – and is – sometime in the past, before memory, we human beings forgot that we are divine and that is the truth of us. We began to create a complex and confusing world. The opportunity is now available to experience the reality of ourselves and create another world as we remember these simple truths.[69]

Meeker had expressed it in more esoteric terms: 'You are the means by which the invisible becomes visible.'[70] But the purpose of the Emissaries, again in his words, is more straightforward: 'to assist in the spiritual regeneration of the human race.'[71]

It all comes down to the individual's relationship with the Divine.

> Divine Action, as it appears through the actions and interactions of the individual, is anything that springs from the desire to bring unity rather than separation, to participate rather than isolate, to create rather than destroy, to understand with the heart rather than attack with the mind.[72]

It is the very individuality of each human being which displays the power and diversity of God; and in a community of such people the whole is greater than the sum of its parts.

> When a group of conscious people each agree to commit themselves to surrendering to the inner impulse, the intensity of the group energy is magnified... This means that Divine energy has a bigger area available, which means that more of it can be made manifest than if the same number of people were surrendering in separate places, unknown to each other.[73]

By 'group energy' or 'Divine energy' the Emissaries mean something almost tangible; at one time they called it 'Pneumaplasm' (Spirit Substance), but now it is simply known as Substance.

As well as appreciating the spiritual value of living in a community, Emissaries teach a practice called Attunement, 'a gentle, meditative technique for aligning subtle body energy with universal energy for increasing Divine Awareness within,' says Kate Hall, former events manager and visitor contact at Mickleton House.[74]

The heart of the beliefs, in Meeker's words, is that:

> God is not just one Being, but God *is* one Being. The Body of God is made up of many God Beings. But we do not have a multiplicity of gods, just one God. All the parts of God are perfectly co-ordinated, perfectly cohesive, and every part of the Body of God is an individualized God Being. That individualized aspect of God is in you, in your body. So it is with every man, woman and child on the face of the earth, good, bad or indifferent.[75]

Hall explains further:

> To Emissaries, this is known as Divine Identity, or True Identity. Most people are not in touch with their own True Identity, but most Emissaries believe that we can begin to become more conscious of our True Identity by choosing to act with greater awareness of the effect of all our actions, great and small, and by consciously taking full responsibility for our behaviour and how it affects everyone around us.

To put it another way, if we were created in God's image then we can each manifest the divine nature on Earth. If hate, fear, anger or other negative emotions or influences get in the way, the divine nature is distorted; we have the choice, however, of accepting divine control, of letting the divine nature and the divine design re-manifest through us in a process known simply as healing. This is what Emissaries aim for, to experience reality (God) and to manifest divine truth and love in a distorted world.

Hall lists the main spiritual principles that Emissaries recognize:

Love: To the degree that individuals fail to let love permeate themselves and all their thoughts, words and deeds, they function outside the realm of the Divine.
Trust: Trust in the Divine process – that no matter how it looks, everything is happening for a reason.
Thankfulness: Be truly thankful for all your blessings, whatever they are.
Acceptance: Accept that everything is just as it is meant to be, without judgement, condemnation or resignation.
Forgiveness: Letting go of our negative feelings towards others and allowing healing to happen. As we each heal our own lives, so the whole world may become healed.

It could perhaps be said that Meeker was a hippie, at least in his ideals, 30 years before anyone else. As Hall says, 'Scratch a middle-aged Emissary and you may well find a Sixties hippie, still full of those peace and love ideals, underneath.' She makes it clear that she is referring to the values of the idealistic youth of the Sixties, not to their supposedly common lifestyle of sex 'n drugs 'n rock'n'roll.

The majority of current members are between 35 and 50, and come from the professions, the arts, media and small businesses. 'Recently more and more young people are joining in as well, most of them with strong and committed concerns about the environment and the state of the planet.'

For 30 years the Emissaries were guided by Martin Cecil. Every community, at its Sunday morning service, would read a transcript of a talk he had delivered the week before to the main community in Colorado; it was a link between all the groups.

Martin Cecil died in 1988, aged 79, and his son Michael (b. 1935) took over. There has now been a transition to a leadership group of eight trustees. Tessa Maskell, Director of the UK Emissary Charity, comments on the change:

Having had one external point of focus, in Uranda [Meeker] and Martin [Cecil], each one now takes responsibility themselves for their spiritual expression and all come together in increased spiritual maturity to bring the Divine expression, Heaven, into the earth now – not in some afterlife!

Very few groups, even companies, have made a successful transition from a one-person focus, guru, to a functional collective body and the Emissaries are well on the way to doing it.

THE 'FLYING SAUCER CULTS'

Idaho businessman Kenneth Arnold has a lot to answer for; to be more accurate, the blame should attach to the reporter who misquoted him in 1947 as saying he had seen 'flying saucers'. Within a year or so, flying saucers (or Unidentified Flying Objects: UFOs) were everywhere.

As UFOs are now part of the global subconscious, it was inevitable that someone would bring the imagination of science fiction to bear on such Bible passages as Ezekiel's vision:

The appearance of the wheels and their work was like unto the colour of a beryl; and they four had one likeness; and their appearance and their work was as it were a wheel in the middle of a wheel.

I heard also the noise of the wings of the living creatures that touched one another, and the noise of the wheels over against them, and a noise of great rushing. (Ezekiel 1:16, 3:13)

Erich von Daniken also has a lot to answer for, with books such as *Chariots of the Gods* and *In Search of Ancient Gods*, which sparked off a host of imitators. But (to misquote the title of a similar book) he was not the first.

For many, the subject of alien visitations, let alone alien abductions, raises only an amused reaction.[76] But there are many religious movements linked to UFOs and extra-terrestrial beings, some more serious than others, and some very serious indeed. Some, particularly perhaps in California, spring up, flourish for a year or two, and fade away; others are longer-lasting. One, British in origin, has been around since 1955 and shows no sign of vanishing into the deep blue sky.

Many outsiders who are quite prepared to accept the sincerity of Moonies and Mormons throw their hands up at the thought of 'crackpots' seriously believing that alien beings have come in flying saucers to bring mankind a message from the gods. But this is really no more unbelievable than the basis of many other religions. As the White Queen says to Alice, 'Why, sometimes I've believed as many as six impossible things before breakfast.[77] Most people, if they are prepared to be honest, do so — at least by lunch.

Several religions have what might be seen as science-fictional elements; but here we shall look briefly at just two of what are sometimes rather unkindly referred to as the 'flying saucer cults'.

It is important to accept that the members of these movements believe in the extra-terrestrial origin of the messages given to them, just as Mormons believe in Joseph Smith's golden plates, and Christians believe that the Creator of the Universe became a man for 33 years; they should not be dismissed as 'UFO nuts'. Their belief is genuine, and their religions are worth as much attention as all the others in this book.

For those who question either the rationality or the truthfulness of these move-ments and their founders, it should be pointed out that there are now many thousands of people who say they have talked with aliens, or have been abducted by them. They don't just claim this; they believe it. For them it is as much a fact as the colour of their car or the name of their home town. So far as other people are concerned, they might well be deluding themselves, but if so they're not doing it deliberately. Psychologists and sociologists have a number of theories — particularly False Memory Syndrome, or the combined effect on our collective world view of Cold War fears, SF films and sexual insecurity — but most agree that such 'abductees' are sincere in their beliefs. So are those whose religions originated in messages from extra-terrestrials.

It isn't just the 'saucer cults' which have some belief in UFOs. Like a number of other Christian groups, the Family see UFOs as a clear sign that we're in the End Times. Some see them as the way that Satan's forces will wreak havoc upon the Earth. But others see their occupants as angels, and their purpose as more benign: to carry true believers away to the glorious next life after death.[78] The Norse myths tell of the Valkyries, shining beings who carried away fallen warriors to their reward in Odin's hall. UFOs are, among other things, today's version of that myth.

An alternative perspective considers that people have been having profound reli-gious experiences, and visions, for millennia; receiving messages from aliens could be seen as simply a modern rendering of the same thing.

It could, of course, be possible that extra-terrestrials *have* spoken to the founders of these movements; in any case, no one can prove otherwise.

THE AETHERIUS SOCIETY

HISTORY

His Eminence Sir George King (1919–1997), born in Shropshire, England, founded one of the first and certainly the longest-lasting of the 'saucer cults' in 1955. His titles included among others Metropolitan Archbishop of the Aetherius Churches, Grand Master of the Mystical Order of St Peter, Count de Florina, His Serene Highness Prince George King de Santorini, and Knight Grand Cross of Justice with Grand Collar in the Sovereign Military Orthodox Dynastic Imperial Constantinian Order of Saint Georges, as well as the rather more mundane Doctor of Science, Theology, Literature, Sacred Humanities, and Philosophy – though according to Richard Lawrence, Executive Secretary of the Aetherius Society,[79] he didn't usually make use of most of his titles and degrees.

His consecration as a bishop was from the Liberal Catholic Church, a Theosophical-Christian movement (see page 192). His knighthood was from the Byzantine Royal House in exile, and was not recognized by the College of Arms in the UK, though apparently it was legally recognized in France and Italy, and appeared on his British passport.

King began practising yoga in 1944, and 'developed his latent powers to such an extent that he attained the much sought-after deep trance state of Samadhi in which many of the hidden secrets of the Cosmos were revealed to him.'[80]

According to his own testimony, King was in his London flat in May 1954 when he clearly heard a voice saying 'Prepare yourself! You are to become the voice of Interplanetary Parliament.'[81] A week later 'an Indian Swami of world reknown' stepped through the locked door of his flat and instructed him to 'form a group of willing helpers'; he should also extend his training in yoga, and 'Pray, be still, meditate and open the doors of your heart and mind to the precious waters of Truth.' Before long, King was receiving telepathic messages: 'A message from Venus was recorded on our tape recorder for the first time.' King hired a room in Caxton Hall, London, and began to deliver in public messages from the Ascended Masters based on other planets. The first Cosmic Master to speak to him, from the planet Venus, used the pseudonym Aetherius. King founded the Aetherius Society in 1955.

Over the next 40 years King received over 600 'Cosmic transmissions', and wrote over 35 books based on them, including *The Twelve Blessings*, *The Nine Freedoms*, *The Five Temples of God*, *The Day the Gods Came*, *Flying Saucers*, *My Contact with the Great White Brotherhood* and others; his last book, co-written with Richard Lawrence, was *Contacts with the Gods from Space: Pathway to the New Millennium* (1996).

King received most of the messages when he was on his own or with a few members of the society. When receiving a Cosmic Transmission in public, King would sit on stage wearing dark glasses, and go into a trance state. First a voice known as Mars Sector 6 (or sometimes Mars Sector 8) would speak through him, giving interplanetary news or warnings of impending troubles on Earth. Then Aetherius, or one of the other Masters, would speak through him, delivering spiritual and moral teaching and messages of hope and encouragement.

George King died in July 1997. The movement, more so than most, had made plans for how they would continue after his death, making sure that there was a clear administrative and ecclesiastical structure in place. According to Lawrence, 'We looked at other groups when their leader died, and learnt from it.' The organizational structure was set up by King; Lawrence says, 'He had a prerogative; we deferred to him by choice, to his authority. It's probably more democratic since he died, but this was set up before he died, and all the people are the same.' The beliefs of the Aetherius Society haven't changed, but Lawrence is clear that there will be no more Cosmic Transmissions; that phase was specific to King's lifetime.

Although George King never made this claim during his life, his followers now believe that he came from another planet, and that he was an avatar of one of the Masters – who, again, include the Buddha, Jesus, and many other prophets and god-figures of other religions. Lawrence says that King is revered, but not worshipped.[82]

The Church hierarchy currently comprises three bishops (of whom Lawrence is one), half a dozen priests, and twenty to twenty-five ministers. There are also ten senior engineering officers (five in Britain, five in the USA) with technical responsibility for the Church's missions. King's widow is on the board of directors in Los Angeles.

Current worldwide membership of the Aetherius Society, according to Lawrence, is 'in the thousands, but not tens of thousands'. The largest numbers of members are in the USA, New Zealand and Africa. In Britain there are 600–700, with about 8,000 on their mailing list. There is an outside impression that the membership is middle-aged and elderly, but Lawrence says that there has been an increasing number of young people in the last few years. The only rule for full members, says Lawrence, is that 'they must attend a certain number of activities'.

BELIEFS AND PRACTICES

The beliefs of the Aetherius Society are Theosophical and New Age, and also include aspects of Christianity and Buddhism, among others; their religious services use both Christian prayers – including a new version of the Lord's Prayer – and Buddhist mantras. They believe in reincarnation based on the Law of Karma – or, in Paul's words, 'whatsoever a man soweth, that shall he also reap' (Galatians 6:7). We progress, life by life, towards perfection. 'Man came forth from God and all things are a part of God. There is nothing but God in the Cosmos, in varying stages of evolution. Everyone will eventually become a Master and will continue evolving from there.'[83] Masters can be male or female.

Although George King often wrote of his journeys in spacecraft to other planets, he made it clear that this was a form of astral travel; his body never left his London flat. The beings whom he met and conversed with on other planets are in some cases the inhabitants of those planets, but they are not physical beings with bodies analogous to ours; even in the 1950s it was thought unlikely that physical Martians or Venusians could exist. These beings live in another dimension, on another plane than the physical. The 'normal' inhabitants are, like us, progressing through their spiritual evolution. But the beings who gave King his teachings are way beyond this; they are Ascended Masters, members of the Great White Brotherhood. This is a belief shared with many other esoteric religious movements, including Theosophy, Eckankar, Benjamin Creme, the I AM movement, and the Church Universal and Triumphant: a living spiritual hierarchy of Masters, who included Jesus, Buddha, Krishna and the other great religious teachers.

Specific to the Aetherius Society is the belief that each planet in our solar system is akin to a classroom, where we learn certain life-lessons before progressing to the next planet.

> A person may have to live on a Planet for thousands of lives before he has learned the required lessons and can pass the 'examination' so that he can graduate to the next higher Planet – the length of time spent in 'school' varying with each individual lifestream, depending on how much effort he puts into living by God's Laws.

The solar system is ruled by a Cosmic Hierarchy, or Interplanetary Parliament.

> This is made up of very highly elevated Masters and is based on the Planet Saturn. This Hierarchy, in turn, is responsible to the Lords of the Sun for the evolution of every lifestream in the Solar System.

Of the great Cosmic Masters who have come to Earth, Jesus and Buddha came from Venus, and Krishna came from Saturn.

> They all taught the same principles or Laws of God. Therefore, man's great major religions sprang from the same source (Masters from other Planets) and the principles were identical.

Some of these Cosmic Masters spoke through King; in 1958, for example, the Master Jesus gave some new teachings entitled the Twelve Blessings, which he urged mankind to accept as their Bible.

A few Masters live on Earth; before long another great one will come, whose 'magic will be greater than any upon the Earth – greater than the combined materialistic might of all the armies. And they who heed not His words shall be removed from the Earth' – not to be destroyed, but to go to another planet to continue their evolutionary process elsewhere, says Lawrence. The coming Master will appear openly, in a flying saucer. There will also be a millennium of peace, but it seems that this depends largely on man's own efforts, rather than being imposed from above.

The Aetherius Society's belief in co-operation with people from other planets is quite sincere. 'We're not out to change existing religions so much as to add a cosmic dimension to them,' says Lawrence.

☼

The Aetherius Society is happy to call itself New Age. It teaches and practises spiritual healing, alternative medicine, yoga and dowsing, among others. Healing is:

the transfer of Prana, the Universal Life Force, from the Healer to the patient. This energy, which flows freely throughout space, when channelled into a person suffering from disease can bring about a state of balance within that person.[84]

Anyone can heal; it is not a special gift, but the birthright of every person on Earth.

The basis of all the Society's teachings is 'service to others'. The most unusual aspect of this work is known as Operation Prayer Power. A group of members invoke spiritual energy by chanting mantras and prayers. This energy is focused and transferred to trained prayer team members, who then pour it into 'a specially designed radionic apparatus' known as a Spiritual Energy Battery. These batteries can store vast amounts of spiritual energy indefinitely; the energy can later be released, specifically to help in times of crisis, such as a war or earthquake.

The Great White Brotherhood is engaged in a battle with evil forces, and the Aetherius Society has a part to play in the fight. It regularly engages in 'Spiritual Pushes' in which, by praying and meditating, they are able to draw Prana down to Earth from a huge spaceship, Satellite Three, in close orbit around the Earth; the spaceship is shielded so that it doesn't show up through telescopes or radar.

In addition to charging Spiritual Energy Batteries, members of the Aetherius Society took part in Operation Starlight, climbing 18 mountains around the world between 1958 and 1961 so that the Cosmic Masters could charge them with spiritual power. Members now make regular pilgrimages to the peaks of these mountains, where the movement's symbol is painted.

☼

Among the evils which the Aetherius Society campaigns against are pollution and nuclear power; they can justifiably claim to have been several years ahead of today's ecology movement.

The Society's literature quotes various prophecies made by the Cosmic Masters through George King, which they claim have since come true. In 1958, for example, their magazine *Cosmic Voice* gave details of an atomic accident in Russia which was not known about in the West until 1976; reporting on this in 1978, the *New Scientist* apparently said it had 'been scooped by a UFO'. Also in the 1950s King was receiving messages warning of the long-term genetic effects of radiation.

However, such problems are symptoms rather than causes.

'The Aetherius Society believes that the only major crisis on Earth is the spiritual energy crisis. If that is solved, all other crises will also be solved,' says Lawrence.

THE RAELIAN MOVEMENT

HISTORY

On 13 December 1973 a 27-year-old French sports journalist and would-be racing driver, Claude Vorilhon (now known as Raël) was contacted by a being from another planet and given a message for mankind; this is described in his first book, *Le Livre Qui Dit La Verité* (1974). The basic message is that mankind was created by an extraterrestrial race, referred to as the Elohim in the Book of Genesis in the Bible. They are not God or gods, but humans just like us – though physically a little smaller, with pale green skin, and thousands of years more advanced.

On 7 October 1975 Raël was contacted again, and this time was invited into a spacecraft and taken to the Elohim's own planet; this is not in our solar system, but is in our galaxy. Raël wrote about this experience in his second book, *Les Extra-Terrestres M'ont Emmené Sur Leur Planete* (1975). These first two books, in one volume, have been translated into English several times, first as *Space Aliens Took Me To Their Planet* (1978), then as *The Message Given To Me By Extra-terrestrials: They Took Me To Their Planet* (1986), and in 1998 as *The Final Message*, a new translation by Anthony Grey, until recently head of the British Raelian Movement. Further teachings were published in the books *Accueiller Les Extra-Terrestres* (1979) – *Let's Welcome Our Fathers From Space* (1986); *La Méditation Sensuelle* (1980) – *Sensual Meditation* (1986); and finally, a book entitled *Geniocracy*, about a new political system.

A Frenchman was chosen for the Elohim's message because France is 'a country where new ideas are welcomed and where it is possible to talk about such ideas openly.' Raël himself was chosen because his father was Jewish and his mother Catholic; 'we considered you an ideal link between two very important peoples in the history of the world.' Also, the world entered 'the Age of Apocalypse' with the first nuclear bomb in 1945; Raël was born in 1946.

Mankind is now sufficiently developed to understand that we were deliberately created by a race called the Elohim who are some 25,000 years more advanced than we are. In Genesis the word Elohim is translated as 'God', but in Hebrew it is actually a plural noun; according to Raël it means 'those who come from the sky'. (Raël means 'the messenger of those who come from the sky'.) Mankind was created, by manipulation of DNA, in the image of the Elohim.

> Leaving our humanity to progress by itself, the Elohim nevertheless maintained contact with us via prophets, including Buddha, Moses, Jesus and Muhammad, all specially chosen and educated by them in order to progressively educate humanity by delivering this message, adapted to the level of culture and understanding at the time. They were also to leave written references to the Elohim so that we would be able to recognize them as our creators and fellow human beings when we had advanced enough scientifically to understand them.[85]

We are now, apparently, at that point. The Elohim have appeared to Raël as the prophet for our age, have explained themselves in late-twentieth-century scientific terminology, and will shortly be returning physically to Earth to greet all of us. However, knowing that Earth has many different nations, and not wishing to be identified politically, morally or culturally with any particular one of them, they have instructed Raël to build an embassy in internationally recognized neutral territory, where they can meet representatives of governments.

'When they land, the only philosophy they wish to endorse is their own, so therefore they will only arrive at an embassy built by the movement they created.'

Once the embassy is built, the Raelians expect the Elohim to return some time between now and 2030 – but they will not return unless very large numbers of people want them to; they respect us as their creations, and will not impose their will on us.

Because 'it is the mission of Israel to welcome the messenger (Messiah) of the Elohim,' says Giles Dexter, former secretary of the British Raelians, 'the Elohim have requested that the embassy should be built on a piece of land given to the Raelian movement by the State of Israel.'[86] This is because the message of the Elohim was first brought to the Jews; also, the Jewish race is descended from when the sons of Elohim mated with the daughters of men (Genesis 6:2). Failing that, the embassy should be built in a neighbouring country – Jordan, Syria, Lebanon or Egypt. As there has been no indication that any Middle Eastern country will offer the land for the embassy, it could now be built in any country; according to Eric Bolou, the current UK leader,[87] it is the responsibility of each country's Raelian leader to approach the government of that country to ask for land to build the embassy.

From its formation in 1973 the Raelian Movement spread initially into French-speaking countries in Europe, Africa and North America (i.e. Québec); it has since spread into over 50 countries, and now claims around 40,000 members – though in Britain the movement is tiny, with only 40–50 full members, and a further 500 sympathizers. Its writings have been translated into over 20 languages so far. Raël himself now lives in Québec.

BELIEFS AND PRACTICES

Raelians say they are not ufologists; they find evidence on our own planet to confirm the messages given to Raël by the Elohim. They don't demand blind faith; 'the Elohim invite us to verify their work of creation referred to in our ancient texts, by our own scientific development, and by our opportunity to rationally understand the universe.'

Raelians don't believe in gods, but say that the God of the Bible, and the gods of all other religions, were mankind's misinterpretation of the Elohim. From time to time the Elohim send messengers to Earth, each one of them born of a human woman with an Elohim father; these include the Buddha, Moses, Jesus, Muhammad and, most recently before Raël, Joseph Smith. Raël is the final messenger.

The Raelian Movement states adamantly that we are not spiritual beings; we do not possess a spirit or soul which continues in any way after our death. We are purely physical beings who have a certain period of time alive; and after death, nothing. However, there is an equivalent of heaven or hell, for some. Each human being since the creation of our race by the Elohim, has a unique DNA pattern and a unique electromagnetic frequency pattern, and the Elohim have a cell from each person's body. On the Elohim's home planet there are vast computers which monitor our lives:

> We observe everyone. Huge computers ensure a constant surveillance of all people living on Earth. A mark is attributed to everyone depending on their actions during their life whether they walked towards love and truth or towards hate and obscurantism.[88]

If our good deeds out-balance our bad deeds, we may be recreated at some time in the future, grown new bodies from our DNA pattern, on the Elohim's planet – 'will have the right to eternity on this heavenly planet.' Those who were neither particularly good not evil will simply not be recreated;

> and for those whose actions were particularly negative, a cell from their body will have been preserved, which will allow us to recreate them when the time comes, so that they can be judged and suffer the punishment they deserve.

The only ritual specific to the Raelian Movement is transmitting the cellular code. A Raelian Guide or leader, already known to the Elohim, places his or her hands on a person's head, receives their unique code, and transmits it to the Elohim. The Raelians say that this does not give their members any advantage when people are recreated scientifically on the Elohim planet; in fact, those who have transmitted their code will be judged more strictly than those who haven't, because it is a sign that they have received and understood the truth of the Raelian message.

The Raelians are now aiming to follow in their creators' footsteps. In 1997 they started a company called Valiant Venture, and a research programme called Clonaid, with the aim of offering cloned children to infertile and homosexual couples, created from their DNA.

Apart from spreading the message, and raising funds (so far over $7 million) to build the embassy, Raelians aim:

> to build a society adapted to the future, not the past. This is done through courses of Sensual Meditation held all over the world, enabling individuals to regain control over their lives by questioning all their habits, beliefs and attitudes and implementing choice to retain only what is useful to their development. As each individual becomes more happy and fulfilled, so humanity as a whole becomes more happy and fulfilled and the society of the future begins to develop.

In some ways this echoes the ideas of, for example, the Transcendental Meditation Movement, which believes that a small number of people meditating together can affect the wider world. This philosophy applies to all areas of life, including education, love, sexuality, work, leisure and self-development.

A distinctive teaching of the Raelian Movement is Sensual Meditation, learning how to gain the fullest enjoyment from every aspect of one's life, including sex. The ultimate experience is a Cosmic Orgasm, though it is not clear how this differs from any other especially good sexual experience.

Sensual meditation is a set of techniques to help us 'link with the infinity that we are a part of.' It enables people to

> understand how our minds and bodies function; question the Judaeo-Christian inhibitions of guilt and the mysticism of Eastern traditions; develop our minds and discover our bodies; and reprogramme ourselves by ourselves into what we really wish to be. Sensual Meditation enables us to love ourselves better and to better love others, to discover our individuality and our common humanity.

Some of the meditation techniques are intended to be used with a partner of the opposite sex. 'No specifically sexual techniques are taught at the seminars,' says Dexter, 'though individuals are encouraged to experiment sexually if they wish, and to develop their sensuality.'

This is a key part of Raelian teaching.

> Sex is an important source of pleasure, which along with 'choice' and 'infinity' (correctly identified) is a very important element of Raelian philosophy. The messages state 'Pleasure is the fertilizer which opens the mind. A life without pleasure is like an uncultivated garden.'

The movement has a completely free attitude towards sexual relationships; it depends entirely on individual choice. They have monogamous heterosexual couples, others 'who prefer to have different partners', homosexuals, transexuals... 'In sexuality, as in all other things,' says Dexter, 'the promotion of choice is all-important; and further-more, that sexually as in every other way (race, appearance, etc.), we more than tolerate, we love the differences... A varied community is essential for the equilibrium of the whole.'

The Raelian Movement holds major 'Courses of Awakening' in France, Canada, Japan, Korea and Australia, and smaller courses in Britain, the USA and other coun-tries. The aim is:

> to create a world of leisure, love and fulfilment where we have rid ourselves of
> the moralistic social inhibitions which paralyse our joy for life, so that everyone
> has the courage to act as they so wish, as long as this action does not harm others.

This last sentiment is the same as one of the main principles of Wicca: 'An it harm none, do as thou wilt shall be the whole of the law.'

The symbol of the Raelians, worn as a pendant by members, is a six-pointed Star of David made up of two triangles, the one pointing upwards representing the infi-nitely large, and the one pointing down representing the infinitely small. A swirling design inside the star represents infinity in time. The symbol can also be used as a focus for telepathic contact with the Elohim.

(From 1990, the swirl has replaced the swastika which was originally in the centre of the star. 'This was done out of respect for the victims of the Nazi holocaust and to facilitate the building of the embassy in Israel, despite the fact that the Elohim's symbol is the oldest on Earth and that traces of it still remain in Israel today.'[89])

Infinity is an important concept in the Raelian Movement; they believe that the sub-atomic particles of atoms are themselves galaxies, containing stars, planets and people; and that our own galaxy is a tiny particle of an atom of a living being on a planet revolving around a sun in a galaxy. This is a concept which has been covered in science fiction, but is not generally accepted in human science, though the Raelians say that the Elohim have proved it to be true.

As in many other religious movements, full members tithe a tenth of their income; in Britain a third of this goes to the British Raelian Movement, and the remainder to the International movement.

The Geniocracy of Raël's fifth book is a proposed political system to be run by the most intelligent for the benefit of all; some critics have alleged that it is implied, if not actually stated, that these will be of the white races, and that the Raelian Movement is therefore white supremacist. Dexter strongly denies this.

The messages clearly state, 'Do not suffer racist fools'... There are people from all the different races of the world in the Raelian movement, whose aim is to break down barriers between peoples of different ethnic and cultural backgrounds, and create a family of humanity.

The aims of the Raelian Movement are similar to those of many others; the difference is that their revelation came from extra-terrestrials rather than from Ascended Masters or God.

SHAMANISM

Shamanism is perhaps the oldest spiritual activity of all. It is usually associated with 'primitive' societies, but in recent years it has become a major part of contemporary Earth-based spirituality or nature religion, closely associated with Neo-Paganism or, more generally, with alternative spirituality.

The modern shaman, like the shaman of early religion, usually works alone. He or she is able, through trance or visions, to enter the spiritual world and communicate with the beings there, working magic or bringing healing back to those in their care. Because it is based on individual experience, there is no single set of beliefs – each shaman finds his or her own way – but there are many courses in learning how to be a shaman. One shaman, Leo Rutherford, describes briefly what Shamanism is about:

> Shamanism is the oldest tradition on Planet Earth of healing, maintaining balance and harmony in society and the individual, and keeping our connection with Mother Earth and All Creation. A shaman knows that all things are alive, lives both in this world and the spirit world, and has understanding of the inner realities. What I like to call contemporary shamanism is the application of these ancient timeless ways to our situation of the present, be it urban, suburban or whatever. Our outer world may be different, but our human inner landscape has the same components it always did. Our outer health and wholeness (holiness) depends on our inner state and the balance between matter and spirit.[90]

The shaman is one who crosses between worlds. 'Using rhythmic drumming, dance, and song the shaman experiences a consciousness-shift which enables her to let her soul journey to what is traditionally known as the Spirit World,' says shamanic teacher Jonathan Horwitz.[91] He refers to shamans as 'stone-age psychotherapists', and healing, both physical and psychological, is probably the main part of the shaman's work.

One of the most prominent schools of shamanism is the Scandinavian Centre for Shamanic Studies, based in Denmark, which holds courses throughout Europe, and also in North America. Its basic course is on The Shaman's Journey, fundamental to the shaman's work; it also teaches courses on, among others, shamanic singing, healing, counselling, and helping people who are close to death.

In the UK, the London Open Drumming Group aims to 'provide a safe and sacred environment for people to practise core shamanic techniques: we work with drum and rattle, with dance and song and of course with the shamanic journey to the Spirit World.'

Shamanism, like other Neo-Pagan paths, is in close touch with nature. Jonathan Horwitz comments:

> As I see it, one of the greatest challenges to the new generation of shamans is to re-establish the contact between human beings and the other inhabitants of the Earth, to network nature, to stop the slaughter of the environment we share, to find out what can be done – spiritually, ritually, and practically – with the damage which has already been done, and to learn once again that the Earth will nourish us – physically and spiritually – if we allow her to do it.[92]

WICCA

Wicca is simply another name for witchcraft, often used to avoid many of the negative connotations of the latter word. Wicca is usually traced back to a Saxon root meaning 'to bend', sometimes to a word meaning 'wit', as in knowledge or understanding, and sometimes, though with less justification, to a word for 'wise', as in 'wise-woman' (it should be remembered that in France, a midwife is still known as a *sage-femme*).

Some, instead of witchcraft or Wicca, prefer to call it 'the Craft'.

The term 'witchcraft' covers a wide range of things. A BBC news story in 1995 reported that over 100 women had recently been burnt to death – often with a petrol-soaked tyre around their necks – in the Transvaal in South Africa; they had been accused by neighbours of being witches. It has been suggested that in the famous Old Testament injunction 'Thou shalt not suffer a witch to live' (Exodus 22:18) the word 'witch' might have had the sense of 'one who poisons wells'; if this is so, it would make some sense for nomadic peoples living in a desert.

Today's witches rarely match the popular image of the toothless old hag living in her hovel. They live in the country and the town, in all Western countries; they are likely to be well educated, and many of them are professional people; they are old and young; and they are as likely to be men as women. Male witches are called witches; terms such as 'warlock' and 'wizard' belong only in fantasy novels.

One point must be made clearly here, once again. Witchcraft has nothing to do with Satanism; witches do not worship Satan. This is still the most common misunderstanding that witches (and other Neo-Pagans) have to cope with, particularly from the media but also, more worryingly, from schools and social services.

Medieval witchcraft, with all its demonic trappings, rather than being any sort of reality, was very largely the creation of the two Dominicans who around 1486 wrote the *Malleus Maleficarum* ('The Witch Hammer'). The book, which became the textbook of the Inquisition, is full of accounts of how succubi and incubi pass semen between men and women. It also puts the burden of witchcraft largely on women:

> they are more credulous... naturally more impressionable... they have slippery tongues... they are weak... since they are feebler both in mind and body, it is not surprising that they should come more under the spell of witchcraft...[93]

Modern witches would tend to disagree.

The book's authors, both men, both highly educated Dominicans, displayed a fear of women which was fairly common at that time, especially among educated religious men. Women, it was believed, had the power to emasculate men, not just metaphorically but physically; the book contains numerous accounts of men claiming a witch had stolen their penis. Here is an early account of multiple Bobbittism:

> And what, then, is to be thought of those witches who in this way sometimes collect male organs in great numbers, as many as twenty or thirty members together, and put them in a bird's nest, or shut them up in a box, where they move themselves like living members, and eat oats and corn, as has been seen by many and is a matter of common report? It is to be said that it is all done by devil's work and illusion, for the senses of those who see them are deluded in the way we have said. For a certain man tells us that, when he had lost his member, he approached a known witch to ask her to restore it to him. She told the afflicted man to climb a certain tree, and that he might take which he liked out of a nest in which there were several members. And when he tried to take a big one, the witch said: You must not take that one; adding, because it belonged to a parish priest.[94]

The serious reason for including this marvellous passage is that many men today believe that they are being emasculated not only by feminism, with its creation of the New Man, but also by Wicca, with its emphasis on the Goddess. There are all-women areas of Wicca, but most Wicca, and most of the wider world of Neo-Paganism, is now taking great care to let men realize that the religion is for them as well. Outsiders may only notice the Goddess, because of the difference from the male Judaeo-Christian God; but a lot of Neo-Pagans worship both Goddess and God.

To quote Shan, Clan Mother or Priestess of the London-based group, the House of the Goddess:

So what does this mean for men? It means a third way, neither bully nor wimp, but powerful, wild, loving, sexual and supportive with room for doubt and uncertainty. This is very much the cutting edge of the Craft today.[95]

To return to the medieval persecution of witches, there is an interesting argument that the Inquisition could not have had so much 'success' in identifying witches if ordinary people had not been willing to turn in their neighbours. In an age of super-stition, if your child was ill or your cow died, you might well put the blame on a woman in your village whom you'd insulted or cheated a few months earlier, getting her own back by cursing you.[96] Another suggested reason for grass-roots public opinion turning against the formerly respected wise-women or herbalists could perhaps be to do with the Black Death, which swept Europe between 1347 and 1350, killing as many as a third of the population. If people asked their local herbalist for a potion against the Black Death and were given, for example, an infusion of willow bark (the forerunner of aspirin), it would have had little effect against the plague. If you ask for help and your loved ones die, you are apt to lose faith in – or even to blame – the person whose help you sought.

RECENT ORIGINS

To a very large extent modern witchcraft is the creation of a retired British civil servant, Gerald Gardner. Before him, however, and providing at the time the powerful backing of academic study, came the anthropologist Dr Margaret Murray. Murray argued persuasively in *The Witch-Cult in Western Europe* (1921) and *The God of the Witches* (1931) that medieval witches didn't worship the Devil, but were followers of an old, pre-Christian Pagan religion 'which appears to be the ancient religion of Western Europe'.[97] Murray called this worship Dianic, after the goddess Diana.

It is likely that Murray's research was sparked off by Charles Leland's *Aradia, or the Gospel of the Witches* (1899), based on the teachings of an Italian hereditary witch called Maddalena. A great deal of doubt has now been thrown on this work.

Murray has also been criticized on many academic grounds. The historian of the esoteric, Richard Cavendish, states 'This brilliant and ingenious theory is unfortunately full of holes and has been demolished time and again.'[98] This didn't stop the Oxford University Press splashing on the 1970 US paperback of *The God of the Witches*, 'The findings she sets forth, once thought of as provocative and implausible, are now regarded as irrefutable by folklorists and scholars in all related fields.'

Other scholars now point out that there is actually no evidence whatsoever for a reli-gion of one Goddess; early Pagan religions were pantheist rather than female monotheist. Murray, they say, came up with her theory, then selected evidence to support it.

Whatever the factual truth, Murray's thesis – with the added weight of Robert Graves' *The White Goddess* (1946), a study of the Moon Goddess in many different cultures, which perhaps contained more poetic than historical truth – became received wisdom for Wiccans for a few decades, making it possible for them to say they were recreating the old religion, not creating something which is solely 'New Age'.

The Dianic Wicca of the 1970s and 1980s stemmed very much from Murray's thesis; it is a religion of the Goddess, and very much a religion for women. It has been argued that Dianic Wicca, and similar religions, are historically more a spiritual expression of the feminist movement than anything else.

There has now been a considerable amount of academic work on the roots of Wicca,[99] showing that it stems as much from nineteenth-century Gothic Romanticism as from anywhere else, and casting major doubts on Leland, Murray and Graves. Wiccans, like Druids and other Neo-Pagans, are often middle class, well educated and well read, and tend to be very self-consciously aware. Most of them today have taken this scholarship on board, but say that the validity or otherwise of Murray and other early 'authorities' doesn't actually matter to them; Murray's thesis can be treated as a 'foundation myth'. They readily accept that their religion is a modern synthesis from many roots; the important thing, for them, is that it works.

Other books significant in the development of modern Wicca, though to a lesser extent than Leland, Murray and Graves, were the fictional and non-fictional works of writers like Dion Fortune, Montague Summers, Charles Williams and Denis Wheatley, which were actually more to do with the occult than with Paganism, but which at least kept esoteric religion in the public eye.

Gerald Gardner (1884–1964) had a lifelong interest in folklore, magic and the esoteric. He belonged to a Rosicrucian group, and was an initiate of Aleister Crowley's Ordo Templi Orientis (see page 361). When he discovered a coven of witches in the south of England in 1939 he was delighted, and joined them. In 1954 Gardner published his book *Witchcraft Today*.

Most British and European witches owe a considerable debt to Gardner. His re-creation of witchcraft was a blend of folklore, Masonic rituals and Crowley-type magic, and had quite a major sexual element; Gardner was into both naturism and flagellation. His handwritten *Book of Shadows*, containing ritual and ceremony borrowed from a number of sources, has formed the basis for much of what came after him – though some of the more overtly sexual parts have been quietly dropped by many of his successors.

After Gardner came Alex Sanders (1926–1988), the self-styled king of Britain's witches, who with his wife Maxine popularized witchcraft in the 1960s; they had a flamboyant style, which may or may not have been good for the 'new' religion, but which certainly caught the headlines. Alexandrian witchcraft is a much freer and more open version than Gardnerian. Maxine Sanders, who separated from her husband in 1973, became a widely respected leader of Wicca.

Today's Wicca, as Stewart Farrar (who was initiated by the Sanders in 1970) points out,[100] has roots in both the old Pagan religions and the nineteenth- and early-twentieth-century occult revival. Many groups, some calling themselves covens, others not, developed their own rituals and their own sets of beliefs over the last decade or so of the twentieth century, based in part on earlier traditions.

'There were really many "old religions" such as various Celtic cults, Nordic ones, Isis, Mithras, and so on,' says Shan from House of the Goddess.

> The 'Old Religion' is actually a bit inaccurate, but a very affectionate name for the Craft. We often argue among ourselves about how much of the Craft nowadays is a modern invention, how much ancient tradition. Some of us say almost all of it is modern – but fine, it works. Some think it's a mix. Some say most of it has been handed down to us.[101]

Today, probably most Wiccans share Shan's free approach; some might still stress the importance of the supposed ancient origins of their beliefs; a few, the comparatively rare self-styled 'hereditary witches', believe that their own family tradition and bloodline is vital.

Most agree that Neo-Paganism's strength lies in its diversity. Though there is sometimes rivalry and mutual criticism between different traditions and groups of Neo-Pagans, Wiccans or witches, there is probably far more commonality between them, and mutual support in the face of opposition, than there is between the many variations and offshoots of Christianity. One organization which helps people interested in Wicca find a local group or coven which might suit them is the Wiccan contact group, Children of Artemis.

Wicca is usually thought of as a 'small group' religion, but its rituals, pathworkings, guided visualizations and so on are also often practised alone.

Many Wiccan groups hold to the 'Charge of the Goddess' which is, in Shan's words, 'the nearest thing the Craft accept as a statement of faith common to all.' The Charge was written by Gardner and Doreen Valiente, with some sections taken from Leland's *Aradia*, and so perhaps going back hundreds of years. There are many different versions of the Charge today; here enough extracts are presented to demonstrate its style and content, the roots of Goddess worship under many different names, and the life-affirming nature of Wiccan belief.

THE CHARGE OF THE GODDESS

> *Listen to the words of the Great Mother, who of old was called Artemis, Astarte, Athene, Dione, Melusine, Aphrodite, Cerridwen, Diana, Arianrhod, Isis, Brighde and by many other names...*

Whenever ye have need of anything, once in the month, and better it be when the moon is full, then shall ye assemble in some secret place and adore the spirit of me who am Queen of all Witches...

And ye shall be free from slavery; and as a sign that ye be really free, ye shall be naked in your rites; and ye shall dance, sing, feast, make music and love all in my praise. For mine is the ecstacy of the spirit, and mine also is joy on earth, for my law is love unto all beings.

Keep pure your highest ideal; strive ever towards it, let naught stop you or turn you aside; for mine is the secret door which opens upon the door of youth, and mine is the cup of the wine of life, and the cauldron of Cerridwen, which is the holy Grail of immortality.

I am the gracious Goddess, who gives the gift of joy unto the heart of man...

Nor do I demand sacrifice; for behold, I am the Mother of all living and my love is poured out upon the earth...

I am the beauty of the green earth, and the white moon among the stars, and the mystery of the waters, and the desire of the heart of man.

Call into thy soul; arise, and come unto me; for I am the soul of nature who gives life to the universe...

Let my worship be within the heart that rejoices; behold, all acts of love and pleasure are my rituals. And therefore let there be beauty and strength, power and compassion, honour and humility, mirth and reverence within thee...

If that which thou seekest thou findest not within thee, thou wilt never find it without thee. For behold, I have been with thee from the beginning; and I am that which is attained at the end of desire.

Blessed be.[101A]

CHURCH OF ALL WORLDS

A number of new religions – Scientology, the Aetherius Society, the Raelians, even the Mormons – have what outsiders might see as science-fictional elements to their mythology. The Church of All Worlds (CAW) is perhaps the only religion for which an SF novel is a prescribed text. CAW was founded in 1962 by Oberon (Otter) Zell – then plain Tim Zell – and three college friends. Although a form of Neo-Paganism, it bases much of its teaching and ritual on Robert A. Heinlein's classic *Stranger in a Strange Land*. 'Thou art God,' its members say to each other. A question in the CAW Membership Handbook, 'Does CAW accept the divinity of Jesus?' is answered,

'Certainly. Why should he be left out? We accept the Divinity of every living Being in the universe!'

CAW has no particular dogma or creed:

we are essentially 'Neo-Pagan', implying an eclectic reconstruction of ancient Nature religions, and combining archetypes of many cultures with other mystic, environmental and spiritual disciplines... Some of our individual paths include Shamanism, Witchcraft, Vodoun, Buddhism, Hinduism and Sufism, as well as science fiction, transpersonal psychology, bodywork, artistic expression and paths of service.[102]

As with many Neo-Pagan groups, CAW's beliefs are spiritual, environmental, social and personal.

We concentrate on healing the separations between mind and body, men and women, civilization and nature, Heaven and Earth. We are fairly all-embracing in promoting general Pagan and Gaian lifestyles and values. We advocate basic feminist and environmentalist principles, including freedom of reproductive choice, ordination of women as priestesses, sacred sexuality, alternate relationships, gay and lesbian rights, legalization and utilization of hemp products, protection and restoration of endangered species, wilderness sanctuaries, green politics, space exploration and colonization, etc. We are also engaged in restoring ancient Mysteries and rituals, such as the Eleusinia and Panathenaia.[103]

The Church has a path of progression from Seeker, an ordinary member, to Scion, those who help run subsidiary branches, to Clergy, ordained priests and priestesses. It generally takes a few years of training and personal spiritual development before anyone is ordained.

CAW has developed slowly and gradually, with a number of ups and downs over the years; compared to many religious organizations, they are refeshingly honest about their failings. 'We try to learn from our mistakes and not make them again,' says Zell.

Most of our most glaring mistakes have been due to either ignorance or arrogance. Mistakes of ignorance can be cured with additional knowledge. Mistakes of arrogance have been far more painful, and humbling. We have had to eat considerable crow as we have evolved over the years. We will probably continue to make mistakes, for we are fallible creatures (a pack of monkeys, actually!) and sometimes our mouths overload our brains. Hopefully we will also continue to get better, but I seriously doubt we will ever attain infallibility!

Membership is currently around 650, 'and growing rapidly,' says Zell; there are over three dozen 'nests' or branches scattered across the USA and Australia, though not yet in the UK. CAW incorporated in 1968, 'becoming the first of the Neo-Pagan Earth religions to obtain full Federal recognition,' he says. It was also the first legally recognized Neo-Pagan religion in Australia. It has 'proto-nests' in Germany, Switzerland and Austria.

As with all US religious organizations, the Church of All Worlds is established as a corporation, with legally established Bylaws. One of these reads:

> To honor Oberon Zell for his many years of service to the Church of All Worlds, and to acknowledge him as co-founder of the CAW, and in recognition of his well-known abilities as an excellent representative of the larger primate family, he shall be known as the Primate, and shall hold this position for life unless he no longer desires to, or if through illness or incapacity he can no longer adequately demonstrate his capability to perform its duties and functions to the membership and the Clergy Council...[104]

In 1998 Zell took a sabbatical from this role as Primate, at the same time as a major reorganization of the Church took place. The headquarters moved from California to Ohio, and a lot of the administrative jobs which Zell had performed were taken on by other people in the Church; he is still an active priest in the Church, leading major ceremonies. At the time of writing he and the Church are re-evaluating his role. It is possible that his new title might be 'Emissary', and one member has said that 'voice and vision should be his major role.'[105]

Some of the terminology and symbolism of the Church of All Worlds is borrowed from Robert Heinlein's novel — neuts, grokking, water-sharing — or other SF works (Zenna Henderson's 'The People' stories are another favourite), and there is a relaxed attitude to sexuality and social nudity, but CAW appears to be somewhat more than a bunch of spiritually minded hippies living in a commune.

The mission of CAW is:

> to evolve a network of information, mythology and experience that provides a context and stimulus for reawakening Gaia and reuniting her children through tribal community dedicated to responsible stewardship and the evolution of consciousness.

Linked organizations are heavily involved in ecology, particularly forestry, scholarly research into history and mythology – and the development of a 'living unicorn', from a goat rather than a horse.

From the start CAW has aimed for communal living, even if a community is only a handful of people. Living in a community, there is more opportunity to put their beliefs into practice.

> Since we are concerned with the emergent evolution of a total new culture and lifestyle, and since we perceive no distinction between the sacred and the secular, we consider every activity to be essentially a religious activity. For us, recycling is as much a religious duty as prayer and meditation... We recognize that the essence of a religion is in the living of it.[106]

But specifically religious or spiritual activities are an important part of their lives.

> The religious aspects include maintaining household altars and shrines (in a Pagan household, every horizontal flat space becomes an altar, just as every wall becomes a bookcase!), meditations, conversations with the Gods, to rituals and celebrations, especially those of the great Sabbats of the Wheel of the Year. These latter often include great theatrical productions, with sets, costumes, props and music, wherein people take on the personas of Gods, Elementals, and other Archetypal beings.

For non-Pagans, the belief in and practice of magic is one of the more worrying aspects of Paganism; for Fundamentalists, it brands Pagans as evil (see page 336). What Zell says about magic is fairly typical of many Neo-Pagan groups:

> The practice of magic is a major component of virtually all Pagan traditions, including CAW. We define magic as 'probability enhancement'. I don't think it is possible to separate out the magical from the religious, as it all seems a continuum. Magical practices run the gamut from simple 'Kitchen Witch' spells and charms – mostly concerned with individual healings, blessings, transformations, and other small workings; through 'Circle Work' involving raising group energy for healings, community service, weather working, etc.; to larger group workings to save the planet – protecting endangered forests, people and species, etc.

One point which separates CAW from many Neo-Pagan groups, particularly in the UK, and which most Christians (except the Family) would condemn as sinful, is their free approach to sexuality. If any two people – or three, or four – want to make love, that's entirely up to them. But the Church is very aware of the possibilities of abuse, and of misinterpretation.

It is *absolutely unacceptable* to attempt to pressure, cajole or coerce another into any sexual activity that they do not wish freely and wholeheartedly to participate in... A loving touch, hug or a massage is not an invitation to coitus, so if your attempts at intimacy or caring make someone uncomfortable, *stop!*[107]

Any form of 'sexually charged interaction', let alone love-making, with youngsters under the age of consent, is forbidden.

CAW is by no means a typical Neo-Pagan group, but most of its principles, and its eclectic approach to building up a belief system, are broadly the same as those of many other Pagans, and it appears to be well respected within Neo-Paganism at large.

DRUIDRY

As a measure of its standing, there are currently around 35 different Druid organizations in the UK alone, according to Philip Shallcrass, joint Chief Druid of the British Druid Order. As with Wicca and other areas of Neo-Paganism, they have very different approaches to their beliefs and practices, but a number of them meet as 'a loose, informal group' in the Druid Forum, 'to discuss the development of modern Druidry in all its forms.' The Druid Forum began in 1996 as a successor to the Council of British Druid Orders.

This entry gives a brief overview of the recent history of Druidry, some of the Orders, and some of the major beliefs.

The traditional derivation of the word 'druid' is from the Greek *drus*, the Irish *daur* and the Welsh *derw*, each meaning 'oak', and the Indo-European word *wid* which is to do with knowing (cf. wit, wise and wisdom, from the same root, and the Sanskrit *veda*). A Druid was one who knew or understood the oak, or perhaps the wise man of the oak – the oak standing for all trees. Interestingly, in both Irish and Welsh the words for 'tree' and 'knowledge' are etymologically connected. It was not that the Druids *worshipped* the oak, or any other tree; but they had a close relationship with nature, their worship took place in groves, and they seemed to see trees as symbolic of wisdom and solidity. 'Although the oak seems to have been favoured by the Druids of Gaul, those of Ireland certainly seem to have preferred the yew or ash as their primary sacred trees,' says Shallcrass.[108] However, most modern Druids, he says, do regard the oak as especially sacred.

Shallcrass also points out that many scholars have now discarded the 'oak' derivation in favour of derivations from either an early Celtic intensive prefix *dru*, which would give the meaning of druid as 'very wise one', or from an Indo-European root, *dreo*, meaning 'true', which would give the meaning 'true [or truth] knower'.

The main problem with recreating the old religion of the Druids is that nothing was written down by the original Druids – or if it was, it is long lost. Nearly all that we know about the Druids is from other writers of their time, such as Julius Caesar, Cicero, Pliny and Tacitus; their reports are likely to be antagonistic, and might well be inaccurate.

Present-day Druids have had to recreate the religion from what is known or surmised about the religious and philosophical beliefs of the Celts. Love and respect for nature were and are clearly central. So is the emphasis on oration and song; many of the original Druids were respected as tale-tellers and bards.

It was this latter aspect which was largely at the heart of the Druid revival of the eighteenth and nineteenth centuries. Bardic schools existed in the Celtic fringes of the British Isles up to the seventeenth century, and Pagan 'folk' customs (including, for example, well-dressing, May Day, Hallowe'en, and decorating houses with greenery at midwinter) have continued in one way or another right up to the present day. Some of the earlier Druid revivals were therefore more cultural and artistic – and more Romantic – than spiritual; the Welsh Eisteddfod, originally a serious bardic assembly, became essentially a music festival with ritual robes.

The revival of Druidry can be traced to several people in the seventeenth and eighteenth centuries. The antiquarian John Aubrey first associated Stonehenge and Avebury with the Druids in the 1690s. Influenced by Aubrey, William Stukeley also studied Stonehenge seriously. John Toland's *History of the Druids* was published in 1726. Later in the eighteenth century a Welsh stonemason, Edward Williams, took the name Iolo Morganwg, and researched and wrote much about Welsh bardic tradition. The historian Stuart Piggot is derisory about Iolo Morganwg 'furthering his nonsense',[109] and even Phillip Shallcrass describes him as a 'scholar, forger and genius'.[110] He not only originated many 'early' Welsh documents, he also created the 'ancient' Gorsedd, or bardic religious ceremony, at Primrose Hill, London, in 1792 and at the Eisteddfod in 1819.

Although most of Iolo Morganwg's work can justifiably be called fraudulent, it was largely responsible for inspiring nineteenth- and twentieth-century interest – and somewhat more scholarly enquiry – into the Celts, and specifically the Druids. In addition, his work should not be dismissed out of hand simply because much of it stemmed from his own imagination. In all areas of Neo-Paganism, the creative use of the imagination is an important part of symbolism, ritual and magic. No one would argue that the entire Arthurian mythos should be thrown away on the grounds that the majority of it is fictional rather than factual; it is not the factual basis of mythology which is important; rather, it is the truths contained, often symbolically, within the myths. The same argument could be applied to Iolo Morganwg's work.

☀

Present-day Druidry includes the **Ancient Druid Order**, said to have been founded in 1717, which holds regular ceremonies at Stonehenge, Primrose Hill and Tower Hill. The **Ancient Order of Druids**, founded in 1781, also holds some ceremonies, but is largely (like the Freemasons, the Rotarians and so on) a fund-raising organization for those in need; the **United Ancient Order of Druids** developed out of it in 1833.

Most of the other Orders are far more recent. One of the most respected, the **Order of Bards, Ovates and Druids** (OBOD), an offshoot of the Ancient Druid Order, was founded in 1964 by Ross Nichols (1902–1975), whose *Book of Druidry* is an imaginative but very spiritual exploration of Druid beliefs. OBOD has a fairly eclectic membership, which includes both Pagans and Christians. The **British Druid Order** was founded in 1979 as a specifically Pagan orientated Druid group, whose teachings are based on the *Mabinogion* and other early British/Celtic texts. The **Secular Order of Druids**, a West Country-based order founded in 1986, is heavily orientated towards environmentalism, and to supporting the civil rights of Druids to meet at places like Stonehenge in the face of police opposition. It seeks 'to enhance the modern-day relevance of Druidry by reviving folk traditions and by taking Druidry to "raves".'[111]

Some groups, such as the **Breton Druids** and the **Cornish Druids**, are more cultural in their emphasis; others, like the **College of Druidism**, based in Edinburgh, are more shamanistic; others, like the **Insular Order of Druids**, founded in 1993 in Portsmouth, are in many ways closer to Wicca. The **Druid Clan of Dana**, based at Clonegal Castle in Eire, and in London, is a well-organized and rapidly expanding Pagan Druid movement, and part of the Fellowship of Isis (see page 410); it publishes the magazine *Aisling*. The **Loyal Arthurian Warband**, led by the colourful self-styled King Arthur Pendragon, campaigns for environmental and animal rights, and against new road building, nuclear and chemical weapons, and the Criminal Justice Act.

The **Gorsedd of Bards of Caer Abiri**, founded in 1993, holds open celebrations of the eight Druid festivals within the stone circles of Avebury in Wiltshire. Shallcrass describes them:

> The Gorsedd well represents the current ecumenical trend in Druidry in that it brings together members of several different Druid orders as well as followers of other Pagan and non-Pagan faiths. Its rituals combine modern Druidic practice with the Iolo Morganwg tradition and elements from the other faiths represented among its membership.

Druids in different Orders generally get on well together; but there are some serious differences in attitude. The **Charnwood Grove of Druids** says 'we are non-hierarchical, we believe in self-initiation when an individual feels that he or she has gained enough confidence and knowledge...' In contrast, the **College of Druidism** offers:

> a comprehensive Initiation Course into the Keltic Druidical Mysteries... The Training Process is structured in seven graduated stages (Degrees), culminating in full Initiation... To complete the Course will take years... There are many pseudo-Druidical Organizations around who will confer the title of 'Druid' or Druidess' upon someone, whether that individual has developed the requisite talents or not. We are different...[112]

Druidry is just as widespread, and just as diverse, in the USA. To take just one example of many, the **Henge of Keltria** is a Neo-Pagan Druid movement based in Minneapolis. Its major beliefs are worth quoting, as a general summary of what many of the more modern Druid orders believe:

> We believe in Divinity as it is manifest in the Pantheon. There are several valid theistic perceptions of this Pantheon.
> We believe that nature is the embodiment of the Gods.
> We believe that all life is sacred, and should neither be harmed nor taken without deliberation or regard.
> We believe in the immortality of the spirit.
> We believe that our purpose is to gain wisdom through experience.
> We believe that learning is an ongoing process and should be fostered at all ages.
> We believe that morality should be a matter of personal conviction based upon self-respect and respect for others.
> We believe that every individual has the right to pursue enlightenment through his or her chosen path.
> We believe in a living religion able to adapt to a changing environment. We recognize that our beliefs may undergo change as our tradition grows.[113]

The eight festivals celebrated by modern Druids are the same as those of modern Wicca: Samhain (Hallowe'en), Winter Solstice, Imbolg (Candlemas), Spring Equinox, Beltaine (May Day), Summer Solstice, Lughnasad (Lammas), and the Autumn Equinox.

Most of the Druid Orders are deeply concerned with the environment. OBOD, which offers a correspondence course in Druidry, is probably speaking for most Orders when it says:

More than ever, we need a spirituality that is rooted in a love of nature, a love of the land. Druidry and the teaching programme of OBOD is based upon this love for the natural world, and offers a powerful way of working with and understanding the Self and Nature – speaking to that level of our soul and of our being which is in tune with the elements and the stars, the sun and the stones. Through the work of the Druids we are able to unite our natural, earthly selves with our spiritual selves while working, in however small a way, for the safeguarding of our planet.[114]

Many of the Druid Orders contain three grades or groupings of members; these focus on different talents and interests, and although they are not necessarily progressive levels, as in the esoteric Mystery Schools (see page 362), those at the third level would normally have passed through the first two. In OBOD, for example, Bards are the keepers of tradition, those who remember and relate the stories, poems and myths. The Ovates are trained in prophecy and divination; they are the seers and shamans of the movement. The Druids are the teachers, counsellors and judges; they are philosophers rather than priests, and will tend to be the older, more experienced members of the Order.[115]

The British Druid Order also has three grades, roughly equivalent to those of OBOD: Bard (Poet/Seer), Ofydd (Philosopher) and Derwydd (Druid).

The essence of the Order's teachings lies in working with the spiritual energy known to the British tradition as Awen. The feminine noun Awen literally means 'flowing spirit' or 'fluid essence'. The Bards of medieval Wales saw it as their primary source of inspiration, and as a gift of the ancient pagan Goddess Ceridwen, 'the Bent White One', who they referred to as Patroness of the Bardic Order.

In the Bardic grade this 'flowing spirit' is directed into creativity on many levels, particularly in the traditional areas of poetry, music and storytelling, but also in all other arts and sciences.

In the Ofydd grade, Awen is used to create windows, or gateways, into unseen worlds, leading to the development of the gift of seership, and knowledge of the Faery realm, the Otherworld, and its inhabitants.

In the Derwydd grade, Awen is related to Earth energies, or Dragon Lines, which run through the landscape, accumulating at sacred sites. The task of the Druid is to learn to work with this energy for the benefit of the land and its inhabitants, human and animal, physical and non-physical.

In all this work, we call upon the aid of the Ancestors, who are both our physical forebears who have passed on, and our spiritual Ancestors, the Druids of all past ages, and also the Gods themselves. Much of our strength and wisdom comes from them, and they give it freely and joyously, because we are part of the same golden chain of age-old tradition.[116]

Present-day Druidry, in all its varieties, is clearly part of the Neo-Pagan revival, but is usually quite distinct from the more Wiccan varieties of Neo-Paganism, though the two traditions generally seem to have respect for each other, and several Druid leaders are also Wiccan priests. According to Shallcrass, Ross Nichols, the founder of OBOD, was a friend of Gerald Gardner, who effectively founded modern Wicca; Gardner, who was a great eclecticist, joined OBOD shortly before his death in 1964.

THE FELLOWSHIP OF ISIS

The Fellowship of Isis has aspects of Neo-Paganism, Druidry and Esotericism. It was founded in 1976 by the late Baron Strathlock, Reverend Lawrence Durdin-Robertson, with his wife Pamela and his sister the Honourable Olivia Robertson, in Eire. They worship the Goddess, but differ from many other Neo-Pagan organizations in emphasizing Egyptian roots as well as Celtic; their priesthood, they claim, 'is derived from an hereditary line of the Robertsons from Ancient Egypt.'[117]

Because they venerate all goddesses (and also gods), members include people from a variety of religions, including Hindus, Buddhists, Christians and Spiritualists. 'The good in all faiths is honoured... The Fellowship accepts religious toleration, and is not exclusivist. Members are free to maintain other religious allegiances.' They claim a membership of 12,500 in 81 countries, with over 450 Iseums (Hearths of the Goddess) in 37 countries. The Fellowship has three 'daughter' societies, the Order of Tara, which has chivalric titles, the Druid Clan of Dana, which works on the development of psychic gifts, and the College of Isis.

In common with esoteric Mystery Schools, the College of Isis offers a correspondence course – 'a structured Magi Degree Course in the Fellowship of Isis Liturgy. There are 32 working degrees, the 33rd relating to spontaneous mystical awakening.'[118]

In contrast with esoteric schools,

> there are no vows required or commitments to secrecy. All Fellowship activities are optional, and members are free to resign or rejoin at their own choice... The Fellowship reverences all manifestations of Life... [and] believes in the promotion of Love, Beauty and Abundance. No encouragement is given to asceticism. The Fellowship seeks to develop friendliness, psychic gifts, happiness, and compassion for all life.

The Druid Clan of Dana, whose London base, the Grove of the Four Elements, is headed by Steve Wilson, will continue to investigate and work with ancient sites, to explore cross-cultural connections amongst ancient peoples and develop an English Druidry in the Irish tradition.[119]

THE NORTHERN TRADITION

Part of the Neo-Pagan revival of recent years has been a renewed interest in the gods and goddesses of native traditions: these include not only the Celtic and Native American, but also the old Norse and Germanic religions – the Northern Tradition. For many people this goes little further than using runes instead of (or as well as) Tarot cards, for divination, meditation and magic; but for some, the religion itself is being revived and reinterpreted for a modern world.

> Heathenism, or the Northern Tradition as it is alternatively known, is perhaps the most diverse of all faiths under the pagan umbrella. It has a structure unlike any other pagan religion but at the same time, a sort of nomadic looseness at worshipper level. Heathens may invoke many gods and goddesses, and yet some may worship only one, such as the shamanic wind god Odin. Heathenism is one religion or many related religions according to your point of view.[120]

As with Neo-Paganism, there are several different 'flavours' in the Northern Tradition. These include the generic terms Odinism, Asatru and the Elder Troth, and movements such as the Ring of Troth, the Odinic Rite and Odinshof, each of which has its own emphasis. All follow the Northern European traditions of the Norse, Germanic and Anglo-Saxon peoples, practised from around 2,000 years ago, and supplanted by Christianity from around 1,000 years ago.

The Ring of Troth is 'a religious organization dedicated to the promotion and practice of the native heathen folk-religion of Northern Europe,' says Freya Aswynn, former Drightinne in the Rune Gild, and an Elder in the Ring of Troth.[121] 'The religious organizations I represent are relatively young and modern; however, the religion itself is old, not new age as some other forms of contemporary Paganism. We therefore distinguish ourselves by naming ourselves Heathen rather than Pagan.'

Heathen originally meant 'the beliefs of the people of the heath', just as 'Pagan' originally meant 'the beliefs of the country people'.

Aswynn stresses the immediacy of religion to her Norse ancestors.

> For them there was no separation between sacred and profane, spiritual and secular. Their faith was intricately interwoven into everything they did, from working in the fields to naming their children. Theirs was a life where the gods

and goddesses were never any further away than their own shadow.

These gods and goddesses include the entire Norse pantheon, known to us through the poetic or *Elder Edda* and the prose or *Younger Edda*; the German equivalent is the *Niebelungenlied*. These myths are familiar to us through Wagner's *Ring Cycle* and other works, and inspired J.R.R. Tolkien's *Lord of the Rings* and related books.

In America the generic term Asatru tends to be used, rather than Odinism. It is named after the Asa or Aesir, one of the two main families of Norse gods; the other family were the Vanir. According to Andrew Clifton, Steersman of the Ring of Troth Europe, Asatru is an Icelandic term, and the revival of the tradition 'was led in Scandinavia some 30 years ago. Asatru was accepted as a legitimate religion in Iceland in 1972.'[122]

> Modern-day Asatru is a religion based on reconstruction from historical sources. It is a polytheistic faith encompassing belief in a multitude of different gods and goddesses. Within Asatru there is the emergence of a sister tradition named Vanatru, centring mainly on the Vanir. This branch takes especial interest in the feminine mysteries and female ancestor work.[123]

The religion has a strong ethical side similar to that of most Neo-Pagan movements.

> Modern concerns of Asatru are environmental issues and the re-establishing of family values. Unlike many other ethnic peoples, we have lost the sense of kinship, community and extended family. Many old people are freezing or starving. Young people drift towards a life of drug abuse, crime, and general uselessness – with little but the dole queue to look forward to. We offer change. We want to give back – especially [to] the young – a pride in ancestors and their achievements. We aim to instil responsibility, respect and care for our elders, and stress the value of education for our youngsters.[124]

The Norse peoples, and their gods, lived life to the full; they were a hot-tempered bunch, but honourable within their own rules. According to Aswynn:

> The concept of Honour is the most vital element of Asatru ethics. Others are Courage, Truth, Loyalty, Self-discipline, Hospitality, Industriousness, Independence, and Endurance. We strive to express these nine virtues in our lives and dealings with people. Forgiveness, loving your enemy and turning the other cheek are tactics with no place in Asatru.

The Odinic Rite also places strong emphasis on honour and self-discipline. 'Each time that we speak out against tyranny, are hospitable to guests or help to protect the environment we are performing a religious act.'[125]

The Odinic Rite, like other Northern Tradition movements, places great emphasis on the family and the extended family, including close friends; it is organized in Hearths, groups of ten to twelve people who usually meet in members' homes.

> Odinism is the organic religion of the peoples of Northern Europe. Our ances-
> tors... reflected their awareness of a unity in which the cosmos is one with man
> and nature... Odinists aim at creating a restored order based on the idea of
> respect for all life and on the explicit recognition of spirituality within ourselves
> and in the world in which we live, to extend our views of nature so that it is
> seen as a true manifestation of the spirit.[126]

The Rune Gild was founded in the USA in 1980 by Edred Thorsson, author of *A Book of Troth*. One of the most influential academic writers is Kveldulfr Gundarsson, author of *Teutonic Magic and Teutonic Religion*. (His *Rhinegold* and *Attila's Treasure*, under the name Stephan Grundy [Michael Joseph, 1994 and 1996] are modern novelizations of portions of the Norse/Germanic sagas.) Freya Aswynn's *Leaves of Yggdrasil* is a study of the runes, the Norse gods and magic.

The structure of the various organizations is democratic, but with leaders.

> One of the weaknesses in some previous attempts at reviving the Elder Troth
> has been the lack of a wise and learned priesthood, a body of persons qualified
> and certified as experts in the lore and work – in theory and practice – of the
> Elder Troth. Too often, uninformed anarchy led to dissolution, where a little
> help from those more experienced and knowledgeable may have brought
> success. As long as the Troth remains an amateur pastime of the untrained
> enthusiast, it cannot achieve its destiny.[127]

Like most other Neo-Pagan movements, the revived Norse religions do not actively recruit new members. 'They find us,' says Aswynn.

> People join us because they want to work with others to contact the gods and
> goddesses. What they get out of it is a closely knit artificially constructed 'tribal
> family' where we support each other in everything. We are mostly bound
> together by personal friendships between us and our enthusiasm for our gods.

Odinshof does not limit itself strictly to the Norse religion. 'The philosophy of the 'Hof is to look back over 2,500 years or so and gain insight from most periods since then,' says Martyn Taylor, co-founder of Odinshof in 1987.[128] Like most of the other new religious movements of the Northern Tradition, its numbers are small. Its members:

want to promote the cult of Odin (Odintru) and learn spiritual truths ('dharma'). Odinshof members do not reject anything from the past but believe strongly in the 'now'... The backbone of the Odinshof is its membership, whether they be working alone or attached to an official hearth or loose group (sometimes called a kindred). Some members feel the need to progress to the level of being at one with Odin – to be 'an Odin'. These are potential Grimserular, or shaman-priests... A Grimesruli is seen by the Odinshof as a healer, pathfinder, rune-master and teacher, all rolled into one.[129]

The roots of Norse religion go back at least 2,000 years. The god most closely associated with the runes is Odin or Woden, the Allfather. The myths tell how Odin hung upside down from the great World Tree Yggdrasil for nine days and nights, impaled on his own spear, in order to gain wisdom.

The Norse were a very down-to-earth people; the mystical, the magical and the religious were seen as a fundamental part of everyday life. The runes were associated with wisdom and well-being, with words and deeds, with the gods and with magical power. They were both practical and mystical; if a particular combination of runes brought good luck or protection, it made sense for a warrior to carry it with him.

Although people might initially be attracted to Odinism by the use of runes, there is much more to the religion than that.

Those who believe that runes and runology are the be-all and end-all of Odinism have a too narrow vision of the runes, a shallow knowledge of their mysteries and ignorance of the meaning of religion. The runes are the essential mystical ingredient of the Odinic Rite and are its spiritual mainstay. But they are not its sum total... The Odinist religion is our way of life, our inherited culture and our patrimony.[130]

Like most mythologies, Norse mythology includes creation myths and end-of-the-world myths; it has interrelated families of quarrelsome gods, who from time to time had dealings with humans, and these gods swap responsibilities to some extent over the centuries as the mythology evolves. These are a few of the better-known gods and goddesses:

• Odin (Woden), sometimes known as the Allfather, was foremost among the gods. He is generally pictured with a wide-brimmed hat sloping over his blind eye, in the company of two ravens, his messengers. He was known for his wisdom, but also for his unpredictability; like many gods, he had a trickster side to his personality.
• His son Thor was the god of weather, particularly thunder, and is often seen wielding a hammer, which he frequently used to slay giants. He was also the

god of the peasants and common people, which might account for the fair way in which Norse rulers treated their people.

- Tyr or Tîw was the original god of war; his prominent position was later taken on by Odin. Tyr was the god of the Thing, the people's assembly, and so of justice.
- Frey, one of the most important gods, was a fertility god, and also the god of summer.
- His sister (and at one point wife) Frija or Freya was the goddess of sexuality and beauty, and also of feminine magic, which she taught to Odin.
- Often confused with Frija, especially in the Germanic versions of the myths, is Frigga, goddess of fertility, but more in the sense of motherhood; she was one of Odin's wives.
- She bore him a son, Balder, who was the most beautiful of all the gods; he was an expert in herbal medicine, and also in the runes – indeed, he had runes carved on his tongue.
- Balder was eventually slain through the treachery of Loki, the god of lies, deceit and trickery – and of fire and leisure.

There are several dozen other gods and goddesses, in addition to giants, dwarves and heroic humans, entwined in Norse mythology. Four of them live on today wherever the English language is spoken around the world, in the days of the week: Tuesday is named after after Tyr or Tîw , Wednesday after Woden or Odin, Thursday after Thor, and Friday after either Freya or Frigga.

As Christianity made inroads into northern Europe, the power of the old gods waned to some extent – but not entirely. For some centuries the two religions existed side by side, and there are many examples of gravestones or crosses with the crucified Christ on one side and scenes from Norse mythology on the other. Very often the inscriptions were in runes, rather than in the Roman alphabet. Runes continued to be used for writing, and for more esoteric purposes, for many more centuries, despite the efforts of the Catholic Church to stamp out their use. As late as 1639 there was an edict in Iceland forbidding their use – which shows that they were in use – and it is said that even in the late nineteenth century pastors in remote rural parts of Scandinavia were required to be able to read and write the runes.

Many elements of the Old Norse language survive today, obviously in the Scandinavian languages, but also in English, Dutch and German. There are still a few valley sheep farmers in south Cumbria who speak between themselves a variant of Old Norse; the closest present-day language is Icelandic. In English, the occasional use of 'Ye' to mean 'The' is a reminder of the rune Thorn, which is pronounced as a soft 'Th' but looks something like a 'Y'.

Do the modern-day successors to Sigismund and the other great Norse heroes actually believe in Odin, Thor, Balder, Frija and the rest of the gods? 'We have no fixed doctrine at all,' says Aswynn. 'Most of us believe on the whole in an objective existence of our gods as spiritual beings, whereas others in our religion perceive the gods more as Jungian Archetypes. Most people have a favourite god or goddess they are devoted to in particular.' Thus there are Odinists, Thorians, Tyrians and others.

The Odinic Rite explain it a different way.

> We know that our gods exist: we can see, feel and sense them. They are manifested in various forms: in the summer and the winter, sunshine and storm, hill and river and plain. Because it is in keeping with our culture and our tradition Odinists give names to the gods who show themselves to us in this way: Thor, Frey, Balder, Odin and many others... There is nothing unusual or illogical in this Odinist use of an ancient mythology. All religions are mythical in their development. It is not the myth that we believe in but the gods whom the myth helps us to understand.[131]

Believers in the Norse/Germanic religions are conscious that they have some seriously bad press to overcome. In the 1930s and 1940s Hitler deliberately drew on Norse/Germanic sources to provide a religious, mystical and magical basis for Nazism. The SS used the rune Sigel as their symbol. The swastika is one of the oldest religious symbols in the world, but has probably been irreparably polluted by its adoption by Nazism. Aswynn comments:

> Unfortunately, some in the past have sought to use the revival of our native folk religion to advance their racial and political agendas. Such activity is not tolerated in the Ring of Troth. The peoples of the North did not achieve great things by fearing, distrusting or hating everyone unlike themselves; rather they attained greatness through their ability, where necessary, to learn from others and to borrow, adapt and improve ideas and technologies which suited their own needs. If the Germanic peoples had hated and feared all that was new and different they may not have achieved all that they have.

A press release on Asatru looks at it from a different angle:

> Attempts to call and control the Northern gods were made in the '30s and '40s.

However the gods had their own agenda, and seeing the subversion of the runes and other sacred signs, extracted the penalties of the perpetrators – who lost!

The efforts of Odinists to distance themselves from Nazism are made more difficult by two things: the fact that the Norse religion *is* an ethnic tradition, and the recent rise of neo-Nazism, which is once again appropriating some of the symbols and which lays claim to the same ethnic heritage.

Odinists, like Wiccans, have sometimes been accused of being too much in love with a rose-tinted past. They disagree.

It is not a spare-time religion providing an escape route from the problems of modern life by invoking visions of the romantic past but an opportunity for the individual to grow in self-reliance, to grow closer to nature in the practice of the ancient rituals of our ancestors and to secure the future.[132]

Odinshof also stress the practical, everyday nature of their beliefs.

There is a danger of members becoming too reliant on written texts and not spending time being involved with hearth activities or out of door rituals. 'Armchair Heathens' do not change society for the better. Again, Tacitus said, 'The Germanic-speaking tribes do not think it is in keeping with the divine majesty to confine gods within walls or to portray them in the likeness of any human countenance. Their holy places are woods and groves, and they apply the names of deities to that hidden presence which is seen only by the eye of reverence.'[133]

Like the other Norse movements, Odinshof is dedicated to nature, and in particular to maintaining areas of wildwoods. It helped campaign against the proposed road through Oxleas Wood in London. In 1992 it set up a charity called Land Guardians to purchase and maintain a wildwood.

It is difficult to say how many followers of the Norse religion there are, but Clifton estimates that 'two or three thousand are seriously interested in the tradition in the UK, and tens of thousands in Europe.'

PAGAN FEDERATIONS

In general, Neo-Paganism glories in its diversity. Shamans, Witches, Druids and others have different approaches, based on different mythological traditions; and within each broad group there are many different aims and emphases. This is both a strength and a potential weakness of Neo-Paganism; the lack of any central organization prevents the movement becoming dogmatic and authoritarian, both of which are alien to the Neo-Pagan way of thinking, but it could also mean that individual groups, influenced by a strong local leader, might wander off in strange directions.

Various umbrella organizations have arisen over the years. In 1981 the **Pagan Federation** grew out of the former Pagan Front, which had begun in 1970. The Pagan Federation 'works to make Paganism accessible to people genuinely seeking a nature-based spiritual path.'[134] A large part of its current work is informational, and it has become effectively the mouthpiece of British Paganism to the outside world; it has established links with the Home Office, the police, social services, the Press, libraries, teachers and Members of Parliament. It is working towards establishing the same rights for Neo-Pagans as for members of any other religion, including, for example, hospital and prison chaplains, and Pagan weddings and funerals.

Initially the Pagan Federation was almost exclusively Wiccan, but by the 1980s, according to Farrar and Bone, it was 'facing increased criticism for its lack of democracy, and its inability to cater adequately for members who followed other paths than Wiccan.'[135] It was also very much centred on the southeast of England, which was a source of irritation to Pagans elsewhere in the country. From around 1991, recognizing these weaknesses, it expanded its work to give more emphasis to non-Wiccan Paganism, and made real efforts to make itself more democratic. Its magazine *The Wiccan* was relaunched as *Pagan Dawn*. Its annual conferences, established in 1989, attract Neo-Pagans from a wider variety of traditions.

The Isle of Avalon Foundation isn't a religion in itself, or even a federation as such; it is more of a study centre, a clearing house for teaching about Neo-Pagan and New Age ideas, set in Glastonbury. It was set up as the University of Avalon in 1991,

> with the vision of creating a recognized University of the Spirit in Avalon within the temenos of Glastonbury, known for centuries as the Isle of Avalon. We are a University in the original sense of the word – meaning an educational establishment concerned with exploring the whole of creation, encompassing spiritual as well as material values and systems.[136]

The British government didn't see it the same way; they were told that they couldn't use the name because they were not an officially recognized university offering academic degrees. In April 1995 they changed to their current name, and reassessed their aims and ideals.

Isle of Avalon Foundation is a spiritual education centre whose main purpose is to make available to visitors and residents the transformative energies of Avalon and the experience of people who live in Glastonbury and elsewhere on the planet.[137]

They offer talks and courses on, among others, personal development, music and magic, healing, runes, numerology, dowsing, shamanism, and the teachings of Dion Fortune. The aim is to develop courses at beginner, intermediate and advanced (mystery school) levels in seven faculties: Consciousness, Health and Healing, Human Potential, Planet Earth, Sacred Arts, Sacred Sciences, and Spiritual Revelation.

Federations and other umbrella groups serve a number of functions: exchange of views, mutual support, general friendship, central information point for the media and official bodies, centralized research and publication, and so on. The Neo-Pagan movement in general is still quite young, and a lot of its vigour seems to come from its diversity. A possible danger, which the leaders of such federations are clearly aware of, could be a shift from what is essentially a mutual support group to a structured, centralized authority which decides who may join and who may not, with a too-rigid codifying of what is or is not a valid and acceptable form of Paganism; if this were to occur, most would see it as being against the overall free spirit of Neo-Paganism.

Notes

[1] Oberon Zell, founder of Church of All Worlds, in correspondence with the author, 14 June 1995.

[2] Elen J. Williams, then secretary of the Pagan Federation, in correspondence with the author, 26 May 1995.

[3] Ronald Hutton commending on Tanya Luhrmann's *Persuasions of the Witch's Craft* (1989) in Hutton 1999: 375.

[4] The classic books were *Michelle Remembers* by L. Pazder and M. Smith, New York, 1980, and *Satan's Underground* by Lauren Stratford, Eugene OR, 1988; the latter was later revealed to be a fake.

[5] Sherril Mulhern, 'Satanism and Psychotherapy: a rumour in search of an Inquisition', in J.T. Richardson, J. Best and D.G. Bromley (eds), *The Satanism Scare*, New York 1991: 145–72.

[6] See La Fontaine 1998, and De Blécourt, Hutton and La Fontaine 1999.

[7] De Blécourt, Hutton and La Fontaine 1999: 131.

[8] Massimo Introvigne, director of CESNUR, in correspondence with the author, 4 February 2000.

[9] *The Mail on Sunday*, 13 February 2000: 42–3.

[10] E.g. J.D. Douglas (ed.), *The New Bible Dictionary*, London: Inter-Varsity Fellowship, 1962; Alan Richardson (ed.), *A Theological Word Book of the Bible*, London: SCM Press, 1957; William Smith, *Smith's Bible Dictionary*, New York: Pyramid edn, 1967.

[11]Smith 1967: 607. (see note 10.)

[12]Douglas 1962: 755. (see note 10.)

[13]Melton 1992: 109.

[14]LaVey 1969: 21.

[15]Justin Woodman, 'Psychologizing Satan: Contemporary Satanism, Satanic-Abuse Allegations, and the Secularization of Evil', *Scottish Journal of Religious Studies*, 18 (2): 134.

[16]Graham Harvey, 'Satanism in Britain today', *Journal of Contemporary Religion*, 10: 353–66, cited in De Blécourt, Hutton and La Fontaine 1999: 108.

[17]Jean La Fontaine in De Blécourt, Hutton and La Fontaine 1999: 108.

[18]Information leaflet: *The Reappearance of the Christ and the Masters of Wisdom*, 1994: 2.

[19]Ibid.

[20]*The Emergence Newsletter*, 1994, no. 3: 3.

[21]Unless otherwise stated, quotations are from Professor Tilo L.V. Ulbricht, on behalf of the Gurdjieff Society, in correspondence with the author, 11 November 1999.

[22] Moore 1999: 319.

[23]Routledge & Kegan Paul, London: 1950.

[24]Moore 1999: 57.

[25]Unless otherwise stated all quotations are taken from a Subud information leaflet, untitled.

[26]'Frequently Asked Questions', on http://www.subud.org.

[27]Ibid.

[28]Subuh, quoted in Lyle 1983: 91–2.

[29]For a more in-depth look at both the origins of Rosicrucianism, and several present-day Rosicrucian Orders, see the author's *Secret Societies*, Blandford, 1997: 78–83, 150–62.

[30]Quotations are from the booklet *An Introduction to AMORC*, 31st edn, n.d.

[31]Booklet: *Mysticism... What it is, What it does, What it offers*, AMORC, Crowborough, E. Sussex, n.d.

[32]Quotations are from H.C. Steinhart, General Secretary of Lectorium Rosicrucianum, in correspondence with the author, 12 July and 30 October 1995, and 22 November 1999.

[33]See Massimo Introvigne, 'Lectorium Rosicrucianum: A Dutch Movement Becomes International', CESNUR '97 International Conference, Amsterdam, on http://www.cesnur.org/testi/RosyCross.htm.

[34]Regardie, one-volume edition 1971, 3rd edn 1989.

[35]François Rabelais, *The Histories of Gargantua and Pantagruel*, The First Book, chapter 57; H.G. Bohn 1849: 279; London: Penguin, 1955: 159.

[36]Unless otherwise stated, all quotations are from the BOTA introductory booklet *The Open Door*, 1989 edn.

[37]Pollack 1989: 137.

[38]Gareth Knight, in correspondence with the author, 10 February 2000. Knight's biography, *Dion Fortune and the Inner Light* (Thoth Publications, 2000), was not yet available when the current book was being prepared.

[39]Leaflet: *The Society of the Inner Light: Work and Aims*, 2000 edn.

⁴⁰The secretariat of the Society of the Inner Light, in correspondence with the author, 7 February 1995.

⁴¹Unless otherwise stated, all quotations are from the introductory booklet *The Society of the Inner Light: Work and Aims*, n.d. (pre-1995).

⁴²Dion Fortune and Gareth Knight, *The Circuit of Force*, Thoth, 1998, and *Principles of Hermetic Philosophy*, Thoth, 1999.

⁴³Leaflet: *The Society of the Inner Light: Work and Aims*, 2000.

⁴⁴Unless otherwise stated, all quotations are taken from the introductory booklet *Servants of the Light School of Occult Science*, n.d.

⁴⁵'Frequently Asked Questions' on the Servants of the Light webpage: http://www.naradek.org/info/faq.html.

⁴⁶'The Third Degree', on the SOL website: http://www.naradek.org/course/degree3.html.

⁴⁷All quotations are taken from the introductory pamphlet *The London Group: Its Aims and Objectives*, n.d.

⁴⁸The Secretary, London Group, in correspondence with the author, 25 October 1999.

⁴⁹This paragraph is based on a discussion between three chaos magicians and the author at Talking Stick (now known as the Secret Chiefs), 19 January 2000.

⁵⁰Quoted in Harvey 1997: 100; also printed at the foot of each page of the magazine *Chaos International*.

⁵¹This and the following quotation are from Pete Carroll, 'Chaoism and Chaos Magic, A Personal View', on http://brainwave.org/~fenwick/chaos/carroll/chaoism.html.

⁵²Throughout this entry 'Prophet' refers to Elizabeth Clare Prophet.

⁵³*Keepers of the Flame: A Fraternity*, 1986: 24.

⁵⁴CUT press release, 3 September 1998. In June 2000 Mrs Prophet left the CUT HQ at Royal Teton Ranch, to move in with and be cared for by Steinman and his wife. (*Heart to Heart* [CUT newsletter] Aug/Sep 2000: 3)

⁵⁵Murray Steinman in telephone conversation with the author, 7 September 1995.

⁵⁶Prophet 1985: 255–6.

⁵⁷Booklet: *Profile: Elizabeth Clare Prophet/Teachings of the Ascended Masters*, 1992: 7.

⁵⁸'The Life of Saint Issa' 4:12–13, in Prophet 1987: 218.

⁵⁹This is Steinman's paraphrase; the actual verse reads, 'Jesus said, "He who will drink from my mouth will become like me; I myself shall become he, and the things that are hidden will be revealed to him."' 'The Gospel of Thomas', verse 108, in Willis Barnstone (ed.), *The Other Bible*, San Francisco: Harper & Row, 1984: 307.

⁶⁰Christopher Kelley, spokesman, Church Universal and Triumphant, in correspondence with the author, 17 March 2000.

⁶¹*Profile*: 9–10.

⁶²*Profile*: 8.

⁶³Video: *Climb the Highest Mountain: A Profile of the Church Universal and Triumphant*, 1994.

⁶⁴*Profile*: 16.

⁶⁵Ibid.: 10.

[66]*Royal Teton Ranch News*, vol. 7, no. 2, February/March 1995: 8.

[67]Lewis and Melton 1994: 62, xii, *et passim*.

[68]Booklet: *The Emissaries*, 1992.

[69]Tessa Maskell, Director of the UK Emissary Charity, in correspondence with the author, 19 March 2000.

[70]Emissary document: *Mickleton House: Guidelines for Residents*, June 1995.

[71]Leaflet: *Lloyd Arthur Meeker; William Martin Alleyne Cecil*.

[72]Emissary document: *Mickleton House: Guidelines for Residents*, June 1995.

[73]Ibid.

[74]Unless otherwise stated, all quotations are from Kate Hall, former events manager at Mickleton House, in correspondence with the author, 24 January, 3 July, 9 August and 9 September 1995.

[75]Lloyd Arthur Meeker, *The Divine Design*, vol. 1, 1952.

[76]In one of Terry Pratchett's *Discworld* footnotes, he says:

> It's amazing how good governments are, given their track record in almost every other field, at hushing up things like alien encounters.
>
> One reason may be that the aliens themselves are too embarrassed to talk about it.
>
> It's not known why most of the space-going races of the universe want to undertake rummaging in Earthling underwear as a prelude to formal contact. (Terry Pratchett, *Hogfather*, London: Gollancz, 1996: 154.)

[77]Lewis Carroll, *Through the Looking Glass*, chapter 5.

[78] See Mikael Rothstein, 'The Family, UFOs and God: A Modern Extension of Christian Mythology', *Journal of Contemporary Religion*, vol. 12, no. 3, 1997: 353–62.

[79]Quotations from Richard Lawrence are from conversations with the author in 1995, 1998 and 1999.

[80]Aetherius Society Information booklet, n.d.

[81]Quotations in this paragraph are taken from Reverend George King, *You Are Responsible!*, Aetherius Press, 1961: 19–23.

[82]When asked by the author, Richard Lawrence said that he himself is not an avatar.

[83]Unless otherwise stated, all quotations are taken from the leaflet *The Aetherius Society: Some basic principles included in its teachings*, n.d.

[84]Aetherius Society Information booklet.

[85]Unless otherwise stated, all quotations are from the leaflet *The Raelian Movement: Information*, n.d.

[86]All quotations from Giles Dexter, then Secretary of the British Raelian Movement, are from correspondence with the author, 17 July 1995.

[87] Eric Bolou, UK Raelian leader, in conversation with the author, 2 December 1998.

[88]This and the next two quotations are from Raël 1998: 153, 154; the same passage in Raël 1986: 210 reads 'paradisiac planet'.

[89]Booklet: *An Embassy for Extra-Terrestrials*: 7.

[90]Leo Rutherford, of the Eagle's Wing Centre for Contemporary Shamanism, course leaflet: *Elements of Shamanism*, 1995.

[91]Jonathan Horwitz, 'All Life is Connected: The Shaman's Journey', http://www.users.dircon.co.uk/~snail/SCSS/Articles/All%20Life.htm

[92]Ibid.

[93]Kramer and Sprenger 1971: 116.

[94]Ibid.: 267–8.

[95]House of the Goddess leaflet, n.d.

[96]See Briggs 1996 for a sensible and thorough historical analysis of 'witches and neighbours'.

[97]Murray 1921: 12.

[98]Cavendish 1987: 159.

[99]See, for example, Hutton 1999, a major study of modern pagan witchcraft by a history professor at the University of Bristol.

[100]Farrar 1971/1991: 20.

[101]House of the Goddess leaflet.

[101A]Shan 1986: 78-79

[102]CAW Membership Handbook n d · 4

[103]Unless otherwise stated, all quotations are from Oberon Zell in correspondence with the author, 14 June 1995.

[104]Bylaws of the Church of All Worlds, Inc., Article 7.1, as amended 8 August 1998.

[105]Oberon Zell in conversation with the author, 21 March 2000.

[106]CAW *Membership Handbook*: 11.

[107]Ibid.: 21.

[108]Unless otherwise stated, quotations by Philip Shallcrass are from correspondence with the author, 9 September 1995 and 25 November 2000.

[109]Piggot 1968: 143.

[110]Letter to *Odinism Today*, no. 18, May 1995: 22.

[111]'Druid Directory' in *The Druids' Voice*, no. 9, Winter 1998/9: 39.

[112]'Druid Directory', ibid.: 38.

[113]Henge of Keltria introductory leaflet.

[114]The Order of Bards, Ovates and Druids, introductory leaflet.

[115]Summarized from Carr-Gomm 1991: 43–64.

[116]British Druid Order introductory leaflet.

[117]Quotations are from the Fellowship of Isis *Manifesto* unless otherwise stated.

[118]*The Handbook of the Fellowship of Isis*: 8.

[119]'Druid Directory' in *The Druids' Voice*, no. 9, Winter 1998/9: 38.

[120]*Odalstone*, no. 10, the news sheet of Odinshof.

[121]Quotations from Freya Aswynn are from correspondence with the author, 5 February 1995.

[122]Andrew Clifton, Steersman of the Ring of Troth Europe, in conversation with the author, 14 March 2000.

[123]Press release: *Asatru – Ancient to Modern*.

[124]Ibid.

[125]Odinic Rite leaflet: *Odinists say Yes to Life.*

[126]Ibid.

[127]The Ring of Troth membership application leaflet.

[128]Martyn Taylor, Odinshof, in correspondence with the author, 4 August 1995.

[129]Odinshof *Members' Handbook.*

[130]Leaflet: *Welcome to the Odinic Rite.*

[131]Odinic Rite leaflet: *Odinists say Yes to Life.*

[132]Ibid.

[133]Odinshof *Members' Handbook.*

[134]Pagan Federation introductory leaflet.

[135]Janet and Stewart Farrar and Gavin Bone, *The Pagan Path*, Phoenix, 1994.

[136]*The University of Avalon Prospectus*, September to December 1994.

[137]*The Isle of Avalon Foundation: Courses and Workshops April 1995.*

CHAPTER 16

Personal Development Movements

I N earlier decades books such as this sometimes included Marxism or humanism as secular equivalents to religion, in that they performed many of the same functions, and sometimes shared some of the same characteristics. In the last few years there has been a clear societal change; on the one hand the significance of Marxism, humanism and rational scientific materialism has waned, and on the other there has been an increased interest in 'personal development'.

In Britain, for example, advertisements in magazines offer 'The Realization System: Private Lessons in Practical Psychology.' For £180, paid in easy stages, a correspondence course (says the promotional letter):

> will start to build the structure of a new and dominant YOU, a serene and successful YOU, a more courageous and capable YOU, a happier, healthier, more wonderful YOU... A triumphant YOU born of Greater Self-Knowledge which THE REALIZATION SYSTEM will bring you, just as it has done for countless others in all walks of life.

Although it says that it is not in any way a religion, later in the course the student is introduced to the concept of 'the Universal Creative Mind' of which we are all a part.

Personal development isn't new. Samuel Smiles wrote his famous *Self-Help* in 1859, with the aphorisms 'he who never made a mistake never made a discovery' and 'the shortest way to do many things is to do only one thing at once'. Dale Carnegie's *How to Win Friends and Influence People*, published in 1936, was a result of courses in which he taught business and professional people 'to think on their feet and express their ideas with more clarity, more effectiveness and more poise'; it had sold nearly five million copies by his death in 1955. L. Ron Hubbard's Dianetics, first launched on the world in 1950, promised 'a condition of ability and rationality for Man well in advance of the current norm' and 'a complete insight into the full potentialities of the mind'. Norman Vincent Peale's *The Power of Positive Thinking* was first published in 1952; its chapter headings include 'Expect the best and get it', and 'I don't believe in defeat'.

More recent books include among many others Bernard Haldane's *How to Make a Habit of Success* (1960), with chapter titles such as 'Open your life to success' and 'Building success into your thinking', and Robert J. Lumsden's *Twenty-Three Steps to Success and Achievement* (1972), with chapters such as 'Make maturity your goal', 'Increased happiness for you' and 'Wider mental horizons'. On a more overtly spiritual level, Will Schutz's *Profound Simplicity* (1979), was 'one of the first books to apply the learnings of the human potential movement to "real life" problems'.

Such books are still being written, but the last couple of decades have seen an explosion in the number of techniques, courses and seminars available, all offering ways to help you improve yourself. A cynic might suggest that a paperback book costing £8.99 will make less than 70p per copy for its author, while a weekend seminar can cost £300 apiece for only a fraction of the contents, and might encourage the attendee to come back for much more of the same – more advanced courses, for more advanced fees.

A man can make millions by telling other people how they might make millions.

Success-orientated America in particular has always been a fertile field for the planting of such self-improvement concepts. It is probably no coincidence that the country which brings up its children to believe that they can and will succeed, achieve whatever they aim for, and be fulfilled, has more adults going to one form or another of therapy than any other. If you don't succeed, if you don't reach the top, if you don't feel fulfilled, then you feel a failure; the opportunities are all there, in the Land of Opportunity, so it must be you who has failed. In America, a therapist will never be unemployed.

It is probably also no coincidence that most of the human potential movements developed there.

Self-improvement seminars often seek to improve a person's awareness of and confidence in himself or herself by awakening and experiencing, in one phrase or another, 'the heartfelt energies' – which is a similar goal to that of many religions, without necessarily involving God. Could it be that such organizations have taken on a role analogous to religions in the past, and if so, is there still a need for religion? Certainly the fervour of many adherents of personal development movements is comparable to the fervour of a religious convert. Perhaps the benefits they gain are also comparable.

Some of the personal development movements – just like some of the alternative religions – have been criticized for their reluctance to let go of people once they have become involved. Some critics also argued that in the flush of enthusiasm as you successfully complete a course, with all the 'gains' you have made, you are easily persuaded to sign on for the next one. Participants often point to the very real benefits they have received from courses; the promise of even greater benefits from further courses is a powerful incentive to continue.

The best known of all these self-improvement movements will be covered at some length. At different times and for different reasons Scientology has claimed the mantle of educative system, health improvement, therapy, philosophy and religion. Other organizations don't mention any spiritual connection though some, such as Insight, do have links to religious movements in their origins. Others, like Landmark Education, make it clear that they have no connection at all with religion.

Such movements, then, are included in this book not with any implication that they are in any way religions, but for the reasons given above.

LANDMARK EDUCATION/ LANDMARK FORUM

Landmark Forum is the basic educational programme offered by Landmark Education. It is:

> a three-day and one evening programme conducted as a philosophical enquiry which deals with fundamental questions and issues which are key to shaping and determining people's effectiveness, creativity and satisfaction... It poses questions and explores issues that are most fundamental in living our day-to-day lives. These questions are about how to be effective in our relationships, how to operate at our peak performance, and how to communicate so that we bring out the best in others.[1]

Landmark's roots can be traced back to est (Erhard Seminars Training), a personal development programme which engendered a great deal of controversy in the 1970s. In the late-1960s Werner Erhard, born John Paul (Jack) Rosenberg in 1935, spent some time in Scientology, and some critics have alleged that est borrowed some of its basic ideas from Dianetics, though in fact there is little if any similarity between the two. It is also thought that some of Erhard's ideas came from the American version of Zen Buddhism developed and taught by Alan Watts.[2] Erhard, a former used car salesman and later an executive for an encyclopedia company, had apparently also been involved in a sales motivation course at William Penn Patrick's

Leadership Dynamics Institute. The Institute was also instrumental in the development of the self-help organizations Mind Dynamics and Lifespring; along with est, all of these were known for their confrontational, verbally abusive style of training.[3] The idea of all of them was to break down the shell of societal conditioning which entraps and encumbers us, in order to help people take charge of their own lives.

The name est not only stands for Erhard Seminars Training, but is Latin for 'it is'. Some of the key phrases and ideas in est were 'learning to be', 'transformation', 'empowerment' and 'responsibility'.

The first est training took place in San Francisco in 1971, after Erhard had what he described as a 'transformational' experience while driving near San Francisco. It has been reported that Erhard initially considered setting up est as a Church (as L. Ron Hubbard set up the Church of Scientology after establishing Dianetics), but decided instead to 'incorporate as an educational firm for profit'.[4] He established the est Foundation in 1973, and est first came to Britain in 1977. In 1981 Erhard reorganized his growing enterprises as Werner Erhard and Associates.

One academic describes Erhard's teachings as 'a combination of American business techniques, Western psychotherapeutic practices, and an Eastern spiritual orientation linked with a Liberal perspective.'[5] In response Art Schreiber, Chairman of the Board of Directors, Landmark Education Corporation, speaking first about the Landmark Forum, stresses that it is:

> an educational programme which is not therapeutic in design, intent or methodology and is not a substitute for psychotherapy or any health programme. People are informed that the Landmark Forum will not address issues that are best dealt with by psychotherapists or other health professionals.
>
> Numerous psychotherapists and psychologists have participated in the Landmark Forum and have given their opinion that the Landmark Forum was nothing remotely like psychotherapy. They have considered that the content of the Landmark Forum is philosophical rather than psychological in nature, with participants challenged to examine their ways of thinking much as they might be in a philosophy course...
>
> In addition, the est Training was not psychotherapy and did not use psychotherapeutic practices.

The est training was criticized mainly for its authoritarian approach. Except at designated breaks, trainees were not allowed to leave the seminar room even to go to the toilet. They would be shouted at and verbally abused. The aim of this treatment was apparently to break down their defences 'and induce an emotional state in which participants would be receptive to an examination of their "essential life principles".'[6]

Various independent spin-off organizations were founded by est 'graduates'. One which became well known in Britain was Exegesis, which was criticized for much the same reasons as est. When in 1984, largely through the efforts of London Tory MP David Mellor, Exegesis folded as a human potential training movement, its staff set up a successful tele-sales company, putting their theory into practice.

In 1984 est also came to an end, but Erhard's teachings continued, first of all in 1985 as the Forum, run by the Centres Network; this was a much more relaxed programme, with more free exchange of ideas between participants and the programme leader, and a greater emphasis on issues affecting all people rather than on the self. The authoritarian aspects of est were dropped. The Forum was aimed at 'the already successful, healthy, committed, accomplished and knowledgeable.'[7]

In 1991 employees of Werner Erhard and Associates set up an entirely new organization, Landmark Education, to which Erhard sold his teachings. Schreiber makes it very clear that there is no connection between est and Landmark Education.

The nature and material of Landmark Education's programmes is based on a technology originally developed by Werner Erhard, which technology has been redesigned and updated by Landmark Education. Mr Erhard had developed the programme known as the est Training which ceased being delivered to the public in 1984, more than six years prior to the formation of Landmark Education. The technology embodied in Landmark Education's programmes is totally different from that embodied in the est Training. Mr Erhard has never been a shareholder of Landmark Education and has never been involved in the management or operations of Landmark Education.

Landmark Education is owned by 'its employees and former employees around the world with no one person owning more than 3 per cent of the stock.' Its president is Harry Rosenberg, Erhard's younger brother. The company has over 40 offices in 14 countries; around 500,000 people have participated in the Landmark Forum programme.

The Landmark Forum seminars, typically with around 150 attendees, are held in university lecture halls or hotel conference rooms. The current UK cost is £235. The three-day sessions start at 9am and go on until midnight, with breaks every three hours and a 90-minute meal break; the evening session on the following Tuesday runs for three-and-a-quarter hours.

Although the course content and structure are different from est, the ultimate aim appears to be similar:

The Landmark Forum provides a technology that enables participants to think and act outside existing views and limits, both in their personal lives and relationships in the wider communities and areas of concern in which they are engaged.[8]

However, Schreiber points out that:

> the est Training and the Landmark Forum are based on very different technologies and are different in their purpose and methodology. The est Training dealt with people's ability to experience, and the purpose was to rehabilitate people's ability to experience so that they were more able to deal with situations that occurred in their lives.
>
> In contrast, the Landmark Forum does not address people's ability to experience and does not have as its purpose the rehabilitation of people's experience. Instead, the Landmark Forum is intended to provide people with the ability to create new possibilities in all aspects of their lives. The Landmark Forum also provides people with the possibility of completing their past so that it no longer determines their present or future, thereby providing them with an opportunity to create a future not determined by the past.

One further difference between est and the Landmark Forum is the method used.

> The methodology of the est Training was very different from that of the Landmark Forum. Extensive processes were used to support people in rehabilitating their ability to experience, which processes were often considered by people to be confrontive. In contrast, the Landmark Forum is conducted as an enquiry or dialogue with the Landmark Forum Leader facilitating the discussion and delivering data, much like what would occur in a university course on philosophy...
>
> The est Training was experiential while the Landmark Forum is an inquiry into issues which are important to what it means to be human.

Landmark aims to be challenging to its course participants, 'to help individuals examine fundamental assumptions that both shape actions and define the parameters of what one considers possible,' says Schreiber. He continues:

> A number of challenging ideas are examined in the Landmark Forum. One idea is that the future shapes a person's reality, not the person's past. The Landmark Forum poses that the quality of our lives is shaped by the future into which we are living, not merely by building on the past. If the past is taken out of the future − by simply being put back into the past where it belongs, or just by virtue of recognizing the past for what it is − then the past would no longer have the influence and impact it has. The Landmark Forum makes possible creating a future not determined by the past, and offers a life referenced against true possibility.

The Landmark Forum also examines people's formulas for success, Schreiber says: ways of being which have worked in the past and which we tend to use again and again.

However, sometimes relying on these formulas keeps us from seeing new, more effective ways of being in difficult situations. In the Landmark Forum, people have an opportunity to look into their formulas for success and discover the origin of people's identity.

Participants are also shown that the way they see something is not necessarily the way it is.

Instead of having things be just what happened, we assign meanings, interpretations and explanations to them... We end up dealing with all the meanings and interpretations we have added, instead of with what actually happened. In doing so, we rob ourselves of much of our effectiveness in life and our ability to create.

Landmark Education points out that numerous cult and sect experts, psychologists and clergy have participated in Landmark Forum, and have stated publicly that the company and its programme are not 'sects or cults, or religions, alternative religions or religious movements.'

NEURO-LINGUISTIC PROGRAMMING

Neuro-Linguistic Programming (NLP) is an approach rather than an organization; it is used by several different human potential movements. The information here was provided by John Seymour Associates, the longest established NLP organization in the UK, which offers NLP consulting and training mainly in London and Bristol.

'NLP is the art and science of personal excellence,' say Joseph O'Connor and John Seymour in their introductory book. It is 'a way of studying how people excel in any field and teaching these patterns to others.'[9]

NLP was developed in the mid-1970s by John Grinder, an Associate Professor of Linguistics at the University of California, Santa Cruz, and Richard Bandler, a psychology student at the university, with input from various others.

There is a perhaps apocryphal story that Bandler came up with the somewhat off-putting name Neuro-Linguistic Programming on the spur of the moment, to give him 'legitimacy' when seeking access to a mental hospital to visit a friend.[10] However, the name encompasses the theory and practice of NLP. 'Neuro' reflects the fact that our experience and our behaviour stem from the neurological processes of our senses and our thoughts. 'Linguistic' refers to the fact that we use language to think logically, and to communicate with others. 'Programming' refers to the way that we order and organize our ideas and actions to produce results.

Put them all together and NLP is a new way of looking at how people think, communicate and behave. It examines how people learn, and teaches more efficient ways of learning, and how to improve the memory; it shows how many of our reactions to events reinforce negativity, and how instead they can be made positive; it teaches how to communicate effectively, and how to understand and interpret the signals from other people. It teaches people to question what they do and what they believe:

1 Why do you do what you do?
2 What does that mean to you?
3 What would happen if you didn't do that?
4 What is that like? What do you compare it to?
5 What is empowering to you about this?[11]

It may use different terminology and perhaps different methodology, but it is in the great tradition of Dale Carnegie and Norman Vincent Peale; in a phrase, it teaches people to be more successful.

The reason for NLP's inclusion here is twofold. First, several movements which do have a spiritual element use NLP techniques and have NLP Masters among their leaders. Second, although it should be stressed once again that NLP itself is a process, a set of techniques, a methodology, and is not a religious movement nor even a religious belief system, yet its function is similar to one function of some religions, particularly many of the 'alternative' religions covered in this book.

NLP identifies and defines how our minds work. By developing a practical understanding of these processes we can learn how to achieve results that often seem magical.[12]

The emphasis is on practicality and usefulness in the real world. 'NLP offers specific and practical ways of making desired changes in our own and others' behaviour. It is about what works.' Similar sentiments can be found in many of the esoteric religious movements, both those within the Western Mystery Tradition, and those which follow a more Eastern path such as the School of Economic Science, and the various Gurdjieff offshoots.

The 'philosophy' of NLP also sounds familiar:

It is about creativity, learning and change, and how you construct your reality. Put simply, the world we each live in is not the real world. It is a model of the world. A model that we each create unconsciously and live in as though it were the real world. Most human problems derive from the models in our heads rather than from the world as it really is. As you develop your practical under-standing of how these inner models work, so you can learn to change unhelpful habits, thoughts, feelings and beliefs for more useful ones.

A Neo-Platonist or a Christian Scientist might say much the same thing, in surpris-ingly similar language – though probably for different reasons.

What ultimately distinguishes NLP from any of these religions or religious philosophies is that NLP teaches you to know yourself and better yourself; esoteric religions teach you to know yourself, and through knowing yourself, the god within, to know better the God without.

$$\approx$$

Rather than targeting people like sales reps, as est did, NLP courses tend to aim for executives, people climbing their way up the corporate ladder, who want to know how to improve their chances. Many major companies, including top banks and building societies, privatized utilities, health authorities, county councils, police author-ities and even government departments, have sent middle and senior management on NLP courses to improve their efficiency and increase their management potential. The self-employed and the non-professional classes are less likely to be able to afford the courses: the two-day introductory seminar cost nearly £300 in 1999.

Like many alternative religions, again particularly the esoteric movements, there is a 'career ladder' within NLP. 'Many people find that experiencing the Introduction Seminar creates an enthusiasm and thirst for more. Practitioner level training is the place to go next.'

The 20-day Practitioner course in London costs £2,937.50; the same course in Bristol costs the same amount, plus residential fees. The 20-day course is recognized by the Association for NLP, and John Seymour Associates are aiming for approval by OCR (Oxford, Cambridge and RSA) for national accreditation; according to Samantha West of John Seymour Associates, this will ensure that both the course and its trainers are 'quality controlled and assured'.[13] There are also 7-day Practitioner courses offered by several NLP companies, but West expresses some doubt about these: 'hundreds and thousands of people are going for the shortest route. It could be said they end up with a completion certificate for attending a training.'

Another set of courses, Trainer Training, is for teachers, lecturers, workshop leaders, or anyone else wanting to improve their presentation skills. It should not be confused with Assisting and Coaching, and Apprentice Trainer, which teach Practitioners to become NLP Trainers themselves. There are certificates and diplomas for NLP Trainers; above that there are certified Accelerated Personal Development Practitioners, Advanced Practitioners, Master Practitioners and Master Trainers.

Interestingly, the brief biographies of NLP Trainers usually give the names of the people they themselves trained under; this could be seen as similar to new Eastern-origin religions tracing themselves back through a progression of gurus, and esoteric movements claiming the authority of authenticity through their descent from previous movements.

INSIGHT

Like other personal development movements, Insight has sometimes been confused with est (Erhard Seminar Training – see page 427). Although, as they offer motivational seminars, there is probably some similarity in their aims and objectives, the two organizations have no connection.

> Insight is very practical, offering a number of powerful yet simple techniques which you can take away and apply to your life daily, to allow you to do more of what you've always wanted to do.[14]

The UK Insight organization currently conducts seminars four times a year, in a central London hotel. These take place on Wednesday, Thursday and Friday evenings, all day and evening on Saturday and Sunday, with a final session on the Monday evening – a total of around 48 hours. It's a cumulative process, and people are discouraged from missing any of the seminar at all.

The seminar includes:

> games and group processes involving the whole group; exercises done with a partner; periods when the facilitator will present information and new concepts; discussion and sharing of feelings; closed eye processes (sometimes called guided meditation or creative visualization). It is very varied, as people learn best when they are stimulated and interested.[15]

Aware of the adverse publicity attached to some similar courses in the past – particularly the early est movement – Insight are keen to stress that attendees at a seminar are free to leave whenever they want, and are allowed 'regular water and loo breaks'.

The aim of the seminars is to help people to 'see who they really are underneath... They also become aware of the fears and limiting beliefs they have, and may also start to drop some of the pretence and outer behaviours.' These 'outer behaviours' are the face we present to the world, which is often not how we really are; an insecure person might project brash self-confidence, for example. We are all a mixture of the person we really are, the person we fear we are, and the person we pretend to be, say Insight.

> On the seminar, people become more aware of how they are living their lives and more aware of how they may be holding themselves back. Often these things are unconscious. At the root of Insight's approach is the belief that each person starts life perfect and unlimited. Yet as life goes on, we have experiences that cause us to limit our expression in the world and to close down on our natural loving, spontaneity and creativity.
>
> These experiences can begin at birth and usually take place in childhood, where the patterns are laid down for later behaviour. An example of the kind of experience would be a small child being scolded for being noisy when it was simply expressing joy...
>
> So, rather than just being our natural unique selves, we develop fears and anxieties about life.

By revealing and dealing with their fears and anxieties, and those early negative experiences which are now limiting them, they can emerge with 'increased self-esteem and a clearer sense of their own unique qualities and strengths.'

Similar ideas are taught, sometimes with variations, by most human potential movements. Indeed, Insight's facilitators 'draw on a number of different approaches, including Gestalt, Core System Psychology and NLP.'

Menis Yousry of Insight Seminars says:

> During the seminar you will learn many powerful techniques and approaches which, when applied to your life, will allow you to have more of what you truly want. Each individual works with their own hopes, dreams and desires – be that better relationships, more self-confidence, a deeper sense of fulfilment and purpose, peace of mind, greater material success, better health, and so on. As well as enjoying the seminar, most people come away with a powerful and memorable reference point of what it is like to really feel content within themselves and with a renewed zest for life.[16]

The Sunday session concludes with a candle-lighting 'graduation ceremony', which friends and family may attend.

Insight's philosophy or 'vision statement' is 'Insight is committed to Loving as a practical reality worldwide.'[17] Its introductory literature suggests that there is a spiritual aspect to all this, but only in a broad sense. 'Where Insight differs from other personal development programmes is that at the centre of our philosophy is the heart, rather than the mind, and that the power of loving can heal everything.' Insight is portrayed as being '"spiritual" with a small "s" in that it deals with the human spirit', but it makes it clear that it is not religious.

Insight trainers or 'facilitators' are people who have been through several levels of training, including Insight IV, a five-week course in the USA; who have done at least two years on-the-job training in the seminar room; and who 'live the training to the best of their ability, and [are] a demonstration of what we teach.' Some of them have therapeutic qualifications, and some are Masters in Neuro-Linguistic Programming.

Insight seminars have an unusual payment system. Attendees pay £95 to reserve a place; 'at the end of the seminar you will be asked to consider the value you have received and to give accordingly. We suggest a figure of £395 as a guideline.' Some give more, some give less, and it's even possible to reclaim the original £95, 'provided you complete the seminar'.[18]

☼

There is no mention in Insight's introductory literature of its origins, beyond 'Insight began in California in 1978, and came to the UK in 1979. It was founded by Russell Bishop, an educational psychologist, and John-Roger, a teacher.' In fact its history goes back some way before 1978, and gives a clue to the spiritual background to Insight's psychological and educational teachings.

Insight grew out of the Church of the Movement of Spiritual Inner Awareness (MSIA) (see page 321). MSIA was founded in 1971 by John-Roger Hinkins (born 1934), with teachings related in many ways to those of Eckankar. As the Mystical Traveller, John-Roger has total awareness on all levels of consciousness, and MSIA aims to teach this same awareness to others. Related organizations include the University of Santa Monica, the Peace Theological Seminary and College of Philosophy, the Heartfelt Foundation – and Insight, which is probably the most public face of John-Roger's various enterprises.

Insight began when Bishop, who had experience as a Lifespring trainer (Lifespring grew out of the same source as est), held a Lifespring seminar for MSIA members. Apparently it was popular among members, but had a number of aspects which didn't seem right. In John-Roger's words,

> Insight came later, after much reflection as to how Lifespring didn't really work for us and how we wanted to put the Spirit into it and, therefore, change many of the Lifespring processes to fit what Insight wanted to do.[19]

Insight and MSIA were quite closely linked for some time, with many MSIA members taking Insight courses. 'One of the reasons that John-Roger gave for why Insight came into being was to "help all these spiritual MSIA people get their lives together".'[20] As more non-MSIA members took Insight courses, the two organizations became more separate, though there is still a vital connection: Insight Transformational Seminars is wholly owned by the University of Santa Monica, an MSIA educational establishment.

It would be wrong to suggest that Insight could be seen as a recruiting ground for MSIA. The relative numbers show that the vast majority of people who attend the basic Insight seminar have no interest in MSIA:

> Over 500,000 people have taken Insight since 1978. There are currently less than 5,000 people actively involved in MSIA and we have never had more than 10,000 actively involved in MSIA at any point. A recent survey of active MSIA participants in the United States showed that about 16 per cent of those responding gave Insight as a point of referral to MSIA.[21]

MSIA and Insight are two separate organizations doing different things. One is a religion; the other runs seminars for people who want to improve their lives. For a small number of people who want to go deeper, it might be that MSIA provides a spiritual development of the more psychological lessons learnt through Insight.

THE EMIN

The Emin are one of the few religious or semi-religious movements to have originated in Britain – though, like several of the other movements in this book, they say that they are not a religion as such: they are a group of people pursuing 'a natural philosophy and way of life.'[22] Like many other movements, they were stung by an article in the *Observer Magazine* (14 May 1995), 'A to Z of Cults', which described them as 'a highly secretive British cult' which held 'clandestine meetings'. In response, they point out that they have been holding public meetings for over 20 years; they have also published an introductory booklet.

HISTORY

The usual media story about the origins of the Emin has its founder Leo, then Raymond Armin, sitting under a tree on Hampstead Heath in London receiving enlightenment. The Emin say that as a boy, like many others, he had a favourite place to go and think about life, but that this story is 'really a simplistic misinterpretation of what, for any human, is a complex process'; in any case, this had nothing to do with the start of the movement *per se*. The Emin began some 30 years later, in 1972, when 'a group of people searching for the meaning and purpose of life, most of whom were widely travelled, academically qualified, and had spent years investigating numerous philosophies and religions' without finding satisfactory answers, happened to meet Armin 'through a chance encounter' in 1972.

The chance encounter was when Armin's son John, then an ambulance driver, picked up a young woman who was carrying a book of Sufi tales. John mentioned that his father read similar books, the two met, a few of the woman's friends joined them, and the Emin began. *Emin* is apparently an Arabic word for 'Faithful One'. The name is pronounced E-min rather than Em-in.

Raymond Armin, born Raymond Schertenlieb in 1924, was the son of a Swiss immigrant to Britain. The family surname was changed to Armin; it was quite common to change Germanic surnames between the wars.

His early years, as told by the Emin, have much in common with other founders of religious movements, from Madame Blavatsky to L. Ron Hubbard:

> His quest to discover the truth about living began as a young boy... During his young adult life he extensively researched and studied world history, science, world religions, philosophy and a whole range of other subjects. National Service took him to the Far East, where he explored Indian and other Eastern religions and traditions. These explorations were not just academic... The paramount quest in his life was to be true and aligned to whatever causes each human to be.

The Emin say that Leo never looked for followers, and they do not see him as their founder or leader, as such, 'but certainly the prime inspiration of those who formed the Emin endeavour.' When the early members of the Emin met him, 'they were staggered to find the great tangible results of his own researches and studies into many of the fundamental questions in living, which they found to be of uttermost use, not only in their own quest, but also in their everyday lives.' They persuaded him to provide them with writings and tapes of his researches, and began to pay him consultancy fees to enable him 'to pursue his research full time for the benefit of the growing number of Emin companions.'

Within two years there were about 70 members; now there are between 400 and 500 in Britain, out of a total of around 2,000 worldwide. These numbers have been stable for well over a decade, as new members balance those who leave. Around 200 of the British members have been in the Emin for over 15 years; Nick Woodeson and David Pearce, leading members in Britain, between them have 'nearly 50 years of experience in the Emin Endeavour.' Leo himself has retired from direct involvement in the Emin, though from his home in Florida 'he continues to provide written work under commission from various groupings.'

Around 1986, seven Emin families established a new Israeli settlement, known as the village of Maalé Tzvia, in Northern Israel.

It is important to bear in mind that the Village is, firstly, a domestic Israeli settlement supported by the Jewish Settlement Agency and the government and, secondly, an Emin village, in the sense that the adults are Emin members who have sought to build a way of life for themselves which recognizes both local custom and Emin principles, tenets and understandings.

The Emin Village has now grown to around 130 families, and is still expanding; because of its success 'it is now often used as a showcase example by the Israeli authorities,' say Woodeson and Pearce.

The movement has had a number of names over the years, which has led to some confusion. These include the Faculty of Colour and the Emin University of Life. The first ten years they now see as experimental, trying out various paths and researching different areas. In 1977 they began 'a more advanced exploration', called the Eminent Way, which 'marked the transition of the Emin from external researches to internal processes, from learning to living.' Although the name is no longer widely used, some individual members still pursue this area of work, which involves meditation.

Like several other movements in this book, the Emin accept that they have made mistakes in the past. 'The whole evolution of the Emin endeavour has been trial and error because it is a real human endeavour,' say Woodeson and Pearce. Even Leo, who is clearly regarded as a wise man rather than anything at all divine, has made mistakes in the way he has guided the movement. In 1978, for instance, he established a Church in America, and wrote a book called *The Poem of the Church of Emin Coils*. 'This was an attempt to establish a foundation upon which a religion could develop. This attempt was abandoned, and the book has long since been withdrawn.'

In 1978 the satirical magazine *Private Eye* alleged that Leo was a fraud; the Emin began the process of suing for libel, but dropped the case because of the expense. There was further controversy in 1983 and 1984 when Tory MP David Mellor tried to prevent the Emin from continuing to use a hall in Putney, London, which they had been using since 1976; a public enquiry ruled that they should be allowed to continue using it. Around the same time there were several articles and interviews with Leo and members of the Emin in local papers, none of which did the movement's credibility much good, though the Emin deny that Leo actually uttered the more sensational quotations attributed to him.

The movement is still developing. Leo's teachings, and the discoveries and researches of members, are gathered in the Emin Archives, 'one of the most extensive and original bodies of philosophical writings in the world.'[23] In 1993 'an effort was made to place all of the research that had taken place up to that time into a cohesive framework. Out from this came the "Emin Loom of research starters", which today forms the basis for the first few years of a person's engagement with the Emin.' Those undertaking this work are known as the Emin Stream. More advanced members follow two different streams, the Gemrod and the Acropolis.

BELIEFS AND PRACTICES

The dictionary definition and the popular use of the word 'belief' implies the acceptance *without proof* of things or statements. No one in the Emin is required to believe anything. People are encouraged to undertake their own research upon which they may prove, or disprove, the content of Emin teaching.

Emin teachings are open to constant revision and development, as members explore subjects more deeply. All their publications bear the statement 'This publication is sold on the condition that the reader understands that the content herein is entirely philosophical until such time as it may be proven as fact.' As well as allowing for continuous revelation, this presumably covers them against any possible errors of fact, and also against the possibility of disgruntled ex-members claiming they have been required to believe any particular principles.

The Philosophical Tenets of the Emin are:

1 That the creation is ordered by natural law and that it grows towards completion and that human life is a high point of this growth.

2 That the human also grows and is pressing toward its own evolution and completion.

3 That the human is spiritual and has a duty to the universe, to itself and to the rest of humanity.

4 That the endeavour of human life is to learn and develop and upgrade the ways and contents of the mental faculty and the whole human potential according to natural law.

5 That the human race is meant to be in unison and agreement concerning the conduct of life on earth.

6 That there is life after death and that this must be planned for and worked for individually.

7 That to be constructive and opportunity engendering is the true way to be properly participant in life.

From these Tenets come material responses, such as:

1 To uphold the rightful elected law of the land...
2 To seek to develop one's own potential to the uttermost and to use one's natural gifts to the full.
3 To be resistant to the lowering of standards...
4 To be constructive in the keeping of good order and stability...
5 To strive to be useful by one's own work... and to be supportive of natural freedoms...
6 To be pathfinder in various ways that unlock situations in learning which otherwise prevent further progress, and to try to expand boundaries of understanding as a duty to the future.
7 To seek to be constantly well informed and increasing so as not to offer hypocrisy or deception to others or to self from the standpoint of ignorance.

Generally there is a slightly old-fashioned courtesy about the Emin; for example, like the School of Economic Science (see page 274) they tend to refer to women as 'ladies'.

The emphasis in the Emin is on individual and group study and discovery; Leo's writings in the Emin Archives are seen more as guidelines than as gospel. The Emin Stream – the first few years of Emin work – is:

a live discovery into an array of subjects from theatre, the arts, barding, oratory, dance, to science, architecture, world history, the natural laws and the whole realm of personal development, behavioural sciences and becoming true to one's natural self.

The 'Emin Loom of Research Starters' is a complex seven by seven chart. Down the left are two Connection Domains – 'Mentality Imagery' and 'Brain Perception'; two Alignment Domains – 'Emotions (Higher and Lower)/Feelings' and 'Process Reasonings/Instinct, Thinking, Moving Centres'; and three Reference Domains – 'Functions, Soul Related/White-Red-Blue, White-Pale Yellow-Pale Blue', 'Groundwork, Headwork, Heartwork, Practice, Meditation', and finally, 'Learning, Understanding, Mixing, Matching'. Along the top are 1 Governing Views – 'Genius'; 2 Governing Reason – 'Genetic'; 3 Governing Intentions – 'Generation'; and four further unlabelled columns.

The contents of the grid are an excellent example of the specialist use of language within a religious movement (Scientology is another good example). Language is used in such a way as to make sense to a member of the movement, who has been introduced to the concepts and terminology gradually and systematically, while being utterly baffling to the outsider. This accounts in part for the accusations of secrecy often made against alternative religious movements.

(Incidentally, this is not necessarily a criticism of such movements. Someone with no familiarity with standard Christian terminology would be equally baffled by such 'technical terms' as salvation, atonement and Trinity, let alone Paraclete, predestination or transubstantiation. When the New Testament was put into Basic English, which has a vocabulary of only 850 words, it was found necessary to use 150 additional words because of the specialist nature of the text.[24])

Quoting just two examples taken at random from the 49 boxes of the Emin Loom will illustrate the point:

> 2–5 That the human complex, carnal and electromagnetic, is plasmagenic theatre allowing, in which the cosmic relation and government is 1/3 expendable, 1/3 maintenance, 1/3 custodial.
> 3–6 That human in planetary domicile is evolutary, individually and/or collectively, in the presence of transference, which is the persuasions of human semiconscious and superior conscious alignment by design and attribute and acumen.[25]

Senior members of the Emin move on from study based on the Emin Loom of Research Starters to two further streams, Gemrod and the Acropolis.

> The Gemrod reflects the movement in a person's journey from learning to a more serious practical application and development... It has an emphasis on behavioural science and the improvement and refinement of attitude and values. [The Acropolis is] the pinnacle of Emin research..., an 'Emin think tank' attempt to pioneer into the unknown and to explore the potential of human evolution.

Leo's books also use language in unusual ways. One of the primary Emin texts, Leo's first book Dear Dragon, begins:

> Hello, another person, whatever is your way and style. My name, self-chosen – for this, in truth, must it be – is POEM. Welcome to my purpose, that is not a story. Within this, you will learn and flavour much, that somehow, in some mysterious way, will move you, touch often something deep and powerful in your person.
> Description of normal kind will not suffice; for the Blue Roses of

Forgetfulness and that very fast something, seen from the corner of the eye, instantly gone, seen, but not understood, are only the path that leads to the first gate of passing through to the Way of the Dear Dragon...

Pemero sends you this gift... And although, you not remembering it in its entirety, I tell you, there are parts of you that will retain its essence eagerly.[26]

Dear Dragon is a mystical, poetical book, and its style of writing reflects this, but the language is strange, at times unwieldy, and often syntactically convoluted. A critic might ask – particularly as members of the Emin (like those of many other alternative religious movements) tend to be intelligent, cultured, middle-class people – why they do not at least tidy up Leo's grammar.

Like several other movements covered in this book, the Emin are clearly, as they say, involved in developing human potential, using different terminology and techniques but perhaps reaching towards similar ends to, for example, Insight (see page 434). Much of their terminology also reveals an esoteric element analogous to, for example, Builders of the Adytum (see page 362) – for example, 'birth on earth is the beginning of a universal organic immortality,' and 'human life is designed to be "living spirit of God" in unquickened universal expansions.'[27]

In addition, among the many areas of study for the Emin are astrology and Tarot. Their own Gemrod Tarot pack (Major Arcana only) is substantially different from traditional designs; some of the titles have been changed, including the Lover to Life, the Hermit to the Searcher, Temperance to 'The Communication (the Searcher reaches Land's End)', the Devil to the Green Man, and the World to the Nymph of Ability; the unnumbered Fool card has been dropped altogether. A later Major Arcana, marketed as the Frown Strong pack, also shows many differences from traditional packs, though this one does have a Fool equivalent, called 'The Card of Negation'.

It is widely recognized that the Tarot has been significantly misrepresented and misused throughout the course of history. Early Emin research included the construction of a pictorial mosaic of understanding, based on the study of the laws and the influences that affect human development. This was an attempt to rediscover the original nature of the Tarot, which constituted a comprehensive encyclopedia of human development... definitely not a fortune-telling tool.

The laws which are often mentioned both by the Emin and in accounts of them include several based on numbers. The law of two includes 'opposites/adjacencies, the male/female principles, energy and matter etc. The law of four concerns cyclic phenomena, i.e. the seasons, the phases of the moon, biorhythms, the four elements. The law of seven concerns the major planets and the spectrum colours, and the law of five concerns the five centres of the human, which are thinking, moving, instinctive, emotional and sexual.'

Although an earlier book on new religious movements asserts dismissively that 'Leo's laws seem to be a bizarre mix of psycho-babble and New Age interests,'[28] it is clear that the Emin, like many other alternative religious, philosophical and personal development movements, take an eclectic approach to their study and their teachings; if they find something useful, they use it. For example, both in their teaching of laws of number, and in their emphasis on dance and music as means of approaching inner truths and exploring human potential, there are strong echoes of Gurdjieffian philosophy.

One of the most visible expressions of their work, for outsiders, is their use of music, dance, theatre and art as means to unlock human potential; the Emin are often first encountered in their theatre or dance work. Different groups of Emin musicians have produced a number of music CDs and cassettes which seek 'to capture and clothe in sound, rhythm and harmony the fine essence qualities and values that can balance, refresh and realign a person to cause much well-being'.[29] The use of colour is also important to the Emin: 'green promotes vigour, yellow promotes value, blue promotes regulation,'[30] and so on.

The Emin Centre in north London, 'the primary meeting place for members and their research and project activities', offers Saturday workshops in art, dance, story-telling and the beauty of nature, in addition to meditation and 'Self Leadership – an ensemble of inner lives'.

One area which might be called 'New Age' is Aura Cleaning. The Emin teach that:

the electro-magnetic radiation of the human constitutes a field known as the aura. As the physical body needs regular cleansing, so does the aura. Headaches and irritability are often caused by imbalances in the aura. There are specific yet simple movements that we have developed to clear the pathways and balance the energy levels in the aura.

Former members mention groups of people flexing their fingers and flapping their arms rhythmically; the Emin say that what they call Electrobics works.

New members, after a few months, often take new names, a common practice in many religious movements both new (ISKCON) and old (Simon becoming Peter, Saul becoming Paul). The names are often colours or precious stones (Emerald, Opal), or qualities on which the member wants to concentrate (Patience, Hope); they can change their names at any point, to reflect their development. They no longer wear a tabard-like cotton tunic and satin sash over their normal clothes at meetings; now, 'people wear what they want'. Members are expected to contribute, depending on their financial circumstances, anything from a small amount up to £25 a week; this pays for 'the hire of halls, the purchase of equipment, and also includes salaries for administrators, consultancy fees for lecturers and commissioned researchers, including Leo.'

Perhaps because the teachings of the Emin are constantly developing, there has been confusion over some matters. For example, in the (now withdrawn) *Poem of the Emin Coils*, Leo inveighed against homosexuality, as one 'unnatural condition or freak practice' among several others; now, according to Woodeson and Pearce, 'the Emin does not refuse entry to homosexuals.' It does, like many of the esoteric schools, refuse to take on drug addicts or people with mental illness.

Some writers have made much of the different activities of men and women in the Emin. The movement stresses that it doesn't follow traditional stereotypes.

> Each gender obviously has its own nature, character, qualities and strengths which we recognise and seek to uphold... both genders are encouraged to be self-reliant and independent... We study extensively the meaning and significance of gender both in its human characterization and its appearance through all planetary life.

The Emin do not consider that they are the only ones with the truth.

> The Emin is not a religion. Personal spiritual development has always been possible for any human life... Emin companions hold their own religious beliefs. Many are Christians, Jews, Muslims etc. We uphold the right of all individuals to pursue their own faith.

On morality they say:

> We uphold anything that is constructive and progressive in the world, and stand against anything that is perverse or corrupt... We believe that common decency and good standards of moral behaviour are essential. We deplore the rapid erosion of these values.

At least in principle, anyone committing a criminal offence would be asked to leave – as would anyone seeking to use the Emin as a political forum.

The terminology of the Emin might at times be unusual, but their aims, and the various paths of study which they follow, appear to be an eclectic mixture of ideas common to many esoteric, New Age and personal development movements; the main difference from most other semi-religious movements is that the Emin started from scratch rather than being based on an already existing tradition.

SCIENTOLOGY

Scientology[31] is probably the most well-known, widespread and wealthy of all the personal development organizations – and the most attacked. Vast amounts have been written about it, internally and externally, pro and con.[32] The books and articles against Scientology are often written by ex-members, and opinion on their worth is divided. Critics of the religion say that some of these writers were members at high levels for many years, and that they have personal experience of what they are writing about. Others, including the Church itself, say that they are embittered apostates, that they have their own agendas, and that we shouldn't believe a word they say. The truth probably lies somewhere in between. The critical accounts of disenchanted ex-members of *any* religious movement are likely to be coloured by all sorts of emotions, and it is wise to treat them with a certain amount of discretion. On the other hand, they *were* members, much of what they say may well be factually accurate, and something unpleasant *might* have happened within the religion to make them so angry and bitter. Unless one is prepared to dismiss authors Cyril Vosper, Bent Corydon, Jon Atack and other former members of Scientology as compulsive liars, then there are many disturbing details in their books which ought not simply to be brushed aside as the embittered rantings of apostates.

Atack describes the method of 'Scientology's self-defence: divert the critic, attack the source not the information.'[33] In addition to the Church providing evidence countering them, criticisms of Scientology, especially by 'apostates', are often countered by negative statements about the critic,[34] with the implication that anything they say is unreliable or tainted by their unsavoury character.

This entry contains several criticisms of the Church of Scientology which the Church strongly denies. In some cases, for the outside observer, it comes down to a question of which side one is more prepared to believe. It would be as irresponsible for this book to accept wholesale all of the Church's denials of these criticisms as it would be to accept every attack on the Church as completely true. In any case, whether Scientology likes it or not, many of these criticisms have become part of the 'mythology' attached to the religion (see page 15), and so cannot simply be ignored. Wherever possible within this entry, where criticisms are made the response of the Church has also been included to provide a balanced account.

BELIEFS AND PRACTICES

Arguments have raged for years over whether Scientology is a religion or not; British sociologist Bryan R. Wilson matches beliefs and practices of Scientology against a list of 20 criteria of religions, and concludes that it is;[36] Australian sociologist Alan W. Black looks at Scientology in the light of Professor Ninian Smart's seven 'dimensions of religion' and comes to the same conclusion;[37] but Canadian sociologist Stephen A. Kent looks at the negative stories attached to Scientology and concludes that it is 'a multifaceted transnational corporation, only *one* element of which is religious'.[38] According to Graeme Wilson, Public Affairs Director of the Church of Scientology in the UK, '28 religious scholars have studied Scientology in detail and concluded that it is in fact a religion.'[39]

Some Scientologists have said that it isn't a religion at all, but simply a very efficient way of helping people deal with their lives. It is usually said that L. Ron Hubbard turned Dianetics, his original psychotherapy system, into the Church of Scientology, but Scientology says that the idea of starting a Church came from members, not from Hubbard himself. Members say that whatever attacks are made on the movement, they believe in Dianetics and Scientology because they work.

The aims of Scientology are: 'A civilization without insanity, without criminals and without war, where the able can prosper and honest beings can have rights, and where man is free to rise to greater heights.'[40]

In furtherance of these aims, the Church of Scientology has set up a large number of different organizations involved in several areas of humanitarian work. These include the drug rehabilitation programme Narconon, the Citizens Commission on Human Rights, Committee on Public Health and Safety, American Citizens for Honesty in Government, Committee for a Safe Environment, National Commission on Law Enforcement and Social Justice, Religious Research Foundation, Concerned Businessmen's Association of America, and The Way to Happiness Foundation – this last to improve society by improving individual morals and manners.[41]

The figures of eight million members, 100,000 of these in Britain, are often quoted.[41A] As these numbers include people who have only had one or two introductory auditing sessions, over nearly half a century, they are cumulative rather than current. There are around 130 Scientology churches in the world, and around 3,500 missions and other assorted small groups, in over 130 countries. The Church does not appear to have clear membership figures itself; one external estimate is that it might have as many as 750,000 members worldwide.[42]

Before Scientology came Dianetics, based on L. Ron Hubbard's new theory of how the mind works. This states that our unconscious or 'reactive' mind stores the trauma of every unpleasant thing that has ever happened to us, in a pictorial form known as an 'engram'. Engrams 'are a complete recording, down to the last accurate detail, of every perception present in a moment of partial or full "unconsciousness".'[43] The *Dianetics and Scientology Technical Dictionary* defines an engram as 'A mental image picture which is a recording of a time of physical pain and unconsciousness. It must by definition have impact or injury as part of its content.' Though we may forget the original incident, the engram is still active, and may be triggered by association.

For example, on a fine, sunny day you step out of a bakery in a seaside town, and begin to cross the road; a blue car pulls out to overtake a red bus; it catches your leg, spinning you round so that you fall and crack your head on the kerb, and black out for a few moments. There's no serious injury, so your conscious mind may eventually forget the incident, but your reactive mind stores every detail. For the rest of your life the sight of a blue car or a red bus, or the smell of freshly baked bread, or the cry of a seagull, or even the fact that it is a fine, sunny day, might trigger a 'remembered' pain in your leg, or cause you to start shaking with shock.

According to Hubbard, some of the most powerful engrams are received while you are still in the womb. The original *Dianetics* book contains graphic accounts of a husband yelling at his pregnant wife and striking her in the belly. The foetus hears its father's words, and the reactive mind stores them; though it cannot understand them at the time, those same words, heard in other contexts by the adult decades later, could trigger the engram, perhaps causing deep feelings of being unwanted or under attack.

Through auditing, such engrams can be deleted. The auditor asks the subject questions, leading him or her back to the original incident which caused the engram; once it is identified, its power is dissipated. The subject, known as a pre-clear (PC), holds two tin cans which are connected to an E-Meter in front of the auditor; this measures electrical skin conductivity and resistance in a similar way to a polygraph or lie-detector – though the Church claims it bears no resemblance to this, and that it measures instead 'the movement of mental masses'; 'mental image pictures... have weight and mass'.[44] After all engrams have been identified and disposed of – and this can be a lengthy process, lasting many months – the pre-clear goes Clear.

Many former Scientologists, who have left the Church for a variety of reasons, still believe in the efficacy of Dianetics. Like all forms of psychotherapy, counselling and confession, it clearly works to some extent, and has some obvious benefits – in Dianetics-speak, 'gains'. At the very least, by unburdening themselves of their guilts and hang-ups, PCs feel better. Although Scientology stresses that Dianetics has nothing at all to do with hypnosis, and that the person is fully aware of everything which is going on around him at all times, some critics and former members have suggested that auditing sessions also seem to induce something akin to the effects of a light trance, leaving the PC feeling a 'buzz' of well-being.

If this were all there was to Dianetics and Scientology few people, except perhaps the psychiatric professions, would find too much to worry about. But disposing of all the engrams acquired during your life, and even since conception, is not enough to enable you to go Clear. You also have to deal with any engrams from previous lives which are still troubling you. Scientology, like many other religions, believes in a form of reincarnation, though they do not usually use that word, preferring instead to speak of 'past lives'. Through auditing, you can recall aspects of your previous lives, and dispose of their engrams. Eventually all engrams have gone, and you have achieved Clear.

The precise meaning and claimed benefits of 'Clear' seem to have changed over the years, but two 1960s definitions were:

WHAT IS A CLEAR?
A Clear is an individual who has himself totally erased the destructive Reactive Mind, thus eradicating the seeming evil in Man. A Clear is wholly himself with incredible awareness and power.
HOW VALUABLE IS CLEAR?
Clear is priceless. This state has never before been achieved by Man. It is a stable state, not subject to relapse or deterioration.
WHAT DOES CLEARING DO?
It erases the Reactive Mind, overcoming the barriers to spiritual independence and serenity. It totally removes the cause of counter-efforts to one's happiness, awareness, goals and abilities.[45]

A person who can be at cause knowingly and at will over mental matter, energy, space and time as regards the first dynamic (survival for self). A Clear is a being who has attained this state by completing the Saint Hill Clearing Course and has been declared Clear by the Saint Hill Qualifications Division.[46]

A simpler (and glowing) description of what it means for someone to go Clear is:

Here is a being who has forever vanquished his own reactive mind, the source of man's misery. He has a very high degree of personal integrity and honesty, and is living proof that man is basically good. His own basic beingness returns and his own personality flourishes. When a person becomes Clear, he loses all the fears, anxieties and irrational thoughts that were held down by pain in the reactive mind and, in short, regains himself. Without a reactive mind, an individual is much, much more himself.[47]

At one time, to go Clear was the ultimate goal. The book *Dianetics: the Modern Science of Mental Health*, first published in 1950, claims that someone who has reached Clear will have better health, better eyesight and hearing, will be able to deal with any psychosomatic illness, and will have greatly increased intelligence. He (or she) will have become the optimum man (or woman).

> A clear, for instance, has complete recall of everything which has ever happened to him or anything he has ever studied. He does mental computations, such as those of chess, for example, which a normal [*sic*] would do in half an hour, in ten or fifteen seconds...[48]

Although it would be possible for two friends to reach Clear by auditing each other for free using the original *Dianetics* book, it is more usual to have professional auditing, and this can work out very expensive. 'You can't say how long it would take for each person,' says Wilson, 'but it would likely cost some thousands of pounds – of the order of magnitude of the price of a car, and very much longer lasting in result!'

Hubbard distinguishes between the lesser state of 'release' and Clear: 'But a clear is a clear and when you see it you will know it with no further mistake.' It is necessary for an auditor to check over the next few months that there are no new engrams in the reactive mind, but if there are not, then 'the clear is definitely and without question, cleared. And he will stay that way.'[49]

Hubbard's book speaks of many 'cases' having been cleared. In the early 1950s there were several well-publicized Clears – and at least one attempted public display of their powers. In 1950, for example, at a packed meeting, Hubbard followed a demonstration of auditing with the presentation of 'the world's first Clear', Sonia Bianca who, he claimed, had 'full and perfect recall of every moment of her life.' Unfortunately, she was unable to answer some questions put to her by the audience.[50] The Church now denies that she was ever referred to as 'the world's first Clear', and claims that this description of the demonstration 'is a misrepresentation of what really happened.'

These early Clears seem to have been forgotten by the mid-1960s. In a magazine published in 1967, we read:

> Saint Hill, February 14, 1967. A year ago to this day exactly, John McMaster completed his auditing on the Saint Hill Clearing Course to become the first Clear. On March 8, 1966 it was made official when John flew back from a Worldwide assignment in the United States and was checked out Clear by the Qualifications Secretary at Saint Hill. Shortly thereafter the news went out to the world in *Auditor* 14 that the last barrier to total spiritual freedom for Man had been vanquished by the incredible technology of L. Ron Hubbard.[51]

According to Wilson, McMaster (who left the Church of Scientology in 1969) 'was declared to be "Clear" before procedures for determining if someone had actually made it to Clear were fully developed and refined... [L]ater developments discovered that many had actually achieved Clear as early as the '50s, so he was not actually the first Clear, if he was Clear at all.' This seems to conflict with Hubbard's writing in 1950: 'But a clear is a clear and when you see it you will know it with no further mistake.'

The Church says, 'Did L. Ron Hubbard go Clear? Yes. In order to map the route for others he had to make it himself,'[52] but in fact at that point Hubbard himself hadn't achieved Clear; he became Clear no. 54, and his wife Mary Sue was Clear no. 208. By the anniversary of John McMaster becoming the first Clear, there were 234 Clears; just over a year later there were a thousand. The Church says that 'something over 44,000' people have now reached Clear.

The word 'technology', usually shortened to 'Tech', is important; Hubbard had developed a process which, if followed exactly by auditors and pre-clears, would lead to Clear. No deviation from the Tech was allowed; auditors could not add refinements; PCs could not short-cut the process.

This is why, says the Church, they are so opposed to anyone else using the methodology Hubbard designed: unless it is done *exactly* as he laid down, it can do more harm than good – Scientology-look-alike organizations, they say, are not only charlatans, but actively dangerous. 'It is important to stress that Scientology itself cannot harm anyone,' says Wilson. 'Some who have a desire to harm others (and unfortunately such people do exist), have *altered* Scientology technology, and added in methods of their own invention, in order to try and cause such harm.' Such people, Scientology refer to as 'squirrels'.

The Church says that the only organization which uses the correct methodology is the Church of Scientology; the Tech is kept pure by the Religious Technology Centre,

> a non-profit organization formed in 1982 to preserve, maintain and protect the Scientology religion. Religious Technology Centre holds the ultimate ecclesiastical authority regarding the standard and pure application of L. Ron Hubbard's religious technologies.[53]

More, perhaps, than in any other religious or semi-religious organization, there is a spiritual career path in Scientology. The road to Clear, known as the Bridge, is 'reached by small certain steps, not by huge leaps'.[54] Not everything is revealed at once. A fundamental precept of Scientology is: 'Be very, very certain you never go past a word you do not fully understand.'[55] As PCs progress up the ladder to Clear and beyond, they learn more and more of the philosophy which makes this a religion rather than just another form of psychoanalysis.

The new Scientologist learns early on that his inner self – what other religions might call his individual soul – is called a Thetan (pronounced with an 'a' sound, not an 'e' sound): 'the person himself... the identity that IS the individual.'[56] Beyond Clear is a further ladder; levels of Operating Thetan (OT) I–VIII were available before Hubbard's death, and there are currently 15 levels, though 14 years after his death OT IX–XV are still marked 'Not yet released' on the *Bridge to Total Freedom*, the Scientology Classification Gradation and Awareness Chart of Levels and Certificates. The Chart itself changes as new courses are added to it. Most of the first eight have apparently been rewritten or refined: OT I and OT IV–XV are described as 'New' on the Chart.

It is vital, in any 'progressive-knowledge' religion, that the information gained at these very high levels is kept secret. If the most junior member were able to find it out, says the cynical outsider, it would remove the entire spiritual career structure. The junior member is not ready for such powerful higher knowledge, says the believing insider.

Operating Thetan III ('The Wall of Fire') is the big revelation. Scientologists at OT III level are allowed access to Hubbard's hand-written notes of his own experience.

Hubbard referred briefly to the OT III revelation in a lecture:

> In the lower grades, one is mainly concerned with himself and his own case or his immediate family, but as one moves up the line one becomes more concerned with the environment and the world in which he lives; and with this concern, comes the realization that all has not been well.
>
> And it is very true that a great catastrophe occurred on this planet and in the other 75 planets which form this Confederacy 75 million years ago. It has since that time been a desert and it has been the lot of just a handful, to try to push its technology up to a level where someone might adventure forward, penetrate the catastrophe and undo it. We're well on our way to making this occur...
>
> It possibly is a bit above your reality to say that we intend to salvage this sector. No one has been able to do it for 75 million years. We are the first. In that period of time there has been nothing but suffering and misery for its populations.[57]

According to SF authority Peter Nicholls:

> Hubbard's SF had always emphasized the powers of the mind and deployed protagonists who maintained to the end a heroic stance against a corrupt Universe... [T]he latter vision may be what sustained Hubbard against the widespread execration he and his movement received from some quarters, both outside and inside SF.[58]

With typical melodrama, Hubbard warns that the knowledge revealed during the OT III course is so explosive it must be kept secret; anyone coming across it without the years of careful training through all the preceding levels would be seriously damaged. (Despite this, it seems that Hubbard had plans for a science fiction film related to the OT III story, for general release; in 1977 he wrote the screenplay for *Revolt in the Stars*, which was 'centred on the supposed incidents of 75 million years ago, providing many new details'.[59] The film was never made.)[59A] Even Hubbard himself nearly died learning of it: 'In December 1967 I knew someone had to take the plunge. I did and emerged very knocked out, but alive. Probably the only one to do so in 75,000,000 years.'[60]

The story at the heart of the OT III course[61] is a brief science fictional scenario involving the evil dictator of a Galactic federation – exactly the sort of thing that Hubbard produced in vast quantities in the 1940s and again towards the end of his life. All religions have their central myths; this is one of the hidden myths at the heart of Scientology – and there are yet further revelations beyond this: OT V is called 'The Second Wall of Fire', and OT VIII 'Truth Revealed'.

There was another whole set of mythology in Hubbard's 1952 book *The History of Man* which, according to psychologist Christopher Evans, was produced by Hubbard while lying on a couch at the Wichita Foundation, an early Dianetics Centre, in company with a tape recorder, an E-Meter and an auditor, Perry Chapdelaine (now a scientist and SF writer, and no longer associated in any way with Scientology). As Evans points out,[62] 'the free association characteristic of a psychoanalytic session', just like the hypnagogic images which can flash randomly across someone's mind when they are falling asleep, are not normally taken at face value by psychoanalysts. Evans comments, 'all was apparently accepted with calm deliberation – the most *outré* fantasies, the most oddball ideas being treated as unshakeable fact'.[63]

The History of Man, according to the introduction a 'factual account of your last sixty trillion years,' details the evolution of mankind through clams, molluscs known as Weepers or Boohoos, sloths, apes, and the by-then-not-yet-disproved Piltdown Man.

Most critics assume that Scientologists are supposed to take this book, and the science fictional stories in the OT revelations, as straight fact, which is after all how they are presented. Some apparently do. According to Chapdelaine, 'The problem for many people involved in Dianetics was that they accepted every word Hubbard said as literal truth, rather than a framework around which you could do things.'[64] Some Scientologists, though, do treat such stories as allegories, or parables, or teaching stories. As Lorraine Bulger, a Scientologist who has reached the very top of the Bridge, OT VIII, says:

Many religions have legends and scriptures which taken out of context can appear strange and misrepresentative, but when studied with wisdom and judgement and in context can give you a deeper insight into the philosophical nature of man.[65]

Hubbard himself may have intended them to be taken this way. In a poem called 'Personal Integrity' he writes:

> Nothing in Dianetics and Scientology is true for you
> Unless you have observed it
> And it is true according to your observation.
> That is all.[66]

The phrase 'true according to your observation' could be interpreted in many ways.

Scientologists at OT level, like those at the highest levels of any esoteric movement, will not talk about the content of those levels (in fact, it's rare for them to speak of their achieving OT at all); but Bulger comments on what the Operating Thetan courses have done for her:

> As an OT I have gained a deeper understanding of myself and other people. It's not what you know about yourself but what you don't know that you can have difficulty with. The advanced courses are an adventure into yourself; and into life. By giving me an insight into what holds people back and prevents them from being happy it's enabled me to help many people – including myself.
>
> It is analogous to the degree that each person gets his own benefit and understanding from researching past experiences. The basic premise of Scientology being, of course, that man is a spiritual being and has existed as such over many lifetimes. This is something you find out for yourself rather than you have to believe in, and can only benefit you to the degree it is *real* and *true* for you.

HISTORY

Scientology was founded by Lafayette Ron Hubbard (1911–1986), a very prolific pulp fiction author of the 1940s, known mainly for his science fiction.

SF experts have pointed out similarities between Hubbard's Dianetics and the fictional 'Science of Nexialism', a beneficial form of intensive psychological training, in some of the earliest stories[67] of SF writer A.E. van Vogt, a close friend of Hubbard in the 1940s. Van Vogt's novels *The World of Null-A* and *The Pawns of Null-A*,[68] popularized the General Semantics ideas of the linguist and philosopher Alfred Korzybski, which are thought to have been influential on Hubbard's development of the theories behind Dianetics. His very first novel, *Slan*,[69] featured 'a new race of supermen' who were 'the next evolutionary step':

> [I]ncreased mental powers would mark the inevitable next step on the evolutionary ladder... The ideas of Dianetics came so close to van Vogt's own notions

of the transcendent superman that in 1950 he stopped writing in order to devote himself full-time to running the Los Angeles Hubbard Dianetic Centre.[70]

There is a widely quoted story, which may or may not be apocryphal, that Hubbard and a friend were talking one night about that perennial preoccupation of writers, money. 'The easiest way to make a lot of money,' Hubbard is reported to have said, and paraphrasing Eric Blair (George Orwell)[71] by design or accident, 'is to found a new religion.' Another version of the tale is that Hubbard said this at a meeting. This is denied by the Church, which has called it 'an unfounded rumour'.[72] In fact, the idea goes back much further than Hubbard or Orwell. The Pagan philosopher Lucian, writing about Christianity some time before 180 CE, said:

> If a professional sharper who knows how to capitalize on a situation gets among them, he makes himself a millionaire overnight, laughing up his sleeve at the simpletons.[73]

Whatever the truth of it, he did found a new religion, and he did make a lot of money, although Wilson insists this came from the success of his books.

Hubbard's life pre-Dianetics, including his military career and his time as an 'explorer', is a source of some controversy.

In January 1946 Hubbard was involved in magickal ritual work with a leading member of the Ordo Templi Orientis, whose British leader was the 'Great Beast' Aleister Crowley. In 1945–6 Hubbard stayed for some months at the home of Jack Parsons, a brilliant rocket scientist and the acting head of the Los Angeles OTO. In a letter to Crowley, Parsons said that Hubbard was 'the most Thelemic person I have ever met and is in complete accord with our own principles.'[74]

Although Hubbard did not join the OTO, Parsons and Hubbard worked some major magickal rituals together. According to Parsons, first they performed a ritual to summon a 'scarlet woman', the future actress Marjorie Cameron; then, in March 1946, Parsons performed sex-magick with her, with Hubbard acting as 'the clairvoyant seer describing the happenings on the astral plane',[75] in an attempt to conceive a 'moon-child' – the antithesis of Christ – as first proposed by Crowley in his *Book of the Law* (1904) and fictionalized in his novel *Moonchild* (1929). The following month Hubbard ran off with Parsons' 19-year-old girlfriend Sara Elizabeth Northrup (known then as Betty), in a yacht he bought largely with Parsons' money. In Parsons' account, he caught up with them in Florida, casting a spell which raised a violent storm that ripped off the yacht's sails and nearly drowned them.

The Church of Scientology is very sensitive about this story. They challenge this account, saying that 'Hubbard was working as an undercover agent for the US Navy to break up black magic in America.'[76] According to Wilson, 'Mr Hubbard was indeed involved with Aleister Crowley – in order to break up Crowley's black magic ring! The Sara episode was part and parcel of his work on this matter.'

Whatever the truth of the matter may be,[77] Hubbard later made reference to both Parsons and Crowley, several years after their deaths. In an article in 1955 Hubbard wrote, 'I have been very fortunate in my life to know quite a few real geniuses – fellows that really wrote their name fairly large in the world of literature and science,'[78] and goes on to talk about Parsons. In a lecture in Philadelphia in 1952, Hubbard described Crowley's writings as 'a trifle wild in spots but is a fascinating work in itself,' and referred to Crowley himself as 'my very good friend'.[79] It should be pointed out that Hubbard never met Crowley, and also that there are no elements of magic, let alone sex-magick, in the teachings and practice of Dianetics and Scientology.

Hubbard claimed to have travelled the world as a young man, and to have been an explorer; the Church has produced glossy publications entitled *Ron: Letters and Journals: Early Years of Adventure*, and *Ron: Adventurer/Explorer: Daring Deeds and Unknown Realms*. Critics have said that although he travelled, his claims of exploration are if not fictitious, at least highly exaggerated.

Hubbard was, by profession, a storyteller; according to fellow SF writers, he could produce detailed plots of SF stories off the top of his head. At American Fiction Guild lunches, everyone told tall stories about their exploits; the difference was, according to one writer, that Hubbard seemed to expect people to believe his.[80] Eventually, some critics say, he came to believe them himself. In response to such criticisms, the Church points to Hubbard's journals and photographs, and awards from institutions such as the Explorers Club.

Whether true or exaggerated, tales of Hubbard's early life, like those of Madame Blavatsky, G.I. Gurdjieff and several other founders of religious movements, have become part of the mythology of the religion. The authorized version of Hubbard's life and endeavours is well documented by the Church.[81] It includes his achievements as an explorer, scholar and scientist.

In response to critics who allege that Hubbard claimed more war decorations than he was actually awarded, and that his naval exploits were similarly over-inflated, the Church produces documentary evidence supporting Hubbard. However, his true role in World War II, they say, was highly classified because of his intelligence work, and so could never be proved by official documentation.

In 1980 Hubbard agreed that an official, Scientology-approved biography should be written by Omar Garrison, and researched by Gerry Armstrong, the stepson of Heber Jentzsch, President of the Church. Armstrong began his research, with full access to Hubbard's personal archives. According to his account, he became disturbed by the disjunction between the 'approved' story and the actual facts. He was still loyal to both Scientology and Hubbard, and in his concern wrote to the Messengers, who were then effectively running Scientology (Hubbard having gone into seclusion), saying:

> If we present inaccuracies, hyperbole, or downright lies as fact or truth, it doesn't matter what slant we give them; if disproved, the man will look, to outsiders at least, like a charlatan.[82]

The Church ordered Armstrong to be 'security checked' (an internal procedure), and declared him to be a Suppressive Person. At about this time Armstrong left Scientology, taking with him copies of sufficient documentary material to support his claims of the vast differences between the fiction and the reality. This was perhaps a mistake. The Church took him to court to make him hand back the material he had effectively stolen. The court cases rumbled on for years. According to Wilson, 'Armstrong turned out to be a dishonest and superficial researcher who never examined more than a fraction of the material available to him, and who was later forced to admit his incompetence in court.'

In the end the Church won; in December 1986 it forced Armstrong to a settlement, part of which was that 'he would not assist any persons litigating any claims against the Church.'[83] Armstrong later said that he had been pressured into signing this, and in 1990 'began to undertake actions which directly violated the agreement he had made.' In 1992, 1995 and 1996 various American courts upheld the settlement, awarding costs of $321,923 against Armstrong, who filed for bankruptcy and left the USA.

Critics see this entire sorry story as a heavy-handed organization using its wealth and the power of the courts to suppress the truth. Unsurprisingly, the Church sees it somewhat differently, as Wilson explains:

> Gerry Armstrong is very far from being a reliable source of information... Armstrong carried out a failed scheme involving the forging of 'incriminating' evidence and the secret planting of that evidence on Church premises... This is a man who was recently found in multiple contempts of court for violating court orders. He now lives in Canada, a fugitive from jail sentence should he return to the US.

When the British TV station Channel 4 screened a *Real Lives* documentary on Hubbard, in part based on Armstrong's material, the Church of Scientology made its own video, *Merchants of Chaos*, in response, painting a very negative picture of Armstrong. It also provides a transcript of a secretly videotaped conversation in which Armstrong says, 'You don't have to prove a goddamn thing! You don't have to prove s——t! You just allege it!' Some critics have suggested that the meeting amounted to entrapment because Armstrong was led to believe that the other person (known as 'Joey') was a disaffected Scientologist wanting to set up a dissident group.[84]

It should be pointed out that the Church's various statements that Armstrong is a criminal on the run from the law, while true, all stem from Armstrong's original claim that the Church was telling lies about its founder.

Back in May 1984, in one of the early court cases which Armstrong won, Los Angeles Judge Paul G. Breckenridge had commented:

> The organization clearly is schizophrenic and paranoid, and this bizarre combination seems to be a reflection of the founder, LRH. The evidence portrays a man who has been a pathological liar when it comes to his history, background and achievements. The writings and documents in evidence additionally reflect his egoism, greed, avarice, lust for power, and vindictiveness and aggressiveness against persons perceived by him to be disloyal or hostile.[85]

The Church says that Breckenridge's opinion was based solely on Armstrong's falsehoods, that Hubbard was never a party to the suit and that Breckenridge never met him.[85A] It views Hubbard very differently:

> Every few hundred or a thousand years, some genius rises and man takes a new step toward a better life, a better culture. Such a man is L. Ron Hubbard, the Founder of Scientology.[86]

Although a short piece about it was published in the Winter/Spring 1949–50 issue of *The Explorers Club Journal* under the title 'Terra Incognita: The Mind', details of the new science of Dianetics were first revealed to the world in April 1950 in a 40-page article in the magazine *Astounding Science Fiction*,[87] to which Hubbard was a regular fiction contributor; its influential editor, John W. Campbell, like many other SF writers and readers at the time, was initially an enthusiastic supporter of Dianetics, and had been plugging it in advance for months. Hubbard's early science fiction, say SF authorities John Clute and Peter Nicholls, 'often came to haunt his readership, and its canny utilization of superman protagonists came to tantalize them with visions of transcendental power.' They continue:

> The vulnerability of the SF community... to this lure of transcendence may help account for the otherwise puzzling success first of Dianetics, then of Scientology itself, which gained many early recruits from SF; for, both as tech-

nique and as religion, these very US bodies of doctrine centrally posited a technology of self-improvement, a set of instructions to follow in order to liberate the transcendent power within one.[88]

SF writer Isaac Asimov was an exception; he thought that Dianetics – 'out of which Hubbard would make his fortune and gain his godhead' – was 'gibberish'; according to Asimov, Campbell 'had broken with Hubbard and was out of the Dianetics movement' by May 1951.[89] SF writer A.E. van Vogt initially ran the Los Angeles Dianetic Research Foundation, but split away early on to run his own version, firmly based on Dianetic principles, but without Hubbard's later religious ideas, with which he openly disagreed. The British SF writer and editor George Hay, as secretary of the British Dianetics Association in the early 1950s, was the first to invite Hubbard to Britain. Hay, no longer involved with Scientology for many years, recalls his first meeting with Hubbard:

> This was in the early 50s, when Dianetics was being transmogrified into Scientology and the whole subject was liable to change overnight. Any scepticism this might have created was cancelled out by the combination of Hubbard's extraordinary powers (I can vouch for it that he could read minds as a matter of routine) and the gains that members of the group were getting.[90]

In May 1950 Hubbard published *Dianetics: the Modern Science of Mental Health*, which laid down the basics of Dianetics, including the removal of engrams by auditing. The book was an immediate bestseller in therapy-conscious America, and small independent Dianetics groups sprang up all over the country, practising the system laid down in Hubbard's book.

Right from the very start there were problems. In 1950 the Hubbard Dianetic Research Foundation was founded; in 1951, when money was short, cash was put in by Don Purcell, who became President of the Foundation. Hubbard sold all his interests to Purcell, including his copyright to the Dianetics book. Then, in 1952, the Foundation went bankrupt. Hubbard founded the Hubbard Association of Scientologists International, and began suing Purcell for using his ideas. In 1954 Purcell, now associated with an early Dianetics splinter group, Synergetics, handed back the Dianetics copyrights to Hubbard.

All of this is related in quite a different light by the Church of Scientology, which has made available a letter from Hubbard to Purcell:

> Purcell, this is a standard oilman swindle whereby one acquires all the rights, through 'voluntary bankruptcy' and thus squeezes out all other interests, to an oil well. It is a legal sort of fraud. Dianetics isn't oil. And it isn't a new way to pad up your already over-swollen fortune. You lost on this swindle because too

many people were too quick for you and your attorneys are too stupid.

Having failed to grab Dianetics for your own profit by this swindle of 'bankruptcy'... you have now made a grab for all the Dianetics books. And you have lost there...

You are a perjurer, Purcell, and you know it well...

You want to know what's wrong with America, Purcell? It's people like you, snatching and gasping [*sic*] for profit and wrecking reputations and lives or anything to seize profit...

You have promised to hurt me so badly I will never recover unless I put Dianetics solidly and forever into your hands...[91]

Whatever actually went on between Hubbard and Purcell, the story is not particularly edifying.

In 1955 the Church of Scientology was incorporated as a non-profit-making society; within three years the US Internal Revenue Service was attempting to withdraw its tax exemption.

In 1959 Scientology began to use the Hubbard Electropsychometer, or E-Meter. According to Scientology, 'The first E-Meter designed and built to Ron's exact specifications is produced,' in 1959.[92]

The device – basically a galvanometer that detects changes in electrical resistance of the skin due to stress (or, in Wilson's words, 'caused by the movement of mental masses') – had actually been developed some years earlier, not by Hubbard, but by Volney G. Mathison, as the Mathison Electropsychometer. This was a technical aid to his own system of 'Creative Image Therapy', which the Church says was created after his association with Scientology.

Creative image therapy is a practical psychical method for the treatment of physical diseases, and for the eradication of unhappy mental states created by anxieties, worries, fears, nervous tension, and the like.[93]

Mathison's system of therapy, which was taught at 'Sequoia University' (which, coincidentally, awarded Hubbard an honorary PhD in 1953 'in recognition of his outstanding work and contributions in the fields of dianetics and scientology'[94]), bore a marked resemblance to Dianetics. It worked by 'bringing up into conscious awareness all major "automatic" negative image patterns in control in the subconscious area of the personality.'[95] (It is not being suggested that either Mathison or Hubbard 'borrowed' ideas from the other, but that two people had ideas for broadly similar therapeutic systems at roughly the same time.)

Mathison showed his Electropsychometer to the Hubbard Research Foundation in late 1950 or early 1951, and Scientology used it until 1955. It was later replaced by the Hubbard E-Meter.

The E-Meter measures the spiritual state or change of state of a person and thus is of enormous benefit to the auditor in helping the pre-clear locate areas to be handled. The reactive mind's hidden nature requires utilization of a device capable of registering its effects – a function the E-Meter does accurately.[96]

Interestingly, by the time Mathison wrote *Creative Image Therapy* in 1954 he was disillusioned with Dianetics and Scientology. He speaks of 'the fictitiously self-assured gabble' of 'some "Scientology" group', and disparagingly describes some of the common features of 'a pseudo-scientific system of something or other' which in context clearly refers to Dianetics auditing sessions.[97]

Although the E-Meter very quickly enabled Dianetics auditors to run their sessions on a more 'scientific' basis, it also got Hubbard into further trouble. In 1963 the powerful Food and Drugs Administration (FDA) raided the Scientology church in Washington, removing E-Meters on the grounds that it is illegal in the USA to practise any form of medical diagnosis or therapy unless qualified. In 1971 the E-Meters were returned to the Church, but a court ruling allowed their use only if they bore:

a prominent clearly visible notice warning that any person using it for auditing or counselling of any kind is forbidden by law to represent that there is any medical or scientific basis for believing or asserting that the device is useful in the diagnosis, treatment or prevention of any disease. It should be noted in the warning that the device has been condemned by a United States District Court for misrepresentation and misbranding under the Food and Drug laws, that use is permitted only as part of religious activity, and that the E-meter is not medically or scientifically capable of improving the health or bodily functions of anyone.[98]

Wilson comments: 'Scientology does not, nor does it claim to, carry out medical diagnosis or therapy. Nor has the E-Meter ever been intended to "treat illness".' Perhaps not now, but the reason for the court's ruling was that it had found that 'the literature of Dianetics and Scientology contains false and misleading claims of a medical and scientific nature.'

According to the Church, all the attacks through the years on Dianetics and Scientology originated from one source. After discussing the 'groundswell of public enthusiasm' which greeted the publication of the original *Dianetics* book in 1950, the Church continues:

There were, however, a scant few among society's ranks who were not quite so enthusiastic, i.e. certain key members of the American medical/psychiatric establishment... They were well entrenched and well connected; and when they decided that Dianetics must be stopped to preserve their kingdom, they were fully prepared to make use of every one of those connections.[99]

'Those connections' apparently included the US intelligence services, the FBI, the Internal Revenue Service (IRS), and the FDA. Thus began a bitter fight between the Church and the authorities.

L. Ron Hubbard was implacably opposed to the psychiatric profession, and the Church continues his campaign today. Most of the chapter 'Those who oppose Scientology' in *What Is Scientology?* is a virulent attack on the psychiatric profession; so is the first third of the 90-page brochure *A Description of the Scientology Religion*.

Two leading medical and psychiatric journals had turned down Hubbard's initial paper on Dianetics. It was perhaps understandable that psychiatrists would not welcome a book on their subject written by a layman who told them that they were completely wrong. But it is more than simply pique on both sides. The psychiatric profession and Scientology appear to view each other as equally dangerous.

The Church campaigns strongly against psychiatric malpractice around the world, including psycho-surgery, electro-convulsion therapy and personality-altering drugs.

Since the Church of Scientology's inception, its parishioners have remained steadfastly opposed to the brutal treatments, criminal practices and human rights abuses which are the stock in trade of the mental health field.[100]

Through its Citizens Commission on Human Rights 'the Church has relentlessly exposed psychiatric criminality and oppression.'[101]

The psychiatric profession, according to the Church, is still attacking them, and is still behind other attacks on them.

Although the more than forty-year assault against Scientology assumed large proportions, the source must be remembered – that small but influential circle of psychiatrists. Nor did the means change over the years: false allegations selectively planted in the media, then seeded into federal files as background 'fact'.[102]

The battles continued. The Church of Scientology has clashed with governments around the world, and is rarely out of the courts. It has been embroiled in legal fights in many countries in its attempts to be classed as a tax-exempt religion. Only a few examples will be given here.

An Australian Board of Inquiry reported in 1965 that:

Scientology is a delusional belief system, based on fiction and fallacies and propagated by falsehood and deception... the world's largest organization of unqualified persons engaged in the practice of dangerous techniques which masquerade as mental therapy.[103]

Despite strong opposition from some politicians, Scientology and the use of E-Meters were banned in Australia, although in 1976, under a different government, Scientology received a public apology from the West Australian Deputy Prime Minister. The ban was lifted, and in 1983 Scientology was ruled to be a tax-exempt religion:

The applicant [The Church of the New Faith, later renamed the Church of Scientology] has easily discharged the onus of showing that it is religious. The conclusion that it is a religious institution entitled to the tax exemption is irresistible.[104]

In 1968 the UK government banned any foreign Scientologists from coming to Britain either as students or to work. This effectively cut Hubbard off from his HQ at Saint Hill, East Grinstead. Three years later Labour MP Richard Crossman commented on the ban on BBC Radio: 'I personally very much regretted it [the ban] had been done without a really thorough investigation... I thought the Scientologists had a legitimate complaint.'[105] The ban was not revoked until 1980.

In a 1984 child custody case in Britain, despite, in Wilson's words, the Church not being 'given any right of audience during the conducting of the case,' Judge Latey said:

Scientology is both immoral and socially obnoxious... In my judgement it is corrupt, sinister and dangerous... it is based on lies and deceit and has at its real objective money and power for Mr Hubbard, his wife and those close to him at the top.[106]

Considering these and many other public criticisms of Scientology, it is hardly surprising that the Church has felt for years that it is under attack. To quote a French saying about human nature, '*Cet animal est très méchant; quand on l'attaque il se défend.*' Scientology sought to defend itself by going on the attack, and proved itself in the process to be somewhat more than merely *méchant* (mischievous, disagreeable).

From the point of view of some ex-members, a Suppressive Person (SP) was any Scientologist who violated Ethics, which could mean something as slight as questioning an order; according to Wilson, SPs are defined as 'those who are destructively anti-social.' SPs were 'bounced' down the career structure, and were effectively sent to Coventry (cf. the Exclusive Brethren, page 163-164). Wilson makes the point that most religions have some mechanism of excommunicating or disfellowshipping seriously troublesome members.

In October 1968, in a Policy Letter to members, Hubbard defined the principle of Fair Game against SPs, or any other perceived threat to Scientology: '[They] may be deprived of property or injured by any means by any Scientologist without any discipline of the Scientologists. May be tricked, sued or lied to or destroyed.'

In response to criticism, Fair Game was officially abolished only a month later. Hubbard signed an affidavit in 1976 affirming that:

> There was never any attempt or intent on my part by the writing of these policies (or any others for that fact), to authorize illegal or harassment type acts against anyone.
>
> As soon as it became apparent to me that the concept of 'Fair Game' as described above was being misinterpreted by the uninformed, to mean the granting of a licence to Scientologists for acts in violation of the law and/or other standards of decency, these policies were cancelled.[107]

Opponents say that 'Fair Game' may have been cancelled, but the principle remained, and still remains. Indeed, Stacey Brooks Young, who worked in the mid-1980s in 'the PR Division of the Guardians Office, which by that time had been renamed the Office of Special Affairs,' has said in court:

> As a result of this work I became very familiar with the policies and practices of Scientology with regard to individuals and groups that criticize the organization. I have personal knowledge that the practices which were formerly called 'Fair Game' continue to be employed, although the term 'Fair Game' is no longer used. These tactics are laid out in many of the key policies that are studied and applied by staff of OSA.[108]

According to Wilson, 'Stacy Young has her own vested interest in attacking our Church'; the Church claims that she is an unreliable source and that what she says is untrue.

Hubbard resigned as Executive Director International of the Church of Scientology in 1966, established the Sea Org (organization), and

> set to sea with a handful of veteran Scientologists to continue his research into the upper levels of spiritual awareness and ability...
>
> Today the majority of Sea Organization members are located on land, but in

keeping with tradition, many still wear maritime uniforms, and all have honorary ranks and ratings.[109]

The 5,000 Sea Org members (around 400 in the UK) are the elite corps of Scientology, a 'fraternal religious order' who sign a billion-year contract 'to symbolize their commitment to the religion as immortal spiritual beings'. They hold the senior ecclesiastic positions, technical jobs and PR posts within the Church, and give the most advanced training and auditing. Like some other religious Orders, they live communally.

While Hubbard was alive, Sea Org members were unswerving in their loyalty to him. 'The Commodore' spent the next ten years sailing around the world, mainly in the Mediterranean and the eastern Atlantic coast.

According to some reports by ex-members, shipboard life in the late 1960s and early 1970s could be hard for everyone except Hubbard, whose Messengers, mainly teenagers brought up in Scientology who were devoted to him, did everything from cooking his meals and washing his clothes (with 17 rinses to remove the smell of soap), to lighting his cigarettes for him. For anyone who stepped out of line, ex-members have said that punishments could be severe, including being thrown overboard. Hubbard may have been charismatic, but apparently he could also be very irascible. Tales by ex-members of unpleasant treatment in the Sea Org can be found in many books and Internet sites on Scientology. According to the Church, however, many Sea Org members and Messengers found their time with Hubbard very rewarding.

One of the criticisms most often levelled against Scientology is that it takes over its members' lives, making them behave in ways they might prefer not to, such as with the forbidding of Sea Org members to have children. There is no doubt that Scientology has rules and regulations laid down for many internal procedures. For example, the Church says that the rigid structure of auditing sessions is because the system has been proved to work, and that auditors should be discouraged from adding 'improvements' or 'refinements' of their own; it is the exact process of auditing which has results, not the personality of the auditor. But Wilson challenges any idea of totalitarianism in Scientology:

> The whole purpose of Scientology is to make the person more able, put him in control of his own life, able to solve his own problems, improve his life, help others... Scientology teaches you how to think for yourself and how to raise your own self-determinism.

The Ethics procedure has also come in for much criticism. This is a description of Ethics from a Scientologist who was in the Church from 1967 to 1992:

Ethics is the method of keeping everyone's mind controlled into thinking and seeing one way only to the point of ignoring major faults in the Scientology leaders, the organizations and the Hubbard technology itself...

Once you have bit the bait and have completely joined Scientology, you are channelled in that vein of thinking from there on out with the use of Ethics procedures.[110]

The Church claims this writer, Mary Tabayoyan, is an unreliable witness. According to Wilson, 'The person quoted in this section has been discredited in numerous declarations.' He provides the somewhat different definition of Ethics in the *Scientology and Dianetics Technical Dictionary*:

Ethics actually consist, as we can define them now in Dianetics, of rationality toward the highest level of survival for the individual, the future race, the group, and mankind, and the other dynamics taken collectively. Ethics are reason. The highest ethic level would be long-term survival concepts with minimal destruction, along any of the dynamics.

For what are judged to be major infringements of Ethics, says another former member, Cyril Vosper, Scientologists have to appear before a Committee of Evidence, which rules on four classes of offence: Errors, Misdemeanours, Crimes and High Crimes. High Crimes include, among many others:

Testifying as a hostile witness against Scientology in public.
Announcing departure from Scientology (but not by reason of leaving an organization, a location or situation or death).
Seeking to resign or leave courses or sessions and refusing to return despite normal efforts.
Continued adherence to a person or group pronounced a Suppressive Person or Group by the Hubbard Communications Office.[111]

According to Vosper, this last includes having any contact whatsoever with your husband or wife if they have been declared a Suppressive Person; the Church denies this.[112]

In 1966 the Guardian's Office (GO) was set up as a sort of intelligence unit; according to a former member who worked in it, this was:

a highly confidential section of Scientology management which was known as the Guardian Office until 1982 and is today called the Office of Special Affairs.

This section of Scientology is responsible for dealing with all external public relations, all matters relating to civil litigation or criminal matters, all governmental relations such as the IRS, and all critics of Scientology.[113]

Unfortunately, like many intelligence agencies, GO took on the role of dirty-tricks department, apparently digging up dirt on its opponents, who included lawyers, politicians, psychiatrists and trouble-making ex-members, with the aim of silencing them or blackening their names. Hubbard's third wife Mary Sue Hubbard, as either Guardian or Controller, had ultimate authority over the GO from 1966 up to her removal in 1981.

GO agents were infiltrated into the American Internal Revenue Service (IRS) and other government departments in what they called 'Operation Snow White' in 1975–6, both to 'borrow' intelligence files on politicians and celebrities and legal files about Scientology (the 'black propaganda' which the Church claimed the US government was using against Scientology), and to plant information themselves. Tens of thousands of official documents were stolen, photocopied and returned.[116]

In 1979, Mary Sue Hubbard, with eight other senior Scientologists, was found guilty of several criminal activities; they were fined £10,000 and imprisoned for between four and five years. The head and deputy head of the Guardians, who had fled to Britain in 1977, received similar sentences when they were returned to the USA in 1980. After many appeals Mary Sue Hubbard eventually went to jail in 1983, serving only one year.

The Church of Scientology now says that the Guardian's Office,

initially created in 1966 as a unit to deal with the Church's legal and external affairs... had been infiltrated and set up to fail in its mission to protect the Church. It was influenced to abandon its original mandate and established itself as an independent autonomous unit, answerable to nobody. It was isolated... even from the Founder of the religion.

By the late 1970s,

the Guardian's Office had abandoned any pretence of following the principles described in Mr Hubbard's writings... a handful of GO staff members had been influenced to adopt an 'anything goes' approach in dealing with government discrimination against the Church. These dupes infiltrated and burglarized several US government offices to obtain copies of files maintained and circulated about the Church. Obviously such activity was illegal and directly violated Mr Hubbard's policies... GO managed to keep its operations secret from Church management, staff and membership.[117]

The Church doesn't say who GO was 'infiltrated' by, or who 'influenced' its most senior staff. According to Atack, at the time when it was 'isolated... even from the Founder of the religion', Mary Sue Hubbard was still living with her husband.[118]

☀

In 1980 Hubbard went into seclusion. Only a handful of senior Scientologists, who did not include his wife, ever saw him again.[119] He began work on his ten-volume 'Mission Earth' science fiction series, most of which was published posthumously, leading to claims that at least some of it was 'ghost-written'; however, Hubbard was always a fast writer.

With the bad publicity of the revelations of criminal behaviour by the Guardian's Office, including Hubbard's own wife, and with Hubbard's hand officially no longer on the tiller, the Church went through a difficult period. Because of the rigid systems laid down by Hubbard in his literally thousands of bulletins, it was easy for Scientologists to find fault with and inform on each other, and for whatever reasons – Wilson says 'for their attempt to usurp the Church' – many senior people, who had devoted their lives and energies to Scientology, were 'busted' to much lower positions. Many left the Church.

Into the chaos, in 1981, stepped 21-year-old David Miscavige, who had been one of Hubbard's most trusted aides as a teenager in the Commodore's Messenger Organization (CMO) within the Sea Org. There are understandable differences in the interpretation of the ensuing events from critical former members who were involved in the traumatic changes of the next year or two, and who left or were expelled, and from today's Church organizations which are the result of those changes. The Church is very sensitive about any questioning or criticism of Miscavige's actions.

Suffice to say that several powerful new organizations were set up. The Commodore's Messenger Organization already existed, consisting largely of young Scientologists who had worked personally for Hubbard and were fiercely loyal to him, and who, for their age, had considerable authority. In May 1979 the Watchdog Committee was set up, consisting entirely of Messengers; in September 1979 it announced that it had control of the senior management of the Church.[120] In 1981 the All Clear Unit (ACU) was set up, ostensibly to fill in for Hubbard and prepare for when he came back to open prominence.[120A] The ACU also became powerful. Various senior members of the CMO and of the GO, for many years two of the most powerful bodies in Scientology, were fired and replaced. Some of those who were deposed had been in Scientology since Miscavige was an infant, if not before he was born, and were highly respected, very senior figures.

In the Church's words, 'Mr Miscavige had the personal courage and the moral certainty to entirely dismantle the GO. Those who had engaged in criminal actions were dismissed from the church, never to be hired again.'[121]

Critics see Miscavige's actions as a coup: the Young Turk clearing out the Old Guard, all those who might challenge his new authority. The Church today sees it differently:

When the GO's criminal activities were discovered by those who today form the core of the Church's leadership, the GO was disbanded, no small feat since it was the GO officials who held corporate control

– which seems to conflict with the previous statement that 'GO managed to keep its operations secret from Church management'. The statement continues:

Sadly, there were also some people in the Church, but outside of the GO itself, who sympathized with the GO... In some cases, it was the Scriptures themselves they wanted to pervert for their own ends. Given these people had proved themselves to be avowed enemies of L. Ron Hubbard and the religion, they were excommunicated... This cleanup of the GO was led by Mr David Miscavige, who removed all corporate control from the hands of the GO, and dismissed all personnel who had been involved in illegalities or attempts to alter Mr Hubbard's technologies. Mr Miscavige and a team of Church executives then set up an entirely new corporate and administrative structure for the Scientology religion which has since served to keep the religion pure and in accordance with the teachings laid out by its Founder.[122]

Two further organizations were set up, the non-profit Religious Technology Centre (RTC) and the external, profit-making corporation Author Services Incorporated (ASI). Hubbard donated all the trademarks of Dianetics and Scientology to RTC, whose role, says Wilson, was 'protecting the orthodoxy of Scientology'. According to the Church:

Mr Hubbard... was concerned that sufficient provisions be in place to prevent attempts to alloy or subvert the purity of the religious teachings of Scientology. He desired that an organization be founded that would carry out this function. This is RTC.[123]

Author Services Incorporated, of which Miscavige became Chairman of the Board in 1982, was set up late in 1981 to control the massive publishing empire based on Hubbard's books, both non-fiction and fiction. These include the Mission Earth 'dekalogy', which Scientologists see as innovative, thought-provoking and inspiring – 'acclaimed as a genuine masterpiece of the genre.'[124] Though some SF writers and critics have praised it as good old-fashioned SF adventure ('heroes and villains on an epic scale'[125]), this is not an opinion universally shared in the professional SF community. The authoritative *Encyclopedia of Science Fiction*, for example, says that its 'farcical overemphases fail to disguise an overblown tale that would have been more at home in the dawn of the pulp magazines.'[126] Perhaps the greatest value in publishing these books, for Scientology, is in spreading Hubbard's name and ideas as far and wide as possible – in essence, religious PR.

By early 1982 Scientology was under the control of RTC and ASI, the former protecting the Tech, the latter protecting all of Hubbard's writings. People who had formerly been in positions of power found themselves without any authority. One of these was David Mayo, who had worked personally with Hubbard to design the highest OT levels. Mayo has often been referred to as Hubbard's right-hand man and heir-apparent to the running of the Church, though the Church now says there was no evidence for this. By the beginning of 1983, along with many others of the old guard, Mayo had been declared a Suppressive Person. He left the Church of Scientology and set up an Advanced Ability Centre – one of several Scientology-look-alike splinter organizations which, unlike the independent Dianetics splinter groups of the 1950s, also taught the higher OT levels.[126A] Bill Franks, whom Hubbard had appointed Executive Director International – effectively 'Ecclesiastical Head' of the entire Church[127] – in early 1981, was deposed after only a few months. Another who left was Jon Atack, who was to write a critical book on Scientology, *A Piece of Blue Sky*; Wilson points out that there is now 'a High Court judgement preventing distribution of his book.' Atack had progressed as far as OT V; Mayo, who had helped write the OT material, even higher.

Most of those who left or were driven out of the Church at this time still believed deeply in Dianetics and Scientology. Unlike those who had left in earlier years because they were unhappy with Hubbard's perceived authoritarianism, many who left at this time still supported Hubbard, believing that he had lost control of his own Church.

Unsurprisingly, Miscavige's 'cleanup' of the entire organization made many enemies for both him and the reorganized Church.

> Today, some of these same people, no longer part of the Church, are loudly and bitterly critical of the Church's current management. It is these few apostates who are most often the ones who spread vitriol in the media about Scientology and Church leaders.[128]

Though some had believed as early as 1983 that L. Ron Hubbard was dead, his death was announced by the Church of Scientology on 27 January 1986. There was no post mortem; his body was cremated, and his ashes scattered on the Pacific.

Since 1987, when Miscavige left ASI to become Chairman of the Board of RTC, 'his duties have been to ensure RTC carries out its function of assuring the orthodox and proper use of the Scientology religious scriptures.'[129]

The Church of Scientology was finally recognized by the US Internal Revenue Service as a tax-exempt religion in 1993, after a several-year investigation of the Church which 'made comprehensive, detailed enquiries of the Church relating to its organization and financial structure as well as research and enquiries into several other areas relevant to our determination...'. These included the 'involvement of prior key church officials in criminal cases, civil tort cases, and other litigation matters.'[130]

In other countries Scientology is still struggling for this recognition. Although the British Home Office accepted that Scientology was a religion in December 1996, exactly three years later Charity Commissioners turned down the Church's application to be registered as a charity. They found that:

the core activities of Scientologists 'auditing' and 'training' were private in nature and in the benefit they deliver. In the absence of public benefit, the Church of Scientology would not be charitable under English law, regardless of whether or not it was a religion or otherwise established for a potentially charitable purpose.[131]

According to the Church, and to sociologist Bryan R. Wilson,[132] the Charity Commissioners made their decision at least partly on the grounds that Scientology is a new religion, and that it does not worship a Supreme Being in any conventional way. The Church is appealing this decision, saying that 'newness' should not disqualify a religion, and that many other religions have a non-anthropomorphic concept of a Supreme Being.

At the time of writing, the Church of Scientology is having major problems in both Germany and France. The German government appears to see Scientology as a threat to democracy, and has banned Scientologists from jobs in the public sector.[133] This has escalated into a major battle, with the Church taking out newspaper advertisements accusing the German authorities of religious persecution. In France, the government is considering banning the Church of Scientology altogether. The actions of both governments have caused concern in human rights organizations.

Scientology has the unfortunate reputation of being one of the most litigious religions in the world, both in its pursuit of religious status and in its legal moves against ex-members and other critics.

For the last few years Scientology has also been embroiled in a controversy over whether members, ex-members, non-members[134] and opponents of Scientology should be allowed to discuss (and thus quote) the beliefs of the Church on the Internet. The Church has taken legal action against writers and operators of the Usenet discussion group alt.religion.scientology, among others; this is despite a clause in its Creed which reads: 'That all men have inalienable rights to think freely, to talk freely, to write freely their own opinions and to counter or utter or write upon the opinions of others.'[135] Wilson responds succinctly, 'This point of the Creed does not countenance violation of copyright laws.' He also comments that 'the Church maintains that it has set precedents for copyright protection on the Internet which benefit all owners of intellectual properties.' Critics point out that it is difficult to discuss a religion if one is not permitted to discuss its beliefs.

For many years the Church was engaged in a fierce battle with the Cult Awareness Network (CAN) in the USA, detailed in its 145-page book *The Cult Awareness Network: Anatomy of a Hate Group*, sub-titled 'An Analysis of Violence and Crime Incited by the Cult Awareness Network'. Following a judgement against it in 1995, involving another religion, CAN was bankrupted and all its assets went to auction – where they were bought by a group including Scientologists, who now run the organization.

Christopher Evans, in his 1973 book *Cults of Unreason*, devotes over 100 pages to Scientology. After detailing some of the above problems, and much else besides, he concludes that:

> Scientology's future, at the time of writing, is very uncertain, but it seems that it has probably passed the low-water mark of public unpopularity... the time has probably arrived when one should concentrate on what Scientology is all about now, and not be too diverted by its tumultuous past.[137]

This was written before the criminal activities of the Guardian's Office were exposed, and before more recent controversies. With the continuing attacks on Scientology, by some ex-members and by some national governments, and the continuing legal action in which the Church is involved, Evans was perhaps a little premature in his optimism.

Notes

[1] Unless otherwise stated, all quotations are from Art Schreiber, Chairman of the Board of Directors, Landmark Education Corporation, from correspondence and conversations with the author, 2–14 March 2000.

[2] Other possible influences on Erhard are explored in Wendy Warren Young, 'The Aims and Methods of "est" and "The Centres Network"' in Clarke 1987: 131–47; and in 'The Skeptic's Dictionary: Werner Erhard and est' on http://wheel.ucdavis.edu/~btcarrol/skeptic/est.htm.

[3] 'Inside Lifespring', *Washington Post Magazine*, 25 October 1987.

[4] 'The Skeptic's Dictionary: Werner Erhard and est': 1–2.

[5] Wendy Warren Young, in Clarke 1987: 134.

[6] Ibid.: 140.

[7] Forum brochure, 1985, quoted in Clarke 1987: 142.

[8]'Landmark Overview' on http://www.landmark-education.com/overvw/default.htm.

[9]O'Connor and Seymour 1993: 1.

[10]Laura Spicer, talk on NLP at Talking Stick, London, 19 January 2000.

[11]O'Connor and Seymour.: 183.

[12]Unless otherwise stated, all quotations are from John Seymour Associates brochures, *Introducing NLP*, 1995, and *NLP Training: Professional Skills for Leading People*, 1998.

[13]Samantha West, John Seymour Associates, in correspondence with the author, 12 December 1999.

[14]Insight course flier.

[15]Unless otherwise stated, all quotations are taken from the leaflet *Everything you always wanted to know about Insight*. n.d.

[16]Menis Yousry, City Director (London), Insight Seminars, in correspondence with the author, 15 March 2000.

[17]Ron Hulnick, head of Insight Worldwide, quoted by Menis Yousry, City Director (London), in correspondence with the author, February 2000.

[18]Insight course flier.

[19]Lewis 1998: 41.

[20]Mark Lurie, one of the three members of the Presidency of MSIA, in his notes on the relationship between MSIA and Insight, which he passed to the author.

[21]Ibid.

[22]Unless otherwise stated, all quotations are from Nick Woodeson and David Pearce, in correspondence with the author, 17 August, 17 and 25 September, and 12 November 1995, and 13 March 2000. Woodeson and Pearce are senior British members of the Emin, but stress that 'the Emin has no spokespeople; the people speak for themselves.'

[23]Emin leaflet, Saturday Amber Workshops, November 1999–February 2000.

[24]*The New Testament in Basic English*, Cambridge, 1941: v–vi.

[25]'Emin Loom of Research Starters', 1995 edn.

[26]Leo 1992: 15.

[27]'Emin Loom of Research Starters', 2–1 and 3–7.

[28]Ritchie 1991: 216.

[29]Essence Music Catalogue, 1993: 1.

[30]Ibid.: 3.

[31]The terms Scientology, Dianetics, E-Meter, The Bridge, Saint Hill, OT, Hubbard and L. Ron Hubbard are trademarks owned by the Religious Technology Centre; Narconon is a trademark owned by Able International.

[32]Marco Frenschkowski of the University of Mainz, Germany, has produced an extremely useful annotated international bibliography of books and articles about the Church of Scientology, from all viewpoints. This is published in the *Marburg Journal of Religion*, vol. 4, no. 1, July 1999, and can also be found on the website http://www.uni-marburg.de/fb11/religionswissenschaft/jounalmjr/frenschkowski.htm.

[33]Atack, 1990: 13. An injunction has been obtained against Jon Atack, preventing his promotion

of his book *A Piece of Blue Sky*.

[34]The Church of Scientology has sent the author such information about, among others, Cyril Vosper, Jon Atack, Gerry Armstrong, Stacy Brooks Young and Mary Tabayoyon.

[36]Bryan R. Wilson's paper 'Scientology: A Secularized Religion' was first published in Wilson, 1990: 267–88. The definition of religion which he uses may be a little awkward – 'a set of beliefs, attitudes and dispositions concerning, and activities directed towards, superempirical entities, states, objects, or places' – but his methodology is interesting. He draws up a 'probabilistic inventory' of 20 features and functions 'frequently found in phenomena that in normal usage we recognize as "religions".' If a movement exhibits a good number of these, it is a reasonable assessment to call it a religion; if it exhibits few of them, then not. Wilson then checks these features, one by one, against equivalent statements about Scientology, looking for accord between them. Of the 20, he found 11 cases of Accord, 4 of Qualified Accord, and 5 of Non-Accord, and concluded 'Our probabilistic inventory suggests that Scientology must indeed be regarded as a religion'. Understandably, the Church of Scientology was so pleased by this that it has reprinted Wilson's paper, with six others by other academics, in its book *Scientology: Theology & Practice of a Contemporary Religion*: 111–45.

Wilson's paper doesn't *prove* that Scientology is a religion. Both his selection of the 20 features and, perhaps as importantly, their wording, could be challenged; so could the degree of accord he finds with each one, which in some cases appears to be a subjective judgement. One suspects that another sociologist, wishing to conclude that Scientology is *not* a religion, could use the same methodology to do so. But even with these caveats, it would be churlish to dismiss Wilson's analysis. He may not have *proved* that Scientology is a religion, but in the social sciences, as in the physical sciences, the word 'proof' is usually avoided. Wilson's analysis, along with those of other academics, provides a strong body of evidence to suggest that it makes sense to regard Scientology as a religion.

[37]Alan W. Black, Associate Professor of Sociology, University of New England, Armidale, NSW, Australia; source: 'Is Scientology a Religion? Yes.' on 'The Interactive Bible' website on http://www.bible.ca/scientology-is-a-religion-black.htm.

[38]Stephen A. Kent, University of Alberta, Edmonton, Canada, 'Scientology – Is This a Religion?', *Marburg Journal of Religion*, vol. 4, no. 1, July 1999, also on 'The Interactive Bible' website on http://www.bible.ca/scientology-not-religion-kent.htm.

[39]Quotations from Graeme Wilson, Public Affairs Director of the Church of Scientology in the UK, are from correspondence with the author, 5 May 1999, 19, 23, 24 and 28 March, 24 April and 1 October 2000, and several very detailed discussions with the author including 17 and 31 March and 3 May 2000. Except where by context (e.g. note 36) it is clear that 'Wilson' refers to the sociologist Bryan R. Wilson, all mentions of 'Wilson' in this entry refer to Graeme Wilson.

[40]Brochure: *The Church of Scientology: 40th Anniversary*, 1994: 56.

[41]This produces a 95-page booklet entitled *The Way to Happiness: A Commonsense Guide to Better Living*, Los Angeles CA: New Era Publications, 1989.

[41A]The figure of eight million is twice given in Scientology's own video *Merchants of Chaos*.

[42]'Major Religions Ranked by Number of Adherents' on http://www.adherents.com/Religions_By_Adherents.html.

[43]*What Is Scientology?*, 1998: 65.

[44]Ibid.: 1998: 539.

[45]*The Auditor: the Journal of Scientology*, no. 21, 1967: 3.

[46] *Scientology: The Field Staff Member Magazine*, vol. 1, no. 1, 1968: 38.

[47] *What Is Scientology?*, 1998: 165.

[48] Hubbard, 1950: 171.

[49] Ibid.: 312, 313.

[50] Miller, 1987: 213–15.

[51] *The Auditor: the Journal of Scientology*, no. 21, 1967: 2.

[52] *What Is Scientology?*, 1998: 534.

[53] *Reference Guide to the Scientology Religion*, 1994: 18.

[54] *Scientology: The Field Staff Member Magazine*, vol. 1, no. 1, 1968: 23.

[55] Hubbard, 1950: vi.

[56] *Scientology: The Field Staff Member Magazine*, vol. 1, no. 1, 1968: 38.

[57] L. Ron Hubbard, Ron's Journal 67.

[58] Peter Nicholls, 'Dianetics', in Clute and Nicholls, 1993: 327.

[59] Atack, 1990: 248

[59A] Wilson points out that the screenplay "is not an auditing level" and claims "It is also not even the same story."

[60] Margery Wakefield, quoted in 'OT III Course, summary and comments', on http://www.bible.ca/scientology-fair-use-ot3.htm.

[61] The teaching matter of Scientology, particularly at the higher levels, is confidential. After representations by the Church, this is being respected by not quoting the story in this book. According to Jon Atack (and this was confirmed by Wilson in conversation with the author, 17 March 2000), 'confidentiality was introduced because the relevant materials are highly "restimulative" (upsetting) to people who are not ready for them' (Atack, 1990: 158–9). This is partly why the Church makes such strenuous efforts to suppress the publication of details of OT III and other material. However, the OT III story has been in the public domain for many years, and versions are widely available, both in books and on the Internet.

[62] Evans, 1973: 42–7. See also Miller, 1987: 254–5. Graeme Wilson disputes this scenario: 'Scientology has nothing to do with "free association images", and this was not how Mr Hubbard did his research.'

[63] Ibid.: 43.

[64] Miller, 1987: 255.

[65] Lorraine Bulger, OT VIII Scientologist, in conversation and correspondence with the author, 24 March 2000.

[66] *What Is Scientology?*, 1998: 57.

[67] First published in *Astounding Science Fiction* magazine in 1939–43 and *Other Worlds* magazine in 1950, and collected into the novel *The Voyage of the Space Beagle* (1950), the same year that Dianetics was launched.

[68] First published in *Astounding Science Fiction* magazine in 1945 and 1948–9.

[69] First published in *Astounding Science Fiction* magazine in 1940.

[70] Paul Kincaid, 'A.E. van Vogt (1912–2000)', *Matrix*, no. 142, March/April 2000, British Science Fiction Association: 3.

[71]George Orwell, *Collected Essays*, vol. 1: 304.

[72]*Reference Guide to the Scientology Religion*, 1994: 42. Wilson now disputes even this phrase from a Scientology publication: 'Mr Hubbard is not the originator of the quote, a fact that was also confirmed by a German court. So it isn't an "unfounded rumour."' Wilson also says the Church 'has signed statements by two convention attendees that Hubbard said no such thing.' This subject is further discussed at http://www.cs.colorado.edu/~lindsay/scientology/start.a.religion.html.

[73]Lucian, *Peregrinus Proteus*: 13–15.

[74]Quoted in Miller, 1987: 153. See also *Fortean Times*, no. 132, March 2000: 34–8, and John Carter, *Sex and Rockets: The Occult World of Jack Parsons*, Venice CA: Feral House, 1999.

[75]Wilson says in a letter to the author that Hubbard was absent from this ritual, while providing an academic paper by J. Gordon Melton from which this quotation is taken (J. Gordon Melton, 'Thelemic Magic in America: The Emergence of an Alternative Religion', *The Conference on Alternative Religions: Research and Study*, Loyola University, 7–10 May 1981).

[76]In support of this, Wilson writes: 'They [the Church of Scientology] point at a December 1969 article in the London *Sunday Times* which described the matter as follows: "L. Ron Hubbard was still an officer of the US Navy [and] because he was well known as a writer and a philosopher and had friends amongst the physicists, he was sent in to handle the situation. He went to live at the house and investigated the black magic rites and the general situation and found them very bad."' In fact, this passage is from a statement sent to the *Sunday Times* by the Church of Scientology, which was quoted verbatim by the *Sunday Times* as a result of legal action.

[77]The evidence supplied to the author by Scientology consists largely of assertions and does not constitute proof of their version of events.

[78]'Professional Auditor's Bulletin' PAB 110, 15 April 1957.

[79]Quoted in Lamont, 1986: 21. Wilson says the remark was "clearly facetious."

[80]Source: Miller, 1987: 86.

[81]See, for example, *What Is Scientology?*, 1998: 25–55; *The Church of Scientology: 40th Anniversary*, 1994: 49–55; *L. Ron Hubbard: A Profile*, 1995: 1–124, etc.

[82]Quoted in Miller, 1987: 5–6.

[83]This and the next quotation are from a Church of Scientology summary document on Gerry Armstrong: 2.

[84]See Lamont, 1986: 138–9.

[85]Quoted in Lamont, 1986: 137–8; see also Miller, 1987: 485–6.

[85A]The Church also produces a number of third-party statements to support their views and counter Breckenridge.

[86]*What Is Scientology?*, 1998: 54.

[87]The fact that Dianetics was unveiled in a science fiction magazine is not mentioned in the 835-page book *What Is Scientology?*, 1998 edn. On page 584 it says only: 'Ron writes *Dianetics: The Evolution of a Science* for magazine publication to promote and accompany the release of *Dianetics*.' Even that is not mentioned in the 593-page 1993 edition.

[88]John Clute and Peter Nicholls, 'Hubbard, L. Ron' in Clute and Nicholls, 1993: 593.

[89]Asimov, Isaac, *In Memory Yet Green*, New York: Doubleday, 1979: 570, 587, 625.

[90]George Hay (1922–1997) in correspondence with the author, 8 August 1995.

[91]Letter from L. Ron Hubbard to Don G. Purcell, 5 April 1952.

[92]*What Is Scientology?*, 1998: 586.

[93]Mathison, Volney G., *Creative Image Therapy*, Mathison Electropsychometers, 1954: 2.

[94]Affidavit of J.W. Hough, President of Sequoia University, 30 July 1968. According to Miller, Hough was 'a chiropracteur [*sic*] and naturopath who ran a successful practice from a large house in downtown Los Angeles and conferred 'degrees' on whoever he thought merited them' (Miller, 1987: 276).

[95]Mathison, 1954: 36.

[96]*What Is Scientology?*, 1998: 83.

[97]Mathison, 1954: 82, 85.

[98]*United States v. Article or Device Etc.: 333 Federal Supplement 357 (1971)*: 364.

[99]*What Is Scientology?*, 1998: 503.

[100]Ibid., 1998: 357.

[101]Ibid., 1993: 290; see also 290–300.

[102]Ibid., 1998: 512.

[103]Anderson, Kevin V., *Report of the Board of Inquiry into Scientology*, Melbourne, 1965.

[104]Ruling of the High Court of Australia, 27 October 1983.

[105]BBC Radio 4, 22 December 1971. Crossman also refers to his misgivings about the ban in his book *The Diaries of a Cabinet Minister*, vol. 3, London: Hamish Hamilton & Jonathan Cape, 1977.

[106]Quoted in Lamont, 1986: 149. The Church says that Judge Latey's statement is untrue, and Wilson points out that 'Latey's decision concerned a case to which neither Hubbard nor the Church was a party. Latey did no study of Hubbard or Scientology and the Court of Appeal ruled that his remarks were not to be taken as a precedent for any other case.'

[107]Affidavit of L. Ron Hubbard, 22 March 1976.

[108]Declaration of Stacy Brooks Young to the United States District Court, Central District of California, 13 October 1994 (www.sky.net/~sloth/sci/young1.affidavit). Wilson points out that 'one of the criteria for tax exemption is that the applicant is not in violation of public policy, and that the US government examined and rejected charges of this kind before granting exemption to Scientology organizations.'

[109]*What Is Scientology?*, 1998: 323.

[110]Declaration by Mary Tabayoyon to United States District Court, Central District of California, 4 April 1994 (www.sky.net/~sloth/sci/mary.tabayoyon).

[111]Quoted in Vosper, 1971: 147–8.

[112]The Church points out that in 1987 Vosper was convicted in Munich of falsely imprisoning a German Scientologist 'in an attempt to persuade her to abandon her religion' (*The Guardian*, 30 December 1987: 3).

[113]Declaration of Stacy Brooks Young to the United States District Court, Central District of California, 13 October 1994 (source: as above). Wilson emphasizes that "the Office of Special Affairs is not an extension of the Guardian Office" which was "completely disbanded." The Church says that the Office of Special Affairs is a different organisation entirely, with a different position in management, different organisational structure and with different responsibilities.

[116]For detailed accounts of the illegal activities of the Guardian's Office, see Atack, 1990: 226–41;

Lamont, 1986: 78–88; Miller, 1987: 440–60.

[117] *Reference Guide to the Scientology Religion*, 1994: 30.

[118] Atack, 1990: 231.

[119] Ibid.: 265.

[120] Lamont, 1986: 91.

[120A] The Church says that this is inaccurate and that the All Clear unit took over the handling of key litigation which the Guardian office had let flounder.

[121] Warren McShane, President of the Religious Technology Centre, in correspondence with the author, 16 April 2000: 3.

[122] *Reference Guide to the Scientology Religion*, 1994: 31.

[123] Warren McShane, President of the Religious Technology Centre, in correspondence with the author, 16 April 2000: 1.

[124] *The Literary Works of L. Ron Hubbard: Foreign Rights Catalogue*, Author Services, Inc., 1996: 11.

[125] Brad Linaweaver, 'A review of the Screenplay for Battlefield Earth', Cinema Confidential, http://www.cinecon.com/reviews/batearthscript.html.

[126] John Clute and Peter Nicholls, 'Hubbard, L. Ron' in Clute and Nicholls, 1993: 593.

[126A] See Atack, 1990: 36–37; Lamont, 1986: 97; David Mayo Affidavit, 14 Oct. 1994, on USENET's alt.religion.scientology.

[127] Corydon, 1992: 198.

[128] *Reference Guide to the Scientology Religion*, 1994: 31.

[129] Warren McShane, President of the Religious Technology Centre, in correspondence with the author, 16 April 2000: 4.

[130] Letter from Department of the Treasury, Internal Revenue Service, Washington DC, to the Scientologist Lord McNair, 4 September 1996.

[131] Press release, Charity Commission for England and Wales, 9 December 1999.

[132] Statement from Bryan R. Wilson, 9 December 1999.

[133] Kevin Boyle and Juliet Sheen, *Freedom of Religion and Belief: A World Report*, London: Routledge, 1997: 13, 312–14.

[134] For many years Scientology referred to non-members as 'wogs', though not so much in Britain where the word is extremely racially offensive.

[135] 'The Creed of the Church of Scientology', para 7, *The Church of Scientology: 40th Anniversary*, 1994: 1.

[137] Evans, 1973: 131, 133.

CHAPTER 17 – CASE STUDY

Schism in a Sect

The Worldwide Church of God and Its Offshoots

The September/October 1997 US edition of *The Plain Truth*, for over half a century the flagship magazine of Herbert W. Armstrong's Worldwide Church of God (WCG), carried a full-page advert for a book by Joseph Tkach, current President and Pastor General of the Church:

> For nearly 70 years the Worldwide Church of God, founded by Herbert W. Armstrong, preached a 'different gospel'. Then in 1995, only ten years after Armstrong's death, the leadership of the WCG publicly renounced its unorthodox teachings and entered the evangelical mainstream. In this fast-paced and exciting record, Joseph Tkach... delivers the plain truth.[1]

This case study examines the background to this unusual transformation in a Church, and examines the resultant fissioning of the Church as many of its members reject the new leadership in favour of the old teachings.[2] But it is not just a study of one relatively small group of heterodox Christian Churches: it is an examination of a microcosm of ideas and events which occur throughout the macrocosm of alternative religions – not just schism, but authority problems, alleged abuse, scandal, millenarian theology and much more can be seen within this one group of Churches perhaps more than in any other.[3] Hence, although it might seem strange to end this book by looking in such depth at what has happened to one movement, this is a fitting conclusion to a book about the variety of alternative religions.

A note on the abbreviations used in this chapter appears on page 480. The following diagram may help clarify the relationship between the various Churches.

PRE-HISTORY: 'CHURCHES OF GOD' BEFORE 1934, AND THE ENTRY OF HERBERT W. ARMSTRONG

The Worldwide Church of God was founded as the Radio Church of God by Herbert W. Armstrong (HWA) in 1937 as an offshoot of the Church of God (Seventh Day) (COG7), which has common origins with the Seventh-day Adventist Church (SDA).

NOTE ON ABBREVIATIONS

The following abbreviations occur both in quotations and in the text of this chapter. Two sets of father and son are distinguished in each case by using the surname alone only for the father.

HWA or Armstrong	Herbert W. Armstrong (the Founder) (1892–1986)
GTA, Garner Ted or Ted	Garner Ted Armstrong (his son) (1930–)
Tkach	Joseph W. Tkach (1927–1995)
Joe Jnr	Joseph Tkach (his son) (1951–)
CGCF	Church of God, a Christian Fellowship (ex-GCG)
CEM	Christian Educational Ministries (ex-CGI)
CGI	Church of God, International
CGOM	Churches of God Outreach Ministry (ex-CGI)
COG (Monrovia)	Church of God (Monrovia) (ex-UCG)
COG (UK)	Churches of God, UK (ex-CGI)
COG7	Church of God (Seventh Day)
GCG or Global	Global Church of God
GTAEA	Garner Ted Armstrong Evangelistic Association (ex-CGI)
ICG or Intercontinental	Intercontinental Church of God (ex-CGI)
LCG or Living	Living Church of God (ex-GCG)
PCG or Philadelphia	Philadelphia Church of God
RCG	Restored Church of God (ex-GCG)
SDA	Seventh-day Adventist Church
UCG or United	United Church of God, *An International Association*
WCG or Worldwide	Worldwide Church of God
WCGR	Worldwide Church of God Restored

With the exception of COG7, SDA and WCG itself, all the above are ex-WCG.

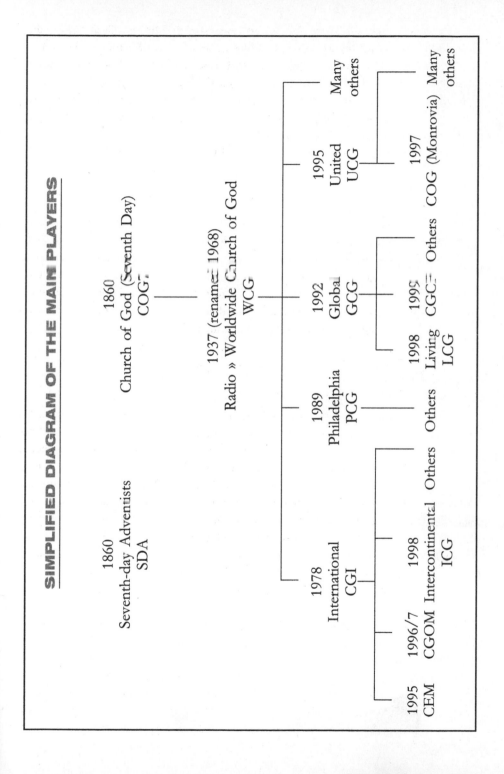

SIMPLIFIED DIAGRAM OF THE MAIN PLAYERS

1860
Church of God (Seventh Day)
COG7

1860
Seventh-day Adventists
SDA

1937 (renamed 1968)
Radio » Worldwide Church of God
WCG

1989
Philadelphia
PCG

1992
Global
GCG

1995
United
UCG

Many
others

1978
International
CGI

1998
Living
LCG

1995
CGC= Others

1997
COG (Monrovia) Many
others

1995
CEM

1996/7
CGOM Intercontinental Others
ICG

After the 'Great Disappointment' of 1844, when Christ failed to return as forecast, the believers who had followed William Miller's Adventist teachings went in several directions, the best known and largest of which, under Ellen G. White's leadership, became the Seventh-day Adventist Church (see page 168). Initially little more than a federation of independent congregations, this movement set up its headquarters in 1855 in Battle Creek, Michigan, where it remained until 1903, when it moved its centre to Takoma Park, Washington DC. Its three most distinctive beliefs were, in brief:

- In 1844 Christ entered his heavenly sanctuary to prepare for the judgement of mankind.
- Christians must obey God's law, including Seventh-day Sabbath observance as stated in the Ten Commandments.
- In the Last Days the gift of prophecy would come upon God's Church, specifically through Ellen G. White.

Mrs White's movement, which was formally organized as a Church in 1863, took the name Seventh-day Adventist at a conference at Battle Creek in 1860. Some there preferred the name Church of God, and the matter was put to the vote. Mrs White made the point that:

> The name Seventh-day Adventist carries the true features of our faith in front, and will convict the enquiring mind...
>
> I was shown that almost every fanatic who has arisen, who wishes to hide his sentiments that he may lead away others, claims to belong to the Church of God. Such a name would at once excite suspicion; for it is employed to conceal the most absurd errors.[4]

Some congregations in the 1860s refused to use the new name; they kept to the name Church of God and retained Saturday worship, but rejected most of the rest of Ellen G. White's theology. They took the name Church of God, Seventh Day, officially, in 1884. In this organization was a church based in Stanberry, Missouri (actually one of the earliest churches in the Seventh-day Adventist movement) – and it had a daughter church in Oregon. It was to this church that Herbert W. Armstrong came in 1927. Armstrong, through his wife Loma, had become convinced of the seventh-day Sabbath doctrine; he also believed that the only valid name for a Church was the Church of God, hence his choice of the Oregon church.

According to Armstrong, the Christian Church had lost its way in 69 or 70 CE. The mainstream of Christianity had been wrong ever since – but there had always been a few, somewhere in the world, who had followed the true way. Among these were Constantine of Mananali around 650 CE and Sergius a hundred years later. Around 1000 CE there were the Paulicians and Bogomils of Bulgaria, and a preacher called Peter de Bruys in the south of France. Even the Gnostic-influenced Cathars are claimed as forerunners of the Worldwide Church of God, albeit with no doctrinal justification. The Waldenses had the truth, said Armstrong, and so did the Lollards. There were Sabbatarians in the seventeenth century; one of these, Stephen Mumford, took the true gospel to America in 1664, setting up in Newport, Rhode Island.[5]

Armstrong's picking out of these particular religious movements and leaders seemed to rest on one or more of four points: their keeping of the Saturday Sabbath, the name 'Church of God', their rejection of the standard idea of the Trinity – and their persecution by the established Church. In reality, few if any of them could be seen in any way as forerunners of the Worldwide Church of God.

In every case, Armstrong said, either mainstream Christianity had destroyed the small group of true believers, or the Devil, seeing God's Truth preached, had encouraged the beliefs to be watered down or distorted. This was the case, Armstrong taught, with the Seventh-day Adventist Church, which under Mrs White's influence had abandoned the only scriptural name for God's Church.

There were other congregations which kept the name Church of God, or Seventh-day Church of God, or Church of God, Seventh-day, or Church of God (Adventist). It is worth noting three points. First, some of the early Seventh-day Adventists, and the Church of God, held numerous doctrines which Herbert W. Armstrong took with him into his own Church. One prominent SDA minister, Greenbury G. Rupert (1847–1922), who knew Ellen G. White for 40 years,

> observed the Holy Days, eschewed unclean meats, held to the name 'Church of God', advocated local autonomy, rejected Christmas, Easter and other pagan holidays, believed in tithing and Church eras, emphasized Bible prophecy in his preaching and taught that the United States was part of Israel.[6]

All of these were to become part of WCG doctrine. Second, over the years the Church of God generally held on to its distinctive beliefs, while the SDA moved closer to standard Protestant doctrines and practices; for example, many early SDA preachers rejected the Trinity, but by the 1930s it had become accepted doctrine. Third, as the following quotations show, the Church of God which Armstrong joined was prone to schisms over doctrinal differences, which included Church organization.

- Throughout the 1860s, the split between the majority who followed the Whites and the scattered remnant who didn't became more and more decisive.
- 1861–2: A portion of us were unwilling to accept these new planks in the platform of our Church...
- In 1905 the Church underwent a serious rupture...
- c. 1922: The issue of organization and government had long been a source of controversy within the Church of God.

- After several years of growing doctrinal disagreement he [G.G. Rupert] left the Adventists in 1902.
- Because of disagreement between Mr Dugger and Mr Rupert over some issues of doctrine, and particularly over the issue of church organization and government...
- In August 1933, Andrew Dugger, the primary church leader for the past 20 years, lost his position by one vote. This precipitated a crisis that split the Church down the middle.[7]

By 1928 Armstrong was preaching, and in 1931 he was ordained a minister by the Church of God. In 1933 he gave a series of lectures around Eugene, Oregon, and in 1934 he began the two activities which characterized his Church for the next half century: *The World Tomorrow* programme on a small, 100-watt local radio station, and *The Plain Truth* magazine – 250 copies of a mimeographed sheet. According to Armstrong, 'The Work from this point grew in power and scope at the rate of 30% per year over the next 35 years.'[8]

During the 1930s, says one internal Church historian, 'Mr Armstrong came into increasing conflict with the Church headquarters in Salem because of his teachings...'.[9] In the late 1930s Armstrong 'was asked to turn in his credentials for continuing to preach contrary to Church doctrine'[10] – particularly on British-Israelism. In 1937 he founded his own Church, then called the Radio Church of God, which changed its name to the Worldwide Church of God in 1968.

Looking back from 30 years later, Armstrong commented on the beginnings of his ministry:

Coincidence? – or DESIGN!
This brings us to a series of almost incredible facts...

First, Jesus Christ began His earthly ministry at about age 30. God took away my business, moved me from Chicago, started bringing me to repentance and conversion preparatory to inducting me into His ministry, *when I was 30*!

Second, Jesus began the actual *teaching and training* of His original disciples for carrying His Gospel to the world in the year 27 AD. *Precisely 100 time-cycles later*, in 1927 AD, He began my intensive study and training for carrying His same Gospel to all nations of today's world...

But *that is not all*. Consider further!

More Amazing Parallels!
... in the year 31 AD. For exactly one 19-year time-cycle this preaching was confined to the continent where it started – Asia. After *precisely one 19-year time-cycle*, 50 AD, Christ *opened a door* for the apostle Paul to carry the same Gospel to Europe!...

God first *opened a door* – that of radio and the printing press – for the mass proclaiming of His original true Gospel *the first week in 1934*! The exact date was January 7, 1934. *Exactly one time-cycle later*, January 7, 1953, God opened wide the massive door of the most powerful commercial radio station on earth, and Radio Luxembourg began broadcasting Christ's Gospel to Europe and Britain!

What startling coincidences! – or *are* they mere coincidences?[11]

(Incidentally, this quotation illustrates Armstrong's usual literary style, with its typographical emphases.)

SOME OF THE DISTINCTIVE DOCTRINES OF THE HISTORICAL WORLDWIDE CHURCH OF GOD

- God is a family, currently consisting of the Father and his Son, Jesus.
- Our ultimate destiny is to become part of (the family of) God ourselves.[12]
- The Holy Spirit is the action of God, not a Person.
- The Trinity is a false doctrine, devised in the second to fourth centuries, which has been the mark of false Christianity through the ages.
- Although salvation is by grace, our reward is according to our works.
- Observation of not only the seventh-day Sabbath but also the seven Jewish festivals is required of all true believers.
- Christmas, Easter etc. are Pagan festivals and must not be celebrated.
- Observation of all Old Testament law is required, including tithing[13] and dietary restrictions – e.g. no pork or shellfish.
- We are in the End Times, and the return of Jesus is rapidly approaching.
- British-Israelism: All the End-Time prophecies in the Bible can be interpreted with specific regard to identifiable countries; Ephraim is Britain, Manasseh is the USA, etc. (This made WCG very much a religion for the USA; cf. the Mormons).
- True believers (i.e. WCG members) will be the rulers of the Earth during the millennium, when other people will be given the chance of salvation.
- After death there is unconsciousness ('soul sleep') until the Resurrection at the Second Coming.
- The unsaved will be destroyed, rather than suffering in Hell.
- The Gospel is the Gospel of the forthcoming Kingdom of God, rather than a Gospel of present salvation and being 'born again'.
- The Bible is literally true, including the Genesis account of Creation.
- Jesus was crucified on Wednesday and rose exactly three days and three nights later, on Saturday – the Sabbath.
- The government of the present Church of God should be hierarchical, not democratic.

Several of these doctrines, such as the composition of God, were debated at great length in the first few centuries of Christianity before the generally accepted formulae of orthodox Christianity were devised. Note the similarities between several of the doctrines and some of those of other non-orthodox Christian religions, such as Seventh-day Adventism, Jehovah's Witnesses, Christadelphians and the 'Christian Identity' movement (see page 78).

Unlike several other new religious movements, the Worldwide Church of God has always been upfront about its beliefs. Every issue of *The Plain Truth* mentioned booklets on a wide variety of doctrinal subjects, which readers could send for, free of charge. Just two of these doctrines will be examined here.

THE LAW

The Worldwide Church of God, like many other movements in this book, was often accused of being authoritarian in practice; it was also accused of being legalistic. While perhaps not using that precise word, the latter is a charge which they would admit to with pride. Mainstream Christianity doesn't exactly dispense with the Law – the Ten Commandments are still read in churches – but it emphasizes the point that before Jesus the Jews lived under the Law, while since Jesus Christians live under Grace. The New Testament is about the New Covenant, which replaces the Old Covenant of rules and regulations.

The balance between Faith and Works can be, and has been, argued endlessly. The usual Protestant formulation is that we are justified by faith, but that our lives should demonstrate the fruits of the Spirit (Galatians 5:22–23); as Jesus said, 'By their fruits ye shall know them' (Matthew 7:20). But then there's that awkward verse, 'Think not that I am come to destroy the law, or the prophets; I am not come to destroy, but to fulfil' (Matthew 5:17), and the even more awkward 'Ye see then how that by works a man is justified, and not by faith only' (James 2:24), which Evangelicals have to use almost Jesuitical reasoning to explain away.

The Worldwide Church of God taught that the Law still holds, that when God commanded Israel to do this or not to do that, he meant it, and he meant it for everyone, and for all time. This applies perhaps most of all to observance of the Sabbath, which must be on the seventh day, Saturday, not on Sunday. It also applies to the seven major annual festivals of Judaism – Passover, the Festival of Unleavened Bread, the Festival of Tabernacles, etc. – which were of major importance to members of Worldwide, and still are in the many offshoots. And it applies to the Jewish dietary rules; no member of Worldwide would eat pork or shellfish; bacon butties and prawn cocktails were forbidden.

This emphasis on obedience to God's Law as laid down in the Old Testament was not just for theological reasons. In a very real sense, Armstrong taught, we are not just the spiritual but also the physical descendants of Abraham, Isaac and Jacob; we are the House of Israel; and so what God told Israel over 2,000 years ago applies to us, today.

BRITISH-ISRAELISM

British-Israelism is the belief that the dispersed 'Lost Ten Tribes' of Israel migrated to Europe, and in particular that Biblical prophecy about the tribes of Ephraim and Manasseh refers specifically to Britain and the USA. The theory was not original to Armstrong; it was first clearly propounded by a Scot, John Wilson, in 1840, and can be traced back a couple of centuries before that.[14] (Even Columbus wondered whether the native peoples of America might be 'the barbarized descendants of the Ten Tribes of Israel.'[15]) But Armstrong, having embraced British-Israelism, made it his own. *The Plain Truth*, *The World Tomorrow* radio programme and numerous books preached this message over and over again. It was the foundation of his prophetic teaching, on which all else hung.

Armstrong taught that the people (Hebrew *iysh*) of the covenant (*beriyth*) became the *British* people; Isaac's sons became the Saxons; the tribe of Dan (remembering that written Hebrew doesn't use vowels) passed through or settled in or around, among many others, Mace*don*ia, the Dar*dan*elles, the rivers *Dan*ube, *Dn*ieper, *Dn*iester and *Don*, and came to the British Isles – in Ireland *Don*egal, Lon*don*derry and *Din*gle, in Scotland *Dun*dee, *Dun*kirk and E*din*burgh, and in England, of course, Lon*don*. The famous Tuatha de Danaan of Ireland were simply the tribe of Dan.[16]

The sub-tribes of Ephraim and Manasseh, Joseph's sons, eventually became the peoples of Britain and the USA respectively – and all the Biblical prophecies about them refer to these great countries in the present day. In addition, James VI of Scotland and I of England was a direct descendant of the royal line of Israel. The Stone of Scone, Britain's Coronation Stone, was the stone which Jacob used as a pillow (Genesis 28:18), and was carried to Ireland by Jeremiah in 569 BCE; Jeremiah was accompanied by a daughter of King Zedekiah, Princess Tea-Tephi, whose descendant is Queen Elizabeth II – and so the throne of Britain is a continuation of the throne of David.[17]

This is only the very briefest of summaries. Accepting a few initial premises and making a few conceptual leaps, the whole theory seems logical, and has a certain appeal for English-speaking Westerners. Britain was for centuries a great world power; and there have been many Americans who have regarded themselves as the Chosen People.

Unfortunately for British-Israelites, independent historians have always dismissed the entire theory as completely false, but this did not stop Armstrong making it the very heart of his message. It enabled him to apply Biblical prophecies to Britain, the then-fledgling European Community, and the USA, particularly with regard to the End Times.

THE ARMSTRONG YEARS

As with many new religious movements, there are several quite different versions of what Worldwide was actually like, with huge differences between public image and insiders' perceptions.

For the outside world, WCG was a glossy magazine, *Plain Truth*, and a very professional radio and TV broadcast, *The World Tomorrow* (in the UK, only the radio broadcast was available, on Radio Luxembourg). Magazines, booklets and a few full-length
books were offered free to anyone who requested them. They contained photographs
of beautiful college buildings, smart young students, and HWA meeting dozens of
world leaders. The main emphases were prophecy of the End Times, Creationism, and
very traditional teaching on morality (books and booklets included *God Speaks Out on
The New Morality* and *The Missing Dimension in Sex*). The End-Time teaching was very
prominent. 'Signs of the Times' were listed – earthquakes, famines, wars, diseases,
assassinations, plummeting morality – to show that Christ's return must be very near.
Many in the Church believed that this would occur in 1972, and though this had never
been preached as a certainty, quite a number left in disillusionment. A booklet entitled
1975 in Prophecy became unavailable from the mid-1970s onwards.

For those who received the more doctrinal magazine, variously entitled *The
Good News of Tomorrow's World*, *The Good News* and *GN*, there were more detailed
teachings on these doctrines, and on the wrong festivals (Sunday, Christmas,
Easter etc.) versus the right festivals (the Sabbath, the seven Jewish festivals), and
on the importance of tithing. The strict requirement for tithing caused much
resentment over the years, as poor members saw HWA flying around the world
in his personal plane, wearing expensive clothes and watches, and living in some
luxury, while they scrimped and saved to pay their tithes. Armstrong's philosophy
(in common with some other American Churches) was that only the best is good
enough for God.[18]

Armstrong was often photographed in *Plain Truth* and elsewhere with great world
leaders – kings, princes, politicians, prime ministers, presidents – which gave him
kudos and credibility. According to some former senior members, these photographs
were intended to show Armstrong's importance by the circles in which he regularly
moved; but very often, it seems, the great world leaders had no idea who this short,
elderly man was, who asked to be photographed shaking hands. Garner Ted
Armstrong disapproved of his father's many trips, calling them 'the world's most
expensive autograph hunt'.[19]

On many occasions Armstrong, as Chancellor of the Ambassador Colleges, is
alleged to have effectively 'bought' meetings and photographs by making donations
to charitable causes supported by a world leader. His son later wrote:

> While I knew his advance man, a Japanese immigrant, was giving away golf
> clubs, gold pen sets, free trips to the United States, and many other gifts to
> various of his contacts through Japanese embassies, in order to *buy* my father's
> way into these various meetings, my father was kept in the dark. Over $900,000
> was spent in only one year by my father's advance man, arranging for him to
> meet various dictators, premiers and presidents, like Jomo Kenyatta, Haile

Selassie, and President Marcos... I could not help feeling this was a terrible waste of tithe-payers' money.[20]

Until the mid-1990s, the most traumatic and controversial decade in the history of Worldwide was the 1970s, though most readers of the *Plain Truth*, non-members, would not have known it. The Church went through 'a very serious financial storm'[21] in 1971. Some ministers and members left in 1972 when Christ didn't return as expected. More left in 1974 when there were disputes over two doctrines: remarriage after divorce, and the true date of Pentecost. Armstrong referred to 'a conspiracy... angry attack... The handful of dissident and disloyal ministers took a certain number of deceived brethren with them.'[22] There were also sexual scandals, some of which leaked out to the wider world.[23] In 1974 Garner Ted was revealed to have had extra-marital relationships; for a time he was suspended from his positions in the Church, and from broadcasting on *The World Tomorrow*. But GTA was a gifted preacher, and the show was nowhere near as successful without him – success being measured not just in requests for literature, but in how much revenue was brought in. This had fallen by 40 per cent before GTA was reinstated.

As Armstrong grew older, Garner Ted increasingly took the helm, doing most of the radio and TV broadcasts and much of the writing, and practically running the Church. Herbert W. Armstrong, however, found it difficult to relinquish the reins, and GTA frequently found his decisions overturned. (Another part of the rift between them was caused by Armstrong's remarriage in 1977 to a divorcée younger than his son; GTA disapproved strongly of the marriage.) In 1978 the clash between them came to a head, and Armstrong expelled his son from the Church. GTA went off to found the Church of God, International, based in Tyler, Texas.

Armstrong ousted his son and heir quite possibly because, among other reasons, he couldn't stand the competition. There were doctrinal differences; Armstrong claimed that GTA had begun 'to water down, liberalize and secularize Christ's true doctrines!' But worse, perhaps, 'I learned that Ted had a somewhat normal attitude of resentment against his father,' and, 'He has accused his father of senility,' and, 'His sole effort has been to destroy his father and God's Church, and draw tithe payers after him!'[24]

Unsurprisingly, Garner Ted's version of the dispute is very different. He had effectively been running the entire organization for several years, while his father spent up to 300 days a year on his trips. He consulted his father on major decisions; but often, after they had agreed a policy and Garner Ted had implemented it, Armstrong would suddenly change his mind and countermand his son's actions.

No, I did not 'try to take over,' but you gave the reins to me, and then continually snatched them back out of my hands until I was once more in a complete power vacuum – every decision second-guessed and suspect wrote Garner Ted in a long and very emotional letter to his father.[25]

In 1977 Armstrong had major heart problems and nearly died. From then on he became more and more forgetful, and also more prone to falling out with his son. According to Garner Ted, among Armstrong's closest aides were several people who deliberately fed his confused father lies about him, which his father believed. 'To most, I am viewed as being very conservative, far-to-the-right. But to some who had my father's ear unbeknownst to me, I was being subtly painted as a "liberal".'[26]

After he had been ousted Garner Ted became, for his father and the Worldwide Church of God, a non-person. In Volume 2 of Armstrong's autobiography, the 143 pages covering the 1970s contain almost no references to any of the troubles the Church went though in that decade. Official histories can be very selective. In the whole of that decade there is one mention of Garner Ted, who was the Church's chief evangelist for most of the decade, and who ran the Church in his father's absence. This was when Armstrong suffered a near-fatal heart failure in August 1977, and reads in total, 'I think Ted anointed me.'[27]

At about the same time as GTA was expelled there was a doctrinal shake-up. The background to this was the Systematic Theology Project (STP), a doctrinal review in 1972–4 'to sift our accumulated teachings'. This had the support of Garner Ted, but the results of STP were largely rejected by Herbert W. Armstrong. Nevertheless, during the 1970s there had been certain shifts in emphasis within the Church. One of the many doctrinal disputes between father and son was over the 'Place of Safety' (Revelation 12:14), which Armstrong thought was probably Petra in Jordan (see page 505), while Garner Ted believed that it was in no physical, geographical place, but rather the believer's faith in Christ the Rock. There were also disputes over matters such as the wearing of make-up by female members; Armstrong had always been against it; Garner Ted allowed it.

Once Garner Ted had been ejected, classic 'Armstrongite' booklets which had been downplayed were brought back into print, including *The United States and Britain in Prophecy* '– back to full length!' Some other leaders and members left with Garner Ted: 'Some 'liberals' who wanted to water down God's truth are being sifted out,'[28] said his father.

This wasn't the end of the problems. In 1979 the State of California put the Church into receivership after allegations of financial impropriety based on 'false charges... by malcontent former members.' With characteristic overstatement, Armstrong referred to this as 'this most monstrous and outrageous travesty of justice ever heard of by any state government!'[29]

According to Roderick Meredith, later to be the founder of Global Church of God and then Living Church of God, Armstrong was often badly advised during this period, his later years.

He did not know fully what was going on... He had been misguided and misinformed. When Mrs Armstrong was alive, she would spot the phonies around him and the bad guys. Once he lost Mrs Armstrong [in April 1967, a few months before their Golden Wedding Anniversary], he tended to have people, and I won't name their names, take advantage of him. As he got older, he couldn't see well or hear well, and those things happened and men took advantage of the situation.[30]

John Jewell, current head of United in the UK, provides another perspective on this. If HWA had a weakness, Jewell says, particularly in a Church where there was a lot of politicking by strong personalities, it was in 'his evaluation and selection of people. He always thought the best of people, and gave them the benefit of the doubt.'[31]

The Worldwide Church of God had always been very authoritarian, very 'top-down', a classic case of establishing and maintaining 'the purity of the truth.' In sociologist Roy Wallis' words, 'its protection... requires extensive control over those to whom access [to the truth] is permitted'[32] – i.e. the Church membership. During the 1970s, and right up to Armstrong's death, there were many abuses of leadership which are still unforgotten and unforgiven by former members today. As senior leaders, powerful, ambitious men, constantly jockeyed for position in the hierarchy, they would suddenly find themselves demoted or even disfellowshipped for what often seemed to be trivial reasons. Six months or a year later they might be back in favour, and the person who had fired them might himself be in the wilderness. One reason for all the many variant offshoots today is the unresolved grievances and lack of trust between people who had worked together for decades.

As for Armstrong himself, who has sometimes been portrayed as authoritarian and arrogant, Jewell disagrees. 'That was not so. He was a very nice man, very humble.'[33] He would take the time, says Jewell, to sit down and chat with his staff, unlike some of his chief lieutenants.

AFTER ARMSTRONG'S DEATH

Herbert W. Armstrong died in January 1986, aged 94.[34] When a prophet/founder/leader dies, as was seen in Chapter 6, there are nearly always problems. In the Worldwide Church of God it had always been believed that as God's End-Time apostle Armstrong would be around to see Christ's return, and receive his reward for his work. His appointed successor Joseph W. Tkach's letter to co-workers announcing Armstrong's death got around this first problem:

Perhaps God saw fit, as He describes in Isaiah 57:1, to spare Mr Armstrong, at his advanced age, from the persecutions and trials prophesied to come as we finish the work of God for this age.[35]

There was no doubt that many in the Church had seen things over the years which needed improvement. Some of the doctrines were perhaps a little awry, some of the literature was perhaps a little over-written, and a lot of members were unhappy about the authoritarianism. Within a year of Armstrong's death a full literature review and a doctrinal review had been initiated by Tkach.

Joseph W. Tkach's son, then known as Joe Jnr, had attended a non-denominational Christian university, Azusa Pacific University, and had started to question the teachings of his own Church. He was very influential on his father; both were eventually converted to Evangelical Christianity, and 'born again'. Initially this remained unannounced. The Tkaches gradually introduced doctrinal changes to the Church, and initially these were accepted by most members, because of the authority of the leadership. (There had been changes in past years, under Armstrong; his authority had guaranteed their acceptance.) But now the changes kept coming, until eventually the Church was taking a diametrically opposed stance on many of its former core beliefs.

The Church was beginning the process of what sociologist Bryan R. Wilson calls 'denominationalization': 'the loosening rigour; the loss of the sense of dissent and protest; the reduction of distance from other Christians; and the muting of claims that the sect's distinctive teachings are necessary for salvation.'[36]

For example, on British-Israelism, the core of Armstrong's entire prophetic teaching, the Church now announced:

> after having carefully researched the tenets and history of its belief that the United States and Britain are the descendants of the ancient Israelite tribes of Manasseh and Ephraim, the Worldwide Church of God no longer teaches this doctrine. While it may be an interesting theory, there is simply a lack of credible evidence, either in the biblical account or the historical record, to support a conclusion regarding the modern identity of the lost 10 tribes of Israel. We recognize that there were hermeneutical and historical inaccuracies in the Church's past understanding of this issue.[37]

Without Ephraim = Britain and Manasseh = USA, the distinctive central plank of Worldwide's message, of Herbert W. and Garner Ted Armstrong's prophetic teaching for several decades, was discarded completely by the Church the father had founded and the son had run.

WCG leaders now also admitted what critics of the old WCG had been pointing out for decades: that Armstrong's *The United States and Britain in Prophecy* (in all its versions) was a direct plagiarization of *Judah's Sceptre and Joseph's Birthright* by J.H. Allen, published c. 1917.

On Armstrong's 'startling coincidences' between the beginnings of the Early Church's ministry and his own, a spokesman for the WCG said in 1995, 'Regarding 19-year time cycles, we no longer have any formal statements or beliefs on this particular topic.'[38]

For decades Armstrong had preached that Christ would return very soon. Like the Jehovah's Witnesses, he pointed to the 'signs of the times': drastic changes in the weather, drought, wars, famines, pestilences. His booklet *1975 in Prophecy* did not say definitively that Christ would return by that year, but it did say, speaking of a major drought, 'the indications of prophecy are that this drought... will strike *sooner* than 1975 – probably between 1965 and 1972! This will be the very *beginning*, as Jesus said, of the Great Tribulation!'[39] Throughout the booklet he emphasizes the imminence of the Great Tribulation: 'But again, I repeat – IT'S LATER THAN YOU THINK!... All this is now only a few years off.'[40]

Again it depended on God's 19-year cycles. In the 1967 edition of his *Autobiography* Armstrong says, 'Today, we are now almost eight years (written in November 1959 – but, as published December 1967, almost 15 years) into the *second* and *last* remaining 19-year cycle!'[41] Although he immediately stresses that 'the year 1972 by no means is indicated as the year of Christ's return', many members came to believe that the Second Coming would be in 1972.

Looking back through its own history, the WCG now says, 'In the 1970s, growth continued, but at a slower pace, as the Church learned important lessons about avoiding predictive prophecies. Christ did not return as expected, but he did lead the Church to a deeper understanding of the Bible.'[42]

Another great passion of both Armstrongs, father and son, had been debunking the theory of evolution. They and their associates wrote dozens of gloriously illustrated articles, many of them reprinted as full-colour A4 booklets, 'proving conclusively' that evolution was a false doctrine. Titles included *Some FISHY STORIES About an Unproved Theory*, *The Amazing Archer Fish Disproves Evolution!*, *A Theory for the Birds*, and *A WHALE of a TALE, or The Dilemma of Dolphins and Duckbills!* Now the WCG says,

We have firm confidence in the inspired declaration of Genesis 1:1, 'In the beginning God created the heavens and the earth.' We do not deny, however, evidence from science that indicates a long history of life on this planet. We do know that only God can create life, and that the Creator has not revealed exactly how he has done this. Therefore we do not presume to speak for him on this subject.[43]

One of the main doctrinal differences separating the Worldwide Church of God from conventional Christianity was its rejection of the Trinity, which it taught was a doctrine invented in the first few centuries of Christianity; the Trinity limited God to three persons instead of the 'God-family' which Armstrong taught. In his last book, Armstrong said of the Trinity, 'by that doctrine, along with others, Satan has deceived all traditional Christianity.'[44] The WCG taught that Jesus is God, but the Holy Spirit is simply the power of God, an It rather than a He.

But by 1994 the Church taught, 'the triune nature of God is an essential part of Worldwide Church of God doctrine',[45] and by 1995 the Holy Spirit was 'the third Person of the Godhead'.[46] As a member of one offshoot said, 'They went from "hypostasis" to "Person", a process which took the Early Church a couple of hundred years, in just six months.'[47]

Although the WCG had always denied that it taught salvation by works, critics pointed to statements like: 'We are not justified BY THE LAW – we are justified by the blood of Jesus Christ! But this justification will be given only on Condition that we REPENT of our transgressions of God's Law – and so it is, after all, only the DOERS of the Law that shall be JUSTIFIED.'[48]

With the changes brought in by the Tkaches, the Church changed to a more standard Christian theology, saying that it 'teaches that salvation is the gift of God, by his grace, through faith in Jesus Christ, not earned by personal merit or good works.'[49]

While mainstream Christians, beginning to take note of the changes, expressed an initially guarded delight that the Worldwide Church of God was coming closer to orthodox Christian doctrine, reaction within the Church was more mixed. By this stage many ministers had resigned, or had been fired for refusing to teach the new doctrines. Many had taken their congregations with them. Those who stayed were having to learn a new terminology, and to teach the need to be 'born again'.

To outside observers, the final straw might seem puzzling. The WCG had long been criticized by Evangelicals and anti-cultists alike for its legalism, its insistence on obeying Old Testament Law; its members were not allowed to eat pork or shellfish; they must observe the seven Jewish Festivals each year; they must tithe a tenth of their gross income to the Church; and they must worship on the Sabbath, not on Sunday. Such were the marks of the true believer; those so-called Christians who talked about being 'born again' and neglected God's clear commands were, Armstrong said, 'deceived by Satan.'[50]

Now all these practices suddenly became unnecessary. Tithing, for example, 'was commanded under the old covenant, but is a voluntary expression of worship and stewardship under the new covenant.' As for the seventh-day Sabbath, the absolutely essential mark of the true believer, members were now told 'Though physical Sabbath keeping is not required for Christians, it is the tradition and practice of the Worldwide Church of God to hold its weekly worship service on the seventh-day Sabbath (Saturday).'[51] To be told that the Law of God which they had taught for so many years was now only 'voluntary' or a 'tradition' was too much. Many of those who had struggled to accept, and even to teach others to accept the new teachings, and who had echoed the headquarters leadership's condemnation of those who had left, now walked out themselves.

The number of members left in the WCG plummeted; and so, as a direct consequence, did the Church's income. Many of those who stayed, now that they were told that tithing was voluntary, simply stopped tithing. With high expenditure commitments on its magazines and radio and TV programmes, the Church found itself having to lose hundreds of employees and sell buildings to make ends meet. Joseph W. Tkach's letters to co-workers in early 1995 included increasingly frantic appeals for financial support. In 1995 the Worldwide Church of God withdrew its funding of its proudest asset, Ambassador University, and in 1997 the University was forced to close.

Joseph W. Tkach died in September 1995, and his son Joe Jnr (now known as Joseph Tkach) became Pastor General. According to a leading member of one offshoot Church,[52] Joe Jnr had effectively been running WCG for some years, under the figurehead of his sick father – a close parallel to the Armstrongs in the 1960s and early 1970s. But where Garner Ted Armstrong had been ousted from the Church, Joe Jnr, according to many internal sources, had been the one to push through all the changes in the Church. At his father's funeral, Joe Jnr was photographed being embraced by Hank Hanegraaff, president of the Evangelical cult-watching organization the Christian Research Institute (see page 104-105).[53]

Many ex-Worldwiders believe that Joe Jnr had planned the whole thing from the start: the conversion (or as they see it, subversion) of Worldwide. He denies this in his own account[54] of the years of turmoil, arguing that they were led, step by step, to the truth; after they had made one change – doubting the truth of British-Israelism – all the others inevitably followed.

How did Joe Jnr and his father turn the Worldwide Church of God around? Sociologist Betty R. Scharf, commenting on H.R. Niebuhr's belief that 'a pure sect-type religion is always transient', says that 'The original leader dies, and his successor may not be able to evoke the same personal loyalty (if he does so among part of the following, there is likely to be a further split in the sect).'[55] While this is certainly true in the case of WCG, the situation here is even more complicated than the 'pure' type which Scharf describes.

Armstrong had inspired strong personal loyalty, and since his death still does among many of the former WCG members. When there had been changes in beliefs and practices (and there were several over the years), Armstrong spoke and his followers followed. Scharf lays the emphasis on the *person* of the leader, and this is undoubtedly true, but this is only part of the story. Although Joseph Tkach had been appointed the successor by Armstrong, the continuing power of the leadership in

WCG did not rest on the succession of *personal* loyalty alone. Armstrong had also enforced a strict top-down form of Church government, and this continued after his death. The Church leadership had its authority directly from God, and must be obeyed *even if it was wrong* (I Peter 2:18). This was why so many loyal ministers struggled with their consciences for so long to teach what they were told they must now teach, even if they personally still believed the old teachings. Some members who completely reject the new teachings are still in WCG today because they believe that God founded that Church through Herbert W. Armstrong, and so they must remain in that Church even if it is now teaching what to them is outright heresy.

The WCG offshoots point out an interesting change over four or five years in the justification given by WCG for the changes they were making. In summary (and paraphrase):

1 'Changes? What changes?'
2 'We haven't changed any doctrines; we're simply clarifying the language in which we describe them.'
3 'Mr Armstrong, on his deathbed, asked Mr Tkach to look into precisely this area/to correct the errors in this book. We're doing exactly what he wanted us to do.'
4 'Although well intentioned, Mr Armstrong sometimes got a little carried away in his enthusiasm.'
5 'Mr Armstrong was wrong.'[56]

Many former members of WCG feel that when the Tkaches and their followers changed their beliefs so radically from the beliefs of the Church they belonged to, it might have been better had they left that Church and gone off to join an Evangelical Protestant denomination. They were very much the minority. It was they who had changed their beliefs. The majority still held to the teachings of Herbert W. Armstrong. The Tkaches rejected his teachings, but because of their position were able effectively to hijack his Church – an emotive term, but this is how it must have felt to those who continued to hold to the old beliefs. If the Tkaches had left the Church Armstrong founded, they could have left the majority of members to remain true to those teachings within the organization founded on those teachings. That would, some feel, have been a more satisfactory, even a more honest, resolution. It would also have avoided what has been for many members the appalling turmoil of the last few years, with loyalties, friends and even families split apart – and also the problems over physical, financial and intellectual property rights: buildings, pensions, HWA's books, etc., including Armstrong's pride and joy, Ambassador University, which might still now be functioning.

By analogy, if the Archbishop of Canterbury became a Roman Catholic, one would expect him to leave the Church of England, rather than to try to take the entire Church with him into Catholicism.

But from the viewpoint of the Tkaches, they had found the Truth, and had seen the error of their (and their Church's) ways, and had an absolute duty to bring the Church out of darkness into light.

THE 1989-95 SCHISM, TO DATE

As the doctrinal changes in Worldwide became more evident, an ever-increasing number of ministers and members holding to the old Armstrongite beliefs left to found new Churches holding to slightly different versions of the old beliefs. At the time of writing these now number over 200. The main players are:

- Worldwide Church of God (membership still falling; in March 2000 it was said to be c. 40,000 – much less than half its pre-schism membership)
- United Church of God (c. 11,500)
- Living Church of God (4,000–5,000)
- Philadelphia Church of God (c. 7,500)
- Church of God, International (less than 1,000)
- Churches of God (location)/Churches of God Outreach Ministries (? c. 3,000)

In addition, there are at least three other types of offshoot. There are smaller Churches, often no more than one or two congregations, which for doctrinal or sometimes personal reasons prefer to keep independent from any of the major offshoots. One of many examples is a church in Texas, which split from United when United's headquarters tried to move their pastor elsewhere. Most of the congregation, and the pastor himself, wanted him to stay, but United imposed a new pastor. At least initially, the congregation held a United Church of God morning meeting, with the new pastor, who was salaried by UCG, and a separatist afternoon meeting, with the old pastor, unpaid, in the same hall. Many members went to both meetings.

Secondly, there are believers who have cried 'A plague on all your houses,' and don't attend any of the Churches. They keep their own faith going with teaching tapes and booklets, and go to whichever festival sites most appeal to them. According to Dixon Cartwright of *The Journal*, there are thousands of these 'living-room Churches'.[57]

Third, there are several new organizations such as Christian Educational Ministries which insist that they are not new Churches, but have set themselves up to provide teaching materials – booklets, tapes, radio programmes – for whoever wants them. At this point, most of these seem to be holding fairly closely to the classical teachings of Armstrong's Worldwide Church, or to the modified version of his son's

CGI/ICG (see below); but in light of the rapid changes since 1995, it would be worth keeping an eye on them to see whether they start taking tithes, having their own festivals, holding their own services, and insisting on their own version of the doctrines – i.e., whether they have become Churches in their own right.

In the midst of all this turmoil, a group of former WCG members produced a monthly newspaper for nearly two years, *In Transition: News of the Churches of God*. When this closed, in January 1997, its editor continued with a similar newspaper, *The Journal: News of the Churches of God*. These papers kept many former members of WCG, whether or not they had joined any of the offshoots, in touch with the wider picture. They also, for the first time in the history of Armstrong's Church, enabled differing beliefs and viewpoints to be aired in detail and in public. Articles and letters in any one issue might hold up Armstrong himself as a great, revered teacher and prophet, God's Apostle, or criticize him for his authoritarianism and inconsistencies. Hotly debated issues such as the precise calendar to be followed to set the dates of the Holy Days each year, or the importance or otherwise of using the Holy Names Yahweh and Yeshua, or (a perennial favourite) exactly how God's Church on Earth should be governed, are set out and argued from many different sides. There is a considerable amount of in-depth theological debate – far more so than is normally available to members of *any* religion, alternative or mainstream; for example, the long and complex arguments of the first few centuries of Christianity were revisited in a series of articles of divergent opinions on the balance of divinity and humanity in Jesus.

The letters pages show how valuable individual members find this free exchange, and also reflect a range of stances from the absolute intransigence of 'We alone have the Truth; all the rest of you are wrong' to 'Why can't we accept the 99 per cent we all hold in common, and agree to differ on the 1 per cent?' (paraphrased comments).

Interestingly, through these newspapers members of the WCG family who had thought that the Church of God and the Seventh-day Adventists had gone in different directions a century ago, discovered that there are still links between the two. A prominent SDA scholar, Dr Samuele Bacchiocchi, wrote a number of articles based on his books, particularly *God's Festivals in Scripture and History*, which takes the stance that the Jewish Holy Days are still to be observed. It should be noted, though, that there is also a range of beliefs within the SDA Church, and that Dr Bacchiocchi's views are not universally held within his own Church. Also, the SDA, like the new-look WCG, now believes in the Trinity, which is anathema to the WCG offshoots that maintain the classical WCG beliefs.

Former WCG members can now 'shop around' for the right Church for themselves. It has been suggested that the main Churches are images of WCG as it was in different decades: the 1950s can be seen in Philadelphia, the 1960s in Global/Living, the 1970s in United, and the 1980s in Worldwide itself.[58]

Most of the minor players fit somewhere into this same general pattern; there are few significant doctrinal differences between the majority of them. A few, though, have a specific focus which marks them out from the rest. Some, for example, stress the Hebrew 'Sacred Names' by which God the Father and Jesus should be known. A few in America have latched on to the right-wing, anti-federal government, conspiracy theories which are shared by both extreme Fundamentalist Survivalists and certain New Age believers. One British group, Midnight Ministries, is run by Malcolm B. Heap, a member of WCG for over 20 years before falling out with his local ministers over alternative health therapies; he was disfellowshipped in 1990. Since then he has devoted much of his time to a prophetic ministry and to attacking Armstrong and Worldwide for their teachings and alleged abuses. Midnight Ministries is effectively a family business; one of Heap's daughters desktop-publishes his newsletters and booklets while, unusually, much of his teaching is based on his interpretation of his wife Helena's dreams.

UNITED

The most moderate old-style members, who accepted that the authoritarianism of Armstrong's WCG had been harmful, and that he might not have been 100 per cent correct in every one of his teachings, tended to join the largest offshoot, United Church of God, *An International Association*. This was founded in 1995 (only after WCG announced it was now an Evangelical Church), and very quickly grew to around 15,000 members (not 20,000, the figure usually quoted), with around 560 in the UK. Its public magazine, *Good News*, is a well produced, rather milder version of the old *Plain Truth*; its internal magazine, *New Beginnings*, focuses on Church news, structure and organization.

United's leaders faced criticism from the start, first of all from those in Philadelphia and Global who had left Worldwide before they did; they were perceived as having hung on to the very last minute, accepting watered down beliefs, making accommodation with the Tkach leadership, hanging on to their jobs rather than having the courage of their convictions and leaving. Only when it became impossible for them to pretend any longer that the new Worldwide had anything at all to do with the Church they had worked in all their lives, only when Tkach actually said that Armstrong had been wrong and that he, Tkach, was now leading them all to the truth, did they leave. They were the last to jump ship from WCG, three years after Roderick Meredith (Global) and six years after Gerald Flurry (Philadelphia) quit or were fired for disagreeing with the new doctrines. As ministers within WCG they had accepted (willingly or unwillingly) and taught the new doctrines, one by one, as they were introduced by the Tkaches. In 1989 and 1992, when members of their congregations had come to them with questions, worries and fears about the new doctrines, wondering whether to follow Flurry or Meredith out of WCG, these ministers had persuaded them to stay under the authority of WCG, and followed the WCG hierarchy line in condemning those who did leave. Then, when the changes became too great to accept, they themselves left and founded United; those members who also joined United found themselves under the authority of the very leaders who had very recently been criticizing them for daring to question WCG. Letters and articles in *The Journal* five years later reveal a considerable amount of lingering bad feeling over this.

In its first couple of years, United seemed to spend as much time organizing its structure – full of checks and balances, boards of elders, doctrinal boards, and numerous commitees and sub-committees – as in preaching their Gospel. The Church was determined to get it right. It would have a collegiate structure of Church government, and would perform its own review of doctrines to prove the truth or otherwise of all its teachings. Both reforming moves were to prove difficult.

Despite its avowed collegiate structure, United was led largely by its Chairman of Elders, Robert Dick, and its President, David Hulme – who, interestingly, was selected by Joseph W. Tkach three days after Armstrong's death to be one of three new TV preachers who 'are dedicated, *humble* ministers of Jesus Christ, who have shown themselves to be *yielded* to Him as *faithful* servants'[59] (emphasis in original). Unusually, in a family of Churches with such a strong American emphasis, Hulme is English. United's UK leader, Peter Nathan, was also very senior in the organization, and on its Council of Elders.

United's name was soon to become somewhat ironic. United's selling point to many of its members was its initial determination to be collegiate in government – almost a voluntary federation of autonomous congregations – in marked contrast to the strict top-down government of classic WCG. But either this was a misunderstanding, or the theory proved difficult to put into practice. During 1997 there were several disagreements between individual congregations and the 'Home Office', causing some congregations to secede from United in protest at decisions from the top. There was increasing talk of splits in United. In response to this, after a five-day meeting in November 1997, the Council of Elders issued a 'Unity Statement' which included a declaration signed by each Council member saying, in part, 'I therefore renounce divisions and schisms as a means of solving our differences,' and quoting Hebrews 13:17, 'Obey them that have the rule over you, and submit yourselves.'[60] This was to be read to each congregation on the following Sabbath. Many saw it as a disturbing response to their concerns about the increasing authoritarianism of their Church hierarchy.

It was to get worse. Within two months the Council of Elders of United removed David Hulme from his position as President; it appears that he had been the main opponent of democratic government within the Church. Rather than stay within United, Hulme founded his own Church of God in Monrovia, California, letting it be known that other disaffected United congregations were welcome to align themselves with him. In June 1998 the UK leader of United, Peter Nathan, led most of his members – around 400 of a total of around 500, and 13 of the 16 UK elders – into Hulme's Church; the remainder stayed with United, with David Fenney as

Chairman and John Jewell as CEO. Nathan's letter to the chairman of United suggests part of the problem. United had offered dialogue with the UK Church; Nathan wrote:

> We feel that such an invitation is very one sided. The purpose of such dialogue would seem to be to help us reach your position, rather than for you to resolve and understand ours. Hence our concern over leadership appears to be misunderstood or evaded.[61]

United was still by far the largest offshoot worldwide, but things were not going well. In its first five years its central leadership had imposed pastors on several congregations – in some cases congregations which had left Worldwide *before* United was formed, and which had voluntarily joined the United fold because of its avowed attitude to collegiate government and respect for local autonomy.

At the end of 1999 United's leaders were also being criticised for their lack of progress on the promised doctrinal review. Especially in view of their far greater resources, they had published far fewer booklets on aspects of their beliefs than either Philadelphia or Global.

United had started big, with well-defined intentions – and then gave the impression to many people that they didn't quite know what to do with them. There is a different view: John Jewell, who joined the United Council after Peter Nathan left, says that they have been pouring a tremendous amount of effort into getting their new doctrinal booklets right; for example, their new booklet on British-Israelism, due out in late 2000, will incorporate much new research and 'will be seen as the definitive version'.[62]

GLOBAL/LIVING

One of Armstrong's closest associates, and one of WCG's most prominent evangelists and writers, Roderick C. Meredith, split away from Worldwide in 1992. In an interview three years later[63] he said:

> One young smart aleck... one of their leaders, he said, 'Mr Armstrong gave the whole Church a bucket of lies!'... When I realized that was their attitude, that those changes were heading in a total opposite direction from everything we had proved was the truth, then I knew it was time to leave.

The last straw for Meredith was WCG's publication of the new *God is...* booklet, which in two editions within six months went from 'the God family' to practically a full-blown Trinity. When he refused to teach the new doctrine, the Church he had been with since the 1940s sacked him.[64]

Meredith founded the Global Church of God, which quickly grew to around 8,500 members (less than 200 in the UK), and was a conscious recreation of WCG: 'All our major doctrines are the doctrines extant under Mr Armstrong at his death in January, 1986.' Global's public magazine, *The World Ahead*, was very close to the classic *Plain Truth*, with articles about how world events show that Christ's return is imminent.

For the first few years the attitude within Global seemed reasonably relaxed; individual members had fairly cordial relations with members of United, the main difference being that Global members wanted strong leadership vested in one man.

But there is strong leadership and strong leadership. There began to be criticism of Meredith in both *The Journal* and *Ambassador Report,* suggesting that he was holding the reins of power too tightly – for example, by not letting other, younger, ministers in his Church speak on his TV programme. At first it appeared that Meredith responded positively to this criticism, but then things changed dramatically over the space of a couple of months.

Global, like any American Church, was set up legally as a corporation; this means, among other things, that there has to be a corporate structure. In November 1998 Meredith suddenly found that his decisions were being challenged by the governing body of his Church. Letters, some private, some public, flew around, each side accusing the other of obduracy, disloyalty, and worse. The half-dozen or so men at the very top of Meredith's corporate structure had turned against him. If Meredith wanted to retain control there was only one way out. He left the Church he had founded and of which he was the head, Global Church of God, and established a new Church, Living Church of God. Something like 80 per cent of Global's members followed him. They had joined Global because they believed in Meredith's strong, top-down leadership. If they had wanted government by committee they would have joined United.

Global was left with a name and a corporate structure, but with no charismatic leader, very few members, and (as when Worldwide started to disintegrate in the mid-1990s), a drastic reduction in income. And there were other problems. Meredith's sermons, articles and booklets were copyrighted by Global, a Church he no longer belonged to. Legally he couldn't use them in Living, and Global wouldn't want to use them with his name on them. There were negotiations about Global licensing Meredith's writings back to him for his own use, but it wasn't even as straightforward as that. As with any leader, much of what he 'writes' is actually written by other people; who, then, has the moral right to be considered the author, the originator?

(This is a problem which has bedevilled all the major offshoots of Worldwide. Many of the booklets from United, Global and Philadelphia are effectively differently worded rewrites of booklets originally published by Worldwide. For an even more complex copyright issue, see page 505.)

The rump of Global also had internal dissension. One of its leading ministers,

David C. Pack, was fired from its Council of Elders in April 1999, in part for complaining that Global was straying from the truths revealed by Herbert W. Armstrong. (He left Global to found the Restored Church of God shortly afterwards.) One of his supporters wrote to the Council; his letter is a damning indictment not just of Global but of much of Worldwide's troubled history:

> You are no doubt aware that there is a high level of suspicion and mistrust of the ministry. It is a widely held sentiment, if not belief, that the ministry – even in Global – cannot be trusted to tell the brethren the truth when it comes to matters of doctrinal aberration, finance and discipline of members and ministers. This suspicion has been nourished for decades, the brethren having witnessed a continual series of scandals at headquarters, beginning in the early 1970s with efforts to conceal the sexual immorality of church leaders, continuing with cover-ups of abuses of tithes in the late 1970s, and culminating with the introduction of heretical doctrines in the 1980s.[65]

There was worse to come for Global. Any corporation, any organization, needs start-up funding, especially if it has an ambitious and expensive publishing and broadcasting ministry. Once it was up and running it could operate on the tithes of its members, but when it began, Global-the-corporation took loans from many of its more well-heeled members. Now most of these had left Global and – quite naturally, from their point of view – asked for their loans to be repaid. Global faced financial crisis. In September 1999 Global 'voluntarily entered into a legal process called assignment for the benefit of creditors (similar to bankruptcy)'.[66] Global as a corporation and as a Church was finished; its remaining members, only about a thousand worldwide, started up a new Church, the Church of God, a Christian Fellowship (CGCF).[66A]

PHILADELPHIA

The Philadelphia Church of God is the most hardline of the major offshoots, and happy to be seen as such. It was founded by Gerald Flurry in 1989, after he asked Joe Jnr why the WCG had withdrawn HWA's final book, *Mystery of the Ages*, about which HWA had written,

> I feel I myself did not write it. Rather, I believe God used me in writing it. I candidly feel it may be the most important book since the Bible... I am now in my 94th year and I feel that this book is the most valuable gift I could possibly give to you.[67]

Joe Jnr told Flurry that the book was 'riddled with error';[68] Flurry refused to accept this, and was sacked.

According to Garner Ted Armstrong, *Mystery of the Ages* was simply a rehash of earlier works, including portions of *The Wonderful World Tomorrow: What it will be like*, which he had co-written with his father in 1966.

> How surprised I was to see page after page, major portions of whole chapters, of my father's book, *Mystery of the Ages*, containing word-for-word excerpts from my half of that booklet.
>
> While millions had been told my father had written a new book; imagined him, as a ninety-one or ninety-two-year-old man sitting there pounding away on a typewriter, the truth was that his books were pieced together from dozens of his old co-worker and member letters, booklets and articles, with various inserts and new material added to tie it all together. While my name does not appear as co-author of *Mystery of the Ages*, I am, in fact, a co-author![69]

The PCG has around 7,500 members, with perhaps 200 in the UK. Its public magazine, *The Philadelphia Trumpet*, is more strident than Global's or United's magazines, and even than the *Plain Truth* usually was in the glory days of Worldwide. The Church is based in Oklahoma, not Philadelphia; its name is taken from the letters to the seven Churches in Revelation 1–3, in which God says of the Church in Philadelphia, 'thou hast a little strength, and hast kept my word, and hast not denied my name' (Revelation 3:8).

Philadelphia sees Herbert W. Armstrong as the End-Time Elijah, as God's true apostle and prophet to the twentieth century. It exemplifies what Bryan R. Wilson says of charismatic leadership – 'In the strong instances we find the messiah-figure, the uniquely endowed guru, or the special vehicle transmitting to mankind a message from beyond'[70] – in this case, after the founder's death:

> Herbert W. Armstrong fulfilled God's end-time covenant concerning the ministry... God gave Mr Armstrong the key of David... Only God's end-time Elijah was commissioned to restore the key of David (Matt. 17:10–11). That is why we print that same booklet by Mr Armstrong. Nobody else was commissioned by God to produce their own version after he died. God is using the Philadelphia Church of God to build on the foundation which Mr Armstrong laid... GOD ESTABLISHED HIS GOVERNMENT THROUGH MR ARMSTRONG – ONE MAN... All of God's Laodicean churches today have rejected that government. That is why God reveals no new truth to them after Mr Armstrong died. But God has deluged the PCG with new revelation, and it will continue to flow to God's very elect.[71]

The Laodicean Church, in Revelation, is the one of which God says, 'because thou art lukewarm, and neither cold nor hot, I will spue thee out of my mouth' (Revelation 3:16).

The PCG not only condemns WCG for its apostasy, but also argues strongly that the other major offshoots, although they have some of the truth, are not following God's will. God's true Church, the Church of God, is only to be found in the PCG.

For its first seven years, the PCG targeted its message at WCG and former Worldwide members. Now it is extending its ministry to the outside world. As in the heyday of Armstrong's *Plain Truth*, Flurry's *Philadelphia Trumpet* preaches an uncompromising message tied in with a prophetic analysis of world political and economic events; the war in Kosovo, for example, was seen (through complex argument) to demonstrate how Germany was once again becoming a potentially imperialist world power. One further distinctive teaching of Philadelphia is Armstrong's mid-1970s belief that the Place of Safety is in the hidden valley of Petra, Jordan; there, God will protect his chosen people (i.e. themselves) from the terrible battles of the End Times.

The Worldwide Church of God no longer publishes *any* of Herbert W. Armstrong's books or booklets. While the other major offshoots are producing their own rewritten and updated versions of the classic books and booklets of Worldwide's Armstrong years, Philadelphia is reissuing Armstrong's own books – despite the fact that their copyright is owned by Worldwide. Worldwide sued Philadelphia for breach of copyright in printing and distributing thousands of copies of Armstrong's final book, *Mystery of the Ages*. The judge's ruling, though ungrammatical, was profound:

> This is admittedly a work by the founder of a religion who has died... This [the Worldwide Church of God] is an entity that has a corporate structure and it also has a religious structure. The people who inherited the corporate structure are not all of the people who used to have religious position. Some of the people that had religious position have now either been taken out of the corporate structure, or they were never in it. The question is – and it is to me a new one – does the surviving corporation, through its board of directors and all such people, have the right to suppress the founder... the right to prevent there from being future printing of the religious founder's work?

The judge discussed briefly the 'Rule of Perpetuity' regarding religions, then went on:

> I do think that if it is, as I suspect it is, that when you're dealing with the first generation after the founder, that you're dealing with very different religious issues. And you are dealing with a founder's work in the first generation after the founder's [death] and you've had a split in the religion, which was by definition different from the corporation... The founder did not dream, I suspect...

that by giving this corporation, which was his corporation that reflected his religion, that those who would come after him would use their corporate power to suppress his religion or to keep any prior practitioners of his religion, or keep any people that were vested with the authority of that religion, notwithstanding they don't have the corporate position, from making that book available on a continuous, freshly printed basis – I don't believe the founder dreamed that.[72]

This legal distinction between the corporate and the spiritual legacy of the founder of a religion appears to be a landmark decision which could have major implications in the future, not just for the WCG family of Churches, but for any schismatic religion, and perhaps most particularly new religious movements.

It is as yet unknown whether the judge's decision will stand; Worldwide dropped their legal action against the Philadelphia Church of God, then promptly filed a new one in a different state. This too was dropped for various reasons; the case then returned to California.[72A]

CHURCH OF GOD, INTERNATIONAL, AND ITS OFFSHOOTS

The story of Worldwide's offshoots is further complicated by Garner Ted Armstrong's Church of God, International (CGI), founded in 1978 when he was expelled from Worldwide by his father. (His hurt and anger over this are evident in his booklet *The Origin and History of the Church of God, International.*) With teachings based on those of his father, but as modified by the Systematic Theology Project of the early 1970s, GTA built his Church up to perhaps 5,000 members in about 100 congregations in the USA and others around the world; many members were new, but others had joined him from WCG, either in 1978 or later.

Leading members of other WCG offshoots have a complex attitude towards Garner Ted.[73] Many of them worked closely alongside him in Worldwide before 1978, and still regard him with friendship and respect, even if they haven't seen him for nearly 20 years. But as one of them said, 'Ted is a great man, and great men tend to have great sins.' GTA was embroiled in sexual scandals in the 1970s, and sex proved his downfall again in 1995.

In brief, a masseuse released a video to the media showing a fully naked GTA in a highly compromising situation. She pressed charges of sexual assault against GTA and, initially, his Church; three years later the case was concluded with an out-of-court settlement. It has been alleged that the masseuse later admitted that she only made the video and decided to take GTA to court once she learned that he was a TV evangelist. (Although GTA's actions are incontrovertible, and appear to be his own fault, this incident does seem to have elements of entrapment.[74])

The elders and ministers of the CGI asked GTA to step down as Church president. When he refused, about two-thirds of them left CGI in February 1996, taking their congregations with them. Initially they intended to be completely independent Churches, known individually as the Church of God (location), but in May 1997 they set up an umbrella organization called Churches of God Outreach Ministries (CGOM), to help co-ordinate literature and other matters. It remains to be seen whether they will eventually reorganize as a Church.

Garner Ted Armstrong continued with a slimmed-down CGI, regularly publishing a newsprint magazine, *Twentieth Century Watch*, and issuing teaching tapes. However, this was only a temporary delay of the inevitable; at the end of 1997 the Council of CGI unanimously voted to remove GTA from all his positions in the Church, including broadcasting and writing. GTA set up the Garner Ted Armstrong Evangelistic Association (GTAEA), and a new Church, the Intercontinental Church of God (ICG).

In personal terms, Garner Ted Armstrong's career as an evangelist has been a sorry downhill path: from effective head and heir-apparent of a thriving, truly world-wide Church with, at its height, 100,000 baptized members, to head of a Church with at most 5,000 members, to head of a Church starting again with only a few hundred,[75] with his moral lapses always on the record. It is perhaps a tribute to his undoubted skills as a preacher[76] and his personal charisma that he still has a band of loyal followers.

It might be thought that the CGOM Churches would have reunited with CGI once GTA was gone. They have the same teachings, and the same heritage. But as with all the offshoots, the history of disputes, often acrimonious, makes reunion all but impossible. Grass-roots members, old friends, might remain in close touch with each other, but leaders remember pain and betrayal.

Garner Ted Armstrong's CGI was never prominent in the UK. According to James McBride, leader of COG (UK) and one of the leaders of CGOM, the remaining CGI 'have about six UK members at present, with a European address in Oslo. COG (UK) are little bigger – we never had a huge following.'[77] An indication of the historical importance of literature to the WCG family is that although COG (UK) has only about 25 members in all, in two congregations, its desktop-published magazine *New Horizons* has a mailing list of 1,750. CGOM publishes a slim pastoral magazine, *Fountain of Life*.

WORLDWIDE

In its beliefs the Worldwide Church of God is now openly an Evangelical Church,[78] welcomed with open arms by Christian cult-watchers who formerly condemned it. Observance of the seven Jewish festivals is being downplayed; Christmas, Easter and other 'Pagan' festivals are now being observed; and most telling of all, the Church has told individual congregations that it is up to them whether to worship on Saturday or Sunday.

Joseph Tkach (Joe Jnr) revels in the new-found freedom. He describes a Church colleague ordering a pepperoni pizza, and continues:

> I've had lunch or dinner with several others who have ordered similar items. I don't know if they're eating these things just to see how I react or if they really want to enjoy the new experience. One friend, a longtime church member, ordered a plate of mussels. Every insect in the ocean was on his plate. And you know what? It really didn't trouble me at all.
>
> I've tasted shrimp, I've tasted pork, I've tasted just about everything now...[79]

After a lifetime of observing the Old Testament laws on 'unclean foods' (Leviticus 11), such a change in attitude is revolutionary.

There are some who still believe Armstrong's teachings, who do not accept the new teachings, and yet who remain in Worldwide because they believe that that was the Church which God established, and they have no right to leave it, even if its leaders have turned away from the truth. They quote I Peter 2:18, 'Servants, be subject to your masters with all fear: not only to the good and gentle, but also to the froward' (RSV: 'overbearing'). The writer of one article in *In Transition* says:

> Without question, Herbert Armstrong taught, preached and wrote more zealously on the subject of government than on any other topic...
>
> Do you realize that the ultimate test is not our willingness to submit to a righteous government. No, that would be too easy. Rather, our acid test involves the proper response to a corrupt government. Are we willing to be under authority to a wicked leader? Will we see God's authority behind the office of that unrighteous leadership?...
>
> Our calling is to involve suffering at the hands of froward (wicked) leaders...
>
> This is exactly what the trial on God's church for the last 10 years has been all about: being under a froward government...[80]

In personal conversations with members of Worldwide in the UK (with the obvious caveat that these might not be representative), the author has gained the strong impression that many are unhappy with the changes – or, at least, with the speed of the changes. One spoke of 'pressure from Pasadena' to follow the new party line. A more objective corroboration is that of the 50 or so Worldwide congregations in the UK, only one meets on Sunday; all the rest meet on Saturday, as they always have done. One member said openly that the main reason she was staying with Worldwide, despite the new teachings, was that this was the Church God had called her to several decades ago.

According to John Jewell of United, some have stayed with Worldwide to fight from within, to attempt a last-ditch attempt to save the Church they spent their lives working for from its apostasy. Some of these attempted to form a semi-breakaway group *within* Worldwide, called Worldwide Church of God Restored (WCGR);[81] this was for 'members who believed in traditional WCG doctrines as taught by the late Herbert W. Armstrong and who... felt they were not free to leave the WCG because of its status as God's church, even if the WCG had altered vital doctrines.'[82] Joseph Tkach (Jnr) agreed that they could hold meetings, but within days had disfellow-shipped them on the grounds that they were teaching what they believed.

Others, too, stayed, including Herman L. Hoeh, one of Armstrong's first four students at Ambassador College in 1947, widely respected in Worldwide as one of the Church's leading doctrinal experts; apparently he was one of the few people whom Armstrong seriously considered for his successor, in the last months of his life.[83] Either Hoeh has turned his back on everything he had studied, believed and taught for nearly 50 years, or he has stayed because, in Jewell's words, he feels 'a duty to defend the people'.[84]

But others, maybe the majority, have stayed in WCG because they approve the changes:

> I am a twenty-year member of the WCG and pleased with the change and believe it is upheld by the Bible. It is such a relief to be out from under the dictatorship of Mr Armstrong's theories, which were very wrong and hard on people. While the people lived like rats trying to live up to his greed, the minis-ters lived like kings. *Never* again will any man get me brainwashed like that. I am very thankful to be free of his teachings.[85]

Yet others have accepted the changes, become born-again Evangelicals, and gone off to join some other Evangelical denomination without all the historical baggage of the Worldwide Church of God.

And some have no doubt dropped out completely.

THE FUTURE?

The Worldwide Church of God has become virtually indistinguishable from any other conservative Evangelical Church; it has become 'denominationalized'. But what of the vast number of offshoots? There is considerable grass-roots contact between indi-vidual members of different Churches, there is a non-aligned news magazine, *The Journal,* covering all the significant developments in the dozen or so most major offshoots, and there are some independent ministries supplying teaching material to any individuals or congregations, whatever their organization. But of the main players, United (at least initially) seemed determined to have a more democratic leadership, Living is very much run by its evangelist Roderick C. Meredith (though he is responsible, as he was in Global, to a Board), Philadelphia believes that it alone is the true Church of God – and no one, apart from his own followers, wants anything much to do with Garner Ted Armstrong.

Even in 1996, when he was still with the Church he founded, CGI, GTA was well aware of this:

> So far as any movement towards ecumenism or co-operation with any of those groups, I am afraid that the major obstacle to all of them would be *me*. I would imagine that the same thing might be said, however, of the leaders of every single one of them, for leaving me completely out of it, I have seen no moves toward any mergers among any of them, but, on the other hand, the desire on the part of each of the individual leaders to maintain a kind of fierce independence.[86]

Some of the smallest players will probably fade away completely; others may join United, or merge with each other; many will remain independent, some in loose mutual fellowship, others becoming a 'Small Remnant', who possess the only Truth. These last would be in competition with the Philadelphia Church of God, which is quite clear on the matter: 'Many wish that the PCG, Global and United Church were all one church again. Do you realize why that cannot happen? All except the PCG have lost the key of David vision.'[87] So far as Flurry is concerned, only the Philadelphia Church of God has the Truth. It is the only legitimate successor to Armstrong's Worldwide Church.

This is disputed by, for example, this letter-writer to *The Journal*, who is referring to an article in a previous issue

> saying that it is well known that the PCG holds more strictly to Mr Armstrong's teachings than any other group. Well, no, that is not well known. In fact, that honour belongs to Rod Meredith and the Global Church of God.

The letter (written before Meredith left Global [GCG], to found Living) refers to God's commission to Armstrong to preach the Gospel of the coming Kingdom of God, and continues:

> Mr Armstrong lived and breathed for that message. The PCG has, and always has had, an entirely different commission. The GCG has always had the same commitment as Mr Armstrong to that commission.
>
> Mr Armstrong's restored truth No 1 was that God's form of government is hierarchical. The GCG teaches the same thing. From the top down means from Christ through the apostle, then through evangelists and then pastors and then teachers (elders).
>
> That means that after the apostle are evangelists, of whom Rod Meredith is

the senior evangelist who has stood up for the truth. To reject that rank (Ephesians 4:11–13) is to reject hierarchical government.

The PCG rejects Ephesians 4:11–13 and so rejects true hierarchical government.

So, when the facts are considered, it is the Global Church of God that continues to teach the truths that Christ restored to His church through his end-time apostle, Herbert W. Armstrong.[88]

For Global, now read Living. Meredith himself, however, is in company with many others in regarding 'other Seventh-day Churches of God, who are keeping the Sabbath and the Holy Days', as brethren, and in hoping that 'God will bring together the vast majority of everyone who is faithful and zealous... together in one place to do one Work before it's all finished.' But it's unlikely that he would ever join up with Garner Ted Armstrong's Intercontinental Church of God or some other offshoots.

I sincerely felt that some of those people had actually been put out of the Church (disfellowshipped) for very good reason. Some of these groups left while Mr Armstrong was still alive, still doing the work and still preaching the truth, and were in fact disfellowshipped properly, and I felt I had no reason to join disfellowshipped members, who left at a time that they should not have left, and left in a spirit of rebellion.[89]

The CGOM Churches, which themselves split away from CGI when Garner Ted Armstrong had his encounter with a masseuse, seem happy to have grass-roots fellowship with members of other offshoots, and are particularly close to Christian Educational Ministries (CEM), another CGI offshoot.

A further disincentive towards union between the WCG offshoots is the heavy hand of history. At least three factors are apparent. First, leaders such as Roderick Meredith, David Hulme and Gerald Flurry go back a long way. They knew Herbert W. Armstrong, they worked with him and for him, and they have many memories, good and bad, of those days. In the 1960s and 1970s there were a lot of ambitious evangelists and elders in various senior positions in the Church; some of that ambition, and pride, is still evident in the way that they speak and write of their close relationship with Armstrong.

Second, a lot of ministers and members still appear to hold grudges about the way they were treated by an authoritarian leadership two or three decades ago, being transferred to new posts against their will, denied promotion, disciplined for alleged misdemeanours, disfellowshipped and then reinstated. Some of those 'abusive' leaders in the old Worldwide are now leaders in the offshoot Churches.

Third, in the great schism of 1989–95, clearly not everyone left Worldwide at the same time. As mentioned above, some members still feel angry that they were criticized and perhaps disciplined by senior ministers for querying the new doctrines, yet those same ministers, having themselves left Worldwide a few months later, now hold senior positions in the offshoot Churches.

Put simply, a lot of former Worldwide ministers and members do not trust, or even like, each other. There is a lot of old pain just below the surface. Former colleagues, former friends, even members of the same families, are now split between different offshoots; some of them may never be reconciled.[90]

The future? Changes were still going on as this chapter was being written, and undoubtedly continued up to and after publication of this book. At the latest count, in March 2000, there were over 200 offshoot Churches. Unless, as they all fervently believe, Christ returns shortly (in which case he would probably crack a few heads together), it is highly unlikely that any of these will merge with each other. It is very likely that there will be further schisms, over doctrinal issues, over personality conflicts, and over the thorny matter of authority.

THE QUESTION OF AUTHORITY

Sociologists of religion use Weber's classic descriptions of traditional authority, rational/legal authority, and charismatic authority. With the first, 'obedience is given to long-standing customary rules, and to men holding traditional positions of leadership in which their first duty is to maintain these rules.' With the second, 'obedience is given to a system of law, and to men holding official positions, whose power derives from, and is circumscribed by law.' With the third, 'obedience is given to a leader... for his personal qualities, not as the representative of a pre-exisiting group, or as the occupant of an office.'[91]

The problem with the Worldwide family of Churches is that they have never resolved the issue of personal or organizational authority, the conflict between charismatic authority and rational/legal authority – or the difference between prophet and priest; this has been a major issue throughout the century or more of the relatively modern history of the Churches of God, since long before HWA entered the scene (see pages 483-484). Effectively, they have tried to have the best of both worlds, with a corporate pyramidal hierarchy under a 'personal-power' leader. The members, in the old WCG, were taught to accept the rulings of the leadership, even if they believed the leaders were wrong, on the grounds that the leaders couldn't be wrong because they were appointed by God, so the member must be wrong. (Or if the leaders *were* wrong, the members must still show obedience; God must be testing them.) So initially, after Armstrong's death, many ministers and members continued in WCG despite the doctrinal changes, because they were conditioned to accept the God-given word of authority. Since the split, some of the leaders of offshoot Churches have continued to believe this of themselves, in contrast to a rather hesitant fresh breeze of democracy blowing through the members.

With hindsight, if HWA had wanted his Church to continue unaltered, he should perhaps have appointed one of his senior evangelists as his successor – perhaps Roderick C. Meredith, who had been with HWA since the 1940s, was one of the very first ordained ministers, and was a fervent believer in HWA's teachings and a charismatic leader in his own right. But there would probably still have been splits: over the decades Meredith had made numerous enemies in the Church, who would have resented his leadership. However, the Mormons and Jehovah's Witnesses went on to greater things under their controversial second leaders – a boost of fiery new blood, of someone taking on the mantle of power and authority of the founder, and running with it. The same could have happened to WCG under Meredith, or another of HWA's close associates.

(In fact, according to one of Armstrong's closest aides in the last months of his life, HWA did not consider Meredith to be a suitable choice: 'Mr Armstrong knew that he showed a strong tendency to want the chief seat, and Mr Armstrong felt he should not be in charge of the church.'[92] Interestingly, neither Gerald Flurry, founder of Philadelphia, nor David Hulme, former president of United and later founder of his own Church, nor Dave Pack, founder of Restored Church of God, was ever considered by Armstrong as his successor.)

If Armstrong had died ten years earlier, of course, his son would still have been his obvious heir – and if GTA had kept both his mouth and his trousers buttoned, he would have made a brilliant second leader of Worldwide: not only his father's son but also very much a driving force, a very gifted evangelist, with the added advantage of being convinced of his own rightness. The irony is that being his father's son made him the ideal heir, but also made it impossible for the two of them to coexist; there inevitably had to be a clash between two such similar strong personalities.

If GTA had succeeded his father it would not have been plain sailing – he had many enemies within the Church, who would have fought and/or left – but he would have had sufficient personal authority to make the changes *he* would have wanted, without destroying his father's Church.

But it was not to be. GTA was ousted, and Armstrong spent his last eight years vacillating over who should succeed him. Again, if he had died six months earlier or six months later, he might have chosen someone else, but fate (or, some in the various Churches say, God) decreed that Joseph W. Tkach was the appointed one – with everything that followed.

The changes in the Worldwide Church of God and its offshoots are continuing to happen; even while this chapter was being drafted, Global fell out with its founder, Roderick C. Meredith, and then collapsed when he left to found Living. So it will almost undoubtedly continue; by the time this book is published, there may have been yet further developments. (see notes 67, 74, 81.) Over the coming years other major players might be forced out; further schisms will almost inevitably occur, for both personality and doctrinal reasons; it is even possible that there might be mergers. This account is accurate and up to date to March 2000.

Notes

[1] *The Plain Truth*, US edition, September/October 1997: 31.

[2] This case study is about the historical Worldwide Church of God up to 1995, the schisms, and the schismatic Churches, rather than about WCG as it now is. Most of the information about recent events is from the schismatic Churches (or 'offshoots'), both from their literature and from interviews – by post, by telephone, and face to face – with senior members of these Churches. Hence there is an obvious bias, both in factual information and in quoted and paraphrased opinions, towards the viewpoint of the schismatic Churches rather than of the WCG. This does not imply any personal bias on the part of the author.

Note also that some of the quotations and paraphrased comments in this chapter are unattributed; these are generally taken from personal conversations with the people concerned, who sometimes asked not to be identified with their comments. This tends to be when they are expressing a slightly cynical view which might not be quite in line with the official stance of their Church; cf. H. Russell Bernard in *Research Methods in Cultural Anthropology* (California: Sage Publications, 1988: 179), who comments that some of the best informants are those who are 'observant, reflective and articulate'. This applies to all those I spoke to. Bernard suggests that, while 'solid insiders... they claim to *feel* somewhat marginal to their culture by virtue of their intellectualizing of and disenchantment with their culture.' Again this applies to many of those I spoke to; their 'disenchantment' with the changes in WCG has caused them to cast a more critical eye over the ongoing story, even within their own Churches. They were also responding, to a greater or lesser extent, to my line of questioning as an outside commentator. To my surprise, most of them appeared actively to enjoy doing this – stepping back to see the wider picture; only one of my informants was clearly uncomfortable with doing so, and rather suspicious of my motives in investigating his Church.

[3] We are fortunate that the process is so well documented, from three types of source: the publications of the various Churches themselves, their booklets, their own successors to *Plain Truth* and their internal magazines; *Ambassador Report*, which was set up in 1976 by a former graduate of the then Ambassador College, to turn a critical and often investigative, but usually fair eye on the Worldwide Church of God; and two monthly newspapers produced from May 1995 onwards by a group of former WCG members to document the schism, *In Transition: News of the Churches of God* and *The Journal: News of the Churches of God*. For some of the background detail, and for many of the leads to assorted organizations and individuals, I am especially indebted to Dixon Cartwright Jnr, editor of both *In Transition* and *The Journal*, and to Barbara Fenney, for supplying me with both papers; and also to John Trechak, editor of *Ambassador Report* (who sadly died while I was writing this book), for supplying several recent issues; and also to certain leaders in the main offshoot Churches both for supplying their magazines and booklets, and for responding to my questions.

Note: emphasis in all quotations is as in the original text, unless otherwise stated.

[4]Quoted in Hoeh 1959: 24.

[5]Summarized from *ibid.*: 18–23.

[6]Richard C. Nickels, 'Writer traces common roots of Church of God and SDA' in *In Transition*, vol. II, no. 2, 19 February 1996: 4.

[7]Ogwyn 1995: 53–63.

[8]*This is the Worldwide Church of God*, 1972: 15. This is typical Armstrong exaggeration: compound growth of 30 per cent p.a. would turn 100 in Year 1 into well over 2,000,000 by Year 35.

[9]Ogwyn 1995: 64.

[10]Ogwyn 1995: 65.

[11]*The Autobiography of Herbert W. Armstrong*, Volume 1, 1973 edn: 366, 373–4.

[12]The relevant book was *The Incredible Human Potential*.

[13]This was a tenth of gross income to be given to God (i.e. God's Church, the WCG). There was a second tithe, to pay for travel to and accommodation at the week-long Feast of Tabernacles, and an occasional third tithe for 'widows and orphans'.

[14]An excellent summary of the development of British-Israelism can be found in Katz and Popkin 1999: Chapter 7.

[15]Ibid.: 80.

[16]Summarized from *The British Commonwealth and the United States in Prophecy*, 1954: 17–20; The *United States and British Commonwealth in Prophecy*, 1967: 115–122; *The United States and Britain in Prophecy*, 1980: 93–102.

[17]Ibid.: 19–22; 118–128; 99–104.

[18]Although Armstrong did not specifically teach 'seed-faith giving' (cf. Oral Roberts and others), he did teach that the more you give to God, the more he will bless you. Another indication of 'the ethos of twentieth-century American religion' was his booklet *The Seven Laws of Success*.

[19]Garner Ted Armstrong, *The Origin and History of the Church of God, International*, 1992: 40. It should be noted that supporters of Herbert W. Armstrong in other offshoots dismiss Garner Ted's claims as those of 'a very embittered man'.

[20]Ibid.

[21]*The Autobiography of Herbert W. Armstrong, Volume 2*, 1987: 496.

[22]*Autobiography, Volume 2*: 548, 550.

[23]There have been many allegations of sexual impropriety by senior evangelists in WCG throughout its history. Such accusations about leaders of new religious movements are not uncommon; sometimes, no doubt, they are blatant slanders, but all too often there is a basis of truth to them.

There were also persistent reports that Herbert W. Armstrong committed incest with one of his daughters for ten years in the 1930s and 1940s. This was revealed by a former senior member of WCG, David Robinson, in his book *Herbert Armstrong's Tangled Web*, six years before Armstrong's death: 'I learned of this in the summer of 1979 from members of his own family' (page 266). Although WCG lawyers managed to block distribution of Robinson's book for a short time after publication, the incest allegations were never confirmed or denied by either HWA or his daughter. The matter was also discussed in several issues of the news magazine *Ambassador Report*; according to *Ambassador Report*, no. 27, April 1984, Armstrong confessed to the incest to at least two named people, including his second wife. Garner Ted Armstrong is said to have confronted his father over the incest in 1978, in what was the last face-to-face meeting between the two. Others, though, dismiss the allegation altogether; United's John Jewell, who knew HWA for many years, describes it as 'absolute nonsense' (telephone conversation with the author, 11 January 2000).

[24]Herbert W. Armstrong, 'Why my son no longer stands "back to back" with me', *The Good News*, April 1979: 25.

[25]Dated 25 April 1979, quoted in Armstrong, 1992: 72.

[26]Ibid.: 52.

[27]*Autobiography, Volume 2*: 591.

[28]*Autobiography, Volume 2*: 598, 602.

[29]*Autobiography, Volume 2*: 601, 603.

[30]Interview with Roderick C. Meredith by Edwin H. Barnett and Sue Ann Pomicter, 24 October 1995, published on the Internet.

[31]Telephone conversation with the author, 11 January 2000.

[32]'The Cult and Its Transformation' in Wallis 1975: 43.

[33]Telephone conversation with the author, 11 January 2000.

[34] When Armstrong appointed Tkach as his successor, the legal document 'gave him all the corporate titles in the organization... and then stated "all my titles except that of apostle."' Despite this, 'Mr Tkach took the title of apostle himself in the first year... yet the spiritual title was never passed on by Mr Armstrong.' (Dave Havir, 'HWA considered several men besides Mr Tkach', *The Journal*, no. 29, 30 June 1999: 1, 10, 13.)

[35]Joseph W. Tkach, letter to co-workers, 16 January 1986, quoted in *Autobiography, Volume 2*: 647–8. (Published posthumously.)

[36]'How Sects Evolve' in Wilson 1990: 109.

[37]'Church's statement regarding the identity of ancient Israel', undated (probably 1994–5).

[38]This spokesman has since left the Worldwide Church of God and joined one of the major offshoots.

[39]Armstrong 1956: 10.

[40]Ibid.: 18, 19.

[41]*Autobiography, Volume 1*, 1967 edn: 408; understandably, this passage is dropped from later editions.

[42]'Where we have been, Where we are going', *Welcome to Our Fellowship*, 1995: 18.

[43]*We're Often Asked...*, 1994: 6.

[44]Armstrong 1985: 42.

[45]*We're Often Asked...*, 1994: 4.

[46]*Statement of Beliefs*, 1995: 2.

[47]Telephone conversation with the author, 21 November 1997. 'Hypostasis' refers to the one person of Jesus combining the two natures of humanity and divinity.

[48]*What kind of FAITH is required for Salvation?*, 1952: 10.

[49]*We're Often Asked...*, 1994: 10.

[50]Armstrong 1985: 224; see also 206–7, 230–2.

[51]*Statement of Beliefs*, 1995: 8–9.

[52]Telephone conversation with the author, 10 November 1995.

[53]Founded by Walter R. Martin, author of the influential Evangelical cults study *The Kingdom of the Cults* (1967 and revisions).

[54]Tkach 1997.

[55]Scharf 1970: 105.

[56]Summarized and paraphrased from conversations with leading members of two of the offshoots, and from Flurry 1992/1994.

[57]Dixon Cartwright, editor of *The Journal*, in conversation with the author, 30 March 2000.

[58]Telephone conversation between a senior member of Worldwide and the author, 6 October 1997.

[59]Joseph W. Tkach, letter to co-workers, 19 January 1986, quoted in *Autobiography, Volume 2*: 649.

[60]Report from the Council of Elders, Compuserve WCG Religion Forum, 18 November 1997, supplied by Bob Devine of Global.

[61]Peter Nathan to Robert Dick, 10 June 1998, quoted in *The Journal*, no. 17, 30 June 1998: 14.

[62]Telephone conversation with the author, 11 January 2000.

[63]Interview with Roderick C. Meredith by Edwin H. Barnett and Sue Ann Pomicter, 24 October 1995, published on the Internet.

[64]Commenting on an earlier version of this chapter, John Halford, Regional Director of WCG in the UK, wrote: '[Y]ou describe Dr Roderick Meredith's split from the Worldwide Church. As you say, you are getting this from his point of view. I assure you, as one who was involved in these events, that the situation was considerably more complicated than that. But I frankly don't think it constructive to wash all the dirty linen in public. The same goes for the situation regarding the formation of United and Philadelphia. Denominational splits are rarely simple.' (Letter to the author, 6 February 1998.)

[65]Letter from David Medici to the Global Church of God Board of Directors and Council of Elders, April 1999, published on http://www.restoredcog.org/medici.htm.

[66]*The Journal*, no. 34, 30 November 1999.

[66A]In June 2000 it was announced that CGCF and United "have begun a dialogue to look for common ground and ways to cooperate with each other." In July 2000 the President of CGCF, Raymond McNair, shocked his Church by resigning from it and joining Living, led by Roderick Meredith, from whom he had split 18 months earlier. (*The Journal*, no 41, 30 June 2000: 1; no. 42, 31 July 2000: 1.)

[67]Letter to co-workers dated 12 September 1985, quoted in Autobiography, Volume 2: 637, 640.

[68]Flurry 1992/1994: 34.

[69]Armstrong 1992: 32–3.

[70]'Factors in the Failure of New Movements' in Wilson 1990: 232.

[71]Gerald Flurry, 'Jeremiah and the greatest vision in the Bible #9', *The Philadelphia Trumpet*, September/October 1997: 5.

[72]Federal District Judge J. Spencer Letts, in the Federal District Court in Los Angeles, 18 February 1997, quoted in *Ambassador Report*, no. 65, May 1997: 3; detailed story in *The Philadelphia Trumpet*, November 1997: 10–27.

[72]This ruling was overturned by a Court of Appeals in September 2000.

[73]The author has discussed Garner Ted Armstrong with leading members of several other offshoots.

[74]*Ambassador Report*, no. 61, March 1996: 4–7; no. 62, July 1996: 7–9; no. 70, October 1998: 3.

[75]As in the past, against all odds Garner Ted Armstrong's new Church is growing. 'We are in the process of attempting to compile a membership list at the present time for ICG which I believe is around 2,000, but this is an approximate figure.' (Garner Ted Armstrong, in correspondence with the author 10 February 2000.)

[76]The author recalls being impressed by his broadcasts on Radio Luxembourg in the mid-1960s.

[77]James McBride, in correspondence with the author, 3 October 1997.

[78]In the USA the Worldwide Church of God was accepted as a member of the National Association of Evangelicals in May 1997. Worldwide in the UK joined the Evangelical Alliance in July 2000.

[79]Tkach 1997: 39.

[80]Philip Neal, "Writer asks: Have we flunked the test on the church?" *In Transition*, vol. II, no. 10, 28 October 1996: 4.

[81]Not to be confused with the Restored Church of God (RCG) founded by former Global minister David C. Pack in June 1999 after he accused the post-Meredith Global Council of Ministers of falling into heresy.

[82]*The Journal*, no. 30, 30 July 1999: 28.

[83]Dave Havir, 'HWA considered several men besides Mr Tkach', *The Journal*, no. 29, 30 June 1999: 1, 10, 13.

[84]Telephone conversation with the author, 11 January 2000.

[85]Ralph and Vivian Milks, letter in *In Transition*, vol. II, no. 9, 16 September 1996: 14.

[86]Garner Ted Armstrong, in correspondence with the author, 29 July 1996.

[87]Gerald Flurry and Dennis Leap, 'The Key of David Vision #8: Royal Spiritual Jews', *The Philadelphia Trumpet*, September/October 1997: 23.

[88]Ellery Burgess, *The Journal*, no. 2, 26 March 1997: 2.

[89]Interview with Roderick C. Meredith by Edwin H. Barnett and Sue Ann Pomicter, 24 October 1995, published on the Internet.

[90]Although this chapter is an outsider's largely objective observation, I am very aware that for those involved in the events of the last few years, this has been an intensely traumatic and troubling time; as a sociological observer I am not belittling the personal pain of members of the Worldwide 'family' of Churches; as a human being I have great sympathy for all those who have found their world turned upside down.

[91]Scharf 1970: 153.

[92]Dave Havir, 'HWA considered several men besides Mr Tkach', *The Journal*, no. 29, 30 June 1999: 13.

Useful Addresses

The addresses of the movements are arranged alphabetically within each chapter. Worldwide Church of God offshoots are grouped together after Worldwide Church of God.

'CULT-WATCHING' ORGANIZATIONS

American Family Foundation
PMB 313, PO Box 413005, Naples, FL 34101–3005, USA
PO Box 2265, Bonita Springs, FL 34133, USA
www.csj.org

Catalyst
Thames House, 65–67 Kingston Road, New Malden, Surrey KT3 3PD, UK
www.catalyst-uk.freeserve.co.uk

CESNUR: Centre for Studies on New Religions
Via Juvarra 20, 10152 Turin, Italy
www.cesnur.org

Christian Research Institute
PO Box 7000, Rancho Santa Margarita, CA 92688–7000, USA
www.equip.org

CCGI: Concerned Christians Growth Ministry
50 Carcoola Street (cnr Carcoola Court), Nollamara, Western Australia 6061
ccgm@ccgm.org.au

Cult Information Centre
BCM Cults, London WC1N 3XX, UK
www.xenu.net/cic/

Dialogue Centre
dcukdci@koral.com

FAIR: Family Action Information Resource
BCM Box 3535, PO Box 12, London WC1N 3XX, UK

INFORM: Information Network Focus on Religious Movements
Houghton Street, London WC2A 2AE, UK
www.lse.ac.uk/experts/inform

Institute for the Study of American Religion
PO Box 90709, Santa Barbara, CA 93190–0709, USA

Liberty Outreach
PO Box 9061, London W3 6GS, UK
Freedom@Liberty.softlet.co.uk

OCRT: Ontario Consultants for Religious Tolerance
www.religioustolerance.org

Reachout Trust
24 Ormond Road, Richmond, Surrey TW10 6TH, UK
reachouttrust.org

The Religious Movements Homepage @ the University of Virginia
http://cti.itc.virginia.edu/~jkh8x/soc257/

Spiritual Counterfeits Project
PO Box 4308, Berkeley, CA 94704, USA
www.scp-inc.org

WORLD RELIGIONS

Buddhism
The Buddhist Society, 58 Eccleston Square, London SW1V 1PH, UK

Church of England
Church House, Great Smith Street, London SW1P 3NZ, UK

Hinduism, Sikhism, Zoroastrianism
Bharatiya Vidya Bhavan (Institute of Indian Culture), 4A Castletown Road, West Kensingtom, London W14 9HQ, UK

Islam
Islamic Cultural Centre and London Mosque, Regent's Lodge, 146 Park Road, London NW8 7RG, UK

Judaism
The United Synagogue, Woburn House, Tavistock Square, London WC1H 0EZ, UK

Roman Catholicism
The Chase Centre, Catholic
Enquiries, 114 West Heath
Road, London NW3 7TX, UK

Sikhism, see Hinduism

Sufism
Sufi Order UK, London Sufi
Centre, Beauchamp Lodge, 2
Warwick Crescent, London
W2 6NE, UK

Zoroastrianism
88 Compayne Gardens,
London NW6 3RU, UK
see also Hinduism

CHRISTIAN ORIGINS

Alpha Course
Holy Trinity Brompton,
Brompton Road, London
SW7 1JA, UK
www.alpha.org.uk

**Anthroposophical Society in
Great Britain**
Rudolf Steiner House, 35
Park Road, London NW1
6XT, UK
www.anth.org.uk

Christadelphians
The Christadelphian, 404
Shaftmoor Lane, Hall Green,
Birmingham B28 8SZ, UK
www.christadelphian.uk.com

Christian Brethren
52 Hornsey Lane,
London N6 5LU, UK

Christian Community
22 Baylie Street, Stourbridge,
West Midlands DY8 1AZ UK

TheChristianCommunity@153.
clara.co.uk
www.newave.net.au/~msamso
n/index.html

Christian Scientists
The First Church of Christ,
Scientist, 9 Elysium Gate, 126
New King's Road, London
SW6 4LZ, UK
The First Church of Christ,
Scientist, 175 Huntington
Avenue, Boston, MA
02115–3187, USA
www.tfccs.com, www.mary-
bakereddy.com

Ellel Ministries
Ellel Grange, Ellel, Lancaster
LA2 0HN, UK
www.ellelministries.org

Evangelical Alliance
Whitefield House, 186
Kennington Park Road,
London SE11 4BT, UK
www.eauk.org

Exclusive Brethren
Bible and Gospel Trust, 99
Green Lane, Hounslow,
Middlesex TW4 6BW, UK

The Family
Postfach 241, Zurich 8021,
Switzerland
www.thefamily.org,
www.thefamilyeurope.org,
family@thefamily.org

**International Church of
Christ**
25 Euston Road, London
NW1 2SD, UK
www.kingdomnewsnet.org,
www.icoc.org.uk,
www.hopeww.org

Jehovah's Witnesses
Watch Tower Bible and Tract
Society of Pennsylvania, IBSA
House, The Ridgeway,
London NW7 1RN, UK
Watch Tower Bible and Tract
Society of Pennsylvania,
Wallkill, New York NY
12589, USA
www.watchtower.org

Jesus Army
Jesus Fellowship Central
Offices, Nether Heyford,
Northampton NN7 3LB, UK
www.jesus.org.uk

Liberal Catholic Church
Drayton House, 30 Gordon
Street, London WC1H 0BE,
UK
PO Box 598, Ojai, CA 93023,
USA

Mormons
The Church of Jesus Christ
of Latter-day Saints, 751
Warwick Road, Solihull, WM
B91 3DQ, UK
The Church of Jesus Christ
of Latter-day Saints, 50 East
North Temple Street, Salt
Lake City, Utah 84150, USA
ldschurch.org

New Apostolic Church
19 Southwell Park Road,
Camberley, Surrey GU15
3PU, UK
PO Box CH-8044, Zurich,
Switzerland

The New Church
c/o The Swedenborg Society,
20 Bloomsbury Way, London
WC1A 2TH, UK

Opus Dei
6 Orme Court, London W2
4RL, UK
www.opusdei.org

Quakers
Society of Friends, Friends
House, Euston Road, London
NW1 2BJ, UK

**Reorganized Church of
Jesus Christ of Latter-day
Saints**
769 Yardley Wood Road,
Billesley, Birmingham B13
0PT, UK
PO Box 1059, River and
Walnut Streets, Independence,
MO 64051, USA
www.rlds.org

Seventh-day Adventists
Stanborough Park, Watford,
Herts WD2 6JP, UK
www.adventist.org.uk

Swedenborgians
The General Conference of
the New Church, Swedenborg
House, 20 Bloomsbury Way,
London WC1A 2TH, UK
www.swedenborg.co.uk,
www.swedenborg-
movement.org

Unification Church
42–44 Lancaster Gate,
London W2 3NA, UK
www.ffwpu.org.uk

Unitarians
The General Assembly of
Unitarian and Free Christian
Churches, Essex Hall, 1–6
Essex Street, Strand, London
WC2R 3HY, UK
www.unitarian.org.uk

**Universal Church of the
Kingdom of God**
232 Seven Sisters Road,
London N4 3NX, UK

Vineyard Churches
www.avc.vineyard.org,
www.vineyard.org

WORLDWIDE
CHURCH OF GOD
AND OFFSHOOTS

Worldwide Church of God
Elstree House, Elstree Way,
Borehamwood, Herts WD6
1LU, UK
300 West Green Street,,
Pasadena, CA 91123, USA
www.wcg.org

**Church of God,
International**
PO Box 2525, Tyler, Texas
75710, USA
www.cgi.org

Church of God (Monrovia)
PO Box 117, Great
Staughton, St Neots PE19
4FH, UK
PO Box 150, Monrovia, CA
91017-0150, USA
www.church-of-god.org

Churches of God (UK)
PO Box 2525, Lincoln LN5
7PF, UK
Churches of God Outreach
Ministries, PO Box 54621,
Tulsa, OK 74155–0621, USA

**Intercontinental Church of
God**
PO Box 1117, Tyler, TX
75710, USA
www.gtaea.org

*The Journal: News of the
Churches of God*
PO Box 1020, Big Sandy, TX
75755, USA
www.thejournal.org
Living Church of God
3 Burnside Tower, Motherwell
ML1 2BA, Scotland
PO Box 501304, San Diego,
CA 92150-1304, USA
www.livingcog.org

Philadelphia Church of God
PO Box 9000, Daventry
NN11 5TA, UK
PO Box 3700, Edmond, OK
73083, USA
www.keyofdavid.com

United Church of God, *an
International Association*
United Church of God –
British Isles, PO Box 4052,
Milton Keynes, Bucks MK13
7ZF, UK
PO Box 541027, Cincinnati,
OH 45254–1027, USA
www.ucg.org

OTHER
RELIGIONS
OF THE BOOK

Bahá'í Faith
National Spiritual Assembly of
the Bahá'ís of the United
Kingdom, 27 Rutland Gate,
London SW7 1PD, UK
www.bahai.org

Holy Tabernacle Ministries
PO Box 7807, London SW11
5ZB, UK
504 West 42nd Street,
Savannah, Georgia 31401,
USA
www.geocities.com/Area51/
Corridor/4978/

Messiah/H'al Mahshiyach
www.messiah.org

Nation of Islam
Box 20083, Chicago IL
60620, USA
www.noi.org

Rastafarians
290–296 Tottenham High
Road, London, UK

EASTERN MOVEMENTS IN THE WEST

Adidam
11 Quantock Gardens,
London NW12 1PJ, UK
750 Adrian Way, San Rafael,
CA 94903, USA
www.adidam.org

**Brahma Kumaris World
Spiritual University**
Global Co-operation House,
65 Pound Lane, London
NW10 2HH, UK
Global Harmony House, 46
South Middle Neck Road,
Great Neck, NY 11021, USA
World Headquarters, Post
Box No 2, Mount Abu,
Rajasthan 307501, India
www.bkwsu.com

Eckankar
PO Box 4496, London SW19
8XQ, UK
PO Box 27300, Minneapolis,
MN 55427, USA
www.eckankar.org

Elan Vital
PO Box 999, Hove, E. Sussex
BN3 1HX, UK
www.maharaji.org

**Friends of the Western
Buddhist Order**
Madhyamaloka, 30 Chantry Road,
Birmingham B13 8DH, UK
www.fwbo.org

**Impersonal Enlightenment
Fellowship**
Centre Studios, Englands
Lane, London NW3 4YD, UK
PO Box 2360, Lenox, MA
01240, USA
www.andrewcohen.org

**International Society for
Krishna Consciousness
(ISKCON)**
Bhaktivedanta Manor,
Letchmore Heath, Watford
WD2 8EP, UK
www.iskcon.com

**Movement of Spiritual
Inner Awareness**
PO Box 513935, Los Angeles,
CA 90051–1935, USA
www.msia.org

New Kadampa Tradition
Conishead Priory, Ulverston,
Cumbria LA12 9QQ, UK
www.kadampa@dircon.co.uk

Osho International
Osho Life Academy, Croydon
Hall, Rodhuish, Minehead,
Somerset TA24 6QT, UK
Osho Commune International,
17 Koregaon Park, Poona 411
001, MS, India
oshobuddhafield.co.uk

Sahaja Yoga
44 Chelsham Road, Clapham,
London SW4, UK
Pandara Road, New Delhi
110003, India
www.sahajayoga.org

**School of Economic
Science**
90 Queen's Gate, London
SW7 5AB, UK
School of Practical
Philosophy, 12 East 79th
Street, New York, NY 10021,
USA
www.schooleconomicscience.org

**Soka Gokkai International
UK**
Taplow Court, Taplow,
Maidenhead, Berks SL6 0ER,
UK
15-3 Samon-cho, Shinjuku-ku,
Tokyo 160, Japan
www.sokagakkai.or.jp,
www.sgi-usa.org

Transcendental Meditation
Roydon Hall, East Peckham,
Tonbridge, Kent TN12 5NH,
UK
www.maharishi.org

ESOTERIC AND NEO-PAGAN MOVEMENTS

Aetherius Society
757 Fulham Road, London
SW6 5UU, UK
6202 Afton Place, Hollywood,
CA 90028, USA
www.innerpotential.org

AMORC
Greenwood Gate, Blackhill,
Crowborough, East Sussex
TN16 1XE, UK
Rosicrucian Park, 1342 Naglee
Avenue, San Jose, CA 95191,
USA
www.amorc.org, www.rosicru-
cian.org

Astara
800 West Arrow Highway,
Box 5003, Upland, CA 91785,
USA

**Benjamin Creme and
Maitreya**
Share International, PO Box
3677, London NW5 1RU, UK
Share International, PO Box
971, North Hollywood, CA
91603, USA
www.shareintl.org

British Druid Order
PO Box 29, St Leonard's-on-
Sea, East Sussex TN37 7YP,
UK
www.druidorder.demon.co.uk

Builders of the Adytum
5105 North Figueroa Street,
Los Angeles, CA 90042, USA
www.BOTA.org

**Children of Artemis
(Wiccan contact group)**
BM Artemis, London WC1N
3XX, UK

Church of All Worlds
127 Carbon Street, Toledo,
OH 43605–1603, USA
www.caw.org

**Church Universal and
Triumphant**
Box 5000, Corwin Springs,
MA 59030–5000, USA
Summit Lighthouse (UK),
65/66 Charlotte Road,
London EC2A 3PE, UK
www.tsl.org/church

College of Druidism
c/o Keltia Publications, PO
Box 307, Edinburgh EH9
1XA, Scotland

Druid Clan of Dana
Clonegal Castle, Enniscorthy,
Eire

Emissaries
Mickleton House, Mickleton,
Chipping Campden, Glos
GL55 6RY, UK
emissary.demon.co.uk

Fellowship of Isis
Clonegal Castle, Enniscorthy,
Eire

**Golden Dawn Occult
Society (Oxford)**
Mandrake of Oxford, PO Box
250, Oxford OX1 1AP, UK

Gurdjieff Society
BM Box 4752, London
WC1N 3XX, UK

Henge of Keltria
PO Box 48369, Minneapolis,
MN 55448–0369, USA

House of the Goddess
33 Oldridge Road, London
SW12 8PN, UK

Isle of Avalon Foundation
The Courtyard, 2–4 High
Street, Glastonbury, Somerset
BA6 9DU, UK

I AM
St Germain Foundation, 1120
Stonehedge Drive,
Schaumberg, IL 60194, USA
www.tsl.org/presence,
www.saintgermainpress.com

Insular Order of Druids
www.insular.demon.co.uk/druids
Lectorium Rosicrucianum
BM LR7, London WC1N
3XX, UK

Bakenessergracht 11–15, 2011
JS Haarlem, The Netherlands
PO Box 9246, Bakersfield,
CA 93309, USA
www.lectoriumrosicrucianum.org

London Group
BM Vixack, London WC1N
3XX, UK

**Loyal Arthurian Warband/King
Arthur Pendragon**
c/o 10 Sine Close, Farnborough,
Hants GU14 8HG, UK
dragons4.demon.co.uk

Midgard's Web
(Heathen networking group)
www.atradyne.co.uk/midgard

Odinic Rite
BCM Runic,
London WC1N 3XX, UK
www.odinic-rite.org
http://odinic-rite.org

Odinism/Asatru
http://www.bcsupernet.com/
users/wodan

Odinshof
BCM Tercel, London WC1N
3XX, UK
www.gippeswic.demon.co.uk/
odinshof.html

**Order of Bards, Ovates and
Druids**
PO Box 1333, Lewes, E
Sussex BN7 3ZG, UK
www.druidry.org

Pagan Federation
BM Box 7097, London
WC1N 3XX, UK
www.paganfed.demon.co.uk

Raelian Movement
BCM Minstrel, London
WC1N 3XX, UK
CP 225, 1211 Geneva 8,
Switzerland
CP 86, Station Youville,
Montreal, H2P 272, Canada
www.rael.org,http://.rael.net

Ring of Troth
BM Troth, London WC1N
3XX, UK
PO Box 212, Sheridan, IN
46069, USA
www. troth.org.uk
http://asatru.knotwork.com/
troth/index/html

Rune Gild
PO Box 7622, Austin, Texas,
USA
www.mackaos.com.au/Gild.
html

Servants of the Light
PO Box 215, St Helier,
Jersey, JE4 9SD, Channel
Islands
www.naradek.org

Society of the Inner Light
38 Steele's Road, London
NW3 4RG, UK
www.innerlight.org.uk

Subud
23 Ashpole Road, Baintree,
Essex CM7 5LW, UK
International Subud
Committee, Jalanl Tegal
Harum No 1, Denpasar
80237, Bali, Indonesia
www.subud.org

Theosophy
The Theosophical Society in
England, 50 Gloucester
Place, London W1H 4EA,
UK
www.theosophical.org

PERSONAL DEVELOPMENT MOVEMENTS

Emin
33-37 Brewery Road, Islington
N7 9QH, UK

Insight
37 Spring Street, London W2
1JA, UK
www.insight-seminars.org

Landmark Education Corporation
353 Sacramento Street, Suite
200, San Francisco, CA
94111, USA
www.landmark-education.com

Neuro-Linguistic Programming
John Seymour Associates, 17
Boyce Drive, Bristol BS2
9XQ, UK
www.hollis.co.uk/jsa

Scientology
Saint Hill Manor, East
Grinstead, West Sussex RH19
4JY, UK
6331 Hollywood Boulevard,
Suite 1200, Los Angeles, CA
90028, USA
www.scientology.org,
www.lronhubbard.org

Bibliography

Most books are listed in the chapters or sections in which they are quoted, or to which they are most relevant. More general books about religion and new religious movements, however, are listed in the general category, wherever they are quoted in the text. This Bibliography also contains books not quoted in the text, but which were useful for background information. Inclusion of a title in this Bibliography does not necessarily imply acceptance or approval of its stance or content by author or publisher.

RELIGION AND NEW RELIGIOUS MOVEMENTS (GENERAL)

Annett, Stephen (ed.), *The Many Ways of Being*, London: Abacus, 1976

Bainbridge, William Sims, *The Sociology of Religious Movements*, London: Routledge, 1997

Barker, Eileen, *New Religious Movements: A Practical Introduction*, London: HMSO 1989, 1992 edn

Barrett, David V., *Sects, 'Cults' & Alternative Religions*, London: Blandford, 1996

Beit-Hallahmi, Benjamin, *The Illustrated Encyclopedia of Active New Religions, Sects and Cults*, Rosen, 1993

Brosse, Jacques, *Religious Leaders*, Edinburgh: Chambers, 1991

Comte, Fernand, *Sacred Writings of World Religions*, Edinburgh: Chambers, 1992

Cozens, M.L., *A Handful of Heresies*, London: Sheed and Ward, 1928, 1974 edn, 1986 impression

Crim, Keith (ed.), *The Perennial Dictionary of World Religions*, San Francisco: Harper & Row, 1981

Davies, Horton, *Christian Deviations: The Challenge of the Sects*, London: SCM Press, 1954, 1961 edn

Deikman, Arthur J., *The Wrong Way Home: Uncovering the Patterns of Cult Behavior in American Society*, Boston Mass: Beacon Press, 1990, 1994 edn

Evans, Christopher, *Cults of Unreason*, London: Harrap, 1973

Evans, John, *A Sketch of the Denominations of the Christian World*, London: Baldwin, Cradock & Joy, 15th edn, 1827

Flower, Liz, *The Elements of World Religions*, Shaftesbury: Element, 1997

Galanter, Marc, *Cults: Faith, Healing and Coercion*, 2nd edn, London: OUP, 1999

George, Leonard, *The Encyclopedia of Heresies and Heretics*, London: Robson Books, 1995

Goring, Rosemary (ed.), *Chambers Dictionary of Beliefs and Religions*, Edinburgh: W. & R. Chambers, 1992

Harrison, Shirley, *Cults: The Battle for God*, London: Christopher Helm, 1990

Hinnells, John R. (ed.), *A Handbook of Living Religions*, London: Pelican, 1984

—, *The Penguin Dictionary of Religions*, London: Penguin, 1984

James, William, *The Varieties of Religious Experience*, New York: The Modern Library, 1902

Jordan, Michael, *Cults: Prophecies, Practices & Personalities*, London: Carlton Books, 1996

Kellett, Arnold, *Isms and Ologies*, London: Epworth, 1965

Larsen, Egon, *Strange Sects and Cults: A Study of their Origins and Influence*, London: Arthur Barker, 1971

McGuire, Meredith B., *Religion: The Social Context*, Belmont CA: Wadsworth, 4th edn, 1997

Martin, Walter R., *The Kingdom of the Cults*, London: Marshall, Morgan & Scott, 1967 edn

Melton, J. Gordon, *Biographical Dictionary of American Cult and Sect Leaders*, New York: Garland 1986

—, *Encyclopedic Handbook of Cults in America*, revised edn, New York: Garland, 1992

—, *Encyclopedia of American Religions*, 4th edn, Detroit MI: Gale Research, 1993

Moran, Sarah, *The Secret World of Cults: From Ancient Druids to Heaven's Gate*, Godalming: Bramley Books, 1999.

Osborn, Lawrence, and Walker, Andrew, *Harmful Religion: An Exploration of Religious Abuse*, London: SPCK, 1997

Otto, Rudolf, *The Idea of the Holy*, London: Oxford University Press, 1923, 2nd edn, 1950

Petersen, William J., *Those Curious New Cults*, New Canaan CT: Keats Publishing, 1975

Puttick, Elizabeth, *Women in New Religions*, London: Macmillan, 1997

Religious Systems of the World, London: Swan, Sonnenschein & Co, 1889, 9th edn, 1908

Richardson, James T. (ed.), *New Religions and Mental Health*, New York, 1980

Ritchie, Jean, *The Secret World of Cults*, London: Angus & Robertson, 1991

Robertson, Roland (ed.), *Sociology of Religion*. London: Penguin, 1969

Sanders, J. Oswald, *Heresies and Cults*, London: Marshall, Morgan & Scott, 1948, 1962 edn

—, and Wright, J. Stafford, *Some Modern Religions*, London: Inter-Varsity Fellowship 1956, 4th edn, 1963

Scharf, Betty R., *The Sociological Study of Religion*, London: Hutchinson, 1970

Shaw, William, *Spying in Guru Land: Inside Britain's Cults*, London: Fourth Estate, 1994

Smart, Ninian, *The Religious Experience of Mankind*, New York: Charles Scribner's Sons, 1969

—, *The World's Religions*, Cambridge: Cambridge University Press, 1989

Smith, Huston, *The Religions of Man*, New York: Harper & Brothers, 1958

Towler, Robert, *Homo Religiosus: Sociological problems in the study of religion*, London: Constable, 1974

Wallis, Roy, *Sectarianism: Analyses of Religious and Non-Religious Sects*, London: Peter Owen, 1975

Wilson, Bryan R., *The Social Dimensions of Sectarianism*, Oxford: OUP, 1990

—, and Cresswell, Jamie (eds), *New Religious Movements: Challenge and Response*, London: Routledge, 1999

Wilson, Colin, The Devil's Party: *A History of Charlatan Messiahs*, London: Virgin Publishing, 2000.

— and Wilson, Damon, *World Famous Cults & Fanatics*, London: Robinson/Magpie, 1992, 1996 edn

CHAPTER 3   SECTS APPEAL

Barker, Eileen, *The Making of a Moonie: Choice or Brainwashing?*, Oxford: Blackwell, 1984

Bromley. David G., and Shupe, Anson D., *The Great American Cult Scare*, Boston MA: Beacon Press. 1981

Clarke, Peter (ed.), *Recruitment Methods and Aims of New Religious Movements*, London: Ethnographica, 1987

Hassan, Steven, *Combating Cult Mind Control*, Rochester, Vermont: Park Street Press, 1988

Hunter, Edward, *Brainwashing: From Pavlov to Power*, New York: 1956

Lifton, Robert Jay, *Thought Reform and the Psychology of Totalism*, London: Victor Gollancz, 1961

Streiker, Lowell B., *Mind-Bending: Brainwashing, Cults, and Deprogramming in the '80s*, Garden City NY: Doubleday, 1984

CHAPTER 6 AFTER THE PROPHET DIES

Miller, Timothy (ed.), *When Prophets Die: The Postcharismatic Fate of New Religious Movements*, New York: SUNY, 1991

CHAPTER 7 IT'S THE END OF THE WORLD AS WE KNOW IT

Bander, Peter, *The Prophecies of St Malachy & St Columbkille*, Gerrards Cross: Colin Smythe, 1969, 1979 edn

Benjamin, Marina, *Living at the End of the World*, London: Picador, 1998

Bynum, Caroline Walker, and Freedman, Paul (eds), *Last Things: Death & The Apocalypse in the Middle Ages*, Philadelphia PA: Penn Press, 2000

Cohn, Norman, *The Pursuit of the Millennium*, London: Secker & Warburg, 1957

Festinger, Leon, Riecken, Henry H., and Schachter, Stanley, *When Prophecy Fails*, New York: Harper & Row, 1956

The Fortean Times Book of UnConventional Wisdom, London: John Brown, 1999.

Hogue, John, *Messiahs*, Oxford: Element, 1999

Katz, David S., and Popkin, Richard H., *Messianic Revolution: Radical Religious Politics to the End of the Second Millennium*, London: Penguin/Allen Lane, 1999

Lieb, Michael, *Children of Ezekiel: Aliens, UFOs, the Crisis of Race, and the Advent of End Time*, Durham NC: Duke University Press, 1998

Maclure, Kevin, *The Fortean Times Book of the Millennium*, London: John Brown, 1996

Mann, A.T., *Millennium Prophecies: Predictions for the Year 2000*, Shaftesbury: Element, 1992

Skinner, Stephen, *Millennium Prophecies*, London: Virgin, 1994

Strozier, Charles B., *Apocalypse: On the Psychology of Fundamentalism in America*, Boston, Mass: Beacon Press, 1994

Thompson, Damian, *The End of Time*, London: Sinclair-Stevenson, 1996.

Weber, Eugen, *Apocalypses: Prophecies, Cults and Millennial Beliefs throughout the Ages*, London: Hutchinson, 1999

CHAPTER 8 CULTS THAT KILL

Elliott, Paul, *Brotherhoods of Fear*, London: Blandford, 1998

Kaplan, David E., and Marshall, Andrew, *The Cult at the End of the World: The Incredible Story of Aum*, London: Hutchinson, 1996

Lane, Brian, *Killer Cults*, London: Headline, 1996

Linedecker, Clifford L., *Massacre at Waco*, London: Virgin/True Crime, 1993

Storr, Anthony, *Feet of Clay: A Study of Gurus*, London: HarperCollins 1996

CHAPTER 9 WATCHING THE WATCHERS

The Cult Awareness Network: Anatomy of a Hate Group, Freedom Magazine, Los Angeles: Church of Scientology International, n.d.

Shupe, Anson D., Bromley, David G., and Oliver, Donna L., *The Anti-Cult Movement in America: A Bibliography and Historical Survey*, New York: Garland, 1984

CHAPTERS 11 AND 12 THE COMPLEXITY OF CHRISTIANITY, AND CHRISTIAN ORIGINS

Alexander, Pat and David (eds), *The New Lion Handbook to the Bible*, Oxford: Lion, 1999

The Book of Mormon, Salt Lake City: The Church of Jesus Christ of Latter-day Saints, 1830, 1950 edn

Bryant, M. Darrol, and Richardson, Herbert W. (eds), *A Time for Consideration: A Scholarly Appraisal of the Unification Church*, New York: Edwin Mellen Press, 1978

A Century of Christian Science Healing, Boston MA: Christian Science Publishing Society, 1966

Cerullo, Morris, *The New Anointing is Here*, Potters Bar, Herts: World Evangelism, n.d.

Chadwick, Henry, *The Early Church*, London: Pelican, 1967

Christie-Murray, David, *A History of Heresy*, London: New English Library, 1976, OUP, 1989

Coverdale, John F., *On the Vocation to Opus Dei*, New Rochelle NY: Office of Communications, Prelature of Opus Dei, 1994

Dawson, Christopher, *Religion and the Rise of Western Culture*, London: Sheed & Ward, 1950

Divine Principle, Thornton Heath, Surrey: HSA-UWC, 2nd edn, 1973

The Divine Principle Home Study Course: 1. The Principle of Creation; 2. The Fall of Man; 3. Mission of the Messiah, New York: HSA-UWC, 1979, 1980, 1980

Doctrines and Covenants; Pearl of Great Price, Salt Lake City: The Church of Jesus Christ of Latter-day Saints, 1876, 1952 edn

Douglas, J.D. (ed.), *The New Bible Dictionary*, London: Inter-Varsity Fellowship, 1962

Eddy, Mary Baker, *Science and Health with Key to the Scriptures*, Boston MA: First Church of Christ Scientist, 1875, 1906 edn

—, *Church Manual*, Boston MA: First Church of Christ Scientist, 1895, 1908 edn

Encyclopedia of Mormonism, New York: Macmillan, 1992

Gilbert, R.A., *Casting the First Stone: The Hypocrisy of Religious Fundamentalism and its Threat to Society*, Shaftesbury: Element, 1993

Gorman, George H., *Introducing Quakers*, London: Quaker Home Service, 1969

Graham, Ysenda Maxtone, *The Church Hesitant: A Portrait of the Church of England Today*, London: Hodder & Stoughton, 1993

Gumbel, Nicky, *Questions of Life: A Practical Introduction to the Christian Faith*, Eastbourne: Kingsway Publications, 1993, 1995 edn

—, *Telling Others: The Alpha Initiative, Eastbourne*: Kingsway Publications, 1994

Hansen, Klaus J., *Mormonism and the American Experience*, Chicago: University of Chicago Press, 1981

Harris, Doug, *Awake! to the Watch Tower*, Twickenham: Reachout Trust, 1988

Hoekema, A.A., *Mormonism*, Exeter: The Paternoster Press, 1973.

Horrobin, Peter, *The Ellel Story*, Lancaster: Ellel Publications, 1998

Hutchinson, Robert, *Their Kingdom Come: Inside the Secret World of Opus Dei*, London: Doubleday, 1997

Jehovah's Witnesses: Proclaimers of God's Kingdom, Brooklyn, NY: Watchtower Bible and Tract Society of New York Inc./International Bible Students Association, 1993

Kim, Young Oon, *Unification Theology*, New York: HSA-UWC, 1980

Lane, Tony, *The Lion Concise Book of Christian Thought*, Oxford: Lion, 1984

Lewis, James R., and Melton, J. Gordon, *Sex, Slander and Salvation: Investigating The*

Family/ Children of God, Stanford CA: Center for Academic Publication, 1994

The Liberal Catholic Church: Statement of Principles and Summary of Doctrine, London: The St. Alban Press, 1986

Lüdermann, Gerd, Heretics: The Other Side of Early Christianity, London: SCM Press, 1996.

Madsen, Louise, The Christian Community: An Introduction, Edinburgh: Floris Books, 1985, 2nd edn 1995

Mankind's Search for God, New York: Watchtower Bible and Tract Society, 1990

Mullen, Robert, The Mormons, London: W.H. Allen, 1967

Robinson, Martin, Rediscovering the Celts: The True Witness from Western Shores, London: Fount/HarperCollins, 2000

Routley, Erik, English Religious Dissent, Cambridge: Cambridge University Press, 1960

Rowley, H.H., The Faith of Israel: Aspects of Old Testament Thought, London: SCM Press, 1956

Seventh-day Adventists Believe... A Biblical Exposition of 27 Fundamental Doctrines, Silver Spring MD: General Conference of Seventh-day Adventists, 1988

Smart, Ninian, The Phenomenon of Christianity, London: Collins, 1979

Steiner, Rudolf, Theosophy: An Introduction to the Supersensible Knowledge of the World and the Destination of Man, London: Rudolf Steiner Press, 1922, 3rd edn 1965

Taylor, Eric S., The Liberal Catholic Church: What Is It?, London: The St Alban Press, 3rd edn, 1987

Tennant, Harry, Back to the Bible, Birmingham: The Christadelphian, n.d.

Tomsett, Valerie, Released from the Watchtower, London: Lakeland, 1971

Urquhart, Gordon, The Pope's Armada, London: Bantam, 1995

Van Zandt, David E., Living in the Children of God, Princeton NJ: Princeton University Press, 1991

Walsh, Michael, The Secret World of Opus Dei, London: Grafton, 1989

White, Ellen G., The Great Controversy, 1911, New York: Pyramid, 1971

You Can Live Forever in Paradise on Earth, New York: Watchtower Bible and Tract Society, 1982

CHAPTER 13 OTHER 'RELIGIONS OF THE BOOK' ORIGINS

The Bahá'ís: A Profile of the Bahá'í Faith and its Worldwide Community, Oakham, Rutland. Bahá'í Publishing Trust of the United Kingdom, 1994 edn

Gleanings from the Writings of Bahá'u'lláh Oakham, Rutland: Bahá'í Publishing Trust of the United Kingdom

The Hidden Words of Bahá'u'lláh, New Delhi: Bahá'í Publishing Trust, 5th edn 1992

Lieb, Michael, Children of Ezekiel: Aliens, UFOs, The Crisis of Race, and the Advent of End Time, Durham & London: Duke University Press, 1998

CHAPTER 14 EASTERN MOVEMENTS IN THE WEST

Brown, Mick, The Spiritual Tourist, London: Bloomsbury, 1998

Cramer, Todd, and Munson, Doug, ECKANKAR: Ancient Wisdom for Today, Minneapolis: Eckankar, 1993 and 1995 edns

Hodgkinson, Liz, Peace and Purity: The Story of the Brahma Kumaris: A Spiritual Revolution, London: Rider, 1999

Hounam, Peter, and Hogg, Andrew, Secret Cult, Oxford: Lion, 1984

Interviews with John Morton and John-Roger, Los Angeles: Mandeville Press, 1999

Janki, Dadi, *Wings of Soul: Releasing your Spiritual Identity*, Deerfield Beach FL: Health Communications, 1999

John-Roger, *The Way Out Book*, Los Angeles: Mandeville Press, 1986

—, *Forgiveness: The Key to the Kingdom*, Los Angeles: Mandeville Press, 1994

Klemp, Harold, *The Secret Teachings: Mahanta Transcripts Book 3*, Minneapolis: Eckankar, 1988

—, *Cloak of Consciousness: Mahanta Transcripts Book 5*, Minneapolis: Eckankar, 1991

Lee, Carolyn, *The Promised God-Man is Here: Ruchira Avatar Adi Da Samraj*, Middletown CA: The Dawn Horse Press, 1998

Lewis, James R., *Seeking the Light*, Los Angeles: Mandeville Press, 1998

Milne, Hugh, *Bhagwan: The God That Failed*, London: Caliban Books, 1986

Prabhupada, A.C. Bhaktivedanta, *Bhagavad-Gita As It Is*, London: Bhaktivedanta Book Trust, 1975

—, *The Science of Self-Realization*, London: Bhaktivedanta Book Trust, 1977

Rawlinson, Andrew, *The Book of Enlightened Masters: Western Teachers in Eastern Traditions*, Chicago: Open Court, 1997

Saraswati, Shantanand, *The Man Who Wanted to Meet God*, Shaftesbury: Element Books, 1996

Sarito, Ma Deva (ed.), *Osho Zen Tarot*, London: Boxtree, 1994

Shah, Idries, *The Sufis*, London: W.H. Allen, 1964

Strelley, Kate, *The Ultimate Game: The Rise and Fall of Bhagwan Shree Rajneesh*, San Francisco: Harper & Row, 1987

Twitchell, Paul, *The Spiritual Notebook*, Menlo Park, CA: Illuminated Way Press, 1971

Wilson, Bryan, and Dobbelaere, Karel, *A Time to Chant: The Soka Gakkai Buddhists in Britain*, Oxford: OUP, 1994

CHAPTER 15 ESOTERIC AND NEO-PAGAN MOVEMENTS

Adler, Margot, *Drawing Down the Moon: Witches, Druids, Goddess-Worshippers, and Other Pagans in America Today*, Boston, Beacon Press, 1979, 1986 edn

Barrett, David V., *Secret Societies*, London: Blandford, 1997

Benjamin, Harry, *Everybody's Guide to Theosophy*, London: Health for All Publishing Co, n.d.

Bloom, William (ed.), *The New Age: an Anthology of Essential Writings*, London: Rider, 1991

Briggs, Robin, *Witches and Neighbours*, London: HarperCollins 1996

Butler, E.M., *The Myth of the Magus*, Cambridge: Cambridge University Press, 1948

Butler, W.E., *Magic: Its Ritual, Power and Purpose, and The Magician: His Training and Work*, 1952, 1959, London: Aquarian Press, 1970

Carr-Gomm, Philip, *The Elements of the Druid Tradition*, Shaftesbury: Element, 1991

Cavendish, Richard, *The Magical Arts: Western Occultism and Occultists*, Routledge, 1967 (originally The Black Arts)

— (ed.), *Encyclopedia of the Unexplained*, London: Routledge & Kegan Paul, 1974

—, *A History of Magic*, London: Weidenfeld & Nicolson, 1987

Climb the Highest Mountain: A Profile of Church Universal and Triumphant, video, Livingston MT: Church Universal and Triumphant, 1994

Cohn, Norman, *Europe's Inner Demons: The Demonization of Christians in Medieval Christendom*, London: Chatto & Heinemann, 1975, London: Pimlico revised edn, 1993

Creme, Benjamin, *The Ageless Wisdom Teaching*, London: Share International Foundation, 1996

Crow, W.B., *A History of Magic, Witchcraft and Occultism*, London: Aquarian, 1968

De Blecourt, Willem, Hutton, Ronald, and La Fontaine, Jean, *The Athlone History of Witchcraft and Magic in Europe, vol. 6: The Twentieth Century*, London: The Athlone Press, 1999

Drury, Nevill, *Dictionary of Mysticism and the Occult*, San Francisco: Harper & Row, 1985

—, *The History of Magic in the Modern Age: A Quest for Personal Transformation*, London: Constable, 2000.

Farrar, Stewart, *What Witches Do: A Modern Coven Revealed*, 1971, 3rd edn, London: Robert Hale, 1991

Farrar, Stewart and Janet, *Spells and How They Work*, London: Robert Hale, 1990

Farrar, Janet and Stewart, and Bone, Gavin, *The Pagan Path: Philosophy of Neo-Paganism*, Phoenix, 1994

Fortune, Dion, *Sane Occultism and Practical Occultism in Daily Life*, Wellingborough: Aquarian, 1987

Gilbert, R.A., *Revelations of the Golden Dawn: The Rise and Fall of a Magical Order*, Slough: W. Foulsham/Quantum, 1997

Greer, John Michael, *Inside a Magical Lodge: Group Ritual in the Western Tradition*, St Paul MN: Llewellyn, 1998

Guiley, Rosemary Ellen, *Encyclopedia of Mystical & Paranormal Experience*, London: Grange Books/HarperCollins, 1991

Harvey, Graham, *Listening People, Speaking Earth: Contemporary Paganism*, London: Hurst & Co, 1997

—, and Hardman, Charlotte, *Paganism Today: Wiccans, Druids, the Goddess and Ancient Earth Traditions for the Twenty-First Century*, London: Thorsons, 1995

Hutton, Ronald, *The Triumph of the Moon: A History of Modern Pagan Witchcraft*, Oxford: Oxford University Press, 1999

Kieckhefer, Richard, *Magic in the Middle Ages*, Cambridge: Cambridge University Press, 1989

King, George, *The Nine Freedoms*, Hollywood, CA: Aetherius Society, 1963

—, and Lawrence, Richard, *Contacts with the Gods from Space: Pathway to the New Millennium*, Hollywood, CA: Aetherius Society, 1996

Knight, Gareth, *A History of White Magic*, Oxford: A.R. Mowbray, 1978

Kramer, Heinrich, and Sprenger, James, *Malleus Maleficarum*, London: Arrow Books, 1971

La Fontaine, Jean, *Speak of the Devil: Tales of Satanic Abuse in Contemporary England*, Cambridge, 1998

LaVey, Anton, *The Satanic Bible*, 1969, London: W.H. Allen/Star edn, 1977

Lewis, James R., and Melton , J. Gordon (eds), *Church Universal and Triumphant In Scholarly Perspective*, Stanford CA: Center for Academic Publication, 1994

Lyle, Robert, *Subud*, Tunbridge Wells: Humanus Ltd, 1983

Matthews, John, and Matthews, Caitlín, *The Western Way: A Practical Guide to the Western Mystery Tradition*, 2 vols., London: Arkana, 1985, 1986

Melton, J. Gordon, Clark, Jerome, and Kelly, Aidan A., *New Age Almanac*, Detroit MI: Gale Research/Visible Ink, 1991

Moore, James, *Gurdjieff: A Biography*, Shaftesbury, Dorset: Element Books, 1991, 1999 edn

Murray, Margaret, *The Witch-Cult in Western Europe*, 1921, Oxford: Oxford University Press, 1962

—, *The God of the Witches*, 1931, New York: Oxford University Press, 1970

Nataf, André, *The Occult*, Edinburgh: Chambers, 1991

Nichols, Ross, *The Book of Druidry*, London: Aquarian Press, 1990

Parker, John, *At the Heart of Darkness*, London: Sidgwick & Jackson, 1993

Piggot, Stuart, *The Druids*, London: Thames & Hudson, 1968

Pollack, Rachel, *The New Tarot*, Wellingborough: Aquarian, 1989

Prophet, Mark L. and Elizabeth Clare, *Saint Germain on Alchemy: Formulas for Self-Transformation*, Livingston MA: Summit University Press, 1985

Prophet, Elizabeth Clare, *The Lost Years of Jesus*, Livingston MA: Summit University Press, 1987

—, *The Lost Teachings of Jesus 1: Missing Texts, Karma and Reincarnation*, Livingston MA: Summit University Press, 1986, 1994 edn

Raël, *The Message Given To Me By Extra-Terrestrials: They Took Me to Their Planet*, Liechtenstein: Raelian Foundation/Tokyo: AOM Corporation, 1986

—, *The Final Message*, London: The Tagman Press, 1998

Regardie, Israel, *The Golden Dawn*, One-volume edition, St Paul MN: Llewellyn, 1971, 6th edn, 1989.

Shallcrass, Philip, *A Druid Directory 1995: A Guide to Modern Druidry and Druid Orders*, St Leonards-on-Sea: British Druid Order, 1995

Shallcrass, Philip (ed.), *Druidry: Rekindling the Sacred Fire*, St Leonards-on-Sea: British Druid Order, 1999

Shan, *Which Craft?*, London: House of the Goddess, 1986

—, *The Pagan Index*, London: House of the Goddess, 1994

Storm, Rachel, *In Search of Heaven on Earth*, London: Bloomsbury, 1991

Sutin, Lawrence, *Do What Thou Wilt: A Life of Aleister Crowley*, New York: St. Martin's Press, 2000

Thomas, Keith, *Religion and the Decline of Magic*, London: Weidenfeld & Nicolson, 1971

West, Kate, *Born in Albion: The Rebirth of the Craft*, Runcorn: Pagan Media Ltd, 1997

White, Ralph (ed.), *The Rosicrucian Enlightenment Revisited*, Hudson NY: Lindisfarne Books, 1999

Yates, Frances A., *The Rosicrucian Enlightenment*, London: Routledge, 1972

CHAPTER 16 PERSONAL DEVELOPMENT MOVEMENTS

Atack, Jon, *A Piece of Blue Sky*, New York: Carol Publishing, 1990

Carnegie, Dale, *How to Win Friends and Influence People*, Kingswood, Surrey: The World's Work, n.d.

The Church of Scientology: 40th Anniversary, Los Angeles: Church of Scientology International, 1994

Clute, John, and Nicholls, Peter, *The Encyclopedia of Science Fiction*, London: Orbit, 1993 edn

Corydon, Bent, *L. Ron Hubbard, Messiah or Madman?*, Fort Lee, NJ: Barricade Books, 1987, 1992 edn

A Description of the Scientology Religion, Los Angeles: Bridge Publications, 1994

Evans, Christopher, *Cults of Unreason*, London: Harrap, 1973

Hubbard, L. Ron, *Dianetics: The Modern Science of Mental Health*, Copenhagen: New Era Publications, 1950, 1981 edn

—, *Scientology 0–8: The Book of Basics*, Copenhagen: Scientology Publications Organization, 1970, 1976 edn

—, *Have You Lived Before This Life? A Scientific Survey*, Copenhagen: Scientology Publications Organization, 2nd edn, 1978

L. Ron Hubbard: A Profile, Los Angeles: Bridge Publications, 1995

L. Ron Hubbard: Education, Literacy & Civilization, Los Angeles: Bridge Publications, 1996

Lamont, Stewart, *Religion Inc.: The Church of Scientology*, London: Harrap, 1986

Leo, *Dear Dragon*, UK, 1976, Israel: Topaz, 1992

Mathison, Volney G., *Creative Image Therapy*, Mathison Electropsychometers, 1954

Miller, Russell, *Bare-Faced Messiah*, London: Michael Joseph, 1987

O'Connor, Joseph, and Seymour, John, *Introducing NLP*, London: Aquarian, 1990, 1993 edn

Peale, Norman Vincent, *The Power of Positive Thinking*, Kingswood, Surrey: The World's Work, 1953

Reference Guide to the Scientology Religion, Los Angeles: Church of Scientology International, 1994

Ron: The Explorer: Daring Deeds and Unknown Realms, Los Angeles: Bridge Publications, 1996

Ron: The Humanitarian: Rehabilitating a Drugged Society, Los Angeles: Bridge Publications, 1996

Ron: Letters and Journals: Early Years of Adventure, Los Angeles: Bridge Publications, 1997

Ron: The Writer: The Shaping of Popular Fiction, Los Angeles: Bridge Publications, 1997

Scientology Theology & Practice of a Contemporary Religion, Los Angeles: Bridge Publications, 1998

'Secret Lives': Merchants of Chaos, video, Freedom magazine, Church of Scientology International, 1998

Smiles, Samuel, *Self-Help, with Illustrations of Conduct and Perseverance*, London: John Murray, 1908

The Scientology Handbook, Los Angeles: Bridge Publications, 1994

The Scientology Religion, East Grinstead: Church of Scientology World Wide, 1974 edn

Vosper, Cyril, *The Mind Benders*, London: Neville Spearman, 1971

The Way to Happiness: A Common Sense Guide to Better Living, Los Angeles: Bridge Publications, 1989

What Is Scientology?, Los Angeles CA: Bridge Publications, 1993 and 1998 edns

CHAPTER 17 CASE STUDY: THE WORLDWIDE CHURCH OF GOD AND ITS OFFSHOOTS

Armstrong, Garner Ted, *The Origin and History of the Church of God*, International, Tyler TX: Church of God, International, 1992

—, *Europe and America in Prophecy*, Tyler TX: Church of God, International, 1994

Armstrong, Herbert W., *The British Commonwealth and the United States in Prophecy*, Pasadena CA: Ambassador College, 1954

—, *Mystery of the Ages*, Pasadena CA: Worldwide Church of God, 1985

—, *The United States and British Commonwealth in Prophecy*, Pasadena CA: Ambassador College, 1967

—, *The United States and Britain in Prophecy*, Pasadena CA: Worldwide Church of God, 1980

—, *1975 in Prophecy*, Pasadena CA: Radio Church of God 1956

— and Garner Ted, *The Wonderful World Tomorrow: What it Will be Like*, Pasadena CA: Ambassador College, 1966

The Autobiography of Herbert W. Armstrong, vol. 1, Pasadena CA: Ambassador College, 1967 edn, 1973 edn, Pasadena CA: Worldwide Church of God, 1986 edn

The Autobiography of Herbert W. Armstrong, vol. 2, Pasadena CA: Worldwide Church of God, 1987

Bacchiocchi, Samuele, *God's Festivals in Scripture and History Part 1: The Spring Festivals*, Berrien Springs MI: Biblical Perspectives, 1995

Bowden, John, *Herbert W. Armstrong and His Worldwide Church of God: An Exposure and An Indictment*, Chippendale, New South Wales: R.Marke/The Rationalist Association of N.S.W., 2nd revised edn, n.d.

Buchner, J.L.F., *Armstrongism Bibliography*, Sydney, Australia, 1983

Campbell, Roger F., *Herbert W. Armstrong: Mr Confusion*, Lincoln NB: Back to the Bible Broadcast, 1962

Flurry, Gerald, *Malachi's Message to God's Church Today*, Edmond OK: Philadelphia Church of God, 1990, 1995 edn

—, *Worldwide Church of God Doctrinal Changes and the Tragic Results*, Edmond OK: Philadelphia Church of God, 1992, 1994 edn

Hoeh, Herman L., *A True History of the True Church*, Pasadena CA: Radio Church of God, 1959

Hopkins, Joseph Martin, *The Armstrong Empire: A Look at the Worldwide Church of God*, USA: William B. Eerdmans, 1974

McNair, Raymond F., *America and Britain in Prophecy*, San Diego CA: Global Church of God, 1996

Ogwyn, John, *God's Church Through the Ages*, San Diego: Global Church of God 1995

Robinson, David, *Herbert Armstrong's Tangled Web: An Insider's View of the Worldwide Church of God*, Tulsa OK: John Hadden, 1980

This is the Worldwide Church of God, Ambassador College, 1972

Tkach, Joseph, *Transformed By Truth*, Sisters OR: Multnomah, 1997

Alphabetical list of entries

This list (against page numbers) includes popular and alternative names for some movements.

Index

Darby, John Nelson 77, 140, 162–3
Darbyites 163
  see also Exclusive Brethren
Das, Master Gopal 318
Das, Shaunaka Rishi 288–9
Davidian Seventh-day Adventists
  see Branch Davidians
Davies, Maureen 104
Dawn Horse Communion 298
De, Abhay Charan (A. C. Bhaktivedanta Swami Prabhupada) 62, 283–5, 287, 309
Deception, recruitment techniques 30–9
Definitions 16–18
  alternative religion 24
  cult 19–27, 28
  New Religious Movements 24
  problems of 19–27
  religions 19–27
  sociological 23–5
Deists 144
Deliverance ministry 216–17
Demonization 94
Denominationalization 42, 59–60, 64, 492, 509
Deprogramming 99–101, 379
Dev, Guru 267, 276–7, 282
Devi, Shri Mataji Nirmala (Shri Mataji) 296–8
Dexter, Giles 393–4
Dharma, Bhagavat 284–5, 287–8
Di Mambro, Joseph 89, 93
Dianetics see Scientology
Dianic Wicca 399
Dick, Robert 500
Disciples of Christ 173
Discrimination, religious 40–1
Dispensationalism 71, 77, 163
Dittemore, John V. 180
Divine Light Mission see Elan Vital
Divine Science of Light and Sound 321
Doctrinal differences, Christianity 126–9
Doctrine 68, 485–7
Drew, Timothy (Noble Drew Ali) 251–2
Druid Forum 405
Druidry 335, 372, 405–10
Drummond, Sir Henry 166
Dugger, Andrew 484
Dunkley, Archibald 259
Durdin-Robertson, Rev. Lawrence 410
Durdin-Robertson, Pamela 410
Dynamic Meditation 290, 296
Dynamic Monarchianism 136

Eastern movements in the West
  Adidam 298–300
  appeal for the West 262–3
  Brahma Kumaris 263–6

Eckankar 279, 312–21, 436
Elan Vital 65, 325–9
Friends of the Western Buddhist Order 307–10
Impersonal Enlightenment Fellowship 300–1
ISKCON (Hare Krishna) 24, 62, 262–3, 283–9, 309, 444
Movement of Inner Spiritual Awareness 321–4
New Kadampa Tradition 310–11
Osho International 290–6, 374
Sahaja Yoga 296–8
School of Economic Science 61, 266–76, 433, 441
Soka Gakkai International 302–7
Transcendental Meditation 26, 267, 272, 276–82, 283
Eaton, Michael 56
Echevarría, Bishop Javier 201
Eckankar 436
  beliefs and practices 279, 314–21
  history 312–14
Eddy, Asa 177
Eddy, Mary Baker 66, 176–81
Edson, Hiram 169
Elan Vital 65
  beliefs and practices 326–9
  history 325–6
Elim 214
Ellel Ministries 214, 233–4
Emerson, Ralph Waldo 144, 147, 149
Emin
  beliefs and practices 440–6
  history 437–40
Eminent Way see Emin
Emissaries of Divine Light 381–4
Emma Hopkins College of Metaphysical Science 179
Emotions, Christian worship 215–16
End Times 167, 385, 487–8
  Branch Davidians 86
  Christian millennium 71–2
  The Family 218
  interpretation problems 125
  Jehovah's Witnesses 186
  Nation of Islam 251
  prophecies 74–7, 80–1
  Second Coming 71–2, 149
English Sangha Trust 307–8
Enlightenment, Age of 144
Enthusiasm, Christian worship 215–16
Episcopi vagantes (Wandering Bishops) 195
Erhard Seminar Training (est) 427–30, 434
Erhard, Werner (John Paul Rosenberg) 427–8
Escrivá de Balaguer y Albas, Monsignor Josemaría 200, 202
Esoteric & Neo-Pagan movements 183, 215, 295, 333–424
  see also Theosophy

Est see Erhard Seminar Training
Eucharist 127
Eusebius 134
Evangelical Alliance 217, 229
Evangelicalism 80, 213–14, 349
  fervent Christian 42–3
  Reachout Trust 103–4
  resurgence 211–17
Evans, Christopher 453, 472
Evans, Heather 326
Evans, John 123, 139
Evans, Thomas Penry 365
Exclusive Brethren (Plymouth Brethren) 77, 140
  beliefs 163–5
  Bible and Gospel Trust 162
  origins 162–3
  services 165–6
  women 166
Exegesis 428–9
Exit counselling 54

FACE see Friends of Andrew Cohen Everywhere
Factors affecting change 66–9
Faculty of Colour see Emin
FAIR see Family Action Information and Resource
Families of members
  advice 40–6
  campaigns against new religions 99–100
  legal action 43, 100
  beliefs and practices 222–7
  history 61, 217–22
  recruitment 221, 224
Family Action Information and Resource (FAIR) 28, 101–2
Family of Love see The Family
Fard, W. D. (Master Fard Muhammad) 251, 253
Farrakhan, Louis (Louis Eugene Wolcott) 252
Farrar, Stewart 338, 400, 418
Father David see Berg, David Brandt
Federal Bureau of Investigation (FBI) 82, 86–8, 93
Federation for World Peace and Unification 203, 207
Fellow Members, The Family 225
Fellowship 54–6
Fellowship of Independent Missionary Communities see The Family
Fellowship of Isis 410–11
Festinger, Leon 79
Ficino, Marsilio 275
Fielding, Charles (Alan Adams) 371
Fillmore, Charles and Myrtle 179
Fiore, Joachim of 75
Firth, Violet Mary (Dion Fortune) 364–6
Florida Church of Christ 230
Fludd, Robert 356

Rabelais, François 361
Radio Church of God 479, 484–5
Raël (Claude Vorilhon) 390–2
Raelian Movement 65, 350
  beliefs and practices 392–5
  history 390–1
Raj, Dada Lekh 264
Rajneesh, Bhagwan Shree (Osho)
  290–6, 374
Rajneesh Movement see Osho
  International
Rajneeshpuram 92–3, 290–2, 374
Ras Tafari Makonnen (Emperor
  Haile Selassie) 259–60
Rastafarian movement 244, 252,
  259–60
Rawat, Prem Pal Singh see Maharaji
Reachout Trust 103–4
Reagan, Ronald 80–1
Recruitment 28–9
  conditioning 53–4
  deceptive techniques 30–9
  example stories 34–8
  the Family 221, 224
  International Church of Christ
  231
  passive 33
  Soka Gakkai 306
  Unification Church 204–5
Regardie, Israel 367–8
Religious discrimination 40–1
Religious Technology Centre 61,
  451, 469–71
Remey, Mason 247
Remey Society 247
Renewed Order of the Temple
  see Order of the Solar Temple
Reorganized Church of Jesus Christ
  of Latter-day Saints (RLDS)
  161
Restored Church of God 503
Richardson, James 84
Rigdon, Sidney 156, 161
Ring of Troth 411, 412, 416
RLDS see Reorganized Church of
  Jesus Christ of Latter-day Saints
Roberts, Oral 215–16, 230
Roberts, Robert 173
Robertson, George 203–7, 209–10
Robertson, Olivia 410
Roden, Benjamin 85
Roles, Francis 267, 277
Roman Catholic Church 192,
  213–14
Rooakhptah, Ammunubi 254
Rosenberg, Harry 429
Rosenberg, John Paul (Jack) (Warner
  Erhard) 427–8
Rosenkreutz, Christian 356
Rosicrucians 196, 355–9, 399
Ruhani Satsang 320
Rune Gild 413
Rupert, Greenbury G. 483–4
Russell, Charles Taze 63, 188–9,
  190

Rutherford, Joseph Franklin 'Judge'
  188, 190
Rutherford, Leo 395

Sabbatarian Movement 85, 172, 483
Sabellianism (Monarchianism) 135–6,
  149
Sahaja Yoga 296–8
St. James Independent Schools 274
Saint-Germain, Comte de 372,
  374–5, 377, 379
Salvation Army 140
Salzmann, Madame Jeanne de 352
Samkara see Shankaracharya of the
  North
Samraj, Ruchira Avatar Adi Da
  see Da, Adi
Sanders, Alex and Maxine 399–400
Sanders, J. Oswald 131, 144
Sangharakshita (Denis Lingwood)
  307–10
Sant Mat 312, 319, 320, 324
Santa Monica, University of 322
Saraswati, Sri Shantanand 267, 269,
  276
Saraswati, Sri Vasudevananda 269
Satanic Ritual Abuse 14–15, 40, 104,
  339–42
  see also Child abuse
Satanism 14–15, 341–3, 396–7
Scandinavian Centre for Shamanic
  Studies 395–6
Scharf, Betty R. 495
Schertenlieb, Raymond see Leo
Schisms 63–4
  Mormon church 160–2
  Worldwide Church of God
  479–514
School of Economic Science 61,
  433, 441
  beliefs and practices 269–76
  history 266–9
School of Meditation 267–8, 277
School of Philosophy 268
School of Practical Philosophy 268
Schreiber, Art 428, 430–1
Science of Creative Intelligence
  see Transcendental Meditation
Scientology 26, 61, 365, 427
  beliefs and practices 441, 447–54
  deprogramming 101
  history 454–72
Scott, Rachel 218–21, 223, 225–6
Sea Org 464–5, 468
Second Coming 71–2, 149
  see also End time beliefs; Shakers
Selassie, Emperor Haile see Ras
  Tafari Makonnen
Self-Revelation Church of Absolute
  Monism 312
Sergius 482
Servants of the Light 367–70
Servetus, Michael 143
Seventh-Day Adventists 33, 63–4,
  76–7, 78

beliefs and practices 126, 140–1,
  170–2
  history 168–70
  offshoots 172–3
Seventh-day Church of God 483
Seymour, John 431
Shakers 67, 140
Shallcrass, Philip 405–7, 410
Shamanism 335, 395–6
Shan 399–400
Shankara see Shankaracharya of the
  North
Shankaracharya of the North 61,
  267–72, 276, 285
Sheela, Ma Anand 291–2, 294
Shepherd's Rod Movement 85
Shoghi, Effendi 247, 249
Sidhi Programme (Transcendental
  Meditation) 277–8, 280–1
Sikhism 118–19
Sinason, Valerie 341
Singer, Margaret 30
Smart, Professor Ninian 447
Smiles, Samuel 425
Smith, Joseph 62, 77, 152–3, 156,
  158, 160–1
Smith, Matthew F. 144–7
Societas Rosicruciana in Anglia 359
Société Spirite 344
Society of Friends see Quakers
Society of the Inner Light 364–7
Society of Jesus (Jesuits) 199, 202
Society for the Study of Normal
  Psychology (Study Society) 267,
  277
Socinianism 143
Socinus, Faustus 143
Socinus, Laelius 143
Soka Gakkai International 302–7
Soka Kyoiku Gakkai 303
Solar Temple, Order of 88–90, 92
Southcott, Joanna 62, 77
Sovereign Order of the Solar
  Temple (Monaco) 89–90
Spaulding, Solomon 154
speaking in tongues (glossolalia)
  214–15
spiritual career path 56–7
Spiritual Regeneration Movement
  277
Spiritus Sanctum 356
Sprengel, Fräulein 359–60
Stanton, Noel 227
Star of the East, Order of 345–6
Stark, Rodney 24, 68
Steiner, Rudolph 196–7, 344,
  346–7
Steinman, Murray 375–7, 379–80
Stella Matutina (Order of the
  Morning Star) 360–1, 365, 368
Stewart, Gary L. 356–7
Storm, Rachel 106
Storr, Anthony 83–5
Strathlock, Baron 410
Strelley, Kate 291–2